Away from the White House

Presidential Escapes, Retreats, and Vacations

Away from the White House

Presidential Escapes, Retreats, and Vacations

LAWRENCE L. KNUTSON
FOREWORD BY BRIAN WILLIAMS

WHITE HOUSE HISTORICAL ASSOCIATION
Washington, D.C.

A laughing President Gerald R. Ford tried to escape the press as he sprinted toward *Air Force One* in March 1975. He had been visiting the Elk Hills Petroleum Reserve in California and was heading back to Palm Springs, where he was on what so many presidents described as "a working vacation."

For Frank Cormier,

Chief White House Correspondent of the Associated Press,

and for the generations of reporters

whose stories make up the backbone of this book

Page ii: The president's helicopter *Marine One* prepares to lift off from the South Lawn of the White House, 2013.

Opposite: In a cartoon entitled "To the Woods," Clifford Berryman captured President Theodore Roosevelt escaping the business of the White House with "Teddy Bear" on November 1, 1906.

First Edition

10 9 8 7 6 5 4 3 2

Library of Congress Control Number: 2013944981

ISBN 978-1-931917-40-7

Printed in Italy

CONTENTS

FOREWORD

I have travelled thousands—perhaps millions—of miles with the author of this book, and I've found that bad meals, long bus rides, cramped airplanes, and the general chaos of White House travel can form a band of brothers as strong as those for whom the expression was coined.

Larry Knutson and I overlapped as colleagues while covering the presidency of Bill Clinton. Very early on in our work, it was clear we had something in common—an eye for detail and an interest in the places we went. Sure, we covered the story of the day, but it was often the destinations—the granularity and texture of our surroundings and what the president was doing there—that got our creative juices going. An example comes to mind from a perfectly awful fund-raising trip to Florida. We members of the press pool who flew on *Air Force One* and were forced to cover the president (a nifty proposition when we're kept out of off-the-record private events in lavish private homes) attended a number of swanky waterfront receptions, all at stately homes with varying dock lengths and boathouse decors. During one particularly grim evening (actually, as I remember, it was a still night on the water with skies clear enough to pick out the constellations), over pre-wrapped sandwiches in one particular boathouse, Larry and I got to talking about the billionaire host in question, the business he owned, the history of the place and the state we were in, and similar homes that similar presidents had traveled to. This story from the road simply proves my thesis here: the intrinsic, intellectual curiosity and sense of history that Larry brings to his work will make this book come to life for all readers.

As long as we've elected presidents, those presidents have elected to get away. My only quibble with the book is that, to mark increasingly intrusive press monitoring and public interest, it ought to contain red dividers printed on robust stock that say:

"THIS IS WHEN IT GOT BAD FOR VACATIONING PRESIDENTS" *and*
"IT GETS REALLY BAD RIGHT ABOUT NOW" *and finally,*
"THIS IS ABOUT THE TIME THE PRESIDENCY BECAME INTOLERABLE
IN TERMS OF PRIVACY"

When it comes to enjoying their leisure time with their families, some presidents have done nothing to hide their lavish, comfortable wealth. Other presidents have done everything to cultivate others with lavish, comfortable wealth—so that they may "borrow" sprawling compounds, homes, beaches, riding trails, vessels—you name it—the necessities required for the Leader of the Free World to feel as though he and his family are "away."

In the modern era, the Kennedys stand out for their access to the water and the casual shirts, tweed blazers, and shabby khakis that go along with their studied old-money New England lifestyle. Jerry Ford enjoyed the relative anonymity of an enormous ski hat while navigating the slopes in his beloved Vail, Colorado. Both Bushes had Walker's Point, and the speedboats that were intended to leave no doubt about their virility or seamanship. While Nixon had his beach walks in black socks, LBJ had his ranch and Reagan had brush to clear. The Clintons, who were accused of relying on public opinion polling before

selecting a vacation spot that would look "the most American," also used their down time to try to repair marital problems that developed—and started to heal—as Larry and I (and thus all of you) looked on.

Mostly though, I hope you will enjoy the past. Pay special attention to my home turf of the Jersey Shore, and the number of presidents who chose to live there when they weren't in the White House (and in Garfield's case, die there). You'll see why Long Island was important to Teddy Roosevelt long before the first Kardashian ventured out to the Hamptons. And you'll read about my favorite subject contained here: the chapter titled "Grover Cleveland: Surgery at Sea." Try to picture that chapter with today's press corps riding along . . . with 24-hour cable, TV expert medical consultants, bloggers, Instagram, and Twitter along for the ride as well. In heavy seas, no less.

We ask a lot of our chief executives. And in our system of government, the job goes to one man (and so far just men) at a time. That means the burdens and hopes and dreams of the nation reside in that one individual, and given the pressures of office, we voters have always been interested in where they choose to go to relax. Larry Knutson takes us there—to each place and in great detail—in this first book of its kind. I always suspected that the author was taking a lot of notes, and not just those pertaining to whatever story we were reporting on that day. Now I know the rest of the story, and upon turning the following pages, so will you. You are in for a great treat, and a wonderful journey.

BRIAN WILLIAMS
Former Chief White House Correspondent, NBC News
Anchor and Managing Editor, NBC Nightly News

The Great Iron and Tubular Pier at Long Branch, New Jersey, is pictured here in 1879. The Jersey Shore was a favorite vacation destination for presidents Ulysses S. Grant, Rutherford Hayes, James Garfield, Chester Arthur, Benjamin Harrison, William McKinley, and Woodrow Wilson.

PREFACE

In April 1995, President Bill Clinton traveled to Georgia for a speech marking the fiftieth anniversary of the death of Franklin Roosevelt at his vacation retreat at Warm Springs. Sitting with other reporters on the grass outside the cottage known as the Little White House, I was told that Clinton's advance team had installed a White House telephone next to the long-disconnected telephone Roosevelt had used during World War II. I was struck by the apparent continuity between two eras of presidential history. The story also underscored a fact: While relaxing at Warm Springs, FDR worked on his stamp collection and drove into the country for picnics. But his responsibilities traveled with him, as they have with every president.

President Bill Clinton delivered a speech from the front porch of the Little White House at Warm Springs, Georgia, on April 12, 1995. The event marked the 50th anniversary of the death of President Franklin D. Roosevelt in 1945.

Much other presidential travel came my way, and a share of it involved vacations. I watched as President Jimmy Carter played softball at Plains, Georgia. And I stood near the first hole of a Martha's Vineyard golf course as President Clinton began a round with the Duke of York. Once, on the slopes of Wyoming's Teton Mountains, I shared a narrow forest path with Clinton, his party, and a rather large moose.

When I could I visited the retreats and homes of early presidents. The list was long but included Poplar Forest, the secluded retreat Thomas Jefferson designed when he felt overcrowded at Monticello. At various times I toured Harry Truman's vacation house in Key West, Florida, and admired his poker table on the south porch. I renewed my acquaintance with Jimmy Carter's hometown, Plains. I walked the streets of Theodore Roosevelt's Oyster Bay and explored Franklin Roosevelt's Top Cottage, Dwight Eisenhower's Gettysburg farm, and Herbert Hoover's Rapidan Camp.

In Washington, the Associated Press asked me to write a weekly Washington history column, and that led to stories about the history of presidential vacations and retreats. The search for ideas and sources led, in turn, to the White House Historical Association. When this book became a possibility, I discovered its underpinnings in more than two

President Jimmy Carter joined his brother Billy's softball team for a game in Plains, Georgia, in August 1978 (*left*).

A bronze sculpture (*below*) unveiled on the grounds of President Lincoln's Cottage at the Soldier's Home in 2008, marked the 200th anniversary of Lincoln's birth. President Lincoln often commuted by horse or by carriage from his retreat at the Soldiers' Home to his office in the White House.

centuries of news stories about presidential escapes, retreats, and vacations. The stories surfaced from stacks of faded newspaper clippings, unreeled from spools of microfilm, and emerged from the recesses of the internet. The documents, logs, photographs, and oral histories held by many of the nation's presidential libraries proved an unequaled resource. Interviews with former presidents Gerald R. Ford and Jimmy Carter provided personal perspectives that can only be got firsthand.

Often an important source was an observant staff member or Secret Service agent, or simply a well-placed person on the street. Walt Whitman, the poet, watched Abraham Lincoln ride back to the White House almost every morning from his summer retreat at the Soldiers' Home. "We have got so that we always exchange bows, and very cordial ones," he wrote in his journal. At times I felt as though I had been doing that as well.—Lawrence L. Knutson, January 2014

ACKNOWLEDGMENTS

This book about presidents away from the White House drew on many sources over a good number of years. Many people and organizations gave help and encouragement and deserve applause. Here are some of them:

The journey began when Sandy Johnson, then bureau chief of the Associated Press in Washington, asked me to write a weekly Washington history column. Inevitably, it often included stories about presidential escapes, retreats, and vacations.

Maria Downs of the White House Historical Association first suggested the possibility of a book. Neil Horstman, the association's president, endorsed the idea and provided valuable support throughout. William B. Bushong, association historian, offered important encouragement and advice. Research librarian Brian McLaughlin of the U.S. Senate Library was of the greatest possible help in locating books, magazines, and news articles. Gregg Harness, then head librarian, kindly permitted the library's use as a base for research. Nancy E. Kervin and other librarians offered enthusiastic encouragement and support throughout.

Calvin Woodward, Associated Press writer and editor, read all chapters on his own time, made editing corrections, and suggested many improvements in the text. Don Ritchie, now the historian of the U.S. Senate, read the text and made important suggestions.

Editor Ann Grogg closely and expertly read and edited the final manuscript for the White House Historical Association. Marcia Anderson, the association's vice president for publications, and Fiona Griffin, Nenette Arroyo, Abby Clouse-Radigan, and Lauren Zook, its production managers, organized countless details and pushed the project forward. Julia Riesenberg ably researched and located images and fact-checked notes.

Former Presidents Jimmy Carter and Gerald R. Ford kindly agreed to interviews. So did George Elsey, who served on Harry Truman's staff during his vacations at Key West; Hugh Sidey, who covered President John F. Kennedy's vacations for *Time* magazine; and Rex Scouten, former White House chief usher. President Ford's daughter, Susan Ford Bales, shared impressions of Camp David and memories of Ford family ski vacations.

John Alan Gable, the late director of the Theodore Roosevelt Historical Association, gave valued and informed assistance. Among many others who did the same are Bob Wolz, executive director of the Harry Truman Little White House Museum at Key West, Florida, and Carol Hegeman, director of the National Park Service's Eisenhower Historic Site at Gettysburg, Pennsylvania.

The late William H. Harbaugh, a distinguished University of Virginia historian and Theodore Roosevelt biographer, shared his considerable and valuable research on Pine Knot, Roosevelt's Virginia hideaway. Amy Verone, curator at Sagamore Hill for the National Park Service, and other staff members provided useful information. Tom Keuhass, director of the Oyster Bay Historical Society, and local historian John E. Hammond led a memorable tour of the town.

Preservation director David Overholt gave an impressive and informative tour of Abraham Lincoln's summer cottage at Washington's Soldiers' Home while restoration of the 14-room residence was still a work in progress. Mary V. Thompson, research historian at Mount Vernon, offered an understanding of the rigors of travel in George Washington's time. The staff of the Franklin D. Roosevelt Presidential Library at Hyde Park, N.Y. made much valuable material available, including the log book recording FDR's visits to Shangri-La, his wartime hideaway in the wooded hills of western Maryland.

Important institutional sources of information include: the Library of Congress and its Periodical Reading Room; the National Park Service and its network of historic sites, including the Adams National Historical Park at Quincy, Massachusetts, and President Herbert Hoover's Camp Rapidan in Shenandoah National Park; the presidential libraries, each a storehouse of essential information; and the privately managed presidential sites, including George Washington's Mount Vernon, Thomas Jefferson's Monticello and Poplar Forest, and James Madison's Montpelier.

President Dwight D. Eisenhower departs the White House for Camp David by helicopter in 1957. Eisenhower was the first president to employ helicopters in his transportation service.

President Warren G. Harding greeted childen in Valdez, Alaska, during his historic "Voyage of Understanding" his famous transcontinetial speaking and sightseeing tour by railroad during the summer of 1923. Harding was the first president to visit Alaska. The tour ended with his sudden death on August 2, 1923.

INTRODUCTION

America's presidents have been trying to get away from it all for more than two hundred years, and never quite succeeding. The job and its responsibilities follow no matter where they are. But whether they escape to a golf course or a trout stream, a sailboat or a ski slope, vacationing presidents find that time away from the White House can clear the mind, rest the body, restore energy, and perhaps add a touch of humanity to a politician's image. After President John Kennedy had cleared his desk, an aide observed, he dedicated "every inch of mind and body to leisure as intensively as he had to work, completely shaking off and shutting out the worries of the world beyond."

Some presidents loved the job and all that comes with it. Others experienced an almost painful isolation. Their thoughts about the office have a touch of melancholy: "a bed of thorns," "a splendid misery," "a dreadful self-inflicted penance," "the loneliest place the world." "This great white jail is a hell of a place in which to be alone," Harry Truman told his White House diary in 1947. When bleak winter set in, Truman broke free and flew south to the sun, palm trees, and evening poker awaiting him at Key West, Florida. "You can get a kind of a bird-in-a-gilded-cage feeling," Ronald Reagan told friends when he mused about White House life. Reagan escaped to his California ranch much more often than top aides thought wise. He made the continent-spanning trip on *Air Force One* not only to change scenery but to shed schedules and ceremony. At the ranch, the president rode horses, built fences, chopped wood, and cut brush.

Vacation was not a concept in anyone's mind when George Washington first stepped into his coach at the president's house in Philadelphia and headed to his Potomac River plantation. He and other early presidents went home to tend to private responsibilities at places with names: Mount Vernon, Peacefield, Monticello, Montpelier, and Oak Hill. It was an era when travel was measured by the speed of a coach and four horses pounding over rutted roads. For them and for many who followed, late summer in the capital's steamy and enervating heat served as a spur to explore cooler surroundings.

The great American vacation wouldn't arrive until the middle of the nineteenth century, when the steamboat and the railroad increased the distances people could safely and comfortably travel. Then the telegraph made long-distance communication easier. The new technologies multiplied the options of presidents and ordinary Americans alike. An overnight steamer brought Andrew Jackson from Washington to the mouth of Chesapeake Bay for days of cold-water bathing. James Polk and later James Buchanan traveled by rail to their favorite spa to "take the waters." Ulysses S. Grant spent long summers in a cottage overlooking the Atlantic on the fashionable New Jersey Shore. The presidential yacht made its appearance, offering comfortable adventures on the river, bay, and ocean.

By the time the new century arrived, the nation's rail network offered new possibilities. A week or so on the train brought Rutherford B. Hayes, Chester A. Arthur, and Theodore Roosevelt to Yellowstone, Yosemite, and the Far West. Roosevelt could board a train in Washington and reach his home in Oyster Bay, New York, in less than a day. Once there, the telephone and telegraph kept him in touch with the White House. The Atlantic and Pacific cables extended his reach around the world. Roosevelt's options were further enhanced by the full staff that he brought with him from the White House. The president juggled all these elements in the summer of 1905 as he brokered a peace agreement between Russia and Japan. The effort won him the Nobel Peace Prize.

William Howard Taft motorized the White House, ending the era in which presidents rode in horse-drawn carriages. Taft greatly enjoyed whizzing down New England roads near his Summer White House while bundled in the backseat of an open touring car. The automobile also permitted visions of a permanent presidential retreat, secluded but located just a few hours' drive from the White House. Herbert Hoover set the pattern with his fishing camp in the Blue Ridge, where bags of official mail were dropped from an airplane. During World War II, Franklin D. Roosevelt established Shangri-La as a presidential hideout in the forests of western Maryland. Dwight D. Eisenhower gave it permanent status and a new name—Camp David.

Over two centuries the White House vacation has acquired the crust of controversy as opposition voices seek to dent a president's political armor by contending his vacations are untimely, too long, too expensive, and in the wrong place. The tactic's first use may date from the summer of 1797 when an opposition newspaper in Philadelphia accused President John Adams of abandoning his post and going home just when the public most needed him at his desk and on the job. Grumbles about presidential vacations have varied widely over the decades. Here are a few of the complaints: Eisenhower played too much golf. Richard Nixon spent far too much money on his vacation homes. Theodore Roosevelt exposed his dangerously reckless nature by diving in a submarine. And Calvin Coolidge fished with worms instead of proper flies. A New York newspaper once proposed that President Arthur have his pay docked every time he went fishing. Because President Grant spent long summer vacations at his seaside cottage in New Jersey, his congressional enemies sought to pass a law nullifying all official presidential actions taken away from the seat of government. That idea fizzled. So did the bid to penalize presidential fishing.

Presidential escapes, retreats, and vacations away from the White House are much transformed from the days when a president traveled with a few coachmen and outriders, a servant or two, and perhaps a private secretary. In the twenty-first century a vacationing president arrives at his destination by U.S. Air Force jet, is transported by motorcade and helicopter, supported by communications staff, shielded by Secret Service and local police, briefed by intelligence and defense officials, and followed by a print and broadcast press corps intent on making the morning editions and the evening news. An urgent call can reach him as easily on a golf cart, a sailboat, or a mountain path as it can in the Oval Office.

Presidential vacations continue despite hurdles and serial criticism. Modern presidents have clearly discovered that frequent escapes offering absorbing activities and a break from the daily schedule can still rest the body, clear the mind, and renew energy for the work ahead.

President Ronald Reagan
and Vice President George
H.W. Bush ride horses
at Camp David in 1981.
Approximately 70 miles
from the White House,
Camp David in the Catoctin
Mountains of Maryland, has
been a favorite retreat for
many presidents since the
time of Franklin D. Roosevelt.

Chapter 1

George Washington: Setting the Example

GEORGE WASHINGTON
First President of the
United States, 1789–1797

From the president's house at Philadelphia, George Washington, his coach and four-horse team, his liveried outriders, and two-horse baggage wagon usually required a full six days to reach Mount Vernon, his Virginia plantation on a bluff above the Potomac River. The early rising president could cut a day off that time if he traveled long hours on sturdy horses and with few companions. When in a hurry, or in need of exercise, he rode the entire distance on horseback. If Martha Washington and her maids traveled with him, the journey required a more sedate pace and might take a full week.

During Washington's first seventeen months in office, the long and time-consuming journey from the temporary captial in New York effectively barred his return to Mount Vernon. That must have been painful for someone as bonded to the land as he was. Travel home became far more practical and realistic after the government moved south to Philadelphia in 1790, cutting many days off travel to Virginia. Over the next six years Washington visited Mount Vernon fifteen times. He made the trip as many as three times in some years, while limiting himself to a single visit in others. His stays ranged from a hasty few days to more than two months. They were often timed for spring and fall when Congress was out of session. By the end of his presidential visit in the fall of 1796,

President George Washington's family owned land along the Potomac River in Virginia for almost a century before he inherited the farm called Mount Vernon in 1754. "No estate in United America is more pleasantly situated than this" he wrote of his home, depicted at right in 1800 by Alexander Robertson.

During his presidency, Washington made fifteen trips from the seat of government in Philadelphia home to Mount Vernon. While at Mount Vernon, he spent considerable time planning the new capital city of Washington, 15 miles north. He often traveled by horseback, as in the painting (*opposite*) by Alfred Jacob Miller titled *George Washington at Mount Vernon*.

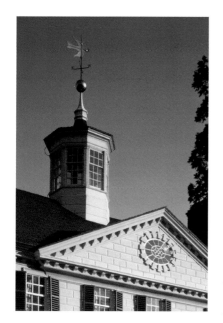

In July 1787 Washington commissioned a weathervane for the top of Mount Vernon's cupola. He specified that he "should like to have a bird (in place of the Vain [*sic*])—with an olive branch in its Mouth." The dove, a symbol of peace, is still mounted above the cupola on Mount Vernon.

Washington had spent an estimated 397 days at home at Mount Vernon. Travel days added significantly to his time away from the seat of government. He did not leave his duties without preparing for contingencies. Before he left Mount Vernon for his extensive 1791 tour of the South, Washington supplied his cabinet with a detailed itinerary, naming the towns and days where a courier with urgent dispatches might expect to reach him. If circumstances warranted, he told them, "I will return immediately from any place at which the information might reach me."

Washington knew that small actions as well as great decisions would set precedents. His visits to Mount Vernon, and occasional sightseeing or fishing trips elsewhere, established the practice that chief executives might step away from the daily pressures of their position to go home, tend to their personal responsibilities, and, if time allowed, enjoy themselves. The responsibilities of the office accompanied Washington on all his travels, as they would with future presidents. Official mail and dispatches arrived by courier and post at Mount Vernon and followed him nearly everywhere. The hours he spent on official correspondence in his library at Mount Vernon show that while the presidential responsibilities might be eased in the familiar surroundings of his own home, they could not be shed.

A principal and unique responsibility, one that consumed as much of Washington's time as any other, was the establishment of a permanent United States capital. After much sectional wrangling, Congress in July 1790 approved legislation moving the seat of government from New York City to Philadelphia for ten years while a permanent capital was built on a site to be chosen on the Potomac River. That October, on his first trip to Mount Vernon since taking the oath of office, Washington spent twelve days visiting possible locations on the upper Potomac above Great Falls. But those who knew his mind believed he had already decided on the navigable stretch of the lower river just north of Alexandria, the Virginia town closest to Mount Vernon. They were soon proven correct.

───────

Travel in the eighteenth century could be an ordeal. An outrider often pressed ahead of Washington's coach to warn of dangerous conditions. The presidential caravan stirred a choking cloud of dust on dry and sandy roads. A long carriage trip in summer was a stifling misery. Washington could expect to be jarred and jolted if the roads were deeply rutted. Recent rain meant coach wheels might sink hub-deep in mud. Once, when his coach became mired on a Maryland road, Washington paid handsomely to have it shoveled free. Mishaps like this were common. On one trip to Philadelphia an inebriated coachman overturned the baggage wagon, not once but twice. In April 1791, as Washington headed south from Mount Vernon to begin a tour of the Carolinas and Georgia, a horse fell into deep water from a river ferry and pulled its three harnessed and frightened teammates with it.

On his trips north and south, Washington became intimately acquainted with the wide range of accommodations offered by roadside inns, taverns, and public houses. His diaries can be read as a mile-by-mile travel guide, including road conditions and assessments of the taverns at which he spent the night and rested the horses. The ratings he assigned to public houses range from good to ordinary to "indifferent," his term for shabby and badly managed. When Washington described an inn as "very indifferent," one can almost feel him shudder at the memory of bad food or uncomfortable straw pallets. Traveling through rural areas during his tour of the South in 1791, Washington endured some of the most disagreeable public accommodations he ever encountered as president. He described them as "extremely indifferent—the houses being small and badly provided either for man or horse." He rejected one Virginia inn when he found it had no stables in which his horses would be comfortable and offered "no rooms or beds which appeared tolerable." But he acknowledged that most tavern keepers made "extra exertions when it was known I was coming."

Washington's life was anchored at Mount Vernon. Despite the discomforts and occasional perils of travel, he felt an insistent need to escape to his Potomac River farms. That need increased as his time in office lengthened, the new government's problems mounted, political factions formed, and opposition newspapers grew bolder. Mount Vernon gave him peace. The first glimpse the traveling president may have had of his house as he turned into the long drive, and approached the trimmed and level bowling green, was a gilded dove in flight, its beak gripping a symbolic sprig of olive. Mounted above the octagonal cupola on the mansion's cypress-shingled roof, the dove of peace had been a final architectural touch. Washington ordered it in 1787 to mark the establishment of peace after American victory in the Revolution.

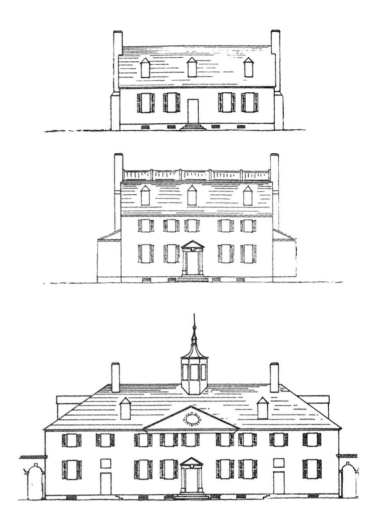

Once at Mount Vernon, Washington immersed himself in the smallest details of farm management and the planting, harvesting, and rotation of crops. He paid close attention to the proper upkeep of flower and vegetable gardens, roads, and fences, the decoration and furnishing of the mansion house, the landscaping of its grounds, and the well-being and performance of the work force of slaves who made all his enterprises possible. Mount Vernon's affairs were a consuming interest that provided mental escape and produced streams of written instructions to his estate managers even when he was commanding his country's revolutionary armies or sitting at his presidential desk.

It was a substantial domain. Washington's land purchases greatly expanded an estate that had been a family possession since 1674. Divided into five farms, his 8,000 acres stretched for miles along the Potomac and took in about 12½ square miles. In a series of building projects that began in 1754 and continued for more than thirty years, Washington expanded and enlarged the existing small house, shaping it into a two-story mansion with a broad and pillared front porch that framed the spectacular view down the steep bluff and across the broad river to the wooded Maryland shore.

During his forty-five years at Mount Vernon, Washington expanded his home to suit his changing needs. The colonial planter on the rise needed a more prominent "seat" than that left to him by an elder half-brother (*top*, c. 1754). He started by raising the structure a full story in height (*center*, c. 1757). In the mid-1770s, prior to the Revolution, he began a second major renovation. The finishing touches were completed before the start of his presidency (*bottom*).

Early in 1791, Washington disclosed his plan to establish the permanent capital in a 10-square-mile federal district on land ceded by Maryland and Virginia. He hoped the central location, midway between Maine and Georgia, would ease North-South tensions and promote the survival of the new nation. Mount Vernon was just a short ride away.

7

The Washington Family, completed in 1796 by Edward Savage, depicts President and Mrs. Washington, with Martha Washington's grandchildren, gathered around a map of the new city of Washington. Savage's notes explain that Martha Washington is "pointing with her fan to the grand avenue," now known as Pennsylvania Avenue. A servant dressed in livery and a vista down the Potomac complete the imaginary scene.

For the rest of his presidency, Washington's visits to Mount Vernon were focused on the city that he knew would bear his name. Although his efforts proved successful, he came to regard the experience as "a *fiery trial*." Over the next six years, the president explored the terrain on horseback, negotiated with suspicious and greedy landowners, dealt with troublesome assistants, fretted over financing schemes, and ignited the city's real estate market as a perpetual topic of dinner table conversation. As the project moved forward, he approved the sites for the Capitol and the President's House, helped select their architects, and endorsed the designs. Eager to demonstrate that actual building had begun, he laid the Capitol's cornerstone.

Washington named military engineer Pierre Charles L'Enfant as the city's chief planner. He endorsed the Frenchman's visionary and expansive city plan that imposed sweeping avenues like sword strokes over a grid of streets and endowed the future capital with a constellation of circles, squares, and triangles. When progress was threatened by L'Enfant's apparently endless quarrels with the city's commissioners, Washington reluctantly fired him. But he kept L'Enfant's map as a guide. Later, when the city's prospects looked bleak, he resisted efforts to change course and locate the capital permanently in Philadelphia or New York. While fully aware of the difficulties, his vision of the city of Washington as commercial "emporium" and capital of the United States never dimmed.

Washington entered the presidency in 1789 determined to travel to every state, using his popularity and fame as a unifying force to build support for the new national government. His journeys began in October when he set out by coach for New England. In a month of travel he passed through nearly sixty towns and villages, drawing throngs of excited citizens who cheered, applauded, and entertained him. In the summer of 1790, after waiting until Rhode Island ratified the Constitution and officially joined the Union, Washington set sail

Building the First White House (1931), by N. C. Wyeth. President Washington selected the architect for the President's House and oversaw much of the construction himself. In this rendition he holds the plans in his hands. The structure was not completed during his presidency; his successor, John Adams, was the first president to live in the White House.

Pierre Charles L'Enfant's 1792 *Plan of the City of Washington* was engraved, printed, and distributed in an attempt to foster the development of the capital city through the sale of lots. It also provided the first notion of the grand plans envisioned by the designer and his patron, President Washington. The Federal City's Board of Commissioners named the city after the nation's first president in the fall of 1791.

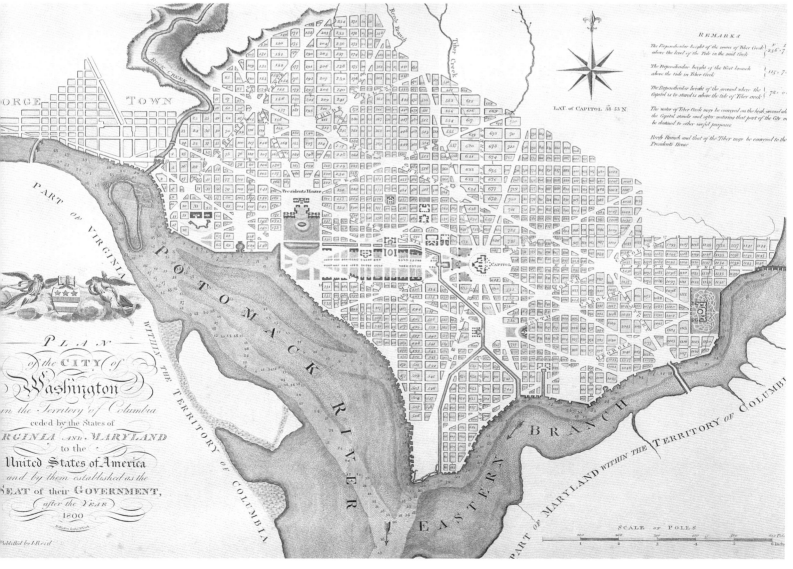

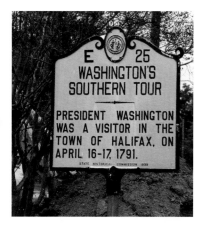

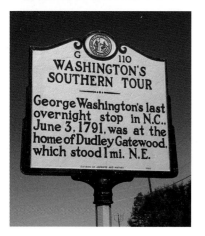

To build national unity, President Washington toured the southern states in 1791. He first traveled down the eastern seaboard, from Maryland to Savannah, and returned on an inland route, from Augusta to Virginia. Today, historical markers commemorate his tour. He traveled in a coach similar to the one pictured above right, which is now in the collection of Mount Vernon Plantation.

from New York to visit Newport and Providence. The president returned to the road in the spring of 1791, visiting Charleston, Savannah, and many other southern cities. He logged 1,887 miles in nearly three months of hard travel and was thankful he had not been delayed by sickness, bad weather, or accidents. Washington believed the activity, exercise, and diversion of travel were necessary for someone whose position tied him to a desk and a sedentary life. A few days before leaving for New England, the president told his sister he was looking forward to the trip as a "relaxation from business and reestablishment of my health."

While these first presidential road shows were fact-finding missions and attempts to gauge popular feeling, they also resembled a triumphal progress. Washington knew what was expected. Leaving his coach on the outskirts of each new town, he slipped into his old uniform as general of the Continental Army, mounted an immaculately groomed white horse, and rode through streets crowded with thousands of cheering citizens. Cavalry escorts, cannon salutes, ringing church bells, and local bands welcomed the hero. The local gentry, war comrades, and members of patriotic and fraternal orders offered laudatory addresses, lavish banquets, extravagant

balls, concerts, and even fireworks. At banquets Washington lifted his glass to fifteen or more patriotic toasts, each punctuated by the firing of a cannon posted outside the windows. The president became so accustomed to the roar of massed artillery salutes that he took note at lesser efforts. After his arrival at Tarboro, North Carolina, he wrote that he had received "as good a salute as could be given with one piece of artillery." On the other hand, he never failed to note with appreciation the number of beautiful and stylish women attending a reception or a ball in his honor. At one affair in Charleston, he counted 256 "elegantly dressed & handsome ladies." Clearly dazzled after a Charleston concert, he noted the audience had included "at least 400 lad[ies], the Number & appearances of. exceeded any thing of the kind I had ever seen."

When he could, Washington took in the local sights, much like a modern tourist although always with official escorts and guides. While waiting for dinner to be prepared at Middletown on the Connecticut River, he strolled around the town and climbed to heights from which he found the view both sweeping and beautiful. Visiting Cambridge, Massachusetts, he and Vice President John Adams toured the campus of Harvard College and saw the library, museum, and the orrery, "a curious piece of mechanism" used to demonstrate revolutions of the Sun, Earth, and other planets. Arriving at Charleston, South Carolina, the high point of his 1791 tour of the South, Washington rode horseback through the main streets and admired the architecture of private homes and public buildings. The next day he climbed to the second tier of the steeple of Saint Michael's Church for a panoramic view of the city and its gardens. After dinner he watched a display of fireworks mounted on a ship in Charleston Harbor. At

Charleston and elsewhere on his tour he visited Revolutionary War battlefields and entrenchments, places he had known during the war only by written reports. In Charleston, he was introduced to James Hoban, an aspiring architect. Hoban later became architect of the President's House in the new Federal City. Future generations would know it as the White House.

At times, Washington escaped from the crowds and just enjoyed himself. One Monday morning during his New England tour, he boarded a large rowboat at Portsmouth, New Hampshire, inspected the harbor shipping, received a thirteen-gun salute from a coastal fort, and then went deep-sea fishing off Kittery, in what would be later become the state of Maine. Although the president caught only two cod, blaming the meager result on the state of the tide, he left a story in his wake. One of those fish was reported to have been hooked not by the president but by Zebulon Willey, a local resident who was fishing from a nearby boat. According to the story, Willey was rewarded with a silver dollar when he handed his line to Washington, allowing the president to land the fish. Washington's next recorded experience was far more successful. In June 1791, while he was still recovering from a near-fatal bout with pneumonia, he joined Secretary of State Thomas Jefferson for a three-day fishing trip off Sandy Hook, New Jersey. "We are told he has had excellent sport, having himself caught a great number of sea-bass and black fish," a newspaper reported. It added the hope that the remarkably fine weather, the sea breezes, and the "wholesome exercise" would result in "a speedy and complete restoration to health."

———

Although Washington traveled north to the edge of Maine and south to the Georgia coast, Mount Vernon remained the president's preferred destination. That was true even when he expected to share it with others. In early June 1796, eager to escape Philadelphia's political bickering, Washington instructed William Pearce, his estate manager, to prepare for a summer season crowded with distinguished guests, including the envoys of France, Great Britain, and Portugal. (As it turned out, he also would be visited by a delegation of a dozen Catawba Indians.) With his usual attention to detail, Washington made it clear he wanted Mount Vernon to look its best for what a later president might have called a working vacation. The president directed that house, gardens, and lawns be put in order with outdoor trash swept and raked from "holes and corners." Fresh white paint was to be applied wherever needed. The servants hall was to be swept and scrubbed and the bedsteads made ready for visiting valets and coachmen. Washington told Pearce to replace the front gate because it was cracked and "scarcely to be opened." Arrangements needed to be made for an abundant supply of beef and veal for the kitchen. "Tell the gardener I shall expect everything that

While visiting Charleston on his Southern Tour, President Washington climbed up into the steeple of Saint Michael's Church, pictured here in 1812, for a view of the city.

President Washington enjoyed fishing both as a gentleman's contemplative recreation and as a practical means of securing provisions while on the frontier. His tackle case, today in the collection of Mount Vernon Plantation, contains hand-wrought hooks, horsehair and silk fishing lines, and wax for preparing the lines.

Mount Vernon with the Washington Family on the Terrace, painted by Benjamin Henry Latrobe in 1796, depicted George and Martha Washington on the riverfront side of the mansion, at ease with children and pets. This is the only known image, created during their lifetimes, of the Washingtons on their Mount Vernon piazza.

The estate remained in the Washington family until 1858, when the Mount Vernon Ladies' Association of the Union was formed to purchase and preserve it. It was first opened to the public in 1860 and remains open to the public today.

a garden ought to produce, in the most ample manner." Since he was bringing eight or ten horses from Philadelphia, and each new guest would bring horses as well, the president had a final instruction: "Take care to keep a sufficiency of oats and the best of your old hay on hand." It all had to be done quickly. The master of Mount Vernon expected his house and grounds to be "in clean and nice order" when he reached home.

Almost a year later, in March 1797, George Washington went home to Mount Vernon, for good. He wrote to his cousin that he was looking forward to "more real enjoyment than in all the business with which I have been occupied for upwards of forty years." Unfortunately, he had less than three years left. On December 14, 1799, Washington died, and he was buried at Mount Vernon, as he directed in his will. In 1831 a new brick tomb replaced the old burial vault. Over the years it was visited by many who came to pay homage to the nation's first president.

Chapter 2

John Adams: Gone Home to Massachusetts

While George Washington reached home by riding south, John Adams headed north to the Massachusetts town of Quincy, formerly Braintree, on the coastal road to Boston. Farming the rocky soil not far from his birthplace, Adams joined his hired hands in building stone walls, cutting fence posts, plowing, cultivating, and reaping. He delighted in nature and was near enough to the sea to train a telescope on ships entering Boston Harbor. "Yesterday mow'd all the Grass on Stony field Hill," Adams wrote in a journal entry on a July day in 1796 when he was still vice president. Two days later he made this note: "I arose by four O Clock and enjoyed the Charm of earliest Birds. Their Songs were never more various, universal, animating or delightful." A few days after that he noted with satisfaction that one of his apple trees had produced enough fruit to make two barrels of cider. Later that year, farmer Adams was elected president.

Stubborn, proud, plainspoken, and well read, John Adams was the many-faceted son of a Massachusetts farmer. A graduate of Harvard College, a lifelong student of the Greek and Roman classics, he married the remarkable Abigail Smith, who was easily his intellectual equal. Adams had been a successful lawyer, a delegate to the Continental Congress, and a member of the committee of five that oversaw the writing of the Declaration of Independence. Dispatched by Congress as a wartime diplomat to Holland and France, he helped negotiate the treaty that brought peace with Great Britain and established the independence of the

A watercolor of Peacefield (*opposite*) was painted by E. Malcolm in March 1798, eleven years after John and Abigail bought the farm in Quincy and before they expanded it. This is the earliest known illustration of the Adams estate.

Sketch of the Mansion (*right*) was drawn in 1820 by Abigail Smith Adams, the granddaughter of John and Abigail Adams, from a point on the south side of what would later be known as Adams Street. It may be the earliest view of the barn and stable added by John Adams in about 1800.

Peacefield, known to later generations as "The Old House," was also home to President John Quincy Adams, U.S. ambassador to Great Britain Charles Francis Adams, and writer Henry Adams. It remained in the Adams family until 1946. Today the Adams family properties in Quincy are administered by the National Park Service as Adams National Historical Park.

United States. Adams had that accomplishment in mind in 1796 when he decided to name the 83-acre farm he and Abigail had purchased shortly before their return to the United States from Europe nine years earlier: "I think to christen my place Peace field, in commemoration of the peace which I assisted in making in 1783, of the thirteen years peace and neutrality which I have contributed to preserve, and of the constant peace and tranquility which I have enjoyed in this residence."

As his presidency became more turbulent, and with Abigail experiencing long periods of poor health, Peacefield's tranquillity may have diminished. Adams later started calling the farm Stoneyfield, perhaps in tribute both to its rocky soil and the harder circumstances with which he was surrounded. But as Abigail Adams wrote, Peacefield remained their "ark of safety." It was a haven in many ways. In the heat of summer, Philadelphia, the nation's capital until Washington could be built, was not only a sweltering "bake house," as Mrs. Adams called it, but a fetid breeding ground for yellow fever, which claimed hundreds of lives each summer. On their way back to the capital from a summer in Quincy, the couple might linger in New York for as long as a month until the epidemic in Philadelphia abated with the return of colder weather.

Adams did not travel in the high style that Washington preferred. At the beginning of his presidency, he purchased a serviceable coach, describing it as "simple, but elegant enough." Instead of a team of four or six, it was drawn by just two "young and clever" horses named Caesar and Cleopatra. While Washington was often accompanied by a retinue of aides and liveried servants, Adams generally limited his traveling companions to his secretary and one other aide. When Mrs. Adams suggested they paint the Quincy family crest on the coach doors, her husband dismissed the idea as "a trifling symbol of aristocratic pretension." Overall, Adams wrote, he preferred to avoid display in his equipage so as not to "excite popular feelings and vulgar insolence for nothing." Even so, he found the expense not insignificant. While he rented the presidential mansion for $2,700 a year, the combined cost of his coach and horses was $2,500.

No amount of style could lessen the inconveniences of travel: bad roads, poor food, small rooms, and lumpy beds. On one trip to Quincy, Abigail became so dizzy in the stifling heat she twice stopped at inns to rest. The distance to home was nearly twice what it had been for Washington. While Adams could make the trip in thirteen days, it often took as many as nineteen. But at times, fortune favored the traveler. Returning to Philadelphia in November 1798, Adams found the skies clear, the temperature cool, the roads dry and hard, and the horses able to make 30 miles a day. He saved further time by traveling unannounced, forestalling welcoming ceremonies, receptions, and banquets. "Our horses go like birds," he wrote to Abigail. "We glided along unforeseen, unexpected, and have avoided all noise, show, pomp, and parade."

Once home at Peacefield, Adams tended to stay as long as he could. As vice president in an era of short congressional sessions, he stayed for as long as nine months. The unhurried visits continued after he became president. In 1797, he reached Quincy on July 19 and remained until early October. In 1798, Adams was at home at Peacefield from late June to mid-November. And in 1799, a year in which his wife fell critically ill soon after they reached Peacefield, he traveled home in late March and remained until September, a full seven months. It was the longest any president has ever been away from the seat of government.

The walls of the long room at Peacefield hold Adams family portraits. Left to right are Abigail Adams, John Quincy Adams, John Adams, and Charles Francis Adams.

Abigail Adams designed a new wing at Peacefield that included a second-story study for John Adams, where, as she insisted, his books could be in order and everything arranged "so that no trouble occurs in searching for papers."

The president's critics fussed over his absences, and even his friends worried. In the summer of 1799, members of the Adams cabinet hinted that he should return and a Federalist ally told him bluntly that "public sentiment is very much against your being so much away from the seat of government." Shortly after had Adams left for New England in 1797, the acidly hostile

On November 1, 1800, when President Adams moved in, the White House was still under construction. In this 2000 painting, the artist Tom Freeman imagined the construction scene, with its mud and littered grounds, that greeted Adams on his arrival. The interior was also unfinished. In some rooms plaster was still drying; in others there was no plaster on the walls at all. The only access to the Second Floor was by a twisting service stair.

Philadelphia *Aurora* aimed a question at its readers: Why has the president "absconded" from the capital just when the critical state of affairs leaves the public "exceedingly agitated"? Many other vacationing presidents would face similar questions in the years to come.

Adams maintained he could accomplish as much at Quincy as he could at Philadelphia, as he was kept fully informed by letter and dispatch. "Nothing is done without my advice and direction," he told one anxious friend. "The post goes very rapidly, and I answer by the return of it, so that nothing suffers or is lost." The grumbles and worries continued, nonetheless.

Adams did work conscientiously at his desk at Peacefield. And when he arrived for a long stay in 1798, he found that Abigail had conspired with local builders to improve his working conditions. Using money saved from household expenses at the president's house in Philadelphia, she added a new wing to the old house, doubling its size and providing a second-floor library or "bookroom" with a fireplace and windows on three walls. Her aim was to create an efficient workspace for correspondence with every government department. She insisted it also be a pleasant place to do business. "I know the President will be glad when it is done," she told her sister. "But he can never bear to trouble himself about any thing of the kind, he has no taste for it."

The papers that crossed the president's desk that summer ranged from routine to urgent: reports and letters from department heads, job applications, requests for pardons, a report on the yellow fever epidemic in Philadelphia, a request to build a lighthouse at Cape Hatteras. There were serious concerns over relations with revolutionary France, which had soured to the point that the deteriorating situation was called a "quasi war" and some feared a French invasion. Adams was at Quincy in October 1798 when American envoy Elbridge Gerry

John Adams was the first president to live in the White House, although his term ended barely four months after he moved in. His portrait by Gilbert Stuart hangs in the Blue Room today.

reached Boston with word that the French were open to negotiations and appeared ready for peace. By the end of the Adams administration, a convention with France enabled the United States to maintain its neutrality.

Near the end of May 1800, Adams's carriage left Philadelphia and rolled through the green farm fields and pastures of Pennsylvania and Maryland. On June 3, eight days after he set out, Adams reached the District of Columbia, the raw construction site that was soon to become the seat of government. He stayed ten days, assessed progress, and inspected the new President's House, still little more than a shell. Then he headed north for his summer in New England. The sandstone President's House was still incomplete when Adams returned from Quincy on November 1. But enough had been accomplished that he could set up an office with windows overlooking the Potomac and become the first president to spend a night in the Executive Mansion. The presidential election would be held within days, and voters would reject Adams and elect Thomas Jefferson in his place. When his coach next rolled toward Quincy, John Adams would be a private citizen.

Once a world traveler, Adams remained close to Quincy for the rest of his long life, maintaining an extensive correspondence, defending his past actions, enjoying his grandchildren, and watching his son John Quincy Adams become president. Although Adams had declined to attend Jefferson's inauguration, they resumed their friendship by mail in 1812 and exchanged hundreds of notable and significant letters over the years. The two former presidents died on the same day, July 4, 1826, fifty years to the day after the adoption of the Declaration of Independence.

Chapter 3

Thomas Jefferson: Looking West

THOMAS JEFFERSON
Third President of the
United States, 1801–1809

Thomas Jefferson entered office well aware of the pounding his predecessor John Adams had taken for his "long and habitual absences" in Massachusetts, so far from the seat of government that even the most routine presidential business had to be conducted by mail. At the same time, Jefferson had no intention of chaining himself to the new capital on the Potomac during the hot, humid, and fever-prone months of late summer, especially when he could ride to his mountaintop at Monticello near Charlottesville, Virginia, in only a few days. The president encouraged members of his cabinet to follow his example, offering his thoughts in a letter to Treasury Secretary James Gallatin: "I consider it as a trying experiment for a person from the mountains to pass the two bilious months on the tide-water. I have not done it these 40 years, and nothing should induce me to do it. As it is not possible but that the Administration must take some portion of time for their own affairs, I think it best they should select that season for absence." Jefferson noted that while Washington had retreated to Mount Vernon for up to two months, Adams had been gone far longer than that. "I should not suppose our bringing it back to two months a ground for grumbling," he wrote. "But, grumble who will, I will never pass those two months on tide-water." It was a promise he kept. The president escaped to Monticello's high ground every August and September for each of his eight years in office.

View from Monticello Looking Toward Charlottesville (1825) by Jane Pitford Braddick Peticolas gives an idea of the panoramic western views that Jefferson so loved. In the distance, the University of Virginia—Jefferson's final building project—is under construction.

Thomas Jefferson at the Natural Bridge, painted in 1801 by Caleb Boyle, depicts the president on a visit to one of the natural wonders of western Virginia. Jefferson bought the land on which the limestone arch stands and described it in his 1785 book, *Notes on the State of Virginia,* as "the most sublime of nature's works."

The View of the West Front of Monticello and Garden by Jane Pitford Braddick Peticolas (1825) shows children playing on the lawn at Jefferson's home.

Rather than copy the official letters he wrote from Monticello, President Jefferson used this polygraph machine to copy them automatically, so he could save one and send one. The polygraph machine was invented by John Isaac Hawkins and produced in America by Charles Willson Peale, who made improvements to it under Jefferson's direction. Jefferson wrote tens of thousands of letters using this machine, from 1804 on.

There were grumbles, just as Jefferson predicted. During his first summer as president, one Boston newspaper, the *Columbian Centinel*, wrote that it would be difficult to determine exactly where the government was because the president and most of his cabinet members had left town. More tolerantly, Washington's *National Intelligencer* pointed out that when Jefferson was at Monticello he was only 100 miles away, far closer to the capital than Adams had been during his absences. Moreover, arrangements were in place for the president to receive official mail within two days and to reply within a week.

Monticello was Jefferson's crowning personal achievement, lifetime architectural project, and the center of his intellectual and family life. Deliberately breaking from colonial styles, he sought inspiration in the classical eras of Greece and Rome and the designs of the Venetian architect Palladio. Taken together, he saw them as a prototype building style for the new republic. He built his house on land granted in 1735 to his father, Peter Jefferson, a planter, surveyor, and mapmaker. As a boy he roamed the 867-foot hill or "little mountain" (which he later translated into Italian as Monticello) and relished the panoramic views. As an adult, Jefferson leveled the crest of the hill to build a redbrick, thirty-five room house that in its final form was capped with a white-topped, octagonal dome. Standing by itself, or filled with its builder's inventions and collections, Monticello was easily the most interesting and distinctive house in America. It was also perpetually under construction, not approaching completion until 1809, the year its owner left office.

Despite Monticello's attractions, the new president quickly discovered there was no way to avoid government business or the never-ending stream of visitors who followed him home, occupied his bedchambers, dined at his table, and competed for his time. "They came of all nations, at all times," a granddaughter recalled. The president told his daughter, Martha, that while at Washington he could dispose of most matters with a few words, at Monticello he had to write a letter. Because he brought no secretary with him, that meant hours dealing with correspondence and making copies for his records.

Even though the distances from Washington were shorter, the journey to Monticello was often troublesome. Crossing the Rapidan River while returning to Washington in the fall of 1807, Jefferson's horse, Castor, still in harness and attached to the shafts of the carriage, fell into waist-deep water and nearly drowned. Jefferson had further reason for exasperation during that trip when he discovered he had left his traveling money at Monticello, probably on the "sopha" on which he had been sitting.

As the years of his presidency lengthened and his privacy at home evaporated under the weight of constant guests and social bustle, Jefferson began planning a retreat 70 miles distant from the retreat he already had. He chose a site at Poplar Forest, the 4,819-acre tract he owned near Lynchburg on the eastern rim of the Blue Ridge. The house at Poplar Forest would not be completed while the president was in office, but it would serve as a welcome haven during his long-anticipated retirement. For the time being, the project offered an outlet for Jefferson's architectural energies.

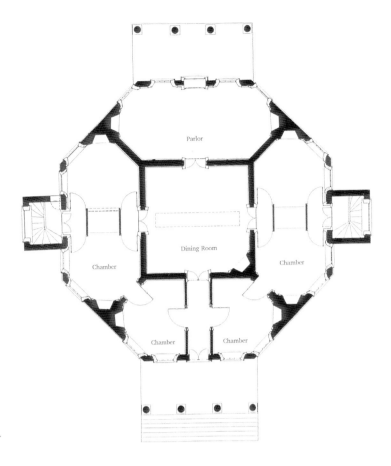

Jefferson designed Poplar Forest while he was still in the White House. It was an octagon-shaped house situated in a circle of trees. He retreated to Poplar Forest after the presidency, visiting several times a year. The house, however, was not completely finished until 1826, the year of Jefferson's death.

Poplar Forest was sold out of the family two years after Jefferson's death. In the mid-1980s it was purchased by local citizens and the work of restoration began. Today, restored to its original design, the house is open to the public. The nonprofit Corporation for Jefferson's Poplar House continues to preserve and restore both the house and the landscape.

Bending over his worktable at the President's House, Jefferson drafted plans and elevations for an octagonal house, the first ever built in the United States. Drawing inspiration from his library of architectural books and his own ideas of what a neoclassical house should look like, he sketched the principal rooms as elongated octagons, grouped around a tall, 10-foot-square central hall with a 16-foot skylight. To complete the geometry, Jefferson placed the redbrick house in the center of a circle edged with trees. He laid out the foundations during a five-day visit in the summer of 1806 and organized construction in a series of letters that specified the dimensions of construction details to the half inch.

Monticello reflected Jefferson's multitude of interests. He rode his fields and attended to the small details of farm and gardens. His library of thousands of books was the finest in America. He corresponded with some of his nation's and the world's greatest thinkers, at times putting their ideas into action. In 1801, during his first visit home as president, Jefferson received smallpox virus from Dr. Benjamin Waterhouse in Boston and inoculated fifty people, including his family and many slaves, against the disease. When a shipment of natural wonders and Indian artifacts arrived from the Lewis and Clark expedition in the summer of 1805, Jefferson took great satisfaction in installing part of the collection in Monticello's two-story entrance hall, which he called the Indian Hall or his "cabinet of curiosities." He hung elk, deer, and antelope antlers and displayed an array of Indian pipes and pottery, bows and arrows, leggings, and a battle scene emblazoned on a buffalo robe.

As the presidency wore on him, Jefferson's determination grew stronger to retire to Monticello with his family, books, and farms. "I am panting for retirement," he told

The entrance hall at Monticello (*left*) was also a museum of sorts, where waiting visitors might see Old Master paintings, busts of Alexander Hamilton and Voltaire, American natural history specimens, and Indian American artifacts. At the White House, President Jefferson installed a similar museum of Western artifacts in the Entrance Hall, depicted in the modern watercolor (*below*) by Peter Waddell, in 2013. Objects brought back by the expeditions of Meriwether Lewis and William Clark and of Zebulon Pike were displayed in the space, along with Indian arrows and headdresses, animal skins, and samples of crops.

Jefferson took a scientific approach to farming, and his gardens at Monticello were divided into square plots and planted methodically according to which part of the plant—fruits, roots, or leaves—was to be harvested. Today his gardens have been re-created and continue to be cultivated.

Monticello, pictured below c. 2000, has been called the "autobiographical masterpiece" of Thomas Jefferson. He called it his "essay in architecture." In 1987 Monticello was designated a UNESCO World Heritage Site.

a correspondent in 1807 when his term still had two years to run. "Never did a prisoner released from his chains feel such relief as I shall on shaking off the shackles of power," he wrote two days before the 1809 inauguration of his old friend, James Madison. A year later he made this report to another old friend: "I am retired to Monticello, where, in the bosom of my family, and surrounded by my books, I enjoy a repose to which I have long been a stranger. My mornings are devoted to correspondence. From breakfast to dinner, I am in my shops, my garden, or on horseback among my farms; from dinner to dark, I give to society and recreation with my neighbors and friends; and from candlelight to early bedtime, I read."

Jefferson's library at Monticello, which housed thousands of books, was considered the finest in America. In 1815 he sold more than 6,000 titles to the government to replenish the Library of Congress collection, lost when British troops burned Washington in 1814. Proclaiming in a letter to John Adams that "I cannot live without books," Jefferson then began accumulating a second collection of several thousand additional books.

Chapter 4

James Madison: Montpelier Summers

JAMES MADISON
Fourth President of the
United States, 1809–1817

This life-size statue of
James and Dolley Madison
(*opposite*) is on the grounds
of Montpelier, in Orange
County, Virginia, the
president's home since
childhood and where he
and his wife are buried.

Montpelier, James Madison's estate in Virginia's Orange County, was a working plantation, an elegant and comfortable retreat, a place of scenic beauty, and the president's lifetime home. The view from the house crossed the Rapidan River, spanned forests, and ended at the mountain wall of the Blue Ridge, 20 miles in the distance. In the crystalline light the mountains reminded one visitor of rolling waves, and the remote and isolated countryside seemed "wild and romantic." The clarity of Montpelier's air always impressed guests escaping the summer swelter of low-lying Washington. More than one guest called the atmosphere "salubrious," as in wholesome, clean, and refreshing.

During his eight years in office, the nation's fourth president rarely missed a summer respite at the estate Mrs. Madison called "our mountain," or simply, "Orange." In a typical year, James and Dolley Madison fled Washington's heat in July or August and remained at Montpelier until late September or early October. Over his two terms, Madison was at Montpelier (or making the three-day road trip to or from it) for at least 600 days, more than a year and a half of his time in office. He took care, as he wrote while visiting Thomas Jefferson at Monticello, to "keep hold of the thread of daily communication with Washington."

Returning to Washington after a summer break at Montpelier was often a jolt. "We passed two Months on our mountain in health & peace," Mrs. Madison wrote to a friend in the fall of 1811, but came back in early October to find the city "sick & afflicted." While the "bilious fever" had now abated, "many died & Congress conven'd in some dread of contagion."

In 1801, the year he was named Jefferson's secretary of state, Madison added a front portico of his own design to Montpelier's facade. He also built a 30-foot extension on the north end of the house for his own use, reserving much of the main residence for his parents and, after his father's death that year, for his aging mother. Madison launched another three-year building project in 1809, the year he succeeded Jefferson as president. Aided by William Thornton, the original architect of the U.S. Capitol, he erected a rear portico and

This watercolor on paper rendering of the west front of Montpelier was made by the Baroness Hyde de Neuville on October 12, 1818. Although the proportions of the portico are not quite correct, the baroness captured such details as Mrs. Madison's macaw on its perch and Nelly Madison, the president's mother, in the window of the north wing.

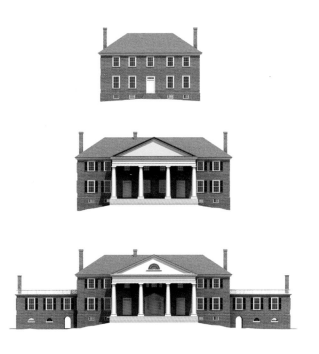

added one-story wings. The resulting symmetry of the Georgian house with its set-back wings, colonnades, lawns, boxwood hedges, spreading oaks, willows, and cedars prompted comparisons to an English country estate. But when visitors walked through the front door, the focus was on America. The thirteen panes in the fanlight window in the entrance hall symbolized the union of the original thirteen states. A large central drawing room called "The Hall of Notables" displayed portraits of the nation's founders by Gilbert Stuart and other artists. Marble busts of George Washington, Benjamin Franklin, Thomas Jefferson, John Adams, and the Marquis de Lafayette stood on pedestals near a wall-mounted bas-relief of Madison himself. Thomas Jefferson had shipped the marble fireplace mantel across the Atlantic as a gift when he was U.S. envoy to France.

Montpelier was built by James Madison's father between 1755 and about 1764, and the president knew he would inherit it. In 1797 he began a series of extensive renovations not completed until about 1812. He expanded the core house and changed its interior configuration. With a new central doorway and Tuscan portico on the west front, a colonnade in the rear, and wings on each side, he converted what had been a Georgian-style dwelling into a Classical Revival mansion. The central door with the acclaimed thirteen-pane fanlight (for the thirteen-state union) was restored to its original condition in c. 2005.

The Montpelier plantation was divided into four farms, each with its cluster of slave cabins. More than one hundred slaves kept the house and worked the fields, bringing in crops of tobacco, wheat, corn, and hay and tending beef cattle, pigs, and sheep. Some of Madison's slaves were skilled artisans: blacksmiths, wheelwrights, carpenters, spinners, and weavers. "All articles that were wanted for farming or the use of the house were made on the spot," a visiting British diplomat observed.

Montpelier's owner was a short, pale, physically unimpressive public servant whose intellectual powers had helped create the republic. Author of the Bill of Rights, he was frequently called "The Father of the Constitution." Shy in public, the president was often humorous, congenial, and lively in private. Seventeen years younger than her husband, Dolley Payne Madison balanced her husband's reserve with style, vivacity, and good humor. The welcoming atmosphere she provided both at the President's House and at Montpelier encouraged people of all ranks and political persuasions to feel at home.

The walls in the large central drawing room at Montpelier "were covered with pictures, some very fine, from the ancient masters, but most of them portraits of our most distinguished men," wrote one visitor in 1828. There was also a sculpture gallery with busts of famous Americans and this bas-relief of President Madison himself, by the sculptor Giuseppe Ceracchi.

When James and Dolley were in Orange County, Montpelier could seem as full of guests as any hotel. In August 1813, Mrs. Madison told a friend to whom she owed a letter that it had been impossible to write sooner "oweing to the croud of company with which our house has been fill'd ever since our return to it." Margaret Bayard Smith, whose husband, Samuel Harrison Smith, was editor of the *National Intelligencer*, found Montpelier bustling and welcoming when she arrived for a short visit in August 1809. When Mrs. Smith confessed she hadn't brought her children for fear of inconveniencing her hosts, Mrs. Madison replied that with twenty-three other guests in the house they wouldn't have been noticed. At breakfast the next morning, the Smiths joined some twenty Madison relatives and friends for a Virginia breakfast of cold ham, chicken, hot wheat bread, light cakes, cornpone, tea, and coffee. Writing in her diary later, Mrs. Smith gave Montpelier an enthusiastic review: "Hospitality is the presiding genius of this house, and Mrs. Madison is kindness personified."

Although somewhat abbreviated, the routine of summer visits to Montpelier continued even after the outbreak of war with Great Britain in 1812. But in 1814, the year the war became a terrifying and personal reality, the Madisons chose to visit Montpelier in the spring, not summer. They arrived at their mountain about April 29, returning to the capital on May 30. A year earlier, after a British fleet on Chesapeake Bay had burned most of the town of Havre de Grace in Maryland, Mrs. Madison shared with her husband's secretary her reaction to the "fears & alarms" that surrounded her. "I have allways been an advocate for fighting when *assailed*, tho *a Quaker*," she wrote. "I therefore keep the old (Tunisian) Sabre within my reach."

Dolley Madison may have been prepared for attack but Washington's defenders plainly were not. On August 24, 1814, a force of about four thousand

Dolley Payne Todd Madison was famous for her ability to put all her guests at ease. At the White House, her social occasions helped dispel political tensions. At Montpelier she welcomed company. "I wish you had just such a country home as this," she wrote to a friend in 1820. "It is the happiest and most independent life."

British regulars, marching from their landing spot on the Chesapeake, brushed aside a larger but ill-trained and poorly led American army. Capturing the city, they burned the Capitol, the President's House, and other public buildings. In the most celebrated moment of her life, Mrs. Madison directed the safe removal of Gilbert Stuart's full-length portrait of George Washington from the Executive Mansion just moments before she fled herself.

After a legendary thunderstorm, the invading army retreated and American fortunes improved. A British attack on Baltimore was repulsed, and a naval bombardment of Fort McHenry in Baltimore Harbor proved futile. After an American victory on Lake Champlain, a British force retreated into Canada. Finally, on January 8, 1815, a hastily assembled American army under General Andrew Jackson routed British veterans at New Orleans. The one-sided battle was fought before word arrived that a peace treaty had been signed at Ghent in the Netherlands restoring relations with Britain to their prewar status. When the treaty reached Washington on February 14, it was clear that if Americans could not declare victory, at least no territory had been lost, nor had any humiliating conditions been imposed. It was, a relieved Dolley Madison declared, "our glorious peace."

On March 21, less than a month after he signed the peace treaty, James and Dolley were again on their way to Montpelier for what they clearly thought was a well-deserved rest. In late April, Madison rode over to Monticello and watched the packing of the more than 6,000 books Jefferson had sold the government to replace the volumes destroyed when the British burned the Capitol and the Library of Congress. Returning to Washington for six weeks and living in a borrowed house, Madison dealt with the details of the war's aftermath. Once assured that peace had restored public confidence, he headed back to Orange County and remained from late July to early October.

The Americans and British had been at war for more than two years when British troops entered Washington on August 24, 1814, and burned most of the public buildings, including the Capitol and the White House. This engraving by Paul de Rapin-Thoyras, entitled *Capture of the City of Washington*, was published in London in 1815.

By the early summer of 1816 America had regained self-respect and a new sense of national identity. Trade and commerce flourished; prosperity returned. Madison left for Montpelier on June 5, not to return until early October. A full four months, it was one of the longest presidential vacations on record. On the Fourth of July, the Madisons extended Montpelier's hospitality to ninety Virginia neighbors at a "profuse and handsome dinner" served in an arbor on the lawn. The president's line of communications with Washington remained open as usual. A French visitor observed in September that while Madison was an excellent host, he also spent many hours a day at his desk. "Work is easy for him; he reads and writes almost all day, and often part of the night." As for Dolley, she was "sweetness, honesty and goodness itself."

On April 7, 1817, delayed for a month by the round of parties in their honor, the Madisons took advantage of new technology to begin their trip home to Montpelier and retirement from public duties. Boarding a steamboat at a Potomac wharf, they set out in comfort to meet their carriage 40 miles downriver at Aquia Creek. As the steamer slipped past Mount Vernon, a fellow passenger noted that the former president was "as playful as a child" as he "talked and jested with everybody on board." The observer was reminded of a schoolboy beginning a long vacation.

Following James Madison's death, Dolley Madison inherited Montpelier. She sold it in 1844, when she returned to Washington, D.C. It had various owners until 1901, when it was purchased by William duPont. Over the years the mansion had been altered and expanded, but the duPonts made significant changes, eventually doubling its size. In 1983 the property was passed to the National Trust for Historic Preservation, which began to restore it to the 1812 Madison-era appearance. The restoration was completed in 2009, and today Montpelier is open to the public.

Chapter 5

James Monroe: Building Oak Hill

JAMES MONROE
Fifth President of the
United States, 1817–1825

The President's House had burned to its sandstone walls. Rebuilding it within those walls demonstrated the resilience of the republic and the permanence of Washington as its capital. Although the stonemasons and carpenters had accomplished much, they were months away from completing their work when James Monroe took the Oath of Office on March 4, 1817.

For that first year, the new president's family continued to occupy a dormered, frame cottage at Oak Hill, his 4,400-acre estate in Virginia's Loudoun County. Monroe had bought it jointly with an uncle years before, then inherited the property outright when the uncle died. At just 33 miles west of the capital city, Oak Hill was an easy day's ride. Monroe became a weekly commuter, riding out most Saturdays, staying through the weekend, and returning to the city early each week. In Washington he and his wife, Elizabeth, lived at his Federal-style townhouse on I Street.

Revolutionary soldier, public servant, and diplomat, James Monroe was the last of four early presidents from Virginia, beginning with George Washington. Over a long public career Monroe served as a delegate to the Confederation Congress, United States senator, governor of Virginia, and envoy to France and Great Britain. Dispatched to Paris by President Thomas Jefferson in 1803, Monroe helped negotiate the Louisiana Purchase, which doubled the size

This early rendering of Oak Hill (*right*) includes the six-room dormered cottage where the Monroes lived during the reconstruction of the White House. The grander mansion (*opposite*) was added to the property in 1822–23. Its most striking feature is a Classical Revival–style portico, which rests on a masonry arcade supported by 30-foot Doric columns.

When James Monroe became president in 1817, the President's House, burned to the walls In 1814, was not yet fully restored. So he and his family continued living in the home he had purchased in 1811 on I Street, NW, a few blocks west of the White House (*entrance hall and entrance, right*). Its parlor (*above*) was the setting for Monroe's first inaugural ball. Today the building is the home of the Arts Club of Washington.

A modern view of Oak Hill.

of the United States. President James Madison employed him as both secretary of state and secretary of war. Friends found Monroe quiet, dignified, and honest. The latter quality drew an endorsement from Jefferson who said Monroe was "so honest that if you turned his soul inside out there would not be a spot on it." In style of dress, Monroe was somewhat of a throwback to an earlier era. He was the last president to wear knee breeches, silk hose, and buckled shoes.

Decades before he became president, Monroe enjoyed a cordial friendship with a young fellow officer in Washington's army, the French nobleman and idealist, the Marquis de Lafayette. The friendship grew stronger in the tumultuous years of the French Revolution while Monroe served as American envoy to France. First he used his influence to extricate Lafayette from a foreign prison. Then he and Elizabeth Monroe intervened to save Madame de Lafayette from the guillotine.

Plasterers and carpenters remained at work at the President's House through the summer of 1817 as Monroe began a tour of New England, which had been a cauldron of wartime discontent. Now Boston and other ports were filled with ships and commerce. Peace and

prosperity transformed public opinion, and for the moment partisan politics had been suspended. Tens of thousands of New Englanders turned out for a glimpse of the new president, hailing him as a symbol of national unity with parades, militia reviews, cannon salutes, and celebratory dinners. There had been nothing like it since Washington made his own unity tour.

The Boston *Columbian Centinel* called the Monroe visit a "presidential jubilee" and endowed his time as president with an enduring catch phrase, "Era of Good Feelings." But the suspension of partisan hostilities could not be sustained. In 1819 an economic depression dimmed the prosperity that marked the opening of Monroe's term. Then Missouri sought admission as a slave state, igniting a fierce debate that threatened to split the country between north and south.

In October 1817, although reconstruction of the White House had not been fully completed, Monroe and his family moved in. Oak Hill became a summer retreat, a place to visit when Congress was out of session. The Monroes also began to see it as a place to spend their retirement when his presidency ended. But the old cottage was clearly inadequate for the broader stage the president now occupied. Monroe began planning a larger, grander house.

Contributing to the design were two of the most significant architectural figures of the time. Irish-born James Hoban played a major role. The original architect of the President's House, Hoban was now in charge of its reconstruction. Design suggestions also came from former president Thomas Jefferson, who had made Monticello his architectural showcase. At least once he used a drawing to present his ideas. In a note, Jefferson modestly voiced hope that "mrs [*sic*] Monroe & yourself may take some hints from it for a better plan of your own."

Local builder William Benton began work in 1822 on a two-story brick house with flanking one-story wings. Its most striking feature was an imposing portico resting on a masonry arcade supported by seven massive 30-foot Doric columns, each 9 feet in circumference and made of stuccoed brick. When completed in 1823, the new house stood at the end of an avenue of trees with a view of the Blue Ridge.

Monroe spent most summers at Oak Hill, maintaining contact with the government through the mails. One or more of his secretaries remained in Washington to review incoming correspondence and forward the most important material to Monroe. But at times that wasn't enough. In June 1817, just months after Monroe's inauguration, Secretary of State John Quincy Adams complained in a diary entry that Monroe had chosen to depart for his Oak Hill farm "though the moment is very critical, and a storm is rapidly thickening. He has not read many papers that I left with him," Adams grumbled. "And he puts off everything for a future time." But in 1823 Monroe worked cooperatively with Adams on the administration's most important and enduring foreign policy initiative: the Monroe Doctrine. While Adams is credited with developing the doctrine's wording and many of its themes, Monroe is said to have worked on drafts while at Oak Hill before including it in his annual message to Congress in December 1823. The doctrine was intended to restrict European expansion into the Western Hemisphere as expressed in one key sentence: "The American continents . . . are henceforth not to be considered as subjects for future colonization by any European Power."

Monroe had been out of office for a few months when in early August 1825 Oak Hill welcomed its most famous visitor. Lafayette had begun a triumphal last tour of the United States a year earlier. A living link to the Revolutionary era and the last surviving general officer on George Washington's staff, Lafayette was celebrated as a hero everywhere as he

The Italian marble fireplace mantels at Oak Hill (*opposite*) were a gift from the Marquis de Lafayette, who visited with his old friend James Monroe during his triumphal tour of the United States, 1824–25.

James Monroe's tomb in Hollywood Cemetery, Richmond, Virginia, is comprised of an elegant cast iron structure (often referred to as "The Birdcage") over a granite sarcophogus.

The view through an elegant entrance at Oak Hill was captured in a recent photograph (*opposite*).

visited old battlefields and met old comrades. On August 7, John Quincy Adams, the new president, accompanied Lafayette to Oak Hill. It turned into one of the hottest days of the year. But they found Monroe in good health and spirits and stayed for several days of quiet conversation. It was Lafayette's final farewell to the American he called his "earliest and best" friend. As an expression of gratitude, Lafayette arranged for two handsome white marble fireplace mantels to be made in Italy for Monroe and shipped across the Atlantic. They were installed in Oak Hill's parlors. After the excitement of the Lafayette visit, Monroe faced the reality that he was deeply in debt, the result of decades in diplomatic positions that paid moderate salaries and imposed heavy spending.

After Elizabeth Monroe died in 1830, Monroe moved from Oak Hill to New York City to live with his daughter, Maria, and her husband, Samuel Gouverneur. He died there at age 73 on July 4, 1831, the third president to die on Independence Day. Monroe's remains rested in a New York cemetery until July 1858. They were moved at the request of the Virginia legislature, which sought the burial in Virginia soil of every president from the state. With great ceremony the remains of the fifth president were placed on board a steamer, moved to Richmond, and buried in Hollywood Cemetery. Oak Hill passed out of the Monroe family. Still standing and still elegant, it is the most important residence of an early U.S. president remaining in private hands.

Chapter 6

John Quincy Adams: The Old House

JOHN QUINCY ADAMS
Sixth President of the
United States, 1825–1829

John Adams had called his New England house Peacefield. His son, John Quincy Adams, simply called it the Old House. Whatever the name, the attraction of the place was equally strong for both. "My native air is as cheering to me as ever," the sixth president wrote in August 1827, shortly after he arrived at the Adams house at Quincy for an urgently needed break from Washington's heat and the troubled state of his presidency. Reared in the cooler climate of New England, Adams found the capital's summer temperatures "insupportable." The heavy humidity of an August evening left him "gasping for breath." Flies and mosquitoes flew through the unscreened windows, adding to the misery and providing another incentive to flee.

The introduction of the steamboat with its speed and convenience made escaping to cooler climes more feasible than ever before. Steamboats cut days off travel time and offered passengers comforts unavailable in a cramped coach jolting over rutted roads. Adams considered the steamboat "one of the greatest and most beneficial innovations of modern ages." Steamboats also offered thrills unavailable elsewhere. On one trip the president's steamer raced another boat and reached the spectacular speed of 10 miles an hour. Adams could find only one drawback: he feared the engine's roar and the slap of the paddles might prove disturbing "to weak nerves."

In 1843, John Quincy Adams (*opposite*) posed for one of the first daguerreotypes made of a former U.S. president. It is believed that this photograph was taken at Peacefield.

This drawing of "The Adams Seat in Quincy" by Mrs. George Whitney, 1828, depicts the Adams family house when it was inherited by John Quincy Adams during his presidency. It is remarkably like the sketch made by Abigail Smith Adams in 1820 (see page 14), but shows the addition of a corn house.

In 1807, following late eighteenth-century experiments, steamboats were introduced for commercial purposes. Robert Fulton's North River Steamboat, known as the *Clermont* (shown here) was the first. By the 1820s, steamboats were carrying passengers on America's rivers and lakes. John Quincy Adams became the first president to travel in this new way. He found steamboats marvelous but noisy.

Adams was still secretary of state in September 1824 when he set out for New England to "take a month of holiday to visit my father and dismiss care" and distract himself from what proved to be a bitterly divisive presidential election. He entered the presidency the next year under a cloud of suspicion. Because none of the several presidential candidates had a majority in the Electoral College, the 1824 election was decided by the House of Representatives. Adams prevailed with votes from backers of Henry Clay, who had run third in electoral votes. But when the new president named Clay as his secretary of state, outraged supporters of General Andrew Jackson accused him of securing office through a "corrupt bargain." Exploitation of the issue over the next four years, coupled with Adams's inability to steer a legislative program through Congress, made Jackson the clear favorite in 1828.

When he returned to Quincy in September and October 1825, Adams found that while his 90-year-old father remained mentally alert, the former president was feeble and could no longer see well enough to read or write. The next July, as America celebrated the fiftieth anniversary of the Declaration of Independence, word reached Washington that John Adams was dying. Hoping to reach home in time, the president was on the road to Baltimore to board a coastal steamer for Boston when he learned that his father had died on July 4. In one of the great coincidences of American history, Thomas Jefferson had died the same day.

New England was gripped in an intense heat wave when the president reached the Old House at Quincy on July 13. "I know not that I ever experienced at Washington a warmer night," Adams told his diary. His father's funeral had already been held; his remains had been interred. But the president felt more strongly attached to the family house than ever before. Thinking of John Adams, he wrote: "It is repugnant to my feelings to abandon this place, where for near forty years he has resided, and where I have passed many of the happiest days of my life." Moreover, he would need a place to return to when he left the presidency. "Where else should I go?" he asked himself. "This will be a safe and pleasant retreat, where I may pursue literary occupations as long and as much as I can take pleasure in them."

The president remained at Quincy for nearly four months as he settled his father's affairs. Ignoring his wife's protests that he was endangering their finances, he took out the large loans needed to pay other heirs and acquire the house and land for himself. He went out with the surveyors to inspect and appraise the property and on one day alone spent "upwards of five hours traversing the woods, climbing rocks, wading through swamps, and breaking through the brakes."

By the summer of 1827, Adams's presidency had proved a bitter personal disappointment. His frustrations led to a decline of his physical and mental health with symptoms that included stomach distress, loss of appetite, fitful sleep, and what he called "an uncontrollable dejection of spirits" and a "sluggish carelessness of life, an imaginary wish that it were terminated." The president's doctor listened to his patient's complaints and prescribed an immediate and lengthy vacation. As Adams expressed it in his diary, he had been ordered to "doff the world

Upon John Quincy Adams's death in 1848, his son Charles Francis Adams inherited the Old House. The next year it was recorded in two images. The first is a daguerreotype (*left*) by the early photographer John Adams Whipple, taken from across Adams Street. The stone wall that appears in earlier images of the house has been topped with a low picket fence. On March 19, 1849, Charles Francis Adams recorded in his diary, "Soon after breakfast M. Whipple, the maker of Daguerrs called to show me the results of his experiment of Saturday. On the Old Mansion he has been remarkably successful." In October of the same year, the painter G. Frankenstein painted the Old House (*below*). Charles Francis Adams also noted this event in his diary, writing on October 6, 1849: "I went out and met Mr. Frankenstein who has come to take a sketch in oils of the old mansion. I wandered with him over the fields examining the effect from various points. We finally fixed upon the end of the Railroad bridge."

aside and bid it pass; to cast off as much as possible all cares, public and private, and vegetate myself into a healthier condition." With that goal in mind, he reached Quincy in August and stayed until early October. He soon reported that he had begun to sleep better. He went swimming every day. He worked in his garden, employing expertise gathered from watching and helping the gardener at the President's House. He joined thirty friends on a fishing trip and caught nothing except sunburn. When the respite was over he confided to his diary that he was still depressed and that his health continued to sag.

After his steamboat docked at Philadelphia on the trip back to Washington, Adams was touched, and a little surprised, to find that a large and friendly crowd had gathered at the wharf to cheer and escort him to his hotel. Another large crowd assembled when it was time for him to leave, swarmed onto the boat, and packed the deck. Adams, a political puritan who detested "electioneering," steeled himself to shake several hundred hands. When the cheers continued he bowed and waved his hand. Passing up the opportunity to deliver a political speech, he limited his response to just four words: "God bless you all!" Privately, he expressed relief there had been no "disorder" and, although pleased, warned himself not to be swayed by "vain or unworthy sentiments of excitation."

The enthusiastic reception was flattering but potentially misleading. The next summer, arriving in Baltimore on his way to New England, Adams found that the crowd gathered to welcome him was out-shouted by members of the opposition who rallied in a public square to listen to speeches on "the unpardonable sins of the Administration and the transcendent virtues of Andrew Jackson." The presidential election that he would lose was just three months away. "A stranger would think that the people of the United States have no other occupation than electioneering," Adams wrote.

His political career apparently at an end, Adams refused to attend Jackson's inauguration and returned to Quincy wrapped in gloom. Then his Massachusetts neighbors intervened, electing Adams to the first of nine terms in the House of Representatives. Once there he too angered members from the South by repeatedly introducing antislavery petitions. At first, attempts to bury his petitions through parliamentary restrictions appeared to have prevailed. But after eight years the House repealed what by then was universally known as "the gag rule." The former president's antislavery speeches caused many to call him "Old Man Eloquent."

Appearing before the Supreme Court in 1841, Adams argued for the freedom of slave mutineers aboard the Spanish ship *Amistad,* and won. On another issue, his insistence eventually persuaded a reluctant Congress to accept a $500,000 legacy from the English scientist James Smithson. That made Adams one of the founders of the Smithsonian Institution.

The former president and his wife continued to spend summers at the Old House in Quincy. Then on February 21, 1848, Adams suffered a stroke at his desk on the House floor. He lapsed into a coma and died several days later. His final words were heard to be: "This is the last of earth—I am composed." John Quincy Adams was 80 years old. The sixth president was interred next to his parents in Quincy's First Congregational Church.

In 1870, Charles Francis Adams constructed a separate library on the grounds of the Old House, to honor his father, President John Quincy Adams, and to serve as testimony to the entire Adams family's love of books.

Chapter 7

Andrew Jackson: Rip Raps and The Hermitage

ANDREW JACKSON
Seventh President of the
United States, 1829–1837

The Rip Raps, a tiny man-made, government-owned, and oddly named island near the mouth of Chesapeake Bay, proved to be a near-perfect antidote to the capital's oppressive summer heat. Located in Hampton Roads near the Virginia Capes, it was a place of Atlantic breezes, diving seabirds, slapping waves, and long views. President Andrew Jackson called it a "beautiful spot, on the rocks." Visiting for the first time in the summer of 1829, he wrote to a friend that he hoped the ocean air and saltwater bathing would improve his often precarious health. While that remained to be seen, one benefit seemed clear from the start. An escape to the Rip Raps freed him "from the bustle of business, and the throng of strangers, that are unusually great at this Season in the city."

During eight turbulent years in office, Jackson often returned to the island spa, enjoying family vacations just an overnight boat ride from the capital. From his first visit he established a custom of vacationing in alternate summers in Hampton Roads and at The Hermitage, his plantation near Nashville, Tennessee. Because of the distance of

This portrait (*opposite*) by
Ralph E. W. Earl, titled
President Jackson at The Hermitage
portrays the seventh
president on the grounds
of his Nashville, Tennessee,
plantation home, c. 1830.

The Rips Raps, seen in the photograph above and the 1861 map at right, is in the mouth of the Hampton Roads Harbor, in Virginia. It began as shoals used as a dumping ground for ships' ballast. In 1817 the U.S. Army began to fill in the island, eventually 15 acres, and to build Fort Calhoun on the site. President Andrew Jackson first toured the island in 1829 and stayed in a frame house there. The fort was decommissioned in 1967 and later developed by the city of Hampton into a park, which can be visited by ferry today.

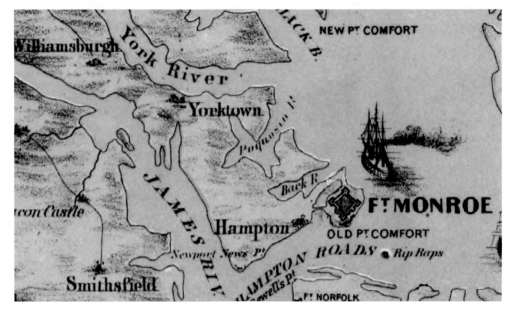

more than 500 miles, trips to The Hermitage required a major investment in time and effort, and Jackson traveled home just four times during his two terms.

Ocean swimming became part of the president's daily regimen at Hampton Roads, beginning with his first trip in August 1829. The fresh air may have been more helpful than cold saltwater. "I cannot yet determine whether I will be benefited by the salt water bath," he wrote after a few days at the island. "It is very cold, tho' this day is clear and fine."

On Jackson's third visit to Hampton Roads in the summer of 1833, the presidential party stayed at the comfortable Hygeia Hotel, at Old Point Comfort just across a narrow navigation channel from the Rip Raps. There they dined well, played games on the shore, and swam in the ocean. The president, his family, and his guests arrived at the hotel on July 27, stayed three weeks and five days, and checked out on August 22. The bill for room and board for the party of twelve totaled $267.75, to which the hotel's manager added $128.00 for dozens of bottles of champagne, red wine, port, brandy, gin, and 3 gallons of "old whiskey," plus bottles of olives.

While no charge was made for the company Jackson entertained during his visit, the presence of visitors might explain the large amount of wines and spirits that were consumed. Returning to Hampton Roads two years later, Jackson and his guests stayed at Fort Monroe for forty-one days at a cost of $576.87. That included a $150 charge "for company" and $40.50 for "wine etc."

With scheduled and regular steamboat traffic, communications with Washington were swift and easy. Jackson spent much time on official correspondence, taking care to have letters ready for the scheduled departures of the steamer *Potomac*. "Business and company follow me everywhere," he grumbled. During his four Hampton Roads vacations, Jackson dealt with a wide spectrum of issues. They ranged from concerns that the grocer supplying the White House might be padding the bill to the president's epic battle to destroy the power of the Bank of the United States and his struggle over South Carolina's proclaimed right to "nullify" federal law.

While the seaside vacations in Hampton Roads provided enjoyable respites, The Hermitage loomed far larger in Jackson's life. He had purchased the property in 1804, first calling it Rural Retreat, then The Hermitage. His much-loved wife, Rachel, died at The Hermitage in December 1828, just weeks after his election as president, and he spent the rest of his life in mourning. The 1,000-acre plantation, its workforce of more than one hundred slaves, and its cotton crop sustained Jackson's way of life. The historical memorabilia and curiosities that filled the house were testimony to Jackson's rise from rural poverty to military fame: the blue-and-yellow uniform he had worn at the Battle of New Orleans, gold medals, presentation swords, and a gallery of portraits of comrades and friends.

On later visits to Hampton Roads, Jackson stayed at the Hygeia Hotel at Old Point Comfort, built in 1822 just outside Fort Monroe and across the navigation channel from the Rip Raps. It was a vacation destination for prominent southerners in the summer and northerners in the winter. The hotel was demolished during the Civil War to make way for batteries, but after the war another grand hotel of the same name was built on the site and continued to serve an elite clientele.

The journey home took three weeks to a month. It generally left both the president and his horses exhausted and ill. Writing to Vice President Martin Van Buren in August 1834, Jackson reported he had reached The Hermitage "worn down with bad health, hot weather and intolerable roads," with the horses in such poor shape they were "scarcely able to get into Port." He had similar complaints two years later, saying it took him seven hours to travel 10 miles. He arrived on August 4, 1836, with a bad cough and a cold, twenty-six days after leaving Washington. Despite constantly replacing worn and broken horseshoes, he found his horses' hooves severely torn. "I am fearful that my fine lead horse may never get over his situation," he wrote. Jackson often made part of the trip by steamboat, but even that could be a misery. Returning to Washington in September 1836, Jackson wrote he had spent five days in suffocating heat in an overcrowded boat, sheltering from squalls and fending off mosquitoes. "You may conclude we are not enjoying much pleasure," he wrote, with considerable understatement. But as miserable as the river trip had been, he said, it was better than going by road.

Jackson's presidency coincided with the development of another innovation in transportation: the railroad. In June 1833, while on a trip to Philadelphia, he stepped from his horse-drawn carriage and into the steam cars of the new Baltimore and Ohio Railroad. The train whisked the presidential party along 12 miles of track and into Baltimore in just a few minutes, making Jackson the first railroading president. The Baltimore and Ohio expanded rapidly. Four years later, after watching Martin Van Buren sworn in as his successor, Jackson boarded the train at Washington to make the first leg of his journey home to Tennessee by rail.

By 1821 The Hermitage, as seen in this print by F. W. Stickland, was a two-story Federal-style mansion. When Jackson first bought the property in 1804, he and his wife lived in a log farmhouse on the site. After the mansion was completed, the log house became slave quarters.

On June 6, 1833, President Jackson became the first president to ride in a train when he took a 12-mile pleasure journey from Ellicott Mills to Baltimore on track laid by the Baltimore and Ohio Railroad Company. The steam locomotive pictured here, nicknamed "The Grasshopper" for its design, was used on the Washington and Baltimore Railway, c. 1835–38.

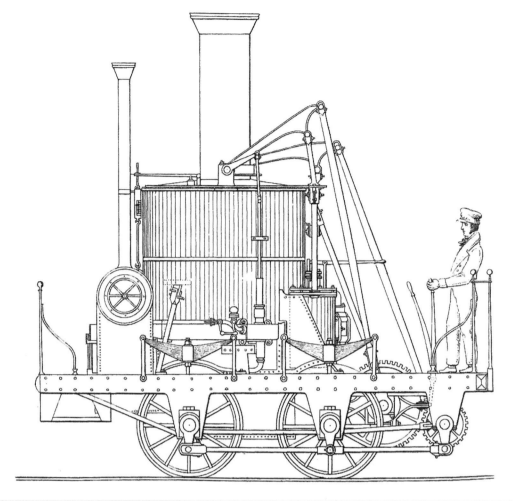

After Jackson's beloved wife Rachel died in December 1828, he ordered a "temple & monument" erected for her in the garden at The Hermitage. Built of local limestone, it is Greek Revival in style and covered with a copper roof. On June 10, 1845, two days after his own death at The Hermitage, the former president was laid to rest beside her. As seen in this 1907 photograph, President Theodore Roosevelt visited the tomb of the former president.

In 1831, the third year of his presidency, Jackson hired a Nashville architect and significantly enlarged his two-story Federal-style house. He added one-story wings, and a two-story entrance portico with simple Doric columns. In the garden he built a graceful tomb with limestone columns and a domed copper roof as a resting place for his wife and himself. But in October 1834, shortly after he had returned from Tennessee, word reached the White House that a chimney fire at The Hermitage had spread to the shingle roof. Except for the dining room, the mansion burned to the walls.

Jackson was determined to rebuild. By the time his carriage rolled into the drive in August 1836, his last visit home as president, The Hermitage had a new facade, two-story front and rear porticoes, Corinthian columns, verandas, welcoming entrance hall, spiral staircase, and new curtains, carpets, and furniture. As always, Jackson was concerned not just with the house but the land, the crops and the livestock. "We must plow better and cultivate less, and we will produce more," he told young Andrew, his nephew and adopted son.

The Hermitage remained in the Jackson family until 1887. When the state of Tennessee proposed turning it into a home for Confederate veterans, prominent women of Nashville —some of them Jackson family descendants—quickly organized the Ladies' Hermitage Association to preserve the property as a memorial to the famous president. They opened The Hermitage to the public In 1889 and began a long series of repairs and restoration efforts. Today the association manages the entire 1,050-acre cotton plantation that Jackson owned when he died.

Chapter 8

Martin Van Buren: Summers at Woodley

MARTIN VAN BUREN
Eighth President of the
United States, 1837–1841

Although he would eventually be accused of living in imperial splendor in the White House, when summer came Martin Van Buren, the nation's eighth president, closed down the Executive Mansion, had the carpets rolled and the furniture draped, and moved across town to a rented house called Woodley.

Even though it was inside the District of Columbia, Woodley in the 1830s was a country mansion. A few miles north of the White House, it was located on higher ground and therefore more apt to catch a cooling summer breeze. The house had been built about 1801 by Judge Philip Barton Key, an attorney and member of Congress from Maryland. His nephew, Francis Scott Key, knew the house well in the years before he witnessed the British bombardment of Fort McHenry in Baltimore Harbor and wrote "The Star-Spangled Banner," the poem that would become the lyrics for the national anthem. Built in the Georgian style, Woodley had Classical Revival porticoes to the front and rear of a three-story central core and fanlights over its doors.

The work of the presidency followed Van Buren to Woodley, and at times the president convened meetings at his summer house. Two of his four sons, Abraham and Martin, acted as aides, keeping track of reports, correspondence, state papers, and books. The president mounted a horse every morning, rode into his office at the White House, and returned to Woodley at the end of the working day. Van Buren paid the costs of his summer rental out of his private funds and probably saved money because the smaller house cost less to maintain and staff and there was little pressure to entertain during the summer months.

The Original Woodley Mansion,
c. 1840s. A Federal-style
mansion, Woodley was
constructed in 1801 by Philip
Barton Key. A few miles north
of the White House, the
mansion served as a Summer
White House for President
Martin Van Buren as well as
for later presidents.

Martin Van Buren,
photograph by Mathew Brady,
c. 1860 (*opposite*).

Woodley stands today on Cathedral Avenue in the Northwest neighborhood known as Woodley Park. It is now the Maret School, a private day school founded in 1911.

A BEAUTIFUL GOBLET OF
WHITE·HOUSE CHAMPAGNE

AN UGLY MUG OF
LOG·CABIN HARD CIDER

During the mud-slinging presidential campaign of 1840, Representative Charles Ogle of Pennsylvania accused President Van Buren of living in luxury in the White House while most Americans struggled through an economic depression. The images at left, from the campaign of Van Buren's opponent, William Henry Harrison, play on this accusation. The first shows Van Buren happily drinking champagne; pull the tab and the champagne turns to hard cider, a beverage indelibly linked to Harrison who, somewhat improbably, became known as the "log cabin and hard cider" candidate.

Of Dutch descent, a widower, and the first president to have been born an American citizen, Van Buren was sociable, red haired, and a professional politician. He had helped engineer Andrew Jackson's election as president and served him so skillfully as secretary of state and vice president that he was dubbed "The Little Magician" and "The Red Fox of Kinderhook," his birthplace in upstate New York. His own administration opened in 1837 with a severe financial panic. And in 1840 Van Buren, hoping for a second term, suffered through an extravagant three-day attack on the floor of the House by Representative Charles Ogle, a Whig from Pennsylvania and a fervent supporter of Van Buren's rival, William Henry Harrison. In what came to be called "The Gold Spoon Oration," Ogle magnified a story about the use of gold or gilt spoons at a White House dinner to portray the president as wallowing in unspeakable luxury at the expense of taxpayers. Under Van Buren, said Ogle, the White House had become "*a PALACE as splendid of that of the Caesars, and as richly adorned as the proudest Asiatic mansion.*" Unfair as it might have been, the speech and other circumstances left van Buren with little realistic chance of winning a second term or having a need to renew his lease on Woodley.

President Van Buren lost his bid for a second term of office to William Henry Harrison, who succumbed to pneumonia after just a month in office.

Chapter 9

John Tyler: Honeymoon Cottage

JOHN TYLER
Tenth President of the
United States, 1841–1845

O n a crisp and bright afternoon in late February 1844, the steam frigate *Princeton*, flags flying and decks crowded with the elite of capital society, headed back up the Potomac after a cruise past Mount Vernon. Among those enjoying the festive occasion were President John Tyler, cabinet secretaries, diplomats, former First Lady Dolley Madison, and members of the Gardiner family of New York. An elegant lunch of roast fowl and hams was over, and champagne flowed in the main cabin. There were bursts of laughter and snatches of song. Raising his glass, President John Tyler offered toasts to the navy while keeping an appreciative eye on one of his guests. She was Julia Gardiner, a beautiful 24-year-old New Yorker known to some as "The Belle of Long Island." Many aboard the *Princeton* had heard rumors that the dazzled president, a recent widower, had proposed marriage, despite their thirty-year age difference. Although the word was that Miss Gardiner had declined, she appeared to enjoy the president's attention and had plainly not returned to her home in New York.

The highlight of the brief cruise had been the test firing of a powerful new naval cannon called the Peace-Maker. Twice passengers had held their ears against the report and cheered as

President John Tyler, portrait by George P. A. Healy 1859 (*opposite*).

The USS *Princeton* played a pivotal role in the private life of President Tyler, as an accident onboard brought him together with his future young wife. The steam frigate, designed by the Swedish naval architect John Ericsson, was the first to be driven by an underwater screw propeller, making it less vulnerable to hostile fire than side wheels. On deck was a 27,000-pound cannon, named the Peace-Maker, capable of hurling a 225-pound iron shot 5 miles.

The cruise of the *Princeton* was intended to be festive, but the third test firing of the new naval cannon resulted in disaster. The heavy wrought-iron breech, unable to withstand the force of the charge, broke in two, sending deadly shrapnel among those on deck. This lithograph print depicting the disaster was published by Currier & Ives.

the heavy iron balls skipped down the river. Now Navy Secretary Thomas W. Gilmer ordered the *Princeton*'s officers to make ready for one last shot. The president lingered below, listening to a sea chantey. David Gardiner, a wealthy New Yorker who had brought his daughter Julia and other family members to Washington for the winter season, climbed to the main deck and joined a cluster of government officials and navy officers near the 15-foot barrel of the wrought-iron gun.

In his own words, John Tyler's presidency had been "tempest-tossed" from its first moments. When President William Henry Harrison died of pneumonia on April 4, 1841, exactly a month after his inauguration, Vice President Tyler, an aristocratic, slaveholding Virginia planter, swiftly established his right to succeed Harrison as the nation's tenth president. Although no previous chief executive had died in office, Tyler stared down those who claimed he was no more than acting president and dismissed him as "His Accidency." He quickly moved into the White House and steered such an independent course that the Whig Party eventually expelled him. By the time of the cruise of the *Princeton*, he was engaged in contentious negotiations aimed at the annexation of the Republic of Texas as a slave state, a condition fervently opposed by abolitionists.

On the *Princeton*'s deck, William Wilkins, a member of Tyler's cabinet, walked away from the knot of passengers gathered to observe the Peace-Maker's firing. "Though I am Secretary of War, I am afraid of these big guns," Wilkins remarked. Then a sailor pulled a lanyard. A deafening explosion shattered the Peace-Maker's breech. Jagged iron shards cut through the

The bell cast especially for the USS *Princeton* survived the explosion. It is pictured here in 2014 on the campus of Princeton University, where a commemorative plaque describes the disaster and the lost lives.

spectators, killing eight and wounding seventeen. The dead included Secretary of State Abel P. Upshur, Navy Secretary Gilmer, a commodore, a U.S. diplomat, two seamen, the president's slave and valet, and David Gardiner, Julia's father. It was one of the worst peacetime disasters in the history of the republic.

Julia Gardiner collapsed when told her father had been killed, and the president carried her across a gangway to another ship. "I fainted and did not revive until someone was carrying me off the boat, and I struggled so that I almost knocked us both off the gangplank," she told a journalist almost forty years later. "I did not know at the time . . . that it was the President whose life I almost consigned to the water." Tyler returned to the *Princeton* and remained there until the last bodies were removed. Miss Gardiner and her sister, Margaret, another *Princeton* passenger, were driven to the White House, where they spent the night.

"After I lost my father I felt differently toward the president," she recalled. "He seemed to fill the place and to be more agreeable in every way than any younger man ever was or could be." This time when the president proposed, she did not refuse. But no announcement was made, and great secrecy was maintained. On June 26, 1844, just four months after the explosion, the two were married at an Episcopal Church on Fifth Avenue in New York City. The groom was 54, three decades older than his bride. Following a light wedding breakfast the party boarded a ferry for an hour or two in New York Harbor. By then the need for secrecy was over, and they were greeted by local politicians, serenaded by a band, and received cannon salutes from forts and warships. One of the ships was the USS *Princeton*. The Tylers spent

Young Julia Gardiner had been carried away from the *Princeton* disaster by President Tyler, and four months later they were married. As first lady she was vivacious, hosting luncheons, suppers, and parties at the White House, where admiring crowds praised her beauty. Her portrait by Francesco Anelli hangs in the White House today.

their wedding night in Philadelphia and stopped briefly in Baltimore before pushing on to Washington. Julia happily reported on their progress in a letter to her mother: "Wherever we stopped, wherever we went, crowds of people outstripping one another, came to gaze at the President's bride. *The secrecy of the affair* is on the tongue and admiration of everyone. Everyone says it was the best managed *thing* they ever heard of."

Two days after the ceremony the new couple held a wedding reception in the Blue Room of the White House. The new secretary of state, John C. Calhoun of South Carolina, helped the bride cut the wedding cake. "I have commenced my auspicious reign and am in quiet possession of the Presidential Mansion," she wrote.

Then Julia and John Tyler left for a month-long honeymoon in a four-room, one-story cottage at Fort Monroe on Old Point Comfort in Virginia, not far from Andrew Jackson's Rip Raps. Their accommodations on a military base offered privacy as well as comfort and also set a precedent. It was the first time a president had used government property as a private retreat. Many other presidential couples would follow the Tylers' example.

"True love in a cottage," Julia Gardiner Tyler called her honeymoon. "It seemed quite as if I had stepped into paradise." Clearly the circumstances and the surroundings exceeded her

Newlyweds John and Julia Tyler spent their honeymoon in a cottage on the grounds of Fort Monroe, near where President Andrew Jackson had also enjoyed the sea air and saltwater of Hampton Roads.

expectations. The president had made the arrangements for the cottage with the fort's commanding officer, Colonel Gustavus A. De Russey, who selected and purchased the furniture in nearby Norfolk. "His taste and I believe his own hand arranged our sleeping apartment," the new bride wrote, describing the bedroom in an enthusiastic letter to her mother: "A richly covered high post bedstead with white lace curtains looped up with blue ribbon and the cover at the top of the bedstead lined also with blue—new matting which emitted its sweet fragrance—two handsome mahogany dressing tables, writing table, and sofa, the room was papered to match and the whole establishment brand new." The fort's officers offered a round of ceremonies and social activities including a review of troops, dinner aboard a revenue cutter, and a tour of the USS *Pennsylvania,* the largest warship ever built in the United States.

In 1842, the year Tyler's first wife, Letitia, died, the president had purchased a 1,600-acre estate on Virginia's James River. By then Tyler's alienation from the Whig Party was so intense that he named his new plantation Sherwood Forest as a wry comment on his outlawed political status. He had already begun to expand the existing house when he married Julia Gardiner. Just one-room deep but stretching more than 300 feet, the

DRAWING ROOM POLKAS.
arranged for the
Piano Forte,
BOSTON.
Published by OLIVER DITSON, 135 Washington St.

Julia Tyler is credited with introducing the polka to the White House. Originating in Eastern Europe, it had been the rage in Paris but, like the waltz before it, was at first considered indecent in elegant circles. Word of Mrs. Tyler's risqué dancing spread quickly in Washington and inspired "The Julia Waltzes," a polka composed and named for her.

Among Tyler's additions to Sherwood Forest was a 68-foot ballroom that he designed, perhaps to please his young second wife, Julia, who loved to host dances at the White House.

In 1842, the year of his first wife's death, Tyler purchased the James River plantation he named Sherwood Forest. The main house had been expanded over the years, as dependencies were added and connected. Today, at 300 feet long, it claims to be the longest frame residence in America. The Tylers retired to Sherwood Forest after the presidency, where they had seven children (adding to the eight children Tyler had with his first wife). The home remains in family hands today. House tours are available by appointment, and a self-guiding walking tour of the grounds offers information about President Tyler's home and life on a nineteenth-century plantation.

completed house would be 132 feet longer than the White House. Additions included an office for the president and a 68-foot ballroom for dancing the Virginia reel.

Tyler brought his bride up the James River from Fort Monroe for a five-day visit to Sherwood Forest and introduced her to his sixty or so slaves. Readily assuming command of her new domain, she mentally selected furniture, shrubs, and trees while inspecting the house and gardens. Carpenters were told "where to make this change and where this addition." Not hesitating to take credit, she wrote that the head carpenter "was amazed at my science and the President acknowledged I understood more about carpentry and architecture than he did, and he would leave all the arrangements that were to be made entirely to my taste." Then she decided to turn a grove of trees into a 25-acre park stocked with deer.

The Tylers returned to the honeymoon cottage but were back in Washington in early August. With her husband's term rapidly coming to an end, Julia Tyler proceeded to write a lively chapter in the social history of the White House. Over the next eight months she offered a long-remembered whirl of activities including morning cruises on the Potomac, luncheons and elegant suppers, State Dinners, and carriage rides into Virginia and Maryland. She enlivened the East Room with waltzes, introduced the polka—Europe's newest dance rage—and lobbied on behalf of the issue her husband believed would inscribe his name in

history: the annexation of Texas. It was accomplished by majority votes for House and Senate resolutions making Texas, formerly part of Mexico, the twenty-eighth state.

A thousand candles lit the East Room at the Tylers' final ball in February 1845. The Marine Band played, wine and champagne flowed freely, and an estimated three thousand people tried to squeeze into the White House. A guest congratulated the president on a happy and entirely successful event. "Yes," he replied, venturing a pun, "they cannot say *now* that I am a President *without a party*."

Chapter 10

James K. Polk: The Spa at Bedford Springs

JAMES K. POLK
Eleventh President of the
United States, 1845–1849

Rising early, the president walked to the springs and sipped a glass or two of the mineral water that made Pennsylvania's Bedford Springs a much-visited and famous health resort. Then, just as the morning fog began to lift, he climbed the serpentine path to the top of the nearby hill and took in the view over the narrow valley. Walking back to the hotel, he had another glass or two of water and then went into the hotel for breakfast.

It was Sunday morning, August 20, 1848. Congress had adjourned a week earlier, and President James Knox Polk, the nation's eleventh president, had felt in urgent need of a rest. He noted in his diary that he had not been more than 3 miles from the White House since returning to the capital from his tour of New England. "And during that whole period (thirteen months) my labours, responsibilities and anxieties have been very great," he added. "I informed the Cabinet that I was so much fatigued and worn down that I proposed to leave on Friday next on a visit to the Bedford Springs for the benefit of my health."

Polk's visit to fashionable Bedford Springs represented a change in the vacation habits of presidents and well-to-do Americans in general. In earlier times many chief executives had simply gone home when they felt the need, sometimes remaining for months at a time. The increased business of government made long absences impractical. That was certainly true for presidents from distant states. Polk, whose home was in Nashville, Tennessee, did not return home at all during his term in office.

In October 1887 former First Lady Sarah Polk greeted President and Mrs. Grover Cleveland at Polk Place (*opposite*), the Nashville home where President James K. Polk's hopes for a long retirement were cut short in 1849, when he died just three months after leaving office. Mrs. Polk lived on at Polk Place for more than forty years, until her death in 1891. In 1901 the mansion, much deteriorated, was torn down.

The Bedford Springs Hotel, 1843 (left). The resort was frequented by political elites, including not only President Polk but, at various times, Andrew Jackson, William Henry Harrison, Zachary Taylor, and James Buchanan.

The resort at White Sulphur Springs, Virginia, depicted here in 1857, could be reached by canal in the 1820s, and after the Civil War, by rail. It offered extended stays in cottages and a large hotel, where guests could enjoy the healthful benefits of mineral waters and fresh mountain air. Among the influential political leaders of President Polk's era who visited in summer were Henry Clay, Martin Van Buren, and John Tyler. In the twentieth century, with the construction of a grand hotel and golf course, the resort became known as the Greenbrier, and the location is now in West Virginia.

At the same time, steamboats, turnpikes, and a growing railroad network had expanded leisure-time options for the well-to-do by making travel faster, more reliable, and more comfortable than before. Many Americans began visiting natural springs and seaside and mountain resorts, asserting they were traveling for their health. Boosters for such watering places as Bedford Springs in Pennsylvania and White Sulphur Springs and Berkeley Springs in western Virginia claimed their mineral waters cured an astonishingly wide range of illnesses. Seaside resorts in Long Branch and Cape May in southern New Jersey made similar pitches for ocean breezes and sea bathing. Bracing mountain air attracted vacationers to resorts in the Catskills and elsewhere. Newport, Rhode Island, had attracted a fashionable summer crowd since the eighteenth century and remained popular for yachting and ocean bathing. Elegant Saratoga Springs in upstate New York had its adherents. Apart from the benefits of clean air and natural springs, these and other resorts offered refuge from the cholera and yellow fever epidemics that often swept through crowded cities. But health resorts also became choice destinations for those wanting to see and be seen. The socially secure and the socially ambitious mixed and mingled on the shady verandas of the great resort hotels. Their numbers included wealthy easterners, southern plantation owners, New York businessmen, clergymen, as well as physicians and Washington politicians, including presidents and their families.

By the summer of 1848, Polk had achieved the ambitious goals he had outlined for himself when he took office four years earlier. He had confronted Great Britain and successfully negotiated a claim to all territory in the Pacific Northwest south of the 49th parallel. That gave the United States the future states of Oregon and Washington and the strategically important harbor at Seattle. Determined to make the United States a continental nation, Polk prosecuted a war against Mexico that resulted in the acquisition of more than 500,000 square miles of new territory, including the future states of California, Arizona, New Mexico, Nevada, Utah, Colorado, and Wyoming. Polk had achieved his ends with an extreme attention to detail, long hours, and incessant work. "In truth, though I occupy a very high position, I am the hardest working man in this country," he told his diary on one occasion. "With me it is emphatically true that the presidency is 'no bed of roses'," he said on another. He worried that entrusting even the smallest matters to subordinates would result in endless errors. "No president who performs his duty faithfully and conscientiously can have any leisure," Polk concluded.

On a typical day Polk rose at daylight and took a short walk before breakfast. He then worked at his desk until dinner was served at 5:00 p.m. After another walk he often worked late into the night. On rare occasions he broke his routine with a picnic at Mount Vernon, a visit to the Navy Yard, a carriage or horseback ride, or a brief Potomac excursion. Unlike his predecessors, he did not vacate Washington in summer, and in his four years as president he traveled outside Washington only four times.

In August 1846, with work on the Oregon settlement completed but with war with Mexico under way, Polk followed President Taylor's example and took a brief rest with his wife and friends at Fort Monroe, where he enjoyed the tangy ocean breeze, explored sand dunes, examined fortifications, and endured a day of ceremonies at nearby Norfolk on "one of the hottest days I ever felt." When he returned to Washington he learned that U.S. forces had moved by land and sea to raise the American flag over California, New Mexico, and the lower Rio Grande.

In late May and early June of the next year Polk took a nine-day sentimental vacation, traveling by rail and road to his alma mater, the University of North Carolina at Chapel Hill. He visited his student room, explored the campus, stayed up late to reminisce with college friends, and attended commencement ceremonies. "Many objects were perfectly familiar to me, and brought up fresh to recollection many of the scenes of my youth," he wrote.

A little more than two weeks later he was on the move again, this time on a tour of the northeastern United States in an attempt to boost his standing in a region that had been the most resistant to the war with Mexico and the most adamantly opposed to the extension of slavery into new territory. He was away for sixteen days and ventured as far north as Portland, Maine, making him the first president to visit after Maine became a state.

At the president's request, John Appleton, the Navy Department's chief clerk, kept a detailed log of Polk's nine-state travels, noting with interest that word of the president's arrivals and departures now reached the country by "the lightning line," the telegraph wires that followed the railroad right-of-way. Samuel F. B. Morse's electric magnetic telegraph had received its first practical demonstration just three years earlier. Now the telegraph kept track of the movements of presidents and relayed battlefield bulletins with unprecedented speed.

Polk traveled mostly by rail and steamboat and leavened a constant diet of ceremonial speeches with tourist sightseeing. At the U.S, Mint in Philadelphia he saw molten gold and silver turned into hard-edged coins. In New York City the president visited a school for the blind and received an extravagant poetical tribute from a student that concluded:

Hark, one united burst of Joy,

By heart and tongue is woke;

One chorus rends the list'ning air,

Hurrah, for James K. Polk!

On the few occasions he did travel away from the White House, President Polk often paid official visits. In 1847 he embarked on a sixteen-day tour, stopping at the U.S. Mint in Philadelphia before heading north, eventually to Maine. In all, he visited nine states.

Just before the end of his presidency, James K. Polk sold this home in Columbia, Tennessee, which his father had built in 1816. It Is the only surviving Polk residence, and today it is open to the public as the James K. Polk Home and Museum.

The dry, stiff, and formal Polk was not always greeted with such enthusiasm and almost certainly enjoyed the flags, banners, cheers, waving handkerchiefs, and the bouquets of flowers tossed at his carriage. Appleton summed up: "We enjoyed facilities for travel, which almost made distance vanish into nothing, and we saw exhibitions of wealth, of enterprise and of culture, which in so new a country seemed little short of marvellous."

As Polk noted in his diary, he did not travel again until the late summer of 1848. His trip to Bedford Springs may have been urged on him by James Buchanan, then Polk's secretary of state and later president. Buchanan, whose home was at Lancaster, Pennsylvania, had been taking the waters at Bedford Springs every summer since 1816.

There were about fifty other guests at the large resort hotel when Polk arrived, and he knew several of them: the editor of a Democratic newspaper, a member of Congress, the colonel who had commanded U.S. volunteers in Mexico. He found the hotel to be pleasantly accommodating, the walks and grounds well-ordered and shaded, and the atmosphere refreshing after a summer in the low-lying and soggy capital.

The spring waters were the resort's reason for existence, and Polk's diary gave them due attention. The resort's boosters credited the waters, used both internally and externally, as being good for the stomach, the intestines, and the skin; for rheumatism and gout; and for curing "derangements of the liver." They were also said to counteract the bad effects of unwise eating or drinking. Polk wrote that the spring with the greatest medicinal value was a bold, strong fountain rising from one of the two mountains that framed the narrow valley. This spring, he reported, contained both magnesia and iron and was said to benefit the kidneys and bowels.

After a day or two of cool weather, Polk welcomed the fires that were built to warm his room. "It is almost too late in the season to visit this watering place," he wrote. "In the hot weather it must be a delightful spot." After breakfast on Friday morning, August 25, he paid his bill and boarded a coach for the first leg of his trip back to Washington. The hotel ledger recorded a charge of $9 for the president's six-day stay plus $4 for a servant and 13 cents for postage.

Polk's term was nearly over. He had vowed he would not seek reelection despite his success in waging war against Mexico and the realization of his vow to make the United States a two-ocean nation. On March 4, 1849, Polk saw General Zachary Taylor, a hero of that war but a member of the opposition Whig Party, sworn in as the twelfth president. In his diary, Polk dismissed his successor as a "well-meaning old man" who is "exceedingly ignorant of public affairs." Then he and Mrs. Polk set out for home by way of a month-long tour of the South, traveling by water and rail. At New Orleans, Polk became seriously ill. He still felt shaken when his steamboat arrived at the dock at Nashville. On June 15, less than four months after leaving the presidency, James Polk died. He was only 53.

Zachary Taylor, Polk's successor and the twelfth president, lived only a year longer. He fell ill after Independence Day celebrations and died on July 9, 1850.

Zachary Taylor, Polk's successor and the twelfth president of the United States, fell ill after Independence Day celebrations in Washington and died on July 9, 1850, in his second year in office. He was succeeded by Vice President Millard Fillmore of New York. In 1852, Fillmore was not renominated by his party, and in November, Franklin Pierce of New Hampshire won the presidency, serving until his term ended in 1857.

Chapter 11

James Buchanan: Bedford Spa, Once More

JAMES BUCHANAN
Fifteenth President of the
United States, 1857–1861

Of the next four presidents, James Buchanan, the last before the Civil War, had the most constant vacation habits. He paid brief visits to Wheatland, his estate at Lancaster, Pennsylvania. He established a summer residence at the Soldiers' Home in hills overlooking Washington. And he spent two weeks in July or August taking the waters at Bedford Springs. Buchanan had visited the health resort nearly every summer since 1816, when he was 25, except for those years when he served as envoy to Great Britain. He saw no reason to change his destination when he became president. Summer after summer he checked into the Springs Hotel, walked the paths up Federal Hill and Constitution Hill, and strolled along the resort's man-made lake. He drank his first glass of mineral water early in the morning and counted up to twenty glasses a day, often augmenting their hoped-for benefits with a soak in the thermal waters. On long afternoons the president joined other guests on the hotel's broad veranda, where they reclined in rocking chairs or strolled from group to group, sharing political news or gossip. In the evenings, many guests moved to the hotel ballroom, where an orchestra played the polka, the schottische, and other lively dance music.

James Buchanan with his books (*opposite*) at Wheatland, his home in Lancaster, Pennsylvania, following his presidency. Photograph by Mathew Brady, c. 1860–65.

Mountain View Near Bedford, Pennsylvania by Augustus Kollner, 1840. James Buchanan visited Bedford Springs almost every summer of his adult life. The resort was proud of its association with the noted congressman, senator, diplomat, secretary of state, and president, and made special arrangements to accommodate him. Bedford Springs remained a resort destination for more than a century and a half, long after mineral water cures passed from favor.

Near Bedford, P.

In 1986, two years after being designated a National Historic Landmark, the Bedford Springs resort closed. In 2007, the hotel was restored and reopened. The connection with Buchanan continues as a matter of pride, and his work desk is displayed in the hotel lobby.

During Buchanan's term of office his niece, Harriet Lane, served as White House hostess. Buchanan, a lifelong bachelor, had been her guardian since she was orphaned at age 11, and he was her favorite uncle. A popular hostess, Harriet Lane was vivacious and gracious, helping to dispel the tensions in the capital city through carefully planned social occasions as the nation careened toward disunion.

When Buchanan arrived at the springs in July 1857, he discovered that the hotel managers had redecorated his customary room to make it worthy of his new position. But he was irritated to find that the mahogany rolltop desk he had become used to over the years had disappeared. Not only did he use it to write on, but its large drawers were just the right size for his clean shirts. The desk was quickly brought out of storage and restored to its place.

A lifelong bachelor, Buchanan was accompanied to Bedford Springs that summer by his niece, Harriet Lane, who served as his official White House hostess. When he returned to Washington in mid-August the *Bedford Gazette*, the local newspaper, took notice: "His health was much improved during his stay at the Springs, his old favorite summer retreat. May he live, often to return to our delightful spa, and to take by the hand his numerous friends in Bedford County who are always glad to meet him and who testified by their votes last fall, that the acts of his life meet their hearty approval." Such accolades would be rare during Buchanan's White House years, which were increasingly dominated by North-South tensions over slavery.

There was comic relief amid the serious preoccupations at Bedford Springs that summer. When the president accepted an invitation from a colonel's wife for a ride in her carriage, a correspondent for the *Baltimore Sun* wrote this account: "Dashing through Bedford Town at a spanking pace, the horses flecked with foam, the lady glowing with excitement, and the President known to everybody, very serious alarm seized the public mind that some aspiring dame had caught up the Chief Magistrate and was eloping with him. As it was observed, however, that the President . . . seemed resigned to the consequences, whether it was a broken neck or matrimony, nobody interfered." Eventually, the newspaper continued, the wild ride concluded and Buchanan was returned "safe and sound."

Buchanan's next vacation at Bedford Springs was remembered for an exchange of telegraph

Visit of the Prince of Wales, President Buchanan, and Dignitaries to the Tomb of Washington at Mount Vernon, October 1860, by Thomas P. Rossiter (1861). A visit to Washington's tomb was a prerequisite for sitting presidents and visiting dignitaries. When the 18-year-old Prince of Wales paid an official visit to the United States in 1860, President Buchanan took him to Mount Vernon. In this oil painting, the president stands behind the young prince, the great-grandson of King George III, and Harriet Lane stands nearby, under a parasol.

messages that was extraordinary not for what they said but for the technological achievement they represented. Final work had been completed on a trans-Atlantic cable linking Europe and North America. J. Buchanan Henry, the president's nephew and secretary, called the cable "the wonderful wire under the sea." On August 17, 1858, a copy of the first message to cross the ocean reached Bedford Springs and was handed to the president:

> London, England. Come let us talk together. American genius and English enterprise have this day joined together the OLD and the NEW worlds. Let us hope that they may be as closely allied in bonds of peace, harmony and kindred feeling. Victoria, R.

Buchanan's reply to Queen Victoria made use of a passage from the Bible:

> Bedford Springs. NEW England accepts with gladness the hand of fellowship proffered by OLD England and if ever discord or diversity of interest should threaten this alliance let our language be "entreat me not to leave thee or return from following after thee for the interests of thy people shall be the interests of my people and thy God shall be my God." James Buchanan, President, U.S.A.

Political and sectional tension was increasing in Washington and the country in July 1859 when Buchanan again traveled to Bedford Springs. Visiting at the same time was a friend, a wealthy Virginia widow accompanied by her three children and a young slave, her personal maid. Abolitionists persuaded the maid to flee and gave her travel money. Some said the incident was an attempt to embarrass the president.

Buchanan had already served notice that he would not seek a second term. But on July 19 the *Pittsburgh Post* ran an editorial endorsing a Buchanan candidacy and implying that he was

In 1858 Queen Victoria (*right*) exchanged
telegrams with President Buchanan while
he was staying at the Bedford Springs
Hotel. They were the first messages sent by
the just-completed Atlantic cable, which
reduced the time of sending a message
across the ocean from ten days or more to
minutes. Presidents could now stay in touch
with overseas developments, even while on
vacation. The 1858 cable quickly deteriorated,
however, and a second one, completed in
1866, is commemorated in this lithograph
by Kimmel & Foster (*below*). The Atlantic
Cable was referred to as the "Eighth Wonder
of the World" in this allegorical scene where
Neptune is portrayed with his trident in the
foreground. A lion representing Great Britain
holds one end of the Atlantic cable and an
eagle representing the United States holds the
other, with the Atlantic between them and
cities behind them. Cyrus Field the American
businessman who created the cable, is pictured
at top center.

THE EIGHTH WONDER OF THE WORLD.

THE ATLANTIC CABLE.

not as reluctant as he pretended. After midnight on July 20, the president summoned the editor of the *Bedford Gazette* to his room at the Springs Hotel and handed him a written response declaring he would refuse nomination. He asked that it be printed and that copies be sent to other newspapers. Buchanan also wrote to friends expressing his "final and irrevocable" determination to leave office.

That determination had been accepted as a fact by August 1860, when local residents gathered for a surprise party to celebrate Buchanan's arrival at the springs for his last visit as president. Because Buchanan had not been told of the event, he did not come when expected. The disappointed crowd dispersed after a four-hour wait. The president showed up the next day and went straight to bed without celebrations of any kind.

At the end of his term President Buchanan retired to Wheatland, a Federal-style house in Lancaster, Pennsylvania, which he had purchased in 1848. It was in Lancaster that he began his legal practice, and he considered it his home. He died here in 1868. In 1936, the Junior League of Lancaster purchased the property and began to preserve it. Today it is a National Historic Site and open to the public.

Chapter 12

Abraham Lincoln: The Soldiers' Home

In this undated sketch by a French amateur artist, President Abraham Lincoln, dressed for warm weather in a white jacket and straw hat, sits on the lawn of the Soldiers' Home (*opposite*), the military facility north of the White House where he spent summers.

In the last three summers of his presidency, Abraham Lincoln commuted to his White House office from a tree-shaded cottage at the Soldiers' Home, a government institution in the rolling countryside roughly 3 miles northeast of the White House. Situated on a hill with an unmatched panoramic view of the capital, the Soldiers' Home was high enough to catch a breeze and generally a bit cooler and considerably healthier than the overheated and fever-prone city. Lincoln traveled the dusty roads to the White House on horseback or by carriage each workday morning, returning to his rural retreat in the late afternoon. In its park-like setting, the cottage offered more serenity than the bustling Executive Mansion, and both the president and First Lady Mary Todd Lincoln grew fond of it.

Lincoln's morning ride took about 30 minutes, and he got an early start. An army officer remembered finding the president up, dressed, and reading when he entered the cottage at about 6:30 a.m. John Hay, Lincoln's young secretary, recalled that "he would be up and dressed, eat his breakfast . . . and ride into Washington, all before 8 o'clock." The president spent the day at his desk and generally rode back to his country retreat after 4:00 p.m., although he might spend the night at the White House if faced with rapidly developing events. During most of the first year the president often rode unescorted and unguarded, or sometimes in

This view of the Soldiers' Home complex by Charles Magnus, c. 1863, shows the cottage that the Lincoln family occupied in the center. It had been built in 1842 by the Washington banker George W. Riggs. In 1851, Riggs sold the cottage and his 250-acre summer retreat to the U.S. government, which added to the acreage and established a home for retired and disabled veterans there. The soldiers lived in the large stone structure to the right of the cottage. While president, James Buchanan retreated to the home for a few weeks during at least two summers.

On his daily morning ride from the Soldiers' Home to the White House, President Lincoln and his mounted guard traveled through sparsely settled rural areas along the Seventh Street Turnpike (now Georgia Avenue). Today this statue on the grounds commemorates Lincoln's association with the facility.

an open carriage, with his son, Tad, trotting alongside on his pony. But as the war intensified and threats to Lincoln's safety became a daily reality, a cavalry unit escorted the president on the road and an infantry company stood guard at the Soldiers' Home itself. On August 12, 1863, the poet Walt Whitman, who spent much of the war years caring for wounded soldiers in the city's many military hospitals, observed the morning cavalcade and made an entry in his journal:

> I see the President almost every day, as I happen to live where he passes to or from his lodgings out of town. He never sleeps at the White House during the hot season, but has quarters at a healthy location, some three miles north of the city, the Soldiers' Home, a United States military establishment. I saw him this morning about 8½ coming in to business. . . . He always has a company of twenty-five or thirty cavalry, with sabres drawn, and held upright over their shoulders. The party makes no great show in uniforms or horses. Mr. Lincoln, on the saddle, generally rides a good-sized easy-going gray horse, is dress'd in plain black, somewhat rusty and dusty; wears a black stiff hat, and looks about as ordinary in attire, &c. as the commonest man.

Whitman heard the clang and clatter of sabers and reins, the officer riding at Lincoln's left and the troopers following two-by-two, and called it an "entirely unornamental *cortège*." From the street, he observed the lines that marked the president's face and was struck by the "deep latent sadness in the expression."

———

Acting on what appears to have been the advice of outgoing President James Buchanan, the Lincolns drove out separately to inspect the Soldiers' Home just days after Lincoln's inauguration on March 4, 1861. But the surge of events proved too strong that year to permit the president even the shortest of summer respites: the South seceded and formed the Confederate States of America, Fort Sumter surrendered, the Civil War broke out, and a Confederate army routed federal troops at the Battle of Bull Run. In the three summers that followed, the Lincolns closed the family quarters in the White House in June or early July and moved out to the Soldiers' Home with a cook, a housekeeper, a valet, and as many as nineteen wagons filled with furniture and supplies. They often remained until the weather turned cool in early November. Lincoln was at home there for 5 months in 1862, 4½ months in 1863, and 3½ months in 1864. In all, the Soldiers' Home served as Lincoln's retreat for 13 months, a quarter of his presidency.

Built of stucco-covered brick, the two-story Gothic Revival cottage had high-pitched gabled roofs and fourteen large, bright, and airy rooms. The thick brick walls helped keep the interior cool in the summer, while seven fireplaces with handsome marble mantels provided welcome heat when temperatures fell in the fall. A portable gas-generating system supplied lighting for all the buildings at the Soldiers' Home, including the Lincoln Cottage.

The cottage offered more privacy than was available at the White House, where seekers of government jobs and presidential favors besieged Lincoln's Second Floor office and total strangers wandered freely through the public rooms, tried out the furniture, or snipped a piece of drapery as a souvenir. At the Soldiers' Home, the Lincolns were freer to be themselves in a setting of shade trees, shrubs, and bright flowers. Mary Lincoln wrote to a friend that first summer: "The drives & walks around here are delightful, & each day, brings its visitors." In other letters she called the place "very beautiful" and "this sweet spot."

Located on about 300 acres, the Military Asylum, as it was originally named, was founded in 1851 as a home for disabled and impoverished soldiers. It is somewhat ironic that Lincoln, who as a congressman opposed the war with Mexico, should find refuge there. The property's purchase price came from tribute money extracted from Mexican authorities by General Winfield Scott during the U.S. Army's occupation of Mexico City. The sponsor of the legislation creating a home for disabled soldiers was Senator Jefferson Davis of Mississippi, now president of the Confederate States of America. And the cottage in which the Lincolns resided was named for the Military Asylum's first governor, Major Robert Anderson, who commanded Fort Sumter in Charleston Harbor when it came under Confederate attack and the Civil War began. There were roughly 150 veterans in residence in Lincoln's time, with some dating their military service to the War of 1812. Scott Hall, the main residential building, was just steps away from the Lincoln cottage. At times during the war, the army used its battlemented central tower as a signal station, sending and receiving coded messages. Fearing that political support for the institution might falter, the home's administrators issued a standing invitation to presidents and secretaries of war to make use of the cottages on the grounds.

The Lincolns' first summer in the country was overshadowed by personal tragedy. Twelve-year-old Willie Lincoln, one of three surviving sons, died at the White House in February 1862, probably of typhoid fever, and his parents were in deep mourning. Mary Lincoln resorted to spiritualism in an attempt to lift the veil between life and death, and at least one séance took place at the Soldiers' Home cottage. Noah Brooks, a journalist and friend of the Lincoln family, said the medium, Charles J. Colchester, performed in a darkened room, and "pretended to produce messages from the lost boy by means of scratches on the

Lincoln's son Tad was 11 years old when he posed for this photograph by Mathew Brady in 1864. Secretary of War Edwin M. Stanton had given him a courtesy commission in the U.S. Army, and he wears a lieutenant's uniform. The Lincolns indulged Tad, especially after the death of their son Willie in 1862.

wainscoting and taps on the walls and furniture." Brooks later exposed Colchester as a fraud, but Mrs. Lincoln continued to consult other mediums in hope of making contact with her son.

Nine-year-old Tad Lincoln became the much-indulged focus of family life and when the Lincolns moved to the Soldiers' Home for the summer. Tad's White House menagerie of ponies, goats, and cats moved with them. As one story had it, Tad once refused to leave for the Soldiers' Home until all his animals were accounted for, compelling his father to walk back into the White House to find a missing cat. On another day, Nanny, Tad's goat, had to be sent back to the White House in disgrace after it ate the flowers in the cottage garden. Once the president and Secretary of War Edwin M. Stanton, whose family also lived at the Soldiers' Home in summer, intervened to rescue a flock of peacocks their sons were raising. According to the story told years later by one of the Stanton boys, soldiers from the president's guard had attached small blocks of wood to the peacocks' legs with long ropes to stop them from flying away. But once when the peacocks settled in the limbs of some cedar trees for the night, the ropes and the peacocks became hopelessly snarled in the branches. According to the story, Lincoln and his war secretary devoted considerable time to untangling the roosting peacocks.

Tad was a lively, active boy and quickly formed friendships with the men of Company K, the Pennsylvania infantry unit assigned to guard his father at the Soldiers' Home. The soldiers awarded Tad the title of "third lieutenant," and he often rode to their camp on his pony to watch them drill. One private remembered that when the dinner bell rang the boy would "get in line and draw his rations the same as the rest of us." Lincoln also visited the camp and chatted with the men. One evening, a soldier on guard near the cottage noticed the president and Tad playing checkers on the veranda. When Lincoln asked the soldier to play a game, he proudly accepted.

Mary Lincoln took separate vacations in all four years of her husband's presidency. In August 1861, with the president tied to the White House after the Union defeat at Bull Run, the first lady traveled to the fashionable seaside resort at Long Branch, New Jersey. Writing to ask a friend to join her, she observed that three hotels had asked her to be their nonpaying guest and that the railroad was offering free passes. "The trip will cost nothing, which is a good deal to us all these times," she wrote. She chose the Mansion House and stayed for about ten days. Local boosters were elated, believing that the first lady's visit showed that Long Branch had arrived as a select national resort. A New Jersey newspaper reported that her presence caused great excitement: "All along the beach, from every hotel, and in every dooryard for miles around, the American flag floated on the breeze. A number of little girls, dressed in white, lined the path from Mrs. Lincoln's (rail) car to the carriage and an immense procession of people followed her from the depot to the hotel." Although she had asked to be secluded, her hosts planned an active schedule, including a cricket match, a grand ball at the Mansion House, and a recital by an opera singer. While at Long Branch, she visited a lifesaving station for a demonstration of the latest devices to help vessels and seamen in distress. Then she moved on to New York City to indulge her passion for shopping. She was joined there by Robert Lincoln, her oldest son and a student at Harvard. The group went on to Saratoga Springs and Niagara Falls before Mrs. Lincoln returned to Washington.

In 1863 the first lady, Tad, and Robert traveled to Vermont for a long stay in the White Mountains. She ascended Mount Washington to Tip Top House, remembering years later that while it was "intensely warm" at ground level, it was snowing when at the summit. She traveled every summer, leaving the president alone at the Soldiers' Home for weeks or even months.

While Mary Todd Lincoln, photographed here by Mathew Brady, traveled to New Jersey and New England during the summers, President Lincoln stayed in Washington. In 1861 Mrs. Lincoln went to Long Branch on the Jersey Shore, where she lodged at the Mansion House, a leading hotel known for its "elegant hospitalities."

———

The cottage offered Lincoln a degree of privacy and a change of pace. What it did not provide was an escape from the war or the president's duties. Captain David Derickson, commander of Lincoln's cavalry guard, remembered that when the president left the White House for the Soldiers' Home, he often carried papers and spent many hours on them in the evening. The disabled veterans, the patrolling military guards, and the cavalry escort to and from the White House were daily reminders of war. So were the fresh graves of the battlefield dead in the military cemetery a short walk from the cottage. At times the fighting was near enough that the Lincolns could hear the thump of cannon fire. The Soldiers' Home was near one edge of a belt of hastily built forts that defended the city like the quills of a porcupine. Army supply wagons rumbled on the road near the cottage. The president's morning ride to the White House took him near military hospitals filled with wounded soldiers. He and the first lady often visited them as well as the camps set up to house slaves freed from their masters by advancing Union armies.

As 1862 unfolded, two central hurdles facing the Lincoln administration seemed increasingly intertwined: preserving the Union and deciding the future of slavery. Lincoln was living in the Soldiers' Home that summer as he amended his thinking about the war and slavery, a process that led to the Emancipation Proclamation, which transformed the Union cause and secured Lincoln a singular place in the history of human freedom. Lincoln sent the first signal of what was in his mind after he had been at the Soldiers' Home for about a month. On July 18, 1862, he told Secretary of State William H. Seward and Navy Secretary Gideon Welles that after much hard thinking he had "about come to the conclusion that it was a military necessity absolutely essential for the salvation of the Union, that we must free the slaves or be ourselves subdued." Four days later Lincoln convened the full cabinet, announced his intended action, and declared he was acting under his authority as commander in chief of the armed forces. He read the preliminary draft, which set January 1, 1863, as the date on which all slaves living in areas in rebellion against the federal government would be "forever free." In the discussion that followed, Seward suggested a delay until Union forces won a clear battlefield victory to avoid leaving the impression the president was acting out of desperation. Lincoln agreed. But for a time the military situation grew worse, not better. On

Following the Battle of Bull Run in July 1861, open fields at the U.S. Military Asylum were set aside as a cemetery for war dead. Pictured here in c. 1990, it was the first national cemetery and just a few hundred yards from the Lincoln cottage. There were dozens of weekly burials, and more than 5,000 by the end of the Civil War.

In 1864, painter Francis Bicknell Carpenter set up a studio in the White House to try to recapture the moment on July 22, 1862, when President Lincoln submitted the first draft of the Emancipation Proclamation to his cabinet. Lincoln was spending the summer at the Soldiers' Home, and he had already broached the subject of emancipation with Secretary of the Navy Gideon Welles, seated on Lincoln's left, and Secretary of State William H. Seward, seated next to Welles. The painting now hangs in the U.S. Capitol.

The Lincoln cottage has been restored and furnished as it was when the Lincolns spent their summers here. President Lincoln and his son Tad enjoyed reading and playing checkers.

August 29–30, the Army of the Potomac was decisively defeated a second time at Bull Run. Confederate General Robert E. Lee then invaded western Maryland. But when Lee's army was repulsed at the Battle of Antietam on September 17, Lincoln, still living at the Soldiers' Home, saw his opportunity. Five days later he issued the Emancipation Proclamation.

The Lincolns began their second summer at the Soldiers' Home on June 22, 1863. Two days later, Lee's army again crossed the Potomac, this time invading Pennsylvania. On July 1, Union and Confederate forces clashed at Gettysburg, opening a three-day battle that became a turning point of the war. Lincoln mounted a long vigil at the army telegraph office near the White House, following the battle report by report. On the morning of the second day of combat, Mrs. Lincoln called for her carriage at the Soldiers' Home and started into the city for news. Suddenly the carriage seat became unfastened; the first lady was thrown to the road, hitting her head on a rock. The wound became infected and she came close to death, keeping to her bed at the Soldiers' Home for weeks. There was speculation later that someone deliberately unscrewed the bolts holding the seat to the carriage hoping to injure the president. Lincoln chose to blame the poor state of the roads. Summoned from Boston, Robert Lincoln found his mother bedridden and his father in great distress that Lee's army had been allowed to escape after the decisive Gettysburg victory.

Visitors to the cottage might find the president padding around in carpet slippers and stirring a breeze with a palm leaf fan. One found him, in stocking feet with one long leg draped over the arm of an oversize chair. A visiting French amateur artist drew Lincoln dressed in a white coat and hat and seated at a table on the grass. Lincoln generally tolerated callers, even those who came late at night. But he lost his patience one evening—perhaps unjustifiably—when a colonel arrived to ask permission to enter an area closed to private travel to retrieve the body of his wife who had been killed in a steamboat collision. "Am I to have no rest?" Lincoln erupted. "Is there no hour or spot when or where I may escape this constant call? Why do you follow me out here with such business as this?" He told his visitor to seek help at the War Department. But the next morning, according to the story, the president unexpectedly appeared at the colonel's hotel, apologized for being "a brute," and agreed to find a way to grant the request.

This oil painting by Francis Bicknell Carpenter, 1865, portrays the president's family in 1861, possibly at the Soldiers' Home. Left to right are Mary Todd Lincoln, Willie (who died in 1862), Robert, Tad, and the president.

On July 11–12, 1864, Confederate cavalry reached the outskirts of Washington and fired on Fort Stevens, very near the Soldiers' Home. Skirmishing ensued, but the fort was quickly reinforced and the Confederates withdrew. In this photograph (*opposite*) a detachment of Company K, normally guarding the U.S. Military Asylum, stands with heavy artillery at the fort. The fort, partly restored, is now maintained by the National Park Service and may be visited by the public.

Other visitors found the president a gracious host, ready to recite a favorite poem or to read from a Shakespeare play. His secretary John Hay kept the president company one night as he visited the National Observatory to gaze through the telescope at the Moon and Arcturus, one of the brightest stars in the night sky. Then they rode out to the Soldiers' Home. "The president read Shakespeare to me, the end of Henry V and the beginning of Richard III, till my heavy eyelids caught his considerate notice and he sent me to bed," Hay recalled.

Lincoln was known for his storytelling. When members of Company K grumbled that the war was passing them by because of their assignment to the Soldiers' Home, the president remarked: "You boys remind me of a farmer friend of mine in Illinois, who said he could never understand why the Lord put the curl in a pig's tail. It never seemed to him to be either useful or ornamental, but he reckoned the Almighty knew what he was doing when he put it there." The men of Company K understood Lincoln's point that it was a soldier's duty to serve where ordered, and they always called the anecdote "The Pigtail Story."

———

At 10:00 p.m. on July 10, 1864, Secretary of War Stanton reached for his pen and dashed off an urgent message, sending it by mounted courier to the president at the Soldiers' Home: "The enemy are reported advancing towards Tenallytown and Seventh street road. They are in large force and have driven back our Cavalry. I think you had better come in to town tonight." A Confederate army under General Jubal Early, sent north to relieve military pressure against Richmond, had marched through Maryland, defeated a Union force at the Battle of Monocacy, and now threatened to break through Washington's undermanned

defenses. Lincoln thought it unnecessary but brought his family back to the White House. Journalist Noah Brooks noted that the Lincoln cottage was only 4 miles from the advance line of Confederate skirmishers and set down his opinion in a dispatch to his newspaper in California: "The lonely situation of the President's summer residence would have afforded a tempting chance . . . of carrying off the President whom we could ill afford to spare just now."

The next day the president insisted on inspecting the city's defenses and rode out to Fort Stevens, less than a mile from the Soldiers' Home. While he was there, the fort came under enemy fire. John Hay told the story: "He was in the Fort when it was first attacked, standing upon the parapet. A soldier roughly ordered him to get down or he would have his head knocked off." The president obeyed. But he returned to Fort Stevens the next day, this time bringing Mrs. Lincoln. Again someone shouted at him to get out of the line of fire, and again the president obeyed. With federal reinforcements arriving, and under close observation from the signal station atop the tower at the Soldiers' Home, the Confederates soon abandoned their assault. But Lincoln's hope that Early's army would be pursued and destroyed was quickly dashed. On July 14, returning to the Soldiers' Home for the first time since the Confederate advance, the president complained sarcastically to Hay that the Union general in charge of the pursuit was dragging his feet "for fear he might come across the rebels & catch some of them." Hay made a final diary note: "The Chief is evidently disgusted."

Rural quiet returned to the Soldiers' Home for the rest of the summer, but dangers remained. Shortly before an August midnight, a soldier at the army camp heard a gunshot. Moments later he saw the president galloping bareheaded toward his cottage. Lincoln explained that his hat fell off when the frightened horse began to run. When the soldier walked down the curving drive to the main road, he found the president's tall top hat with a bullet hole through the crown. That led to speculation that Lincoln had narrowly escaped an assassin. When the soldier returned the hat the next morning, the president dismissed the incident as the work of "some foolish gunner" and said he wanted it "kept quiet."

This monument located atop the parapet of Fort Stevens commemorates Abraham Lincoln's presence on the second day of the Battle of Fort Stevens. On July 12, 1864, Lincoln stood atop the parapet to witness the battle and came under direct fire of Confederate sharpshooters. It is the only time in American history in which a sitting president came under direct fire from an enemy combatant. The monument was dedicated by the veterans of the Battle of Fort Stevens on July 12, 1920. .

Lincoln clearly intended to use the Soldiers' Home as a summer retreat during his second term, although with the war at an end he probably would have felt free to join his wife on her vacation travels to the White Mountains and elsewhere. On April 13, 1865, a treasury official encountered the president on the road to the Soldiers' Home even though he had not yet moved his household there. The next evening, while he watched a play at Ford's Theatre not far from the White House, Abraham Lincoln was assassinated.

A year later, still torn by grief, Mary Lincoln looked back with longing on her family's summers in the country: "How dearly I loved the 'Soldiers' Home' & I little supposed, one year since, that I should be so far removed from it, broken hearted, and praying for death, to remove me, from a life, so full of agony." She placed a photograph of the Soldiers' Home cottage in the Lincoln family album. More than 140 years later, it was used in restoring the building to its appearance when the Lincolns made it their summertime haven.

James Buchanan and Rutherford B. Hayes also used the Soldiers' Home cottage as a summer retreat. Chester A. Arthur was the last president to stay there. It subsequently served as a dormitory, infirmary, guest house, bar and lounge, and office. In 2008, after a $15 million restoration by the National Trust for Historic Preservation, the Lincoln cottage was opened to the public. The 272-acre campus, with its complex of buildings, is still an Armed Forces Retirement Home.

Chapter 13

Andrew Johnson: Enjoying the Grandchildren

On April 15, 1865, the day of
President Lincoln's death,
Vice President Andrew
Johnson took the Oath of
Office (*opposite*) in a private
ceremony in the small parlor
of the Kirkwood House, the
Pennsylvania Avenue hotel
where he lived. The oath was
administered by Chief Justice
Salmon Chase, who then said,
"You are President. May God
support, guide, and bless you
in your arduous duties."

ndrew Johnson took no vacations. Thrust into the White House by Abraham
Lincoln's murder, he became consumed by events and his own affinity for hard
work. Even if he had not become president, Johnson was an anomaly. A Democratic
senator from Tennessee, he was a Union loyalist who remained in the Senate when his state
seceded. In 1862 President Abraham Lincoln appointed him military governor of Tennessee
and in 1864 selected him as his running mate on the National Union Party ticket, a temporary
name used by the Republican Party to attract war Democrats and others who would not
normally vote Republican. At first Johnson's full attention was claimed by the aftermath of
the assassination, the end of the Civil War, and the fate of the Confederacy's defeated leaders.
Then he battled Congress over the shape of Reconstruction in the rebellious states and staved
off an impeachment conviction in the Senate by a single vote.

Johnson never used the Soldiers' Home cottage that offered Lincoln refuge and solace.
He never sought out the fashionable watering holes that James Buchanan and other chief
executives had favored. He had no interest in beach resorts like Long Branch or mountain
hideaways in the Appalachians. Johnson's home at Greenville, Tennessee, was too distant
for easy visiting, especially for a president caught in the riptide of post–Civil War politics.
Instead, the president submerged himself in work and fended off his enemies. He remained
unmovable and absorbed in work until the end of his term. Decades later, one veteran
member of the White House domestic staff remembered Johnson as about the hardest
working president in the second half of the nineteenth century. A recent biographer describes
Andrew Johnson as a man for whom work meant everything and recreation counted little.
Contemporaries classed him as incorruptible since he accepted no favors or gifts of any kind.
How could you influence someone who wouldn't even accept a weekend in the mountains?

In early July 1865, after Johnson had been president for no more than three months, Navy
Secretary Gideon Welles became alarmed that the heavy load risked the president's health.
Welles intervened when he learned that Johnson hadn't ventured outdoors since moving into
the White House in May. "I told him this would not answer—that no constitution would
endure such labor and close confinement," he wrote in his diary. Welles proposed a relaxing
cruise on the Potomac, and for once Johnson agreed. On an overcast but otherwise pleasant
Sunday morning, the president and his guests boarded a steamer at the Navy Yard and cruised
past Mount Vernon to Aquia Creek. Welles thought Johnson benefited from the break and
the fresh air.

Although such outings were infrequent, the president's routine changed a bit when
his entire family arrived from Tennessee early in August. After that he often bundled his
grandchildren into a White House carriage for an afternoon ride into the country or along
nearby Rock Creek. There were frequent stops to allow time for wading in a stream or

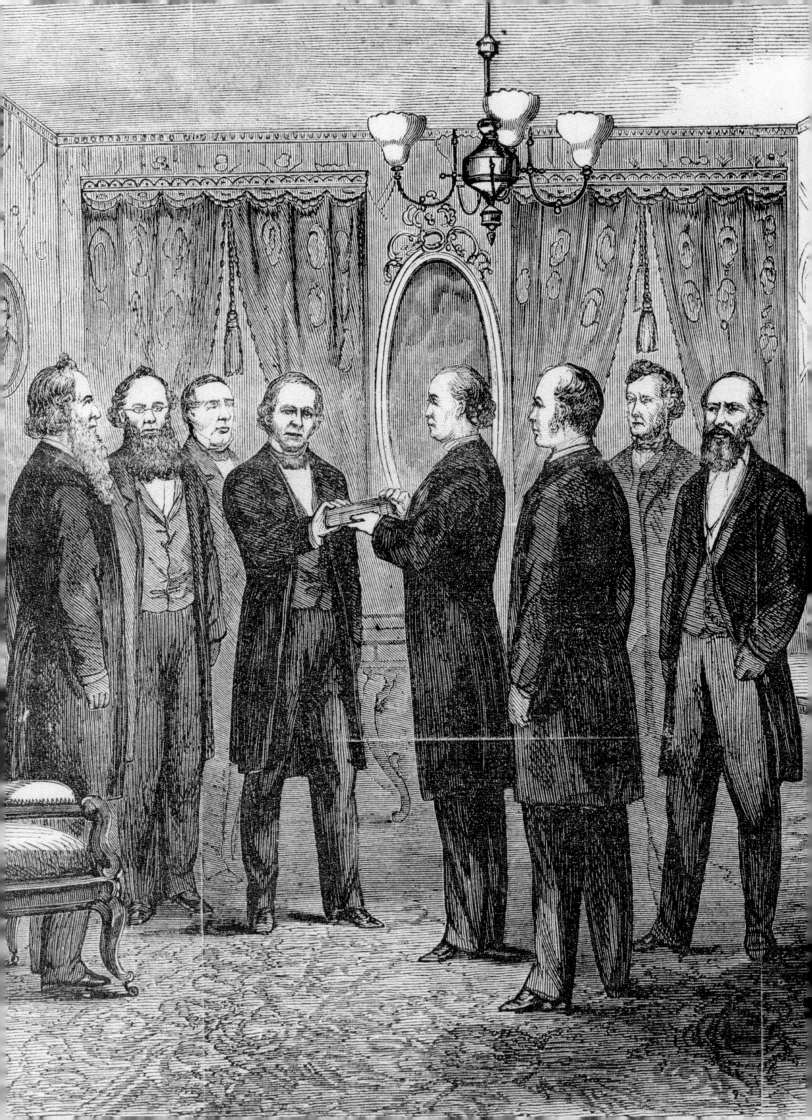

Spring in Rock Creek Park

The only respite from work President Johnson ever took was in occasional carriage rides in the countryside or along Rock Creek, which, just a mile from the White House, splashed over boulders to the Potomac. The creek is depicted by Robert Latou Dickinson's pencil and pastel drawing *Spring in Rock Creek Park* (1918). Much of the forested area through which the creek flows was denuded during the Civil War, as trees were felled to build the sixty-eight forts, batteries, and other fortifications that that surrounded the capital city and to provide clear sight lines for artillery.

The Johnsons' two daughters lived with them in the White House, bringing grandchilden to lighten their lives. Seen here in two photographs taken during Johnson's presidency are the children of his daughter Mary Johnson Stover (*near right*) and the children of his eldest daughter Martha Johnson Patterson (*far right*).

picking flowers along the bank while the president skipped stones across the water. Johnson continued the afternoon rides even when the children could not join him, and one excursion led to an often-repeated story. One day a heavy shower overtook the president's carriage as it rolled back to the White House from Rock Creek. Spotting a young woman trudging through the rain carrying a baby, Johnson invited her to join him for the ride back to town. He delivered her to a modest frame house and bowed in farewell. She apparently never knew that she had been spared a long walk through a rainy afternoon by the president.

Johnson mostly stayed close to the White House until it was time for him to return to Tennessee. His term was marked by social engagements near the end, one of them an evening reserved for children. On Christmas Day 1868, Johnson granted pardons to all who had rebelled against the authority of the United States. That included Jefferson Davis, the former president of the Confederacy, whom he had once threatened to hang as a traitor.

By then Johnson was waiting out the weeks until General Ulysses S. Grant took the Oath of Office as his successor. Grant was the leading military hero of the Civil War, but he and Johnson had long been at odds. On Inauguration Day, Grant made clear he would not ride to the Capitol in the same carriage as the outgoing president, or even speak to him. Johnson chose to remain at his White House desk. He signed bills as they arrived instead of performing that last-minute task in the President's Room of the Senate, as was the custom. At a few minutes past noon, as the ceremonies were beginning at the other end of Pennsylvania Avenue, Johnson put down his pen and said farewell to his cabinet. Then he walked downstairs, waved good-bye to the White House staff, stepped into his carriage, and began the long journey home to Tennessee.

Andrew Johnson was born in North Carolina but settled in Greenville, Tennessee, where he opened a tailor shop (*above*) in the mid-1820s, married, and prospered. In 1851, by then a congressman, he purchased a brick house (*left*), where his family lived until the Civil War. After Tennessee seceded, his properties were confiscated and his wife and family sent away as refugees. The family returned to this house in 1869. Today it is a National Park Service Historic Site and, together with the tailor shop, open to the public.

Chapter 14

Ulysses S. Grant
Long Branch on the Atlantic Shore

President Ulysses S. Grant's
vacations at Long Branch
were enjoyed by his entire
family. In this photo (*opposite*)
taken in the 1870s, Grant sits
on the left. Standing from
left to right are First Lady
Julia Grant, daughter Nellie,
Ferdinand (a valet), sons
Jesse and Buck, and Willie
Coles, a friend of Jesse.

Long Branch, on New Jersey's Atlantic shore just south of New York City, had long been among the smartest, most fashionable resorts on the East Coast. Ulysses Simpson Grant liked it from his first days there and once told a friend he had never seen a place better suited for a summer residence. The Grants first summered at Long Branch in 1867 and 1868, when he was still America's ranking general and not yet president. The family stayed first at the Mansion House, where Mary Todd Lincoln had been a guest in 1861, and then at the equally fashionable Stetson House. When he returned as president, Grant's presence gave the resort the ultimate seal of approval. Thousands of vacationers streamed off boats at the Long Branch pier to stroll on the beach, splash in the water, spend an afternoon at the races, and perhaps catch a glimpse of the president and the socialites, millionaires, and Broadway stars who had built the cottages and stayed at the best hotels.

On August 3, 1869, the first summer of his presidency, Grant attended a Long Branch reception in his honor and announced, "I have purchased a cottage here by the seaside, where I shall make the summer home of myself and family." The Grant family soon took

Long Branch, a beach resort on the Jersey Shore, had long attracted those who sought refreshment in salt air and saltwater, and in 1869 President Ulysses S. Grant acquired a summer home there. Following Grant's example, six later presidents and their families—Rutherford B. Hayes, James A. Garfield, Chester A. Arthur, Benjamin H. Harrison, William McKinley, and Woodrow Wilson—enjoyed at least part of the summer season at the Jersey Shore. The famous pier was depicted upon its opening in 1879 in *Harper's Weekly* (*above*) with an image captioned "The Great Iron and Tubular Pier at Long Branch."

The Grant "cottage," was a mansion in all but name. A reporter from the *New York Herald* who gained access in 1870 described walking up the broad front steps and through the front door to discover on the first floor the president's office, a sitting room, and a large parlor with fireplace mantels, mirrors, sofas, chairs, tables, and a piano. Dumbwaiters in a butler's pantry led to the basement kitchen, where there was also a servants' dining room, a drying room and storerooms, and a passage to an underground icehouse capable of holding several hundred pounds of ice.

possession of the cottage and returned summer after summer.

The Grant cottage at 991 Ocean Avenue occupied a high point on the 5-mile-long bluff overlooking the beach and the Atlantic. "It commands a vast sweep of ocean view," the *New York Herald* told readers in the summer of 1870, adding that "the situation could not have been better chosen for comfort and an extensive prospect." The twenty-eight-room house had two main floors and a full third floor plus a finished basement. The outer walls were built of cement with beams arranged in a distinctive diamond pattern. Living areas and ten bedrooms opened onto deep porches that wrapped three sides on the first- and second-floor levels. With their railings and supports, they gave the cottage an almost lacy appearance. The cottage had sufficient room for the secretaries and aides who moved in during the day as Grant presided over government business from his office on the first floor or from a chair on the veranda.

Newspapers began calling Long Branch "The Summer Capital," but for Grant, the greatest military hero of the age, Long Branch was essentially a place of peace or, as he once put it, "recreation from official duty." Julia Grant summed up the spirit of their visits to the shore in her memoirs: "What a boon our cottage at Long Branch was to the President! Tired and weary as he was with his monotonous official duties, he hastened with delight, as soon as Congress adjourned, to its health-giving breezes and its wide and restful piazzas." The Grants generally arrived in Long Branch in July or even earlier and stayed into September. There, said Julia Grant, the president "gathered new strength and vigor for the ensuing winter's campaign in Washington." From their first summer on the shore, the president and his family visited with friends, rode out in the carriage, walked on the beach, and bathed in the ocean. A large white banner was hoisted when the sea was considered calm enough for safe bathing, as swimming was then called. A local guidebook advised that morning was the best time because of the incoming tide: "The full force of the sea is shoreward and if taken off your feet you are thrown on the beach—a frolic in which many indulge." The trip from the Long Branch pier to Lower Manhattan took an hour by steamer, and the Grants often reserved Thursday for shopping expeditions to the city. The president set aside Friday night for poker with friends.

A skilled horseman since his days at West Point, Grant enjoyed driving a team of Thoroughbreds on the beach or out into the country. Julia Grant remembered with fondness the "glorious drives" along "that enchanted beach." At times the president joined the afternoon cavalcade of summer visitors and their stylish carriages and handsome horses on Ocean Avenue, Long Branch's social artery. The president brought his own horses with him from the White House stables and often drove two favorites, Egypt and Cincinnati. Writing to order a new carriage on the day after Christmas 1876, Grant's secretary asked that it be ready by the time the president left for Long Branch for the summer. Spelling out the requirements, he said it should be "suitable in width and strength to carry two heavy persons (say 200 pounds each)." After Monmouth racetrack opened, the Grants were often seen at the afternoon races.

The four Grant children were an important focus of summers at the beach, and the president set aside evenings for them. Fred and Ulysses Jr., known as "Buck," and their sister, Ellen, known as "Nellie," spent their holidays at the Long Branch cottage. Jesse, the Grants' youngest son, rode his pony along the beach and went out with a shotgun for birds. "As soon as we reached Long Branch my cousin and I were out shooting sandpipers or taking long jaunts after yellow legs and plover," he remembered. He also remembered how ships passing along the Jersey Shore headed into Long Branch to salute the vacationing president. "At first we responded by running up a flag," Jesse recalled. "Later, I acquired a small cannon and would fire that, and then run up the flag." The tribe of small boys who lived nearby found much to admire in the crack and bang of the blank charges fired by Jesse's

Grant and Bonner Dexter's Best Time 2:16 1/4. President Grant enjoyed riding even when it wasn't a necessity. At the White House, he visited the stables every day to inspect his horses. He took Cincinnati and Egypt with him on vacations to Long Branch, where he rode along the beach. He was also a regular in his box at the resort's Monmouth Park, a racetrack that opened in 1870.

In another Long Branch family photo, President and Mrs. Grant sit outdoors with their son Jesse, c. 1872. After his presidency, Grant and his family continued to vacation at Long Branch, and it was here, in 1884, that he agreed to write a series of articles on his Civil War campaigns for *Century* magazine. After Grant's death the cottage was updated and expanded, then demolished in 1963 to make way for an upscale subdivision.

Descriptions of the Grant cottage interested people around the country, and soon they could buy stereographic views of it, some showing the president and his family seated comfortably on the lawn outside. A stereocard's nearly identical double photographs blended into a single three-dimensional image when seen through an optical viewer. Peering at them had become a popular parlor pastime.

Scenes at Long Branch.

G. W. PACH, Photographer, 858 Broadway, New York.

cannon, and a nonlethal arms race developed. "Cannons multiplied," Jesse wrote. "No small boy could resist such an opportunity as that. In time the saluting boats were answered with a salvo of small cannon fire."

The atmosphere of family fun was infectious. Julia Grant had always struck Jesse as "dignified, slow moving, never frustrated or hurried." One day, as she was rocking quietly on the veranda with her family gathered around her, Buck Grant suddenly leaped over the railing and disappeared. The president began to tease his wife and her measured and unhurried pace: "Did you see that, Julia? Now if you were sitting here alone, and the railing extended across the steps, and the cottage caught fire, you must be rescued or burn." With that, the first lady stood up and vaulted the railing "as lightly as Buck had done."

Frederick Dent, Julia's elderly father, lived at the White House and spent summers with the family at Long Beach. He died in 1873 at age 87, and his daughter believed the "delightful sea air" at Long Branch "prolonged his life for years." Her daughter, Nellie, was married in a ceremony in the East Room of the White House in May 1874 to Englishman Algernon Sartoris. A year later, on July 11, 1875, Nellie gave birth at the Long Branch cottage to Grant Sartoris, the president's first grandchild.

———

Although the setting at Long Branch was relaxing and the sea breeze welcome, presidential business rarely lagged. Grant's open nature provided little protection from the hundreds of people who hoped for government jobs and did not mind interrupting his vacation to make their case. The Grant cabinet held meetings at Long Branch and officials arrived by train to pursue their interests in person. Old army comrades, admirers, and outright celebrity seekers sought out the president. Official mail flowed to and from Long Branch. From his summer home Grant dealt with racial violence in the South, which was still occupied by federal troops, and considered appeals for assistance from Republican state officials. Grant monitored Indian affairs from Long Branch as well as from Washington and in the summer of 1876 dealt with the aftermath of the massacre of George Armstrong Custer's cavalry command at the Little Big Horn River in Montana Territory. In an interview he said he regarded "Custer's massacre as a sacrifice of troops, brought on by Custer himself, that was wholly unnecessary."

The president's cottage was high on the list of local sights for many Long Branch visitors, and with Grant its most prominent summer resident, Long Branch enjoyed a giddying success in drawing the celebrated, the wealthy, and the socially prominent to its beaches. Grant's presence on the bluff attracted other famous military figures, including General George Gordon Meade, General William Tecumseh Sherman, and Admiral David Farragut. Society flowed into the cottages and hotels. The bearers of famous names included Astors, Fisks, Goulds, Biddles, and Drexels as well as the flamboyant "Diamond Jim" Brady. Broadway sent its stellar attractions, among them Lily Langtry, Lillian Russell, and the Shakespearian actor Edwin Booth. Henry Ward Beecher, the most famous preacher of the day, often visited Long Branch. So did newspaper editors Horace Greeley and James Gordon Bennett and authors Robert Louis Stevenson and Bret Harte. The family of Garret A. Hobart, who would become William McKinley's vice president, had a cottage there. At one time so did Frederick Douglass, the former slave who became the nation's foremost civil rights leader.

Evidently Grant apparently considered purely social affairs a personal trial and was reputed to have said at a grand ball, "Madam, I had rather storm a fort than attempt another dance." Nor did the always restless president always stay put at "The Branch," as he and many others dubbed the resort. During 1874, for example, the Grants spent a June weekend at Cape May, New Jersey, and made a separate trip later in the month to White Sulphur Springs, West Virginia. They arrived at Long Branch on Independence Day amid fireworks, salutes, and parades. But they soon left for a regatta and a Harvard-Yale baseball game at Saratoga Springs, New York. They returned to Long Branch for most of August. But late in the month they steamed up the coast for Newport, Rhode Island, making stops to attend a Methodist camp meeting on the Massachusetts island of Martha's Vineyard as well as Cape Cod and Nantucket Island. The Grants returned to the White House in September but were on the move again in October, traveling west by rail to the Chicago wedding of their son, Frederick.

The artist Winslow Homer painted *Long Branch, New Jersey,* in 1869, the year Grant bought his cottage. Elegantly dressed young women peer down at the beach from the bluff while holding parasols aloft to protect their delicate complexions from the midday sun.

Inevitably, Grant's lengthy vacations made some people unhappy. On a summer day in 1873, Representative (and future president) James A. Garfield of Ohio wrote in his diary: "The President left for [Long Branch] at 8 o'clock yesterday, leaving a great many Congressmen with fingers in their mouths, waiting to complete business at the Executive Mansion. The President has done much to show with how little personal attention the government can be run." The *Chicago Tribune* had a similar complaint on September 16, 1874: "President Grant left Washington last night for Long Branch. He is not the kind of man who allows business to interrupt his vacation." In the context of his scandal-ridden administration, these concerns were coupled with questions about Grant's Long Branch cottage. While the *Chicago Tribune* said Grant had paid $30,000 for the Long Branch property, and the *New York Herald* said $32,000, including furnishings except silver and linen, some newspapers asserted that various combinations of wealthy admirers had pooled their funds, bought the cottage, and presented it to Grant as a gift. Some of these articles appeared as Grant sought a second term in 1872 and were denounced by pro-administration journals as "campaign slanders."

Nevertheless, in the spring of 1876 the House of Representatives demanded detailed information about Grant's long presidential vacations and questioned the legitimacy of the official actions he had taken away from the capital. Presidential holidays had caused periodic grumbling since the earliest days of the republic, but now they were a political issue and the target of a congressional investigation. On April 3, on a voice vote with no recorded opposition, the House, where Democrats held a majority, adopted a resolution by Representative Joseph Blackburn of Kentucky. It called on the Republican president to disclose the dates and duration of all travel outside Washington and to explain and defend all executive actions taken by him away from "the seat of government established by law" in 1790. The Blackburn resolution suggested such actions were "incompatible with the public interest." It appeared to leave open the possibility they might have violated what is more commonly known as the Residence Act.

For Grant, the year 1876 was the most difficult of his presidency, as his administration was under attack from many quarters. Orville Babcock, his private secretary, was on trial in St. Louis for alleged involvement in the so-called Whiskey Ring, a conspiracy to divert revenue from federal alcohol taxes for personal gain. On March 2, Secretary of War William W. Belknap abruptly resigned to head off impeachment by the House on charges of accepting bribes from traders at army posts on the western frontier. Undeterred, the House voted the same day to impeach Belknap anyway, even though he no longer held a government office. It also voted to reduce Grant's salary.

Grant's response was prepared by Secretary of State Hamilton Fish and sent to the House on May 4. Evidently Grant and his advisers suspected the purpose of the Blackburn resolution was to obtain information to support a future impeachment resolution. He invoked executive privilege and his own constitutional right to avoid self-incrimination in refusing to give the requested details, either about his own absences from the capital or about executive actions he had taken during his travels. Grant devoted the rest of the message to a history of presidential vacations and to the work presidents had accomplished away from the seat of government. He freely acknowledged he had taken vacations and been absent from the capital in each of the previous seven years. But he added that, beginning with George Washington, all but two of the seventeen presidents who preceded him had traveled away from the seat of government

In 1884, President Grant agreed to write a series of articles on his Civil War campaigns for *Century* magazine. He is seen here in June 1885 at work on the project, which turned into two volumes of memoirs that he finished just days before his death in 1885.

on personal business. One of them, William Henry Harrison, died only a month after his inauguration. The other, Abraham Lincoln, was tied to his post by the Civil War, traveling only to visit army units in the field.

Grant said that during his own time away from the capital, "I did not neglect or forego the obligations or the duties of my office, but continued to discharge all of the executive offices, acts and duties which were required of me as the President of the United States." He credited the speed of rail transportation and reliability of the telegraph for allowing him to do that nearly as quickly as if he had remained in Washington. He contended that presidential actions were valid no matter where they took place and that it made no difference where he signed a bill or issued an executive order. Even if a Confederate army had driven Lincoln from Washington, "it is manifest that he must have discharged his functions, both civil and military, elsewhere than in the place named by law as the seat of government," Grant declared. Certainly, he added, President Washington did not interpret the law as restricting his exercise of the powers of his office to the city of Philadelphia alone, where the seat of government was established until such time as the site for the capital could be selected. Grant pointed to the hundreds of official acts performed outside the capital by presidents of all parties in an unbroken line from Washington onward and concluded: "No question has ever been raised as to the validity of these acts."

Grant's message laid out the historical record: John Adams was away from the seat of government for more than a year during his four years in office and "discharged official duties and performed the most solemn public acts at Quincy." These included nominating John Marshall as a justice of the U.S. Supreme Court. Thomas Jefferson was away from the capital for more than two years during his two presidential terms and signed and issued seventy-five military commissions from Monticello, his home in Virginia. James Madison and James Monroe both spent long periods away from Washington, and Monroe transacted public business "wherever he happened to be . . . and sometimes while traveling." President Andrew Jackson, a frequent traveler and vacationer, signed the executive order removing federal deposits from certain banks while visiting Boston. Grant also cited routine absences from the capital by Presidents Martin Van Buren, John Tyler, James K. Polk, Zachary Taylor, Millard Fillmore, Franklin Pierce, and James Buchanan.

Grant's defense took the air out of the House inquiry. No further questions were asked on the House floor about presidential vacations. The *New York Times* called Grant's response an effective and "severe rebuke" to House Democrats and labeled the Blackburn resolution "impudent" and a "blunder." The *Chicago Tribune* described Grant's message as a "simple lesson in history." Senator Oliver P. Morton of Indiana wrote Grant that his message was "a complete answer to a multitude of slanders" and that "no sensible person ever believed for a moment that the public interest suffered in the least because of your absence at Long Branch or elsewhere."

By midsummer Grant plainly thought that this particular tempest had run its course. The president and his family left the White House for their annual vacation in Long Branch on August 19. They made side trips to view the Centennial Exhibition in Philadelphia and to visit their son, Jesse, then a student at Cornell University at Ithaca, New York. It was the Grants' last presidential vacation, and they did not return to the White House until October 6.

———

In May 1877, shortly after leaving office, Ulysses and Julia Grant set out on the journey of a lifetime. Over the intervening months, their epic trip around the world quickly became a nonstop celebration of Grant's Civil War leadership and the restoration of the United States as a unified nation. The trip began in England with dinner with Queen Victoria at Windsor Castle. It concluded more than two years later with an audience with the emperor of Japan. Over the intervening months the couple viewed the Alps, the Pyramids, and the Great Wall of China. It was "the very grandest of grand tours." It was "an experience that one can never hope to see again," wrote John Russell Young, a correspondent for the *New York Herald* who filed dispatches throughout the trip.

President and Mrs. Grant on the piazza at Drexel Cottage on Mount McGregor in the Adirondacks with his doctors c. 1885. Terminally ill, Grant completed his memoirs at the Mount McGregor cottage just days before his death. Its royalties secured his family's financial future. The Mount McGregor cottage is today a New York State Historic Site, open to the public.

Back in the United States, the Grants continued to vacation at their Long Branch cottage. But in 1880 the general's bid for a third term as president failed on the thirty-sixth ballot when the Republican National Convention in Chicago nominated James A. Garfield. Needing to support his family, Grant invested in a Wall Street firm, Grant and Ward. It was a mistake. The firm collapsed. Grant was left mired in debt when his partner went to jail for theft and fraud.

Then, in the summer of 1884, the general, a habitual cigar smoker, was diagnosed with throat cancer. Doctors held out little hope. At the urging of Mark Twain and others, Grant began a personal memoir centered on the Civil War. He built his narrative with pen on paper in clean, clear, easily understood sentences. The *Personal Memoirs of U. S. Grant* was completed just days before Grant died on July 23, 1885. Published in two volumes, it became an instant best seller and rescued his family from financial ruin.

Chapter 15

Rutherford B. Hayes: "Rutherford, the Rover"

President Rutherford B. Hayes
and his family toured the
Yosemite Valley in the fall of
1880 as part of a seventy-one-
day trip across the country. He
was the first sitting president
to visit the Pacific Coast. In
this photograph (*opposite*) the
tourists pause in a meadow
with Bridal Veil Falls in the
background.

Shortly after the special train entered Utah, two of the president's sons and three of their friends scrambled onto the locomotive's cowcatcher and rode the rails through the steep-walled slot of Echo Canyon. Rutherford and Lucy Hayes enjoyed the same 25-mile stretch of rugged scenery from the more sedate vantage point of the engineer's cab. It was early September in the summer of 1880, and Hayes was heading west. Within days he would become the first president to visit California and the Pacific Coast while in office.

Hayes traveled so far and so often in his four years as president that the *Chicago Tribune* dubbed him "Rutherford, the Rover" and his wife teased that he was "scenery mad." A former Union Army major general and Republican governor of Ohio, Hayes toured the South, ranged north to New England, and west to the Great Plains. He saw wheat fields in North Dakota and Minnesota. He traveled to state and county fairs and to as many military reunions and ceremonial events as he could fit into his schedule. Just before Christmas in 1877 he took the train to New York City to help inaugurate the American Museum of Natural History. He returned for dedication ceremonies at the new building for the Metropolitan Museum of Art. He traveled to Chester, Pennsylvania, to launch a steamship. He and Lucy sailed up the Hudson to visit West Point. He traveled to accept honorary degrees at Harvard, Yale, and Johns Hopkins Universities.

Impelled by an antiquarian interest in the American past, the president and first lady steamed down the Potomac to George Washington's Mount Vernon and spent two nights in the room once occupied by Lafayette. They visited Montpelier, President James Madison's estate in Virginia's Orange County, where the president admired the "large pillars" of the old manor house, the large and ancient trees, and the "noble view of the Blue Ridge."

In early July 1879, accompanied by two of his sons, Webb and Rudd, and by the attorney general and the secretaries of treasury, war, and the navy, plus some of their families, Hayes boarded the steamboat *Tallapoosa* and cruised into Chesapeake Bay, reaching Fort Monroe on Independence Day. After watching a live-fire demonstration, the party returned to the ship, steamed past Cape Henry, and spent three hours in the open ocean. Returning for evening fireworks, they passed the Rip Raps, where Andrew Jackson had once vacationed. On the way back to the capital the next day, the party stopped to explore the remains of Washington's birthplace at Pope's Creek in Virginia's Westmoreland County. When the water near shore proved too shallow for a small boat, the president and his cabinet officers were carried to dry land by the *Tallapoosa*'s sailors.

In all four summers of his presidency Hayes followed Abraham Lincoln's example and moved his family to the Soldiers' Home on the heights overlooking Washington, finding it "an agreeable abode for the hot weather." Hayes followed Grant to Long Branch and the Jersey Shore. He and Lucy stayed at the Elberon Hotel but never acquired a cottage of their own

and attracted little of the attention lavished on Grant, the hero of Appomattox.

When his friends worried that he was away from his White House desk too often and for too long, Hayes replied that travel renewed his energies and lightened his load and said of his trips: "You have no idea how much they are needed. Eight months of wearying worry over details is enough to kill

a strong man. Every month a man in this place ought to shake off its oppression." And nothing did that better for the nineteenth president than a journey.

Rutherford Birchard Hayes became president in 1877 after an election that was so close many thought Hayes had lost to Democrat Samuel Tilden, who won the popular vote. Hayes was installed in the White House after a commission appointed by Congress decided twenty disputed electoral votes in his favor and named him the winner by a single vote, 185 to 184. It was one of the most controversial elections in U.S. history. Some said Hayes deserved to be titled "His Fraudulency" or renamed as "Rutherfraud B. Hayes." Once established in the White House, the first lady initiated an active and effective social schedule but earned her own nickname—"Lemonade Lucy"—when she refused to serve wine or other alcoholic beverages. As president, Hayes ended the military occupation of the South and dealt with an economic depression and a nationwide railroad strike, but he was unable to sweep aside the spoils system and create a civil service based on merit, not patronage.

Of all of Hayes's journeys, the trip west was the most extended and the most absorbing. It resembled the kind of sightseeing vacation that was just becoming popular with increasing numbers of affluent Americans. With Hayes due to leave office in less than a year, the trip had mainly symbolic importance, demonstrating the unity of a once-divided nation and the increasing economic importance of the Pacific slope. Hayes left on September 1 from Spiegel Grove, his estate at Fremont, Ohio. He would return just in time to vote for fellow Ohioan James Garfield in November's presidential election.

The tour was organized and managed by General William Tecumseh Sherman, whose enduring fame was based on his army's march through Georgia to the sea during the Civil War. For this less epochal but still demanding task, Sherman drew on army posts throughout the West for logistical support. In its various stages the party traveled by train, stagecoach, carriage, army ambulances, ferries, and oceangoing steamships. The presidential train had five cars: one for baggage, one for dining, a Pullman sleeping car, and two luxurious railroad director's cars, one reserved for Sherman and Secretary of War Alexander Ramsey and one for the president. One member of the party described it as "the finest car which I think I ever saw, its upholstery was of the richest, and all its appointments complete."

The USS *Tallapoosa*, a dispatch vessel that was available to the president for cruises, had been built and commissioned in 1863 for service in the Civil War. After the war it was part of the Gulf Squadron, and in 1872 moved to Annapolis to serve as a training ship for the U.S. Naval Academy. In the summer of 1879, President Hayes and two of his sons, together with other Washington officials, toured the Chesapeake Bay on this wooden-hulled steamer.

In the White House, the Hayes family sought to present themselves as models of decency and public service. In private, they were equally dedicated to each other. They are pictured here at the Spiegel Grove estate in Fremont, Ohio, which President Hayes had inherited from his uncle in 1874 (*opposite*).

Following the adventure in Echo Canyon, the train rolled on to Salt Lake City, where the young people in the party swam in the lake's saltwater. The train crossed the Sierra Nevada, stopped at Lake Tahoe, and reached San Francisco for a ceremonial welcome on September 9. After a stop in Sacramento, the party traveled in separate stage coaches into Oregon with General Sherman "riding shotgun" on the president's coach in the seat next to the driver. The sightseeing soon began in earnest. "What beautiful country we have passed through—what magnificent scenery grand majestic trees and of fruits the most luscious I have ever tasted," Mrs. Hayes wrote in a letter. "The grandeur of the views has not been exaggerated," the president wrote after riding a steamboat up the Columbia River. Throughout, the president used the telegraph to stay in touch with Washington in case some unforeseen emergency required his immediate return.

Moving into Washington Territory, the party cruised in Puget Sound for a week and arrived at Seattle by sea. Laura Platt Mitchell, the president's niece, described the voyage in a letter home to Ohio:

> We had a whole week of beauty and delight on Puget Sound following its blue inlets in and out among the many islands and around the rugged fir-hung promontories or gently sloping shores. The Olympic Range seemed attending us in the blue distance, and Mt. Ranier rose in the sky, a snow-crowned shrine for our admiring worship, from time to time. As we drew near Seattle, a fleet of seven vessels—the flag-strung revenue cutter and big and little steamboats, came to meet us, first circled round us, and ranging themselves on either hand, escorted us into port.

Returning south to Oregon, the president's party boarded another ship and steamed down the coast back to San Francisco. "The sea is smooth, almost nobody sick," the president informed his daughter Fanny back home in Ohio. Laura Mitchell offered a more vivid description in her own letter to Fanny Hayes and her brother, Scott:

> Your Mama wishes me to tell you what a superb sailor she has become. For twenty-four hours we have been on the ocean, and she sings, and talks, and laughs like the jolliest Jack Tar of them all . . . the ocean seems holding its breath, or rising and falling with the gentlest sighs. . . . We saw a pair of whales, yesterday, tossing up their sun-lit spray quite near our steamer. . . . To be a whale and spout must be the next best happiness to being a little boy and blowing bubbles.

The sightseeing was far from over. From San Francisco the president and the others rode a train to Yosemite, where a team of six horses pulled their open stagecoach through the valley. They moved farther south to Los Angeles, visiting orange groves, vineyards, and the new campus of the University of Southern California. They then turned east for home, pausing in Tucson, Arizona Territory, for a military parade and moving on to the end of the rail line in New Mexico Territory. Leaving the luxuries of their special train, they boarded army ambulances and, shielded by a cavalry escort, pushed into rugged country still subject to raids by hostile Apaches. They spent one night at an army post, another in a camp on the Rio Grande, and finally reached the tracks of the Atchison, Topeka & Santa Fe Railroad, where another train waited. On November 1, 1880, at

the end of the longest journey undertaken by a president up to that time, Hayes reached Spiegel Grove.

Hayes neglected his diary during the long trip. But when he returned to the White House he provided a one-paragraph summary: "We left W[ashington] on our Pacific tour Thursday evening 26th August and returned Saturday morning 6 November after an absence of Seventy one days. Our trip was most fortunate in all of its circumstances. Superb weather, good health and no accidents. A most gratifying reception greeted us everywhere from the people and from noted and interesting individuals."

In March 1880, looking forward to returning to Spiegel Grove, First Lady Lucy Webb Hayes wrote to her husband, "We will grow old together and lead a happy life at Fremont." They did. They expanded the house for their family and guests, doubling the size of the front porch, or veranda, which the former president especially loved.

In 1912 the Hayes Speigel Grove property was donated to the state of Ohio by the Hayes children, although the family continued to live in the house until 1965. Today the house and the adjacent Rutherford B. Hayes Presidential Center are open to the public.

Chapter 16

James A. Garfield: Death of a President

Bursting with fun and energy, President James A. Garfield teasingly tugged his teenage sons around the White House bedroom while singing snatches from Gilbert and Sullivan's *HMS Pinafore*: "Oh, bitter is my cup! However could I do it? I mixed those children up, and not a creature knew it." On a dare from the youngest, the 49-year-old, 200-pound president leaped over the bed. Then he did handsprings across the floor. Still laughing, he returned to his own room, put on a light gray summer suit, slipped a flower in his buttonhole, and walked downstairs for breakfast. It was the morning of July 2, 1881. The president was leaving Washington for a long summer vacation. He clearly felt liberated.

A Civil War major general and a member of the House of Representatives from Ohio, Garfield won the Republican nomination on the thirty-sixth ballot as a dark horse, humbling former President Ulysses S. Grant, who sought a third term. But both politically and personally, Garfield had found the four months since Inauguration Day frustrating, anxious,

This artistic half-length, profile photograph of President James A. Garfield (*opposite*) was taken in the 1870s by Napoleon Sarony, a Fifth Avenue, New York City, photographer who specialized in theatrical portraiture.

The Garfields were a close, affectionate family, devoted to one another and determined to preserve their family life despite the duties of the White House. James Garfield's mother, Eliza Ballou Garfield, resided with the family. James and Lucretia Garfield are pictured here in 1881 with their five children: Harry, age 17; Jim, 15; Mollie, 14; Irvin, 10; and Abram, 8. Notice the image of former president Abraham Lincoln prominently displayed on the wall.

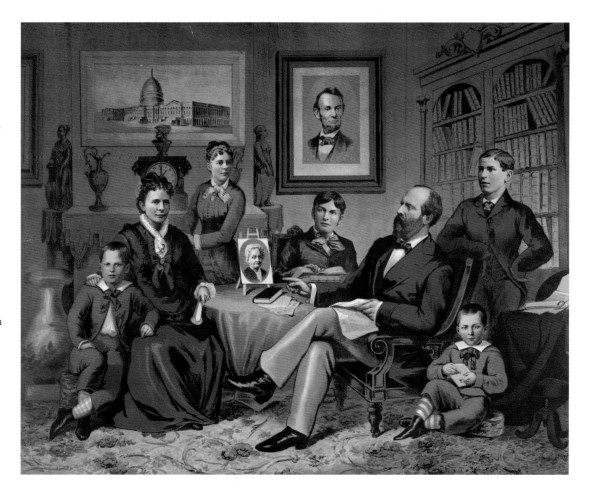

Like the Grants before them, the Garfield family vacationed at the Jersey Shore, at Elberon, just south of Long Banch. The shore communities were connected by Ocean Boulevard, which was lined with luxurious summer homes, called "cottages" by their wealthy owners. Recovering from illness, First Lady Lucretia Garfield was staying at the Elberon Hotel when she heard that her husband had been shot.

Built in 1873, the Baltimore and Potomac Railroad Depot was located at the corner of 6th Street and Avenue B (now Constitution Avenue) in Northwest Washington, approximately where the National Gallery of Art stands today. It was replaced by the current Union Station in 1907.

and wearing. He became embroiled in a bitter fight over patronage with powerful factions inside the Republican Party. Then his wife, Lucretia, was stricken with a serious illness. Her temperature reached 104 degrees and stayed high for so long that her doctors feared she might die. But on this July morning, the road ahead looked clear and the future, promising. Garfield's opponents were in disarray. His wife appeared to be well on the road to recovery. She was waiting for him at the Elberon Hotel near Long Branch on the Jersey Shore, where he had taken her to complete her recuperation within sound of the surf. The president believed fervently in the healing powers of the ocean.

Garfield had charted an active summer. Meeting his wife and their daughter Mollie at Elberon, he planned to sail up the Hudson on the yacht of millionaire Cyrus Field and spend the night at Field's estate. From there the family would travel to Williamstown, Massachusetts, to enroll Jim, 15, and Harry, 17, as freshmen at the president's alma mater, Williams College. After receiving an honorary degree at commencement ceremonies, Garfield planned to tour New England, ending with a weekend visit at the home of Secretary of State James G. Blaine and his wife, Harriet, in Augusta, Maine. The family would spend August at the Garfield farm in Mentor, Ohio, a comfortable distance from the capital's steamy heat. In the fall the president would attend centennial ceremonies at the Yorktown battlefield in Virginia, tour the South, and get down to the business of setting directions for the government.

Secretary Blaine waited with a State Department carriage at the White House door, and he and the president chatted as they were driven to the Baltimore and Potomac Railroad Depot, a redbrick structure with a massive corner tower not far from Capitol Hill. A private parlor car had been added to the regular 9:30 a.m. train and was ready for Garfield to board. They arrived with ten minutes to spare and entered the building. Still talking, they walked side-by-side across a waiting room. A man in a dark business suit and a slouch hat moved in behind them. He was short, slim, and 39 years old, with a dark mustache and a beard. His name was Charles J. Guiteau.

Guiteau drew a revolver and fired. Garfield felt a sting in his right arm and threw back his head: "My God! What is this?" Guiteau fired once more. This time the bullet struck the president squarely in the back, about 4 inches to the right of his spinal column. The impact crumpled him. Walking next to the president, Blaine heard "a very loud report of a pistol discharge, followed in a brief interval by a second shot." The secretary of state looked around. He saw a dark-haired man with a pistol running toward the street door.

On the morning of July 2, 1881, President Garfield was on his way to meet his wife in Elberon, New Jersey, and then to travel extensively throughout the summer. He was deep in conversation with Secretary of State James G. Blaine as he entered the Baltimore and Potomac Railroad Depot. There Charles J. Guiteau stepped behind the president and fired twice, the second bullet lodging near Garfield's spine.

Guiteau was arrested on the spot. Americans soon learned he was a self-educated lawyer and a religious fanatic. Many came to believe he was mentally unstable. After involving himself in the 1880 presidential campaign, he became obsessed with the notion that his street-corner speeches for Garfield entitled him to be named to head the U.S. consulate in Paris. Guiteau had thrust a copy of his speech at Garfield at a White House reception. At another

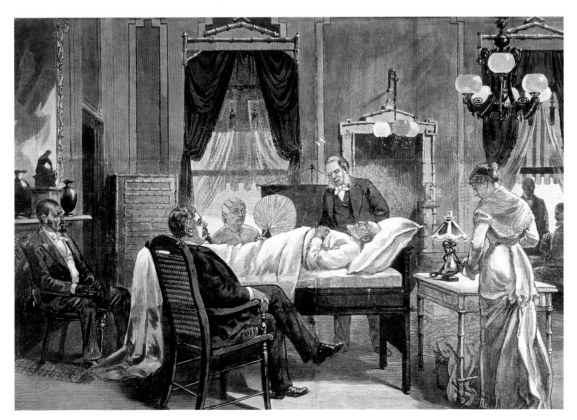

Brought back to the White House, Garfield lay on his back two months while the bullet wound grew infected. Fans were little use in the stifling summer heat, but the president got some relief through a navy-engineered "air-conditioning" system that used an electric blower to pump ice-cooled air through cotton filters and a canvas hose to the sick room. Meanwhile, doctors continued to probe for the bullet. Alexander Graham Bell tried to assist them by using an electrically charged needle, but Garfield's doctors told him to look in the wrong place; it was later suspected that the heavy iron springs in the president's bed distorted the findings.

At Elberon, men worked through the night to lay track close enough to the Francklyn cottage that the gravely ill president could be carried directly from his railcar to his bed. Locomotive headlights, lanterns, and flaming torches lighted their way.

event, he had tried to make his case to the first lady. When he was told the president could not see him "today," he took that as an invitation to return tomorrow. He pursued his quest with such dogged zeal that he was soon considered a nuisance, and White House clerks were instructed not to admit him. Some time after that, Guiteau decided to "remove" the president. He stalked him for weeks before taking advantage of his departure on vacation. He had detailed letters in his pocket explaining his crime and political motivations. The *Boston Daily Globe* and other newspapers gave him an enduring label: "Disappointed Office Seeker."

Throughout July and August the heat built and the city sweltered. Fetid odors from the Potomac River flats drifted through the White House windows. The president lay on his bed in a darkened room, surrounded by screens, cut off from most visitors, even members of his cabinet. His many doctors proved unable to locate the bullet in his back. They repeatedly probed the wound with unwashed fingers and unsterilized instruments, and it became infected. The temperature in the sickroom reached 90 degrees, and the moist, hot air became so stifling Garfield experienced difficulty breathing.

By the end of August, Garfield's weight had fallen to 130 pounds. Infections were widespread. He experienced fevers, then chills. Even the slightest movement was painful: no thoughts now of handsprings. But Garfield chafed at the social isolation imposed by his doctors. Increasingly he wanted to leave the White House, go to his Ohio farm, or visit the seashore with its bracing ocean breezes. After much discussion the doctors agreed. He would be moved to a private and luxurious cottage on the bluff above the Atlantic beaches at Elberon, his destination on the day he was shot.

Moving the ailing president from the White House to the Jersey Shore required the technical precision of a military operation. Beginning on the afternoon of September 5, surveyors laid out a right-of-way for a 3,200-foot spur track from the Elberon station to the Elberon Hotel and the door of the cottage reserved for the president. Within hours, 2,000 men were at work. Trains delivered ties, rails, spikes, sledgehammers, and shovels. Wagons carried away the excavated dirt. Crowds of vacationers from the hotels and cottages watched from the sidelines as the new track moved forward. "Hot coffee and sandwiches, furnished by Col. Jones, of the Elberon, are served to the industrious workers at frequent intervals, and

every man is working with a will to get the road in readiness," the *New York Times* reported. The first tie was laid at 6:00 p.m. in the evening. The last spike was driven at 6:00 a.m. the next morning, just as the president was leaving the White House to board the train.

Arrangements in Washington had been just as pressured. Track layers built a 300-yard spur line from Sixth Street to the main track in less than three hours. A special train was assembled near the depot where Garfield had been shot. In the lead was Pennsylvania Railroad Engine 658, described in news accounts as "one of the finest and most powerful owned by the company." For this run it would burn anthracite to reduce coal dust. Lucretia Garfield and family members were to ride in parlor car of the president of the Pennsylvania Railroad. Just behind was Car 33, a baggage-passenger car chosen because its door was wide enough to accommodate a full-size mattress. Converted overnight to a hospital car, it had been fitted with wire gauze over the windows to keep out dust. The interior was lined with heavy curtains and carpets to reduce noise. A new false ceiling provided space for air to circulate and cool, and ice in chests further reduced temperatures. The president's doctors and a squad of soldiers to carry the stretcher rode in the train's last car, a Pullman. Preceded by a pilot engine, the presidential special had a clear run to the station at Elberon. All southbound trains were ordered to pull into sidings or switches and stay there until the president's train passed. Medical stations were set up along the route in case the president's condition grew worse.

At 6:00 a.m. on September 6, the president was placed on a stretcher, carried out of the North Portico of the White House and up a wooden ramp, and placed on a mattress on the floor of a curtained express wagon. Hundreds watched in silence as it left the grounds. Soldiers walked next to the horses to prevent sudden movements. At the train, a squad of soldiers carried the mattress from the wagon and placed it on a waiting bed in the hospital car. En route the Garfield train reached speeds of up to 60 miles an hour. Standing along the

FRANK LESLIE'S ILLUSTRATED NEWSPAPER

Entered according to Act of Congress, in the year 1881, by Mrs. Frank Leslie, in the Office of the Librarian of Congress at Washington.—Entered at the Post Office, New York, N.Y., as Second-class Matter.

No. 1,357.—Vol. LIII. | NEW YORK, OCTOBER 1, 1881. | [Price 10 Cents. $4.00 Yearly. 13 Weeks, $1.

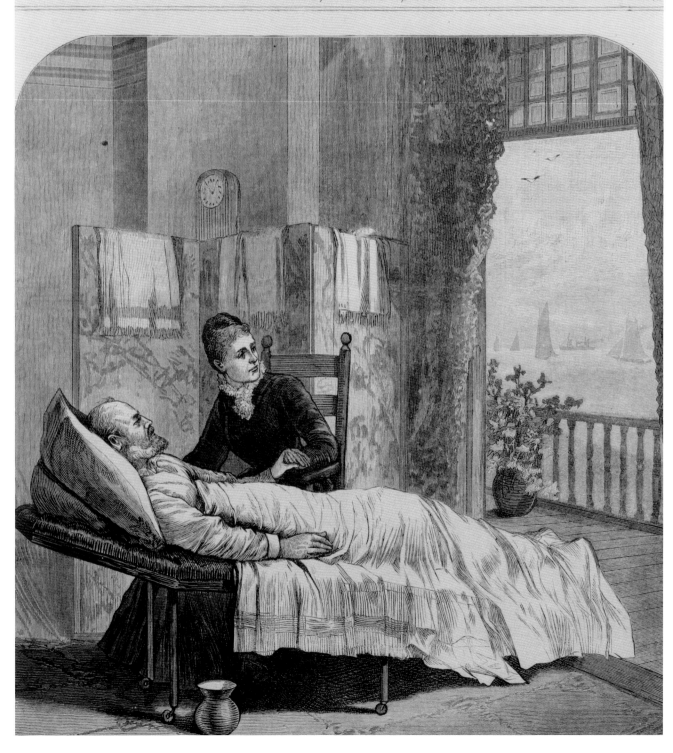

tracks, men held their hats in hand and women waved their bonnets. The train made the 230-mile trip in seven hours, arriving at the Elberon station in mid-afternoon. Shortly thereafter, the president was brought to rest in the twenty-room cottage owned by New York financier Charles G. Francklyn, which stood at the rear of the Elberon Hotel and was within earshot of the splash and tumble of the surf. "The rooms are large, the ceilings high, and the furnishings sumptuous," the *New York Times* reported.

At first, Garfield's optimism and trust in the ocean's healing powers seemed justified. While the first few days had been uncomfortably warm, by September 9 temperatures had cooled. Garfield appeared to be rallying, and the doctors were optimistic. The president's principal physician, Dr. Willard Bliss, called him "convalescent." "The President's condition is so generally satisfactory that it does seem as if nothing could prevent recovery," the *Washington Post* reported. Secretary of State Blaine sent an advisory telegram to the U.S. mission in London: "The medical reports were all favorable to-day, morning, noon and night. The president has not for many weeks done so well for so many consecutive hours." But another cabinet member advised caution: "We had better wait awhile before we toss up our hats."

The optimism began to fade two days later. "Not So Well As Saturday," the *New York Times* reported in a headline. "He has held his own, but that is all," the newspaper observed. Day by day the president's condition declined. The medical bulletins issued by the president's doctors remained as upbeat as possible even as the patient's fever rose and he suffered chills, vomiting, and a severe cough. On September 17, Dr. Silas Boynton of Cleveland, the president's cousin, told a reporter that the president had lost ground after every relapse. He was even more candid in dispatch to a friend: "I have no hopes of his recovery."

By Monday morning, September 19, Garfield was extremely weak. He could raise a glass only a few inches. He made motions as if to play a hand of cards but lacked the strength to hold them. He slept on and off throughout the day and into the evening. At about 10:00 p.m. he awoke, put his hand on his chest, and cried out to a friend: "I am in terrible pain here." Dr. Bliss entered the room moments later, found Garfield unconscious, searched for a pulse, administered stimulants, heard a flutter, and sent for Mrs. Garfield. The group stood at the president's bedside for twenty minutes. Then all breathing stopped. "It is over," the doctor said. It was 10:35 p.m., and eighty days after Garfield set out from the White House for a summer holiday.

———

Vice President Chester Arthur was at his home in Manhattan. He was quickly advised by telegram of Garfield's death. At midnight a wire from the cabinet advised him to take the Oath of Office as quickly as possible. The national flag hanging from a window of the Elberon cottage was draped in black crepe. Church bells tolled for the slain president coast to coast as he was returned to Washington in the same rail car that had brought him to the shore. His casket lay in state for two days in the Rotunda of the Capitol. More than 100,000 people filed past.

In a eulogy delivered at a joint meeting of Congress, Secretary of State Blaine recalled that as they left the White House on that morning in July the president had been gleefully anticipating a welcome vacation and had been "joyfully, almost boyishly happy." Garfield felt "that trouble lay behind him and not before him," Blaine remembered. He had not had even a momentary premonition of what the next few minutes held in store.

At Elberon, as reported in *Frank Leslie's Illustrated Newspaper* on October 1, 1881 (*opposite*), Garfield was surrounded by his family and able to see the ocean. He told his doctors, "It is refreshing to get where I can look at the sea." He observed "the fishermen at sea, the vessels on the ocean, and the bathers on the surf," and whispered, "I am myself again."

Chapter 17

Chester A. Arthur: The Elegant Angler

A gentleman in manners, a peacock in style, a fisherman by inclination, Chester A. Arthur traveled anywhere a trout or a bass might be tempted by an artfully cast fly, a gleaming lure, or a wriggling minnow. Thrust into the presidency by the assassination of James Garfield and privately suffering from a life-threatening illness, Arthur found he could unwind best with a fishing rod in his hands. Arthur angled so often and journeyed so far that the *New York Sun* accused him of neglect of duty and urged Congress to dock his pay every time he left the White House on a fishing vacation.

As president, Arthur fished for pike and bass in the Thousand Islands on the St. Lawrence River in upstate New York. He cruised along the New England coast aboard a navy steamer, fishing whenever possible. He held a record for an Atlantic salmon caught before his presidency. He mingled with the nation's social elite—and fished—at fashionable Newport. He checked into a beach hotel at Coney Island after sending word he wished to avoid politicians and go deep-sea fishing. Arthur fished in New York's Catskills and in Florida's rivers. And in the greatest outdoor adventure of his presidency, he joined a government expedition, rode through the Rocky Mountains, and caught trout by the dozens in the sparkling streams on the way to Yellowstone National Park.

In October 1882, slightly more than a year after James Garfield died and Arthur entered the White House, the *Sun* dispatched a reporter to follow the president at Alexandria Bay on the south bank of the St. Lawrence River near the Canadian border. Arthur fished four to eight hours a day from the steam yacht *Minnie*, a long narrow launch. At times he and his guides transferred to one or more of the three light and graceful canoe-like skiffs tied

President Chester A. Arthur (*opposite*) was one of a long line of American presidents who found refreshment in fishing. An angler long before he ascended to the presidency, Arthur went on his first fishing vacation in the fall of 1882. Reporters followed him to Alexandria Bay in the Thousand Islands region of upstate New York, where a photographer caught him standing in a fishing skiff.

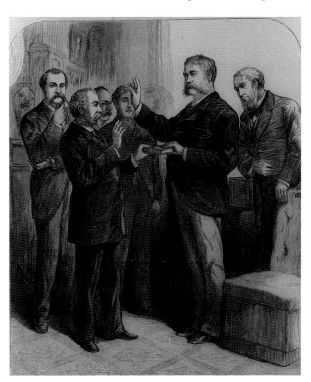

The front page of *Frank Leslie's Illustrated Newspaper* (*left*) carried this image of Vice President Arthur taking the Oath of Office. He was at his home on Lexington Avenue in New York when he learned of President James A. Garfield's death late in the evening of September 19, 1881. A few hours later, at 2:30 a.m. on September 20, he was sworn into office by Justice John R. Brady of the New York Supreme Court.

to the *Minnie*'s stern. The skiffs were loaded with fishing gear: hooks, spoons, lines, snells, extra reels, scissors, knives, nets, gaffs, and even a container of silver polish. The reporter noted admiringly that Arthur's own split bamboo rods had nickel-plated joints and reels and that each was as "slender as a carriage whip."

A night owl, Arthur went fishing when he was ready, to the despair of guides who believed in early morning starts. On Monday, October 2, Arthur boarded the *Minnie* at noon, stylishly attired in a gray suit with a loose jacket and a pearl-gray derby. He settled into a comfortable armchair on the forward deck, simultaneously fishing and reading a book. At first there was no action, and the president's eyelids drooped until they nearly shut. Then a pike swallowed the bait. "When he felt a tug at his line he waked up and played with the fish artistically," the *Sun*'s reporter noted. "He had a pretty battle with a big pickerel, and tired him and brought him in three minutes." Altogether, the president netted eleven fish that day: nine bass and two pickerel. The fishing was even better on other days, and Arthur once caught a 35-pound muskie.

It was fishing with a dollop of luxury. The picnic hampers overflowed with broiled chicken, chops, cold meats, and potatoes. Arthur brought a robe lined with otter and mink to fend off the October chill. There was an ice chest filled with bottles to ward off thirst, a collapsible table for dining on shore, cushioned lockers for an afternoon nap, and a double-barreled shotgun in case a duck flew over. The *Sun* reported the president spent little time on official business, read no newspapers, and received no important visitors. While he did get daily mail delivery, he sent few telegrams. But the reporter concluded that as far as the president was concerned, the trip had been a success. "President Arthur has got what he came to the border for—rest and improved health," he wrote at the trip's end. "He goes away feeling very much better than when he came, and wholly satisfied with the efforts of those who managed to turn every day to account in producing rest and pleasure for him."

In their editorial, written before the reporter arrived on the scene, the *Sun*'s editors demonstrated no concern for a president's need for relaxation. The newspaper branded Arthur's frequent travel "culpable absenteeism and criminal neglect of duty" and extended its wrath to the wanderlust of cabinet members. "The President and Secretaries take oaths to perform their duties faithfully. They are supposed to be present to perform them," the *Sun* contended. "They draw the pay with punctilious regularity, whether sporting with fashion at Newport, or cruising in public vessels, or luxuriating at Long Branch." In their absence, it thundered, the corrupt and the venal hold "high carnival" in government departments.

Disregarding the constitutional ban on amending a sitting president's pay, the *Sun* made its suggestion: "We propose that Congress shall pass a law at the next session to correct this shameful abuse. The terms of it may be very simple, and need only a few plain but direct words, forbidding any public officer from receiving pay while absent from duty at his own request or by any recognized practice of vacation. Stop the salary, and reform will follow as naturally as day succeeds night." Congress passed no such law. Arthur and his cabinet members and those who followed them in office continued to travel and vacation as they saw fit.

———

A lawyer and machine politician removed by President Rutherford B. Hayes as collector of customs in New York, Arthur was chosen as James Garfield's running mate at the 1880 Republican convention in Chicago as a consolation prize for the disappointed Stalwart wing of the party. A recent widower, he considered the vice presidency a higher honor than he had

ever hoped to attain, but his reputation was as a willing cog in the system of party patronage and political spoils. No one thought of him as a presidential contender in his own right. After Garfield was shot, the *New York Times* called Arthur "about the last man who would be considered eligible" for the presidency. Once in office, however, Arthur surprised the skeptics, proving himself an able and honest administrator. In the most important act of his presidency, he signed into law the Pendleton Civil Service Reform Act of 1883. Although it left many positions untouched, it laid the foundation for reform by establishing the principle that merit, not political influence, should be the primary qualification for a public service position.

At 6 foot 2 inches, Arthur was the tallest president since Lincoln. He kept his silky, wavy hair carefully combed and cultivated a full mustache and cascading sideburns. A clotheshorse with as many as eighty pairs of trousers in his wardrobe, Arthur wore a coat with an elegant fur collar for an official photograph. Once in office he found the White House run down and out of fashion and transformed it into a showcase for Louis Comfort Tiffany's stained glass. During most summers, Arthur resided at the presidential cottage on the grounds of the Soldiers' Home, and on many evenings could be seen sitting on the porch, puffing on a cigar, and chatting with friends.

A frequent traveler, Arthur mingled with John Jacob Astor and Cornelius Vanderbilt at elegant banquets at Newport. He used the USS *Despatch*, a sleek, 174-foot navy steamer, as a presidential yacht for cruises on the Potomac River and Chesapeake Bay and up the Atlantic coast to New England. Some newspapers accused him of "junketing" at taxpayers' expense. But the president had his defenders. "A few able editors are greatly distressed about this 'junketing expedition'," the *Washington Post* commented in September 1882 as the president visited Newport on the *Despatch*. "But, it really seems to us, the commander-in-chief of the navy is not guilty of a great wrong in making a tour in a vessel that is only fit for duty of this sort, especially as the mess bills of officers, passengers and guests are not paid for out of the public purse."

The USS *Despatch*, a commercial steamer purchased by the navy in 1873, saw service in the Caribbean and eastern Mediterranean before being recommissioned as a training vessel for cadets at the U.S. Naval Academy. During his administration, President Arthur made use of the *Despatch* as a presidential yacht, visiting Bar Harbor, Maine, where this photograph was taken on September 10, 1882.

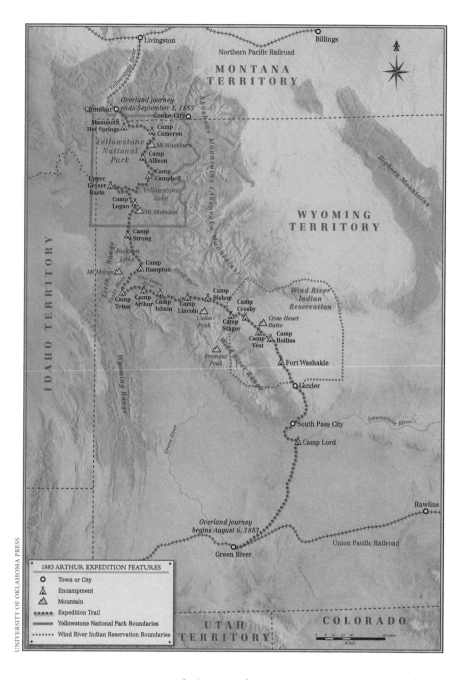

The next spring, Arthur became the first president to vacation in Florida, a newly fashionable destination. But the heat, humidity, swarming mosquitoes, and his own sudden illness prevented it from becoming the pleasure cruise the president had hoped for when he left Washington. Arriving in Jacksonville, he boarded a streamer and headed south for fishing on the St. John's River but soon became overheated, edgy, and irritable. Eventually he boarded the navy steamer *Tallapoosa* for Savannah, where he took a long drive under an intense sun. Returning to the ship, he retired to his cabin. But at about 2:30 a.m. he became desperately ill. The ship's doctor found the president in such extreme pain he thought he might die. Arthur's condition had previously and privately been diagnosed as Bright's disease, the late nineteenth-century name for a serious kidney disorder. Arthur swore the *Tallapoosa*'s doctor to secrecy. When reporters learned of the president's illness, and the *New York Times* accurately described it as "sudden and violent," they were told Arthur had experienced a slight indisposition due to overexposure to the sun and indigestion. Returning to Washington, Arthur appeared well enough when he stepped from his railroad car. "I am

President Arthur's 1883 expedition through Yellowstone National Park was planned and led by General H. Philip Sheridan. This map shows the route.

feeling perfectly well, as well as ever, in fact." he told a friend. "I have not been sick at all." He maintained that stance for the rest of his administration.

———

Arthur continued to travel. In midsummer the White House announced that the president would take part in an ambitious western adventure: an expedition to Yellowstone National Park in Wyoming Territory led by General Philip H. Sheridan, the Civil War cavalry officer who commanded on the western frontier. The president was at Cape May, New Jersey, when someone asked if the western trip would be part of his vacation. Arthur erupted: "Vacation! That is the way all the newspapers talk. They speak of my journeys as junketings. I need a holiday as much as the poorest of my fellow-citizens, but it is generally supposed that we people at Washington do not want any rest."

The president's newspaper critics, including the *New York Sun*, continued to fume. It declared the trip was a further and expensive example of Arthur's absenteeism and neglect of duty. But other journals responded that in the age of the telegraph and telephone, a president could manage official business and stay in touch from almost anywhere. Reporters were told that

President Arthur's expedition to Yellowstone Park in the summer of 1883 involved more roughing it than might have been expected of a president known for his fine taste in clothes and White House furnishings. At Upper Geyser Basin, the presidential party posed on army campaign chairs. General Philip H. Sheridan, the leader of the expedition, is third from left. Standing behind him is General Anson Stager. President Arthur sits to Sheridan's left, in the center of the photograph. Sitting to his left are Secretary of War Robert Todd Lincoln and Senator George G. Vest, a great promoter of Yellowstone Park.

Arthur's presence would cause no extra expense because the expedition would leave for the West whether or not he was along. "It is not to be a pleasure party gotten up for the benefit of the President, but an official exploration party and the President is to accompany it as an invited guest," the *Hartford Daily Courant* reported. But the mutterings did not entirely fade. Following Arthur's return to Washington, one newspaper ran a one-sentence comment: "It appears that a junketing expedition, reported officially, becomes an 'exploration'."

Yellowstone's supporters had strong motives for wanting the president to view the park's waterfalls, geysers, and elk with his own eyes. Created in the Grant administration, the park seemed threatened by developers, miners, and other private interests. Congress was reluctant to provide necessary appropriations. One chief supporter, Senator George G. Vest of Missouri, a member of the expedition, hoped to enlist the president as an important ally. For his part, Arthur may have made the trip hoping that the mountain air would improve his uncertain health.

Members of the expedition met in Chicago on August 1 and headed west by train. They included President Arthur, Senator Vest, and Secretary of War Robert Todd Lincoln, son of the late president. Reaching Wyoming Territory, they rode wagons to Fort Washakie in the Shoshone Reservation near the Wind River, where 500 tribesmen staged a war dance and sham battle. After a day of rest, they rode horses into rugged terrain, crossing the Continental Divide, skirting the Teton Mountains, passing Jackson Lake, and arriving at Yellowstone's Upper Geyser Basin. They made the distance in easy marches, pausing for fishing and hunting. At Sheridan's order, no newspapermen were permitted to join the expedition. But seventy-five troopers from the Fifth U.S. Cavalry rode along for protection. The president stayed in daily communication with Washington through a relay system of mounted couriers who ran messages to and from the nearest telegraph line.

Once under way, the travelers rose before dawn, ate a campfire breakfast, rode until early afternoon, and camped near a trout stream. For Arthur, the value of any trip depended on

In Yellowstone Park the presidential party traveled by horseback, crossing Gros Ventre River escorted by Troop G of the Fifth Cavalry, and the Snake River at Lewis Fork. They saw and photographed wonders not yet familiar to Americans: the Great Falls of the Yellowstone, Old Faithful, and the Grand Teton.

the quality of the fishing, and Wyoming's streams and lakes did not disappoint him. An early dispatch from the trail, written for newspapers by army officers accompanying the expedition, described the experience:

> Buffalo Lake, Wyoming Territory, August 12, 1883: The president spent the entire afternoon fishing in the cool water of the lake, one of the most picturesque on the continent. He had no difficulty in hooking any number of speckled trout. They bite with any kind of tackle or bait. One has only to double up a pin, attach it to a string on any kind of stick, with a piece of red flannel, a grasshopper, or anything else for bait, and the trout bite in these mountain streams and pools as fast as they can be hauled out.

Most of the accounts were vividly descriptive and at times almost lyrical:

> Camp Strong, Wyoming, Aug. 21, via Bozeman, Montana, Aug. 23—The reveille call at 5 o'clock awoke us all from a refreshing sleep, although the ice in our buckets showed that three blankets had been none too many during the night. Half-past 6 o'clock found all the tents struck and packed on the mules and the Presidential party in the saddle. Our route to-day of 30 miles lay nearly northward, over the foot-hills of the Shoshone mountains. . . . It was rough and rugged country, covered for nearly a quarter of the distance by dense tracts of burned and fallen timber. At noon we reached a sparsely timbered knoll, which commanded a view of Jackson Lake, with the snow-covered hills rising from its shores in the background. The scene was wild and grand, and repaid us for our severe, hot, and dusty march in the early part of the day.

Even though a simple pin on a string would suffice to hook a trout, Senator Vest remembered that at first neither he nor the president had much success with their bamboo rods and expensive gear. The cavalry troopers and mule drivers did much better with the crudest of make-do equipment. Close observation revealed their secret: approach the bank with extreme stealth so as not to alarm the fish, allow the bait to be carried away in eddies and currents, and then yank the lunging trout out of the water "without a second's delay." After employing those methods, Arthur and his companions caught as many trout as they could pull in. When he read the accounts, Eugene Field, the Chicago poet, envisioned a luckless Shoshone chief vowing to move farther west "where presidents didn't come fooling about / Turning the heads of the giddy trout."

By the time the party reached the railhead of the Northern Pacific Railroad, boarded a waiting train, and headed east, Arthur had ridden 350 miles on horseback and was reported to have caught more than 100 pounds of trout.

———

Although the Yellowstone trip was the outdoor adventure of a lifetime, it made no long-term improvements in either Arthur's health or his political prospects. His symptoms returned shortly after he did. Even though Arthur appeared willing to run, the Republican National Convention nominated former Secretary of State James G. Blaine as its 1884 presidential candidate. Blaine lost the fall election to Democrat Grover Cleveland. Arthur returned to New York and resumed his law practice but was soon compelled to retire because of illness. He died on November 18, 1886, at age 57.

President Arthur's big catch from a day of fishing on Gros Ventre River was captured in this photograph.

Chapter 18

Grover Cleveland: Surgery at Sea

The reporters arrived at daybreak, spilling off a train at Deer Park in Maryland's western mountains just an hour after the president's arrival. Soon they were peering through binoculars at the honeymoon cottage tucked into a grove of oaks several hundred yards away. Only a line of determined railroad detectives kept them at a distance and prevented them from approaching the porch and knocking on the front door.

Grover Cleveland, 49, former governor of New York, had been a bachelor president until early the previous evening, June 2, 1886. Then, shortly after 7:00 p.m., John Philip Sousa led the Marine Band in the "Wedding March" and the president married 21-year-old Frances Folsom. She was dark haired, slim, beautiful, and a recent college graduate. The engagement had been unexpected and caused a sensation. Apart from their 28-year age difference, the bride, the daughter of Cleveland's late law partner, had been his legal ward. Curiosity about the president's wife and their May-December marriage was clearly insatiable, and much of the nation's press was determined to do its best to satisfy it. The pursuit began as the newlyweds left the White House, drove to the railroad station, and boarded a special two-car train for the seven-hour, 200-mile ride to Deer Park.

By early morning, a honeymoon watch had opened outside the Deer Park resort's Cottage No. 2, so named because it was the second in a direct line from the station. "The President had hoped that he would not be followed, and was greatly surprised to find that the leading papers of the country had their representatives here almost as soon as he arrived," the *Washington Post* reported. It didn't take long for Cleveland to feel he was under siege and to bristle about prying newspapermen. "I can see a group of them sitting on a bridge, which marks one of the limits, waiting for some movement to be made which will furnish an incident," he wrote to Colonel Daniel Lamont, his private secretary.

The newlyweds' first day as a married couple began with their arrival in a chilly rain at dawn attended by a valet and a maid. Newspaper readers learned that there was no sign of activity until 10:00 a.m., when the window curtains were opened. Reporters watched as waiters from

On June 2, 1886, President Grover Cleveland married young Frances Folsom in a White House ceremony (*left*). The public's fascination with the couple was insatiable, and reporters pursued the newlyweds on their honeymoon trip to the Deer Park resort in western Maryland. As this drawing from *Harper's Weekly* illustrates, newspapermen were on hand, taking notes and making sketches, as the president introduced the new first lady to fishing (*opposite*). She caught no fish, and the president was infuriated by the invasion of privacy.

THE PRESIDENT'S VACATION.

HOW SWEET IS SOLITUDE.

The Deer Park hotel and resort complex in western Maryland where the Clevelands spent their honeymoon was owned and operated by the Baltimore and Ohio Railroad. It offered mountain air, views of the Blue Ridge, wooded drives, and nearby fishing. The newlyweds stayed in a two and one-half story cottage, painted gray with red shutters. It had running water, a bathroom, gaslights, and several fireplaces. For five days it was the most talked about house in America.

Souvenir cards and mementos testify to the popular acclaim for the Cleveland marriage and interest in the young bride. Newspapers reported what she wore for every occasion and subjected the presidential household to a scrutiny that was altogether new and unwelcome by both the president and first lady.

PUCK'S CONGRATULATIONS.

the hotel dining room carried in breakfast on trays, and then removed them. Shortly after that they got their first glimpse of the president as he walked, cigar in hand, onto the porch. Then his bride joined him and they strolled on the lawn, taking in the views. The observers started taking notes. She wore "a pretty dress of blue tulle," the *New York Times* recorded. "A white morning shawl was drawn across her shoulders." Reporters were still watching in the afternoon as the couple drove out for a two-hour sightseeing ride. "The bride had replaced her morning costume with the traveling dress of gray, and wore a peak chip hat of black straw, with a long flowing plume to match the dress."

Cleveland was one of the nation's most dedicated fishermen, and it surprised no one that he took his fly rods on his honeymoon. "If I am going to keep my reputation as a fisherman, I must go where there are plenty of trout," he declared. The trout were abundant, and Cleveland pursued them with relish, even enlisting his wife as an angler. On the third day of the honeymoon, the couple rode to Deep Creek, a mountain stream several miles from the cottage. Here Mrs. Cleveland was said to have threaded an angleworm onto her hook "with more enthusiasm than experience." The president found a comfortable log and happily pulled several trout from the stream. But the newspapermen who followed them reported the afternoon this way: "Mrs. Cleveland Fishes: But She Does Not Succeed in Catching Anything."

The close scrutiny continued, and Cleveland vented his indignation against the newspapermen in a letter to the *New York Evening Post*:

> They have used the enormous power of the modern newspaper to perpetuate and disseminate a colossal impertinence, and have done it, not as professional gossips and tattlers, but as the guides and instructors of the public in conduct and morals. And they have done it, not to a private citizen, but the President of the United States, thereby lifting their offence into the gaze of the whole world, and doing their utmost to make American journalism contemptible in the estimation of people of good breeding everywhere.

Some denounced the prying and intrusive coverage of a newly married couple as "keyhole journalism." But for better or worse, the surveillance of Cottage No. 2 at Deer Park represented a turning point opening a window for coverage of all a president's activities, private as well as public. Reports on a president's vacations and recreational activities were becoming standard newspaper fare. A few months later, in August, when some journals planned extensive coverage of the Clevelands' first vacation, a month-long fishing and hunting sojourn in the Adirondacks in upstate New York, many newspapers saw nothing to apologize for. The *Philadelphia Inquirer* announced: "Mr. Cleveland wants to know why he can't take a vacation trip without publicity or newspaper fuss just like any other citizen. Because he's the President; that's why. We have only one President at a time, and it won't do to lose him."

Not all newspapers agreed. "Let Him Alone," the *Washington Post* retorted. It contended that much had changed since the wedding: "The frenzy of public curiosity, which amounted almost to insanity, has passed away." Newspapers that sent correspondents to roost in trees or hide in the grass "deserve the reprobation and contempt of the community," the *Post* said. But that did not mean the *Post* intended to ignore the president's vacation. On the first page of the same edition in which its editorial ran, it detailed the Clevelands' train journey to

To protect his young wife and family from the glare of White House life, President Cleveland purchased a house and small farm 3 miles north of the White House, in what is now the Cleveland Park neighborhood of Washington. He hired an architect and remodeled the house in the fashionable Queen Anne style, expanding it with an extra story, broad porches on two levels, and an addition for the kitchen and servants' quarters. Called Red Top for its red roof, it is pictured here in 1887. Defeated for reelection in 1888, Cleveland sold the house in 1890. It was demolished in 1928.

the Adirondacks, their transfer to a carriage, and their arrival at a cottage on Lake Saranac. "Tonight, at Mrs. Cleveland's request, the whole party were rowed over the lake by two trusty guides," it revealed to its readers.

———————

Cleveland worried from the beginning that the fishbowl atmosphere of life in the White House might overwhelm his bride and that too much public exposure might turn her head. What he wanted, he declared, was not a distinguished first lady but "a sensible domestic American wife." So in the days before his marriage, he paid $21,500 for a house and 23 acres on Tennalytown Road amid the woods and farm fields of sparsely settled Northwest Washington. There, he hoped, his wife could live as she pleased, free of scrutiny. The property was about 2 miles north of Georgetown and a bit more than 3 miles from the White House. Cleveland named the place Oak View for the trees near the house and the view of the city. But for reporters, who were kept at a distance, the house's newly painted red roof was its most visible and prominent feature. They gave the place its popular name: Red Top.

Red Top was the first residence in Washington ever designated by a president as a year-round alternative to the White House. The couple used it full-time in summer, but it was ready whenever they wanted to come out for a fall weekend or a winter afternoon. Cleveland valued it both as a place where he could work without interruption and as the center of family life. Frances Cleveland happily turned the place into her private menagerie, presiding over a collection of ducks, quail, kittens, foxes, white rats, a dachshund, a beagle, a St. Bernard, and a French poodle.

The Clevelands enjoyed their pastoral home for the rest of his term. Sitting down to breakfast at Oak View on his second anniversary, Cleveland found a large centerpiece of red roses on the table with the numeral 2 fashioned in white rosebuds. A small one-room cottage was built that summer for the president's use as a summer office. On November 4, 1888, the newspapers reported that Cleveland had taken a day off from work to go squirrel hunting in the nearby woods with a neighbor. Two days later he was defeated for reelection by Republican Benjamin Harrison of Indiana.

Most Americans assumed they had seen the last of the Clevelands in the White House. But to Frances Cleveland, the election was not the final word on her husband's future in politics. As she was leaving the White House on Harrison's Inauguration Day, March 4, 1889, she told a White House footman that she wanted to find everything in good repair when she returned. He was startled but managed to ask when that might be. She had a ready answer: "We are coming back just four years from to-day." She was right.

———

Early in his second administration, Grover Cleveland used the pretext of a summer vacation, the privacy afforded by a friend's yacht. and the denials of his closest associates to conceal one of the most daring medical procedures in presidential history. Shortly before noon on July 1, 1893, the president walked into the main cabin of the 150-foot steam yacht *Oneida* as it cruised Long Island Sound, and he took a seat on a chair lashed to the mast. A dentist and a team of surgeons stepped forward and administered anesthesia. What happened next would remain a secret for the next twenty-four years despite determined efforts by reporters to uncover the facts.

Back in Washington, the press, White House staff members, and all but one member of Cleveland's cabinet were given a cover story: The president had taken the train to New York to begin a much-needed vacation. After spending the night of June 30 aboard the *Oneida* at her anchorage in the East River he would cruise up the East Coast for several days. Then he would join his wife, Frances, and their infant daughter, Ruth, at Gray Gables, his Cape Cod fishing retreat.

That much was the truth. But only Dr. Joseph Bryant, the president's personal physician, and a select team of surgeons, as well as Cleveland's closest associates and friends, knew that just days before, a rough and painful patch on the roof of his mouth had been diagnosed as a malignant tumor. It needed to be removed at once. The president's medical emergency was complicated by the onset of serious economic woes. The stock market had collapsed, triggering a severe depression then called a panic. As the economy spiraled downward over the next four years, hundreds of banks closed, thousands of businesses failed, and an estimated 4 million workers lost their jobs. On June 30, the morning of his departure for New York, Cleveland called on Congress to convene on August 7. He kept his surgery secret lest it deepen the crisis by destroying public confidence in his ability to act. Cleveland assigned planning for the surgery and its aftermath to Dr. Bryant and Colonel Daniel Lamont, who had served as the president's private secretary in the first Cleveland administration and was now secretary of war.

On board the *Oneida*, the president woke from a full night's sleep, enjoyed a leisurely breakfast, and then was examined by the doctors. At 56, Cleveland was corpulent and at risk for a stroke or a heart attack. While the doctors found no reason not to proceed, they may have been more nervous than their patient. If the president died, how would they explain subjecting him to surgery at sea instead of operating with all the safeguards of a hospital? "If

Gray Gables

In 1891, Cleveland purchased another property and expanded it for his family's use. It was a summer house, on Buzzards Bay, south of Boston, on the neck of land where Cape Cod begins. Called Gray Gables, the house offered privacy and comfort—and direct access to bathing and fishing. These views of summers at Gray Gables are from a family album in the collection of the Grover Cleveland Birthplace in Caldwell, New Jersey.

you hit a rock, hit it good and hard, so that we'll all go to the bottom!" Dr. Bryant told the yacht's captain.

The doctors administered nitrous oxide, commonly called laughing gas, and later switched to ether. As a first step Dr. Ferdinand Hasbrouck, the dentist on the surgical team, removed the two bicuspid teeth on the upper left side. Then Dr. Bryant made incisions in the roof of the mouth. The tumor was larger than expected. The hollow cavity in the jaw was filled with a gelatinous mass later found to be a sarcoma. In the end the entire upper left jaw was removed along with part of the soft palate. With the use of a cheek retractor the entire operation took place inside the patient's mouth, leaving no visible scars.

The surgery was complete by 1:55 p.m. "What a sigh of intense relief we surgeons breathed when the patient was once more safe in bed can hardly be imagined!" Dr. William Keen, a prominent member of the surgical team, remembered. Cleveland was out of bed briefly the next day and walked on deck on July 3 as the *Oneida* made its way up the Atlantic coast. Late in the afternoon of July 5 the ship reached the end of Buzzards Bay and dropped anchor off Gray Gables. Cleveland walked unassisted from the dock to the house where he was once more put to bed.

Despite the explanations offered at the White House, reporters found the president's five-day disappearance suspicious at best. They peppered officials with questions: Where had he been? Had anything happened to him? Was anything wrong with his health? Why had no one seen him since his arrival at Buzzards Bay? Acting as spokesman and conciliator, Secretary Lamont calmly spun out a plausible lie. The president had suffered a bout of painful rheumatism in his foot and knee. He would stay in his room until his condition improved. The attack had undoubtedly been brought on by the work and stress he had encountered since his inauguration. When the questioning grew insistent, Lamont also conceded that the president was in pain from a toothache. In any case, he needed absolute rest.

Speculation was rampant, especially after Dr. Bryant admitted that the president had had a tooth extracted. But the *New York Times* rejected the suspicions and accepted the official story. "The assertion that President Cleveland is seriously afflicted with any malady is all nonsense," the *Times* maintained. It complained that intense competition in the newspaper business "demands that all such reports shall be magnified, and not corrected or stopped." It summed up in a headline: "Alarming Stories About His Illness Without Foundation."

On July 10, Dr. Bryant, Lamont, and the president went fishing in Buzzards Bay. They stayed out several hours and brought home a good catch of bass and other fish. The expedition added to the impression that reports of surgery at sea had been a fabrication.

After a New York orthodontist produced a made-to-measure prosthesis of vulcanized rubber that replaced the missing jaw and palate, Cleveland began to speak normally. A second operation on July 17, in New York, removed all suspect tissue and cauterized the entire surface. The president returned to Gray Gables two days later to resume his recovery and to work on the message he would send Congress in August. He let the word be passed to reporters that the sea air had worked wonders, that he was in splendid health, and that his rheumatism pains had entirely disappeared.

Cleveland returned to Washington for the opening of Congress on August 7, and then went back to Gray Gables to rest for the remainder of the month. He left a statement behind him: "My day's doings will be devoid of interest to the public, and I shall be exceedingly pleased if I can be free from the attentions of newspaper correspondents." That hope was not entirely realized. A reporter for the *Philadelphia Press* had interviewed Dr. Hasbrouck and published a highly accurate account of the removal of the president's jaw.

Bryant and Lamont repeatedly and emphatically denied his story. Aided by the skill of the surgeons and his close-fitting rubber jaw, Cleveland proved to be his own best ally. He simply did not look or sound much different than he had before surgery, even when he spoke before an audience. Widely dismissed as a sham and a fraud, the surgery at sea story faded into obscurity. It remained that way until the fall of 1917, when Dr. Keen, one of the most prominent surgeons of his day, described the procedure in

For President Cleveland, summers at Gray Gables meant fishing, as portrayed in another photograph from the Cleveland family album.

a lengthy and detailed article in the *Saturday Evening Post*. Cleveland, by then, had long since died of causes unrelated to his 1893 cancer surgery. Keen declared that his disclosure was motivated by fear that the story might otherwise be lost to history. However gratifying it may have been, Cleveland's success at keeping his surgery a secret had no influence on the outcome of the national economic crisis. The economy stayed in depression for the next four years.

In his second term as in his first, Cleveland felt the need for private quarters in the capital where he, his wife, and their children could enjoy life outside the White House fishbowl. Instead of buying a property as he had before, he rented Woodley, a manor in Northwest Washington with a long presidential history. Martin Van Buren, John Tyler, and James Buchanan had all used it as a summer retreat.

But Gray Gables remained Cleveland's favorite retreat and fishing his preferred remedy for stress. Living up to its name with many gables and weathered shingled walls, Gray Gables

Gray Gables sat high on a hill overlooking Buzzards Bay. From his office, the president commanded a view of the approaches to the house and a new lodge at the entrance to the grounds. The view from the water side took in the sailboats across Buzzards Bay. After the Clevelands' time, the house was enlarged. It eventually became a tourist inn, but was destroyed by fire in the 1970s.

faced Buzzards Bay from several wooded acres on Monument Point. It was a short walk from the Crow's Nest, the home of Cleveland's good friend Joseph Jefferson, one of the most famous actors of the era. When Cleveland first arrived, the only access was by water or a 6-mile carriage ride through woods and fields, and that helped preserve the privacy he treasured. He was a hospitable host, but when visitors came bearing cameras Cleveland told them plainly he wanted no photographs made of his family or the interior of the house.

In 1894, the Secret Service was detailed for the first time to keep watch over the president and his family. According to newspaper reports, three agents were assigned to Gray Gables when the president's family moved there for the summer. The president was said to have reason to fear a kidnapping, and the agents gave special attention to Mrs. Cleveland and her two daughters. "The facts in this matter have just come to light and it shows what a careful man President Cleveland is for the safety of his family," the *Chicago Tribune* declared. The president's children had received wide publicity. Ruth, the eldest, had been promptly dubbed "Baby Ruth" by the press and was easily the most famous child in America. Her sister, Esther, was the first child born in the White House.

Richard Watson Gilder, the editor of *Century Magazine* who had introduced Cleveland to Buzzards Bay, was convinced that outdoor activities helped his friend deal with the tensions of his job: "His fishing and hunting excursions, while entered upon with appetite, were also considered by him a duty; for it was only on these little vacations that he was able to

Some Fishing Pretenses & Affectations.

The Mission of Fishing & Fishermen.

A Defence of Fishermen.

The Mission of Sport & Out Door Life.

In retirement, former President Cleveland continued his devotion to fishing. In 1906 he wrote *Fishing and Shooting Sketches*, an autobiographical and philosophical account of the joys of his favorite outdoor hobbies. The book included illustrations of Cleveland by Henry S. Watson (*left*). He was also photographed fishing at age 67, in 1904 (*opposite*). While in office, he had fished with a fierce determination, as fishing helped him forget his public responsibilities and worries. But after the presidency, he philosophically concluded that fishing was its own best reward: "If we catch fish we shall add zest to our recreation. If we catch none we shall still have the outing and the recreation—more healthful and more enjoyable than can be gained in any other way."

obtain the exercise, and release from mental strain, that kept him alive." Gilder observed Cleveland fishing in "hunger and heat, lightning and tempest." He once saw him refuse to be driven from a Cape Cod pond "by the worst-hailstorm I have ever witnessed or suffered." He watched as Cleveland hauled bass from Buzzards Bay during a furious thunderstorm. Cleveland once said that while he was in a boat with a fishing rod in his hands he could forget his public responsibilities and worries, but the moment he stepped ashore they came crashing down on him.

So Cleveland took the sport quite seriously. "If you want to catch fish, attend strictly to business!" he barked after catching Gilder daydreaming. He could also dispense a dry sense of humor, as in this 1890 letter written to his friend from Gray Gables:

> I started the fishing branch of the firm business today and am glad to report that the season promises well. I found here a feeling of depression in the trade and on every side there seemed to be the greatest apprehension for the future. I determined to test the condition and am entirely satisfied that if the industry is properly cared for and prosecuted with zeal, industry, and intelligence, satisfactory returns may confidently be relied upon.

On that day Grover Cleveland caught twenty-five fish.

Chapter 19

Benjamin Harrison: The Gift Cottage

Benjamin Harrison enroute by train to Washington, D.C., during his 1888 presidential campaign (*opposite*).

Summer "loiterers" (*right*) await the arrival of the luxury steamboat *Republic*, which between 1878 and 1903 provided round-trip transportation from Philadelphia to Cape May for $1. Even in the eighteenth century, this fishing and whaling village at the southern tip of New Jersey was a destination for Philadelphians seeking the health benefits of Atlantic sea air. Cape May claims to be the nation's oldest seaside resort.

In early June of 1890, a delegation of wealthy Philadelphians called at the White House and presented first lady Caroline Harrison with the deed and keys to a large, elegantly furnished, and newly built seaside cottage. It was located at Cape May Point, an affluent summer community at the southern tip of New Jersey, a place where many of the donors had real estate interests. Surprised and delighted, Mrs. Harrison immediately accepted. President Benjamin Harrison may have had reservations but said nothing in public as word of the gift circulated. This proved to be a mistake. In little more than a month, he found himself the target of a scorching newspaper attack, accused of conflict of interest and worse.

The Harrisons had spent about a week on Cape May the previous summer as the guests of Postmaster General John Wanamaker, whose Philadelphia department store was one of the nation's great mercantile emporiums. Mrs. Harrison had clearly enjoyed the beaches, ocean views, sea breezes, and Cape May Point's attractive cottage community. Pleased with her enthusiasm, Wanamaker enlisted a syndicate of local friends to build a cottage for the Harrisons, whose presence would make Cape May Point the nation's Summer Capital.

An Indiana Republican with an illustrious family history, Harrison was the last Civil War general to attain the presidency. His great-grandfather and namesake had signed the Declaration of Independence. His grandfather, William Henry Harrison, had served as president for a single month in 1841 before his life was cut short by illness. The new president

By the late nineteenth century Cape May was a full-fledged resort, with grand hotels, a boardwalk, and elaborate "cottages" owned by the nation's elite.

Benjamin Harrison stayed in a guesthouse named Congress Hall (pictured here c. 1900–1915), which was rebuilt in brick following a fire in 1878 that also destroyed much of Cape May. Though devasting, the fire also provided an opportunity for the building of many new mansions, and today Cape May is known for its well-preserved Victorian architecture.

was pleased to have returned Republican rule to the White House but felt pent up and confined by the job and the place. "There is my jail," he told a friend as they returned to the White House from a walk in the city.

Caroline Harrison found the eight rooms reserved for the president's use on the Second Floor of the White House too small for their extended family. Besides the Harrisons themselves, their quarters accommodated a changing cast of family members including her 90-year-old father, her niece, the Harrisons' married daughter, Mary Harrison McKee, and two grandchildren. One of them, Benjamin Harrison McKee, gained instant recognition

when the press dubbed him "Baby McKee." With space a constant issue, the first lady had plans drawn up to vastly enlarge the residence's official, ceremonial, and living space. When those plans stalled in Congress, she refurbished and redecorated the mansion's shabby interior, reclaimed the damp and dirty basement, and installed the first electric lights.

The sudden prospect of having a house large enough to hold all members of the Harrison clan comfortably may have been a factor in her decision to accept the gift cottage. There is no indication that she considered whether others might find such a gift inappropriate. The story broke on June 7, 1890, when the Harrisons' hometown newspaper, the *Indianapolis Journal*, reported the presentation of the cottage by a group of anonymous donors. The president, the newspaper said, "was greatly surprised."

Then a partisan storm swept in. Opposition newspapers contended that far from being just a friendly gesture, the gift was intended to exploit the Harrisons' presence at Cape May Point to promote the fortunes of a group of real estate speculators. The attack was led by Charles Dana's *New York Sun*, which in earlier years had questioned the legitimacy of

President Harrison served as an Army general in the Cival War. He is pictured in this lithograph, titled *Come on Boys!*, at the Battle of Resaca, 1864. The lithograph was published during Harrison's presidential campaign.

official actions taken by President Ulysses S. Grant while on vacation at Long Branch and suggested that President Chester A. Arthur's salary be docked when he went fishing. "Who are those generous individuals," the *Sun* asked sarcastically, "that have bestowed upon MRS. BENJAMIN HARRISON a cottage at Cape May Point, clear of encumbrance and with floors swept clean for BABY MCKEE to creep over this summer?" It insisted the donors' names be made public and demanded the cottage be immediately returned. "The President who takes a bribe is a lost President," it declared. *The Los Angeles Times* noted that newspaper advertisements promoted Cape May real estate as located "near the President's home," and drew a wry conclusion, "It is just possible that there is a little real-estate speculation as well as patriotism in this donation."

———

Public interest was intense when the first lady, her daughter, her niece, two grandchildren, two servants, and the White House chief steward arrived at Cape May Point on June 19 and were escorted to the cottage by William McKean, the editor of the *Philadelphia Ledger* and a principal donor. The *Washington Post* covered the arrival and described the interior of the "gift cottage" room-by-room, from the well-stocked butler's pantry to the third-floor billiards room. "The big lower hall seems yearning for guests, and the wide galleries, with their bright settees, hammocks, and big rush rocking-chairs, suggest all manner of summer comfort," the

The Harrison cottage at Cape May Point was described by the *Boston Daily Globe* as a "Present Fit for a Queen." It had wraparound porches on the first two stories, a gabled roofline on the third, and "substantial elegance" overall. Situated on a large lot next to the beach, the cottage looked south and was about 100 feet from the water at high tide. "The view of the ocean, bay and valley from the upper rooms is extremely beautiful," the *Globe* wrote. The Harrison grandchildren were included in vacations to Cape May. Grandson Benjamin Harrison McKee (*opposite*), known as "Baby McKee," was photographed with his dog and pet bird in a tent erected on the lawn of the cottage in c. 1889.

Post observed. It also noted that the spotlight had begun to shine on Cape May Point: "Already excursions have been started and curious sightseers are haunting the cottage beach."

At the end of the first week in July, Mrs. Harrison invited a reporter to her breezy and quiet retreat. She made clear she was delighted with her new cottage and not at all repentant. She complained that the private quarters assigned to the president at the White House were cramped. Moreover, during the summer the Executive Mansion was so overheated and uncomfortable that her grandchildren could not possibly remain there. But she told the interviewer that just as she and the president were considering where to move the family for the summer, "I was surprised by the gift of this beautiful cottage, fully equipped and ready for our occupation. Its acceptance seemed to me to be the best which could be done. . . . It is a beautiful place, retired and pleasant, and I think will be a benefit to the health to those who are near and dear to us." Asked about the financial benefits the donors stood to reap from the Harrisons' presence at Cape May Point, she replied that the only benefits that concerned her were those her family might realize by spending the summer in a healthy climate. "How others may be benefited does not concern us. If our presence at Cape May Point will be a benefit to any persons they are welcome to it."

The Harrisons made the White House a home for their extended family. In 1889, four generations posed for this photograph. First Lady Caroline Harrison sits on the left holding grandson "Baby McKee," her daughter Mary McKee stands behind her. Mrs. Harrison's father, Reverend Dr. John Witherspoon Scott, a Presbyterian minister and college professor, holds granddaughter Mary McKee.

Events were moving faster than Mrs. Harrison may have realized. She might not have known that on July 2, almost a week before she granted her interview and described the cottage as a gift, the president claimed ownership of the property in his own right. He wrote Wanamaker a check for $10,000 and asked that the various donors be compensated. "Be good enough to see to the right disposition of the check enclosed," he wrote.

Newspapers friendly to the Harrison administration did not learn of his action for more than two weeks. When their articles did appear, they cast the story in a favorable light: the president did not decide to keep the cottage until his wife visited Cape May Point and said she was happy with it; Harrison then determined its cost and wrote his check for that amount. "So far as the main point is concerned, it is enough that he promptly declined to accept the property as a gift," the *Washington Evening Star* declared. "The President's 'Gift Cottage' Bought with Hard Money," the *Hartford Courant* asserted.

But the *New York Times* regarded the development with suspicion. It noted that Harrison had written his check only after he had felt the sting of criticism. And it said that when she told her interviewer that the cottage had been a gift, Mrs. Harrison had either "been led into making an erroneous assertion" or had not been privy to all of the facts. There may have been, it wrote, an attempt "to join the ragged edges of the business together so that they appear to fit." The *Boston Daily Globe* let Harrison off with a light jab: "President Harrison's second thought concerning that Cape May cottage was right. He has done well to refuse it as a gift. But he ought not to have thought twice about it."

After that, newspaper comment mostly confined itself to the usual fare of presidential vacations: walks on the beach, romps with the grandchildren, plunges in the surf, outings in search of crabs, blue fish, and sea bass, and the return to the inevitable deskwork. "To President Harrison this day has been a mixture of crabs, picnic, Indian appointments, minor Post Office appointments, and beach promenading," the *New York Times* reported.

But the furor over the cottage had left Harrison with a dent in his reputation. And it had at least a passing influence on popular culture. In September 1890 an opera singer in Chicago wrote and performed a new and pointedly political verse for a Gilbert and Sullivan operetta:

The President said a vacation he'd take;

Said he to himself, said he,

Down by the blue sea, where the high breakers break,

Said he to himself, said he;

For the place needs the boom that my presence will bring,

And my friends who belong to the real estate ring

Have promised a cottage, to which I shall cling;

Said he to himself, said he.

Harrison wrote the last chapter of the drawn-out saga himself. In 1896, three years after his presidency ended, he sold the Cape May Point cottage to Wanamaker for the same $10,000 he had paid for it. His friends pointed out that he made no profit on the transaction. By then the former president was a widower. Caroline Harrison died of tuberculosis in the White House just weeks before the 1892 presidential election that returned Grover Cleveland to the presidency. Harrison remarried in 1896 and spent vacations among the lakes and forests of the Adirondacks in upstate New York, not at the seashore.

After the presidency, Benjamin Harrison returned to his law practice and family home in Indianapolis, Indiana, shown here in the winter of 1895. Like other Ohio presidential candidates, in 1888 Harrison had conducted a successful "front-porch" campaign from this house, addressing large crowds of people who gathered on the front lawn to hear him speak. Today, as the Benjamin Harrison Presidential Site, the home is open to the public as a museum.

Chapter 20

William McKinley: Beyond the Front Porch

WILLIAM MCKINLEY
25th President of the United
States, 1897–1901

President William McKinley
(*opposite*) liked no place so
well as his own front porch
in Canton, Ohio, where he
was photographed sitting in a
rocking chair in the summer
of 1901.

Hotel Champlain, pictured
here in 1907, stood on a solid
rock bluff overlooking Lake
Champlain near Plattsburgh,
New York. Built in 1890, it
was 400 feet long and five
stories high, with towers and
verandas on three sides. There
were dining rooms, bar rooms,
and a wine room; lounges
and billiard rooms; and five
hundred sleeping apartments
with fireplaces. Presidents
William McKinley and
William Howard Taft were
among its guests. In 1910, the
hotel was destroyed by fire
and later rebuilt on a smaller
scale.

nlike Grover Cleveland or Chester Arthur, William McKinley cared nothing for fishing. "He told me the other day that he liked to eat the trout much better than to catch them, and that fishing was not his way of getting rest," a newspaper correspondent reported in 1897. Golf was gaining popularity, but some of the younger guests at a resort hotel on Lake Champlain had little success when they tried to rouse the president's interest in the game. McKinley watched the play for ten minutes, politely excused himself, and returned to the hotel to curl up on a sofa and nap until dinnertime.

The age of the horse was near its end but not yet over, and McKinley enjoyed handling the reins and driving a team. He went out for short walks and had been known to play croquet. He took an occasional cruise on the dispatch boat *Dolphin*, which served as a presidential yacht. But no one could imagine him swinging at a tennis ball or tramping through the woods to shoot a deer. "He enjoys his friends, and likes a good cigar" and occasionally spends an evening at the theater, the *Chicago Tribune* recorded in July 1900. "But no other form of entertainment seems to appeal to him particularly, and he cares nothing at all for sport of any kind." Although his formal photographs conveyed a mask-like stolidity, those who saw him at close range said he had a mobile and expressive face. A reporter at Lake Champlain observed that when the president turned from social to official conversation, the change in his face was like watching clouds pass over the sun: "The pleasant look deepens into one of care, and the duties of the office which he has temporarily put aside are again full upon him."

The USS *Dolphin* was the first gunboat built of steel, a part of the new American steel navy. It served in the blockade of Cuba during the Spanish-American War but afterward, because of its small size, was generally assigned to presidential transport and ceremonial activities. In this role it was used by both President McKinley and President Theodore Roosevelt.

In the late nineteenth century, the members of the Jekyll Island Club, including some of America's wealthiest businessmen—Marshall Field, J. Pierpont Morgan, Joseph Pulitzer, and William H. Vanderbilt—built grand homes on this island off the coast of Georgia. In March 1899, President and Mrs. McKinley, along with the vice president and speaker of the House, were invited to the island as guests of the club. The McKinleys stayed at Solterra, a cottage in the Queen Anne shingle style. The home burned in 1914.

McKinley's personal life revolved around his chronically ailing wife. The daughter of a Canton, Ohio, banker, Ida Saxton was beautiful and young when McKinley married her in 1871. The early deaths of two children had marked her transformation into an invalid who was subject to fainting spells, nervous prostration, severe headaches, and epileptic seizures. Her care and well-being were the president's constant concern.

The president and the first lady returned to Lake Champlain in 1899, enjoying the scenery, eating in the hotel dining room, and cruising on the lake. McKinley set up an office and a reception room near the hotel ballroom to conduct business and received a stream of visiting cabinet members. Earlier that year the McKinleys had traveled to Florida and Georgia, visiting Jekyll Island off the Georgia coast and the home of Mark Hanna, the Ohio industrialist who was the president's principal political adviser and promoter. "This is a fine place," McKinley told a reporter in Thomasville, the Georgia town where Hanna spent winters. "It is good for one like me, who needs to get away where he can have rest and quiet."

Four turbulent years had followed McKinley's 1896 victory over Democrat William Jennings Bryan. The United States challenged the fading power of the Spanish Empire and invaded Cuba. The U.S. Navy destroyed two widely separated Spanish fleets, one in

Cuban waters and the other across the Pacific in Manila Bay. American forces occupied the Philippines and then fought a guerrilla war with Filipinos seeking independence. The United States annexed Puerto Rico in the Caribbean and Hawaii, a formerly independent kingdom in the Pacific. McKinley had decided against an extensive vacation in 1898, the year of the war with Spain. The *Chicago Tribune*, for one, thought that was a good idea, despite a president's natural urge to escape Washington's summer heat: "In remaining at the post of duty he sets an example worthy of imitation by all holding positions of responsibility." By the time McKinley was ready for summer travel in 1901 he had been elected to a second term and his country had emerged, somewhat to its astonished dismay, as a formidable player on the world stage.

―――――――

Notwithstanding extensive travels elsewhere, McKinley often returned to Canton, his Ohio hometown. He had marched away as a Union army private in 1861 and returned four years later as a major. He had married in Canton and begun his legal and political careers there. He felt rested at the end of a visit to his Ohio home, and his wife often seemed to do better there.

By the summer of 1901 the president had become one of Canton's principal sights as he sat on the front porch of his house on Market Avenue North, chatting with neighbors, stirring a breeze with a palm leaf fan, and waving his hat to people on the sidewalk. Although the McKinley house was comfortable and tastefully furnished, there were many other Canton houses that were both larger and more expensively fitted out. "It is simply the home of an American citizen," mused a columnist for the *Washington Post*, "who, as he sits upon his porch, manifests a kindly interest in the men who are engaged in trimming the trees."

The Market Avenue house had played an important role in McKinley's personal and political life even though it had not always been his. The future president and his bride received it as a

This 1896 carte de visite shows President and Mrs McKinley and their home on Market Avenue North in Canton. The house had been a wedding present to the couple from Ida McKinley's father. McKinley subsequently sold the house, then rented and repurchased it during his presidency.

wedding present from her father and lived there during the first five years of their marriage. They sold the house when McKinley, then a Canton attorney, was elected to Congress in 1876. For the next twenty-three years they did not possess a home they considered their own. But in 1895, after serving two terms as Ohio's governor, McKinley rented the old house. After he received the 1896 Republican presidential nomination, the house on Market Avenue became a magnet for political pilgrims. Hundreds of delegations and tens of thousands of supporters poured off the trains, marched with drums and trumpets through streets bright with flags, shuffled onto McKinley's lawn, listened to his speeches, and made his vine-shaded, banner-draped veranda the most talked about front porch in America.

McKinley failed in his efforts to buy the house after his successful "front-porch" campaign. He didn't succeed in doing so until 1899. He paid $14,500, setting aside an additional $3,000 to repair, improve, and furnish it as a place where he and Ida could enjoy quiet vacations from the White House and use it as their permanent residence when he retired from public life.

Owning the house gave McKinley enormous satisfaction, as he explained to George Bruce Cortelyou, his executive secretary: "We began our married life in that house; our children were born there, one of them died and was buried from there. Some of the tenderest memories of my life are centered there, and some of the saddest. I am as happy as a child to have it back. It's a fine old place." McKinley, who had spent most of his political life in hotels and other people's houses, described the improvements he intended to make and continued: "Now I

Between 1877 and 1892, while William McKinley served in the U.S. House of Representatives and then was elected governor of Ohio, his family lived in Mrs. McKinley's family's home. The house has since been restored to the McKinley era and is open to the public as part of the First Ladies National Historic Site.

shall have a home, what I have wanted for so long; a home I can go to. If I have a place like that I can get away any time, and could take you with all the help we need, and we could transact all the executive business there."

Transacting executive business at the Market Avenue house became easier in the summer of 1900 when workmen installed a long-distance telephone line in McKinley's library. A newspaper noted the vacationing president could now consult with Secretary of State John Hay or Secretary of War Elihu Root "as readily as if they were close at hand." The telegraph and the Atlantic cable further extended his reach and "put him in touch with all parts of the civilized world."

In April 1901, following his second inauguration, the president and first lady left the White House for a great circle tour of the United States intended to celebrate the accomplishments of the first term and set new directions for the second. The presidential party took the southern route to the Pacific Coast and planned to return

When McKinley ran for president in 1896, he continued the midwestern tradition of "front-porch" campaigns, whereby the candidate remained at home and spoke from his front porch to the crowds that traveled to hear him. They came as individuals and delegations—750,000 in all. McKinley won the election over William Jennings Bryan, who had conducted a "whistle-stop" campaign, traveling 18,000 miles by train and speaking to millions.

After Theodore Roosevelt was nominated as McKinley's running mate in the summer of 1900, the two candidates posed for photographs on the front steps of McKinley's Canton home. Roosevelt, the master of Sagamore Hill, was unimpressed and agreed with those who found it too humble a dwelling for the chief executive of an emerging world power. The McKinley house, he wrote to a friend, struck him as just the sort of place that might be owned by the retired division superintendent of a railroad. But the McKinley front porch was the setting for another successful presidential campaign, and Roosevelt became vice president.

through the northern tier of states, ending the long trip with a flourish on June 13 at the Pan-American Exposition at Buffalo, New York. But as the president's train approached San Francisco, Mrs. McKinley became seriously ill. A surgeon lanced her forefinger to treat an infection, but that failed to bring relief. She became feverish and exhausted. She was put to bed in San Francisco and appeared to be sinking toward death. The deeply worried president rushed through his schedule, then cut the trip short to bring her back to Washington. When she was ready, they went to Canton for a long and restful summer vacation. They would remain until the first week in September and then travel to the Buffalo exposition, where President's Day had been rescheduled for September 5.

Staying mostly close to home, the McKinleys visited with friends and enjoyed carriage rides through town and into the countryside. The president often handled the horses himself as he drove his wife about. She grew steadily stronger and soon was much improved. Friends joined them at times for a game of euchre. One evening, a neighbor put on an amateur musicale. The president walked to church or strolled through Canton's business district without protection. "So accustomed did the people of Canton become to his presence unattended that the reverse was considered worthy of comment," the *Washington Post* later reported. McKinley scoffed at danger and told close friend that he couldn't imagine anyone wanting to hurt him. He often walked out from the White House free of police or Secret Service escorts. In Canton, no guards watched the McKinley home at night. But threatening letters had come in during the 1900 campaign, and those close to the president worried about his security.

The house had been changed over the past year. A porte cochere had been built for the McKinley carriage. The north end of the porch had been built out to form a gazebo that offered views of the lawn and garden. The president now had a home he could improve

MC. KINLEY RESIDENCE, CANTON, OHIO.

This 2 cent postcard shows President McKinley's Canton home after renovations that included, most notably, an extension of the famous front porch to include the gazebo, on the far right in this image. Mrs. McKinley returned here after her husband's assassination. After she died in 1907, the new owner donated the house to Sisters of Charity for a hospital, and in 1935, as Mercy Hospital expanded, the home was razed. Today the Stark County District Library is located on the site.

On September 6, 1901, President McKinley was in Buffalo, New York. The previous day he had given a speech at the Pan-American Exposition, and he would later this day return for a public reception. But before the event he climbed a hill toward an overlook, where he would turn to view Niagara Falls. Later that day he would be shot.

COPYRIGHT 1901. BY O.E. DUNLAP.

Electric lights illuminated the Temple of Music at the Pan-American Exposition. The exposition was intended to promote commerce and goodwill among the American republics. President McKinley's speech on September 5, 1901, was a highlight: "Expositions are the timekeepers of progress," he began. "They record the world's advancement. They stimulate the energy, enterprise and intellect of the people." Praising trade and friendly commercial relations, he concluded with a prayer "that God will graciously vouchsafe prosperity, happiness and peace to all our neighbors, and like blessings to all the peoples and powers of earth."

as he pleased. "It is really so comfortable here that unless I am needed I shall be in no hurry" to return, he wrote Secretary of State Hay. "Washington is such a hot place, and you know Canton . . . is perpetually cool."

Callers steadily arrived throughout the summer. Hay was the highest ranking, but there were many others: Senator Hanna, a member of the Hungarian parliament, a Kentucky politician, an army lieutenant seeking a consular appointment, and a man who had translated "The Star-Spangled Banner" into Spanish and sought to have it introduced to schoolchildren in Puerto Rico and the Philippines. Toward the end of the summer McKinley began looking ahead to the policy speech he intended to make at the Buffalo exposition. One evening in his library he told Cortelyou: "Expositions are the timekeepers of progress." The speech was built around that sentence.

The McKinleys' peaceful and happy summer at Canton would never be repeated, although the visit to the Pan-American Exposition began agreeably enough. The president's speech calling for reciprocity in world trade was well received. McKinley toured the exhibits in the domed and towered buildings, admired the unprecedented displays of electric light, and saw his portrait etched against the sky in a nighttime fireworks display. The next day,

September 6, 1901, the McKinleys boarded a train for the short ride to Niagara Falls, where they toured the gorge and walked halfway across the suspension bridge to view the cascading water from a Canadian perspective without actually setting foot on foreign soil. They returned to Buffalo and at 4:00 p.m. the president began pumping hands at a public reception inside the architecturally flamboyant Temple of Music. Seven minutes later, an anarchist who had wrapped his hand in a large handkerchief to conceal a .32-caliber revolver shot the president twice. McKinley at first appeared to rally. His doctors issued a series of optimistic bulletins. Then infection set in, and optimism vanished. William McKinley died on September 14, eight days after being shot.

On September 6, 1901, President McKinley was shot at close range by Leon Czolgosz, an anarchist, at the Temple of Music. T. Dart Walker's wash drawing of the event was published on the cover of the September 21, 1901, issue of *Leslie's Weekly*. McKinley died eight days after the shooting, on September 14, 1901.

Chapter 21

Theodore Roosevelt: Oyster Bay White House

THEODORE ROOSEVELT
26th President of the
United States, 1901–1909

Alocomotive's piercing whistle announced the arrival of the presidential special at Oyster Bay at 5:14 p.m. on July 5, 1902. Despite an earsplitting thunderstorm, more than three hundred thoroughly soaked townsfolks showed up to cheer, wave small flags, and shake the president's hand. On that July afternoon, as Theodore Roosevelt exchanged the sizzle of a Washington summer for the ocean breezes of Oyster Bay, he forever transformed the nature of the presidential vacation. While earlier chief executives did conduct official business away from the White House, they usually did so with only minimal resources at their disposal. Their ranks included William McKinley, whose assassination the previous September had vaulted Roosevelt into the presidency. Times and circumstances had changed. Roosevelt carried the presidency with him wherever he went, whether to Sagamore Hill—his Oyster Bay home on the North Shore of Long Island—bear hunting in the Colorado Rockies, or watching nimble mountain goats at Yellowstone National Park. Although he conducted almost no business while at Pine Knot, his retreat in the western Virginia woods, he worked steadily on the train rides out and back.

———

For the next seven years, Roosevelt's Sagamore Hill became the Summer White House in fact as well as name. Through its doors passed a dazzling parade of cabinet members, senators, ambassadors, potentates, envoys, generals, admirals, industrialists, and labor leaders. They mingled with the writers, historians, poets, architects, philosophers, artists, former Rough Riders, naturalists, and big game hunters whose company Roosevelt relished. Through it all, Sagamore Hill remained the home of a large and lively family and the center of Theodore Roosevelt's life.

The pattern for the summers to follow was set in 1902 by George Bruce Cortelyou, Roosevelt's efficient executive secretary, soon to be promoted to the president's cabinet. Presiding over a staff of White House stenographers, typists, telegraphers, and messengers, Cortelyou charted the president's daily agenda, screened his appointments, and dealt with a platoon of reporters questing for news. Rising early to deal with cable traffic with Washington, Cortelyou appeared in Roosevelt's Sagamore Hill library each weekday morning, bringing with him the leather mail pouches that held the letters and documents needing immediate attention. Dictating to a stenographer, Roosevelt generated a stack of outgoing mail. Over his lifetime he would produce an estimated 150,000 letters.

Telephone and telegraph lines linked the Summer White House at Oyster Bay to the government in Washington. And on July 4, 1903, the president inaugurated the new trans-Pacific cable with a telegraphed message that took just 12 minutes to circle the Earth. Now the president could issue orders to the fleet in Manila Bay or contact his ambassador in Tokyo while sitting at his desk watching guests alight from carriages on Sagamore Hill's broad drive.

In April 1903, President Theodore Roosevelt stood at Glacier Point in Yosemite National Park, with Yosemite Falls in the background. He was on an eight-week, twenty-five-state speaking tour of the West. In between speeches, he camped in the backcountry and toured Yellowstone with the naturalist John Burroughs. Five years later Roosevelt assembled the state governors in a conservation conference in the East Room of the White House, resulting in the National Conservation Commission.

As a young boy, Theodore Roosevelt had spent summers in Oyster Bay, Long Island, and as a young man he purchased farmland there. The Queen Anne mansion (*above*) he built was his permanent home. During his presidency, it was also the Summer White House. In 1905 he added a new North Room, with richly paneled walls, a beamed ceiling, and a great stone fireplace, where he worked every day (*right*). Roosevelt died at Sagamore Hill in 1919, and his wife Edith lived there until her death in 1948. Today Sagamore Hill is a National Park Service National Historic Site, open to the public.

The Summer White House was well enough established by 1903 for newspapers to chronicle the break with the past. McKinley and other recent presidents had taken only a secretary and a stenographer with them when they fled Washington's notorious summer heat. "The increase in the scope of governmental affairs, now that Uncle Sam has become a world power, renders impossible a continuance of this simple plan," said the *Brooklyn Standard Union*. "It has remained for the resourceful Mr. Roosevelt to meet . . . the new conditions by virtually removing the White House offices during the summer months." The change was complete by the summer of 1904 when Roosevelt's executive secretary William Loeb Jr. assured the public that the "regular business of the administration will be carried on the same in Oyster Bay as if

the President were in Washington."

"It was the rule, rather than the exception, to burn 'midnight oil,' in the Summer White House," wrote Albert Loren Cheney, editor of the *Oyster Bay Pilot*. In the first summer alone, the president conferred at Sagamore Hill on myriad issues: a possible canal through the Isthmus of Panama, problems in the newly acquired Philippines, cattle ranching in the West, tariff reform, and efforts to curb the trusts Roosevelt accused of monopolizing business. On August 11, 1902, after lunch with a Chinese prince, the president nominated Massachusetts jurist Oliver Wendell Holmes Jr. for a seat on the Supreme Court. Two days later he ordered the army to substitute comfortable soft-

collar shirts for the high stiff collars that had chafed the necks of generations of soldiers. "The existence at Oyster Bay was decidedly different after father became President," Roosevelt's spirited elder daughter Alice remembered years later. "We were hardly ever alone. Droves of people came down to call, or to lunch, or to spend the night. . . . The *Mayflower*, *Dolphin* and *Sylph*, three government boats, were one or another, as a rule, anchored off Sagamore. The newspapermen were camped in the village."

By the time he became the youngest president in American history, Theodore Roosevelt had graduated from Harvard, been elected to the New York State Assembly, operated cattle ranches in the Dakotas, hunted elk, buffalo, and grizzly bear in the West, fought crime as New York City's commissioner, served as a reform-minded civil service commissioner, and molded the United States Navy into an effective combat force. Thirsting for action at the outbreak of the Spanish-American War, he raised a calvary regiment and then led his dismounted troopers up Cuba's San Juan Hill. The exploits of Roosevelt's Rough Riders won the attention of press and public and assured his election as governor of New York. When that state's political bosses tired of his reformist leanings, they steered him into the vice presidency, an office they viewed as a harmless backwater.

On September 6, 1901, with Roosevelt about to end a speaking tour and go on vacation, an anarchist shot President William McKinley at a public reception at the Pan-American

At Sagamore Hill, rowing was a favorite outdoor tonic. "I always, especially, welcome anything in the boats, because it gives me a chance to row with Edith, so I get some exercise without having tired her out," Roosevelt told a friend.

Exposition at Buffalo, New York. Assured the president would recover, the vice president joined his family in the Adirondacks. Just before noon on September 13, a messenger found Roosevelt on the slopes of Mount Marcy and delivered news that McKinley's condition turned critical. After a wild ride through the night he arrived at the special train waiting for him at the town of North Creek and further news: McKinley was dead. Theodore Roosevelt, 42, was the twenty-sixth president of the United States.

———

Sagamore Hill stood near the center of Cove Neck, a thumb of land separating Oyster Bay Harbor from Cold Spring Harbor. Green tunnels through the trees led to a sandy beach and a pier where the family row boats were tied. From the water they could look back at the raking roof of the house that Roosevelt had named for "old Sagamore Mohannis, who, as chief of his little tribe, signed away his rights to the land two centuries and a half ago." By the time he became president, Theodore and Edith, the former Edith Kermit Carow, presided over a tribe of spirited children. The eldest, Alice Lee Roosevelt, was named for her late mother, Roosevelt's first wife, who had died at a tragically early age in 1884. Theodore and Edith had five children of their own: Ted Jr., Kermit, Ethel, Archie, and Quentin.

Perpetually in motion, Roosevelt only slowly resigned himself to the cordon of Secret Service operatives that surrounded him. He liked to strike off unguarded and alone, claiming the revolver he carried gave him adequate protection. Captain Archie Butt, the president's military aide, said it was impossible for the agents to predict what the president would do next. "He never takes them unto consideration, and he darts from the house sometimes and is well a mile away before they have a chance to follow him." But the agents were not deterred. "They do not allow his feelings in the matter to change their feelings at all and one always tries to keep him in view," Butt said. The agents watched the house when Roosevelt slept and installed trip wires on the grounds to warn of intruders.

Still, the president's family remained concerned about his safety. On Monday, September 15, 1902, near the end of his first presidential vacation, Theodore and Edith threw open the grounds at Sagamore Hill to the people of Oyster Bay and Nassau County. At least 8,000 people shook the president's hand, drank his lemonade, ate his ginger snaps, "and carried away as souvenirs the cups from which they had drunk." Although the Secret Service and private guards handled security, that didn't satisfy the president's eldest son, Ted. Mindful that McKinley had been shot at a public reception, he stood next to his father and carefully "watched every hand before it was extended to the President."

At about 4:00 p.m. on most days Roosevelt shed business for strenuous fun: tennis, horseback riding, swimming, hiking, rowing on the bay, or romping with the children. Once, when Roosevelt was engaged with an official visitor, a boy with a grievance appeared in the doorway. "Cousin Theodore, it's after four," said the boy. "By Jove, so it is! Why didn't you

President Roosevelt promoted "the strenuous life," and he did not believe that leisure should be spent in idleness. During summers at Sagamore Hill he led his family in hiking, picnicking, and horseback riding. His children were as interested in exploring their world as he was.

call me sooner?" the president replied. Then, to his guest: "I must ask you to excuse me. . . . I never keep boys waiting. It's a hard trial for a boy to wait."

While the late afternoon outings took many forms, point-to-point obstacle walks were favorites. Often as many as twenty boys trailed their presidential leader on the cross-country "scrambles," following the rule of "'over or through' any obstacle but never 'around'," explained Corinne Robinson, the president's sister. That meant climbing

rocks and tearing through thickets and brush. "If they came to a wall they had to climb it. If they came to an inlet in the bay they had to swim it," said James Amos, Roosevelt's valet and butler. Corinne Robinson recalled a day when the direct line led through a bathhouse with a steeply pitched roof. Surely her brother would have the sense to go around. "Needless to say, he did not, and I can still see the somewhat sturdy body of the then President of the United States hurling itself at the obstruction and with singular agility chinning himself to the top and sliding down on the other side." Roosevelt himself shook his head, however, over the birthday romp his daughter Ethel had asked him to organize in the barn: "Of course I had not the heart to refuse; but really it seems, to put it mildly, rather odd for a stout, elderly President to be bouncing over hay-ricks in a wild effort to get to goal before an active midget of a competitor, aged nine years."

The adventures continued summer after summer. In July 1906 the president took his younger children and their friends on an all-night camping trip, putting them under overturned boats when it rained. "It only kept them dry in spots. However, not one of them complained," he said. On other jaunts the president told ghost stories at an evening campfire, keeping his youthful audience hanging on each word. Around the dinner table, he told friends that he wanted no weak and misty emanations but active, vigorous ghosts, "the kind that knock you over and eat fire." Archie Butt said that in his dinner-table conversation Roosevelt was like "a perfect flying squirrel," changing subjects so fast that listeners could scarcely keep up.

At Sagamore Hill, the president often walked out with his ax, exuberantly chopping down trees blocking a favorite view. "I think Mr. Roosevelt cuts down trees merely for the pleasure of hearing them fall. Just as he swims and plays tennis merely for the pleasure of straining his muscles and shouting," observed Captain Archie Butt, the president's military aide.

With the first lady's encouragement, Noah Seaman, Sagamore Hill's farm manager. often called on the president when extra help was needed at haying time. "He joked and talked with his fellow workers, drank from the same bucket and dipper and always insisted on Seaman . . . putting his name on the payroll and paying him for his day's work," recalled James Amos, Roosevelt's valet and butler.

President Roosevelt on the "Mayflower," reviewing the Naval Parade off Long Island. Copyright 1903 by Underwood & Underwood.

For newspapers, the Roosevelt family at Oyster Bay became the summer story. Readers everywhere eagerly followed not only the news that emerged from the president's vacation but also accounts of picnics, row-boating, tree-chopping, summer haying, and obstacle races. Reporters eagerly pursued the smallest details, sometimes exaggerating and often annoying the president in the process.

President Roosevelt aboard the *Mayflower* (*above*) reviewed a naval parade off Long Island, 1903. The *Mayflower* (*below* in 1909), a steam yacht built in Scotland, had been purchased by the U.S. Navy during the Spanish-American War. It was afterward converted for service as a presidential yacht and used by five presidents: Theodore Roosevelt, William Howard Taft, Woodrow Wilson, Warren G. Harding, and Calvin Coolidge.

The USS *Plunger* was one of the first U.S. submarines, and President Roosevelt, ever the adventurer, wanted to experience what it was like to be submerged. On August 25, 1905, he joined the crew on maneuvers off Oyster Bay, including a fifty-five minute dive. In this 1905 photograph, the *Plunger* is partly submerged in Oyster Bay, with four members of its crew standing on top.

In the summer of 1905, Roosevelt found himself and Sagamore Hill at the pivot point of international politics. For a year, Russia and Japan had grappled for control of northeast Asia, a contest that saw Japan win stunningly one-sided military victories. After much maneuvering, the two nations agreed to meet at Portsmouth, New Hampshire. Roosevelt opened the conference at Oyster Bay and, from a distance, acted as mediator. Baron Komura, the chief Japanese delegate, was one of the first visitors under the new North Room's beamed ceiling. He was quickly followed by Sergei Witte, the chief Russian envoy. On August 5, the two delegations met for lunch on the presidential yacht *Mayflower* in Oyster Bay Harbor. Launches darted between warships, pennants fluttered, cannon boomed, and bands played national anthems while a flotilla of private craft lay back to watch the show. But American diplomats worried that a presidential misstep could sink the talks. To the surprise of some, Roosevelt handled the protocol with the finesse of an otter slipping into a stream. He propelled the touchy, easily offended chief delegates into the *Mayflower*'s salon before either could check whose highly polished shoe had entered first. A cold buffet was consumed while standing, removing concerns about the protocol of seating arrangements. The president's toast was a showpiece of smoothly crafted neutrality: "To the welfare and prosperity of the sovereigns and people of the two great nations, whose representatives have met one another on this ship." The most audacious gamble of Roosevelt's presidency was under way. Many would accuse him of overreaching if the talks collapsed. "I am having my hair turned gray by dealing with the Russian and Japanese peace negotiators," Roosevelt wrote to his son Kermit

Roosevelt clearly needed a diversion, and one awaited on the choppy, turbulent waters of Oyster Bay Harbor. On the afternoon of August 25 a carriage rolled from Sagamore Hill to a pier jutting into the bay. The rain fell in slanting, wind-driven sheets, and waves washed over the pilings. Roosevelt clambered into oilskins, boarded a navy launch, and headed out toward Long Island Sound. Waiting for him were the officers and crew of the torpedo submarine boat USS *Plunger*. Roosevelt wedged himself through the hatch and disappeared below. The *Plunger*'s log recorded the time as 3:30 p.m.

Two miles out the submarine's conning tower and periscope vanished from sight. For the first time ever an American president had dived in a submarine. While the submarine held steady 20 feet under the surface, its commander, Lieutenant Charles Preston Nelson, showed Roosevelt the grid of dials and gauges, the steering device, the electrical and air supply systems, and the torpedo firing mechanism. The president spoke with the gunners and looked through the periscope. Then he took the controls himself and steered the submarine close to the bottom. "I have never seen anything quite so remarkable," he later stated.

The president's undersea exploit earned him a newspaper scolding. "He really ought to restrain himself from doing those 'stunts' of adventure," lectured the *New York Times*. As president, Roosevelt had no right to risk his life in "some new-fangled, submersible, collapsible, or otherwise dangerous device." Roosevelt offered private explanations. "I went down in it chiefly because I did not want to have the officers and enlisted men think I wanted them to try things I was reluctant to try myself," he wrote to a concerned friend. But his first reaction as he stepped from the *Plunger*'s streaming deck may have been closer to the mark: "I've had many a splendid day's fun in my life but I can't remember ever having crowded so much of it into such a few hours."

There was soon good news on the treaty. On August 29 the Associated Press reported that Russia and Japan had agreed to compromise on all points. "This is splendid! This is magnificent," Roosevelt roared. The gamble had paid off. "It's a mighty good thing for Russia, and a mighty good thing for Japan," he said. "And a mighty good thing for *me* too!"

Soon the North Room had still more trophies to display: a tankard from the czar of Russia and a magnificent, gold-mounted samurai sword from the emperor of Japan. Then another trophy arrived. In December 1906 Roosevelt's diplomatic success earned him the Nobel Peace Prize, making him the first American to win the Nobel in any field.

Aboard the *Mayflower*, President Roosevelt, the mediator in the peace treaty that ended the Russo-Japanese War, posed with the diplomats from Russia and Japan. From left: Count Sergei Witte, chief Russian envoy; Baron Roman Romanovich von Rosen, Russian ambassador; President Roosevelt; Baron Jutarō Komura, Japanese foreign minister; and Kogorō Takahira, minister of Japan.

———

No president has been more closely linked both to the preservation of nature and the thrill of the hunt than Theodore Roosevelt. The contradictions were evident even in his own time. Over the years of his presidency, Roosevelt rode through snowdrifts to shoot bear in Colorado, chased coyotes on the Oklahoma plains, and laid plans to shoot lions and elephants in an epic African safari once he left the White House. But he also took pleasure in the outdoors even when he left his rifles in their racks in the Gun Room at Sagamore Hill.

John Burroughs, the distinguished naturalist, said Roosevelt kept his promise to shoot no living thing even as the two surveyed the elk herds in Yellowstone National Park in the spring of 1903. One morning, summoned from his tent with his face still covered in shaving lather, Roosevelt watched mountain goats leaping down impossibly narrow trails. He spent a day entirely alone, walking the trails and watching herds of elk. At other times he and Burroughs sought out birds. Moving on to California, Roosevelt joined John Muir, naturalist and champion of California's Yosemite, for another outing undisturbed by gunfire. Muir and Roosevelt slept on fir boughs under the looming trunks of the sequoias. It was, Roosevelt said, "like lying in a great solemn cathedral, far vaster and more beautiful than any built by hand of man."

Burroughs called Roosevelt that "rare combination of the sportsman and the naturalist." In the nearly eight years of his presidency Roosevelt added about 150 million acres to the national forests and created the National Forest Service to protect and manage them. The lifelong bird lover and big-game hunter created fifty-one federal bird sanctuaries and four national game reserves. He set aside five new national parks and eighteen national

In April 1903, President Roosevelt embarked on an eight-week, twenty-five-state speaking tour of the West. In between speeches, he camped in the backcountry. In Yellowstone he traveled with the naturalist John Burroughs and helped lay the cornerstone for new gateway arch to the park at Gardiner, Montana. "The geysers, the extraordinary hot springs, the lakes, the canyons, the mountains, and cataracts unite to make this region something not wholly to be paralleled elsewhere on the globe," he said. "It must be kept for the benefit and enjoyment of all of us."

Theodore Roosevelt (center) poses with other gentlemen in front of the "Grizzly Giant," the oldest sequoia tree at Mariposa Grove, Yosemite National Park.

President Roosevelt at Liberty Cap in Yellowstone National Park.

monuments, including California's Muir Woods, the grove of sequoias named for his companion at Yosemite in 1903.

Roosevelt also called on hunters to him preserve wildlife. "All hunters should be nature lovers," he wrote, and he took several hunting vacations. He hunted coyotes in Oklahoma and bear in Colorado, always with appreciation for the wildlife he saw in camp: the four-striped chipmunks, white-footed mice, a "brushy tailed" pack rat. "There were eagles and ravens in the mountains, and once we saw sandhill cranes soaring far above the highest peaks," he observed.

But of all Roosevelt's hunting trips, the one he considered the least successful was the one that did the most

President Roosevelt and party, Inspiration Point, Yosemite Valley, California, 1903. In Yosemite, the president toured with naturalist John Muir.

for his reputation. In November 1902, the president spent five days pursuing bear through Mississippi's marshes and didn't get a shot. "Simply exasperating," he groused. It was the first hunt Roosevelt had allowed himself since becoming president, and to satisfy the demand for stories he granted three reporters once-a-day access to his hunting camp. They were eager for any development. On the morning of November 14, the hounds picked up a scent. After a long chase they drove a scrawny and exhausted female bear into a pond. Since Roosevelt was miles away, a guide roped the bear, slammed its head with a rifle butt, and waited for

Clifford Berryman's cartoon of President Roosevelt choosing not to shoot a bear cub is titled *Drawing the Line in Mississippi*. Published in the November 16, 1902, issue of the *Washington Post,* it enhanced public affection for the president and inspired the creation of the Teddy Bear.

In mid-April 1905 President Roosevelt set off on a bear hunt in Colorado with a hunting party that included guides, wranglers, and twenty-six hounds. Undeterred by deep snow, Roosevelt killed three bears.

the president. Arriving, Roosevelt found a dazed and exhausted black bear tied to a tree. He refused to shoot. "Put it out of its misery," he told the others, who ended the bear's life with a knife.

Back at camp, the tale was told and news stories written. While Roosevelt continued his fruitless hunt, his countrymen were reading of the sportsman president who refused to shoot a defenseless creature (the ultimate fate of the luckless bear was somehow glossed over). At his drawing board, *Washington Post* cartoonist Clifford Berryman read the articles and created a legend. He sketched an appealing bear with big ears and eyes. He drew the president turning his back, holding up his hand, refusing to shoot. The delighted public demanded more bear cartoons. Soon the little bear became Berryman's cartoon mascot, offering side commentary on the issues of the day.

That winter, Brooklyn storekeeper Morris Michom produced a few stuffed bears and placed them in his window with the sign, "Teddy's Bears," using the popular nickname Roosevelt disliked. They sold quickly. At roughly the same time an American toy buyer in Germany discovered the Steiff Toy Company had a new line of stuffed bear cubs with plush fur, button eyes, and moveable arms and legs. He ordered 3,000, and they, too, sold out. Soon millions of Teddy Bears were in the hands of children.

———

The house in the Virginia woods was as free of sham as the farmworkers for whom it had been built. Roosevelt first saw it in early June 1905 and called it "the nicest little place of the kind you could imagine." Edith Roosevelt called it perfect for the "rest and repairs" they both needed. The name she chose was as unadorned as the house: Pine Knot.

Pine Knot's best feature was the broad front porch that framed a view of rolling meadows and the Virginia Blue Ridge. Made from unpainted pine boards, the house itself lacked electricity, plumbing, and a telephone. The single ground floor room, measuring 12 by 32 feet, could have been dropped in the center of the new North Room at Sagamore Hill with space to spare. One newspaperman said it was "probably quite the most unpretentious habitation ever owned by a president of the United States." Another called it "a right crude place."

But Pine Knot met the Roosevelts' needs for a refuge from the White House and a more peaceful alternative to Sagamore Hill with its stream of visitors, curious reporters, ringing telephone, and sacks of urgent mail. The first lady made the arrangements, paying $280 for the house and 15 acres of pine and white oak in Albemarle County, 17 miles south of Charlottesville. Roosevelt took to it immediately, found an ax, and began cutting down trees to improve the view. The Roosevelts brought no White House servants with them that first weekend, left the Secret Service agents at the Charlottesville railroad depot, and fended for themselves. On Saturday evening the president fried two chickens for dinner and served them with biscuits and cornbread. They had cherries and wild strawberries for desert. After dinner they sat on the porch he had grandly named the piazza, then moved inside and read by the light of kerosene lanterns.

In the nearly four years remaining in Roosevelt's term, he and Edith visited Pine Knot eight times. They stayed for just a weekend or for as long as six days. In the spring they ate breakfast around 10:00 a.m., looked for birds and wild flowers in the meadows and woods, and rode horses along the red dirt roads. In the fall the president hunted and was often in the woods before dawn. Roosevelt almost never conducted business at Pine Knot, but he dictated to a stenographer on the train rides.

At Pine Knot Roosevelt immersed himself in nature but continued to enjoy hunting. By the fall of 1906 he was determined to bag the famously elusive wild turkey, which he considered "the king of American game birds." Reporters for the *Richmond Times-Dispatch* followed his progress through the woods until a headline could report, "President Gets His Wild Turkey." Roosevelt provided his own description of the 13-hour hunt: "The turkey came out of the cover not too far off and sprang into the air, heading across the valley and offering me a side shot at forty yards as he sailed by. It was just the distance for the close-shooting ten-bore duck gun I carried; and at the report down came the turkey in a heap. . . . It was an easy shot."

Pine Knot, President Roosevelt's rustic retreat in rural Virginia, offered simplicity and quiet he could get nowhere else. In Roosevelt style, the porch was grandly named the piazza. "It was lovely to sit there in the rocking chairs and hear all the birds by daytime and at night the whippoorwills and owls and little forest folk," the president wrote to his son Kermit. "There was no one around the house to bother us at all." Today Pine Knot is on the National Register of Historic Places. Restored by the Roosevelt Pine Knot Foundation, it is open to the public by appointment.

In May 1908, Roosevelt welcomed John Burroughs to Pine Knot. He was so eager to show off his knowledge of local birds that he took the naturalist on a mad dash through the fields, woods, briers, and marshes, seeing little for all their sweat. They set off at a slower pace the next morning, stopping to watch a Bewick's wren dart in and out of a fence, listening to a gray gnatcatcher singing in a plum tree, and puzzling out the identity of blue grosbeaks in an open field. In four days they observed and listed more than seventy-five species of birds and fowl.

Burroughs said he was worried about the president's security. In the darkness, a mile from another house, Pine Knot seemed vulnerable. Roosevelt slapped his pocket. "I go armed, and they would have to be mighty quick to get the drop on me." Stepping outside, Burroughs heard sounds in the brush. The next morning Mrs. Roosevelt told him that at her request a pair of Secret Service men arrived at 9:00 p.m. each day, stood guard through the night, then retreated to a nearby farmhouse during the day. "She did not let the president know of this because it would irritate him," Burroughs said.

One night, with both men reading by the light of a kerosene lamp and Mrs. Roosevelt occupied with needlework, Roosevelt suddenly slammed his hand on the table with explosive force. Recalled Burroughs: "He had killed a mosquito with a blow that would almost have demolished an African lion."

Sooner than Burroughs may have imagined, Roosevelt would have a real African lion in his rifle sights. Looking to the future in his final White House year, Roosevelt campaigned successfully for William Howard Taft as his presidential successor. He also began planning his next great adventure: a lengthy hunting safari in Africa. Sagamore Hill, and American politics, would be waiting when he returned.

169

Chapter 22

William Howard Taft: Golf on the Gold Coast

WILLIAM HOWARD TAFT
27th President of the
United States, 1909–1913

William Howard Taft,
pictured here in Hot Springs,
Virginia, in 1908, was an avid
golfer. As president, he always
maintained a predictable
schedule during his vacations
that included a daily round of
morning golf.

William Howard Taft's weight, passion for golf, and devotion to the automobile set him apart from earlier presidents. At 350 pounds, he was easily the heaviest chief executive in history. An eager athlete despite his bulk, he simply would not be denied his escapes to the fairways. And as the first president to embrace the automotive age, his delight in fast cars had few limits, including speed limits.

With his handlebar mustache, ready smile, and formidable girth, William Howard Taft was the essence of jovial rotundity. But his bubbling good spirits were strained in the presidency. Theodore Roosevelt's all-guns-blazing personality would prove an impossible example to follow. As Roosevelt's secretary of war, Taft had been an ever-loyal and efficient lieutenant. Roosevelt handpicked him as successor to the White House. But the two men's views of the presidency differed sharply. Roosevelt stretched the institution to its limits; Taft, a lawyer, U.S. solicitor general, and appeals court judge who longed to be on the Supreme Court, felt bound by the limits imposed by the Constitution and by Congress. Setting an independent course in the White House would be seen by TR's followers, and ultimately by TR himself, as a betrayal of the Roosevelt legacy.

———

Perhaps because he never fit comfortably into the presidency, Taft fled the White House as often as he could, preferably to a golf course. He and First Lady Helen Herron Taft—the family called her Nellie—began planning their first summer escape from Washington shortly after the icy, snow-swept day in March 1909 when Taft took the oath of office and Theodore Roosevelt departed on a year-long shooting and collecting safari to Africa. TR had also enjoyed long breaks from steamy summertime Washington, often conducting the presidency from the shores of Oyster Bay from early July through the middle of September. But Taft faced a problem. His family had vacationed for years in Canada, spending sixteen happy summers at Murray Bay on the St. Lawrence River north of Quebec City. And there is an unwritten rule, armored by public opinion, that no American president shall vacation outside the territorial limits of the United States and its possessions. So the Tafts began a serious search for an all-American Summer White House.

Finding the right balance proved difficult. The president's family wanted a place on or near the ocean. The president clearly would not be happy if he could not play golf. The demands of the presidency required first-class rail connections, nearby office space, and sufficient telegraph and telephone lines to connect the traveling White House to Washington and the world. Finally the search narrowed to the Massachusetts coast and the old seafaring town of Beverly on the North Shore, 18 miles north of Boston. After looking at houses over three spring days, the first lady settled on a fourteen-room "cottage" called Stetson Hall, on Woodbury Point. There were many attractions. Lush, elm-shaded lawns swept down to the sea wall. A broad veranda wrapped around the dark-green, shingled house and offered a view across Salem Harbor to Marblehead. The house was large enough for servants, guests, and the Tafts' three children, Robert, Helen,

Summer Residence of Pre

In 1909 and 1910, the magnificent Stetson Hall (*above and below*) in Beverly, Massachusetts, served as the Summer White House. Beverly and neighboring seaside towns north of Boston were so favored as a summer retreat by the wealthy that the region was known as the Gold Coast.

and Charlie. The location offered at least a chance to hold the president's duties at arm's length. "I didn't think it would seem like having a vacation at all if the Executive Offices could not be somewhere out of sight so that they might sometimes be out of mind," the first lady recalled. The cottage was owned by Robert Dawson Evans, the retired president of U.S. Rubber and one of the North Shore's most prosperous residents. He and his wife, the imperious and aptly named Maria Antoinette Evans, lived at Dawson Hall just across the lawn and through the elms. She dreaded the loss of her summertime privacy and was known to have opposed renting their property to anyone, including the president.

The first lady who made Beverly the "Summer Capital" was widely credited with supplying the ambition that helped propel her husband into the presidential race. Once in the White House,

H. Taft at Beverly, Mass.

Copyright 1909 Wm. Mills & Son, Prov. R.I.

Helen Herron Taft became the first president's wife to adopt a public cause: improving the lot of working women. Her White House years would be chiefly remembered for her signal contribution to the beauty of the national capital: the planting of the cherry trees around the Tidal Basin. But on May 17, 1909, shortly after the presidential yacht *Sylph* pulled out of the Washington Navy Yard for an afternoon cruise on the Potomac, the first lady collapsed. Unable to speak and showing signs of facial paralysis, she was quickly rushed back to the White House. Her slow recovery from a stroke kept her on the sidelines for a year and seriously unsettled the president just as his administration was getting under way. He hoped the sea breezes of the North Shore would help her recovery.

The presidential train arrived at Beverly's Monserrat station for the first time on July 4, 1909. Local police and a half dozen Secret Service agents restrained the curious as Taft escorted his veiled and still ailing wife from their private rail car to a waiting White House limousine and drove to the Evans cottage. Standing on the broad veranda in a cool, salt breeze, they took in the vista of woods and sparkling water. The *Sylph* lay at anchor off Woodbury Point. The white sails of hundreds of sloops flecked the blue water. Later, as a rainbow arched over the harbor, the Tafts took the first of many afternoon drives in the largest of the four automobiles they brought with them on vacation.

Although worried about his wife's health, the president reluctantly left her to recuperate in Beverly while he battled with Congress in Washington over the terms of a hotly contested tariff bill. When he returned to Beverly in August, he was relieved to find her much improved, but her speech was slurred, her gait hesitant, and she kept her face veiled in public. Soon the president was a daily player at the 18-hole golf course laid out among the hills and valleys of the Myopia Hunt Club, considered by golf experts as one of the most challenging courses in the country. On fine afternoons he and the first lady bundled into their White steamer and, with a chauffeur at the wheel, explored local roads and byways, covering more than 2,000 miles that summer alone. The president devoted at least half of each day to his wife, talking with her to help her regain normal speech. Mostly, the Tafts kept out of the public eye. Military aide Major Archibald Butt explained that the president "feels that he has earned a good rest and will take it in his own way. . . . He likes to do the same thing in the same way every day and resents any effort to estrange him from this course."

The Taft family outside of Stetson Hall, 1909 or 1910. All three Taft children enjoyed their Beverly summers. Robert (*far right*), then finishing Yale, played golf and tennis. Helen (*far left*), a student at Bryn Mawr, drove around town in an electric runabout. Young Charlie headed for the water in the sailing dory *Bandit*.

The following summer, Charles R. Macauley, a cartoonist and writer for the *New York World*, shared one typical day at Beverly with the president. He found Taft to be an early and energetic riser. Shortly after 6:45 a.m. the president walked the 300 yards from the house to the stables where his physician, Dr. George W. Barker, had assembled a makeshift gymnasium with pads laid across the floorboards. A pair of boxing gloves and a medicine ball were soon put to use. The doctor's goal: making the president slightly less of a heavyweight by shaving 20 pounds off his waistline by the end of the summer.

Following a brisk thirty-minute workout the president returned to the house for a cold shower and a rubdown. He then moved to the breakfast table where he may have overcome the desired effects of shadow boxing and ball tossing. "The presidential appetite leaves little to be desired," Macauley reported. By then it was approaching 9:00 a.m., time for golf at the Myopia links, easily the most enjoyable item on the daily agenda. Macauley said the day was perfect, with a gray but unthreatening sky that tinted Myopia's hills and valleys in soft grays, greens, and purples.

The contest was a rough-and-ready affair. Balls were sliced into the woods, hit into the rough, and missed altogether. When Taft's ball skittered into a sand trap he needed seven strokes to get it back on the green. It took two and a half hours to play the 18 holes, and the final score was not divulged. Taft took a shower at the clubhouse, then climbed into his car for the ride to the cottage. The Secret Service followed in a second auto, eating the dust churned up by Taft's White steamer.

The first lady presided over lunchtime conversation. But the president's workload claimed the rest of the afternoon. Charles Dyer Norton, the assistant to the president, steered Taft through the piles of letters, the dictation, and the forty-five afternoon visitors, including a U.S. senator and a former governor. "Nobody found it inconvenient to come to Beverly to see the President and he was just about as busy there as he ever was in Washington," Mrs. Taft recalled years later in the first autobiography ever written by a first lady. "Nearly always one could find four or five men sitting on the verandah waiting to see him. He had a game of golf every day on the Myopia links," she said. "But for the most part he seemed always to be attending to the business of being president."

Taft believed in the restorative powers of lengthy vacations. In the summer of 1910, he told an audience in Bar Harbor it was not enough to escape the office for a mere ten days or two weeks. The American people, said he, "have found out that there is such a thing as exhausting the capital of one's health and constitution, and that two or three months vacation . . . are necessary in order to enable one to continue his work the next year with that energy and effectiveness which it ought to have." Taft's prescription included a long rest, a change of air, and exercise in the open.

Exercise in the open was certainly on Taft's agenda at Beverly. Golf, preferably on a course that kept insurgent congressmen and the curious world at bay, offered relaxation and escape. For Taft, there was no better way to elude what one writer called "the whole army of peace-destroying, nerve wracking, fearsome isms that lurk around the dark places of Washington, D.C." If not on the golf course, the president might be found in his motorcar, escaping the pressures of office with a drive in the country.

The automobile was, in fact, Taft's great contribution to presidential mobility and style. Roosevelt had spurned automotive transportation as an extravagance of the idle rich. As president, he only rarely rode in a car, and there was a sign at the entrance to Sagamore Hill, "No Automobiles Allowed." Taft used cars everywhere. One of his first moves as president was to banish the horses from the White House stables and replace them with steamers and electric runabouts. At Beverly, the Tafts had four White House cars. Their chauffeur was known as a "daredevil," "famous all about Washington for his fast work at the wheel." The president, too, enjoyed speed: "He likes

A GOOD LONG DRIVE.

At left, President Taft was photographed on the green at a golf course in Chevy Chase, Maryland, in 1909, and at right, captured in a cartoon titled "A Good Long Drive" by Charles R. Macauley. A cartoonist and writer for the *New York World*, Macauley shadowed Taft for a day in the summer of 1910 and drew this image to accompany his article. A writer for *American Golfer* also followed the president on the course at Beverly and analyzed his game: "He stands very straight, keeps his head still and swings through the ball, sweeping it away. Possibly it is more of a baseball stroke than a golf string, but it answers the purpose nobly." .

President-elect Taft was photographed with his family in a rented White steamer automobile in December 1908. The president and his family brought several of their personal cars with them to Beverly, and they enjoyed regular drives in the countryside.

PRESIDENT TAFT AND HIS FAMILY
IN THEIR WHITE STEAMER

to sit well back on the rear seat and see the trees whizz by," claimed the *New York Times*. "He won't admit it, but he has the real speed fever." Taft himself called a brisk ride in an open car "atmospheric champagne."

The president generally ignored speed limits, but the law never held him to account. His car was stopped, the president was recognized, the policeman apologized, and Taft was free to go. During his first summer on the North Shore, Taft's car ran into a speed trap in the town of Newbury. It took a while for the constables to realize the identity of the large man in the rear seat. When they did, and he promised to have his chauffeur drive more slowly for the rest of the trip, he was on the road once more. In May 1910, in western Pennsylvania, the president was reported by the *New York Times* to be traveling at "such a hot speed that he was not recognized at all." It is only human to enjoy speed, the newspaper said. But when the president breaks the speed laws "he sets a rather bad example for the people who lack his immunity from arrest."

Setting a more sedate example, Taft could board one of the two presidential yachts that were always ready for his use. Both the 273-foot *Mayflower* and the smaller *Sylph* were operated and maintained by the navy. But cruising along the Maine coast in the *Mayflower* in July 1910, Taft discovered that even his sailing vacations drew criticism. The presidential party had come ashore for a quiet Sunday with church in the morning followed by a drive through the woods to a lake for a lunch of fish chowder, baked beans, and brown bread. Later, lounging under the trees after a row on the lake, they leafed through the Sunday papers. A front-page *New York World* headline proved impossible to ignore: "Use of Naval Vessels by Presidents and Others Cost $1,465,261 in Five Years." The newspaper claimed that the use of the *Mayflower* and *Sylph* by Roosevelt and Taft were unauthorized "junkets" and "pleasure cruises." The article noted Taft's calls for economy in government spending and strongly implied the president was a hypocrite. Archie Butt recorded the details in a letter and gave his typically honest reaction: "It was one of those sensational articles put out for political effect, but which are none the less annoying when you know there is some ground for the criticism."

By that time, Taft had grown increasingly concerned over his relationship with Theodore Roosevelt, once his closest friend. Following his year-long African hunt, Roosevelt had embarked on a triumphal tour of Europe as a guest of monarchs from Berlin to Madrid. Now he was coming home. When he stepped off the ship in New York, he received a tumultuous and earsplitting welcome. Ship whistles screamed and horns honked. Crowds estimated at more than half a million lined Broadway and Fifth Avenue as Roosevelt passed. "One continuous heartfelt ovation," Butt called it.

Roosevelt's opinion of his handpicked successor had changed drastically from the days in which he said there was no one in the entire country better fit to be president. Privately, he thought the Taft administration had been a "rather pitiful failure." But on June 30, 1910, he set off with Henry Cabot Lodge to spend an afternoon with Taft at Beverly.

Taft was standing on the veranda as Lodge's touring car pulled into the drive. A throng of newspaper reporters and photographers waited outside the gates in numbers that Butt found astonishing. "I never saw as much interest manifested over any one event in the administration of either man," he said. The encounter opened on notes of friendship and cordiality. "For a full minute this afternoon President Taft and Col. Roosevelt stood on the broad veranda of the Evans Cottage with hands upon each other's shoulders, while evident delight shone in every line of their smile-enwreathed countenances," reported the *New York Times*. At lunch, the talk quickly shifted to Roosevelt's experiences in Africa and Europe. Piling anecdote on anecdote, offering thumbnail sketches of kings and emperors, Roosevelt charged ahead for more than two hours. "He was in his best vein, and I never heard him more witty, more humorous, and more incisive than on this occasion," Butt recalled. Mrs. Taft wrote in her autobiography that Roosevelt "gave us as merry an afternoon as we ever spent with him." For the moment he "succeeded in convincing me that he still held my husband in the highest esteem." Then she added: "I was not destined to enjoy this faith and assurance for very long." Two weeks later, Butt observed that Taft was convinced it had always been Roosevelt's purpose to seek reelection in 1912. "Things have become so bitter at this end that I do not see how they will ever get together now," he said.

Taft stayed on at Woodbury Point late into September as his doubts about Roosevelt's intentions deepened. But he soon discovered he was not the only person in Beverly with a grievance. Maria Antoinette Evans, owner of the Summer White House, was simply fed up with the constant stream of visitors and automobiles, the crowds of reporters, the surveillance of the Secret Service, the crush of sightseers, and all the other intrusions on her summertime pleasures. She not only served notice the cottage would not be available for a third summer season, but she also ordered drastic measures: workmen cut the house in half, loaded it onto a barge, and towed it across Salem Bay to Marblehead, veranda and all. There it was reassembled on a new site, never again to offer hospitality to a vacationing president.

The Tafts' search for vacation quarters began anew with the first lady inspecting more than forty cottages. Not long after their return to Washington it was announced that the new Summer White House would be Parramatta, an eighteen-room mansion a bit inland from Woodbury Point. It was leased for two seasons from the widow of the Boston and Salem merchant Henry W. Peabody. The house had no direct water access. But it did have a Japanese garden, artificial pond, tennis courts, and a 9-hole golf course.

When Taft arrived in Beverly for the 1911 season, he plunged at once into golf in the mornings and long auto rides in the golden afternoons. But he was edgy and irritable. According to Butt, he began speculating on the Democratic nominee for the 1912 election. "I am beginning to fear that by some stroke of genius they may nominate Woodrow Wilson," he said.

Major Archibald Butt, President Taft's devoted military aide, made himself indispensable to the smooth running of the White House in Washington and the Summer White House in Beverly. He had been equally close to Theodore Roosevelt and his family. Butt played tennis with Roosevelt and golf with Taft, and said he developed a different set of calluses for each sport. In a long series of private letters still valued by historians, Butt provided a unique insider's view of two presidents at work and play and recorded his sadness over the growing rift between them.

Maria Antoinette Evans, owner of Stetson Hall, not only refused to rent her mansion to the Tafts for a third summer but uprooted it, ordering it split in half (*right*) and towed across Salem Harbor to Marblehead (*below right*). In Its place, she built an Italian garden (*below left*)..

When the Summer Capital returned to Beverly in 1912, a familiar face was painfully absent. Archie Butt, heeding the president's urgings to take a rest, had departed for Europe early in the year. He was returning to the United States on the liner *Titanic* when, on April 14, 1912, the ship struck history's most infamous iceberg. Major Butt was not among the survivors. "He was like a member of my family," Taft mourned.

By this time, the festering resentments between the president and Roosevelt had broken into open warfare. After a failed bid to take Taft's nomination at the Republican Convention in Chicago, TR bolted and mounted a third-party challenge. Fulfilling Taft's prophecy, the Democrats nominated Wilson. The New Jersey governor quickly opened an aggressive campaign for the White House. Soon it became clear that the contest was between Wilson and Roosevelt, with Taft little more than an unhappy bystander. As Roosevelt and Wilson barnstormed the country that fall, Taft brooded. He stayed close to Beverly, golfing in the mornings at Myopia, driving the country roads with Nellie in the afternoons. In September the *New York Times* summed up Taft's four summers in Beverly. The president, it said, confides in friends that his golf game at Myopia is not much better than it was four seasons ago and that he rarely breaks 100. But the exercise is worth the effort: "The playing course is over four miles long, and, with the walks, chasing a ball now and then, takes him daily on a six-mile jaunt, which does him a world of good." And office work was not neglected, as Taft signed an average of seventy-five commissions, executive orders, and other documents daily; read and answered one hundred letters; and used the telegraph and telephone to keep in touch with the State Department on developments in Mexico, then gripped by revolution.

———

On Election Day, November 5, Wilson won the presidency with more than 6 million popular and 435 electoral votes. Roosevelt tallied more than 4.1 million. Taft came in third with less than 3.5 million. He told friends he was satisfied he had at least prevented Roosevelt from returning to the White House. The big man from Ohio was relieved to be leaving the presidency behind. Eventually he would obtain the only government job he had ever wanted, chief justice of the United States. For now, he was free to vacation wherever he wished. No one would complain if a former president spent his summers at Murray Bay in Canada, which Taft promptly and happily did. Reflecting on his years in the White House, and perhaps his summers at Beverly, Taft offered this summing up: "I have come to the conclusion that the major part of the President is to increase the gate receipts of expositions and fairs and bring tourists into the town."

"Parramatta" Montserrat, Beverly, Mass.
Summer Home of
President Taft.

For the summers of 1911 and 1912, the Tafts rented Parramatta, a spacious mansion on a secluded 60-acre estate in Beverly. An interior view of Parramatta, taken in 1911, is seen below left.

Chapter 23

Woodrow Wilson: Summers in New England and on the Jersey Shore

Woodrow Wilson's pensive mood matched the weather as he settled in at the New Jersey Shore two weeks before the 1912 Democratic National Convention. His future rested on the nomination contest ahead in Baltimore. In the meantime, he was determined to make the best of his family vacation, if only the elements would cooperate. "Here we are at Sea Girt," he wrote to a friend on June 17. "The day is gray and drizzly; the sea makes a dismal voice across the bleak camp ground in front of us; we have had to light a fire in the huge fire place to keep our spirits (and our temperature) up; but here we are a home group with that within us that can defy the depressing influences of the weather. What we now look forward to with not a little dread are the possibilities of the next fortnight in politics."

Wilson, the Democratic governor of New Jersey, was 55 years old. Behind him were a creative but stormy tenure as president of Princeton University and a distinguished academic career as a student of American government. Lying directly ahead was the Democratic Convention, where he hoped his growing national reputation would help him win his party's presidential nomination. In the custom of the time, he would wait out the contest from afar. At the breakfast table that June morning with his wife, Ellen, and their daughters, Margaret, Jessie, and Eleanor paying close attention, Wilson said that two weeks from that day they would either be spending yet another tranquil Sunday or finding an army of reporters camped on the lawn. Which would you prefer? his wife wondered. "Need you ask?" her husband replied.

The big white house at Sea Girt had served as the New Jersey pavilion at the 1893 Columbian Exposition in Chicago. Moved in sections, it was reassembled on state-owned land south of Long Branch. Flooded with light and air, it reminded Eleanor Wilson of a summer boarding house with its row of rocking chairs on the long front porch. The mansion at Sea Girt was the only official residence New Jersey offered its governors.

The house was calm and quiet as the convention opened 165 miles away. After an indecisive nine ballots, Wilson predicted "a ten-inning game." The front-runner was Champ Clark, of Missouri, the Speaker of the House of Representatives and a favorite of party conservatives and big city bosses. But Wilson, an antiboss progressive, was clearly a contender. And the throng of reporters he had hoped for arrived at Sea Girt in force. Workmen pitched a telegraph and press tent on the lawn to accommodate them, and they walked in and out of the house at will. When the governor and his wife emerged for an afternoon auto ride, a moving picture cameraman and a dozen photographers crowded into the drive to record the scene.

Phone calls from Baltimore reported the struggle on the convention floor as one ballot followed another. A turning point came when William Jennings Bryan, the three-time presidential candidate, switched his vote from Clark to Wilson. But the balloting continued, and Wilson broke the tension with a humor few suspected he had. He told funny stories,

On April 20, 1916, President Woodrow Wilson threw the first pitch for the Washington Senators' season opener, continuing a tradition started by his predecessor William Howard Taft. Wilson enjoyed watching baseball, as his smile clearly indicates. Portrayed as professorial and aloof, Wilson was seen differently by his family, who knew him to be warm and fun-loving.

recited limericks, and teased an aide by humming snatches of Clark's campaign song.

At 2:48 p.m. on July 2, with delegates midway through the forty-sixth roll call, Wilson was summoned to the telephone. He listened, then walked upstairs to tell his wife his nomination was assured. Ellen Wilson called the result a happy ending to "a hard, pounding battle." Wilson stressed the serious responsibility he now faced. "As it has seemed more and more likely that I might be nominated I have grown more and more solemn," he said. But his supporters would not be denied a celebration. Soon a brass band marched across the lawn and people waving flags and shouting slogans spilled out of buggies and automobiles and headed to the house. Wilson walked out on the lawn to thank the crowd and chat with reporters who noticed he had a new name for the house at Sea Girt. He called it, presumptuously, "The Little White House."

On the opening day of the 1912 Democratic Convention, the Wilson family, on vacation at the Jersey Shore, departed from Sea Girt for an afternoon drive.

With Sea Girt as headquarters, Wilson campaigned across the country, steadily drawing larger crowds and using his speeches to call for ending business monopoly and granting organized labor the ability to bargain collectively for better pay and working conditions. He was at his home in Princeton on election night as it became clear that the split in the Republican Party between Theodore Roosevelt and William Howard Taft guaranteed his election. In March 1913, he and his family moved into the Executive Mansion.

Ellen Wilson had shown artistic talent since childhood, attended art school, and painted whenever she found time. The summer of 1913 would prove one of her most creative seasons. Before his presidency, Wilson and his wife often vacationed at the artists' colony at Old Lyme, Connecticut, valuing it as a place for Ellen to paint in congenial company. In 1913 they rented Harlakenden House, a magnificently appointed mansion on a 200-acre estate at Cornish, New Hampshire, another summer colony of artistic and affluent men and women. The house belonged to Winston Churchill, an immensely successful American novelist unrelated to the British soldier and statesman whose name he shared. Elizabeth Jaffray, the White House housekeeper, brought up a staff of eight servants to clean, cook, and wait on tables. The novelist's house would be a center for the Wilson family in both happy and sorrowful times over the next three summers.

Because he had insisted Congress stay in session through the summer, Wilson could manage only brief escapes to Cornish. He had planned to join Ellen on July 2 for the announcement of their daughter Jessie's engagement to Francis B. Sayre but found he was expected to speak at the fiftieth anniversary of the Battle of Gettysburg. "I must choose always as a President," he wrote, bitterly describing his position as much like that of "a superior kind of slave."

Although she missed her husband and would return to Washington in August to spend a few days with him, the first lady enjoyed her idyllic surroundings and her interesting neighbors. Among them were the painters Maxfield Parrish and Kenyon Cox, the artistic family of the late sculptor Augustus Saint-Gaudens, and her own former teacher at the Art Students League, George de Forest Brush. She set up her easel on the terrace at Harlakenden

On August 7, 1912, Woodrow Wilson, then governor of New Jersey, officially accepted the Democratic Party's nomination for the presidency while vacationing with his family at the Governor's Cottage in Sea Girt on the New Jersey Shore. In anticipation of the candidate's appearance, a large, respectful crowd assembled on the lawn.

Prior to his presidency, Wilson vacationed three times in Bermuda with his family. He relished the slow pace, pedaling a bicycle to the market and enjoying the company of such illustrious friends as Mark Twain, pictured here seated with Wilson and other companions. As president-elect, Wilson took his family to Bermuda for a winter holiday, but the quiet, private times he had formerly enjoyed had vanished, as he was now a celebrity.

First Lady Ellen Wilson painted this view of the side porch of the Griswold House, where the Wilsons often stayed during summers in Old Lyme, Connecticut.

House and experienced an outpouring of creativity. By summer's end she had added many new canvases to an output that had already resulted in her inclusion in juried exhibitions in Chicago and Philadelphia. That fall the *New York Times* gave her an encouraging review: "Mrs. Wilson is a serious art student and she observes in nature aspects that appeal to the lover of outdoor life. . . . [Her work] is the honest student work of an amateur in the good sense of the word, and holds its own effectively."

The president was able to visit Cornish for eight days in mid-July and again in September, when he watched Eleanor and Margaret perform in an outdoor pageant. He joined Ellen for automobile rides in the countryside, their heavy car raising dust on dirt roads. With the president on hand, his staff operated out of executive offices established in the courthouse above the post office in Windsor, Vermont, just across the Connecticut River. Cables were strung so newspaper correspondents could file reports, mostly on baseball games and afternoon drives. A direct line to Washington kept the president in touch with events.

With his family away for the summer, Wilson kept "Bachelor Hall" at the White House in the company of his doctor, friend, and golf partner, Rear Admiral Cary Grayson, and Joseph Tumulty, his executive secretary. Wilson had readily agreed when Grayson put him on a healthy diet and recommended a daily round of golf for fresh air and exercise. Now the two golfed nearly every morning. Golf was a satisfying diversion, Wilson said, "because when you are playing golf you cannot worry and be preoccupied with affairs. Each stroke requires your

Dr. Cary Grayson was President Wilson's physician and close friend.

In the summer of 1913, President and Mrs. Wilson posed with their three daughters (left to right) Margaret, Jessie, and Eleanor, at Harlakenden House in Cornish, New Hampshire. Mrs. Wilson and their daughters spent entire summers at the house, enjoying the countryside and the company of friends and artists. The president visited when his schedule permitted.

whole attention and seems the most important thing in life." Grayson said Wilson had taken up golf too late in life to become a good player but was at his best where accuracy and carefulness counted. Wilson delighted in quoting a definition of golf as "an ineffectual attempt to put an elusive ball into an obscure hole with implements ill-adapted to the purpose."

Unlike Taft, who enjoyed the camaraderie of the game, Wilson was not a social golfer. He generally visited clubhouses only to pass through them. He

President Wilson playing golf (*left*, c. 1916; *right*, c. 1910s). President Wilson was advised by Dr. Grayson to take up golf. As president he golfed every season, and in the summer he managed to golf almost every day.

did not stop to chat and played with few partners other than Grayson. "The fact of the matter is that he did not want business mingled with his recreation," Grayson explained in his memoirs. Wilson golfed year round and in almost any weather, and said he played six times a week during the summer. After a winter snowfall the Secret Service painted his golf balls red to make them easier to spot. His game was marked with a chronic slice and for all his practice never really improved. He generally shot about 115 and rarely broke 100. One writer called him "a fidgety player who addressed the ball as if he would reason with it." But none disputed the joy he found in the game.

In late 1913, Wilson golfed on Mississippi's Gulf Coast during the first extended vacation of his presidency. A string of successes had begun in March when he addressed Congress in person for the first time since Thomas Jefferson abandoned the practice more than a century earlier. By the end of the long session he had secured passage of the most sweeping overhaul in the protective tariff system in more than sixty years and the creation of a new Federal Reserve System with powers to set interest rates and regulate the money supply. He also clearly needed a rest.

So, as Christmas approached, Wilson acted quickly when Dr. Grayson recommended Pass Christian, named after French explorer Christian L'Adnier. But when Wilson's train rolled in the day after Christmas, the air was unseasonably icy. It was still icy the next morning when the president drove 8 miles to

This mansion in Pass Christian, Mississippi, became "The Dixie White House" when the Wilson family spent their 1913 winter vacation as guests of the owner. President Wilson enjoyed golfing in the warm weather and became a local hero when he alerted a neighbor, astonished to find the president knocking at her door, that her house was on fire.

This crayon-on-paper sketch of Ellen Louise Axson Wilson was made by the British artist Fred B. Yates during a Wilson family vacation in the Lake District, about 1908. The future first lady took art lessons from Yates, and he became a family friend. When Ellen Wilson died on August 6, 1914, in the White House, the president was bereft.

a golf course at Gulfport. "I'm nearly frozen," he said. The chilly weather soon moderated, however, and one warm and sunny day followed another, restoring the president's energy and leaving him relaxed and ready for what would prove a difficult year.

———

Woodrow Wilson's world changed forever in August 1914. The great powers of Europe were rushing to war, and Ellen Wilson, the Presbyterian minister's daughter he had married twenty-nine years earlier, was dying of Bright's disease, a fatal kidney ailment. On August 6, as he sat by her bedside, Wilson wrote a letter in shorthand offering the services of the United States to mediate the European conflict. That afternoon, with the end approaching, the first lady spoke to Dr. Grayson: "Please take good care of Woodrow." She died at 5:00 p.m. with the president holding her hand. "Oh my God," Wilson cried, "What am I going to do?"

Cary Grayson did his best to honor Ellen Wilson's dying request. He persuaded the grieving president to resume his automobile rides in the countryside, to cruise on the *Mayflower*, the presidential yacht, and to return to the golf course. But Grayson knew that these were "only temporary diversions, and that at heart he was desperately lonely."

At Dr. Grayson's urging, Wilson returned to Cornish, still in mourning and beset with alarming news from the battlefields of Europe. He had dispatched his personal emissary, Colonel Edward M. House, to assess the situation, and on August 30 House arrived at Harlakenden to report privately on his meetings with European leaders. In the evenings they talked, read, and played pool. On the second afternoon they sat on the terrace looking out over the Connecticut Valley, and the president confessed the despair he felt at the loss of his wife. "Tears came into his eyes," House recalled, "and he said he felt like a machine that had run down, and there was nothing left in him worth while."

Woodrow Wilson often came across as a calculating and aloof intellectual most at home in the lecture hall and the stacks of a research library. But he asked friends not to be misled, adding that his inner nature was equally divided between his Scots and Irish heritage: one cool and canny, the other warm and spirited. "It is no compliment to me to have it said that I am only a highly developed intellectual machine," Wilson told Tumulty. To those who observed Wilson at close range, the president's warmth showed most clearly in the embrace of his family. On vacation, and during the evenings at the White House, they played charades, operated a Ouija board, guessed at the authors of mystery quotations, and read poetry aloud. Wilson relaxed by reading detective stories, attending the burlesque theater, reciting his favorite limericks, exercising his considerable talent for mimicry, and telling funny stories, often in Scottish or Irish dialect.

In early 1915, Dr. Grayson, arranged an introduction to Edith Bolling Galt, an attractive, independent, and quick-witted Washington widow from an old Virginia family. The president found her charming, and she was soon a frequent guest for dinner at the White House. In the summer of 1915, traveling separately to avoid the attention of the press, Mrs. Galt joined the president at Harlakenden House under the pretext of a visit to his daughters. They took drives together, held hands, walked in the moonlight. "Things are looking very serious," Elizabeth Jaffray, the White House housekeeper, confided to her diary. "The president's daughters were delighted with the match," she recalled. "Very soon the girls were calling Mrs. Galt by her first name, Edith, and she was taken into the bosom of the family."

Years later, Edith Wilson remembered that summer as a symphony of color and sound composed of bright flowers and the "music made by the river where nearly every day we walked." The president came as often as he could and drew her into his official as well as his personal life. In the evenings the family pulled the curtains, gathered by the fire, and listened as Wilson read dispatches from Europe, described the problems, and explained how he intended to deal with each one. In the mornings, on the terrace, Woodrow and Edith worked together on the daily pouch of White House mail. The president proposed, and on December 18, 1915, they were married in a small, private ceremony in the bride's Washington home.

Knowing that reporters were waiting to follow the newlyweds to Union Station and perhaps beyond, Colonel Edmund Starling, head of Wilson's Secret Service detail, arranged an escape to a private railroad car waiting in a rail yard across the Potomac River in Virginia. A series of unexpected turns and a dash through darkened streets left journalists in the dust and enabled the couple to depart on their honeymoon trip with their privacy secure. The next morning, as the president's private railroad car crept into a siding at Hot Springs, Virginia, Starling opened the door to the private sitting room and saw the president, in top hat, tailcoat, and gray morning trousers, whistling and dancing a jig. Starling was familiar with the tune. He had heard it late at night as the president skipped down a Washington street after leaving his fiancée's home. Now Wilson clicked his heels in the air and hummed it again: "Oh, you beautiful doll! You great big beautiful doll!"

Mr. and Mrs. Woodrow Wilson registered at the Homestead, a fashionable resort that had long experience with presidential guests. A wood fire burned in their suite's inviting living room, which offered sofas and chairs covered in English chintz. American Beauty roses filled vases there and in the dining room and two bedrooms. Outside, the mountains were wrapped in snow, and there was a crisp bite to the clear air. It took some days for the Wilsons to emerge from their comfortable quarters, but when they did they played golf and scouted snowy back roads in the presidential Pierce Arrow. Wilson wrote to a friend: "We are having a heavenly time here. Edith reveals new charms and still deeper loveliness to me every day and I shall go back to Washington feeling complete and strong for whatever may betide."

World events do not stand still, even for presidential newlyweds. On December 30, 1915, a German submarine in the Mediterranean Sea torpedoed and sank, without warning, the British liner *Persia*. Several Americans were feared to be among the hundreds of casualties. Wilson cut short his honeymoon and returned to Washington by special train. The United States remained officially neutral in the war throughout 1916, despite provocations and growing pressure to intervene. The day he returned from his honeymoon, Wilson told Tumulty he would not be stampeded into intervention and that if his reelection depended on his getting into the war he no longer wanted to be president. At the same time he took preliminary steps to ensure the United States would be prepared militarily for all contingencies. The

This oil portrait of Edith Bolling Galt Wilson, by the Swiss-born American artist Adolpho Müller-Ury, was a wedding present from Colonel Edward M. House. A Washington widow, she had been introduced to the president by Dr. Grayson, and they were married on December 18, 1915. She outlived her husband by almost thirty-eight years.

Shadow Lawn, the mansion the Wilsons rented on the Jersey Shore in the summer of 1916, was enormous and, at first glance, First Lady Edith Wilson thought it pretentious and generally "awful." A large room—like a hotel lobby—took up much of the lower floor. In the center stood a white marble statue that so offended the first lady she ordered it draped.

The editorial cartoonist John T. McCutcheon plays on the name of the Summer White House—Shadow Lawn—to illustrate the many political challenges faced by President Wilson during the summer of 1916, when he was both president and candidate for reelection.

Shadow Lawn served as President Wilson's campaign headquarters. Delegations arrived every Saturday, and Wilson addressed them all. On October 7, 1916, he greeted delegates from the Young Men's Democratic Clubs (*left*). News conferences were also a frequent event on the lawn at Shadow Lawn.

U.S. attitude toward the conflict would clearly be a paramount issue in the 1916 presidential elections, and Wilson's supporters offered a long-remembered slogan, "He Kept Us Out of War."

———

The president thought it improper to run for reelection from the Executive Mansion, and in early September 1916 the Wilsons moved to a new Summer White House, a rented mansion on the New Jersey Shore called Shadow Lawn. There he received delegations on the front lawn, gave speeches from the veranda, and conferred in the study with party leaders, government officials, and distinguished guests. He began campaign swings around the country from Shadow Lawn. When he wasn't engaged in campaigning, Wilson turned to governing and the bulging leather mail pouches that arrived daily from the White House. He dictated responses to his stenographer, who quickly produced stacks of letters and directives ready for signing, marking those requiring priority attention with red cardboard squares. When the president moved on to the thousands of army commissions awaiting his signature, the first lady blotted the ink and slid a fresh commission in front of him as fast as he could sign. Soon Dr. Grayson ordered the president to slow down, and the Wilsons began enjoying a few evenings alone, the president reading aloud as they sat near the fire. They went for drives along the shore and played golf nearly every morning while obliging Secret Service agents doubled as caddies.

Ida Tarbell, perhaps the nation's best-known female journalist, interviewed the president in early October. They were seated outdoors, and she felt the breeze, "soft and fragrant through the trees." She called Wilson a man of principle and a "fine, humorous, cultivated American gentleman." The president told her he thought of war as a future scholar might, weighing his own actions against the verdict of history. The immediate verdict would come not from history but the voters, and the signs were ominous.

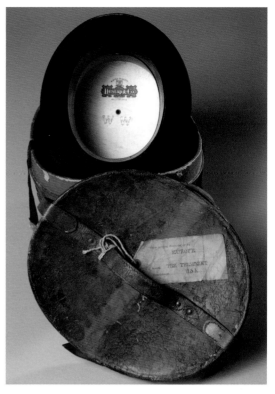

The president and Mrs. Wilson attended the
Longchamp races (*left*) during their extended
stay in Paris for the Peace Conference that ended
World War I. For formal events during the Peace
Conference, 1918–19, President Wilson wore
this top hat (*above*), now in the collection of the
Woodrow Wilson House.

On the evening of election day, as they waited for returns at Shadow Lawn, the president's
family and guests played a game of Twenty Questions, ignoring for a few moments the only
question they cared about. Initial results from eastern states showed Republican Charles
Evans Hughes making impressive inroads. The possibility of defeat settled in like a fog, and
Wilson went to bed without issuing a personal statement.

In the morning it was apparent that Hughes had swept much of the Northeast, carrying
New York and Wilson's home state of New Jersey. But more favorable trends were developing
farther west, and California was clearly the key. The reporter David Lawrence followed
Wilson to the golf course as he played with Dr. Grayson. "How's your game, Mr. President?"
Lawrence shouted. "Grayson's got me three down, but I've picked up four states!" Wilson
replied.

That wasn't enough. The nervous waiting continued into the evening when the Wilson
family drove to Sandy Hook and boarded the *Mayflower* for a cruise up the Hudson River.
Starling rose at 5:00 a.m. on Thursday morning and went to the galley for a cup of coffee.
Half an hour later Arthur Brooks, the president's valet, rushed in waving a wireless message
and shouting, "The boss has won!" California had gone for Wilson. Starling turned back to
Brooks: "It was a funny election. The Republicans celebrated and the Democrats won."

Following his term of office, President and Mrs. Wilson lived at 2340 S Street, NW, on Embassy Row in Washington, D.C. Today, the Woodrow Wilson House is a National Trust Property and is open to the public for tours.

Shadow Lawn was the last Summer White House of the Wilson presidency. After Germany resumed unrestricted submarine warfare, American intervention in the Great War in Europe became inevitable. On April 2, 1917, Wilson appeared before Congress to ask for a declaration of war. From then on his only escapes were at Washington-area golf courses and on board the *Mayflower*. When the war ended in November 1918, Wilson went to Paris for peace talks and emerged in triumph with the framework for the League of Nations. Returning to the United States, he set out on a national speaking tour to rally support for U.S. membership in the League. On September 25, 1919, he collapsed, forcing his return to the White House where, on October 2, he suffered a severe stroke that paralyzed his left side. He remained an invalid for the rest of his term and was unable to act effectively as the Senate rejected U.S. participation in the new world body.

Chapter 24

Warren G. Harding: A Final Journey

WARREN G. HARDING
29th President of the
United States, 1921–1923

Early on a July Sunday in 1921, a middle-aged man with distinguished gray hair stood in his undershirt near the tent he had slept in and shaved with the aid of a small mirror wedged in a tree. President Warren G. Harding had spent the night roughing it at Licking Creek in the mountains of western Maryland with a trio of the nation's most celebrated campers: automaker Henry Ford, tire manufacturer Harvey S. Firestone, and Thomas Alva Edison, who had invented so many things that he could almost be said to have invented the modern era itself.

A year before, Harding, the owner of the *Marion Star*, his hometown Ohio newspaper, and the state's junior U.S. senator, had been no better than a long shot for the 1920 Republican nomination. Skillful maneuvering at the Republican convention in Chicago made him the party's nominee. In the campaign that followed, conducted largely from his front porch in Marion, Harding appealed to an electorate weary of war and presidential crusades. He famously promised "not heroics, but healing; not nostrums, but normalcy." An advertising campaign pumped out his message, almost as if he were a breakfast cereal, and he won with an impressive 60 percent of the popular vote.

A return to normalcy happened quickly at the White House, where the Hardings dropped wartime restrictions, reopened the doors, and resumed the old traditions of Easter Egg rolling, garden parties, gala dinners, weekly receptions, and presidential vacations. Ignoring Prohibition, they served drinks for themselves and select guests in their private quarters.

———

As president, Harding kept company with the rich and the powerful, even if their annual back-to-nature adventures required sleeping on a cot in a canvas tent near a muddy mountain creek. The camp might be a bit primitive, but the Ford and Firestone limousines were parked nearby. So was the radio car able to send and receive the coded messages that linked the president to the State Department in Washington.

Edmund Starling, chief of Harding's White House Secret Service detail, spent most of the July 1921 weekend swatting flies and scoffing at the arrangements made by Firestone, the host for the well-publicized excursion. The camp lacked privacy, Starling grouched. The tents were badly arranged, the ground too low, the river too sluggish, and the mess tent miserably hot. Only cold water was available for shaving. There was no way to take a bath. And the flies were everywhere. "With a jack knife and ten dollars I could have built a better camp," he grumped.

Shaved and dressed, Harding joined the circle of millionaire campers relaxing on folding chairs under the trees. He leafed through a newspaper, then regaled Edison with his still-fresh memories of tarpon fishing in the Gulf of Mexico. Since the 74-year-old inventor was quite deaf, the president raised the volume of his voice. As a result, a newspaper reported, everyone within earshot became fully informed on "the nature and customs of tarpon."

Harding's acquaintance with tarpon first occurred just days after the November election when he boarded a train for a fishing and golfing vacation along the Texas Gulf Coast. The trip

President Harding was the first president to travel to Alaska. At Sitka he visited the Great Alaskan Totem Pole (*opposite*).

The millionaire campers at Licking Creek enjoy lunch in the shade of a tent, July 1921. President Harding is sitting in the back (one right of center), wearing a bowtie. Thomas Edison (one over from Harding's right) and Henry Ford (one over from Harding's left) are also seated at the lunch table.

President Harding and his fellow campers relax in lawn chairs with daily newspapers at the Licking Creek campsite in western Maryland, July 1921. From left to right: Henry Ford, Thomas Edison, George Christian (standing), President Harding, Harvey S. Firestone, and Bishop William F. Anderson.

offered Americans an informal look at the man who would soon succeed the ailing Woodrow Wilson in the White House. The Hardings' wealthy socialite friends, Edward "Ned" and Evalyn McLean, attached their private car to the Harding train. Reporters, photographers, White House stenographers, and Secret Service agents found seats in the car they shared. The trip also gave newspaper readers a chance to become more closely acquainted with Florence Kling Harding, the woman whose sharp eye and strong hand had made the *Marion Star* a success and who had been the prodding force behind her husband's political rise. At 60, she was five years older than her handsome, amiable husband. In a nickname that matched her regal character, Harding called her "The Duchess."

In a second fishing trip before his inauguration, Harding cruised for two weeks off Florida's east coast. He also gave Miami a tourist boost by staying at developer Carl Fisher's new Flamingo Hotel. At St. Augustine the president-elect worked on his cabinet appointments. The top of the roster was impressive: Charles Evans Hughes, a recent Republican presidential candidate, for secretary of state; financier Andrew Mellon as treasury secretary; international engineer Herbert Hoover as commerce secretary. But the president also found room for friends and cronies, making Harry M. Daugherty, his chief political adviser, attorney general, and Senator Albert Fall of New Mexico, secretary of the interior. Ultimately, both would be indicted and stand trial. Fall would be convicted and serve a prison sentence.

But in the heady days before Harding's inauguration, scandal was not even a cloud on the horizon. And as Harding vacationed, enjoying the applause of the crowds he met and the deference and ceremony accorded a president-elect, he began to shed at least part of the self-doubt he had long harbored. Evalyn Walsh McLean noted the change as it occurred: "The constant adulation of people was beginning to have an effect on Senator Harding. He was, more and more, inclined to believe in himself. He cherished an idea that when a man was elevated to the presidency, his wits, by some automatic mental chemistry, were increased to fit the stature of his office."

Warren Harding's mental chemistry was far removed from that of Woodrow Wilson. A lifelong scholar, Wilson enjoyed intellectual parlor games, poetry, and serious reading. A conscientious worker at his desk, Harding in his free time played poker, bet on the results, and relaxed with a drink and a long cigar or a chew of tobacco. He romped with Laddie Boy, his instantly famous Airedale. Golf was one of the few leisure activities Harding and Wilson had in common. But Wilson was a loner on the greens; Harding enjoyed the camaraderie of a large cast of golfing partners.

Relaxing in Florida the winter before his inauguration, President-elect Harding golfed at the Flamingo Hotel Golf Course, where Carl II, pet elephant of the resort's developer Carl Fisher, served as caddie.

Laddie Boy, the president's famous Airedale, greets Harding on his return from a trip to Florida, 1923.

Prohibition was now in force and in his Oath of Office Harding had sworn to uphold the Constitution, which included the Eighteenth Amendment banning the manufacture and sale of alcohol. But in his private conduct, Harding held to personal standards. Drinks were served at Harding's frequent White House poker games, in his private quarters, and in the clubhouse at the end of a golf game.

Agent Starling found that his duties on the golf course went far beyond providing the president with a protective shield. Harding wagered on all aspects of the game, using Starling as his accountant. "He played as if his life depended on every shot, and he made so many bets that sometimes he was betting against himself," Starling said, listing wagers on low score, individual holes, and even on individual shots. "I had to keep accounts, and it was a job for a Philadelphia lawyer." The president accepted no favors on the golf course. When his ball landed on difficult ground, he played it where it lay, even when his opponents offered to move it. "Forget that I am President of the United States," he told them. "I'm Warren Harding, playing with some friends, and I'm going to beat hell out of them."

Harding's frequent golf drew editorial criticism, just as President William Howard Taft's had. But he said the relaxation he found on the greens did him good. "I may not know everything about being President," he said. "But I do know that a lot of decisions can be made on golf courses." And he had his defenders. When it was reported he had played 36 holes on a single Florida vacation day, the *New York Times* chose to be generous: "After all, 36 holes a day is very good preparation for the 10 times that number of problems he will have to deal with when he resumes the day's grind at Washington."

There was no Summer White House in the Harding administration. Harding and The Duchess cruised on the *Mayflower*, visited the homes of wealthy friends, and returned quite often to Florida. The Harding administration's first year was widely hailed as a success and the president's popularity soared. Congress ended the state of war with Germany, gave him the tariff legislation he wanted, and established the Bureau of the Budget he proposed for the efficient management of executive branch finances. Harding convened a naval disarmament conference acclaimed at the time as a major move toward world peace. To the public, the president's horizons seemed darkened only by his wife's poor health: in the fall of 1922 a chronic kidney disorder brought her close to death. But there were also symptoms of an investigation of suspicious oil leases at Teapot Dome, Wyoming. The leases had been approved by Harding's friend, Interior Secretary Albert Fall. As 1923 opened, Fall resigned. A few weeks later another Harding friend, Charles R. Forbes, resigned as head of the Veterans Bureau, also amid allegations of widespread graft.

But Harding's popularity remained high. With his wife slowly recovering, and he himself recuperating from a stubborn and fatiguing cold, the president set out on another winter vacation in Florida. By then he was halfway through his first term, and *Time*, the new weekly news magazine, summed up: Harding was not a superman and should not be judged by the lofty standards set by presidents like Roosevelt or Wilson. On the other hand, "Almost everyone in Washington likes

Harding golfed two or three times a week, always stylishly turned out in knickers, knee socks, and a tweed cap or a straw hat. Celebrities lined up to walk the greens with him. For all the energy Harding put into the game, he rarely broke 100. Critics focused on his swing: too rushed and too short. Although his playing was often ragged, Harding once drew cheers from the gallery when he hit a drive straight and true down the fairway. The president shrugged it off: "A blind sow will find an acorn once in a while," he said. Clockwise from top left: 1921; President Harding played in a foursome at the Newspaper Men's Golf Tournament, 1923; 1921.

President Harding in Florida, January 1921. With several weeks remaining before his inauguration, Harding enjoyed a two week vacation in Florida that involved golfing as well as a two-day fishing trip. While fishing, he landed a 4-foot barracuda and a 6-foot sailfish.

President and Mrs. Harding (left) stand with Edward ("Ned") Beale McLean, his wife Evalyn (right), and their son on a pier in Palm Beach (early 1920s). On several Florida vacations, Harding was a guest of the McLeans and rented the luxurious houseboat the *Pioneer* from them. Ned McLean owned the *Washington Post*; Evalyn, whose father made his fortune in western gold mines, owned the steel-blue, 67-carat Hope Diamond and the even larger Star of the East. Their opulent Washington estate, Friendship, was spacious enough for its own private golf course. The McLeans had been favorites of the Hardings since shortly after Harding arrived in Washington to begin his Senate term in 1915.

him and admits he is a 'good fellow.' And to be a 'good fellow,' handshaker and amiable 'regular guy' and still occupy the President's chair is, in the national mind, the realization of the highest American idealism."

In 1923 Florida's president-watchers kept track as the 120-foot houseboat *Pioneer,* rented from the McLeans, meandered southward from Ormond Beach to Miami. Presidential whim and the availability of golf courses largely dictated the *Pioneer's* course and schedule. The *New York Times* explained: "having been tied down to a year's White House routine he has no liking for a vacation cruise on a time-table basis." Reaching Miami Beach, the president ventured out to try the fishing

President Harding during a 1923 trip to Florida.

at tiny Cocolobo Island but was frustrated by high winds and a rolling, white-capped sea. Reporters saw signs Harding was "quite tired." The president stretched out on a cot set up on the forward deck, covered himself with a blanket, and napped until the island was reached.

Back in Miami, Attorney General Daugherty called in reporters and produced the biggest news story of the vacation, announcing, "President Harding will be a candidate for renomination." Daugherty went on to predict, "The President will be renominated and re-elected because the country will demand it." A reporter asked if there were circumstances in which the president would not run. Daugherty said only an unexpected change in Harding's health would stand in the way. *Time*

President Harding loved tarpon fishing. He is shown here, on another fishing trip in the early 1920s, at Cocolobo Cay Club, Adams Key, Florida. He stands with his fishing rod and the results of what appears to be a successful fishing trip.

said the surprise announcement forcefully dispelled rumors that Harding was tired of the job and worried about his wife's health, and perhaps his own.

———

For more than a year, Harding had been planning an ambitious transcontinental trip to include the first presidential visit to Alaska Territory. The journey would be part speaking tour, part political fence-mending, part sightseeing extravaganza; the final half would be almost entirely a vacation. Opening with a train ride across the United States, the two-month, 15,000-mile excursion would include a steamship voyage to Alaska and a goodwill stop in Vancouver, Canada. After visiting cities along the Pacific Coast, Harding would go deep-sea fishing at the Catalina Island estate of chewing gum magnate William Wrigley Jr., an early political supporter. Then he would cruise south, go through the Panama Canal, and visit Puerto Rico before steaming for home. By eliminating a second transcontinental rail crossing, Harding would cut by half the number of speeches he would have to make.

Harding coined a name for the trip: "The Voyage of Understanding." It was an elastic concept, but the president hoped to use it to win national acceptance for a foreign policy idea he hoped would become his legacy. As an alternative to U.S. membership in the League of Nations, Harding now proposed joining the League's Permanent Court of International Justice, using it as a forum to arbitrate disputes and avoid war.

As the time for departure approached it was clear the president was more than usually tired. He ran out of energy after a dozen holes of golf. He complained of shortness of breath. Arthur Brooks, the president's valet, told Agent Starling that Harding couldn't sleep unless he propped himself into a sitting position. Some in the presidential circle remembered that Woodrow Wilson had become desperately ill on just such a trip. As Starling was leaving to arrange for the president's security on the road, the first lady took him aside: "I want you to promise me something. Wherever we are to stop I want the doctors . . . as close to the President's room as possible." She made clear she was unconcerned about her own recent illness. "Are you sure you understand? It is not for myself that I want this done, but for Warren." Harding himself told Starling to eliminate all unnecessary events from his schedule, to "cut every program to the bone." Starling said it was the first time he had ever heard the president express such concerns. "He looked more weary than I had ever seen him," he said.

In the background was the nagging possibility of future scandal. Rumors circulated linking the attorney general's close friend, Jess Smith, with the illegal sale of bonded liquor to bootleggers. Harding struck Smith's name from those traveling with him to Alaska and said he wanted him out of Washington as well. Smith committed suicide shortly before Harding's departure.

The president and Mrs. Harding boarded their private car, the *Superb*, on June 20, 1923. At least sixty-five people were with them on the seven-car Presidential Special: cabinet members, the president's doctor, stenographers, secretaries, messengers, Secret Service agents, reporters, and photographers. The train was equipped for telephone and telegraph communication. Radio gear would allow the president's speeches to be broadcast to a national audience. Loudspeakers were in place to amplify track-side speeches.

The westbound trip was a political and personal triumph. The crowds started large and grew much larger. Harding made his first appeal for the World Court before an audience of 12,000 in St. Louis: "My passion is for justice over force. My hope is in the great court." He defended his farm policies in Kansas City and at Hutchinson, Kansas, drove to a farm and shocked sheaves of wheat. The Presidential Special rolled on to Denver and to Cheyenne, Wyoming, where, according to *Time*, five airplanes flew over the train and pelted it with roses. In Salt Lake City, where he also played golf, Harding turned again to the keystone of his new foreign policy: "I am seeking American sentiment in favor of an international court of justice. I want America to play her part in helping to abolish war."

President Harding gave fourteen speeches in all. But he also enjoyed more relaxed moments. The president rode horseback through the dusty canyons at Zion National Park, returning red-faced in the heat. He spent a weekend at Yellowstone National Park in Wyoming, where he saw the geysers and pleased the ever-hungry photographers by feeding gingerbread to a black bear and her cub. At Tom Thumb Junction he was happily ambushed by a dozen or so youthful waitresses from the Old Faithful Inn who crowded onto the running board of his car, strummed guitars, and sang. Leaving the park, Harding took the engineer's seat while the locomotive ran a dozen miles down the St. Joseph River and through the Bitterroot Mountains.

On the afternoon of July 4, after speaking in Tacoma, Harding boarded the army transport ship *Henderson*, ready at last for Alaska. The Navy Band was aboard. The ship had laid in a supply of seventy-five motion pictures. A glass-enclosed observation deck provided comfortable viewing of the spectacular coastline. But Harding only wanted to play bridge, almost nonstop. The first cards were shuffled shortly after breakfast; the last, shortly before midnight. Herbert Hoover, the commerce secretary, felt he had been dragooned into the game: "There were only four other bridge players in the party, and we soon set up shifts so that one at a time had some relief. For some reason I developed a distaste for bridge on this journey and never played it again."

Despite the undoubted success of his speaking tour, Harding struck some of his fellow passengers as edgy and morose. One morning, after the *Henderson* had been at sea for a few days, Harding asked Hoover to join him in his cabin and hit him with a question: "If you knew of a great scandal in our administration, would you for the good of the country and the party expose it publicly or

President Harding's 1923 transcontinental train trip included visits to several National Parks. At Zion National Park, in Utah, he forded a stream on horseback (*above*). At Yellowstone National Park he visited Inspiration Point and fed Max the bear (*left*), a photo opportunity that endeared him to Americans who were following his journey.

would you bury it?" Recalling the conversation in his memoirs, Hoover replied: "Publish it, and at least get credit for integrity on your side." That might be politically risky, Harding said. Asked for details, the president mentioned Jess Smith's activities at the Justice Department. Hoover asked if Attorney General Daugherty was involved. But the president "abruptly dried up and never raised the question again," Hoover said.

On July 8, the Hardings' thirty-second wedding anniversary, the *Henderson* entered the bay at Ketchikan and was escorted to the dock by a chorus of hoots and whistles from tugs, fishing boats, motorboats, and other craft. From that moment the tour quickly became a crazy-quilt blur of mountains and water, welcoming committees, impromptu speeches, Indian delegations, dense forests, and glistening glaciers. At Wrangell the president said he had come as "an apostle of understanding; that is what the world and the nation most need." Reaching Fairbanks on a newly constructed rail line, Harding found himself just 150 miles south of the Arctic Circle. It was, said *Time*, the northernmost point ever reached by a U.S. president.

On the return voyage, the *Henderson* anchored at Vancouver, and thousands of Canadians turned out to celebrate the first official visit of an American president to their soil. But Harding was again beginning to tire. At a Vancouver golf club he stopped at the 6th hole and cut across to the 17th so that he would be seen finishing the course. "Just can't get on my game today," he told one of his doctors. "I don't feel too well."

Scenes from the
Voyage of Understanding

This collection of stereographs features images captured of President Harding during his journey west across the United States and into Alaska during the summer of 1923. *Clockwise from below right*: President Harding drove a tractor binder in Hutchinson, Kansas, and rode in the cab of the Great St. Paul electric locomotive in Falcon, Idaho; President and Mrs. Hoover were shown the wonders of Yellowstone Falls by Park Superintendent Horace Albright in Yellowstone National Park, Wyoming; in Alaska, the President admired a dog-sled team and posed aboard a train with members of his entourage including Secretary of Commerce Herbert Hoover (second from right); and he was photographed in contemplation aboard the USS *Henderson* in Alaskan waters. The full-size stereograph (*top center*) shows the president greeting children during a warm welcome in Valdez, Alaska.

In Seattle, Harding reviewed the massed ships of the Pacific fleet in a rolling barrage of 21-gun salutes. Then he spoke before 40,000 people at the University of Washington stadium, saying that Alaska's natural resources and unspoiled beauty must be forever protected from exploiters. Standing under a hot sun, he appeared worn and listless. At one point, he misnamed the territory he had just visited, calling it Nebraska. At another, he dropped the pages of his speech. When he boarded the train that evening Harding called himself "an exhausted man." Harding's doctors, consulting with the first lady, cancelled the rest of the schedule. The train slid past Portland, Oregon, and headed south to San Francisco. Reporters were told the president had a slight case of ptomaine poisoning, probably from eating tainted crabs.

At San Francisco's Palace Hotel, medical specialists began to worry, not about food poisoning but heart disease or a possible stroke. Then the president developed pneumonia. The medical bulletins set off alarms when they called his condition "grave." But Harding seemed to rally, and the doctors held out hope for recovery. Agent Starling visited the sickroom on Thursday afternoon, August 2, and found the president sitting up in bed, alert and still hoping for deep-sea fishing in the Pacific off Catalina Island. Encouraged, Starling headed across town to keep a social engagement.

The Associated Press had installed a telegraph operator and a staff of reporters in a room on the seventh floor of the hotel, just below the president's quarters. That evening, AP reporter Steve Early, who had covered the Voyage of Understanding from the beginning, stood watch on the eighth floor. The end came suddenly and with a jolt. At about 7:30 p.m., the sickroom door flew open. Mrs. Harding burst into the corridor, calling frantically for a doctor. Early asked questions, raced downstairs, and dictated a series of bulletins reporting the president's condition had suddenly worsened. Again he sprinted upstairs. He was back in minutes, breathing hard but able to dictate a flash, the news service's highest priority bulletin: FLASH—FLASH SAN FRANCISCO—PRESIDENT HARDING DEAD.

Harding's cause of death has never been pinned down with confidence, in part because his wife would not allow an autopsy. Modern theories suggest a heart attack; at the time, an epileptic stroke was suspected. The president's sudden death eclipsed visions for the future that he had spelled out on his Voyage of Understanding. Despite his advocacy during that trip, the United States never joined the World Court.

On vacation across the continent, Vice President Calvin Coolidge was visiting his father at his childhood home in the green hills of rural Vermont. The hamlet of Plymouth Notch had no telephone or telegraph, and the vice president did not learn the news until he was roused from bed by reporters. At 2:43 a.m., August 3, 1923, by the light of a kerosene lamp, Coolidge repeated the words of the Oath of Office as they were read to him by his father, a notary public. Only seven people were in the room as Coolidge became the thirtieth president of the United States.

After leaving Alaska, President Harding delivered a speech to thousands of Canadians at Vancouver, British Columbia (*opposite*). While in Vancouver he was fatigued and expressed feelings of illness.

Following his death in San Francisco, President Harding's body was returned to Washington, D.C., by train. His casket was placed in the East Room of the White House and later moved by the traditional horse-drawn caisson (*above*) to the U.S. Capitol for his state funeral on August 8, 1923.

Chapter 25

Calvin Coolidge: Summer in the Black Hills

Newspapers in the summer of 1927 offered their readers some of the most unusual and entertaining photographs ever made of an American president: Calvin Coolidge posing gamely in ten-gallon hat, cowboy boots, and flapping chaps; the dour New Englander draped in the cascading eagle feathers of a Sioux war bonnet. In darkened theaters, newsreels showed the vacationing president wading through the trout streams of the Black Hills of South Dakota, watching a rodeo, riding horseback, and panning for gold. And in one of the startling moments in a surprising summer, the penny-pinching president endorsed the spending of government money on one of the most colossal monuments ever to emerge from an artist's imagination.

When the president and Grace Coolidge, his friendly and admired wife, headed for South Dakota in mid-June, the president's prospects were as bright as those of his thriving country. In nearly four years in office Coolidge had scrubbed away Warren Harding's comet trail of scandal and corrupt associates and fostered an era of government rectitude and thrift. Coolidge himself became something of a national good luck charm, affectionately linked with "Coolidge prosperity."

The future would show it was a prosperity built on shaky foundations. But for many Americans in the summer of 1927, getting rich seemed as close as the next upward tick of the stock market. If Coolidge thought the bubble might ever burst he didn't say so. Good times, the Model T Ford, flaming youth, and bathtub gin eclipsed the acrid memory of the world war. Prohibition was in force but many ignored it. Babe Ruth hit his 60th home run in 1927, setting a record. And in the year's supreme moment, Charles A. Lindbergh, a lone pilot in an airborne eggshell, flew nonstop to Paris in 33 ½ sleepless hours and electrified the world.

The occupant of the White House was decidedly out of step with the syncopation of his times. The public Coolidge was a tight-lipped and self-regulated Vermonter who rationed words as though the supply was running out. Alice Roosevelt Longworth offered a contrast, observing that the atmosphere of the White House after Coolidge took over from Warren Harding was "as different as a New England front parlor is to a speakeasy."

Coolidge welcomed Lindbergh home in a celebration at the temporary presidential residence on Dupont Circle, where he was staying while renovations were under way at the White House. Then he boarded his train and set out for a three-month vacation in the Black Hills. No Summer White House had ever been established so far west. The train's eight passenger cars were occupied by White House staff members, Secret Service agents, White House servants, and a contingent of reporters, photographers, and news reel cameramen, all of whom had to be housed when the train reached Rapid City. Also on board were the Coolidges' handsome white collies, Rob Roy and Prudence Prim, two chows, and a lively raccoon named Rebecca. Coolidge was fully aware of the effort and planning it took to move a president. The Secret Service advanced each trip, checking out "every street and location which he is to visit," he wrote in his memoirs. "Every switch that he

During the summer of 1927, President Calvin Coolidge vacationed in the Black Hills of South Dakota and posed in cowboy attire.

goes over is spiked down. Every freight train that he passes is stopped and every passenger train slowed down to ten miles per hour."

Although the moment of departure was cheerful, the president was privately troubled. Most political commentators believed Coolidge would be re-elected in 1928, but that would mean ten years as president. George Washington had gone home to Mount Vernon after two four-year terms. No president had ever served longer. Coolidge respected the two-term tradition even though some argued it really didn't apply to him.

Moreover, the Coolidges carried a personal burden that had drained their zest for further public service. In July 1924, 16-year-old Calvin Coolidge Jr. died of blood poisoning from an infected blister

The Swearing in of Calvin Coolidge by His Father, by Arthur I. Keller, c. 1923. Awakened in the middle of the night to be told of President Harding's death, Vice President Coolidge took the Oath of Office in the sitting room of his childhood home in Plymouth Notch, Vermont, August 3, 1923.

on his right toe, raised while playing tennis on the South Lawn. Coolidge told the story in the most emotional passage of his autobiography: "When he went the power and the glory of the Presidency went with him. . . . I do not know why such a price was exacted for occupying the White House."

———————

Before their son's death, the Coolidges had planned to spend most of the summer of 1924 at the White House, preparing for the fall campaign and cruising every few days on the *Mayflower,* the presidential yacht. Instead, they joined John Coolidge, the president's father, at the family home at Plymouth Notch, Vermont, where the president had taken the Oath of Office after President Warren G. Harding's death a year earlier.

Folded into a crease in the green hills, Plymouth Notch held a store, a church, a cheese factory, a blacksmith shop, the Coolidge home, and not much else. An office for the summer White House was established on the second floor of the store the Coolidge family had once run. The leather mail pouches followed the president from Washington. So did the reporters who traveled with

Among the visitors to Plymouth Notch the summer of 1924 was that trio of American achievement: Thomas Edison, Henry Ford, and Harvey S. Firestone. They brought kitchen chairs out onto the grass and discussed the world. Left to right: Harvey Firestone, President Coolidge, Henry Ford, Thomas Edison, Russell Firestone, Grace Coolidge, and Colonel John Coolidge, the president's father. Because Ford was interested in the American past, Coolidge autographed an old pine-and-ash sap bucket and gave it to him: "My father had it, I used it, and now you've got it."

him. They explored his early life, noting the room in which he was born and the artifacts remaining in the store: the tobacco cutter, the spice cabinet, the cheese box, and the scales.

For their vacation in 1925, the Coolidges chose White Court, a twenty-eight-room seaside mansion at Swampscott, Massachusetts, where broad lawns sloped down to a rocky coast. There were gardens to walk in and a pool for swimming. Fifty U.S. Marines helped the Secret Service provide security. The *Mayflower* was ready for cruising at nearby Marblehead. The presidential offices were established in an office building 3 miles away at Lynn. The White House mail arrived in a 2-bushel leather bag said to have served vacationing presidents for twenty-five years, including William Howard Taft at Beverly, Massachusetts, and Woodrow Wilson at Shadow Lawn on the Jersey Shore.

In 1926 the Coolidges spent the summer at White Pines Camp, an estate in the Adirondacks overlooking Lake Osgood. There, under the amused but expert guidance of Edmund Starling, chief of Coolidge's Secret Service detail, the president became an enthusiastic fisherman for the first time in his life.

In the summer of 1924, President Coolidge returned home again to Plymouth Notch, where he relaxed by doing farm chores.

Starling, a member of the protective detail since the Wilson era, had become fond of the president, privately dubbing him "the little fellow." But he became concerned that Coolidge had few outside interests. The president didn't golf, fish, hunt, swim, ride, sail, bowl, or play billiards. Other than a daily walk, he got little exercise. Now the agent had a lake full of fish as an ally. Using his own fishing skills to set an example, he captured the president's interest. He was so sure of himself that he bet other White House staff that he would make a fisherman out of Calvin Coolidge.

The president's first fish in the Adirondacks was a 6-pound northern pike, hooked on a copper spinner polished on Starling's sleeve. Coolidge proudly carried the catch to the house, calling for his wife, "Mama! Mama! Look what I've caught!" "You never caught that fish!" the first lady said. "Yes, he did, Madam," Coolidge's guide attested. And reporters soon were headed for the telegraph office to trumpet the news. "Thereafter we fished everyday, rain or shine," Starling recalled. "The conversion was complete. The little fellow became one of the most ardent fishermen I have ever known, and I collected all my bets."

———

At summer's end, Coolidge announced he would vacation somewhere in the West the next year. Civic boosters in sparsely populated South Dakota and the state's congressional delegation opened a campaign to lure the president with tales of beauty of the Black Hills and reports on the abundance of trout waiting to be caught there.

White Court, the seaside mansion that served as the Summer White House in 1925, was in Swampscott, a short distance outside of Boston. It offered seclusion and the possibility for long walks with the dogs, Rob Roy and Prudence Prim.

Located at the center of the continental United States, the Black Hills rise like ancient battlements out of the flat plains around them. Their weathered granite was long ago sliced by streams, furrowed by valleys, and cloaked by trees. Ponderosa and lodgepole pine, juniper, and aspen deepen the color of the hills and give them their name. It is a place that the Lakota Sioux revere as holy ground, the province of the Great Spirit. It was also a place wrested from the Sioux by the government after Colonel George Armstrong Custer and army surveyors discovered gold in 1874.

Stepping up the campaign, the South Dakota legislature passed a resolution assuring Coolidge that "the population in and about the mountains are intelligent and moral, with whom neighborly relations are most safe and pleasurable." Coolidge sent Starling west to check out the Black Hills. His search quickly narrowed to the twenty-room State Game Lodge inside the 125,000-acre Custer State Forest in the southeastern corner of the hills. A promising trout stream ran just outside its door. When told the president had a shuddering fear of snakes, local organizers mounted a "rattler extermination hunt." Starling returned with an enthusiastic report: "You can fish all day. You'll sleep well at night, and you can ride into the Executive Offices at Rapid City three or four times a week. You'll come back to Washington a new man."

In 1926 the Coolidges spent the summer at White Pines Camp in the Adirondacks. There, under the guidance of Secret Service agent Edmund Starling, President Coolidge learned to fish, and fishing soon became a presidential passion.

Coolidge agreed, and Starling headed back to South Dakota, huddled with state officials, and got to work at setting up the Summer White House. Road menders spread fresh gravel on the 32-mile route between the game lodge and Rapid City. The government set up executive offices in the Rapid City High School. The president's office was established in a freshman English classroom, three of its walls covered with blackboards. A telephone switchboard linked the president with the White House. Linesmen strung telephone wires from the high school to the game lodge. The army organized a tag-team of airplanes to deliver the president's mail, cutting a full day off rail delivery. The lodge's water supply was tested for safety, and gasoline pumps were installed for the president's automobiles. The government built a military camp and staffed it with fifty troopers, three officers, a surgeon, and a medical detachment from a nearby cavalry squadron.

Because this was a fishing trip, state officials made sure there were fish to catch. Game wardens, chosen for their discretion, netted 1,500 of the largest trout at the state's Spearfish hatchery and released them into the creek. Steel mesh nets concealed by a layer of logs prevented the trout from swimming elsewhere. But while there would be plenty of time for fishing, sightseeing, and relaxation, the president and his staff made clear this would be a "working vacation." This may have been the first use of the term, much favored by later presidents. "It is seldom quiet where the President is," said Coolidge en route to the Black Hills with a full staff of presidential assistants, secretaries, stenographers, and clerks.

Log fires burned in the stone and timber game lodge when the Coolidges arrived. Buffalo skins and elk antlers hung under the beamed ceilings. A small herd of buffalo raised their heads as the limousines drove up. The pine-covered ridges reminded Grace Coolidge of Vermont's Green Mountains. Reporters, exploring on their own, found no flies, no mosquitoes, and, thankfully, no snakes. The president quickly got his fishing tackle in order. The elegant white collies explored the trails under the pines, but Rebecca, the president's pet raccoon, was banished to a hayloft in disgrace after leaping through the treetops for more than two hours while the president's men tried to coax her to the ground.

The State Game Lodge in the Black Hills of South Dakota was the Summer White House of 1927.

211

Presents began arriving: a buffalo robe, a peace pipe, horses, sheep, fishing gear, moccasins, eighteen Chinese pheasants, agate jewelry, a gold paper knife with a handle shaped like a wheat sheaf, a 90-pound watermelon, a 25-pound tub of butter, and a buffalo roast certified by a state game warden as "pure and wholesome." Landmarks took on new names: Sheep Mountain, a 6,000-foot peak, became Mount Coolidge; Squaw Creek, the stream that ran past the game lodge, became Grace Coolidge Creek.

Coolidge was soon hip deep in the creek where the captive trout performed hungrily. He wore a business suit, high starched collar, tie, and brown fedora and, except for his waist-high rubber wading boots and a fishing creel, appeared much as he did at his White House desk. A reporter asked an innocent question: What bait are you using? "Worm," the president replied. Then he displayed a coffee can full of wrigglers. With that, Starling said, a first-class "hullabaloo" broke out. Claiming outrage, the nation's fly fishermen denounced the use of common worms as unsportsmanlike, unethical, and just unseemly. The ruckus drew bipartisan scorn on Capitol Hill. "Nothing but an imbecile trout would bite a worm," said Senator William Borah, an Idaho Republican. "Any trout that would lie in the bottom and bite a worm is a degenerate trout," said Senator James A. Reed, a Missouri Democrat, who claimed that no self-respective trout would bite a worm, even for a president.

Clifford Berryman's 1927 cartoon, which ran on the front page of the *Washington Evening Star*, shows just how much the "worm issue" had wriggled into the popular imagination. Some suggested that by advertising his use of worms, and by vacationing in the heart of the agricultural Midwest, Coolidge was trolling for the votes of disaffected farmers. Senator La Follette of Wisconsin speculated that "the President is attempting to make farmers forget his veto of farm relief legislation by wearing a ten-gallon hat and catching trout with milk-fed worms."

Starling thought the fuss was silly, but decided it would be in the president's best interest to wean him from worms. A few days later, when the trout were snubbing Coolidge's live bait, Starling hooked a lunging trout with a fly, "an old, dilapidated Black Gnat." The president got so excited that "he tangled his own line up in his rubber boots. He called to me, 'Don't lose him! Don't lose him!'" Then Coolidge waded into the creek, netted the trout himself, and walked off with it. Mission accomplished: from then on Coolidge fished with flies. Governor William J. Bulow, who had authorized the transfer of fish hatchery trout to Grace Coolidge Creek, observed, "The two miles of creek became the best trout fishing in all the world." The president, he proclaimed, "became the nation's foremost trout fisherman."

The enthusiastic mood seemed to peak on July 4, 1927, Independence Day and the president's 55th birthday. He was flooded with birthday greetings. *Time* reported that on a single day, 6,801 letters arrived, along with a 4 x 6 foot birthday card from the governors of the forty-eight states. The president's willingness to pose for news photographers seemed to herald a reelection campaign and, as the Sioux nation planned to invest the president as a chief, more photo opportunities were on the horizon. Speculation over the ceremonial name Coolidge might receive was rampant. *Time* reported that "Still Waters" was under consideration. The *New York Times* said the Sioux had tentatively settled on "Sullen Warrior," explaining that when fully translated the name referred to a deliberative leader, someone "in no hurry to 'get a move on'." Some politically inclined observers suggested, "Man-Who-May-Be-President-Two-Years-Longer-Than-Washington."

Coolidge had indeed been mulling his political future. In late July, he called executive secretary Everett Sanders into his office in the Rapid City High School. In a dry, matter-of-fact tone, he

President Coolidge was made a member of the Sioux Tribe while on vacation in South Dakota in 1927. The tribal ceremony took place during the Frontier Days festivities in Deadwood, the state's most famous frontier town. It was reported that 10,000 Indians witnessed his induction. Coolidge's Sioux name was Wanblee Tokaha, meaning "Leading Eagle."

President Coolidge posed for the cameras in the Black Hills on his 55th birthday, July 4, 1927. His western attire was a birthday gift from local cowboys.

said: "Now—I am not going to run for President." Sanders was astonished but said nothing. The president continued: "If I should serve as President again, I should serve almost 10 years, which is too long for a President in this country." Coolidge passed over a slip of paper. Written in blue pencil was a twelve-word sentence: "I do not choose to run for President in nineteen twenty-eight." Sanders suggested the announcement wait for a few days. Coolidge said he would be ready on August 2, the fourth anniversary of Harding's death and his succession to the presidency. He kept his decision quiet and waited for the appointed date.

The days passed rapidly. Visitors continued to arrive in caravans in hopes of sighting Coolidge or his wife. Cabinet members, senators, and the entire South Dakota state legislature also visited. So did publishers, industrialists, union leaders, five hundred newspaper editors, members of the Republican National Committee, railroad barons, two hundred South Dakota Methodists, and an Indian delegation claiming ownership of the land on which the game lodge stood. A delegation from the National Woman's Party arrived at Coolidge's office in Rapid City to urge passage of the Equal Rights Amendment.

When a horse-drawn wagon in which he was riding threatened to stall on a steep mountain road, Coolidge pulled off his coat and helped in pushing. When Rebecca Raccoon escaped again, the president, whistling loudly, joined the pursuit himself. And when the president sat on the front porch while his valet cut his hair, an audience of tourists watched from the nearby road.

On Tuesday morning, August 2, Coolidge pushed away from the breakfast table. "I have been president four years today," he told his wife, then drove to the office in Rapid City. When he arrived, Sanders asked if he still intended to make his announcement. Coolidge replied with a yes. At 9:00 a.m. reporters filed in for a scheduled morning briefing. One newsman asked Coolidge to list the accomplishments of his administration. Peace, Coolidge said, followed by prosperity, specifically low unemployment, a reduced national debt, and lower taxes. When the questions ended the president said he would have an additional statement at noon.

At noon, after the reporters had assembled, Coolidge handed each a slip of paper on which his stenographer had typed his simple, twelve-word sentence: "I do not choose to run for president in nineteen twenty eight." This was bulletin news, the biggest news story on the White House beat since Harding's death. *Time* called it "a twelve-word shock." Much effort went into analyzing the word "choose," though fellow Vermonters saw no grounds for confusion. "I do not choose," they said, meant "I ain't gonna do it and I don't give a dern what you think."

The uproar caused one Black Hills resident momentary fear that his plans to exploit the president's vacation might be derailed. Gutzon Borglum, an ambitious sculptor, was determined to confound his many detractors and carve a monument to the American spirit out of an unforgiving 500-foot granite wedge called Mount Rushmore. The sculptor had invited the

president to dedicate the work of carving the faces of George Washington, Thomas Jefferson, Abraham Lincoln, and Theodore Roosevelt into the sheer rock. The fate of the project probably rested on Coolidge's endorsement. The sculptor certainly thought so. The president's choice of the Black Hills as a vacation spot "meant everything to the monument," Borglum said. But there was no guarantee the president would attend, let alone speak. Borglum's talent for self-promotion took over. He hired a local pilot to buzz the game lodge and drop a wreath with the message: "Greetings from Mount Rushmore to Mount Coolidge." Mrs. Coolidge sent an encouraging reply, and the president agreed to speak.

Arriving for the dedication of Mount Rushmore in 1927, President Coolidge dressed for the occasion. In western hat, cowboy boots, fringed gloves, and a business suit, Coolidge rode horseback 3 miles from town to Mount Rushmore. *Time* said it was the first time he had ever been photographed on a horse. Coolidge's speech (*below left*) bestowed national legitimacy to the project. Below right, Mount Rushmore is shown in mid-winter, a work in progress.

This 1928 cartoon, by Clifford Berryman, plays on President Coolidge's decision to "choose not to run" again for the presidency and on his love of fishing.

CHOOSIN' TO RUN ISN'T AS RESTFUL AS THIS

Ever theatrical, Borglum saluted the president's arrival by detonating explosives under twenty-one tree stumps. The president's opening words exceeded expectations: "We have come here to dedicate a cornerstone that was laid by the hand of the Almighty." Coolidge recounted the virtues of the presidential giants whose stone faces would look out from the granite wall. The completed memorial, he said, would become a national shrine "to which future generations will repair to declare their continuing allegiance to independence, to self-government, to freedom and to economic justice." For a parsimonious chief executive, what came next was exceptional. Coolidge endorsed enough federal financing to supplement private and state money and ensure the monument's completion. He then walked to the edge of the stage, raised a dipper from a water bucket, and took a long drink.

With his decision to leave the White House behind him, Coolidge happily returned to fishing. "His mind was now free of any particular worry about the future, and he enjoyed every day of his stay at the Game Lodge," Starling said. Some of Coolidge's eastern friends worried he was making himself look ridiculous by allowing photographs while wearing war bonnets and 10-gallon hats. One opposition newspaper said newsreel audiences "roar with laughter as this bewildered little man teeters down the steps in his vaudeville chaps and timidly grasps the reins of the gift horse he fears to mount." Coolidge's reaction: "Well, it's good for people to laugh." Starling had his own explanation: "If he had fallen asleep over a Buffalo Bill dime novel at the age of 12 and it had all come true, he could not have been more tickled. I had the impression . . . that he was living a boyhood that had been put off 40 years."

In early September, after the Coolidges had returned from an excursion to Yellowstone National Park, the drumming of an airplane engine was heard over Rapid City. The town responded with screeching mill whistles and wailing fire sirens. Coolidge stood quietly outside the high school with a group of Sunday School children, all looking up. He waved a white handkerchief. An

engraved card fluttered from the cockpit. It announced that the pilot was touring the country to promote commercial aviation. The signature was scrawled in pencil: "Charles A. Lindbergh."

"I have had a good time," the president said of his vacation in the Black Hills. But there was one sad moment. Prudence Prim, the first lady's white collie, died of distemper. "We lost her in the Black Hills," Coolidge wrote in his memoirs. "She lies out there in the shadow of Bear Butte, where the Indians told me the Great Spirit came to commune with his children."

———

A year later, as the presidential train headed for northwestern Wisconsin and another fishing vacation, word came that Commerce Secretary Herbert Hoover had received the 1928 Republican nomination. Coolidge, who dismissed Hoover as "that superman," showed little enthusiasm.

Starling had again scouted out a vacation retreat: Cedar Island Lodge, a 4,160-acre estate centered on a private island in the Brule River with pools packed with a reported 500,000 hatchery-raised trout. Built of oak logs, the lodge had eight bedrooms, four baths, and a circular living room. A separate dining room featured a table large enough for thirty guests. Sixty infantrymen from Fort Snelling, Minnesota, provided security. Executive offices were set up in a high school in Superior, and the president went there twice a week. The usual menagerie of Coolidge pets, including five White House canaries, made the trip. But the central attraction was the river and the fish. "The Brule River, fed by springs, was cold and clear and full of wily trout," Starling wrote. "Nature could not have been improved upon, and every luxury of civilization was also available."

In the summer of 1928, President Coolidge fished day and night on the Brule River in northwestern Wisconsin. One day he fished until nearly midnight. *Time* said that by now he had learned his fly book by heart.

217

Calvin Coolidge's boyhood home is today a National Historic Landmark and Vermont Historic Site, open to the public. The village of Plymouth Notch, largely unchanged since the nineteenth century, is a Historic District.

At first nature did not cooperate. "Curtains of rain descended upon the northwest corner of Wisconsin," *Time* reported. "All week they brushed the forests, slowly, monotonously." But the skies cleared on July 4, Coolidge's 56th birthday. Real fishing began, often stretching from first light to long after dark. Starling kept watch: "One day he lost a fish he had been playing and I heard him say, 'Damn!' Then he turned to me and with a shy smile said: 'Guess I'm a real fisherman now. I cussed'."

———————

Coolidge returned to Northampton, Massachussetts, the town he had served as mayor near the beginning of his long political career. The former president and his wife moved back into the unpretentious duplex house at 21 Massasoit Street, where they had been living when he was nominated for vice president in 1920. It was a mistake. Platoons of what one neighbor called "motorized gawkers" drove by, hoping for a glimpse of its famous occupant. The unwanted attention soon prompted the Coolidges to move to The Beeches, a larger, much more private house on 9 acres in another part of town.

The former president spent part of each weekday in his former law office, issued a well-received autobiography, and for a year wrote a syndicated newspaper column, "Calvin Coolidge Says." In the fall of 1929 he watched from the sidelines as the Coolidge prosperity collapsed with the stock market crash and the onset of the Great Depression. Near the end of his life he told a friend, "I feel I no longer fit in with these times." Calvin Coolidge died suddenly on January 5, 1933, and is buried under a simple headstone in the family plot at Plymouth Notch Cemetery in Vermont.

A memorial statue of Calvin Coolidge on the Presidential Walk in Rapid City, South Dakota, is a lasting reminder of the president's 1927 summer vacation in the Black Hills.

Chapter 26

Herbert Hoover: Trout on the Rapidan

HERBERT HOOVER
31st President of the
United States, 1929–1933

By every measure, the rocky wedge of land folded between two prongs of Virginia's Rapidan River met the tests the president had set. At a bit more than 100 miles, it was an easy three-hour drive from the White House. At 2,500 feet above sea level, the site on the eastern rise of the Blue Ridge offered cool air, low humidity, deep woods, mountain views, and freedom from mosquitoes. And for Herbert Clark Hoover, 45 years an angler, the mountain streams served up all the speckled trout a fly fisherman could ask.

There had never been anything quite like Hoover's fishing camp. Other presidents escaped Washington's summers at country homes or seaside cottages. Abraham Lincoln spent summers in a cottage at Washington's Soldiers' Home. Edith Roosevelt provided her husband a farmhouse near Charlottesville as an occasional refuge. But Rapidan Camp added a new dimension, evolving into something close to a private presidential resort and entertainment center.

The idea of a permanent presidential country retreat came from Calvin Coolidge as he considered summertime Washington's sea-level heat, sweltering humidity, and the complex and demanding logistics involved in moving a president from place to place. "For these reasons it seems to me that some place should be provided in the hills within easy striking distance of Washington where the President might go for two or three days at a time when he was so disposed with conveniences for entertaining members of the Government and other guests, where he could have that freedom of action which he has only at the White House and where he could get a complete change of atmosphere," Coolidge advised.

Love of trout fishing drew President Herbert Hoover to the Blue Ridge Mountains of Virginia, where in 1929 he established a fishing camp on the Rapidan River, the first permanent presidential hideaway. As the nation descended into the Great Depression, fishing was about the only thing that brought him joy. In August 1930, as the Depression deepened, President and Mrs. Hoover posed on one of the Camp Rapidan bridges (*opposite*).

Coolidge found a ready audience in Hoover, who had his own assessment of summer in the nation's capital: "Washington's exhausting summer heat is known to several million people from acute experience. Eggs have been fried on the pavement." Moreover, Hoover had decided to retire the *Mayflower*, the luxury yacht that had offered a quick escape to every chief executive since Theodore Roosevelt. But the new president was less excited about Coolidge's recommendation that a "Country White House" be located at Mount Weather, a government weather station 60 miles west of the capital. He found it too formal.

220

At first, early in the summer of 1929, Camp Rapidan was just a series of raised canvas army tents. By August the tents were being replaced with permanent structures as the presidential cabin, with its huge stone fireplace, was rushed to completion.

An orphan who had earned a fortune as an international mining engineer, Hoover won worldwide acclaim when he used his organizational skills to shape European relief efforts during and after the Great War. His visibility at home rose further when he became an active secretary of commerce. Although he had never held elective office, Hoover, "The Great Engineer," easily defeated Democrat and longtime New York governor Al Smith in 1928, in part for his perceived ability to solve any problem that might cloud the American horizon.

———

Hoover's search for a summer White House began even before his inauguration. When William E. Carson, head of the Virginia State Conservation and Development Commission, discovered that the president yearned for a place to catch mountain trout, he promoted Virginia trout streams. Soon Hoover's secretary, Lawrence Richey, a brawny former Secret Service agent who had once guarded Theodore Roosevelt's family, was driving down back roads in the Blue Ridge, where he was regarded with suspicion and presumed to be a revenuer. But, said *Time*, Carson wasn't looking for homemade whiskey. "He was looking for, and asking for, and prepared to pay for, the right to catch—brook trout." The time was short. Virginia's three-month trout season was at hand.

In early April, Richey brought the president and First Lady Lou Henry Hoover out to explore where Mill Prong and Laurel Prong splash over boulders to form the Rapidan. Forced by the rough country to abandon their cars, they made the final 5 miles on horseback. The Hoovers had lived and camped in many parts of the world and knew what they wanted. Dr. Joel Boone, the White House physician, was in the party and said Hoover did not take long to make up his mind. The president pointed to the pie-shaped patch of land between the two prongs and said, "That's where I want my camp."

The Rapidan meanders through Virginia's Madison County, below the spine of the Blue Ridge in a region that is now Shenandoah National Park, before flowing into the Rappahannock, which in turn empties into Chesapeake Bay. Oak, maple, hemlock, chestnut, and flowering laurel climb the hills and line the riverbanks. "It is really away from civilization, really a place where a man may rest from the cares which beset the head of a complicated democracy," the *New York Times Magazine* reported. Hoover spent his first night in the camp toward the end of May and returned in early June, helping catch enough trout to serve at both dinner and breakfast in the canvas mess tent erected by U.S. Marines. The first lady, also quick to see the possibilities of the place, rode 5 miles on horseback and picked wildflowers on a ridge overlooking the Shenandoah Valley.

Rapidan Camp began as a cluster of canvas tents with raised wooden floors. By the time construction of the cabins began, the president had bought the 164-acre campsite, paying a reported $5 an acre. He eventually spent $114,000 of his own money on building the camp and clearing 75 miles of hiking trails and bridle paths. He later announced his intention to make it part of Shenandoah National Park, then in the planning stages.

The country through which the Rapidan flowed was tangled with underbrush, bristling with rocky outcroppings, and totally unimproved. Marine Major Earl C. Long, who supervised building the camp and then ran its day-to-day operations, called the job one of the most challenging he had ever faced: "It would have been easier to have moved an army of 10,000 men across the Blue Ridge than to have built this camp. I have been amazed to find so wild an area existing here so close to the eastern cities."

Telephone service arrived in June 1929 with the completion of 15 miles of pole and cable. A radio transmitter was installed. Air mail service began in July with military aircraft dropping mailbags in a clearing marked with a circle of stones. Electric power was connected in September with the completion of a 12-mile high-voltage line. A blasting crew cut a footing for road construction equipment. Then tractors and heavy graders roughed out a roadbed from one blast hole to another. Workers laid more than 1,000 feet of culvert for drainage. A dozen substantial

To build Camp Rapidan, new roads had to be carved out of rugged mountain wilderness, as shown here in August 1929.

bridges were built across nearby streams, and a landing field for military aircraft was constructed several miles away. Tons of supplies were hauled in by truck. "The fish are close at hand and the President may lie in his bed and listen to the water tumbling over the rocks," said the *New York Times* when the work was done.

Most commentators applauded the effort. "It is the kind of camp which cries aloud for old clothes and stout boots, for blue veils of wood smoke drifting through the trees," one journalist wrote. "The whole thing is incredibly simple. All the houses are built of pine boards, stained outside a warm wood brown that fits them into the mountain color scheme."

Hoover was riding a crest of popularity and economic prosperity in the summer and early fall of 1929, and few begrudged him the comforts and outdoor pleasures of a fishing camp. While there was a tremor of nervousness about stock market speculation, the economy was booming, employment robust, and the world at peace.

One small problem Hoover could take

By August 1929, cabins had replaced the army tents. Most had a bedroom, living room, bathroom, and porch, and all had names, such as Creel and Owl. Some cabins were for guests; others housed staff and offices. Wooden bridges traversed gullies and streams, and everyone spent most of their time outside, even when just talking or walking or reading the newspaper.

pleasure in solving arrived at Rapidan Camp as the president celebrated his 55th birthday. Fourteen-year old William "Ray" McKinley Burraker, born and raised in the Blue Ridge, appeared with a captured opossum as a gift for the president. Hoover handed over $5 for the animal, and he and the boy talked. Young Burraker, it developed, could not read or write. He had never been to school because there was no school within 20 miles of nearby Dark Hollow, where he lived. A few weeks later Hoover announced he and several friends would buy the land and build and equip a schoolhouse and community center if the Commonwealth of Virginia would provide a teacher. Agreement was quickly reached, and Hoover School opened in early 1930.

Thousands of Virginians crowded into the Madison County fairgrounds on August 17, 1929, to welcome the Hoovers as their new neighbors. Squirrel stew was served in 5,000 tin cups on tables heavy with fried chicken, country ham, and barbecued beef. Harry Flood Byrd, Virginia's governor, arrived in an army blimp, and the celebration was broadcast by radio and filmed for the newsreels. Hoover thanked Virginia for its hospitality and said he had found in the Blue Ridge a natural antidote to Washington's hurry and stress. "I have discovered that even the work of government can be improved by leisurely discussions of its problems out under the trees where no bells ring or callers jar one's thoughts," he said. Inevitably, he turned to fishing, which he called a fully valid excuse for retreat from a hectic world. "Fishing seems to be the sole avenue left to Presidents through which they may escape to their own thoughts and may live in their own imaginings and find relief from the pneumatic hammer of constant personal contacts." Fishing teaches lessons in democracy, humility, and human frailty, Hoover contended, "for all men are equal before fishes. And it is desirable that the President of the United States should be periodically reminded of this fundamental fact—that the forces of nature discriminate for no man."

Two months later, the bottom fell out of national prosperity in a series of violent Wall Street jolts. The crash began on October 24, 1929, a day that would be remembered as Black Thursday. The Great Depression soon became the Hoover administration's preoccupation. Other than weekends in the Blue Ridge, Hoover rarely traveled. He twice canceled planned vacations in the West and did not see his own home in Palo Alto, California, until the week of the 1932 election.

Medicine ball was Hoover's one concession to his doctor's demands that he get a daily dose of exercise. At first he told his physician, Dr. Boone, that his day was too busy and his calendar too full. The doctor persisted, rounded up a roster of senior officials willing to arrive at the White House before breakfast, and marked out a 30 x 60 foot court on the South Lawn. A 9-foot net divided the court, and the only gear was a 6-pound leather ball. Boone said the effort paid off. Hoover lost weight, and his condition improved. *Philadelphia Inquirer* reporter Thomas F. Healey said an extra benefit came with "the fresh air, the fun of the thing, the hearty appetite that follows." What is more important, he added, "is the fact that during that half-hour of strenuous exercise Mr. Hoover forgets he is President of the United States."

By the time the trout season opened on April 1, 1930, Rapidan Camp was a well-established presence in the Blue Ridge. Designed by James Yardley Rippin, a Hoover friend who had done architectural work for the first lady's beloved Girl Scouts, the camp with its thirteen widely spaced buildings was low-slung, simple, and restful. "The camp buildings harmonize wholly with the rustic surroundings," Virginia writer Thomas Lomax Hunter observed in 1931. "They are plain, pine-board structures, adequate and comfortable, but without the smallest pretense of architectural elegance, and fit into the scenery like the pines and lichened boulders." In addition to the president's cabin, there were cabins for twenty-five guests, a mess hall, offices, a community center, servants' quarters, stables, and a dog kennel. Boxes of hardy flowers enlivened the porches.

The president's physician convinced him to get some exercise by organizing daily games of medicine ball. Participants called it "Hoover Ball." The games began about 7:00 a.m. every morning except Sunday and lasted half an hour, with players throwing and trying to catch the heavy ball. "It required less skill than tennis, was faster and more vigorous, and therefore gave more exercise in a short time," Hoover wrote in his memoirs. The game pictured here is from 1933.

The Hoovers and their guests were served breakfast and dinner at tables in the mess hall. Lunch was often an outdoor affair, served under the trees. Main courses at dinner included steak, broiled fish, hamburgers, lamb chops, Virginia ham, or fried chicken. Orange juice was the most common cold drink. Unlike the Hardings, the Hoovers served no alcohol.

The camp's recreational and social life, thought out and planned by Mrs. Hoover, centered on Town Hall, a large, L-shaped structure featuring two stone fireplaces that served as places for conversation. It had comfortable seating and circular braided rugs on the floors. Town Hall was equipped for rainy days, offering jigsaw puzzles, a ping-pong table, two radios, and shelves filled with books, including the mysteries Hoover favored. When Ike Hoover, chief usher of the White House (and no relation to the president), toured the camp in 1931, he was clearly astonished: "I had no idea such a place could possibly exist up in those wilds. . . . As a camp it is just as complete as the White House is as a place of residence. There is not a detail lacking."

While fishing provided the reason for the camp's existence, many other outdoor activities were offered to guests. For some, horseshoe pitching became a mild addiction, with games beginning after breakfast and continuing into the early evening. Archery was available, as were lawn tennis, croquet, and even baseball. Horses were brought up from the stables after breakfast and again after lunch and were always available on request. Peeled balsam walking sticks were offered to hikers.

Aides to the president and first lady acted much like social directors on an ocean liner, encouraging the flow of conversation, taking part in games, acting as guides, and planning special events. Although Hoover preferred to fish alone, once out of the stream he sought company, not solitude. "He always wants to have people around him," his wife told friends. The president was rarely disappointed. Thousands accepted the Hoovers' Rapidan hospitality, including governors, bankers, lawmakers, scientists, authors, educators, industrialists, lawyers, government officials, generals, admirals, and friends. British Prime Minister Ramsay MacDonald brought his daughter, Ishbel. When Charles A. Lindbergh and his wife, Anne Morrow Lindbergh, visited, they gave the Hoovers a lamp with a signed parchment shade showing the route of the *Spirit of St. Louis* on its 1927 flight across the Atlantic.

The first lady, an avid botanist, directed the landscaping, keeping the setting simple and natural and using local flowers and shrubs. "The President is very fond of color in gardens," she noted. "So where possible and appropriate to the species, arrange the flowering shrubs and flowers so as to give mass effects of color." She asked for honeysuckle, huckleberry, dogwood, and rhododendrons, also for morning glories, wild cucumber, black-eyed Susans, asters, jack-in-the-pulpits, columbines, lady slippers, iris, and larkspurs. So that no live trees would be cut unnecessarily, she asked that only dead wood be used for firewood, most of it from chestnuts killed by blight.

For all the camp's attractions, it was trout that brought Hoover to the Rapidan and trout that brought him back. Four days after trout season opened in 1930 the president tied a Royal

President Hoover's cabin, also called the Brown House (in contrast to the White House) had a 60-foot-long living room centered around a stone fireplace. Rows of windows framed forest views and slanted inward to invite the mountain breezes. Unpainted rafters supported the roof. There were Navajo rugs on the floor, Pueblo pottery on the tables, and a fisherman's creel hanging from a hook. In this photograph, guests enjoy tea on the sofa.

Coachman to his line and explored the river's pools and currents. Later he changed to a Grizzly King. "Almost as soon as he had cast a gayly colored fly into the stream a fish rose to the hook," a newspaper reported. He was back in early May, again using the Royal Coachman but later changing to a Yellow May. Newspaper readers learned that the president "carries a fly-book full enough to meet almost any angling emergency." By nightfall he had caught the legal limit of twenty trout. In early June, a 16-inch rainbow trout rose to Hoover's Black Gnat. At 2 pounds, it was the prize catch of the season. If the fish were plentiful, there were reasons. Government agents often stocked the Rapidan with thousands of good-size trout months before the fishing season opened.

Fishing was never a casual affair for President Hoover. He carefully dressed for camp and stream in white flannel trousers, a blue sports coat, white shirt with tie, and a broad-brimmed Panama hat, as shown here in 1932. Home movies, taken by the first lady, show him in hip boots over his trousers and a fishing creel at his side. He casts, casts again, and every so often lifts a trout from the water and drops it in the creel.

As the Depression deepened, newspaper accounts of Hoover's Rapidan weekends increasingly portrayed the camp less as a fisherman's paradise and more as an alternative workplace. "Sticks to His Camp Desk," a headline reported in August 1930, when a severe drought burned up crops across a vast swath of farm country and the camp turned into a virtual "drought relief headquarters." Hoover met so often with cabinet members at the camp that some stayed in their own cabins about 2 miles away. When the president wanted to cut agency budgets in 1931, processions of officials drove out from Washington for discussions on the Rapidan. So much business was being conducted at the camp by the spring of 1930 that an editorial in the *Washington Post* said the "place in which to get away from it all" had become "a place for concentrated attack upon affairs of state." Now, the newspaper said, "it bids fair to become a permanent 'deputy capital'" and a bustling "presidential city." That would be a shame, the *Washington Post* said: "The woods are meant for leisure. The streams are meant for fishing. The president should have been permitted to retain the privacy of his retreat."

Secret Service agent Edmund Starling, watching Hoover on the Rapidan, said that as the Depression grew more serious the president became progressively more nervous, even while fishing. "His hands would tremble as he worked with his tackle," Starling said. "I have seen him catch a fishhook in his trousers, his coat, and then in his hat. It was odd to see this, for he looked like a man without a nerve in his body."

Despite the public's intense interest in his activities, and although fishing stories made him seem more human, Hoover refused to share his private life with the press. With only a few exceptions, reporters were barred from Rapidan Camp. But in August 1932, with the November election approaching and his aloof and distant reputation in need of repair, Hoover admitted twenty-three newspaper correspondents, photographers, and newsreel cameramen, and in seventy-five minutes reenacted camp life while the shutters snapped. He cast for trout, rode horseback along a mountain trail, posed on his porch while Mrs. Hoover knitted, strolled in the woods, showed off a waterfall, and played with his two dogs, Weegie and Pat. The news crews ran cables for motion pictures and set out microphones to record the sound of splashing water, the barking of dogs, and the clatter of hoofbeats. But the attempt at naturalness fell flat. Hoover was stiff, unresponsive to

In August 1932 President Hoover fished from a navy boat on the Chesapeake Bay near Crisfield, Maryland.

For President Hoover, horseback riding was definitely second to fishing, but he enjoyed exploring the mountains around Camp Rapidan. On one Blue Ridge Crest ride with the director of the National Park Service, the two discussed the possibility of a crest road, and groundbreaking for the Skyline Drive began in 1931. The road was at first intended as a relief project, a means to employ Virginia farmers and apple pickers suffering from the severe drought of 1930. In 1933, President Franklin D. Roosevelt's Civilian Conservation Corps took over the project.

First Lady Lou Hoover's attention to detail is evident In this photograph from 1930, where the deck of the presidential cabin has been graced with a bowl of fruit and a vase of flowers. In the guest cabins she hung maps of the area and information sheets with an array of practical advice, including suggestions for chilly nights: "After all blankets and eiders are exhausted, put on your camel's hair dressing gown, wrap your head in a sweater, and throw your fur coat over everything!"

questions, clearly restive and ill at ease. "It was very difficult for the President to be a showman," his physician, Dr. Boone, remembered. "A great opportunity for particularly good publicity had been missed."

The Reconstruction Finance Administration, Hoover's response to the Depression, was said to have been shaped at the Rapidan. During a long Rapidan weekend in June 1932, Hoover worked into the night to arrange the loans needed to stop a run on endangered banks. But there was one policy line Hoover refused to cross. As demands grew in Congress for massive public relief programs, Hoover dictated a 2,500-word letter from the Rapidan decisively rejecting the idea: "The back of the Depression cannot be broken by any single government undertaking. . . . We cannot squander ourselves into prosperity. . . . Such a program as the huge Federal loans for 'public works' is a fearful price to pay in putting a few thousand men temporarily at work."

By then Hoover's election contest with New York Governor Franklin Delano Roosevelt was taking shape. In his acceptance speech at the Democratic National Convention, Roosevelt pledged "a New Deal for the American people." Hoover campaigned on his record, a balanced budget, and volunteerism, contending that FDR's New Deal would "destroy the very foundations of the American system." Roosevelt's appeal proved far stronger, and he won by more than 6 million votes, with 472 electoral votes to Hoover's 59.

On December 4, Mrs. Hoover drove out to the camp to supervise the packing of personal belongings. Her husband did not join her. On New Year's Day, 1933, Hoover kept his promise to deed his 164 acres on the Rapidan to the commonwealth of Virginia for eventual transfer to Shenandoah National Park. But his hope that the camp would be a weekend retreat for his presidential successors was never realized. President Roosevelt drove out to the camp in April 1933 and picnicked there. Although ramps were built for the president's wheelchair, Roosevelt found the rocky terrain too rough for easy movement and the mountain stream too chilly for swimming. By the end of the decade the camp began to deteriorate. Then, with Hoover's encouragement, the Boy Scouts of America signed a lease and camped on the Rapidan through the 1940s and 1950s. In the summer of 1954, 80 years old, Hoover returned for dinner with the scouts and walked along the river, visiting his old fishing holes. It was his last visit. He died in 1964 at age 90.

In 1958, the National Park Service resumed maintenance responsibility and determined that decay and termite damage made it necessary to tear down most of the camp buildings. But three cabins, including the president's, were rehabilitated and opened to high-level guests at nominal cost. In November 1979 President Jimmy Carter and his wife, Rosalynn, inspected the cabins and the river in the first presidential visit since the FDR picnic in 1933. The next May, the Carters and their daughter, Amy, returned for a weekend of hiking and fishing. Vice President Walter Mondale used the camp frequently, and it served as a retreat for senior government officials until VIP privileges were revoked in 1996. In 1997, Shenandoah National Park began restoring the three cabins to their Hoover-era appearance. Many of the trails, bridges, and trout pools survived, and today, in summer months, park rangers give tours.

Shortly after his 80th birthday, former President Hoover visited President Dwight D. Eisenhower in Fraser, Colorado, where they grilled and fished together.

Visitors tour the president's cabin at the Rapidan Camp in 2002.

231

Chapter 27

Franklin Delano Roosevelt: Country Squire

President Franklin D. Roosevelt's famous smile gave comfort to Americans as he guided them through the Great Depression. In this photo, taken in 1935, he waves from the wheel of his automobile in Warm Springs, Georgia, where he first went for therapeutic swimming during his recovery from polio and later built a cottage known as the Little White House.

On the morning of June 18, 1933, Franklin Delano Roosevelt trimmed the sails of the two-masted schooner *Amberjack II*, glanced at the dark blue Presidential Flag snapping in the northwest breeze, sailed out of the harbor at Marion, Massachusetts, and headed north up the Atlantic Coast. Congress had just ended one hundred days of the most astounding burst of legislative action in presidential history, laying the foundation of Roosevelt's New Deal. Soon a brigade of freshly minted federal agencies would begin tackling the economic challenges posed by the Great Depression: job creation, protection for bank deposits, supports for faltering farm income, stock market regulation, home ownership protection, and relief for financially strapped state and city governments. With that cascade of legislation now law, the president escaped to blue water and the dictates of wind and weather.

Roosevelt's 400-mile cruise aboard the white-hulled, 45-foot schooner marked the opening of a nautical odyssey unique in presidential history. Until war and the threat of enemy submarines closed the sea lanes to pleasure cruising, Roosevelt's yearning for sea breezes, salt spray, and genial shipmates carried him as far north as the Bay of Fundy, into the sapphire waters of the Caribbean, through the Panama Canal, along the Pacific Coast of Central and South America, and as far west as Hawaii. He crossed and recrossed the Equator, inspected lonely islands and bays once frequented by whalers and pirates, visited Indians indigenous to those lands, and reeled in a staggering variety of fish. Throughout the 1930s Roosevelt sailed on a friend's luxury yacht, two chartered schooners, two presidential yachts, and a flotilla of U.S. warships, using their launches as fishing boats and their code rooms as presidential communications centers.

Once war curtailed his ocean travel, the president could summon up the sea just by glancing at the ship models and maritime prints in his White House quarters, in the Roosevelt family home at Hyde Park, New York, and at his retreat in the piney woods of Warm Springs, Georgia. When he established a secret wartime hideout in the cool but landlocked mountains of western Maryland, he called each of his brief visits a "cruise" and produced a ship's logbook for guests to sign.

The 1933 cruise of *Amberjack II* set the pattern for future ocean journeys and had important personal significance for FDR. Campobello Island, just off of Maine and part of the Canadian province of New Brunswick, was the final port on the eleven-day cruise. Roosevelt had spent his childhood summers there, perfecting his mastery of small craft. He hadn't visited since the summer of 1921 when he was carried to a boat in a canvas stretcher, his legs paralyzed by polio. The dozen intervening years proved unexpectedly productive. After determined rehabilitation improved his health but failed to restore his ability to walk, Roosevelt made the buoyant waters of Warm Springs into a treatment center for other polio victims. After reestablishing himself in Democratic politics, he won two terms as governor of New York and became the first Democrat

After little more than two months in office, President Roosevelt set sail aboard the schooner *Amberjack II* from Marion, Massachusetts, to Campobello Island, New Brunswick. Sailing a small craft gave the paralyzed president mobility, control, and a sense of freedom. When the schooner entered port, Roosevelt was the confident skipper at the helm of his ship, trimming the sails and gauging the wind and tide. His affliction was, for the moment, invisible. It was a perception Roosevelt fostered throughout his presidency, both at sea and on land.

to win the presidency since Woodrow Wilson secured a second term in 1916.

Two navy destroyers, a Coast Guard cutter, and a pair of press boats shadowed Roosevelt's schooner up the New England coast on its way to Campobello Island. They hovered nearby as a squall drove *Amberjack II* into the harbor at Edgartown on the Massachusetts island of Martha's Vineyard. With no radio, Roosevelt talked with the escorting destroyers by wigwag signal flags. The seas were still heaving the next day, with waves cresting to 8 feet, as Roosevelt, his oilskins glistening with spray, brought the schooner into Nantucket Harbor for the night. He kept his mainsail furled but broke out a foresail and two jibs. "Perfect navigation was required, for in these waters shoals frequently reach the surface of the water, and the tide was bad and the channel narrow," the *New York Times* reported. Then it was on to Gloucester, Massachusetts. Old salts in the boats following the president's schooner found themselves impressed. "That's not yachting, that's Gloucester fishing sailing, by all that's holy," exclaimed Captain Irwin Hall on the press boat *Mary Alice* as the *Amberjack II* scudded along the Maine coast in a stiff breeze, shifting sail as the wind required, the schooner's lee rail awash.

Advisers arrived by seaplane, and FDR conferred with one of his ambassadors at Mount Desert Island, Maine, before again heading off on a northeasterly course. But progress stopped at Roque Island, where the schooner and its escorts found themselves wrapped in fog for three days, penned in a rocky cove. Edmund Starling, veteran chief of the president's Secret Service detail, found the president lounging on deck in dirty flannel trousers, an old gray sweater, a creased and dented floppy hat, and a three-day growth of beard. "I am having a wonderful time," Roosevelt said. "I don't care how long this fog lasts."

But on the third day Roosevelt grew weary of waiting, raised sail, and crept through the fog bank to open water and the final leg of the trip. The skies were clear and the sun bright when *Amberjack II* reached Campobello on June 29. A crowd gathered at the docks cheered the neighbor and friend who had fought against his infirmity and returned to the scenes of his boyhood with his Presidential Flag flying. "I remember I was brought here because I was teething 49 years ago, and I have been coming here for . . . many years until about 12 years ago," Roosevelt told the crowd. "Since then there has been a gap," he said, which needed no further explanation. After resting in his cottage on the island, the cruiser *Indianapolis* sped him back to Washington.

Roosevelt let the navy handle the sailing when on July 1, 1934, he boarded the USS *Houston* for the first of four trips he made aboard the heavy cruiser. In a 14,000-mile marathon, the 600-foot *Houston* headed south to the Caribbean, called at Haiti, Puerto Rico, and the Virgin Islands, stopped at Colombia on the coast of South America, and made its way through the Panama Canal and west across the Pacific to the naval base at Pearl Harbor, Hawaii. The navy had fitted out a 34-foot tender as a fishing boat and Roosevelt used it throughout the voyage. On July 13, the *Houston* anchored off Cocos Island

On June 25, 1933, after a week sailing the *Amberjack II,* President Roosevelt was joined by family and friends in Southwest Harbor, Maine. Here, aboard the schooner, Roosevelt sits between his wife, Eleanor, and their son, James. Two of Roosevelt's other sons are in the second row.

President Roosevelt took several vacation journeys aboard the USS *Houston*, a navy cruiser that was outfitted for his needs. At top, he stands on deck near Pensacola, Florida, in 1938.

in the eastern Pacific, where the president and his party landed pompano, bonito, swordfish, ono, and snapper while curious dolphins trailed the boats and frigate birds floated overhead. The waters off Cocos Island became his favorite fishing grounds, and the president returned three more times on board the *Houston*. The next year he wrote to Margaret "Daisy" Suckley, his distant cousin and close friend, that his voyage had been "perfect for this mood of pushing away all the dreary facts and actions of many months—it gives me a mental peace and a sense of proportion which is much needed."

By then the president's vacation preferences were clear. "President Roosevelt loves the sea for its own sake, and for the sake of all the things there are to do on it or in it," *New York Times* writer Mildred Adams observed. "He likes intimate contact with it—the feel of salt spray, the motion of a rolling ship, sticky oilskins and tricky winds." While at sea the president mixed cocktails for his guests, watched movies on deck, read mysteries from the ship's library, and worked on his stamp collection, carrying a stamp catalogue, magnifying glass, hinges, and other supplies in a square and battered wooden box.

The navy made sure the president stayed comfortable, mobile, and able to work whenever he traveled on a warship. Holes were punched through the deck for an elevator. Ramps were built over obstacles so he could move about in his wheelchair. An extra long bed was placed in his stateroom to accommodate his 6 foot 3 inch frame, and steel rails were installed in the bathtub to provide a grip. Whenever possible the White House mail was delivered by seaplane. Radio operators maintained contact with the White House and Roosevelt's advisers in Washington.

No matter how far he sailed, national and world events followed in the president's wake. Cruising to Hawaii in 1934, Roosevelt fretted over a threatened labor strike in San Francisco and followed events from radio reports and newspapers delivered by seaplane. On board the *Houston* in October 1935 he received a stream of coded wireless reports on the invasion of Ethiopia by the forces of Italian dictator Benito Mussolini, an early signal of the aggressiveness of Europe's fascist dictators. Late one evening in November 1936 he watched from the deck of the cruiser *Indianapolis* as the homeward-bound German airship *Graf Zeppelin* appeared off the port bow and circled the ship, causing jitters in the president's Secret Service detail. A few days later he read news bulletins reporting the abdication of Great Britain's King Edward VIII and later listened with fascination to the former king's broadcast explanation that he had acted because he could not give up "the woman I love."

Embarking on the *Houston* in July 1938, Roosevelt explored the natural treasure house of the Galapagos Islands, some 600 miles west of Ecuador in the eastern Pacific, and wrote his name into the annals of science. Among the president's guests were Dr. Waldo L. Schmidt, a naturalist at the Smithsonian Institution, who led *Houston* crew members in a search for unrecorded species. Hundreds of specimens were collected, and thirty previously unknown species were given Roosevelt's name to honor his sponsorship of the scientific fieldwork. That gesture "tickled him as much as if he had carried a hitherto Republican county in an election," the president's son, James, wrote years later. On the list were *Merriamium roosevelti*, a sponge; *Thalamita roosevelti*, a crab; *Neanthes roosevelti*, a worm; and *Rooseveltia frankliniana*, a new type of royal palm.

There were other seaborne adventures. Roosevelt inherited the presidential yacht *Sequoia* from Herbert Hoover, and used it on the Potomac River and Chesapeake Bay for private discussions and a quick change of scene. In 1936, the navy converted the 165-foot Coast Guard cutter *Electra* into the presidential yacht USS *Potomac,* with an elevator for the president's wheelchair hidden in a false stack on the main deck. The president used the *Potomac* for longer jaunts in the Gulf of Mexico, the Caribbean, and in June 1939 to escort Britain's King George VI and Queen Elizabeth to Mount Vernon. With war approaching in August 1941, FDR employed the yacht in a nautical flim-flam. Using a New England fishing expedition as cover, he slipped away to a meeting at sea with British Prime Minister Winston Churchill. Conferring off the coast of Newfoundland, the two leaders drafted the Atlantic Charter, which defined Allied goals for a postwar world.

President Roosevelt with his catch on the USS *Houston,* at Cocos Island, his favorite fishing ground, 1935. On another trip here he landed a 235-pound shark after a 90-minute struggle. Ross McIntire, his physician, witnessed the fight and called it "an exhibition of strength and endurance without parallel when it is considered that he had no legs with which to brace himself, and depended entirely on arms and shoulder muscles."

President Roosevelt with the shark he caught while fishing from a small boat near the navy cruiser USS *Houston,* in the Galapagos Islands, 1938. In a letter to his cousin, he recounted his fishing adventures aboard the Houston: "I hadn't been out in the launch for an hour before I hooked one—110 lbs. and 9 feet 6 in. long—and it took me 40 minutes to get him alongside and into the boat."

In December 1937 President Roosevelt, shown here fishing for tarpon with companion, took the USS *Potomac* down to the Florida Keys. During this cruise Assistant Attorney General Robert H. Jackson (a future Supreme Court justice) took part in a Roosevelt ritual: a small-stakes pool on the largest fish and the most fish caught by each fishing boat. Jackson's barracuda proved the biggest and the one-dollar prize was split three ways: 34 cents for the president, 33 cents each for Jackson and the president's son, James.

President Roosevelt with family on the USS *Potomac*, near Hyde Park. Just before leaving for Washington and his inauguration, Roosevelt told his Hyde Park neighbors: "I think you all will continue to see a great deal of me." And Hyde Park did continue to see a great deal of Franklin Roosevelt.

Fieldstone fences, weathered over centuries and lying stone on stone, were Hyde Park's inheritance from the Dutch and English farmers who settled the Hudson River Valley. Fieldstone was part of Franklin Roosevelt's inheritance as well. A frequent and enthusiastic builder, Roosevelt favored both the simplicity of the Hudson Valley houses built by his Dutch ancestors and the ruggedness of the stone they often used.

In 1915, Roosevelt asked for fieldstone for the new wings when he and his mother, Sara Delano Roosevelt, transformed Springwood, the family's turreted Victorian villa, into a Colonial Revival mansion. He used fieldstone in 1925 at Val-Kill, the cottage he built for his wife, Eleanor, when she wanted a place of her own, separate from her difficult mother-in-law. So, too, with the Dutch Colonial style post offices built in Hyde Park and elsewhere in Dutchess County during FDR's presidency, with his presidential library on the family estate, and with Top Cottage, his daytime retreat from the mansion known as the Big House. "I have a lot of old walls in the woods that were put in there about 150 years ago to keep the cattle in and I am just using the fieldstone out of those walls," he told reporters in 1938. He estimated Top Cottage would need "about half a mile of wall."

For someone so much at home on the ocean, Roosevelt had a strong bond with the land, its history, and the trees rooted in it. He planted trees in groves at Hyde Park and raised Christmas trees for sale. When asked to state his occupation when he voted for the last time in 1944, the president chose to call himself a "tree grower."

James Roosevelt, the president's father, bought the Hyde Park estate in 1867. While Springwood was clearly his mother's realm, the house was crammed with reminders of the president's interests from his earliest days. Hundreds of the birds he had mounted as a youthful taxidermist filled the cabinets in the entry hall. The shelves in the new wing's library held some of the thousands of books he had collected. Nearby chests held coins and medallions and political memorabilia. The high-backed leather chair he had used as governor of New York was the president's favorite place to sit while mixing cocktails at the end of the day. FDR's maritime prints and paintings competed for space with Roosevelt ancestors, including Gilbert Stuart's portrait of his great-great-grandfather Isaac Roosevelt hanging over the fireplace in the library. Upstairs, Roosevelt's

James Roosevelt, the president's father, bought Springwood (*above*), the Hyde Park estate, in 1867. He was the most recent owner in a line of Roosevelts stretching back to 1697. *Far left:* President Roosevelt and his mother, Sara Delano Roosevelt at Hyde Park, 1933. *Left:* President and Mrs. Roosevelt at Hyde Park, 1933.

commission as assistant secretary of the navy hung in the hallway near his bedroom door. A pair of small naval cannon flanked the door on the outside terrace, further reminders of his executive service in the navy.

Hyde Park was Franklin Roosevelt's vacation capital; he generally declined invitations to spend holidays elsewhere. His train rolled north along the Hudson River more than one hundred times during his presidency, more frequently as time went on. And like all chief executives since his Oyster Bay cousin, Theodore Roosevelt, he brought the presidency with him. Executive offices were established in an office suite in a seven-story building on Market Street in Poughkeepsie, 4 miles south of Hyde Park. A telephone switchboard connected the White House to the desk phone in the president's small study. Private telegraph lines linked the president to cabinet members, advisers, and staff in Washington.

On a typical Hyde Park day, early in his administration, Roosevelt woke around 8:00 a.m. and breakfasted in his room while examining five to ten newspapers, paying attention to editorials commenting on his policies. By 9:30 or 10:00 a.m. he was shaved and dressed and in his cramped study consulting with a senior White House aide—often Marvin McIntyre or Steve Early. White House aides reported on overnight telephone and telegraph messages and delivered the morning mail pouch dropped by airplane at a field near Poughkeepsie. Action was taken as needed. Bills and papers were signed. And by noon the president was ready for a quick lunch. During the afternoon

he often dictated to a stenographer or worked on speeches. He generally stopped work around 4:00 p.m. for a short drive, followed by a swim in the pool at the Val-Kill cottage and perhaps another drive. On some evenings he watched newsreels and movies shown on a screen set up on the lawn.

"No president, even in placid times, has ever found it possible to enjoy a vacation in the full sense of the word, with complete freedom from all business or professional cares," the *New York Times* observed in the summer of 1933. "Far less is it possible for Mr. Roosevelt to indulge in the luxury of idleness at a time when new and vast forces are being brought into play, when precedents in government are being set daily and when a nation of 130,000,000 persons is being shaped into a new economic mold." The president's vacation, the newspaper said, was merely a change of scene, "a brief transition from the artificially cooled office and living quarters of the White House to the green acres of Hyde Park and the cool breezes that blow down the Hudson River." But Roosevelt's holidays often served their intended purpose. "He again has become deeply tanned, the circles disappearing from under his eyes and his vitality appearing as great as when he entered office," a newspaper reported after one of Roosevelt's famous picnics in early September 1934.

Hyde Park, where Roosevelt was born on January 30, 1882, witnessed both the beginnings of his

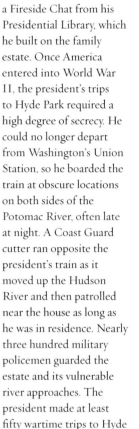

President Roosevelt almost always spent holidays at Hyde Park, and his Scotch terrier, Fala, always traveled with him. On Christmas Eve, 1943, he delivered a Fireside Chat from his Presidential Library, which he built on the family estate. Once America entered into World War II, the president's trips to Hyde Park required a high degree of secrecy. He could no longer depart from Washington's Union Station, so he boarded the train at obscure locations on both sides of the Potomac River, often late at night. A Coast Guard cutter ran opposite the president's train as it moved up the Hudson River and then patrolled near the house as long as he was in residence. Nearly three hundred military policemen guarded the estate and its vulnerable river approaches. The president made at least fifty wartime trips to Hyde Park.

political career and his life-changing struggle with polio. His neighbors sent him to the New York State Senate in 1910, and reelected him two years later. In 1920, after eight years of service at the Navy Department, Roosevelt ran for vice president, and lost in a Republican year. The next year, while vacationing at his summer home at Campobello Island, he contracted polio. Brought home to Hyde Park, he began a long, ultimately fruitless, effort to regain use of his paralyzed legs. But he rejected his mother's pleas that he retire to the comfortable life of a gentleman farmer. And in time there were more election nights with the returns tabulated on the dining room table and the neighbors carrying flaring torches up the tree-lined drive to greet the victorious "squire of Hyde Park" at his front door.

By 1937, the Big House seemed too small, the encroachments on Roosevelt's holidays too constant. "I found that on my trips to Hyde Park from Washington, it was almost impossible to have any time to myself in the big house," Roosevelt wrote in a private memo in 1942. He said he viewed his Hyde Park vacations as opportunities to read, sort his books, and make plans for roads and tree plantings. This proved impossible, he said, because of the torrent of telephone calls and visitors. He began thinking about building a cottage "to escape the mob."

The president selected a site on Dutchess Hill, one of the county's highest points and more than a mile east of Springwood. The trees framed the view, which reached west over the Hudson River to the rise of the Catskills on the distant horizon. Roosevelt often drove to the hill with his cousin Daisy Suckley. In her letters she called it "the nicest hill in Dutchess County" and, more personally, "our hill."

Top Cottage can be compared to Poplar Forest, the retreat Thomas Jefferson built at Lynchburg, Virginia, to escape the throngs seeking him at Monticello. Like Jefferson, Roosevelt was his own architect, sketching a large central block with two setback wings on whatever scraps of paper came to hand. His designs called for a deep, stone-floored porch from which to enjoy the view on pleasant days. Pocket doors paned with glass slid into the walls to reveal a large, vaulted living room centered on a fireplace framed in stone. Architect Henry Tombs, who had worked with the president on other projects, produced detailed plans from Roosevelt's designs. Tombs called the cottage "homelike, personal, unpretending, livable" and full of the elements Roosevelt enjoyed: "a bright fire, always a cluttered room of books, papers, a few ship models & odds & ends."

President Roosevelt built Top Cottage (*right*) at Hyde Park as a hideaway from Springwood. At his direction, it had no telephone, although he could always be contacted through Secret Service radios in cars parked nearby. Sitting on the porch at Top Cottage in August 1941, he was photographed by his cousin Daisy Suckley as he held Fala, the Scottish Terrier she gave him, and talked with Ruthie Bie, the granddaughter of a caretaker (*below right*). This is one of the few photographs of the president in his wheelchair. Roosevelt also built a cottage, called Val-Kill, for his wife, Eleanor, so she could have her own hideaway (*below*).

In June 1939, after a State Visit to the White House that included a cruise to Mount Vernon, Britain's King George VI and Queen Elizabeth visited Hyde Park for a weekend. The queen said she would never forget her ride with the president. "He was conversing more than watching the road and drove at great speed. There were several times when I thought we would go right off the road and tumble down the hills," she remembered. "It was a relief to get to the picnic." Sitting on the porch at Hyde Park (*below*) are, left to right, Eleanor Roosevelt, King George VI, Sara Roosevelt, Queen Elizabeth, and President Roosevelt.

Top Cottage was one of the first American buildings to be constructed barrier-free, inside and out, in keeping with a disabled owner's desire for independent living. It had no door sills or ground-level steps to obstruct Roosevelt's wheelchair. The windows were set low to allow him unimpeded views from wheelchair or sofa. An electric outlet near the president's chair allowed for a favorite activity: plugging in a toaster and buttering toast for his guests. Daisy Suckley said in her diary that the cottage gave the president many happy hours in the company of "people with whom he did not have to make an effort—who did not demand anything of him, & always loved every little joke."

The fieldstone house on Dutchess Hill was not Roosevelt's only building project as the 1930s came to a close. The Franklin D. Roosevelt Library, a repository for his presidential papers, official and unofficial gifts, and his personal collections, was under construction on the Hyde Park estate. He brought in furniture and paintings from the Big House and used it for meetings and radio broadcasts, including four Fireside Chats.

With war threatening in Europe, the Big House at Hyde Park and the little cottage on Dutchess Hill received their most celebrated guests. In June 1939, after a state visit to Washington aimed at cementing ties with the United States, Britain's King George VI and Queen Elizabeth arrived at Hyde Park for the weekend. The president prepared by gathering the ingredients for cocktails near his chair in the library. "My mother does not approve of cocktails and thinks you should have a cup of tea," he said. "My mother would have said the same thing," the king replied. "But I would prefer a cocktail." The clinking of martini glasses soon followed, and the king and the president talked through the night.

A picnic during the royal visit quickly became the talk of the country. The president, determined to serve typical American outdoor fare, offered hot dogs to the king and queen. Steak, ham, turkey, and salad also were available. But for those who chose to be outraged at the alleged insult to the national dignity, hot dogs were the scandal of the hour.

During the war years, Springwood became a guesthouse and way station for exiled European royalty. From Greece, the Netherlands, and Norway they came to enjoy Roosevelt hospitality. Winston Churchill came, too, and lived up to his reputation as a consumer of scotch whiskey. At Top Cottage, the prime minister and the president sat on the porch, possibly expanding on earlier

The name of this novel's hidden sanctuary and the name of FDR's secret retreat in the mountains of western Maryland were clearly in the president's mind at a news conference in April 1942. Responding to questions, he jested that the American warplanes that had just bombed Tokyo had flown from "our secret base in Shangri-La." The remark caught the public's imagination and inspired a drive to give the name to a new aircraft carrier. The Navy agreed. The USS *Shangri-La* was launched early in 1945 and saw action in the Pacific for the rest of the war. At right, a guard was photographed posted near the entrance to the retreat in 1945.

discussions of Anglo-American cooperation in the urgent effort to build an atomic bomb. The British called that effort Tube Alloys. The Americans would soon name it the Manhattan Project.

Invisible under a screen of oak, maple, flowering dogwood, and camouflage, the mountaintop camp satisfied both the president and Secret Service officials concerned that German submarine warfare made further use of the presidential yacht unwise, even reckless. Their search for an alternative resulted in the creation of a top-secret and secure retreat in the stubby Catoctin Mountains of western Maryland. With some basic remodeling, a former boys camp quickly became a place for a wartime commander in chief to escape for a quiet weekend just two hours from Washington.

Yielding to fancy, Roosevelt called it Shangri-La. He adopted the name from the popular 1933 James Hilton novel *Lost Horizon*. Its Shangri-La was a fictional sanctuary in the mountains of Tibet, isolated from the cares and alarms of an increasingly turbulent world. The government had less romantic names for FDR's retreat: Hi-Catoctin, Camp No. 3, and Naval Support Facility. A later president called it Camp David.

Shangri-La was about 60 miles west of the White House and a short drive up a tree-shaded road from the quiet town of Thurmont. The camp was one of three built by the Civilian Conservation Corps in the early days of the New Deal as summer camps for needy boys. During the war, one camp served the detachment of Marines assigned to guard the president's retreat. Another was a center specializing in sabotage and commando training for the Office of Strategic Services (OSS), the wartime intelligence agency and the forerunner of the CIA. The third camp was Roosevelt's hideout.

With Roosevelt giving architectural advice and offering sketches for the camp, several small cabins were joined to form a lodge that aides quickly dubbed the Bear's Den. At its center was a roomy living and dining room paneled in natural oak. A wagon-wheel chandelier hung over the dining table near a cheerful fieldstone fireplace flanked by the U.S. and Presidential Flags. A side table held a telephone with a direct line to the White House switchboard. A telescope on a tripod enabled visitors to inspect the view through a cut in the trees to the valley below. Inside the lodge there were a kitchen, two baths, and four small bedrooms, each with its own fireplace. The Secret Service installed a pressure-activated escape hatch and ramp in the outer wall of the president's bedroom to enable a quick exit in case of fire, the president's one abiding fear.

In May 1943 Winston Churchill visited Shangri-La, where he had a chance to observe Roosevelt working on his stamp collection. The prime minister recalled that he watched him "with much interest and in silence for perhaps half an hour as he stuck them in, each in its proper place, and so forgot the cares of State."

A 10-foot-high barbed-wire fence topped with a 3-foot barbed-wire overhang enclosed the compound. The Marine guard provided the outer rim of security, patrolling with attack dogs and manning sentry booths linked to a central alarm system, including floodlights that could illuminate the grounds with a single switch. The Secret Service, under Michael Reilly, head of the presidential detail, formed the security system's inner core. Bombing raids were a fear early in the war, and Reilly said the Secret Service hid parts of the camp with camouflage and prepared a slit trench to which the president could be moved in case of attack. As many as a hundred men and women staffed the camp when the president spent the weekend. Beyond the Marines, the Secret Service detail, and *Potomac*'s mess crew—given this new assignment when their ship was turned over to wartime service—there were secretaries, radio operators, cryptographers, telephone operators, the president's doctor, a navy medical corpsman, chauffeurs, the president's valet, and the projectionist who screened the movies that were shown each night.

The president felt at ease at his private Shangri-La. "There were no luxuries at all, yet I believe FDR loved that camp more than any other place he frequented, except his own home at Hyde Park," said William M. Rigdon, then a navy lieutenant and Roosevelt's stenographer and secretary on wartime trips. Roosevelt first visited on July 5, 1942, recording the event in a black and gold log book nearly 15 inches high and stamped with the Presidential Seal and the words "U.S.S. Shangri-La." Deprived by the war of access to the sea, he called that first inspection a launching and led off brief accounts of most of his twenty-two other visits, usually called "cruises," in nautical terms. Guests signing into the Shangri-La logbook included Harry Hopkins, perhaps FDR's most trusted adviser; diplomat Averell Harriman; Archibald MacLeish, the Librarian of Congress; speechwriters Robert Sherwood and Sam Rosenman; Admiral William Leahy, chief of staff to the commander in chief; FDR's cousin, Daisy Suckley; his daughter, Anna; and his secretary, Grace Tully. While Eleanor Roosevelt did not visit often, the Shangri-La log records her presence on four weekend visits.

The United States was grimly fighting a defensive war when Roosevelt first visited Shangri-La in the summer of 1942, just months after Pearl Harbor. Japanese torpedoes had sunk the USS *Houston*, the cruiser that had often served as a floating White House during the 1930s. The anxiety was quite evident on a Saturday evening after dinner in early November 1942 when the president took the phone call he had been waiting for. As he listened the tension drained from his face. "Thank God! That sounds grand. Congratulations. Casualties are comparatively light—much below your predictions. Thank God!" Then he turned to his guests: "We have landed in North Africa. We are striking back." Later, as he prepared to return to the White House, he made an entry in the Shangri-La logbook: "On this cruise . . . came the news of the American landing at Algiers . . . and near Casablanca, thus establishing a second front." When war reports came in, Roosevelt and Hopkins often read them on the porch, dictating responses and messages to Churchill, Joseph Stalin of the Soviet Union, and China's Chiang Kai-shek. In May 1943 Churchill himself visited, for the "first cruise" of the year. Writing in the logbook, Roosevelt noted that reports of the fall of the fascist regime in Italy had proven false, "much to our regret."

There were lighter moments, and Roosevelt encouraged them. "The president always knows how to dismiss care and worry when he is host, and kept us laughing with a succession of jokes and stories," Hassett confided to his diary after a visit in August 1942. Roosevelt relished the company of bright, genial, and nondemanding friends who were ready to laugh. In late afternoons he insisted on his cocktail-shaking ritual, enjoying the mellow period before dinner as much for the banter as for the drinks. After dinner there were card games. While he dealt with the war when he had to, Shangri-La was a rest area and the president used it as intended, often staying in bed until nearly noon. Shangri-La remained Roosevelt's secret until the summer of 1943 when a society gossip columnist for a Washington newspaper broke the story, annoying the reporters who covered the White House and had also known about the presidential retreat but had written nothing about it.

But by then the chances of an enemy air raid were remote, and Roosevelt visited Shangri-La a few more times. He was there in late May 1944 a week before D-Day. The log's last entry, the "Third Cruise of 1944," is for the weekend of June 25. There is no entry for the last trip, which he made in July following a visit to the White House by France's Charles de Gaulle. An intense round of international conferences and work lay ahead as the end of the war approached. The bear had made his final visit to the "Den" at Shangri-La.

———

The Little White House At Warm Springs in west central Georgia was a by-product of Franklin Roosevelt's determination that he would one day walk again despite legs withered by polio. By 1931, the year construction began on the simple frame cottage, FDR had been seeking relief and a possible cure at Warm Springs for the better part of a decade and had decided he needed permanent quarters there. He was in his second term as governor of New York when a local carpenter began work on the six-room cottage and was a presidential candidate when work on was completed. He arrived for his first overnight visit in late November 1932 as president-elect. Set on the brow of a hill and shaded by pines, the cottage met Roosevelt's requirement that it be "flush with the ground in front but in back over the ravine a porch as high as the prow of this ship." The deck would be "wonderful for sunsets," he said, while the cottage itself, "a home for all the time I'll spend here."

The combination living-dining room was paneled in pine, displaying some of FDR's ship models and nautical prints. The president worked at a card table drawn up to his armchair. When the weather was good, the table was placed on the sundeck overlooking the ravine. In colder weather it was moved inside near the fieldstone fireplace. Much like the cottage Roosevelt would build at Hyde Park, this one was designed without door sills or steps to accommodate his wheelchair. A telephone was connected to a long cord and could be plugged into any of seven jacks, allowing the president to make or receive a call wherever he might be.

Roosevelt first saw Warm Springs on October 3, 1924. Over the next twenty-one years he visited forty-one times, sometimes just for a day or two but often for several weeks. He traveled there sixteen times as president, but managed only three visits after the Japanese attack on Pearl Harbor. Still, except for 1942, he visited at least once a year.

When Roosevelt first explored Georgia's dusty roads, Warm Springs was a shabby resort community far removed from its days as a fashionable spa in the late Victorian era. Roosevelt called it "a perfectly good down-at-the-heel summer resort and nothing else." The enduring attraction was the water that gave the resort its name. It flowed from nearby Pine Mountain at a year-round temperature of 88 degrees. As Roosevelt told the story, his doctor had seen evidence that swimming helped polio patients and that those who swam in warm water appeared to benefit more than those who swam in cold. Roosevelt soon heard the story of a polio victim whose leg muscles had become strong enough after months at Warm Springs that he could walk easily in the waters of the pool and with canes outside of it. Roosevelt traveled south to see for himself.

The Little White House in Warm Springs was, like Top Cottage, built to the president's design. It was a low-lying, Greek Revival structure covered in local pine boards painted white. Long windows were flanked with dark green shutters. French doors led out to the deck, which was covered with awnings. A small portico that sheltered and framed the front door was supported by four simple white columns, entwined with red roses in season. The duties of the presidency followed Roosevelt to Warm Springs, where he worked on a table set on the porch in good weather (*below left* in 1932) or beside the fireplace when it was cold.

Roosevelt already enjoyed a national political reputation when he first tested the waters bubbling out of Pine Mountain. Not long after he arrived, an article in the *Atlanta Journal* declared he was "swimming his way back to strength and health." "He swims, dives, uses the swinging rings and horizontal bar over the water, and finally crawls out on the concrete pier for a sunbath that lasts another hour," the article said. And then it quoted Roosevelt: "I am deriving wonderful benefit from my stay here. See that right leg? It's the first time I have been able to move it at all in three years." The article was widely reprinted, and polio victims all over the country took notice. People in need of hope began arriving unannounced in Warm Springs. Soon Roosevelt used a significant share of his private fortune to buy the old resort and establish the Georgia Warm Springs Foundation to treat victims of polio and other crippling diseases.

While his treatments at Warm Springs never fulfilled Roosevelt's highest expectations, his overall physical condition greatly improved by the time he became president in 1933. Although still unable to walk unaided, his upper body and arms were strong and muscular, his health robust. By then, Warm Springs had become a central part of his life. In time, its relaxed atmosphere and distance from Washington's political tumult became as important as the treatment it offered. He looked forward to the frequent picnics and relished the active evening social life where he could sip a cocktail and talk and laugh without restraint.

At Warm Springs, President Roosevelt swam daily as pictured here in 1929. He established the Warm Springs Foundation to help children who had been paralyzed by polio, and he made it a point to befriend them and boost their spirits during events the foundation held in his honor. President and Mrs. Roosevelt talked with four of the young guests attending a foundation luncheon (*above*) in 1938.

Warm Springs quickly became a place where Roosevelt could think through his decisions. He was there in September 1928 when he let his name be placed in nomination as a candidate for governor of New York. He was in his second term as governor when the campaign opened to make him president. He traveled to Warm Springs just after the 1932 election, arriving to learn that he had carried its surrounding Meriwether County 2,900 votes to 37. Early planning for the New Deal took place at Warm Springs. As president, he often visited at Thanksgiving and continued to visit all through the buildup toward war in Europe and after the United States, too, was at war. By the spring of 1945 the war's end was in sight.

When President Roosevelt visited Warm Springs at Thanksgiving in 1938, he used the occasion to reflect in a radio address on the war clouds in Europe and Asia. "I am grateful," he said, quoting a telegram that he received from the comedian Eddie Cantor "that I can live in a country where our leaders can sit down on Thanksgiving Day to carve up a turkey instead of a Nation."

For Franklin Roosevelt, Warm Springs with its buoyant waters and bright Georgia sunshine was a place for recovery, optimism, and hope. Such was the expectation when he arrived in Warm Springs on the afternoon of March 30, as exhausted as he had ever been. He had recently returned from a grueling conference with Churchill and Stalin at Yalta in the Crimea. He delivered his report to Congress on the results of that conference while sitting in a chair. For the first time in public, he spoke of the weight of the iron braces necessary for him to stand. Staff members and friends noted how worn, thin, and ashen gray he looked, how deep and dark were the circles under his eyes. Agent Reilly was startled to find Roosevelt "absolutely dead weight" when he and other agents struggled to lift the president into his blue Ford at the Warm Springs depot. People in the crowd were surprised when their usually genial neighbor neither smiled nor waved. But, as usual, the car with its "FDR 1" tag drove into the foundation grounds and passed Georgia Hall, where patients in wheelchairs were gathered to greet him.

Within days the magic of Warm Springs seemed to be doing its usual good work. Cheering news from the battlefronts in Europe may have helped. Allied forces were closing in on Berlin, and Germany's Nazi regime appeared to be in its last days. In the Pacific, the net was tightening on the Japanese homeland. Some thought the president's color grew better. His energy and appetite improved. He became more animated, and his familiar laugh was heard again. He began to look to the work ahead and the planning for a world at peace. He confirmed plans to speak at the opening session of the United Nations in San Francisco on April 25 and approved the design of a commemorative postage stamp to be issued there. He began planning a State Visit to Britain, confident the war in Europe would be over when he arrived. He met with the president of the Philippines and again pledged the U.S. territory would soon be granted independence. He accepted an invitation from local citizens to attend a barbecue on Thursday, April 12. Ruth Stevens, the manager of the Warm Springs Hotel, promised to serve Brunswick stew and other favorite southern dishes.

On April 10, driving his blue Ford on the dusty Warm Springs roads, the president hailed Merriman Smith, White House correspondent for United Press, who was riding a rented horse, with a hearty "Heigh-O, Silver." "His voice was wonderful and resonant," Smith recalled. "It sounded like the Roosevelt of old." On April 11 Roosevelt approved a final draft of an optimistic and forward-looking Jefferson Day radio speech. The last typed sentence read: "The only limit to

Whenever President Roosevelt arrived at Warm Springs, a crowd was there to greet him. The president would wave, flash his smile, and, remembered one of the local residents, shout "Hi-Ya, Neighbor!" In 1938, the people of Warm Springs even prepared a banner of welcome.

our realization of tomorrow will be our doubts of today." Roosevelt added nine words in his own hand: "Let us move forward with strong and active faith." But Hassett was worried. On the day after the president arrived in Warm Springs he confided to his diary, and to Dr. Howard Bruenn, Roosevelt's cardiologist, that he thought the president was "slipping away."

The sun was warm. Dogwood and honeysuckle were in bloom. The fruit was forming on the peach trees. And the president was surrounded by admiring women. He had been joined at Warm Springs by Lucy Mercer Rutherfurd, an old and trusted friend. Their affair decades earlier had strained his marriage to the breaking point. Eleanor Roosevelt did not know they were again in contact. His other guests were: cousins Daisy Suckley and Laura Delano, known as Polly. A fourth guest was Madame Elizabeth Shoumatoff, an artist who had been commissioned by Mrs. Rutherfurd to paint Roosevelt's portrait.

At the cottage, Roosevelt worked on his stamps, read mystery novels, and chatted with the women. At breakfast he read and commented on the war reports carried in with the morning newspapers. "He has the whole western front in Europe in his head, knows exactly where each army is at any one moment," Daisy wrote in her diary. After a leisurely lunch on April 10 the president drove with Lucy in his blue Ford to Dowdell's Knob, a favorite picnic site with a view over Pine Mountain Valley. They sat in the sun and talked for an hour as a detachment of troops maintained security and Fala scurried about. "The best thing he could do," Daisy commented. Later that day, preliminary sketching for the portrait began with the president wearing a double-breasted gray suit, a vest, a Harvard-red tie and his dark blue navy cape. "Very smiling and handsome," Daisy thought. Fala lay on the floor, often with his head on the president's foot.

That night, the president read himself to sleep, marking his place at page 78 in John Dickson Carr's mystery, *The Punch and Judy Murders.* In the morning, while waiting for his daily medical check by Dr. Bruenn, he interrupted a conversation the maid, Lizzie McDuffie, was having in the kitchen.

President Roosevelt held a press conference at the wheel of his car in Warm Springs, March 1937.

Learning that the subject was reincarnation, Roosevelt asked her if she believed in it. She wasn't sure, she said. "But if there is such a thing, I want to be a canary bird." The president stared. "A canary bird!" he roared. "Don't you love it? Don't you just love it?"

By mid-morning Madame Shoumatoff was ready with her easel and watercolors, standing before the president, who was seated in his leather chair, the light on his face. She was struck by Roosevelt's "exceptionally good color." "That gray look had disappeared." Daisy, too, thought her cousin's "colour was good." "He looked smiling & happy & ready for anything," she wrote in her diary. "He looked so good looking." But Hassett, who came in around noon with a stack of papers that needed FDR's signature, thought the president looked ill and should have been spared the ordeal of sitting for a portrait.

On Pine Mountain, preparations were well under way for the late afternoon barbecue at the cabin of Frank Allcorn, the owner of the Warm Springs Hotel and the town's mayor. The president was expected at 4:30 p.m. and planned to stay for about an hour before going on to watch dress rehearsals for a minstrel show at the polio foundation. Ruth Stevens had been in motion for days, preparing two 150-pound hogs and a 100-pound lamb for the barbecue and gathering the dozen chickens needed for the Brunswick stew that would simmer in a large iron pot. She arrived at the

FDR was an avid stamp collector. After his death commemorative postage stamps included a green one-cent stamp picturing Hyde Park and a red two-cent stamp featuring the Little White House at Warm Springs.

President Roosevelt worked at a table in the living area of his house at Warm Springs.

Allcorn cabin at 5:00 a.m. to get the fire started in the deep barbecue pit. Most of the forty-five guests would be seated on benches on either side of a long table decorated with a crock full of white azaleas and sprays of green huckleberries. A wooden armchair was waiting for the president in the shade of an oak tree. A local fiddler was ready to play "Comin' Round the Mountain" when he arrived.

Inside the Little White House lunch was over. The president leafed through a stack of signed letters, reading some intently. Madame Shoumatoff resumed work. Although she asked the others not to look at the unfinished sketch, Daisy discovered she could steal glances in an oval mirror hanging near the president's bedroom door. She went back to her crocheting, then looked up. The president appeared to be fumbling, as if he had dropped something. "He looked at me with his forehead furrowed in pain and tried to smile. He put his left hand up to the back of his head & said: 'I have a terrific pain in the back of my head'." Then he collapsed in the chair.

Nearly four hours went by. A few local guests had gathered at the Allcorn cabin. The pungent smell of cooking drifted through the trees. But none of the White House staff had arrived. There was no sign the president's car was moving. Smith, of United Press, reached Louise Hackmeister, chief White House operator at Warm Springs: "Why aren't you people on the way?" She said she didn't know, but Hassett wanted all three press association reporters in his cottage immediately. Smith said the speedometer hit 90 miles an hour once their car reached the paved road leading to the foundation grounds. Hassett at Warm Springs and press secretary Stephen Early in Washington were ready with simultaneous announcements. As a young Associated Press reporter, Early had broken the news of President Warren Harding's death. Now he and Hassett had an official announcement to make: "It is my sad duty to inform you that the President died at 3:35 this afternoon."

President Roosevelt sat for Elizabeth Shoumatoff (1888–1980) twice, in 1943 in the Oval Office and again in 1945 at Warm Springs, at the time of his death. The watercolor she made during development of the final portrait is shown here. Today it is displayed in the Little White House, which is managed as a historic site by the state of Georgia and open to the public.

Chapter 28

Harry S. Truman: Truman Beach at Key West

HARRY S. TRUMAN
33rd President of the
United States, 1945–1953

The shirts were loose, comfortable, and bright as a Florida sunset. They represented a break from the blue-suit, white-shirt formality that was Harry Truman's sartorial hallmark. They proclaimed temporary independence from the regimen of the White House appointments and social calendar, from the mansion Truman called "The Big White Jail." Some people called them loud, garish, and unpresidential. Others called them Harry Truman shirts. When photographs of Truman wearing them hit the newspapers, people showered the Winter White House at Key West, Florida, with gift shirts. Since there were far more shirts than the president could wear, he had dozens laid out on the lawn for anyone on the staff who wanted one. The "Key West uniform" spoke to the breezy informality of all of Harry Truman's Florida vacations.

Truman visited Key West eleven times from November 1946 to March 1952, vacationing there in good times and bad for a total of 175 days. He timed his escapes for fall or late winter, trading Washington's damp cold for warm breezes, emerald water, and what the newspapers called the rustling palms.

At the end of the island chain stretching southwest into the Gulf of Mexico from the Florida peninsula, the coral island of Key West, 4 miles long and a mile wide, is the southernmost point in the United States. Coconut palms, purple and red bougainvillea, frangipani, red and pink hibiscus, and elegantly tinted oleanders thrive in the frost-free tropical climate. Truman found the waters of Key West perfect for swimming. Farther out, the cobalt-blue reaches of the Atlantic offered deep-sea fishing for yellowfin, grouper, amberjack, mackerel, and barracuda.

Key West's naval base gave Truman a degree of privacy, security, and freedom unavailable in most vacation spots. The president could swim on his own at "Truman Beach"—which the navy enhanced with tons of sand—nap in the afternoon, sip bourbon if he felt like it, and play poker until midnight. "Down there the President felt that he could step out of the house and walk

Informality reigned at Key West, and President Truman received so many of his tradmark "tropical" shirts as gifts (*right*) that in 1951 he laid them out on the lawn of the Little White House in Key West so his staff and reporters could help themselves.

Swimming was a daily part of President Harry S. Truman's routine in Key West (*opposite*). Shown here in 1946, he always swam with his glasses on.

around the base without every person he encountered wanting to stop him and talk to him," said Commander William M. Rigdon, who managed the president's vacation workday. "From the first day he saw the advantages it offered."

Truman quickly settled into a routine and maintained it on each of his Key West vacations. He rose as early as 7:00 a.m. and took a bracing morning walk, ranging the

The Little White House was a ten-room, West Indian-style structure built by the navy in 1890 to house the commandant of the Key West naval base. The screened and louvered porches filtered the midday sun, welcomed the ocean breezes, and assured privacy. The president slept in the northeast bedroom on the second floor.

LITTLE WHITE HOUSE, KEY WEST, FLA.—K47

tree-shaded streets of the naval base and sometimes venturing into town. The presidential yacht *Williamsburg* was docked nearby and its mess crew had breakfast ready when he returned, usually around 8:00 a.m. The president was often joined at the breakfast table by members of his senior staff, who might include Fleet Admiral William Leahy, his military chief of staff; William D. Hassett, his correspondence secretary; or Clark Clifford, his chief counsel. After breakfast the president worked on his mail until about 10:00 a.m., then gathered a troop of aides and walked to Truman Beach to soak up the sun, tell stories, discuss the news or government business, and watch games of beach volleyball or darts. When he was ready he took off his sun helmet and went in for a swim. "If the weather was cool, he swam anyway, to the shivering horror of Secret Service men who had to stay in the water as long as he did," said Rigdon, who, along with his other duties, kept a detailed log of the president's vacation activities, not neglecting humorous incidents and adding an occasional wry comment.

Returning to the Little White House for a 1:00 p.m. lunch, Truman generally allowed himself the luxury of an afternoon nap, followed by a two-hour poker game at 4:00 p.m. and dinner at 7:00 p.m. Unless First Lady Bess Truman and their daughter, Margaret, were with him, the president most often skipped the nightly screenings of first-run movies and adjourned to the south porch for a second poker session that wound up near midnight. When Rigdon noted in his vacation log that the president had spent the evening visiting with friends on the south porch, insiders knew that meant poker.

Although he valued the opportunities for rest and relaxation, Truman could not shed his responsibilities. "Wherever I happened to be, that's where the office of the President was," he observed. While at Key West he dealt with a coal miners' strike, the Cold War, the communist takeover of China, and the shooting war in Korea. Events followed the president, even under the palms. "I do not know of any easy way to be President," Truman said in his memoir; "It is more than a full-time job." He insisted that Key West and the yacht *Williamsburg* were less vacation spots than convenient hideaways, "very useful when I wanted to catch up on my work and needed an opportunity to consult with my staff without interruptions."

As in Washington, President Truman began each day in Key West with a "constitutional," a brisk, 1–2 mile walk for which he always carried a walking stick, as shown here in 1951. After breakfast he read and answered mail (*middle row, left*), before walking to Truman Beach, where he swam and aides played volleyball (*bottom*). Relaxation intermingled with responsibilities, such as the occasional press conference (*middle row, right*).

257

Truman's search for a private retreat began in 1946 as his presidency moved into its second year. He had never warmed to Shangri-La, the heavily wooded retreat FDR had enjoyed in the mountains of western Maryland. He found the presidential yacht *Williamsburg* had disadvantages for anything longer than weekend trips in sheltered waters. But he did feel the need for brief escapes in a peaceful setting.

In November 1946, a Republican explosion in the midterm election reversed Democratic majorities in the Senate and House. The Truman administration reached so low a point some said it would never recover. *Time* said the president held an office that had "proved too much for him." Truman ended the dispiriting campaign with a persistent cold that turned into a hacking cough. His doctor ordered a vacation in a warm climate. A search began for a place that could accommodate not only the president but fifteen staff members, fifteen or so Secret Service agents, and up to thirty White House reporters and photographers. Truman never regretted the final choice: the navy's submarine base at Key West.

The president's aircraft flew out of Washington on a cold, rainy November day and headed for a week in the Florida sunshine. Upon landing, Truman quickly called his wife, Bess, to report his safe arrival. Rising the next morning, he scanned the newspapers, listened to radio newscasts, and dipped into a book before going for a swim. "My cough and cold are nearly gone already," Truman wrote to his mother and sister. Then he added one more thought: "I am seeing no outsiders. From now on I'm going to do as I please and let 'em all go to hell. At least for two years they can do nothing to me and after that it doesn't matter." He had cards printed to get the point across: "Don't Go Away Mad . . . Just Go Away."

For months the navy had been experimenting with a war trophy, the U-2513, a fast German submarine seized by the British in 1945. On a morning shortly after his arrival, the crew raised the

President Truman enjoyed flying and was the first president to travel regularly by plane. He named the presidential aircraft *The Independence*, after his hometown, and had its nose painted to resemble a stylized eagle. *The Independence* was a four-engine DC-6 with a cruising speed of 358 miles per hour and a presidential stateroom in the rear.

presidential flag, piped Truman aboard, headed out to sea, and rigged for diving. The prospect of a dive put Truman's Secret Service agents on edge. "There were quite a few people who had beads of perspiration as big as marbles on their foreheads," Rigdon said. The U-boat disappeared beneath the waves at 9:30 a.m., stopping its descent at 450 feet below the surface. Truman had just become the first president to dive in a submarine since Theodore Roosevelt submerged in the USS *Plunger* forty-one years earlier. The sub resurfaced after forty-four minutes. Later that afternoon, the president boarded the navy crash boat *Dolphin* for three hours of deep-sea fishing. At day's end photographers recorded his catch: a Spanish mackerel, a 5-pound barracuda, and a grouper.

The next morning Truman combined blue water and history. Boarding the destroyer *Stribling*, he headed out at 28 knots to Fort Jefferson, the moated and six-sided, brick-and-stone fortress that dominates the Dry Tortugas, specks of land surrounded by diving sea birds. That afternoon the party set off in two small boats for more fishing. Bets were placed on which boat could haul in the most impressive catch. Truman did his share for his boat, hooking a 6-pound grouper and three yellowtail.

The sun, palm trees, Truman Beach, and the easy atmosphere made the vacation memorable and ensured the president's return. "The sun shines with terrific force down here," he happily reported in a letter to Bess. "My face and head are as red as a beet, but the rest of me is brown except for a strip around the middle which is white."

On his first morning in Key West, November 18, 1946, President Truman slipped a purple robe over his pajamas and walked two blocks in bedroom slippers to the officers' swimming pool, no doubt startling those used to presidents in more formal attire.

From the very first trip, the government made sure Key West met the president's needs, starting with direct, rapid communication with the White House. Workers linked teletype equipment

President Truman tried out a pair of German-made binoculars aboard the captured German submarine U-2513, November 21, 1946. He and his staff were given a full tour of the submarine, including a 450-foot dive below the surface.

President Truman displayed his first day's catch, Key West, November 19, 1946. Never an eager fisherman, he claimed he lacked the necessary patience, but he felt obliged to not disappoint Florida boosters who expected him to try his luck.

On a visit to Fort Jefferson in the Dry Tortugas, November 22, 1946, President Truman made a point of inspecting the prison cell of Dr. Samuel Mudd, the Maryland physician who set the broken leg of Abraham Lincoln's assassin, John Wilkes Booth. An avid student of history, the president enjoyed discussions of famous battles with his aides, and once he and press secretary Charlie Ross reenacted fourteen military campaigns with four sets of silverware spread out on a table.

to Washington through a landline, adding a radio backup in case the landlines failed. Rigdon, an expert stenographer who had begun his navy career as a ship's clerk, managed the office routine and kept the official logs for each trip. "To keep things running at Key West required that I be on the job before the president came down in the morning, and to remain on call until he retired at midnight," he said. "Just before he retired he would brief me on any plans he had for the next day. These eighteen-hour days at times were tedious, but never disagreeable."

Assistant press secretary Roger Tubby described a day at the Little White House as starting with mail deliveries, informal staff discussions, phone calls to Washington and the 10:00 a.m. walk to Truman Beach. "The President suns in a deck chair for a while, talking business or pleasure," Tubby wrote. "There are jokes and laughter, comparing of sea shell collections, stories of Missouri . . . . observations by the press, the state of the Nation, health, educational problems—almost anything and everything. After a while, several phone calls and telegrams, come into the beach house and telegrams go out. [Then] Mr. T takes his dip for about ten minutes, swimming neither far nor fast, but pleasant splashing." Truman, who swam with his glasses in place, called his head-out-of-water style "the Missouri sidestroke."

Key West's attractions quickly gained favor not only with Truman but his staff. Rigdon said that on Truman's first visit in 1946, his needs were met by sixteen cooks, stewards, secretaries, clerks, and communications personnel. On his eleventh and final visit in 1952, the support staff had increased to fifty-seven people, and more space had to be found to house them. Rigdon's logs also expanded, growing from a slim seventeen pages for the 1946 vacation to profusely illustrated productions of more than one hundred pages each.

Truman returned to Key West in the late winter of 1947, his arrival delayed a week by a congressional speech in which he drew the line against further Soviet expansion in Europe, a "containment" doctrine that became the bedrock of U.S. foreign policy. He felt drained. "No one, not even me . . . knew how very tired and worn to a frazzle the Chief Executive had become,"

Truman wrote to his daughter after he settled in. "This terrible decision I had to make had been over my head for about six weeks."

More fishing followed, this time off American Shoal, about 25 miles from Key West. But for the president the clear highlight of the vacation came after Sunday dinner on March 16, when the staff joined him to listen to Margaret Truman's professional debut as a coloratura soprano in a radio concert broadcast from Detroit. "The reception was perfect and the program was intently followed and thoroughly enjoyed by all hands," Rigdon reported. Others were less charitable. *Time* said the president's daughter had "a good, choir-average soprano voice," but added that 15 million Americans had joined her proud father in listening as she sang.

Following a Key West visit in December 1947, Truman returned the next February amid speculation about whether he would run for election in his own right in 1948. Most pundits told him not to bother. *Time* said the Democrats "seemed to be heading toward the ditch," with voters apparently ready "to dump the whole Truman administration." But *Time's* reporter was surprised to find no evidence of concern on Truman Beach. The president was tanned, carefree, smiling, he reported.

At a shirt-sleeves news conference on the lawn of the Little White House, Truman maintained he was not wasting time while on vacation:

> I have been in touch with the State Department every day since we have been away. . . . I have talked personally to nearly every member of the Cabinet since I have been away. The only thing that is different from the White House is just the change of scenery. We have direct wires that go there [the White House], and I get a pouch nearly every day, and sign just as many documents and make just as many decisions as if I were sitting at the desk in the Executive Office.

On March 15, 1947, following a day of competitive fishing in what was grandly named the Key West International Fishing Tournament, Truman and Admiral William Leahy weighed and measured the catch. Leahy won the honors, for a 20-pound amberjack. Clark Clifford's boat won for the most fish caught, and the president landed a 4½-pound mackerel.

Following Truman's surprise success in the presidential election of 1948, First Lady Bess Truman and their daughter, Margaret, joined the president on Key West for a celebratory holiday. The date of this photo is November 24, 1948.

Perhaps he was a bit more candid in a letter to Bess: "The weather here is ideal. It is hell to have to go back to slavery and the bickerings that I'll have to face from now on, but it must be done."

―――――――

Until the votes were counted almost no one, except Harry Truman, believed Harry Truman had won. "The little old voter fooled everybody," *Time* reported after the election of 1948 was wrapped up for the history books. Truman produced his astonishing upset in a 31,700-mile trek by train across the country, speaking wherever crowds gathered. He made 356 speeches, 16 in one day. The crowds grew. So did the enthusiasm for the dogged campaigner. When at one speech a voice from the rafters called out, "Give 'em hell, Harry," Harry obliged. Assured by the polls that he could coast to the White House, Republican Thomas E. Dewey ran a lofty and colorless campaign. And there were few who took seriously Truman's last words as Americans voted: "Why, it can't be anything but a victory." Soon after the voters ratified that claim the president boarded the *Independence* and flew to Florida for a rest.

"Key West never before had such a celebration," said the *Miami Herald*. The *New York Times* ran the headline "Key West Greets Truman as a Hero" and said Key West's welcome fit the president's role as "election day miracle man and this town's No. 1 vacationer." The president grinned when the mayor of Key West announced that Division Avenue would be renamed Truman Avenue. At the submarine base hundreds of sailors lined the route to the Little White House. Truman was glad to step inside. "I didn't know I was so tired until I sat down," he told his sister.

Clark Clifford remembered that Key West vacation as a succession of happy days. "He had pulled off the greatest political coup, I believe, in American history, and had done it practically single handedly. . . . He was relaxed and happy and we were greatly amused by people getting back on the wagon. . . . That caused great merriment." The campaigners may have been happy, but they

The people of Key West gave President Truman a hero's welcome when he arrived after winning the election of 1948. Perched on the folded top of his Lincoln convertible, he happily waved at the crowds—estimated at 25,000—as loudspeakers pumped out "The Missouri Waltz."

were also exhausted. "I doubt I've ever been as tired in my life," Clifford said. "I remember, I went . . . without shaving just as part of the general celebration. . . . And we loafed; we didn't discuss any business. I don't know how the government ran during that time; we all were utterly exhausted! I remember going down for awhile, sleeping about fourteen hours a day and then lolling around on the beach." He also remembered that vacation as "one of the few times when government service was just plain fun." Key West, he said, "seemed as far as one could get from Washington and still stay in the U.S., and after those endless days and nights on the [campaign] train, we loved it."

Rigdon remembered that for the first several days Truman seemed unable to shed the tensions of the long campaign. "I had never seen the president so taut," so "unable to be still," he wrote. "He couldn't work, he couldn't rest. He would start signing mail, suddenly push it aside, explaining to me, 'It can wait, Bill'." Truman also didn't touch a razor for days. "The only time I ever knew him to miss a daily shave," Rigdon said. The stubble did not go unnoticed. When a reporter asked if he was growing a Vandyke, Truman responded, "No . . . it's a Jeff Davis," and he stroked his chin as he invoked the memory of the bearded Confederate president. Bantering with newsmen, Truman asked if they were comfortable in their quarters, saying of his staff that he would "give them the devil" if anything was wrong. "Give 'em hell," suggested the colonel in charge of the press plane. "I'm through giving them hell," Truman replied, with perhaps too much optimism. "From now on we'll work together." A *New York Times* reporter in Key West said Truman was "like a man who has just put down a heavy pack and straightened up." *Time* detected "an air of firmness, a new confidence in his bearing" and an apparent determination "to run his own show in his own way."

Five days into his vacation Truman finally had cause to reach for his razor. Bess and Margaret were joining him, sharing a Key West vacation for the first time. The president's restless mood changed when they arrived. He was "once again his old self," Rigdon said and added a final note: "It was observed that Mr. Clifford's five-day growth of beard had [also] disappeared." Ken Hechler, then a young presidential aide and later a Democratic congressman from West Virginia, called the growing and shaving of beards "the most important developments during the entire two weeks of almost total inactivity and complete relaxation."

———

But in fact, Truman was looking ahead at Key West to the crucial policy decisions he faced on his return to Washington. White House staff member George Elsey recalled that Truman decided at Key West to devote his Inaugural Address to foreign policy and his separate State of the Union Address to his domestic agenda. That structural decision led to the use of the Inaugural Address to launch the Point Four plan for scientific and technical assistance to the poorest nations on earth, an undertaking that became a key element of the administration's Cold War strategy. The State of the Union Address contained Truman's "Fair Deal" initiative, which encapsulated the president's economic ideas on the domestic front. "So there was thinking going on, if not many hours of laborious paperwork," Elsey said. "He didn't just go into a vacuum and stop thinking just because he had won the election."

The two most important women in Harry Truman's life also were ready for a vacation. "We needed a rest almost as much as he did," Margaret Truman recalled. Shortly after she and her mother arrived, reporters and other members of the Key West gang mounted a mock victory parade wearing what Miss Truman called "the wackiest costumes you have ever seen in your life." Charlie Ross, the gaunt press secretary and a Truman friend since high school, topped his swimming suit with an Abe Lincoln stovepipe hat. "The whole thing was a surprise, and someone snapped a picture of me and Mother laughing like a couple of lunatics," Margaret Truman said.

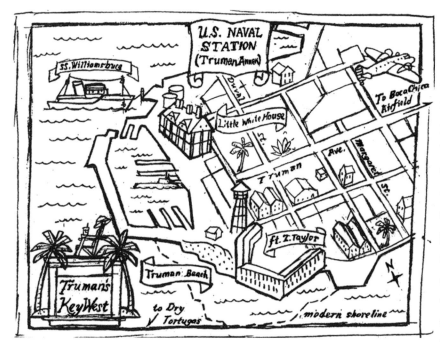

"It *was* funny, and wholly in the spirit of that triumphant vacation."

Congratulations poured in, four and five mail sacks at a time. Truman signed thousands of responses. There were letters from politicians privately astonished that Truman had won and thousands more from farmers and union members and wage earners who said they were glad he had. Some well-wishers showed up in person. Slogging across America, Truman had invited dozens of people to visit Key West. Two sleeping car porters, a railroad policeman, a railroad maintenance engineer, and two White House messengers were among those who accepted. High-ranking visitors also arrived: chairman of the Democratic National Committee, a governor, an ambassador,

Map of Key West, highlighting the sites associated with Truman. Locations are approximate.

and Defense Secretary James Forrestal. Vice President–elect Alben Barkley and House Speaker Sam Rayburn delighted Truman by quickly adopting the Key West uniform.

Truman had won the election. But it would be three years before he would again live in the White House. Nearly a century and a half old, the Executive Mansion was worn by time and weakened by hard use. "In the summer of 1948 the old house just started to fall apart," Margaret Truman said. An engineering study determined that the White House was "little better than a fire trap, so weakened by age and by stresses set up as a result of haphazard patching and alteration that it could not be made safe without major repairs," *Time* reported. "By the time we came back from Key West, the experts . . . decided that there was nothing that could be saved but the outside walls," Margaret Truman recalled. Until reconstruction was complete the Trumans would live at Blair House, just across Pennsylvania Avenue.

The Little White House at Key West had been completely redecorated and refurnished when Truman returned in March 1949. Maritime paintings and prints borrowed from the Naval Academy hung on walls freshly painted gray, green, and blue. The navy renovated the beach house at Truman Beach, installed a shuffleboard, and planted palm trees and oleander bushes to reinforce the tropical air. "Wish you and Margie were here," a wistful Truman wrote to Bess. "They have fixed you up a palatial bedroom next to mine. You've never seen a nicer one. The place is all redecorated. . . . I've a notion to move the capital to Key West and just stay."

Harry Truman stamped his Key West vacations with his personality. Except for rare, short visits by Bess and Margaret, it was a masculine world. He liked the easy banter at the beach, in a fishing boat, or at the poker table, which was the true center of a Truman vacation. Poker, he told friends, is "my favorite form of paper work." Coming downstairs after his afternoon nap, Truman often told Rigdon, "Bill, round up a quorum." Soon the president and seven other men were pulling up chairs around the poker table made for him by sailors at the submarine base. The game adjourned for dinner, then continued until near midnight as Truman sipped bourbon.

Many thought the president loved the game mostly for the ribbing and joshing that punctuated play. "Getting together with his old friends with whom he was completely comfortable was *the* greatest relaxation he had," Clark Clifford remembered. Truman bet freely and often, liked wild cards, oddball variations, and an occasional bluff. Fellow players said he enjoyed himself even while holding losing hands.

Ken Hechler concluded Truman sometimes used poker for more than just relaxation. "Although the conversation was never very heavy, I did observe several occasions when the President sized up prospective appointees and other people by measuring how well they stood up to ribbing," he said. George Elsey said the stakes were set so that "nobody would get hurt if his luck or his skill were particularly bad."

On June 25, 1950, with the president at home in Independence, Missouri, war exploded across the 38th parallel dividing the Korean Peninsula. Truman committed American forces to prevent a Communist takeover of South Korea. The war cast a shadow over the rest of Truman's years in office, including his vacations. After his eighth Florida holiday in early 1950, Truman did not return to Key West for more than a year. He resisted when his doctors again insisted he take a vacation. "He would get a lot of sniping from his critics if he relaxed while U.S. soldiers were fighting in Korea," *Time* observed. But Truman's resistance crumbled as he grew more tired and tense. Finally, and without using the word "vacation," the White House announced the president would temporarily "transfer his base of operations" to Key West. The presidential aircraft would stand by to hustle him back to Washington in case of emergency.

President Truman and members of his staff played poker during a Fourth of July cruise aboard the USS *Williamsburg* in 1949. Clockwise from Truman (standing): Clark Clifford, Stuart Symington, Oscar Ewing, Tom Clark, Clinton Anderson, George Allen, and Mon Wallgren.

The weather was sullen and uncooperative when Truman arrived on March 2, 1951. "Angry grey-green rollers thundered up against Truman Beach, thick black clouds scudded across the sky, and a misty rain dripped down the shutters of the Little White House," *Time* reported. When the sun finally appeared, Truman celebrated with a new blue shirt with white border, green slacks, and white buckskin shoes. He wore the snappy outfit at an outdoor news conference where reporters asked him to assess his place in history. Truman said he wanted to be remembered as having made a sincere effort to establish world peace and to prevent World War III. "All a President of the United States can do is to endeavor to make the Government—the executive branch—run in the public interest," he said. "I have striven very hard to accomplish that purpose." But fixing his place in history would have to wait: "No President can be evaluated during his term, or within 25 or 30 years after that term. . . . It takes an objective survey of what has happened and what was trying to be accomplished to decide whether a President has been a success or not. And you can't decide that now or here, and neither can I."

By vacation time in November 1951, questions were mounting about whether Truman would seek reelection in 1952. He had been president since FDR's death in April 1945. Although a new constitutional amendment limited future chief executives to two four-year terms, it exempted the sitting president. Truman had proven in 1948 that he could defy heavy odds to win the office on his own. The odds were again long. The war in Korea was costly and increasingly unpopular and showed little sign of ending soon. At an informal news conference on the lawn of the Little White House, Truman said he had "no intention" of announcing his plans.

During his Key West visits, President Truman occasionally boarded the USS *Williamsburg* for tours around the Caribbean. It is at anchor here in 1946 in Bermuda, with the president aboard. When at Key West, the *Williamsburg* served as a galley and floating communications center in addition to offering cabin space for extra guests.

That didn't mean he hadn't been thinking about the future, at least in private. On November 19 he gathered members of the senior White House staff in the Little White House, pledged them to secrecy, and read from a private memo written nearly a year earlier. The first line answered the question: "I am not a candidate for nomination by the Democratic Convention." The memo affirmed the two-term tradition established by George Washington, even though that tradition had twice been broken by Franklin Roosevelt: "In my opinion eight years as President is enough and sometimes too much for any man to serve in that capacity. There is a lure in power. It can get into a man's blood just as gambling and lust for money have been known to do." Truman told his staff he was giving them notice so they could chart their own futures, but he wasn't ready to make the news public.

This was Truman's tenth visit to Key West's sand and sun. The publicity given his Key West vacations, and the obvious pleasure he took in the tropical surroundings, had created a tourist boom, transforming a shabby town filled with cheap bars catering mostly to sailors. Air-conditioned motels were rising along the beaches outside the naval base. "New stores are opening, restaurants are crowded, the sidewalks are flowing with women in shorts and halters and men in atom-flash sports shirts," *Time* reported.

Truman's secret held when he arrived for his eleventh Florida vacation on March 7, 1952. "All you fellows have been trying to set a date for me," the president told reporters. "And I will set my own date." Privately, he and his staff drafted a speech setting out his plans. Then he had time to relax. "He managed to keep his work to a minimum and cut the number of visitors to a new low," said *Time*. "The temperature was amiable, the water warm, and the poker brisk and profitable."

On March 27, after Truman flew from Florida, his limousine drove directly to the White House and stopped under the North Portico. After more than three years of demolition and reconstruction, the old house stood strong and was ready for the president. A couple nights later, the Key West speech lay on the president's podium at the annual Jefferson-Jackson Day Dinner. The telling line, handwritten on a separate sheet of paper, came near the end: "I shall not be a candidate for re-election. . . .I do not feel that it is my duty to spend another four years in the White House."

As he left the podium and strode off to begin his final year in office, Truman fully expected to vacation at the Little White House in the fall or winter. Events kept him in Washington until his term ended. Although he would often return to the Florida Keys as a private citizen, Harry Truman had completed his last presidential vacation at Key West.

––––––––––

Truman Beach no longer exists, at least as Harry Truman knew it. Deprived of its shoreline in a 1960s harbor dredging and landfill project, it is now essentially a landlocked field. The U.S. Naval Station at Key West closed in 1974, and its office buildings, workshops, and officers' quarters became the core of an upscale condominium development. Truman's Little White House, however, still evokes the memory of the 33rd president. Now owned by the state of Florida and privately managed, it opened in 1990 as the Harry S. Truman Little White House Museum. The desk Truman used is in his old study. The piano on which he played Chopin and Mozart is in the living room. Margaret Truman's voice can be summoned with a flick of the switch from a living room radio, just as her proud father heard her in 1947. Truman's poker table, with ashtrays made from the cutoff ends of 50-millimeter artillery shells, stands ready for a game on the south porch.

On March 26, 1952, the last day of what turned out to be his last Key West vacation, President Truman posed with his staff on the lawn of the Little White House. Today the Little White House is owned by the state of Florida and is open to the public as a historic site and museum.

Chapter 29

Dwight D. Eisenhower: Playing the Course

DWIGHT D. EISENHOWER
34th President of the
United States, 1953–1961

Opposite: President Dwight
D. Eisenhower liked to golf
with the pros. In 1960, at the
Gettysburg Country Club, he
and Arnold Palmer shared a
laugh. His golf pro once said
Eisenhower's face turned a
deep red when he got angry
after flubbing a shot: "But he
plodded ahead and the next
good shot brought a smile
back to his face."

On September 25, 1959, President Eisenhower and Soviet
Premier Nikita Khrushchev
flew by helicopter to Camp
David. The Eisenhower
administration introduced helicopters to the White House,
a change dramatized by the
airborne tour Eisenhower
arranged for Khrushchev.

As the president's helicopter skimmed over the Washington suburbs on a September morning in 1959, Dwight David Eisenhower leaned toward Soviet Premier Nikita Khrushchev and jabbed a finger toward the grass below, "a big green field where he told me he played golf," Khrushchev recalled in his memoirs. "He asked me whether I liked this game. I didn't have the slightest idea what it was all about. He told me it was a very healthy sport."

By then, late in his second term, few Americans would have been surprised that President Eisenhower would try to awaken an interest in golf in so unlikely a prospect as the leader of the Soviet Union. They knew Eisenhower as the most devoted and ardent presidential golfer since William Howard Taft hefted his bulk across the greens near the beginning of the twentieth century. Ike's spirits sank when he could not escape the pressures and confinement of his job and work at perfecting his game. His mood rose and fell depending on how near or far he was from perfection.

Eisenhower putted on the velvety green installed for him by the United States Golf Association just steps away from his West Wing office. He drove iron shots down the South Lawn as his valet scrambled to shag the balls, each identified with the words, "Mr. President." Once or twice a week, weather and health permitting, he escaped to the Burning Tree Golf Club in suburban Maryland, almost certainly the "big green field" he had shown Khrushchev. In the early spring and late fall he flew to Georgia to play daytime golf and evening bridge at the Augusta National Golf Club and dabble at painting in the studio of the well-appointed house that club members had built for him. During his first term he spent summer vacations at his mother-in-law's home in Denver and golfed at his favorite course, the Cherry Hills Country Club. He drove into the Rockies, expertly cast for trout in well-stocked mountain streams, then dusted his catch in seasoned flour and demonstrated his considerable abilities as an outdoor chef. After the president and First Lady Mamie Eisenhower transformed the deteriorating nineteenth-century house on their Gettysburg, Pennsylvania, farm

into their first permanent home, the president golfed on many weekends at the Gettysburg Country Club. In his second term he vacationed three times at Newport, Rhode Island, playing the challenging course at the Newport Country Club. Eisenhower's passion for golf kindled a national interest in the game. The number of American golfers doubled to more than 8 million during

268

President Eisenhower golfed again with Arnold Palmer, this time at the Augusta National Golf Club. The Eisenhowers clearly appreciated the comfort and privacy afforded them at the club, where fifty club members chipped in anonymously to build a spacious home for them (*below*). While the house remained club property, the Eisenhowers were invited to use it for their lifetimes.

his eight years in office, spurring a boom in golf-course construction. Ike was "the greatest thing that ever happened to the game," said Fred Corcoran of the Professional Golfers' Association of America.

But the frequency with which he played also opened Eisenhower to complaints that golf absorbed too much of his time. While Ike worked on his putt, the critics claimed, the Soviet Union launched *Sputnik*, the world's first Earth-orbiting satellite. During Eisenhower's first term, Senator Wayne Morse, the Oregon independent, told the Senate it was time the president started showing more interest in unemployment and less in his golf score. Democrats taunted that the Eisenhower era had been little more than eight years of puttering and putting. The Associated Press calculated Eisenhower had spent an average 112 days a year on trips and vacations, compared with President Harry Truman's 86, and one scholar later documented nearly 800 rounds of golf during Eisenhower's two terms. Eisenhower did not let the carping get under his skin. "It is not the criticism that keeps me awake at night—it is the Suez," he told an army friend during the international tug of war over Egypt's Suez Canal.

Those closest to Eisenhower concluded golf gave him important mental and physical benefits. "We want the president to have all the rest and relaxation he can," said Major General Howard Snyder, Eisenhower's White House physician. "People sometimes forget that his job is more than a matter of eight in the morning until six or seven in the evening. Those are just his office hours. His job goes on all the time. Golf is fine for him, so I say he should play whenever he gets a chance." Eisenhower certainly agreed, telling a questioner at a 1958 news conference that golf, coupled with fishing and quail shooting, let him be outdoors and get "mild exercise, the kind that an older individual probably should have." On top of that, those activities forced him to focus on "the bird or that ball or the wily trout." "Now, to my mind it is a very healthful, beneficial kind of thing, and I do it whenever I get a chance, as you well know."

A constant stream of political cartoons, photographs, and news stories contributed to the image of a president obsessed with his game. In what a later era might call "spin," White House press

On a day of fishing in June 1955, President Eisenhower posed at the Mountain Top Inn, Chittenden, Vermont, with his companions Presidential Assistant Sherman Adams (at left) and Judge Milford K. Smith (at right).

President Eisenhower's golf balls and tees were "personalized." His aides fretted that too much golf would not sit well with voters and tried to curb publicity about Eisenhower's golfing and fishing. That did not stop the president from his favorite pursuits. In 1957 (*above right*), he relaxed at the 18th hole of the Newport Country Club.

secretary Jim Hagerty used the term "working vacation" to dilute the impression of idleness. In Hagerty's mind, at least, "working vacation" more clearly described what the president was doing and conveyed the realities a president faced. The press secretary made sure reporters covering Eisenhower's vacations were kept busy writing stories about policy announcements, appointments, and bill signings, all intended to enforce the impression that Eisenhower was hard at work, even if he was working mostly on his back swing.

U.S. News and World Report told readers that on a typical vacation in Denver, where the White House set up a vacation headquarters at Lowry Air Force Base, Eisenhower got about ten days of complete rest, golfing at Cherry Hills and fishing in the Rockies. Office hours took up at least part of the day for the rest of the vacation, the magazine said. Official mail arrived in chained and padlocked leather pouches as it had since Theodore Roosevelt's time. "A president is president no matter what his location," Eisenhower said, recalling that during the eight weeks in 1954 that he vacationed in Denver he saw 225 visitors, made four official trips, delivered six speeches, made three television appearances, and considered 513 bills, approving 488 and vetoing 25. He also campaigned for Republican candidates during that year's congressional elections. "Every time I see the word 'vacation' in the press as applied to what I am now doing, I feel like turning loose a little barrack room language," he told a friend.

Inevitably, events—both gratifying and disturbing—sought out the vacationing president. At Augusta, in November 1953, shortly after the truce that ended the Korean War, Eisenhower gathered his family at a candlelit table, carved a 39-pound turkey, and said that for the first time in four years he and other Americans could celebrate Thanksgiving "without the fear of the casualty list hanging over us."

The mood was different five years later during one of the chillier periods of the Cold War. John Eisenhower, then one of his father's White House aides, remembered joining the president in his office above the pro shop at Augusta. Khrushchev had just reopened the status of the Allied occupation of West Berlin, setting off tremors in the NATO alliance. The Soviets were holding up convoys headed to the city. A crisis seemed likely. The president, dressed for golf, slouched in his chair, as reports made clear U.S. allies were sharply divided on how to respond. His son remembered him "chewing on the bow of his glasses, gazing over the first tee," musing that it was up to him to make sure that this new threat did not shatter Western unity.

In Newport, on a gray and humid morning in September 1957 and with a civil rights crisis brewing in Little Rock, Arkansas's Governor Orval Faubus flew in for a private word with the president. They talked alone for twenty minutes in Eisenhower's small office, then moved to a larger room for a two-hour session with Attorney General Herbert Brownell and Sherman Adams. The meeting ended with smiles and handshakes for the cameras. But *Time* said the cordiality masked the president's steely message: federal court orders requiring the racial integration of Little Rock High School would be enforced; Faubus "must bow to the law and withdraw from his position of rebellion." When events made clear Faubus was not prepared to do that, Eisenhower ordered the armed forces to uphold the court's decisions. Then he flew to Washington so he could use the backdrop of the White House, not the golf course, for a television address explaining his actions. The next morning he flew back to Newport to resume his vacation.

Eisenhower golfed with intensity and persistence. "Dad had a powerful swing but a horrendous slice to go with it," John Eisenhower remembered. Norman Palmer, the pro at the Newport Country Club, concluded that the slice resulted mostly from the knee injury that decades earlier had ended Eisenhower's West Point football career. Ike got much advice. When he told Sam Snead that he was losing sleep over his backswing, Snead bluntly instructed, "Stick your butt out more, Mr. President." Ben Hogan, another golfing legend, said the president's trouble began with his downswing. "If the President would straighten out his right foot, it would help him initiate his downswing properly," Hogan told *Look* magazine in 1953. Three years later news reports about the uneven quality of Ike's game were so prevalent that a bumper sticker declared: "Ben Hogan for President. If we're going to have a golfer, let's have a good one."

Eisenhower owned the world's most famous grin but also a temper so intense that White House aide Bryce Harlow likened it to looking into a Bessemer furnace. Both were on full display on the golf course. The smile was never broader than after a long drive down the center of the fairway.

Second to golf, President Eisenhower loved fishing. Here he displays a trout caught during a fishing trip at Hianloland Farms, Rhode Island, in 1958.

For President Eisenhower, the February 7, 1956 game at Glen Arvin Country Club in Thomasville, Georgia, was a milestone. After suffering a heart attack in 1955, he was considering a campaign for reelection in the fall and testing his strength. At the end of 18 holes reporters were told the 65-year-old heart patient had shown "no evidence of fatigue." Convinced he was fit enough to run for president again, Eisenhower won a second term.

But the furnace door could swing wide open after a slice into the woods, repeated attempts to escape a sand trap, or a putt determined to avoid the hole.

Eisenhower's temper flared memorably on September 23, 1955. The president was playing at Cherry Hills near Denver where he was vacationing after a meeting with Soviet leaders in Geneva. Play was repeatedly interrupted as the White House switchboard tried to get a call through from Secretary of State John Foster Dulles. "His anger became so real that the veins stood out on his forehead like whip cords," Dr. Snyder recalled. When Eisenhower was called to the secure phone in the clubhouse a third time and was told it was a mistake, he abandoned the game and drove to his mother-in-law's house. He woke about 1:30 a.m. the next morning with severe chest pains, received emergency treatment from Dr. Snyder, and was later taken by car to Fitzsimmons Army Hospital in Denver. There Dr. Snyder's suspicions were confirmed. The vacationing president had had a heart attack.

Months later, after a hospital stay and rest at his Gettysburg home, Eisenhower was allowed to resume his game, on one condition. "My doctor has given me orders that if I don't start laughing instead of cussing when I miss those shots, then he's going to stop me from playing golf," the president told the club pro at the Glen Arvin Country Club at Thomasville, Georgia. "Every time I miss a shot you're going to hear me go haw, haw, haw." In April 1957, Cliff Roberts, investment banker, friend, and co-founder and chairman of the Augusta National Golf Club, sent him a plaque recognizing him in tongue-in-cheek fashion as the "most even-tempered golfer of the year."

President Eisenhower was sensitive about his golf score. In April 1953, at Augusta, he scored an 86 in a game with Senator Robert A. Taft of Ohio. Before the game began both the president and the senator displayed buttons whose red letters read: "Don't Ask What I Shot!"

Yet days later, Eisenhower let his temper show in a televised news conference. The White House was preparing to introduce the first presidential helicopters. A reporter asked if, in the interest of budget cutting, Eisenhower would forgo "that pair of helicopters that have been proposed for getting you out to the golf course a little faster than you can make it by car." The president stiffened. "His face bleached, and then a flush of red spread upward from his neck," *Time* reported. "Well, I don't think much of the question," he said, turning his back, "because no helicopters have been procured for me to go to a golf course." Hagerty issued a statement that the helicopters were intended primarily as a means of evacuating the president in an emergency. But once the helicopters entered service, Eisenhower did use them to reach his Gettysburg farm and was often on the golf course within minutes of his arrival. On June 9, 1960, after 18 holes at Burning Tree, he was shuttled back to the White House by helicopter. By then helicopters were part of the White House scene. There was little press comment.

But Ike's touchiness about his golf scores continued to the very end of his term. He cheerfully responded to a questionnaire submitted by a high school history class in Montclair, New Jersey, until he came to the last question, a request for his best golf score in the previous eight years. "The answer to question number nine is still classified as TOP SECRET," the president replied.

President Eisenhower's grandson David Eisenhower posed beneath his name on the sign at Camp David, 1960. According to Press Secretary Jim Haggerty, President Eisenhower renamed the retreat after his grandson and father, both named David, and David was his own middle name. President Franklin Roosevelt's name, Shangri-La, "was just a little fancy for a Kansas farm boy," according to the president.

On a May morning in 1953, working quickly in the green hills above Thurmont, Maryland, government carpenters removed the roadside sign whose Chinese-red letters identified the place as "Shangri-La" and swapped it for another. The new sign read: "Camp David." The name change sent two signals: Eisenhower would keep the retreat Franklin Roosevelt had established in Maryland's Catoctin Mountains, but the new name set the tone for a new era for Eisenhower and future presidents as well. It would provide not only quiet and privacy in a relaxed, comfortable, and attractive atmosphere but a secure, unpressured place to confer with advisers and foreign leaders.

Mamie Eisenhower was not as pleased with Camp David's rough and rustic nature. She objected to the unpainted wood paneling and the heavy furniture, much of it scavenged from navy warehouses in FDR's time. Discovering there was no money for decorating in the presidential budget, she sought advice from Howell Crim, the White House chief usher. Since the navy ran the camp, Crim said, he didn't see why the navy couldn't pay to make it more comfortable. The first lady brightened: "I think I'll just pass a hint along to the commander-in-chief." The redecoration was soon under way. FDR's "Bear's Den" took on the look of 1950s suburbia with floral prints and a color scheme that included Mamie's favorite shades of green, yellow, and pale pink. There were other touches. For a president who liked movies, carpenters built a booth to hide the movie projector and installed a screen that rolled back into the ceiling. A picnic area and grill were also built for Eisenhower, the outdoor chef.

Camp David had a pool where the president's grandchildren, including 5-year-old David, could splash in the summer. A hill offered them sledding and skiing in winter. There was a bowling alley, an archery range, and a skeet range where Eisenhower could sharpen his aim with a shotgun. There was also room for him to paint. He worked on canvas after canvas, retaining only the few which met his standards. What Camp David did not have was a practice green for the nation's

President Eisenhower painted this view of a lodge at Camp David. First Lady Mamie Eisenhower asked that the lodges and cottages at Camp David be named for native trees, erasing their Roosevelt-era names. The conference center became Laurel Lodge. Other new names included Dogwood, Hickory, Witch Hazel, and Sycamore. At Eisenhower's suggestion the presidential lodge was renamed Aspen for the state tree of Colorado, Mamie's home state.

Right: An outdoor chef with considerable talent, Eisenhower is seen here cooking for friends at Camp David in 1960. He was known to clean and prepare his own catch after a day of fishing.

When not outdoors fishing or quail hunting, President Eisenhower spent his leisure time at Camp David painting (*below*). The president did not save all of his completed paintings, only those he deemed worthy.

most famous golfer. This was soon remedied. Cliff Roberts, who ran the Augusta club, contacted Robert Trent Jones, a leading golf course designer, who laid out a green including a sand trap. Eisenhower friends and wealthy Republicans paid for it. "It is a nice green, with quite a lot of rough, and protected from two sides by a large trap," said Ellis Slater, Eisenhower's friend from the business world.

When he didn't feel like painting, and the weather was too cold, windy, or rainy for golf, Eisenhower turned to the bridge table. White House correspondent Merriman Smith of United Press said Ike played better bridge than he did golf, and experts in both games agreed. "So deep is his concentration at bridge that the rest of the world seems to fall away . . . when he picks up his hand," Smith said. But Ike said he enjoyed the company. "I get more fun out of the wise cracks that shoot back and forth across the table than I do out of holding aces and kings."

Carved deep into the rock near Aspen Lodge was a bomb shelter. Eisenhower got his first look at it on July 12, 1957. Later that year he took visiting British Prime Minister Harold Macmillan on a tour. Macmillan described it in his diary as "a sort of Presidential Command Post in the event of atomic war." It could hold fifty presidential aides in one location, 150 Pentagon officials in another, and it cost $10 million, the prime minister said.

One Camp David guest unlikely to have received a bomb-shelter tour was Nikita Khrushchev, who visited Camp David in the fall of 1959 at the end of a cross-country tour. For his part, the Soviet leader was highly suspicious when he discovered his invitation to the United States included two-

Scrabble with Mamie Eisenhower was another leisure activity at Camp David, in July 1954. For the president, Camp David was both a relaxed place to meet with foreign leaders and a retreat for recreational weekends.

days of talks at a place called Camp David. "I couldn't for the life of me find out what this Camp David was," Khrushchev said in his memoirs. He remembered that when Western officials first met Bolshevik leaders after the 1918 Russian Revolution, they were invited to an island where, newspapers reported, "stray dogs were sent to die." "I was afraid maybe this Camp David was the same sort of place, where people who were mistrusted could be kept in quarantine," Khrushchev said. He eventually discovered that Camp David was the president's personal "dacha," and "far from being an insult or an act of discrimination . . . it was a great honor for me to be invited to spend a few days at Camp David with Eisenhower." "On the outside it looked just like a barracks," he later observed, "but on the inside it was luxuriously decorated, yet at the same time very businesslike—typically American." Later, in Moscow, Khrushchev spoke frequently and optimistically of the "Spirit of Camp David," encouraging the thought that his meetings with Eisenhower had fostered a potential thaw in the Cold War.

The following May 1, with preparations for the Paris summit far advanced, the president was again at Camp David. When a morning rain lifted he knocked golf balls across the green. That afternoon a call came in from General Andrew Goodpaster, the White House staff secretary: a U-2 high-altitude spy plane was missing over Soviet territory and had probably crashed. The State Department issued a cover story about an unintentional border crossing by a weather research plane. Then Khrushchev pounced, announcing the U-2 had been shot down, the wreckage recovered, and the pilot captured. The Spirit of Camp David—and the summit—dissolved.

———

During Khrushchev's visit to Camp David, Eisenhower suggested a helicopter ride to inspect his farm at Gettysburg, about 15 miles to the north. A strobe light beamed from a high window in the barn guided the presidential helicopter, and it landed in a field a short walk from the front door of the president's country home. At the farm, Khrushchev frolicked with the four Eisenhower grandchildren, translated their names into Russian, and passed out red star pins. He was one of many visiting heads of state and wartime comrades that the president welcomed to Gettysburg. After talks on his glassed-in porch and a visit to his prized herd of black Angus cattle, he escorted them through America's most famous Civil War battlefield. One by one, Sir Winston Churchill, British Field Marshal Bernard Montgomery, West German Chancellor Konrad Adenauer, French President Charles de Gaulle, and Indian Prime Minister Jawaharlal Nehru added their signatures to Mamie Eisenhower's Gettysburg guest book. On tours of the battlefield, the military men rehashed Union and Confederate military strategies and tactics.

For the first lady, the white brick and stone house at Gettysburg was a cherished and long-awaited milestone. The Eisenhowers had moved as many as forty-seven times since setting up housekeeping at Fort Sam Houston in Texas in July 1916. From dingy army quarters to the splendor of the White House, all their temporary homes had been rented or assigned. Inevitably, reporters called the Gettysburg house "Mamie's Dream House." "What makes it really charming is Mamie's enthusiasm over the whole place and her own pride and delight in having created her first home of their own," said Slater, Ike's golf partner and business world friend.

Ike and Mamie began looking for a country place in the fall of 1950 while he was president of Columbia University. Eisenhower said Mamie wanted a house "that conformed to her notions of what a home should be." He sought "escape from concrete into the countryside." They were intrigued when their friends, George and Mary Allen, described the old house they were restoring on a farm near Gettysburg. Perhaps they could be neighbors? Soon Mamie Eisenhower was walking through a century-old farmhouse at the end of a half mile private lane a few fields away from the Allens. She took a long look at South Mountain and "plain fell in love with the view," said *Collier's* magazine.

Ike also admired the vista but hesitated when he considered the demands the house and farm would make. "The buildings had seen better days," he said. "So had the soil." Improvements would take significant work and money. But Mamie had decided. When she told him, "I must have this place," Ike agreed. They bought the farm from Allen S. Redding and his wife for $40,000 which included $16,000 for livestock and farm equipment. That made the Eisenhowers the owners of the house, the massive 1887 barn, two silos, two poultry houses, a brooder house, a machinery shed, some cows and chickens and 189 acres of Pennsylvania farmland.

But it would be years before they could call the place home. When President

British Field Marshal Bernard Montgomery made headlines during a 1957 tour of the Gettysburg Battlefield with President Eisenhower when he said both Robert E. Lee and his Union opponent, George Gordon Meade, should have been "sacked."

President Eisenhower gave Prime Minister Winston Churchill a tour of his Gettysburg farm in a golf cart on May 8, 1959. Observers feared for the elderly Churchill as the president drove the golf cart over the bumpy farmyard.

Truman named Eisenhower supreme commander of NATO forces in Europe, Ike and Mamie moved to another temporary home, a chateau outside Paris. In 1952 he resigned, declared himself a Republican, received the GOP nomination, and won election as the thirty-fourth president.

While living in the White House, the Eisenhowers began to renovate and update the Gettysburg farmhouse. But when a building survey discovered that it had been built around a worm-eaten, structurally unsound log cabin, little could be saved. The first lady preserved a two-story section of exterior wall and salvaged some of the old bricks, timbers, and beams. She had the president's study built around a fireplace with an old Dutch oven, then beamed and paneled in the old wood. The architect Milton Osborne designed a new and much larger house around the remnants of the old. He called its style modified Georgian.

While carpenters, electricians, masons, and plumbers worked on the house, the Secret Service made its own alterations: a gate and guardhouse at the entrance to the long private lane, electric eyes along the fences, and infrared scanners for nighttime use. In time, the agency set up a closed-circuit surveillance system with cameras positioned to scan approaches to the property. Agents watched from an office in the old milkhouse of the barn.

The fifteen-room house was completed and furnished by the summer of 1955 with the walls and fabrics that displayed the first lady's favorite colors: pink and light green. There were eight bedrooms and eight full or partial baths. The tile, tub, toilet, and towels in the first lady's bathroom were all pink, as was the telephone on her dressing table. The dining room table downstairs had been purchased early in the Eisenhowers' marriage, as had the silver tea service, which Ike had presented to Mamie piece by piece as his army paycheck permitted. A few steps away, a formal and little-used living room served as a depository for a lifetime accumulation of small gifts and mementos, including the first lady's collection of porcelain birds.

Eisenhower himself oversaw the repainting of old barn, which loomed over the house, its deep red color making it appear even larger and closer. He was, after all, a painter, and one afternoon spent 45 minutes supervising the mixing of paint. His color choice was a light, less conspicuous grayish green.

The Gettysburg farmhouse was expanded and remodeled after the Eisenhowers purchased it in 1950. It was the first home they owned, and they lived there until they died. The property was then turned over to the National Park Service, and, as the Eisenhower National Historic Site, it is open for tours. The house is fully furnished, much as the Eisenhowers left it.

The president's Gettysburg retreat quickly became America's most talked about farm and the president the nation's best-known farmer. While the house was Mamie's domain, Ike made the farm his own, improving the run-down soil, growing corn, oats, barley, red clover, timothy, and alfalfa, and building a blue-ribbon herd of registered Aberdeen Angus cattle. With a farm manager, a herdsman, and three full-time hands to carry out his plans, Eisenhower studied scientific farming and cattle breeding with something like the concentration he had devoted to planning the Normandy invasion. "He talks crop rotation as if he had been a farmer all his life," a neighbor said. Eisenhower said that while he couldn't claim total success, "there are enough lush fields to assure me that I shall leave the place better than I found it." *Time* described him in the summer of 1955, delightedly inspecting rows of corn standing 9 feet high. As reporters watched, the president demonstrated a Kansas-style hog call: "Soooooooey, soooooooey, hoh, peeg, peeg, peeg."

For the White House staff, the frequent visits to the Gettysburg farm became exercises in logistics. Traveling with the president and his wife were a driver, the president's valet, the first lady's maid, a cook, two housemen, and the president's doctor, as well as the Secret Service detail and the Signal Corps staff that maintained communications. Housing and meals had to be arranged for all of them. Food and other supplies were taken from White House stores and delivered to Gettysburg. Linens were packed for each trip and trucked back to the White House daily for laundering.

The glass-enclosed sunporch quickly became the most used, most appreciated room in the house. The Eisenhowers enjoyed it from early morning breakfast to late evening. "Both Mamie and I find it an oasis of relaxation," Eisenhower said. He often set up an easel and painted. They talked, read, and watched television. She favored soap operas and demanded silence during episodes of *As the World Turns*. Ike liked *Gunsmoke*, *Bonanza*, and other Westerns. He could see his cattle grazing from his seat on the white wicker couch. When they entertained, the men would

President Eisenhower took great pride in his Aberdeen Angus cattle. Arriving at the farm in daylight, he often rode a golf cart to his barns to admire the newest additions to his herd, chat with his farm manager, or check the progress of the large vegetable garden.

often play bridge at one end of the porch, while the women played bolivia, a form of canasta, at the other. When Ike and his friends walked onto the putting green, a gift from the Professional Golfers' Association, Mamie could watch through the porch windows. Gettysburg basked in its role as Summer Capital when the president chose to spend his 1959 vacation on the farm, golfing at the Gettysburg Country Club.

At times the house served other needs. The president used it as a place to recuperate after three illnesses, notably after his September 1955 heart attack, but also after his abdominal surgery in 1956 and his 1957 stroke. And it was a place to be with grandchildren, especially after their son moved his family to the old converted Pitzer schoolhouse nearby. The kids—David, Anne, Susan, and Mary Jean—rode ponies and romped with the dogs. As he grew older, David fished, shot skeet, and golfed with his grandfather.

On the afternoon of January 20, 1961, following the inauguration of John F. Kennedy as his successor, Ike and Mamie again set off for Gettysburg, this time traveling by car instead of helicopter. A half century of public service as soldier and president was behind him, as were all the temporary homes. The house Mamie Eisenhower had built at Gettysburg was now their permanent address. Adjusting to the sudden absence of official responsibilities would be difficult. But the former president had a herd of Aberdeen Angus to manage, his backswing to perfect, and the memoirs of his White House years to write.

Ike and Mamie agreed before his death in 1969 that the farm would eventually be turned over to the National Park Service. She continued to live on the farm until she died in 1979. Today, as the Eisenhower National Historic Site, the house is open to tours.

Chapter 30

John F. Kennedy: White House Sailor

President Kennedy, aboard
Honey Fitz on Labor Day
weekend at Hyannis Port,
August 31, 1962, kept in
touch with world events. A
vacationing president might
succeed in reducing the
pressures, even in enjoying
himself, but, as White House
correspondent Hugh Sidey
observed, "He must remain
always remain at the end of
those insistent cables from
around the world."

One bright and breezy afternoon, as the *Honey Fitz* cruised the deep blue waters of Rhode Island's Narragansett Bay, John Fitzgerald Kennedy saluted the last of a flotilla of navy ships and let a grin spread across his face. "You know," he told a friend, "this job might even be fun if the world weren't such a mess." In those moments when the world and the Cold War offered him a chance, Kennedy clearly enjoyed his escapes from the pressures of the White House.

Family wealth and the trappings of office offered the new president much to choose from when he wanted to change scenery: the Kennedy family compound at Hyannis Port on Cape Cod; Joseph P. Kennedy's beach-front mansion at Palm Beach, Florida; Hammersmith Farm, Jacqueline Kennedy's family estate at Newport, Rhode Island; Glen Ora, the Virginia Hunt Country estate the Kennedys rented for the first two years of his administration; and Wexford, the country house Jacqueline Kennedy built after Glen Ora's lease expired. Other houses at Cape Cod and Palm Beach were rented or borrowed as the president needed them.

The patterns of Kennedy's vacation and weekend journeys were set early in his administration: north to Cape Cod and Newport in the summer, south to Palm Beach in the winter, west to the Virginia Country in the spring and fall, back to Hyannis Port for Thanksgiving. The frequent escapes owed much to Jacqueline Kennedy's quest for privacy: her desire to shield herself and her young children, Caroline and John Jr., from prying eyes and intruding photographers. Being away from the White House allowed the Kennedys more time with their children in an atmosphere she considered more normal and more fun. It also allowed her to avoid the rounds of handshakes and polite small talk she detested. She called Glen Ora "the most private place I can think of to balance our life in the White House."

At 43, Kennedy was the youngest man ever elected to the presidency. His image of youthful vitality persisted despite a chronically aching back and other ailments. A former navy lieutenant, he was more comfortable at the tiller of a sailboat than any chief executive since Franklin Delano Roosevelt and never happier than when he was steering a course, meeting the challenges of wind and weather. He felt free when he was on the *Honey Fitz*, the 92-foot presidential yacht, or on the *Manitou*, a 62-foot racing yawl borrowed from the U.S. Coast Guard.

Kennedy's time in office was dominated by the Cold War abroad and the struggle over civil rights at home. Wherever he was, he was linked by phone to the White House switchboard, received a daily intelligence briefing, conferred with senior officials, signed bills and executive orders, and gave interviews. He was followed everywhere by an army warrant officer carrying a black briefcase with the codes needed to launch a nuclear strike. "The President's office is wherever the President may be," said Theodore Sorensen, Kennedy's special counsel and speechwriter. "For unlike the Congress and the Supreme Court, the Presidency never recesses or adjourns."

Nevertheless, Kennedy believed in frequent breaks, and they were indeed frequent. White House records for Kennedy's nearly thirty-five months in office show thirty-four vacation and

The Kennedy family home in
Hyannis Port, Massachussetts,
was only one of the venues for
President Kennedy's escapes.
His father, Joseph P. Kennedy,
bought the sprawling house
on Cape Cod in 1929, and
the family has used it and
other houses in and near the
compound for generations.
The president and his
photogenic family (seen
here in 1962) caught the
public imagination. Throngs
of camera-clutching day-
trippers pressed as close to the
compound as local and state
police would allow. According
to Kennedy confidante Arthur
Schlesinger Jr., the approach
to the compound, past the
tourists, the barricades,
the officials demanding
identification, was "like
crossing a frontier."

weekend trips over 111 days in 1961; thirty-two holiday trips and weekends over 104 days in 1962; and thirty-four weekends and vacations over ninety-four days in 1963. With partial days included, the total is 310 days away from the White House. Kennedy was away so often that when he stayed in town it was news: "Kennedy to Week-End in the White House" ran a headline in April 1962. The first lady was away even more frequently, staying weeks or months at a time at Hyannis Port, Palm Beach, Newport, or the Virginia Hunt Country, with the president joining her on weekends. Once he had cleared his desk, he devoted "every inch of mind and body to leisure as intensively as he had to work," said Sorensen, "completely shaking off and shutting out the worries of the world beyond."

———

On May 27, 1961, the dark blue Presidential Flag rose for the first time on the flagpole inside the Kennedy compound at Hyannis Port. Back at his family's summer home for the first time since his inaugural, Kennedy was on his way to Vienna to confer with Soviet Premier Nikita Khrushchev over the status of Berlin. The presidential helicopter landed repeatedly at Hyannis Port that summer. Kennedy was in residence on thirteen successive weekends from June 30 through September 24, joining his family, who spent the entire summer on Cape Cod, and then returning for Thanksgiving.

Joseph P. Kennedy first brought his large family to Cape Cod in the early 1920s. FDR's prewar ambassador to Great Britain and founder of the family fortune, he bought the big house overlooking the harbor in 1929 and made it an even larger summer home for his wife, Rose, and their eight children. "The Tenuvus," he called the family tribe. But as his sons and daughters married and raised families of their own the large house proved not large enough. By 1960, the compound held three Kennedy houses. Robert and Ethel Kennedy had one house; Jack and Jacqueline Kennedy bought another in 1956. Other family members had summer homes a short walk or drive away: Jean Kennedy and her husband, Steve Smith; Eunice Kennedy and her husband, Sargent Shriver; Ted Kennedy, the youngest son, and his wife, Joan. "We were all close enough to see one another as easily and often as we wished," Rose Kennedy remembered.

At his own residence in Hyannis Port, President Kennedy held an unprecedented two-hour interview with Alexei Adzhubei, Nikita Khrushchev's son-in-law and editor of the Soviet newspaper *Izvestiya,* on November 25, 1961. Dodging bursts of Soviet propaganda, the president renewed calls for a realistic settlement of the status of Berlin and pressed for negotiations to achieve a nuclear test ban. The interview was published in full in Moscow, another milestone. Some Western commentators said it raised a flicker of hope for better communications between the two superpowers.

Hyannis Port and its larger sister, the town of Hyannis, lie in Barnstable County on the south shore of Cape Cod, a sandy peninsula of scrub oak and pine that reaches east into the Atlantic before bending abruptly north. Hyannis Port had long been the haven of wealthy families from New England and elsewhere who relished the sailing and golf, the sandy beaches and water views, the privacy and the informal tranquillity.

The unruffled nature of the place changed rapidly after Kennedy won the presidential nomination and then the presidency. Arthur Schlesinger Jr., a historian and Kennedy confidant, described the formerly quiet village as part street fair, part military occupation. "Everywhere were roadblocks, cordons of policemen, photographers with cameras slung over their shoulders, children selling souvenirs, tourists in flashy shirts and shorts waiting expectantly as if for a revelation," he recalled.

Closer to the commotion than the compound's other houses, the president's residence on Irving Street was soon enclosed with a high wooden palisade fence and protected by a Secret Service detail working out of a command-post trailer parked on the grounds. Invited inside the house, guests found a modest retreat, simply but tastefully furnished with white-painted rattan furniture and bright floral patterns on sofas and chairs. "Off the living room was a beautiful patio, bathed in sunlight during most of the day, where the President liked to sit and read his newspapers," said Pierre Salinger, Kennedy's press secretary.

At Hyannis Port Kennedy rose about 9:00 a.m., an hour or so later than usual, conferred with Salinger about the daily press briefing, received his daily intelligence summary from a military aide, and tore through a stack of newspapers. Then, working with his secretary, Evelyn Lincoln, he handled the mail flown in daily by courier planes. That out of the way, he often boarded the *Marlin*, his father's 52-foot cabin cruiser, or the *Honey Fitz*, for lunch and a cruise with his children. He napped later in the afternoon, or stretched out on his bed to read reports and papers carried from Washington in his battered briefcase.

President Kennedy posed with the family's youngest generation in Hyannis Port, in 1963 (*opposite*) and gave the children a ride around the Hyannis Port compound in 1962 (*left*).

In good weather the Kennedy compound was filled with children riding bikes, bouncing on a trampoline, and running from one game to another. The president would sometimes join them to toss a football across the lawn or scramble on the grass with Caroline and John. On many visits the president led as many as eighteen children on a stroll or a golf cart ride to a neighborhood store for penny candy: licorice, chocolates, lollipops. "On Friday he's regular," the store owner said. "He isn't down in that chopper fifteen minutes before he's over here."

Not since the days of Theodore Roosevelt, *Time* reported at the beginning of August 1962, had America seen such an active first family or such a "heart-pounding, muscle-aching" round of activities. The president, the first lady, Caroline and John Jr., and a myriad of other Kennedy uncles, aunts, cousins, and guests set a fast pace. It was more like a small-scale Olympics than a kick-back-and-rest vacation. "Since sitting down is somehow considered bad form, touch football fills in the 'rest periods' between tennis, swimming, waterskiing, sailing and 'dragging'," *Time* observed. It defined "dragging" as desperately attempting to avoid drowning while clutching life preservers towed by the president's schooner, *Victura*. Two touch footballers won a dollop of presidential praise when they galloped after a spinning football, pitched into a thick patch of rose bushes, and spent the rest of the day plucking thorns from their arms and legs. As an alternative to rash bravery, a generous measure of "brute stamina" was acceptable, *Time* observed. John Glenn, the astronaut, was credited with admirable Kennedy-style endurance after a day in which he rode a bike, swam, played baseball, competed in touch football, and barely ducked a swinging boom while obeying a presidential order to haul down *Victura's* mainsheet. "It's not the way you play the game that counts: it's whether you survive," a Kennedy friend concluded.

When the president needed to break free from the cycle of urgent cables, insistent telephones, and fact-filled meetings, he headed to open water. John Kennedy had sailed from his earliest years:

Politics had a foot on the scale when Kennedy rejected the suggestion of his naval aide that he acquire a yacht capable of ocean travel. Instead, he stayed with the two cabin cruisers Eisenhower had named for his granddaughters. Kennedy renamed the larger, 92-foot yacht the *Honey Fitz* shown here on the Potomac River, in 1961, and the smaller craft the *Patrick J.*, honoring both of his grandfathers.

winning racing honors as a teenager, commanding PT-109 in the Pacific during World War II. History had come alive for him when grandfather John Fitzgerald, the fabled mayor of Boston and the original "Honey Fitz," took him to see the frigate *Constitution* at her berth in Boston Harbor. When he got a chance to name a presidential yacht he called her *Honey Fitz*.

Built in 1931 for Montgomery Ward executive Sewell Avery, the boat had seen Coast Guard service during World War II, then became an escort for Harry Truman's *Williamsburg*. President Dwight D. Eisenhower had named it for his granddaughter, *Barbara Ann*. Kennedy had been tempted to return the *Williamsburg* to presidential service, but Eisenhower had branded the seagoing yacht a needless luxury and Kennedy decided that bringing her out of mothballs would be politically reckless.

The *Honey Fitz* could carry as many as forty guests, seating eleven of them at dinner. An armchair for the president's use was located on the afterdeck, and a print of the frigate *Independence* hung over a television set in the white-walled lounge. Its relaxed setting wrung the formality out of many official cruises. The president set the pace in early April 1961, assessing the state of the world with British Prime Minister Harold Macmillan as they cruised on the Potomac. That July, the *Honey Fitz* became a social butterfly, joining a flotilla of four small yachts and other craft carrying 140 guests to a lavish State Dinner on the lawn at George Washington's Mount Vernon to salute President Ayub Khan of Pakistan. White House correspondent Hugh Sidey said the weather cooperated in setting a romantic mood: "Beyond the western bank of the Potomac a huge orange sun was setting in a cloudless sky. With such lighting, even the silty river became a golden ribbon."

At times the gravity of discussions onboard the *Honey Fitz* belied the casual atmosphere. Cruising on Lake Worth during his 1962 Christmas vacation at Palm Beach, Kennedy received a bleak and blunt report from Senate majority leader Mike Mansfield on the situation facing the United States in South Vietnam, which Mansfield had just visited. Kennedy, in a blue sport shirt and white slacks, took a chair on the shaded afterdeck and began turning pages. The senator saw the president's neck and face flush red with anger as he reached the conclusions. Mansfield added to the tension by strongly advising the phased withdrawal of all U.S. troops. "I got angry at Mike for disagreeing with our policy so completely," Kennedy later told aide Kenneth O'Donnell. "And I got angry with myself because I found myself agreeing with him."

The *Honey Fitz* ran down the coast to await Kennedy's winter visits to Palm Beach. In Florida he often ordered the yacht out to the warm waters of the Gulf Stream and went over the side for a swim. The boat stood off a hundred yards or so while the president was in the water, then edged closer when he signaled to be picked up. Unable to see Kennedy from the bridge, the skipper relied on a crewman's hails to move the boat into position. Once, when he asked for the president's location, he got a startling reply: "He's under the boat!" The captain bolted from the pilot house to discover Kennedy alongside and laughing. He had been hidden from sight by the slope of the yacht's bow.

One afternoon, as the *Honey Fitz* cruised off Cape Cod, Caroline climbed onto the president's lap and demanded a story. He obliged with a favorite, about the White Shark that followed boats at sea and made its living by eating people's socks. Kennedy surveyed his guests and saw that Franklin Roosevelt Jr., son of another presidential sailor, was wearing worn and dirty sweatsocks but no shoes. Old dirty sweatsocks, he said, were exactly what the sock-eating shark liked most. Kennedy "reached over and grabbed a sock off of Franklin's foot and threw it over the stern," said Bill Walton, a family friend. Kennedy then declared that the only thing the shark liked better was another sock, and in seconds Roosevelt was barefoot. "Caroline watched with absolute rapt fascination as the socks disappeared into the water" because she thought the shark had them, Walton recalled. Lem Billings, an old Kennedy friend, said guests soon learned "that when Jack began telling Caroline about the White Shark it was time to move to another part of the yacht."

The press tagged along on Kennedy's nautical excursions, using rented boats to trail the *Honey Fitz* while being kept at a distance by Secret Service chase boats and Coast Guard escort vessels.

The president and his family celebrated Christmas with friends in Palm Beach in 1962. At Easter the next year, the Kennedys were in Palm Beach again, here outside the private chapel at the president's father's residence..

Reporters took notes as the wind whipped the pages of their pads; photographers aimed telescopic lenses. Kennedy regarded them all as an unwarranted intrusion on his private time. He often deliberately turned his back on the photographers. "He demanded privacy," observed UPI's Helen Thomas, "and, like all other Presidents, he got angry with reporters who ignored his wishes."

But sailing offered a sense of liberation that was hard to match, no matter the conditions. Kennedy went out in weather cold enough to make his passengers shiver. He sailed in seas so heavy that other boats remained snugly tied to their moorings. On an afternoon in late July 1962, with a 30-knot wind whipping Nantucket Sound into a washboard of 3-foot waves, Kennedy set *Victura's* mainsail and cast off. His parents had given him the 26-foot sailboat for his fifteenth birthday, and it was always his favorite. "With the president at the tiller, the boat scudded out beyond the breakwater on the starboard reach," wrote E. W. Kenworthy of the *New York Times*. "As soon as she cleared the jetty, she heeled over sharply with her port gunwales awash." On that day, or another just like it, Kennedy had a mishap as he headed into the jetty. "The whole top of the mast gave way and the sail and rigging collapsed around the surprised sailors," the president's naval aide recalled. Watching from shore, Robert Kennedy couldn't suppress a younger brother's wry comment: "I always wondered how exactly we lost PT-109 and after that performance I suggest we have a new inquiry into it."

With Hyannis Port filled with tourists, Jacqueline Kennedy's family home at Newport quickly became an alternative vacation destination. Kennedy was the eighteenth president to visit Newport in a line of chief executives that began with George Washington and extended through Dwight Eisenhower. In the late nineteenth century Newport had acquired a stately procession of "cottages," modest names for the Gilded Age summer palaces built for America's wealthiest families. Kennedy established his Newport Summer White House at Hammersmith Farm, the waterfront estate of Jackie's stepfather, Hugh Auchincloss. The house had been the setting for the Kennedys' 1953 wedding reception, attended by two thousand guests. The broad porches of the twenty-eight-room house framed views of Narragansett Bay. A herd of Aberdeen Angus cattle grazed behind split-rail fences. *Time's* Hugh Sidey reported that a Marine helicopter had flown in Kennedy's extra-firm

An alternative family getaway was Jacqueline Kennedy's family estate, Hammersmith Farm, in Newport, Rhode Island. Set on Narragansett Bay, it offered swimming, sailing, golfing, and privacy. Here the Kennedys arrive by helicopter, September 26, 1961.

mattress and backboard from his Hyannis Port house, to make sure his ailing back had proper support. Although he didn't golf as often or as doggedly as his predecessor, Kennedy followed Eisenhower on the greens at the Newport Country Club. The president also swam at private Bailey's Beach, where he was apparently relieved to be left alone.

The America's Cup Races were the main attraction by far for the presidential yachtsman. In September 1962 the *Joseph P. Kennedy Jr.*, was in port, and Kennedy boarded the destroyer named for his elder brother, killed in World War II, to view the first race. Just a month later, when the Cuban Missile Crisis erupted, the *Kennedy* was ordered to sea to help blockade the communist-ruled island in the Caribbean. But that evening no one could have predicted such a mission. Attending a dinner given by the Australian ambassador at The Breakers, once Cornelius Vanderbilt's summer residence, Kennedy spoke of the bond between humanity and the sea:

President Kennedy was at the helm of the *Manitou*, sailing off the coast of Maine, August 12, 1962. He was never happier than when at the tiller of a sailboat, steering the course, chomping on a small cigar, lunching on fish chowder, and bantering with family and friends.

> I really don't know why it is that all of us are so committed to the sea, except I think it's because in addition to the fact that the sea changes, and the light changes, and ships change, it's because we all came from the sea. And it is an interesting biological fact that all of us have, in our veins the exact same percentage of salt in our blood that exists in the ocean, and, therefore, we have salt in our blood, in our sweat, in our tears. We are tied to the ocean. And when we go back to the sea—whether it is to sail or to watch it—we are going back from whence we came.

The next day Kennedy eagerly followed the race from the destroyer's deck while two thousand boats of all sizes darted nearby. "The love of the man for the sea and ships was never more apparent," said Captain Tazewell Shepard, the president's naval aide. "It was good to see him sit back, light one of his slender cigars, adjust his binoculars, and study the racing yachts—or push his sunglasses back on his forehead and laugh with those around him." Shepard remembered quieter moments with Kennedy "gazing out over the sea, lost in thought and idly chewing on the frame of his sunglasses."

At Newport, off Cape Cod, at Palm Beach, and once for a long weekend in Maine, Kennedy sailed a sleek, 62-foot, two-masted racing yawl, borrowed from the U.S. Coast Guard Academy. Her name, spelled out in gold leaf, was *Manitou*. Her mainmast reached 82 feet above the waterline. "He enjoyed sailing in a knock-down wind with the deck aslant, even though it was a strain on his back," said fellow sailor Julius Fanta. When his back ached Kennedy asked to be relieved from the helm and sat on the bow, holding on to the forestay. "He loved the view from there and seemed to listen to the sound of the water being parted by the bow into a rush of surging white that swept aft along both sides."

In the spring of 1963, as Jacqueline Kennedy began planning to celebrate her husband's forty-sixth birthday on May 29, the *Honey Fitz* developed problems. "She's got rotting stern timbers," Kennedy told his friend, Benjamin C. Bradlee, then a *Newsweek* reporter. So the *Sequoia*—the motor yacht Herbert Hoover and Franklin Roosevelt had used—was commandeered for the event. The invitation read, "Come in Yachting Clothes," and the party of relatives and friends obliged. Cocktails were served on the *Sequoia's* fantail, dinner in the lounge below. Toasts were offered. And when Kennedy insisted, his friend Red Fay did a vaudeville turn, singing "Hooray for Hollywood." Presents piled up at the president's feet, and he was photographed tearing off the wrappings. The band played Chubby Checker's tunes, causing Bradlee to mutter that no one had gotten the word that "the twist" was passé. "The weather was dreadful most of the evening, as one thunderstorm chased us up and down the river all night, and everyone was more or less drenched," Bradlee recalled. At length the yacht tied up at the Navy Yard and the celebrants departed. John F. Kennedy had celebrated his last birthday.

———

As his presidency opened, Kennedy took a two-year lease on Glen Ora, a wooded estate in the Virginia Hunt Country about 40 miles due west of Washington, a half-hour hop by helicopter. In doing so he bowed to his wife's passion for horses and riding. There wasn't a sailboat within miles. He didn't care for fox hunting and was allergic to horses.

Covered in tawny stucco, its windows framed with white shutters, Glen Ora's six-bedroom main house had been repeatedly expanded since its central section was built in 1810. The grounds offered an Olympic-size pool, a tennis court, a children's playhouse, and a guest cottage. A helipad was installed. The Army Signal Corps brought in a communications trailer. The Secret Service erected guard posts and gates. Most important to Jackie were the stables and pastures for her horses. Arriving for the first time in mid-February 1961, she was soon in the saddle, riding her bay gelding, Bit of Irish, along slushy, snow-lined trails.

Glen Ora's 400 acres lay in the woods and fields of Virginia's estate country within 2 miles of Middleburg, the horse-loving capital of a region *Time* called a place of "tweedy elegance." Some of America's most distinguished and most expensive horses grazed beyond white-painted wood fences and fieldstone walls. Dogwoods exploded in clouds of white in the spring. Deer, wild turkeys, and foxes populated the oak woods. The first lady clearly loved Glen Ora and was soon galloping with the Orange County Hunt. She rode to hounds at least twice a week during the winter season, telling old friends that she rode mostly to exercise outdoors with animals and people and that Glen Ora gave her time to be with her children. It offered her the privacy she sought. "I appreciate the way people there let me alone," she said.

Glen Ora, a Hunt Country estate near Middleburg, Virginia, was leased by the Kennedys for two years, primarily to provide First Lady Jacqueline Kennedy with a place to ride in the country and get away from the reporters and photographers who attempted to record the family's every move. Here, in January 1962, Charlie, a Kennedy family dog, stands on the front lawn. The following month, President Kennedy carried his daughter Caroline from the White House enroute to Glen Ora.

A stealth golfer, President Kennedy vigilantly kept his game out of public view while he campaigned for the presidency. Democrats had blistered President Eisenhower for his time-consuming passion for golf. But on July 7, 1963, Kennedy snuck in a game at the Hyannis Port Country Club. *Newsweek* reporter Ben Bradlee said Kennedy didn't take the game seriously, kept up running commentary, and was fun to play with.

In November 1961, while riding with the Piedmont Hunt, the first lady's horse balked at a rail fence and threw her. A local photographer caught her midair, her custom-made riding boots aimed at the sky, her white-gloved hands reaching to break the fall. She was not hurt but her pride was dented. She asked her husband to somehow stop publication of the photograph. "I'm sorry Jackie," he told her. "But when the first lady falls on her ass, that's news." The *Fauquier Democrat* told the story in a more gently worded headline: "First Lady Joins Grass Club at Piedmont Hunt Meet."

Although the estate was rented, not owned, the first lady spent a reported $10,000 in redecoration, bringing in Sister Parish, the fashionable interior designer who also helped redesign the State Rooms of the White House. After a judicious application of paint and wallpaper and the installation of curtains, rugs, and furniture, the house met Mrs. Kennedy's standards. The drawing room was now a soft green with a sofa covered in flowered chintz. The dining room walls were painted green-gray. Much of the furniture came from the Kennedys' former house in the Georgetown section of Washington. It added up, said one enthusiastic commentator, "to an impeccable background for living, . . . a well-servanted atmosphere, capable of bracing itself to the whirlwind pace of the Kennedys."

Although Jack Kennedy often found Glen Ora boring, the family spent much time there, visiting on fourteen weekends in 1961 and twenty in 1962, mostly in the colder months. The president was at Glen Ora on the weekend of April 15–16, 1961, as an invasion force of CIA-trained Cuban exiles approached Cuba's south coast at Bahia de Cochinos, soon to be famous as the Bay of Pigs. On Saturday, Kennedy watched part of the Middleburg Hunt races with Jackie but appeared nervous and restless. At 2:00 p.m. on Sunday, working the phones from Glen Ora, he gave the invasion the green light. As he waited for news he slammed golf balls across the pasture, then played three holes at the Fauquier Springs County Club. The telephone awakened him early on Monday morning. Told the brigade was ashore, he flew back to Washington to follow events. They came quickly. Fidel Castro's forces, aided by a lack of American air cover, counterattacked. By the end of the week the operation had failed. Stung, the new president sought counsel from his

predecessor, Dwight D. Eisenhower, conferring with him the next weekend at Camp David.

As 1962 ended, Glen Ora's owner refused to renew the lease. She also insisted that the house be restored to its pre-Kennedy appearance, another expensive undertaking. But the first lady had no wish to abandon the hunt country. She acquired 39 acres on Rattlesnake Ridge near the hamlet of Atoka, about 60 miles west of the capital, and began to build her own house, one even more secluded than Glen Ora. Hoping to please her husband, she named it Wexford for the Irish county from which the Kennedys had sprung.

The 3,500 square foot ranch-style house was taking shape by early 1963, its costs rising from an estimated $45,000 to more than $100,000. As planned by the first lady, it would be covered in pale yellow stucco with an interior courtyard. There would be seven bedrooms, five full baths, and a spacious living room and dining room, with back-to-back fireplaces serving both. Other rooms included a library, den, and breakfast room. There was also a Signal Corps switchboard and a fallout shelter similar to those being added to thousands of houses across the country. Outside were stables for the horses and workspace for the Secret Service. "The idea of the new home is to make it as cozy as possible—nothing elaborate," said Pamela Turnure, the first lady's press secretary.

With Glen Ora unavailable and Wexford unfinished, the Kennedys began spending frequent weekends at Camp David. They had not liked it formerly, complaining of the fog and the heavily armed Marines guarding the place. Mrs. Kennedy dismissed it as a collection of "motel shacks with their bomb shelters churning underneath." But now Camp David suited them. Mrs. Kennedy found there was stable space for her horses and that the riding was as good as in Virginia. The president swam in the heated pool, golfed on the tiny course, and had the navy build a riding ring for Caroline's pony, Macaroni. Young John was fascinated with his father's helicopter, and the president took him to the hangar, put him in the pilot's seat, and let him waggle the controls. On Sundays, the family rode an electric golf cart to Roman Catholic mass in the Marine mess hall. "If only I'd realized how nice Camp David really is, I'd never have rented Glen Ora, or built Wexford," the first lady told White House chief usher J. B. West.

The Kennedys spent sixteen weekends at Camp David in 1963, visiting in the spring and the fall. They returned even after their house on Rattlesnake Ridge had been completed. Ben Bradlee wrote in his journal that his friend liked the privacy, the heated swimming pool, and "the separate houses where guests can be alone, and out of his hair."

The first family at the ocean-side house they rented on Squaw Island, Hyannis Port, summer 1963. By many accounts, the summer of 1963 was a happy time for President Kennedy. But tragedy struck in August after the First Lady gave birth to a son, Patrick Bouvier Kennedy, five weeks prematurely. The baby had a serious breathing disorder and was quickly transferred to Boston Children's Hospital where doctors struggled to save his life. The president was with his son when he died on August 9, just thirty-nine hours after his birth. He is buried alongside his parents in Arlington Cemetery.

The Kennedys built Wexford (*below*) in the Virginia Hunt-Country after losing their lease on Glen Ora. They spent one weekend here in November 1963.

On a hill in Arlington Cemetery (*above*), the slain president is buried, now with his wife, an unnamed stillborn daughter, and their tiny son Patrick, who was born prematurely on August 7, 1963, and died two days later. *Time* magazine recalled "The Moment that Changed America" in November 2013 on the 50th anniversary of the assassination (*left*).

The Bradlees were guests at Camp David the day after the president's forty-sixth birthday party on the *Sequoia*, riding on his helicopter. "Do you think you could get used to his kind of life?" Kennedy grinned. "Pretty hard to take, isn't it?" Kennedy drove his guests to the skeet range. "The president shot first, and he was as lousy as we all turned out to be. He hit about four of the first twenty," Bradlee said. They swam in the pool, then recessed for Bloody Marys on Aspen's terrace, overlooking "a valley that extends forever."

On November 10, 1963, the Kennedys began a three-day weekend at Wexford. Sitting with guests on a stone wall on the new terrace, they talked about any number of things, including the president's plans to visit Texas near the end of the month. Bradlee remembered it as a cool but sunny fall day, still warm enough to be outside. White House photographer Cecil Stoughton shot Jackie riding Sadar. But the pony, Macaroni, stole the show, walking onto the front lawn to munch grass, and, remembered Bradlee, "nudging the presidential rear end." The guests doubled up in laughter.

———

Two weeks later, bullets were fired at Kennedy's motorcade in Dallas and the United States had a new president. Lyndon Baines Johnson would spend his vacations on the banks of the Pedernales River in the Hill Country of Texas.

Chapter 31

Lyndon B. Johnson: The Texas White House

LYNDON B. JOHNSON
36th President of the
United States, 1963–1969

President Lyndon B. Johnson,
still in his Washington
uniform of suit and tie, did
not hesitate to get to work on
his Texas ranch. He is astride
his favorite horse, Lady B, in
1967.

Texas sagebrush replaced New England ivy so quickly that the change of landscape seemed nearly as stunning as the change of administrations. America now had a Texas White House, and new territory to explore. Lyndon Baines Johnson anchored his life on the banks of the Pedernales River and in the Texas Hill Country of his birth. Improving the LBJ Ranch, enriching its soil, and nurturing his herd of white-faced Hereford cattle became Johnson's passion and pride even as he rose to the highest levels of politics and government. The land, and the saga of the generations of his family who had lived on it, were his "rich inheritance." As president, he reconstructed and made a personal museum of the simple house in which he had been born in Stonewall, Texas, on August 27, 1908. His boyhood home in nearby Johnson City, founded by an earlier Johnson, became another personal museum, a tribute to the hometown boy who thrived in the world beyond. Johnson showed visitors all those places, and he told them of ancestors who had fought for Texas independence, driven cattle on the Chisholm Trail, and hid under the cabin during Indian raids. He often walked among the red-granite markers in the stone-walled family cemetery where his parents and grandparents lay buried in the shade of gnarled and ancient live oaks.

Although the presidency had long been his goal, Johnson grumbled about being locked up behind the iron fence on Pennsylvania Avenue and called the White House "Lonely Acres." Rufus Youngblood, the lead agent in Johnson's Secret Service detail, called the LBJ ranch the president's safety valve. "It was the place he went when he felt the mainspring beginning to wind too tight," Youngblood said. When the new president couldn't be in the Hill Country, he talked about it. "The sight and the feel of that country somehow burned itself into my mind," he said one day when the White House was newly his. "All my life I have drawn strength, and something more, from those Texas hills. Sometimes, in the highest councils of the nation, in this house, I sit back and I can almost feel that rough, unyielding, sticky clay soil between my toes, and it stirs memories that often give me comfort and sometimes give me a pretty firm purpose."

The LBJ Ranch was some 60 miles west of Austin, the Texas capital, and about 70 miles north of San Antonio, site of the state's most storied landmark, the Alamo. Johnson City was 14 miles east. The Hill Country was a place of extremes, a rugged, unforgiving landscape where flash floods often followed drought so severe that worried ranchers could watch the thin soil turn to dust and count the ribs of their suffering cattle. But even at its driest, the sagebrush, mesquite, and scrub cedar lining the eroded limestone ridges teemed with life: white-tailed deer and rattlesnakes, jack rabbits and horned toads, wild turkeys and armadillos. In spring, the harsh hillsides softened in the vivid tint of the wildflowers Lady Bird Johnson so much admired. Masses of bluebonnets burst through the grass and colored the fields.

"From now on, the words 'meanwhile, back at the ranch' are likely to pop up frequently in stories about America's first family," the *New York Times* observed early

For Lyndon Johnson, the LBJ Ranch on the Pedernales River in the Texas Hill Country was the one place he wanted to be when he could break free from Washington. For Lady Bird Johnson, it was "our heart's home." Johnson had acquired the farmhouse and 250 acres along the Pedernales River from an aunt in 1951, and the Johnsons lived there the rest of their lives. A doormat greeted visitors with the words "The Whole World Is Welcome Here," and a "Friendship Walk" of stepping-stones was inscribed with the names of those who came, including John F. Kennedy, who added his name in 1960.

in the Johnson administration. Presidential jets and helicopters carried LBJ home seventy-five times during the five years of his presidency, for a total of 484 days. He stayed for anywhere from two days to most of a month. He tended to remain for longer stretches in July and August and celebrated all but one of his August birthdays at the ranch. LBJ, Lady Bird, and their daughters Lynda and Luci were often home at Christmas. During the rest of the year he returned whenever he could.

Johnson also brought the yacht *Sequoia* back into presidental service and cruised the Potomac, entertaining important guests and lobbying members of Congress. He went to Camp David, mostly on weekends, twenty-nine times in all. But somehow, all of his time away from the Oval Office never became the issue it had for other recent presidents. Perhaps that was because reporters often wrote about the volume of work Johnson tackled at the ranch. Charles Mohr of the *New York Times* noted that when the president went to the ranch for the Christmas and New Year's holidays in 1964 he brought his budget director and cartons of budget documents with him. Over two weeks he met with eight of his ten cabinet members, summoned heads of the government's most important agencies, and held three news conferences. While meetings were often informal—hammocks and chairs on the patio and walks along the river—"Mr. Johnson did almost nothing but work," Mohr wrote. Pointing out the two picnic tables in the yard where he and his economic advisers had met, Johnson told reporters: "That's where I got the budget down, and a sun tan—right there." But White House business never got in the way of Johnson's love affair with the Hill Country.

"Here the sun seems to be a little brighter," said Johnson, "and the climate a little warmer, the air a little fresher and the people a little kinder and more understanding." The president was the Hill Country's greatest booster. "I'm going to show you the greatest thing you ever saw, the greatest treasure that no money in the world can buy—sunset on the Pedernales," he told guests (Texans added an "r" and pronounced it "Pur-den-alice"). Lady Bird Johnson, who called the ranch "our heart's home," could be just as effusive: "In the long twilight the big clouds come rolling up, first pink and then fading through every shade to silver gray. The katydids make the music of summer and it is the time of fireflies, especially in the grove of trees down by the river."

It was Lady Bird's business sense and enterprise, not her love of nature, that made the LBJ Ranch possible. In 1942, she dipped into a family inheritance to buy KTBC, a struggling Austin radio station, and she made it profitable. In 1949, the year Johnson eked out an 87-vote election victory and advanced from the U.S. House to the Senate, she expanded into television, eventually

President and Mrs. Johnson loved the Texas Hill Country, he for the breezes and the sunshine, she for the wildflowers. "We don't have dreariness," he said. "We don't have those dull gray skies when you look up. Here you have birds singing, flowers growing, girls smiling."

President Johnson met with his Joint Chiefs of Staff at the ranch during the 1964 Christmas holiday. The LBJ Ranch had become an international meeting spot during President Johnson's vice presidency and remained so throughout his presidency.

achieving a lucrative TV monopoly in the Austin area. KTBC became the keystone of a regional broadcasting and investment empire that made the Johnsons wealthy just as he began his rise to Senate leadership.

By the early 1950s, the Johnsons had the means to acquire, improve, and manage their own Hill Country ranch. For sentimental reasons one property was high on LBJ's list. He had spent many Christmas holidays at the two-story limestone and clapboard house on the Pedernales that belonged to his Aunt Frank (his father's sister) and her husband, Clarence Martin. He remembered hanging Christmas stockings on the stone mantel. He and his brother and their sisters had stood on

The helicopter in the distance beyond the Herefords evidences the many transportation, communication, and security requirements of the presidency that brought changes to the LBJ Ranch, much to Lady Bird Johnson's dismay. "I hardly recognized my own home," she told reporters. There were satellite dishes, cables, guard posts, a Secret Service trailer, and powerful searchlights that stabbed across the dark fields at night.

the raised hearth to recite poetry for a family audience that included his mother, Rebekah Baines Johnson, and his father, Sam Ealy Johnson Jr., once a state legislator. Decades had passed but memories remained fresh. And in 1951 his widowed aunt was aging, the ranch was unprofitable, the soil was eroded, and the house needed repair. Since his aunt was eager to move to town, they made a deal: Johnson gave her lifetime use of his family home in Johnson City and an income of $100 a month. LBJ got the ranch and named it for himself. It would take work and money to make the property—just 250 acres at the start—all he wanted it to be. But Senator Lyndon Johnson was now a rancher. Back in Washington, House Speaker Sam Rayburn told him: "Thank goodness, Lyndon, now you will have something to talk about besides the Congress."

Lady Bird's first concern was to preserve the grove of ancient live oaks and the shade they cast. Later the Johnsons expanded the house and improved the grounds, adding bedrooms, an office, a private landing strip, a hangar, barns, and a heated swimming pool. Johnson used the ranch to shape his public image as a rugged, self-made man who drew inspiration from the land of his birth, "a man who," said his biographer, "still had his roots firmly in his native soil." The senator soon invited Eastern journalists to Texas. He posed for them on horseback, waving a Stetson. He showed off his crops, cattle, prize bulls, and even his pigs. "Every man in public life should own a plot of land," he told one interviewer. Ranching grounded him. He said it linked him to the realities most Americans face.

During Johnson's presidency, the LBJ Ranch was both a working ranch and an alternative White House. It was a place where cowboys tended cattle and mended fences while officials crafted government policy and wrote speeches, both groups curiously eying—or ignoring—the other. The landing strip just behind the house buzzed with aircraft. At times Johnson used the hangar for news conferences. A homing beacon signaled incoming helicopters from its perch in the oak grove. A flick of a switch could summon popular music from speakers hidden in the spreading branches. The LBJ Ranch, said *Time* as it named President Johnson its "Man of the Year" for 1964, "is an oasis of expensive Stetson hats and tailored twill trousers, herds of sleek Herefords, Angora goats and blooded horses, a fleet of Lincolns and a landing strip with a gleaming private plane, meals of venison steak, homemade bread and pecan pies, a heated pool and Muzak piping in 'The Yellow Rose of Texas'."

Now that the ranch was a presidential command post, the government installed a communications network worthy of the White House itself, spending more than $3.5 million to create it. Three microwave towers provided 120 channels from the ranch to Austin. The White House switchboard set up shop in a trailer. Another held a communications center with teletypes, top-secret cryptographic gear, and a link to the hot line between Washington and Moscow. A chrome-plated, 50,000-watt emergency generator, originally intended for the 1964 World's Fair in New York City, provided backup in case of power failure. Underground telephone cable was installed not only at the ranch but at five other properties President Johnson owned in the Hill Country.

The telephone had become an extension of Johnson's personality long before he became president. "He could practically crawl through that [telephone] wire," said longtime aide George Reedy. Now a telephone waited wherever the president reached out a hand. There was a phone in Johnson's bathroom, one at his place at the dining room table, another at the swimming pool. Radio-telephones were installed in Johnson's many cars and in the power boats he kept at the newly named Lake Lyndon B. Johnson, a thirty-minute helicopter ride north of the ranch. An eager follower of television news, Johnson had TV sets in nearly every room, three in his bedroom alone. He wore an alarm wristwatch to alert him five minutes before the 7:00 p.m. and 11:00 p.m. evening newscasts.

On the LBJ Ranch, telephones were within easy reach wherever President Johnson happened to be, even out on Lake Johnson. Because he demanded a permanent record of conversations, recording devices were installed on phones in the bedroom and office.

Nearby roads were redesigned, including a new spur that allowed tourists to see the Johnson house from across the Pedernales but kept them at a distance. Security was strengthened with new fences and electric entry gates. Housing was provided for staff and guests. The ranch runway was paved and extended to make it long enough for small jets, although the soft soil could not support the weight of *Air Force One*. A portable control tower and the air controllers needed to staff it were brought in to handle the traffic.

From the first days of his presidency, Johnson mustered the ranch and the Hill Country into duty for policy conferences and bill signings. The president's top economic advisers sketched the underpinnings of the Great Society, the centerpiece of the new administration's antipoverty program, while huddled around the kitchen table in the ranch guest house. Education was the foundation stone of the program, and Johnson chose to sign the new Elementary and Secondary Education Act where his own education had begun, at the one-room Junction School, a short walk from the house of his birth. The LBJ Ranch also witnessed state visits and diplomatic events. A bit dismayed, Lady Bird said the ranch was "a revolving door." Planes landed on the private runway, "disgorging Cabinet members with important, difficult decisions, budget estimates, crises." Government business consumed daily life. "Visitors pour in and news pours out," she said. "And these old walls are bursting at the seams!" Through it all, she marveled, "the ranch manages to be restful to Lyndon."

On April 11, 1965, President Johnson signed the new Elementary and Secondary Education Act on a picnic table in front of the one-room school he himself had attended. "No law I have signed or will ever sign means more to the future of America," the president said, after presenting the pen he had used to his first teacher, Kathryn Deadrich Loney.

When President Johnson was at the ranch and in good spirits, he was its grandest, earthiest, most irrepressible spectacle. Most people who described the president's energy reached for the forces of nature: a one-man earthquake, a Texas whirlwind, a volcanic eruption. "Relaxing with LBJ is like getting a massage on a rollercoaster," said Liz Carpenter, a Johnson aide.

Once at the ranch, the president's Washington uniform—tailored dark suit, white shirt, conservative tie, polished city shoes—soon vanished. In its place were tooled leather boots, an open-neck khaki shirt, khaki pants, and a cream-colored "five gallon" Stetson. Clark Clifford said most of the stories about Johnson at the ranch would "sound like Texas fables" to those who did not know the president. But "for the most part, they are true."

In April 1967, President Johnson hosted the Latin American Ambassadors Weekend. He often used the LBJ Ranch as a stage for diplomatic events.

The Texas welcome provided to West German Chancellor
Ludwig Erhard (*right*) in December 1963 involved signs
reading "Willkommen" and a boisterous Texas barbecue.
White House staff passed out Western hats for the
German delegation to take home to Bonn. There had
been nothing remotely like it, *Newsweek* said, since Franklin
Roosevelt served hot dogs to the king and queen of
England at a Hyde Park picnic in 1939.

Johnson's exuberance was overflowing when he flew home in April 1964. "The cows are fat,"
He gleefully told reporters, "The grass is green. The river's full, and the fish are flopping." Then
he piled four of them into his cream-colored Lincoln Continental, gripped the steering wheel
with one hand and a cup of beer with the other, and took off in a spray of pebbles. Although the
reporters in Johnson's car considered themselves guests and the ride "off the record," *Time* pieced
together the story of what happened next.

Driving at high speed, Johnson swung into the left lane to pass two cars "and thundered on over
the crest of the hill—squarely into the path of an oncoming car," forcing it to veer violently off the
road and onto the shoulder, the news magazine said. "The president charged on, his paper cup of Pearl
beer within easy sipping distance." Still nursing his beer, the president pulled up to a cluster of cattle,
reached under the dashboard, and mashed the button of an electronic cow horn under the hood. The

President Johnson wanted people to see him as a genuine Texan and a genuine rancher, and he was glad to accommodate photographers who snapped pictures of him at work on the ranch. During a 1964 tour he held a squirming piglet (*above*). He drove trucks and rode horses to check his livestock and fields and roped his own calves (*right and below*).

heifers galloped toward the mournful sound, inspiring the president to provide what one female reporter described as "a very graphic description of the sex life of a bull." When his beer ran out, *Time* said, Johnson "took off at speeds up to 90 m.p.h. to get some more." When a passenger protested, he flopped his broad-brimmed hat over the speedometer. The magazine's conclusion: "The president may exude slow-spoken, sobersided sincerity during his public appearances in Washington. But let him get a whiff of a spring-fresh Texas range dotted with cattle and Angora goats, and suddenly he comes on like a cross between a teen-age Grand Prix driver and a back-to-nature Thoreau in cowboy boots."

President Johnson treasured an oddly varied fleet of vehicles. The collection included his Lincoln Continentals; a 1915 fire engine, a gift from a Texas town; a 1934 Ford Phaeton touring car with a steel plate underneath to prevent damage from rocks and rough ground; a Ghia Jolly 500, a gift from the Fiat motor company, which Johnson used between the ranch's outbuildings; several golf carts to ferry guests to and from their airplanes; and a small green wagon, often filled with children and pulled by a pair of donkeys named Soup and Noodles. He valued a small, light blue convertible for the way it surprised and even alarmed unsuspecting passengers. When Joseph A. Califano Jr. arrived at the ranch in July 1965 to accept the post of chief domestic adviser, Johnson took him for a ride in it. The day was hot. Califano clutched a soft drink. Johnson sipped a scotch and soda in a white plastic cup, which was periodically refilled by Secret Service agents. At the top of a steep incline, at the edge of a lake, "the car started rolling rapidly toward the water. The President shouted, 'The brakes don't work! The brakes won't hold! We're going in! We're going under!'" Califano started to scramble to safety, then stopped himself. The car was floating, and moving smoothly across the water. It was, he realized, a watertight Amphicar with controls that shifted the power from the wheels to two propellers tucked under the rear bumper. Johnson laughed and shouted at another guest: "He didn't give a damn about his President. He just wanted to save his own skin and get out of the car."

An Amphicar ride became something of an initiation rite for Johnson's Washington associates. Defense Secretary Clark Clifford said he and his wife, Marny, leaped up onto the back seat ready to swim to safety after Johnson drove the car into a lake. Even relatives were not exempt. Secret Service agent Youngblood was in the Amphicar's rear seat late one summer afternoon when Johnson took Oriole Bailey, his elderly cousin, for a spin. He headed for the ramp at the pond behind the dam on his ranch. Oriole started shouting: "Slow down! Stop! The water!" As the watertight car drifted out onto the pond, Cousin Oriole screamed, "Lyndon! You know I can't swim!"

Johnson also enjoyed driving his own boats headlong across lakes he had helped create. As a young congressman, he fostered a regional system of federally financed dams that had transformed rural life in the Hill Country by bringing inexpensive electric power to thousands of homes and ranches. Califano remembered the afternoon Johnson persuaded him to go waterskiing. "He drove faster and faster, zigging and zagging around the lake and between the concrete pillars" of a bridge, Califano recalled. "He was going so fast that I thought I'd split apart when I flew off the skis and hit the water."

After Senator Hubert H. Humphrey of Minnesota was selected as Johnson's running mate in 1964, he, too, was invited to the LBJ Ranch. Johnson soon had Humphrey clad in a tan twill Western outfit identical to his own. As shutters clicked they mounted horses and waved their Stetsons at the cameras. Humphrey got the full tour. He admired the ancient oaks at the Johnson family cemetery and got smudged with soot when he put his head inside the fireplace of the reconstructed birthplace home. Walking across a pasture,

President Johnson at the wheel of the floating Amphicar, with guests, 1965. Defense Secretary Clark Clifford was Johnson's guest for another Amphicar ride. He remembered that "Just as I was about to abandon ship, [President Johnson] turned to me and said, rather calmly, 'What's the matter Clark, are you afraid you're going to get wet?'" Then he engaged the propellers and steered the amphibious car back to shore, gleefully reciting the names of others "who had abandoned their commander-in-chief in wild jumps for safety."

Humphrey stepped on a pile of cow dung. "Mr. President, I just stepped on the Republican platform," he said. Johnson roared with laughter.

A nightly after-dinner walk down the river to the house of Cousin Oriole became part of the ritual, and lore, of a visit to the LBJ Ranch. Bailey was "a little zany lady" whom Johnson loved, and loved to tease, said Lloyd Hand, a lawyer who became Johnson's chief of protocol. "He'd just knock on her door—ten thirty, eleven at night and shout, 'Cousin Oriole, got some friends I want you to meet—come on out—no, no, you come on out here in your nightgown'." Helen Thomas of United Press International made the older woman furious when she described her house as "ramshackle" and said she had come to the door in her bare feet. "Does Helen Thomas sleep with her shoes on?" Bailey asked the president. Johnson wrote the reporter a note saying her story had made Cousin Oriole's house not only a tourist attraction but "the most famous landmark of all." His cousin, he said, now sleeps with her shoes on, so no one will ever catch her barefoot. "And after UPI referred to her house as 'ramshackle,' she's hit me up for a paint job."

Tom Wicker of the *New York Times* recalled a moonless night in 1964 with Johnson, flashlight in hand, leading the way down a path near the river. Reaching Oriole's small house, he rattled the latched screen door, rousing his cousin from bed, where she had been reading a horoscope magazine. She told him that it predicted he would be a good president—but would not be reelected. Johnson laughed, then pointed to a white telephone near the door: "Cousin Oriole, what are you doing with a White House telephone?" he asked. "They just come and put it in 'cause you're down here so much," she replied. And he joked, "Well, don't you pick that thing up if it rings. Khrushchev might answer."

———

By 1964, President Johnson had done much to make the LBJ Ranch a modern agricultural showplace. Under the day-to-day direction of 33-year-old Dale Malechek, a graduate of Texas A&M, the ranch had become "a nothing-wasted layout that almost glows with care and scientific management." Malechek said Johnson demanded "a dime's worth for every nickel he spends" and expected the enterprise to earn its own way. By then the home ranch had 438 acres, and Johnson owned, leased, or controlled more than 10,000 additional acres in Gillespie, Blanco, and Llano Counties. When the Pedernales was high, water backed up behind Johnson's dam for nearly a mile, and pumps irrigated 100 acres planted in winter oats, alfalfa, Sudan grass, and coastal Bermuda grass. Johnson fenced his pastures to allow his cattle to graze in rotation, constructed ponds for watering them, and terraced fields to prevent soil erosion. He built one of the area's first liquid fertilizer plants and had the soil analyzed to determine the correct composition of the fertilizer.

Much of this effort at scientific farming was focused on the president's herd of four hundred or so white-faced and red-bodied registered Hereford cattle, which Johnson sold as breeding stock. The best were raised as show animals and judged at local fairs and livestock shows. Johnson enjoyed pointing out the loading chute near the show barn and telling guests, "That's where the cattle go out and the money comes in." He also kept hundreds of Angora goats and Rambouillet and Columbia sheep; the goats for their mohair, the sheep for their wool and lamb chops. Pigs supplied ham, sausage, and bacon. A flock of more than two hundred hens produced eggs that sold locally in distinctive red, white, and blue cartons. A garden furnished corn, potatoes, okra, green beans, and black-eyed peas. The president often loaded sacks of fresh potatoes onto *Air Force One* and flew them back to Washington for his White House table.

Johnson claimed that "the best fertilizer for a piece of land is the footprints of its owner." It was a rule he lived by. Arriving by helicopter, he often toured the ranch before walking inside his house, inspecting cattle and barking orders to Malechek into his car radio as he drove. Lady Bird wondered what Eastern reporters, city bred for the most part, might take away from their Texas experience as they followed a president "who stops to telephone instructions to a foreman about a sick cow or a cattle guard or a fence crew or seeding a pasture." It must be, she said, "as unintelligible as Urdu to them." Johnson stayed engaged with life on the ranch even when he was back in the White House. He demanded daily weather reports by phone or telex and expected hourly updates during bad weather. Malechek learned to expect frequent and lengthy telephone calls from the White House on details of ranch operations. "He expected 110 percent 120 percent of the time," Malechek once said.

President Johnson was proud of the well-managed, profitable ranch and kept his hand in every detail, inspecting grasses (1963) and his herd of white-faced Herefords (1964).

———

The euphoria of Johnson's 1964 landslide election faded as casualties mounted in Vietnam and opposition to the war increased at home. Antiwar demonstrators protested in cities and on college

Unveiled at the ranch, the 1965 official presidential portrait by Peter Hurd (*left*) was disliked by both President and Mrs. Johnson. Lady Bird disliked the figure and the background and thought "the hands were not Lyndon's gnarled, hardworking hands." While she searched for redeeming features, the president "could find nothing good about the portrait at all." Later Hurd complained that Johnson had refused to take sufficient time to pose, that in one session he had fallen asleep and in another he was either deep in conversation with a hand obscuring his face or jumping up to pace the floor. Although the Johnsons rejected the painting and chose another for the White House, the Hurd portrait did not disappear from view. It is now part of the presidential collection of the National Portrait Gallery, Smithsonian Institution, Washington, D.C.. Herbert Block satirized Johnson's response in his 1967 cartoon, "That's a Little Better, But Couldn't You Do It in Luminous Paint?" (*right*).

campuses across the nation and at the LBJ Ranch. There, in September 1967, the president spent eight hours with John Connally, who had recently stepped down as governor of Texas, and Representative J. J. "Jake" Pickle, who held Johnson's old congressional seat. Lady Bird said they were "riding and talking about Lyndon's big decision—when and how to announce that he is not going to run again for the Presidency." Her husband, she said, wanted to devote all of his remaining time in office to bringing the war to a successful conclusion and to resolving the problems of cities hit by rioting and racial tension. Then Lady Bird offered her views: She simply did not want to face another campaign; she feared for Lyndon's health—that he might become incapacitated and unable to do his best. She ordered dinner on trays and continued talking, "trying to help my husband and two good friends decide his future." On March 31, 1968, Johnson announced his decision to the nation: "I shall not seek, and will not accept, the nomination of my party for another term as your President."

When the Democratic National Convention met in Chicago in August, its turbulent proceedings quickly became part of a televised spectacle: political turmoil, clamorous antiwar protests, and a ferocious police crackdown. Johnson spent most of the month at the ranch, hoping until nearly the last moment to fly to Chicago on—or just after—August 27, his 60th birthday, for a dramatic farewell. Although Johnson had taken himself out of the 1968 presidential race, Califano said it was apparent to aides that he "hoped, and probably anticipated" delegates would attempt to draft him as their party's candidate. He intended to turn them down, Califano said, but believed the offer would validate his presidency. Aides at the White House began to prepare a speech. The president revised drafts as they reached him at the ranch. The opening line anticipated a prolonged welcoming ovation and was ready for delivery: "For a moment there I closed my eyes and thought I was back in Atlantic City," where the Democrats had nominated him for a full term in 1964.

President Johnson tried to relax in the pool at the LBJ Ranch during the 1968 Democratic Convention, but neither his dog Yuki nor his grandson Patrick Lyndon Nugent could divert his attention. He was still hoping to be called to Chicago at the last minute.

But the news from Chicago gave those at the LBJ Ranch little hope for such a reception. On August 27, the morning of Johnson's birthday, Lady Bird told her diary that she felt the entire week had been "suspended-in-space time." She noted the speculation that her husband would fly to Chicago to make a valedictory speech and receive a birthday tribute but thought the odds were against it. Instead, the Johnsons flew to Austin and cut a one-candle birthday cake at the home of their younger daughter, Luci, as the president held his grandson, Patrick Lyndon Nugent, in his lap. Then they took the helicopter back to the ranch for another party. But all the TV sets were on and no one could pull away as the convention debated the Vietnam plank and prepared to nominate a candidate. Dinner was served buffet style with guests balancing their plates on their knees while watching the "three-ring circus" in Chicago. It had been, the first lady said, "probably as strange and dramatic, and, in a way, sad a birthday as any he will ever have."

Then it was November and the 1968 election was over. Richard M. Nixon defeated Vice President Humphrey and became the first Republican president since Dwight D. Eisenhower. The Johnsons were at the ranch for Thanksgiving. Lady Bird thought it was just about a perfect day, cool, crisp, and sunny. There had been rain and the Pedernales was splashing over Lyndon Johnson's dam. "There are green velvet patches of oats here and there, and the Spanish oak outside the picture window of the dining room is a blaze of red," she said. The Hill Country oaks were turning from red to darker burgundy.

The war in Vietnam continued. But as their guests prepared to sit down for Thanksgiving dinner, Lady Bird hoped, too optimistically as it turned out, that Vietnam was "at last maybe on the long slow way toward peace." "There are just fifty-two days left until our time in this job is over," she told her diary. "It seems like an eternity, and yet, only yesterday when it began."

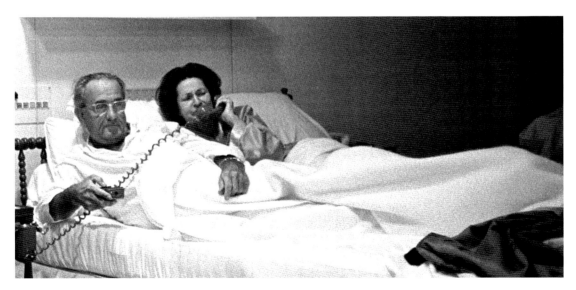

President and Mrs. Johnson watched as the 1968 Democratic Convention descended into chaos. "From afar," Lady Bird wrote in her diary, "the Convention seemed like a seething cauldron of emotions and striving cliques—of every stripe of Democrat—and hippies and yippies and police standing by."

After his term of office ended, the former president, shown here in 1972, concentrated on running the LBJ Ranch. He demanded evening reports from his hands, "I want each of you to make a solemn pledge," he told them, "that you will not go to bed tonight unless you are sure that every steer has everything he needs."

Returning to the Hill Country, this time as a private citizen, Johnson threw himself into running the LBJ Ranch, making sure his cowhands hustled, his Herefords were healthy, his chickens productive, his irrigation efficient, and his fences in good repair. He ran the ranch much as he had run the government, convening morning staff meetings to set priorities and issuing marching orders although he was now addressing just four or five cowboys, not his cabinet. He ordered Malechek and the others to write memos each evening outlining all they hoped to accomplish the next day. It was not a popular move. "Cowboys aren't very good at writing memos," said Malechek's wife, Jewell. Jokingly, but perhaps a bit wistfully, Malechek asked visitors if there was any chance Johnson might run for president again.

Although he mostly stayed away from the public arena, Johnson's eye remained fixed on his place in history. He presided over the writing of his memoirs, *The Vantage Point*, as well as the opening of his presidential library in Austin and the establishment of the Lyndon Baines Johnson School of Public Affairs at the University of Texas. In December 1972, he donated the LBJ Ranch to the National Park Service. He and Lady Bird retained the use of the house for their lifetimes, but Johnson had made sure the ranch, his reconstructed birthplace down the road, and his boyhood home in Johnson City would keep the LBJ story alive. The National Park Foundation also opened to the public the log cabin in Johnson City where his grandfather had lived in the days of the cattle drives, and it acquired the one-room Junction School that Johnson had attended when he was four years old.

The former president let his hair grow shoulder length, played with his grandchildren, rooted for University of Texas football teams, swam in his pool, and rode horseback with Lady Bird. "We can ride for hours—ride over that eroded hillside country of Texas—and be at utter peace," she said. But Johnson's heart condition worsened, and his doctors grew pessimistic. On January 22, 1973, after a morning spent inspecting fences, Johnson suffered a fatal heart attack. He was 64 years old and had been out of office for four years and two days. After lying in state at the LBJ Library and in the Rotunda of the U.S. Capitol, the thirty-sixth president was buried under the oaks in the walled family cemetery on the Pedernales where he had often walked under the big and bright stars of Texas.

For Lyndon Johnson, here c. 1915 (*right*) the Texas Hill Country was home. "It's the one place where they know if you're sick and care if you die," he said. The former president died on January 22, 1973, and was buried in the family cemetery (*opposite*) near his parents and grandparents.

Chapter 32

Richard M. Nixon: White House on the Pacific

RICHARD M. NIXON

37th President of the
United States, 1969–1974

President Richard M. Nixon
walked with his wife Pat
on a Pacific beach near San
Clemente, California, in 1971.
In 1969, Nixon purchased a
mansion in San Clemente, re-
naming the Spanish-style villa
La Casa Pacifica. The press
quickly dubbed it the Western
White House, and Nixon
promoted the idea of governing from the West Coast.
He spent as much time as he
could away from the White
House, and, following his
resignation, August 9, 1974, he
retreated to San Clemente.

Richard Nixon planted outposts of the White House at San Clemente on California's Pacific Coast and at Key Biscayne, a coral island in Florida's warm waters. He visited the presidential mountaintop at Camp David more frequently than any president before him, treasuring its solitude and freedom from interruption. He used all of his retreats as places to think out the problems of war and peace, and to make what he called "the great decisions," often with a fire crackling in the fireplace and his Irish setter, King Timahoe, stretched out at his feet.

The serenity Nixon found at these retreats contrasted sharply with the tumult and tensions of the times. His first term saw his diplomatic opening to China and the pursuit of detente with the Soviet Union. The war he had inherited continued in Southeast Asia. So did massive antiwar protests near the White House and on college campuses across the country. Seeking to bring North Vietnam to the bargaining table and to achieve what he called "peace with honor," Nixon intensified bombing raids and expanded the conflict into Cambodia and Laos. Lengthy and fitful negotiations spanned his first term and resulted in a January 1973 agreement for the withdrawal of U.S. combat forces from South Vietnam.

As Nixon's second term began and the Watergate scandal consumed the nation, he sought the privacy of his retreats so often that some accused him of isolating himself from reality. He moved restlessly from one retreat to another, a study in perpetual motion. In September 1973, *Time* cited reports that the president had spent only one night out of every three in his official residence since entering the White House more than four years earlier. "For a man who spent most of his adult life struggling to get to the White House, and much time after his re-election struggling to stay in the White House, it was ironic how little Nixon liked to spend his time there," said William Safire, a Nixon speechwriter who became a *New York Times* columnist.

Nixon said it was meaningless to count his days away from the Executive Mansion because the office and its responsibilities moved with him. Getting away, he said, helped him "to change the pace, to rest the mental muscles used for work and exercise others." But some wondered if Nixon's Watergate troubles hadn't stemmed in part from his frequent absences. The president had spent so much time "thinking great thoughts on a mountain top," wrote Safire, that he had lost touch with the day-to-day management of the government.

No matter how often Nixon traveled, those closest to him said he found it difficult to relax. When Nixon visited Key Biscayne and San Clemente he was "band-box crisp and pointedly presidential." "He's the kind of guy who wears shoes on the beach," the photographer Ollie Atkins said. Nixon all but abandoned golf because of the time each game consumed. He bowled occasionally, both at the White House and at Camp David. He played the piano when the mood struck. He swam and boated with friends in Florida and the Bahamas. He enjoyed a

President Nixon read by the pool at La Casa Pacifica in 1971, but he was not relaxing. According to his speech writer, James Keogh, when he rests "he's resting to work; when he reads, he's reading to work; when he's relaxing, he's relaxing to prepare himself to work."

movie in the evenings. At times he was joined by his wife, Patricia, their daughters, Julie and Tricia, and their husbands, David Eisenhower and Ed Cox. But he often went away to be alone with a fire flickering in the fireplace, analyzing problems and writing notes on an endless supply of yellow legal pads.

Nixon, observed *New York Times* columnist James Reston in 1970, travels "with more support troops than most armies" but remains an essentially lonely and private man: "He goes away but never gets away." "What do we do with him?" H. R. Haldeman, chief of staff, asked: "He knows he needs to relax, so he comes down to Florida. He likes to swim, so he swims for 10 minutes. Then that's over. He doesn't paint. He doesn't horseback ride. He doesn't have a hobby. His best relaxation is talking shop, but he knows he should not be doing that because that doesn't seem to be relaxing. So what do we do with him?"

Quiet Key Biscayne, a coral island rimmed by sandy beaches, shaded from the Florida sun by coconut palms, and linked to Miami by a long causeway, had been explored by Spanish conquistador Juan Ponce de León in 1513. Richard Nixon discovered Key Biscayne after his election to the Senate in 1950, invited there by Senator George Smathers, a Florida Democrat. Smathers also introduced him to Bebe Rebozo, a local banker and real estate

President Nixon's compound in Key Biscayne, Florida, began with the purchase in 1969 of two waterfront houses next door to his close friend and confidante Charles "Bebe" Rebozo. The compound came to be known as the Florida White House, or the Winter White House, As with the Western White House, the government made a significant investment in security for Key Biscayne.

investor. Long before Nixon won the White House in 1968, Rebozo had become his closest friend and Key Biscayne his most frequent vacation destination. After the election, Nixon purchased two small houses next door to Rebozo, visiting more than fifty times during his presidency.

Charles G. "Bebe" Rebozo, the son of a Cuban immigrant cigar maker, had profited from Florida's land boom after a long string of jobs, including airline steward, filling station operator, and tire salesman. By the 1960s he had large real estate holdings, ran a chain of coin laundries, and was the largest stockholder in the Key Biscayne Bank. "Nixon has always found it effortless to be with Rebozo," said presidential aide John Ehrlichman, adding that Rebozo made no requests or demands, was totally loyal, and "does not gossip." Rebozo and Nixon took long, often silent, walks on the beach, listened to show tunes, and watched football games on television. "We do some fishing, some swimming and a lot of sunbathing," Rebozo once said of their cruises on his boat, *Cocolobo*. "We work, too. Dick takes his brief case and I take mine."

Once at Key Biscayne, Nixon was not always content to stay there. By the early fall of 1973 he was reported to have made twenty-one side trips to Grand Cay, the 125-acre island in the Bahamas owned by Robert Abplanalp, a friend and political supporter whose invention of the aerosol spray valve had made him a multimillionaire. Government money provided a reliable communications system, but Abplanalp said later he spent $1 million of his own money to upgrade and secure the island for his presidential guest.

The security at Key Biscayne was impressive. The government soon leased two adjoining houses, one for a communications center, the other as a Secret Service command post. Together with Rebozo's house, they formed a compound, secured by an iron fence and surrounded by an 11-foot hedge. A Secret Service gatehouse guarded the drive into the compound. Loudspeakers

This Key Biscayne sunset seen from the Nixon compound. "While he was in his lofty retreats conceiving the grand designs for East-West détente and for revenue sharing, the people he left in charge of the White House were running amuck," observed *Time* columnist Hugh Sidey.

President Nixon and his friend Bebe Rebozo walked the boat ramp at the Kay Biscayne Yacht Club following a cruise aboard the yacht *Julie*, March 8, 1969. The president's daughter, for whom the yacht was named, thought of Rebozo as a favorite uncle.

317

Julie Nixon Eisenhower and her husband David Eisenhower fished at Key Biscayne on May 22, 1971. She remembered Key Biscayne's slow pace as idyllic. "A perfect day," she wrote, "was reading in deck chairs . . . a morning swim, always a walk on the beach, and finished with one of Bebe's delicious steak and Cuban black-bean dinners." The island, she said, "remained half wild mango groves, half modest one-story homes, each with its yard of thick emerald-green grass."

hidden in the hedges warned those who approached too closely. Electronic sensors were ready to detect intruders. A new helicopter pad made arrivals and departures more secure. Bulletproof glass was installed in the Nixon houses, and security lights were added on the grounds. A shark net was rigged to protect the president when he swam.

Pat Nixon found security at Key Biscayne so confining she frequently chose not to accompany the president when he visited. "Guards sat in straight-backed striped beach chairs on either side of and in between our two modest-sized houses on Biscayne Bay and got into the water with us whenever we swam with my father," Julie said. And because the yards were small, "one had to speak softly or the guards could not help but hear the conversations."

One conversation at Key Biscayne did not involve the president or any member of the Nixon family. But it was clearly not meant to be overheard. On March 30, 1972, former Attorney General John Mitchell, vacationing a few doors from the Nixon compound, reviewed thirty decision papers prepared for the Committee to Re-Elect the President (later nicknamed CREEP), which Mitchell now headed. They had been delivered by Mitchell's deputy director, Jeb Stuart Magruder, until recently a White House aide. Some were routine: a direct-mail program and an advertising strategy. The last item on the agenda was a plan for political espionage drafted by G. Gordon Liddy, the reelection committee's security coordinator and counsel of its finance committee. The plan was code-named "Operation Gemstone."

What happened next was later disputed even by those who were in the room. Magruder said in a published account that they discussed the proposal for about ten minutes, with everyone expressing doubts. "We feared that it might be a waste of money, and also that it might be dangerous," he recalled. But in the end, a scaled-down version was approved. It was

In the living room at Key Biscayne, President Nixon entertained (left to right) Bebe Rebozo, FBI Director J. Edgar Hoover, and Secretary of State William P. Rogers, in December 1971.

agreed that Liddy would go ahead with wiretapping phones in the offices of the Democratic National Committee. The mission would involve a break-in at party headquarters in the Watergate complex overlooking the Potomac River.

More than three months later, on June 18, Nixon and Rebozo returned from a weekend on Abplanalp's island. Lying on a kitchen counter was a copy of the Sunday *Miami Herald* with this headline: "Miamians Held in D.C.—Try to Bug Demo Headquarters." "I scanned the opening paragraphs," Nixon said in his memoirs. "Five men, four of them from Miami, had been arrested in the Democratic National Committee headquarters at the Watergate, a fashionable hotel, office and apartment complex in Washington. . . . I dismissed it as some sort of prank."

The next day, when Nixon boarded *Air Force One* for an evening flight to Washington, "The Watergate break-in was still the furthest thing from my mind," he asserted. But there had been developments. Haldeman told him investigators had discovered links between the arrested burglars and the president's re-election committee. Nixon said he hoped none of his people were involved because the break-in was "stupid" and politically pointless. But the story continued to unfold. Soon newspapers had a name for it: "Watergate."

———

At Camp David, Nixon could board a golf cart at the helipad, roll past the moss-green cabins sheltered under the trees, and pull up at Aspen Lodge where a fire burned, even in warm weather. In the crisp air of fall evenings, white clouds of steam rose from the president's heated swimming pool. On winter mornings the long view from the lodge windows surveyed miles of leafless trees, sometimes sheathed in ice and gleaming in the sun.

For Nixon, Camp David was a decompression chamber, less than thirty minutes by helicopter from the South Lawn of the White House, but it felt farther away. "The Camp David air smells different," said William Safire. "There you are on top of a mountain, closer to God or whatever it is that moves people about mountaintops." Nixon was clearly captivated

President Nixon said that after a weekend in wooded seclusion at Camp David, "I came back the next week with a totally new perspective and renewed energy."

by the lofty isolation of the place. "I find that up here on top of a mountain it is easier for me to get on top of the job," he told reporters. At Camp David, he said, a president could "think objectively with perception about the problems he has to make decisions on."

Nixon wrote many of his major speeches in the quiet of Camp David, ordering the air conditioning turned up in hot weather so he could have a fire as he worked. He made key choices there about the war in Southeast Asia, relations with the Soviet Union, the course of the American economy, and his own defense in the Watergate crisis. During five and a half years as president, Nixon visited Camp David constantly, 149 times by October 1973. That was three times the number of visits Eisenhower had made during eight years in office. In the first ten months of 1972, President Nixon flew to Camp David thirty-four times, staying for a total of sixty-four days, according to newspaper reports. He was there mostly on weekends but at times for as long as two weeks.

Camp David was where President Nixon often focused on the choices he faced and the direction of his administration. White House aides provided him with black-bound notebooks that set out opposing views and offered options. "In general," explained Nixon's policy coordinator John Ehrlichman, "he works best off the written page."

Roosevelt had named the mountain hideaway Shangri-La, and Dwight

Eisenhower renamed it for his grandson, David. But when Nixon's presidential limousine first rolled through the gates after his inauguration he found the name on the sign outside had reverted to an even older designation: "Camp Three." Since Nixon's daughter Julie had married David Eisenhower, Nixon had a family connection to the name Ike had chosen. He spoke with the camp commander, and by sundown the words "Camp David" were again displayed outside the gate.

The first lady found security inside Camp David far less irritating than at her husband's other retreats. "All day we walked and bowled and swam and walked some more. Even in light rain or on bitter cold days, we were outdoors," Julie remembered. In the evenings the lights would be dimmed in Aspen's living room and movies shown. Nixon liked historical epics: *War and Peace*, *A Man for All Seasons*, *Young Winston*. He could always watch *Carousel* and *South Pacific*. Aides said he had watched *Around the World in Eighty Days* so many times he knew every scene and every line of dialogue. "Working until five, an hour's swim, a movie, and to bed—that was a Nixon Camp David day," Safire said.

At Camp David, President Nixon often was often joined by King Timahoe, his Irish setter. After the dog balked at boarding the presidential helicopter, he made the trip in the backseat of a White House car, arriving two hours or so after the president.

Although five previous chief executives had used Camp David as a hideaway, Haldeman found it insufficiently "presidential." There was at least some justification: a study found some cabins had deteriorated from age and termite and water damage. Haldeman essentially ordered the place rebuilt. In the six months after Nixon's 1969 inauguration most of the buildings from FDR's era were replaced or renovated. Aspen Lodge, FDR's "Bear's Den," became a well-decorated, luxurious house. Laurel Lodge was rebuilt with a paneled conference room and staff dining room. One rebuilt cabin, New Maple, had a large living room with a fieldstone fireplace, vaulted ceiling, and a glass wall overlooking a patio. Nixon moved his offices into a new, three-room lodge called Birch. "It was designed with

President Nixon hosted eleven foreign officials at Camp David, including the leaders of the Soviet Union and Great Britain. On June 20, 1973, his guest was Soviet General Secretary Leonid Brezhnev.

In April 1973, President Nixon summoned his two closest aides, H. R. Haldemen (left) and John Ehrlichman (third from left) to Camp David and told them they must resign. In this photo, from May 13, 1970, they consult with him in the Oval Office.

an air-conditioning system that makes it possible for him to keep a log fire burning, even in summer," wrote Maxine Cheshire of the *Washington Post*. Building the heated swimming pool proved unexpectedly expensive, as the site was immediately above Orange One, the presidential bomb shelter. Once called rustic, Camp David became an exclusive recreational preserve with first-class accommodations. "It's like a resort hotel where you are the only guests," Tricia once said. Safire groused that the Nixon-Haldeman refinements had gone too far. "A hideaway should be a hideaway, not a Catoctin Hilton," he said. "And Nixon's building program up there smacked of the sumptuous spreads of the nouveau riche. FDR, born to wealth, appreciated rusticity; Nixon, born poor, appreciated a heated swimming pool right out front."

As the president's Watergate troubles intensified and Nixon spent more time at Camp David, the security measures—the double row of fences topped with concertina wire, the armed Marines, the guard dogs—made some visitors acutely uncomfortable. Nixon's aide Charles Colson compared Camp David to a secret hideaway in a James Bond movie and told a colleague he could hardly wait to leave: "I feel like I'm being watched all the time, guards everywhere, even hiding behind trees."

By the early summer of 1974, Nixon knew that he could be heard on an audiotape, recorded one week after the Watergate burglary, in which he instructed Haldeman to order the CIA to intervene and halt the FBI's Watergate investigation. The tape would later be called "the smoking gun," evidence that Nixon had ordered a cover-up. The president refused to make that tape and many others public on grounds of executive privilege. As the Supreme Court was deciding whether Nixon could refuse to release the tapes on grounds of executive privilege, Nixon walked a "very muddy" nature trail at Camp David. Then he returned to his study to dictate an entry in his diary on "the unbelievable battle in which we are engaged." The thing to do, he concluded, "is to just treat every day as basically the last one and not to be constantly concerned about what may happen in the future." Then he added one more thought: "We simply have to stick it out."

———

Once past the screen of shrubs and trees, the heavy gate, and the uniformed guards, some visitors to Richard Nixon's Western White House at San Clemente were struck by its air of sheer perfection: flawlessly trimmed trees, lawns and gardens, blooming roses, efficient staff, gleaming limousines and helicopters. The centerpiece was La Casa Pacifica, the president's Spanish-style villa with a red-tiled roof, a fountain splashing in the central courtyard, and a memorable view of the Pacific Ocean through the royal palms. "You sense that you have left one world and entered another," said Magruder, remembering his first visit.

The perfection that impressed Magruder had been created in an urgent and expensive burst of activity during the three months before Nixon's first visit in the late summer of 1969. Even

as the government installed shark nets, bulletproof glass, a helipad, and a communications system at Nixon's houses at Key Biscayne, it was doing much the same at the Western White House, only on a larger scale. Nixon and his aides justified the effort as broadening the perspective of the presidency. "Government is not an exclusively Eastern institution," Nixon aide Herb Klein told reporters. "The San Clemente operation gives Westerners a symbolic share in the business of government, . . . unifying the nation." Henry Kissinger said that since Nixon "insisted that he never took vacations," moving the working White House to the West Coast was a way of justifying his stays there.

La Casa Pacifica sat atop a 75-foot bluff overlooking the Pacific on the southern edge of San Clemente, an Orange County community of some 17,000 residents located midway between San Diego and Los Angeles. The fourteen-room house occupied a 5.9-acre parcel, part of a larger 26-acre tract. The president's study was reachable only by a staircase from the central courtyard. Wide windows overlooked the ocean. A working fireplace, a must in any working space Nixon used, was set into a wall. Offices at the Western White House were located in a pair of single-story prefabricated buildings erected at a former Coast Guard radar station next to the president's estate; soon its grounds, too, were bright with flowers. Nixon and three top aides had offices in Building A, each with patios and expansive ocean views. Building B, just to the east, held a conference room, dining room, and staff and secretarial

President Nixon commuted between his villa and office compound at San Clemente by golf cart. Cushman golf carts were highly valued and jealously guarded status symbols among his inner circle. The president's was known as "Cushman One."

An aerial view of the Western White House. Watergate struck many as murky intrigue, but outlays of tax dollars on private homes were easy to grasp. Journalist Dan Cordtz wrote in a much-quoted 1973 *Fortune* magazine article that "the contrast between the typical homeowner's need to economize and the open-handed expenditure of tax funds on the San Clemente estate is too striking for anyone to miss."

offices. The villa and the office compound were about 400 yards apart, separated by cypress trees and a high white wall. The president commuted by golf cart, often with King Timahoe as a passenger.

La Casa Pacifica was Nixon's anchor in his native southern California, a symbol of how far he had risen beyond the limited world he had known as a boy. His father's modest frame house still stood at Yorba Linda, a short drive away. The gas station his family had operated was in the nearby town of Whittier, as was Whittier College, his alma mater. So was the hotel where he had been chosen to run as a Republican candidate for Congress at the beginning of his political career. Watching and listening as Nixon conducted a driving tour of these places in the summer of 1970, Kissinger saw the president in a new light. "The Nixon in the backseat was not the convoluted, guarded, driven politician I knew from the Oval Office, but a gentler man, simpler in expression, warmer in demeanor," he said.

Nixon's San Clemente villa had been built in 1926 by a wealthy California real estate developer. When they first saw it more than forty years later, the house struck the president's daughters as musty. But Pat Nixon had the dark woodwork painted over. With new carpets and wallpaper, wrote Julie, "Each room was light and beautiful."

Although the estate was elegant and serene, there were reminders of the fretful world outside. The Marine Corps trained recruits for combat in Vietnam at Camp Pendleton, just south of San Clemente. "Nightly, along with the steady pound of waves, we could hear clearly the sound of gunfire and shelling," Julie recalled. Other reminders of the war marched right up to the gates. Antiwar protests were staged nearly every time Nixon visited. While most attracted one hundred or fewer people, some drew as many as 5,000. The *Washington Post* reported in December 1973 that there had been three dozen San Clemente demonstrations over the previous five years.

In June a visit by Soviet leader Leonid Brezhnev gave Nixon a respite. The burly Soviet leader was placed in Tricia's room, a bower of delicate white-wicker furniture with a wallpaper garden of pink, blue, and lavender flowers. "It was amusing to picture a bear of a man like Brezhnev ensconced amid such feminine decor," Nixon recalled. Hollywood turned out for an afternoon cocktail party on the patio adjoining the pool. A mariachi band played as some 175 guests sipped margaritas and filled small plates with snow crab claws, shish kebab, and guacamole salad. Standing in line for a Brezhnev handshake were Frank Sinatra and former Hollywood actor Ronald Reagan, at the time California's Republican governor.

During the next year, the Western White House struggled to project a business-as-usual image despite the clamor in Washington. Reporters were swamped with the routine announcements and appointments while aides had little or nothing to say about the Watergate investigation. The *Wall Street Journal* called it the

Under First Lady Pat Nixon's redecorating scheme, the living room at San Celemente became a sunny yellow with white-beamed ceilings, gold carpets, and a blue-tiled fireplace. But visitors were most impressed by the view of the ocean, framed by three long, arched windows.

On June 24, 1973, President Nixon and Leonid Brezhnev signed a joint communiqué at La Casa Pacifica following the Soviet general secretary's official visit to the United States. The communiqué addressed the general state of U.S.-Soviet relations, arms limitation, and the reduction of international tensions generally.

"we're-too-busy-for-Watergate ploy." But Kissinger was struck by the president's faraway look and the "frozen melancholy" of his features.

Shortly after 8:30 a.m. on Wednesday, July 24, 1974, bells rang on the AP and UPI news tickers in Building B of the presidential compound. Voting 8 to 0, the Supreme Court had ordered the president to surrender the tapes of sixty-four conversations subpoenaed by the Watergate special prosecutor. "As details of the decision came in, it was clear to everyone that it left him no course other than to comply," said his speechwriter Raymond Price. Early that afternoon Nixon asked Price over to the house to discuss an economics speech. He found the president in his second-floor study, the windows framing the blue Pacific. The president

During Brezhnev's visit to La Casa Pacifica, he and President Nixon met in the library. The Senate Watergate Committee postponed scheduled testimony by one week so that the president could host Brezhnev's visit to San Clemente.

Frank Sinatra with the Nixons at the Western White House. The Nixons hosted parties for both Hollywood celebrities and political figures. One party, in honor of Leonid Brezhnev, was attended by singer Burl Ives, Gene Autry, Frank Sinatra, radio comedian Edgar Bergan, singer Pat Boone, comedian Red Skelton, and movie stars Rosalind Russell, Barbara Stanwyck, and Glenn Ford. When the irrepressible Skelton asked Brezhnev if he was a "card-carrying Communist," Brezhnev laughed, pumped Skelton's hand, and admitted he was.

struck the speechwriter as subdued, downcast. Nixon said prospects in the House were now shaky. "He remarked that there were going to be some rough days ahead, and we had all better be prepared for some setbacks."

———

The Watergate investigation opened the floodgates to many separate inquiries, including a close look at the money spent by the government at Nixon's private retreats. Not in all the decades since Theodore Roosevelt moved summertime White House operations to Oyster Bay had government outlays on presidential vacations and out-of-town hideaways been so rigorously and suspiciously examined.

Press reports the previous year revealed that Nixon had acquired and improved the $1.4 million estate with the help of $625 thousand in loans from his two best friends, millionaires Bebe Rebozo and Robert Abplanalp. He then sold most of the property to a holding company owned by Abplanalp, retaining the house and the 5.9 acres surrounding it. While some called the transaction "a sweetheart loan," *Time* said the audit buttressed White House claims that nothing illegal had occurred, but it did raise questions about the propriety of a president becoming so obligated to anyone, including his friends. At the same time, pressured by investigators and journalists, the General Services Administration made a series of disclosures regarding government expenditures at San Clemente and Key Biscayne. When the White House stated that $39,525 had been spent on security-related projects at San Clemente, reporters checked local building permits and discovered more than $100,000 in construction costs. GSA reported $456,352, then $703,367 for the Western White House and $1,180,322 at Key Biscayne. A final GSA accounting set the spending total at nearly $10 million for both properties, the great majority of it for communications, executive offices, and security. Adding in salaries, travel expenses, and routine maintenance, the House Government Operations Committee upped the total to $17.1 million, an

On June 13, 1971, National Security Adviser Henry Kissinger, just returned from a mission to Beijing, briefed President Nixon and Secretary of State William P. Rogers at Nixon's home in San Clemente.

The Nixons welcome California Senator George Murphy and California Governor and Mrs. Reagan to dinner at the Western White House.

outlay of more than the combined salaries of all U.S. presidents.

Price claimed "they were the routine costs of operating the presidency away from Washington," like the costs incurred at the LBJ Ranch in Texas, Eisenhower's Gettysburg farm, and the Kennedy compound at Hyannis Port. But the spending on Nixon's presidential retreats hit a public nerve. Julie said her mother believed "that nothing hastened the turning of public opinion against the Nixon presidency more than the suggestion of profiting at the taxpayers' expense." "And there was no denying," she continued, "that the Nixons' life-style had benefited from the by-now routine perks." Business journalist Dan Cordtz concluded, "The deliberate expansion of presidential benefits tends to confirm and reinforce a monarchial vision of the office," making it harder for the president to "avoid the appearance of enriching himself at the taxpayers' expense."

Nixon tried to avoid that appearance. "Unfortunately," he said, "the American people have been misled into believing that the funds for the office complex were spent on my home." Then he announced that he and the first lady would give La Casa Pacifica to the American people "at the time of my death or that of my wife, whichever is later." The house could be used as a conference center, guesthouse for visiting foreign leaders, or West Coast base for future presidents. Such uses, he said, would "help maintain a truly national perspective for the Presidency."

By August 1974, Nixon's long battle to stay in office was nearly over. The court-ordered disclosure of his tape-recorded conversations tied him to the cover-up. The House Judiciary Committee had approved three articles of impeachment. His support in the Senate had evaporated. On August 9, 1974, Nixon resigned the presidency and flew to California. La Casa Pacifica became his full-time home. He was there a month later when President Gerald Ford, saying he hoped to move his new administration beyond Watergate, issued Nixon a full pardon for any crimes he may have committed.

In his time away from the
White House, President
Nixon sought not relaxation
or entertainment but seclusion. In August 1971, he stood
alone on the beach at San
Clemente.

Nearly five years later, in the spring of 1979, Nixon sold La Casa Pacifica to a group of Orange County investors, reopening the question of his promise to give his estate to the nation and opening a new round in the old dispute over whether government spending at his retreats had been excessive. That September, he wrote a $2,300 check to cover the cost of the flagpole the government had installed at La Casa Pacifica. Everything else, he said, had been "requested by the U.S. Secret Service for security purposes and the expenditures were approved by the appropriate congressional committees."

President Nixon died in April 1994 and is buried beside his wife Pat on the grounds of the Richard Nixon Library and Birthplace, in Yorba Linda, California. The site is open to visitors.

Chapter 33

Gerald R. Ford: Downhill Skier

GERALD R. FORD
38th President of the
United States, 1974–1977

S now matted the president's eyebrows. His cheeks were windblown and ruddy. His breath rose in plumes in the cold air, 12 degrees below zero. Slightly winded, he snowplowed to a halt and managed a brief report: The skiing had been "super!" The snow, "just perfect!" The mountain scenery, "absolutely gorgeous!" It was Christmas Day, 1974. Gerald R. Ford, president for little more than four months, had just completed his second 2-mile run down Simba Trail on Colorado's Vail Mountain, elevation 11,250 feet. The sky was clear blue; the sun bright. Thirty inches of dry and crusty new snow covered the ground and wrapped the firs and lodgepole pines. To one dazzled White House reporter it looked "like a coat of marshmallow frosting, with diamond sparkles in it."

Others were equally impressed with the new president's style on the slopes. The 61-year-old skier rocked back on his heels at the turns, taking them as swiftly and aggressively as if he were competing in a downhill race. "He constantly shoves himself faster," one reporter wrote. A boyhood friend from Grand Rapids called the president "the kind of guy who likes to get up early, stay out late and just ski the hell out of that mountain." The president's ski instructor summed up: "When he goes out there, let me tell you, he's all for skiing. He goes and goes and goes. He has excellent control. He doesn't fall down much. . . . I classify him as a good recreational skier."

Although Ford would leave office saddled with a reputation as an accident-prone bumbler, few who knew him disagreed when *U.S. News and World Report* called him the most athletic of the nation's thirty-eight chief executives. *Time* echoed that, describing Ford as "the most strenuously physical man to occupy the White House since Teddy Roosevelt." A high school and university football star, Ford was the first skiing president. He enjoyed tennis. He was easily the most zealous presidential golfer since Dwight D. Eisenhower. His devotion to swimming prompted private donors to build an outdoor pool at the White House.

Jerry Ford's competitive spirit remained alive after Michigan voters sent him to Congress in 1948 and as he rose to become House Republican leader. But by 1972, with Democrats in firm control of Congress, it seemed unlikely he would ever achieve his highest ambition: election by a Republican majority as Speaker of the House. He promised his wife, Betty, he would run once more and then retire when his term ended in 1977. But Ford's life changed abruptly in October 1973: Spiro Agnew resigned as vice president and President Richard M. Nixon nominated the popular Michigan congressman to replace him.

Ten months later, on August 9, 1974, a day heavy with heat, humidity, and history, Gerald and Betty Ford grimly watched as Nixon walked across the White House's South Lawn to a waiting helicopter. Nixon turned, forced a smile, and gave his familiar two-armed, V-sign wave. Then the thirty-seventh president's era ended in a whirl of rotor blades. With Nixon's resignation, Ford became America's first unelected chief executive. Ford's new beginning generated rave reviews. Journalists rated the new president as genial, low-key, unassuming, and open. *Time* found that good

President Gerald R. Ford, seen here on the slopes in Vail, Colorado, was a good skier, "by far the most athletic president within memory," claimed his press secretary, Ron Nessen.

sense had returned to the Oval Office and summed up in a headline: "Off to a Fast, Clean Start."

The honeymoon lasted barely a month. On September 8, 1974, Ford granted Nixon a full and unconditional pardon. Ford explained that he wanted to move the country out of the shadow of Watergate, which he had earlier called "our long national nightmare." He explained that he wanted to avoid the "ugly passions" and polarization of public opinion that would be stirred during a prolonged effort to bring the former president to trial. But many Americans thought the pardon short-circuited the legal process. *Time* told readers that Ford had undermined "efforts to restore confidence in the presidency and opened his own credibility gap." The president's approval ratings in national public opinion polls dropped by 21 points.

The Ford administration was struggling to regain lost momentum when the president reached Colorado for a winter holiday. Ford was in his best form, "skimming the powder" with ease, *Newsweek* observed. But another news magazine noted that he faced serious problems when he returned to the Oval Office, including an energy crisis and high inflation. A Gallup poll issued during Ford's vacation pegged his approval rating at 42 percent. Some newspaper editorials suggested it was a poor time for a vacation. Ford told reporters on *Air Force One* that while he needed a break he planned to work at least half the time while at Vail.

The Ford family had been Vail regulars for eight seasons by the time the former Michigan congressman became president. Susan Ford, his 17-year-old daughter, considered the annual trek to Vail absolutely "mandatory." The excursion would not be canceled or curtailed just because her father had become president: "We were still going to do that. We weren't going to stay in Washington. We were still going to go skiing."

Vail won its place on the family agenda, Ford told an interviewer, because his children, Susan and her three brothers, Michael, Jack, and Steven, were bored with midwestern skiing and eager for more challenging terrain. "They were all good skiers, better than their old man," Ford remembered. And Vail was not only a premier ski resort but also "a great place to develop family solidarity." Asked for a Vail word picture his daughter had an instant response: "Cold. Fun. Usually great skiing. Christmas. Lots of laughs. Lots of family laughs."

The Ford family had taken skiing vacations in Vail for years before Gerald Ford became president. They were often there at Christmastime. In 1974, First Lady Betty Ford and her friends Sheika Gramshammer (left) and Gloria Brown (right) enjoyed a laugh on a Christmas Eve a shopping trip.

Framed by mountains at an altitude of 8,200 feet, the town and resort of Vail spreads out along Gore Creek Valley in west-central Colorado about 100 miles west of Denver. Vail had boomed since its founding in 1962. With cars banned from its narrow walking streets, it had become a Rocky Mountain version of an alpine ski village with echoes of Bavaria, Switzerland, and Austria in its architecture. Chairlifts and gondolas ran up Vail Mountain, linking the village to miles of ski runs. But some reporters, waiting for Ford in frigid temperatures, called the place "Ski Biscayne" and developed an acute nostalgia for Nixon's warm-weather retreats. "Why couldn't he be a bowling nut?" one shivering correspondent griped. Most agreed that Vail was no "Winter White House" in the way Nixon's residential and office complex at San Clemente had been the Western White House. Local businesses voted to sell no presidential souvenirs when Ford asked that his presence be kept as quiet as possible.

The Ford family had purchased a three-bedroom, three-bath Vail condominium in May 1970 when Ford was House Republican leader. They used it over the Christmas holidays in 1973 when Ford was vice president. Now, however, the Secret Service found itself unable to provide presidential-level security for a third-floor

President Ford was interviewed by UPI reporter Helen Thomas, December 26, 1974, at the Basshaus, where he and his family were spending a two-week vacation.

apartment on a busy street. The search for more secure quarters resulted in a house swap. The Ford family spent their 1974 holiday in a four-story cedar chalet with a rock foundation and turquoise trim. It offered spectacular mountain views and a new enclosed and heated swimming pool. The owner, Richard Bass, a Dallas oil millionaire and ski-resort developer, moved his family into the Ford condominium and Ford paid $75 a day in rent differential. Basshaus, as Betty Ford called it, was located on an easily secured cul-de-sac a short walk from Gondola Number 1, the main ski lift up Vail Mountain. The government rented the houses on either side, using one as a Secret Service command post and the other as a guesthouse for administration officials.

Compared with the more modest family condo, Susan Ford considered the Bass ski lodge "the lap of luxury, a really nice house." A granite fireplace reached up and through the living room's 29-foot beamed ceiling. The room was comfortably stocked with sofas and chairs and ready for a party or an informal business meeting. The house had seven bedrooms and seven baths, a piano, a sauna, mounted deer heads on the walls, a bearskin rug in the study, and at least five cords of firewood stacked outside. But the *New York Times* wrote that the rented house at Vail seemed "quite austere" compared with Nixon's retreats in Florida and California.

Communications lines were run all over Vail, connecting the president's ski chalet with the White House. Ford could be reached on the slopes through Secret Service, police, and ski patrol

President Ford and assistant Donald Rumsfeld huddled over bills during a work session in Vail, December 24, 1974. The president's two-week family vacation was for him a working holiday. He signed fifteen bills into law and vetoed two.

frequencies. He noted in his memoirs that even though he was far from Washington, presidential pressures were never far behind. When Donald Rumsfeld, then the White House chief of staff, appeared with paperwork and a meeting schedule, Ford announced his arrival with a mock complaint: "Rumsfeld has a lot of work for me." "Scrooge came with Santa Claus," he continued, citing Rumsfeld. Ford's staff estimated that presidential duties took up more than half of the president's holiday time, including sessions with energy and economic advisers. Susan Ford witnessed cabinet meetings at the dining room table and saw a lot of work going on. But she thought the change of

In Vail, President Ford wore this red, white, and blue Norwegian-style gift sweater. It had the acronym WIN repeated in its design, for Whip Inflation Now, the motto of the administration's anti-inflation campaign.

location was important: "He could get out and ski for a couple of hours and go back to work."

Vail was no place for three-piece suits. Reporters described one of Ford's ski parkas as "fluorescent orange," while another parka sported "Flash Gordon black and yellow streaks." At work, with a fire crackling in the stone fireplace, Ford wore turtleneck sweaters, plaid trousers, and moccasins. At Vail, observed the *Washington Post*'s Carroll Kilpatrick, "it's strictly thermal underwear, heavy boots, turtleneck sweaters and parkas whether one is working, skiing or partying."

The informality extended to church and to the president's contacts with reporters. Rather than push his way through a crowd at the Vail chapel on Christmas Eve to claim his front-row pew, Ford simply stood in the back. Most reporters had rarely seen or spoken to Nixon at Key Biscayne or San Clemente. At Vail all one had to do was dress warmly and wait for Ford to ski by. Kilpatrick's conclusion: No presidential holiday had been as relaxed, open, or good humored since Harry Truman vacationed at Key West.

———

Ford acknowledged that his aggressive style on the slopes made an occasional spill inevitable. He enjoyed trying new runs and noted that one friend, a highly skilled skier, "was always giving me the devil for trying to ski in rugged places." But when he returned to Vail for another skiing vacation in December 1975, he arrived burdened with a reputation for trips and stumbles. It got its start in May 1975, when he tripped and fell down the ramp of *Air Force One*. After that, shutters clicked when the president hit his head on the top of a helicopter doorway, slipped on a sidewalk, hit a spectator with a golf ball, or fell while skiing. He became the butt of jokes for television comedians and cartoonists. *Saturday Night Live* comedian Chevy Chase repeatedly lampooned the president simply by falling on his face. Now, no matter how well he skied, photographers and television camera crews were interested mainly in shots of the president tumbling into a snow bank. Because Ford had decided to seek election to a full term, his image grew increasingly important. The *New York Times* quoted political experts as agreeing that in order to win, the president had to overcome the perception that he was "an amiable, vacillating, accident-prone bungler who is sitting in

During a 1975 State Visit to Austria, President Ford slipped and fell down the steps of *Air Force One.* Though he did not hurt himself, the fall established his reputation as accident-prone.

Photographs from President Ford's ski holiday in Vail, December 1974. When he finished a run, Ford chatted easily with reporters and bystanders. A half dozen Secret Service agents, all chosen for their skiing skills, stood by. When an onlooker told him everyone was proud to have him in Vail, the president grinned. "You make me justice of the peace and I'll quit"—and he meant the presidency! Although he was a good skier, press photographers tended to focus on his falls. Nevertheless he smiled for the camera after a fall, as his ski instructor, Denis Hoeger, stopped to help him get up.

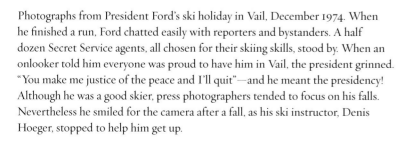

the Oval Office until a real President can be elected."

When his staff suggested he limit his time on the slopes to avoid adding to those perceptions, the president drew the line. "I had skied for most of my life, and I wasn't about to stop doing something I loved to do just because reporters and photographers might be there." Ford fell just twice in a week of skiing, yet, he noted ruefully, "Every picture that ever appeared in the paper was when I was on my fanny falling down." Although Ford professed not to be disturbed by such reports, the columnist David Broder of the *Washington Post* reported that in private the president neither liked nor accepted his portrayal, "not the stumbling ski bum caricature or the bumbling accidental President part, either."

––––––––

As president and first lady, Gerald and Betty Ford swept away the air of mystery that had enveloped the Camp David mountaintop in the final years of the Nixon era. On the Labor Day weekend shortly after he took office, they invited a score of reporters and photographers to take a look at the presidential retreat. The *Los Angeles Times* reported that it was the first time in twenty years that reporters had been allowed to see enough of Camp David to write a firsthand description of it. Their articles noted the moss-green color of the low-slung guest cottages and the goldfish pond surrounded by flowers near Aspen Lodge.

It's a "nice place to work," the president told them. Betty Ford was more enthusiastic. "If I get to return to this world, I'd like to come back to Camp David," she wrote in a diary note at the end of August 1974. "The air, the trees, the sky—it's paradise that place . . . the best thing about the White House." Talking about it years later, her husband agreed: "It was a beautiful location to get away from the trials and tribulations of the White House. Betty and I loved going up there for a weekend or a day or two. There was something unique about it. It gave you a chance to relax and enjoy yourself."

Susan Ford was similarly appreciative. "Camp David was convenient and close; we could get the helicopter right out the back door [of the White House] so that was a quick escape for the weekend." She valued the privacy the place afforded. For her, Camp David represented "someplace you could go and have fun and be silly and not end up in the press." She continued:

> What Camp David meant to me was total relaxation out of the eyes of the press and the public. It's woodsy. It's cabiny. It's more what our family was like. We were not dressed up people. We were a very informal, casual Midwest family. So Camp David fit our lifestyle more than the White House. A lot of it was long walks—and just being quiet. You couldn't hear the protesters out on Pennsylvania Avenue screaming through the megaphones at you.

Over the next twenty-nine months, the Fords visited Camp David seventeen times, mostly on weekends. On one Thanksgiving holiday the president invited his brothers for a family reunion, providing a separate cabin for each family. For the president, Camp David offered a chance to sleep later than he did at the White House, play tennis, drive a snowmobile in winter, chip away on Eisenhower's three-hole golf course, and romp with Liberty, his golden retriever. "Liberty got to really be a dog, run in the woods, do what dogs do," Susan Ford recalled. Liberty swam in the pool, chased deer, and went to the office with the president.

Ford opened Camp David to cabinet members and their families when he wasn't using the retreat. Guests received a checklist of amenities they could choose from during their stay. Swimming suits, hair dryers, irons and ironing boards were available from the camp duty officer.

For the Fords, Camp David offered a time and place to relax together. On visits in 1974 and 1975 (*clockwise from top right*) President Ford and his daughter Susan played tennis, the president played golf, and the entire family bottle-fed a 10-week-old fawn named Flag that had been adopted by the camp commander.

Like many presidents, President Ford used the relaxed setting of Camp David to meet with staff and entertain foreign dignitaries. On July 5, 1974, he met with Secretary of State Henry Kissinger (*right*) and hosted a working luncheon for Indonesian President Suharto at Laurel Lodge (*below*).

Bicycles were parked outside each cottage. An archery range could be set up on request. Movies could be chosen from a list. The shuffle board could be found behind the water tower. Guests were free to explore the nature trail that looped through the woods. The camp swimming pool was available, although the president's pool was off limits. Despite Liberty's free roaming ways, other pets were discouraged. And no photography was allowed.

———

Gerald R. Ford, weekend golfer, possessor of an 18 handicap, happy when he broke 90, adjusted his glasses, leaned forward, and smashed the ball 270 yards down the right side of the fairway at North Carolina's Pinehurst Country Club. Gary Player and Arnold Palmer hooked left into the rough. Of the four golfers playing with Ford that day, September 11, 1974, only Jack Nicklaus managed a longer drive. Ford never forgot the thrill of that drive under the eyes of the legends of golf, including not only his own partners but Sam Snead, Arnold Palmer, Bryon Nelson, and Gene Sarazen. "I had a helluva drive on the first tee; I was out there with the pros, past the pros," he told one interviewer. "Can't say that much for the rest of the game," he told another writer. "But I hit a good one on the first tee."

Golf with the stars represented a relaxed moment in an anxious time. Just three days earlier, Ford had pardoned Nixon, and protest signs peppered the outdoor crowd at Pinehurst: "Is Nixon Above the Law?" "Be a Ford, Not an Edsel." Ford mentioned neither Nixon nor the pardon as he spoke at dinner that night. But some heard an appeal for understanding when he told his audience that golf offered an important lesson:

> I have never seen a tournament, regardless of how much money, or how much fame, or prestige, or emotion was ever involved, that didn't end with the victor extending his hand to the vanquished. The pat on the back, the arm around the shoulder, the praise for what was done right, and the sympathetic nod for what wasn't. These are as much a part of golf as life itself, and I would hope that understanding and reconciliation are not limited to the 19th hole. . . .This afternoon for a few hours, quite unsuccessfully, I tried to make a hole in one. Tomorrow morning I will be back in Washington trying to get out of one.

The *New York Times* ran the headline, "Ford Uses Golf as Example in 'Reconciliation' Plea." The pardon "was much on his mind throughout the day," it concluded. But as he recalled the speech three decades later, Ford insisted he never intended to link the pardon to his golf game: "Any connection that the press saw is clearly unwarranted."

By this time Ford had acquired the reputation as an erratic golfer and had learned to use humor to deal with that side of his game. He began the Pinehurst speech with a nod to the hundreds of fans who followed Arnold Palmer on the greens: "We have all heard of 'Arnie's Army'; my group is called 'Ford's Few'." His problem, he continued, was a "very wild swing," so wild it qualified his Secret Service detail for combat pay. "Back on my home course in Grand Rapids, Michigan, they don't yell, 'Fore,' they yell 'Ford!'"

On a brief winter break early the next year, Ford played the Pro-Am tournament at the Jackie Gleason Inverrary Classic near Fort Lauderdale, Florida. With Gleason and comedian Bob Hope in his foursome, Ford struggled through 18 holes with a disappointing 100, 28 strokes above par. Jack Nicklaus, his professional partner, set a course record with a 63, 9 under par. "Jerry, we all have our bad days," one sympathetic viewer told him. Another dismissed him as "just another Sunday duffer." Nicklaus offered a more diplomatic opinion: "He's very strong, but his principal problem is his grip. He could be a solid six or seven handicap if he played more."

Those were kind words. But Ford had already taken his place in the public mind as a golfer just as likely to hit a spectator as the fairway. Bob Hope, a frequent golfing partner, had an apparently endless reserve of presidential golfing gags:

Ford was the first President to use a lethal weapon—a golf club.

Ford doesn't really have to keep score; he can just look back and count the wounded.

The last time I played golf with President Ford, he hit a birdie—and an eagle, a moose, an aardvark.

Ford conceded his biggest problem was direction, not distance. But some golf writers blamed the huge crowds that gathered when he played. "The almost inevitable result led to all the publicity about his errant shots ricocheting off spectators," the authors of a history of presidential golf

President Ford was repeatedly photographed playing golf. In the summer of 1974 he was at Mackinac Island, Michigan (*top*). At Vail (*bottom*), his golfing outfit included a shirt inscribed "Mr. President—Boogie Buster" and slacks emblazoned with red, white, and blue eagles, similar to the Presidential Seal.

asserted. Just as Eisenhower had done, Ford sometimes tried to sharpen his game by practicing shots on the White House lawn. "I enjoyed golf as a competition," he told an interviewer. "It was a way to relax and enjoy yourself in a competitive environment." In another mood he focused on the camaraderie and the banter and noted that golf creates lasting friendships. Those who played with him saw both elements. "He plays for fun but he loves to win and hates to lose," a friend told *U.S. News and World Report* in the spring of 1975. "I've seen him break his back to win a 50-cent bet."

———————

There was no snow on the ground when Ford returned to Vail in mid-August 1975 for golf and tennis. His summer vacation was billed as two weeks of decompression, even though he planned a five-city speaking tour at the end of the first week. By that time, he had also played golf every day.

Late one night, the scene shifted to a discotheque in Vail Village, where the Fords listened to the Ink Spots re-create the songs that made them famous in the 1940s and 1950s. Soon the couple was dancing cheek-to-cheek to the old tunes: "You Always Hurt the One You Love," "Blueberry Hill," "I Don't Want to Set the World on Fire." The tempo picked up in the next set. The Ink Spots played "Choo Choo Down the Street" and the Fords happily responded with what a newspaper called "first family jitterbugging." Reporters counted eleven numbers that brought the Fords to the dance floor during the evening. As the vacation ended, Press Secretary Nessen produced a virtual time sheet as evidence that Ford had not shirked his duties. Golf, tennis, and swimming had accounted for 44 hours and 20 minutes. But recreation had been more than balanced by nearly 108 hours of work: 39 hours on White House business, 35 hours in staff meetings and sessions with energy and economic advisers, and 33 hours and 55 minutes at public events during short swings away from Vail.

———————

A week after his painfully narrow loss to Jimmy Carter in the 1976 presidential election, Ford was back on a golf course at Palm Springs, California, leaving the headlines to the president-elect and minding his own advice to reporters: "Relax, have a good time, no pressure." When he played the Bing Crosby Pro-Am tournament at Pebble Beach, California, Ford was followed on the greens by an enormous crowd. "Where were all these people on Election Day?" he quipped.

In retirement, the former president and first lady built a winter home on a golf course at Rancho Mirage, near Palm Springs. They spent summers at Beaver Creek, near Vail. Ford remained active, swimming and playing golf. He scored three holes-in-one over the years. But he told one writer that his most satisfying experience was establishing the Jerry Ford Invitational, which raised $3 million for charity over twenty years.

The former president died on December 26, 2006. He was 93.

Chapter 34

Jimmy Carter: Escaping the Crowds

JIMMY CARTER
39th President of the
United States, 1977–1981

In this photo from
September, 6, 1978,
President Jimmy Carter sits
deep in contemplation at
Camp David, where he was
leading difficult diplomatic
negotiations between the
hostile states of Israel and
Egypt. The presidential
scholar Stephen Hess
described Camp David as
an essential antidote to the
tensions of the modern
presidency. "A president
should be able to walk in the
woods on a weekend if it
helps him restore his spirit or
rethink his concerns," Hess
wrote. The setting proved to
be also conducive to peace.

As Jimmy Carter marched from obscurity to the Oval Office, the village of Plains in southwest Georgia became both a political stage set and the measure of his achievement. It vaulted into the public imagination as the most famous small town in America. The new president's bond with his hometown was so strong that most people—Carter included—assumed Plains would be his most frequent destination when he needed a break from the strains of the White House.

Carter's roots were embedded in the red soil of Georgia's Sumter County. His living came from its peanut fields. Carter's peanut warehouse, founded by his father, was the largest business in Plains. His spiritual life centered on the Plains Baptist Church. His career in Georgia politics had begun in Plains, and the peanut was a symbol of his political rise. He and his wife, Rosalynn, the hometown girl he married after graduation from the U.S. Naval Academy, plucked Indian arrowheads from his fields and caught fish in his ponds. The redbrick, tree-shaded house on Woodland Drive was the only home they had ever owned. When the former one-term Georgia governor opened his campaign for the White House, his Sumter County neighbors formed a "peanut brigade" and traveled to snowy New Hampshire and other primary states to help him make his case. A billboard on a Main Street storefront proclaimed his success and theirs: "Plains, Ga., Home of Jimmy Carter, Our President."

There were many Carters among the 683 residents of Plains, beginning with the president's strong-willed, plainspoken mother, Lillian Carter. A former nurse, Miss Lillian joined the Peace Corps in 1966 when she was 67. When her eldest son ran for president a decade later, she greeted one and all in his symbolic campaign headquarters, the town's old railroad depot. The president's spirited sister, Gloria, lived on a nearby farm with her husband, Walter Spahn, and a pair of Harley Davidson motorcycles. Carter's younger brother, Billy, always good for an audacious and irreverent quote, ran the peanut business, owned the town's only filling station, and kept beer on ice in a washtub behind the seat of his pickup truck. Billy often said that he wished his brother had moved out of tiny Plains to sprawling Atlanta before the campaign opened because Georgia's capital was already ruined.

Life as an instant tourist attraction altered the rhythms of this once sleepy town. "Things in Plains were not as quiet and pleasant as they used to be" before the election, Carter lamented. Bus tours showed visitors the sights for a fee. The first traffic lights in town history regulated the flow of cars, and thirty-minute meters rationed Main Street's suddenly scarce parking spaces. For Carter, his ritual Main Street walk now meant wading through throngs of eager tourists, reporters, and television cameras. Most stores sold political and peanut souvenirs to tourists, including the "Happy Mouth Bottle Opener" that displayed a cartoonish version of Carter's toothy smile. A hand-painted political button offered a smiling peanut and the slogan: "Win with the Grin." A news magazine toured Main Street and discovered peanut jewelry, peanut butter, peanut T-shirts,

Plains, the small farming town in south-west Georgia where President Carter was born, had a population of 638 when he was elected president. He had expected to find a haven in Plains, but it was so overwhelmed by tourists that he usually vacationed elsewhere. The shops on Main Street were stuffed with what Carter's son Chip called "Jimmy junk." The campaign pins were photographed in one the downtown Plains store displays.

and just peanuts: fried, candied, boiled, roasted, gold-dipped, and raw. "They've got all the Jimmy junk you want," Chip Carter grumbled as he followed his father on a Main Street walk.

Plains quickly became a hub for protesters, attracted not only by the president but by the television cameras that followed him home. Fifteen hundred discontented farmers and their tractors blocked Main Street when Carter arrived in December 1977 for his first Christmas holiday as president. Although he eventually met with a protest delegation, the farmers remained unhappy with government policies and returned to Plains when he did for Christmas. By then they no longer had the streets to themselves. Hundreds of chanting Taiwanese protesters marched through town waving flags and displaying banners critical of Carter's diplomatic recognition of China's communist government. Creek Indians in feathered clothes and body paint performed a war dance to dramatize tribal grievances. "This is better than Disneyland," a bystander commented. Murray Smith, Rosalynn Carter's brother, rode up on a bicycle, saying it was the only way he could get around. Billy Carter, as usual, offered an opinion: "I wish the hell they would stay out of Plains."

It seemed, President Carter thought, that every state trooper in Georgia had been called on to manage traffic and block side roads as his motorcade drove the 90 miles from Warner-Robbins Air Force Base for his 1977 Christmas visit. "The cameras were always in our faces, practically surrounding whatever house we were visiting, and attempting to film our every move," Carter complained. No activity went unnoticed. When a reporter asked how many birds he had bagged after a day of quail hunting, Carter held up seven fingers. "It was on the evening news; the next Sunday there were more than one hundred (anti-hunting) protesters outside as we arrived for church." Increasingly, the president felt confined to the secured area around his home. Even there he could hear blaring horns and roaring engines as protesting farmers circled their tractors. "It was almost impossible for us to walk down the town's only sidewalk to visit our old friends and neighbors," Carter recalled. Back at the White House, the Carters decided as a family that "despite our love for Plains, it was counterproductive for us to seek any kind of relaxation or normality there." Except for Christmas holidays and other short visits, President Carter would look elsewhere for relief from the pressures of his job.

————

Carter's own austerity policies closed off at least one avenue of escape. Shortly after his inauguration he ordered the sale of the presidential yacht *Sequoia*, which had served as a refuge for Presidents Herbert Hoover, Franklin Roosevelt, John Kennedy, Lyndon Johnson, Richard Nixon, and Gerald Ford. Carter deemed the yacht a needless expense and symbol of the imperial presidency he wanted to dismantle. But Carter also believed that recreation, exercise, and relaxation helped a president clear his mind, refresh his spirits, and prepare for the work ahead. Years later, an interviewer asked Carter if he thought it possible for any president to survive a four-year term without relief from White House tension and strain and an occasional change of scenery. "There might be a president so ill-advised as to do that," he replied. "But it is important for any person to get away from the job, to relax, to take a vacation."

A tennis player since he was a boy, Carter played regularly as president, both at the White House and on the courts at Camp David, where he also bowled, swam in the heated pool, and took up cross-country skiing in winter. He jogged as often as he could. While president, Carter became a skilled fly-fisherman, tying his own flies and seeking out choice trout streams. Fishing was best pursued alone, and that suited Carter. For a vacationing president, Carter maintained, "pleasure comes in being away from the news media and the pressing duties of public service, if possible in relative solitude with one's family or close friends."

Carter initially sought relaxation and solitude in a place he already knew well: the Sea Islands hugging the Georgia coast just north of Florida. Carter had vacationed at St. Simons Island when he was governor of Georgia. He returned as president-elect, staying at Musgrove Plantation, the 1,300-acre estate of Smith Bagley, an heir to the R. J. Reynolds Tobacco Company fortune. The president swam with his 9-year-old daughter, Amy; shot pool with his sons; picnicked with his family; and worked on his transition from private citizen to chief executive. Musgrove Plantation offered palms and palmettos, towering oaks draped with Spanish moss, marshes alive with birds, and views across blue water. Set back 2 miles from the nearest public road, the estate also offered freedom from uninvited television cameras, demonstrators, and the other annoyances that had followed Carter home to Plains. He returned several times as president, keeping mostly out of sight.

But St. Simons, connected to the Georgia mainland by a causeway, was becoming a place of luxurious second homes, condominiums, and vacationers. Feeling the need for even more privacy, in 1979 Carter moved his vacation retreat to nearby Sapelo Island. The 10-square-mile island was sparsely populated, largely undeveloped, and owned and managed

To escape the crowds, President and Mrs. Carter vacationed on the secluded Sea Islands along the Georgia Coast. In 1978, they fished off of Sapelo Island, which was off limits to reporters and other outsiders. Coast Guard boats patrolled offshore to protect Carter's privacy.

by the state of Georgia. Presidential vacation headquarters became a spacious villa with an elaborately decorated indoor pool that made swimming possible even on cool days.

"We would drive all over the island, take a boat out and fish in the ocean, and sail and hike," Carter remembered. For him, a leading attraction was the hamlet of Hog Hammock, the home of descendants of the slaves who had tended the island's rice plantations. They spoke with a Gullah accent, communicated with the mainland by boat, and welcomed the Carters at barbecues, oyster feasts, and fish fries. Attending services in a small, cinder-block church, Carter told the gathered community how much he cherished the island's solitude: "This morning I was alone. I'm not often alone these days. I gave a prayer of thanksgiving."

Most reporters and photographers got no closer to the vacationing president than the press center on Jekyll Island, some 30 miles to the south. That was clearly what Carter preferred. "There's no doubt that he does like to get off by himself," said Phil Wise, the president's appointments secretary. "Anyone who goes as hard as he does just needs that." Later, Carter echoed that thought: "It was a good vacation. We were all by ourselves."

———

The walkie-talkie on the press raft crackled, then transmitted a three-word message: "Deacon is fishing." Updates followed. "Deacon," the president's Secret Service code name, had caught three cutthroat trout.

It was late August 1978. The presidential party was beginning a three-day, 80-mile, white-water run down the Middle Fork of Idaho's Salmon River, a wilderness area 25 miles by horseback from the nearest paved road. Two miles back, mostly out of sight and nearly out of mind, were three rafts carrying rotating teams of reporters, photographers, and television crews. Still farther behind were more rafts and dinghies with backup Secret Service agents, the rest of the press corps, and the tents, stoves, and supplies needed for overnight encampments.

The year had been nearly as turbulent as the river. After an acrimonious national debate, the Senate had approved Carter's timetable for transferring the U.S.-built Panama Canal to Panama. Bitterness lingered. Reporters covering the president's Western trip spotted bumper stickers reading, "Keep the Canal—Give Away Carter." Inflation and energy shortages remained acute. Carter's approval rating in the Gallup Poll stood at 39 percent. The Camp David summit meeting between Israel and Egypt would open soon after his return, testing both his personal effectiveness and American prestige. But *Newsweek* reported that when an aide suggested he scrub the river trip and stay at his desk, Carter resisted: "I need time to unwind. I've been working hard. I'm going to go off and enjoy myself."

True to his studious nature, Carter prepared by examining topographic maps of the river gorges and reading accounts of the history of the Middle Fork. He called the stream "one of the most undisturbed rivers in the nation." The solitude the president preferred was not easy to obtain, even while floating through a wilderness on an 18-foot raft. The roster of the president's party included the first lady, their daughter, Amy, and their adult sons, Jack and Chip. Interior Secretary Cecil Andrus, a former Idaho governor, had urged Carter to make the trip, and he and his wife were along as guests. Other rafts carried guides, a White House communications team, the White House doctor, a White House photographer, Carter's Secret Service detail, and the military officer carrying the "football" holding the president's nuclear attack codes. It had been waterproofed for the occasion.

For the summer of 1978, President Carter took his family on an extended vacation in the wilderness of Idaho and Wyoming. For three days they rafted down the Middle Fork of the Salmon River, camping and fishing (*opposite*). "We were all holding on for life during the more steep and powerful rapids," the president recalled, "and casting flies in the more placid stretches of the stream."

347

President Carter and his family spent the last week of their 1978 summer vacation in the Teton Mountains fishing cutthroat and brown trout. Casting for trout awakened the president's interest in fly-fishing, and he was soon taking lessons from an expert park ranger.

Communications experts made sure Carter's contact with the White House remained unbroken. Radio transmitter stations, positioned on the bluffs above the riverbanks, relayed signals to a Strategic Air Command aircraft circling somewhere overhead, allowing secure two-way transmissions with Carter's raft. Carter disclosed one further precaution as he joked with reporters on the flight to Idaho: "I have issued a directive that there be no crises."

The weather soon turned foul. Thunder rolled over the mountains. A cold drizzle was followed by drenching rain, then stinging hail. With rain still falling, the rafts pulled ashore and the party slipped into a lodge to dry out, warm up, and sip hot coffee. But the trout were biting, and Carter was soon back on the river. "It was a nice day, and nice that I caught a lot of fish, and nice that I don't have to make comments to the press," the president observed as the guides set up camp for the evening. The sun came out brilliantly on the second day. The Carters spotted bighorn sheep on the high bluffs and tracked a soaring golden eagle with a 6-foot wingspan. The fish continued to bite.

The excursion ended the next day at the point where the Middle Fork meets the Salmon. The last 16 miles were marked by an almost unbroken span of white water. Competitive fishing continued. Carter reported that 111 trout were taken and released, 59 by his raft alone. "We came in a little ahead of the others," he boasted. At one point the Carters walked up a rocky bank to inspect ancient Indian cave paintings. When the press raft floated by, Carter was ready with a comment: "I don't want to leave here." Later, he called his time on the river "the best three days I have ever had."

Continuing the vacation, the Carters flew to Wyoming and settled into the four-bedroom Brinkerhoff Lodge in Grand Teton National Park, enjoying views of Jackson Lake and the Grand Teton Mountains. Carter took a sailboat out on the lake and fished in a creek running into the Snake River. Then he moved north to a remote corner of Yellowstone Lake. Back at the lodge, the president and Amy picked huckleberries in a grove of aspen.

But the president's thoughts were moving from wary trout to the hazards of Middle East diplomacy. Working late at Brinkerhoff Lodge, he studied the psychological profiles prepared for him on the two principals in the Camp David talks: Prime Minister Menahem Begin of Israel and President Anwar al-Sadat of Egypt. Carter absorbed details of their lives and backgrounds and evaluated their strengths and weaknesses, their attitude toward one another, and their likely reaction to a crisis. Then he considered negotiating strategy. Finally, he cut short the vacation and returned to the White House. "If he is simply going to sit here and spend all day and a good portion of the night working on these domestic concerns, he might as well be in Washington," Press Secretary Jody Powell told reporters. In an interview twenty-five years later, Carter supplied another reason: "I went back because I wanted to make sure my staff shared my vision of making Camp David as far-reaching as possible. I found most of them were very cautious."

———

Although history would remember Camp David as the site of the most important foreign policy achievement of the Carter years, the presidential retreat was low on Jimmy Carter's priority list when he entered the White House. Some thought Franklin Roosevelt's retreat might be declared excess baggage, along with the yacht *Sequoia*. Richard Nixon became so concerned that he urged Carter to make no decision before he saw the mountaintop retreat for himself.

Carter asked budget director Bert Lance to take a look and received a "glowing" report. Soon Carter took his family to Camp David for the first of many weekends and found it easily met his first requirement: "close to near complete isolation." He came to think of Camp David as "one of the most delightful surprises" of the presidency.

Stepping off the helicopter on a pleasant afternoon, Carter handed his briefcase to an aide and walked hand-in-hand with his wife along the narrow road to Aspen Lodge, a mile away. Trailing them through the thick woods, just far enough behind to give a sense of privacy, were the presidential limousines, a Secret Service detail, and a handful of military and civilian aides. The retreat offered all the recreational features an active first family could want: tree-shaded trails for hiking, jogging, and bicycle riding, tennis courts, a bowling alley, and a heated swimming pool. As a bonus, Carter discovered Hunting Creek, a "very attractive" nearby trout stream. He and Rosalynn rode their bikes down the mountain, fished for hours, and brought their catch back to be cooked for dinner.

Carter described the presidential quarters at Aspen Lodge as "typical of a marvelous resort, a luxurious villa that a wealthy family might lease for a week." The well-decorated lodge had a built-in projector and a roll-down screen. The Carters, like their predecessors, often enjoyed an evening movie. The meeting space and communications facilities were also first rate. "The ability of the president to stay in touch with the outside world was the equal at Camp David to that of the White House, and perhaps even superior," Carter observed.

The Catoctin Mountains were snow-covered in winter, and the Carters rode sleds on the slopes and snowmobiles along the trails. They discovered cross-country skiing and spent hours exploring the countryside. An avid jogger, Carter often ran during Camp David weekends and said he averaged 40 miles a week. On September 15, 1979, wearing the number thirty-nine and a yellow headband, he entered the 6.2-mile Catoctin Mountain Race. The 54-year-old jogger pushed himself. Near the 4-mile mark he wobbled, gasped, and all but collapsed. Widely published press photographs showed the president's ashen and contorted face. He soon recovered and returned to hand out awards for that day's race. Over four years, Carter visited Camp David ninety-nine times. The White House

On September 15, 1979, President Carter entered the Catoctin Mountain Race, and toward the end he showed signs of fatigue, almost collapsing. But he recovered and was on hand at the end of the race to give out the awards.

In August 1978, President Carter chose Camp David as the setting for historic peace talks between Prime Minister Menahem Begin of Israel and President Anwar al-Sadat of Egypt. With its opportunities for walking, biking, and informal conversation, Camp David facilitated the peace process and gave its name to the famous accords. Clockwise, from top left: the Carters and Begins take a stroll through Camp David; President Carter confers with advisers Zbigniew Brzezinski and Cyrus Vance; the president meets with Menahem Begin and Anwar al-Sadat on the Aspen Lodge patio; Begin and Carter meet with Brzezinski and Vance after a tennis match; Carter meets members of the Israeli delegation.

To break up the intensity of the Camp David talks, President Carter led an excursion to the Civil War battlefield at nearby Gettysburg. It was a tour filled with symbolism: the failure of politicians to prevent a war, the bitter costs of the war itself, and the eventual reconciliation of the armies that did the fighting. Unlike Sadat, Begin displayed little interest in terrain or tactics. But as the party approached the battlefield cemetery, he recited Abraham Lincoln's Gettysburg Address. "He seemed to know it by heart, and considered it one of the best and simplest speeches ever made," Carter remembered.

calculated he was in residence at the camp for a total of 6,647 hours and 50 minutes, or more than three-quarters of a year.

The question of where to hold the Begin-Sadat talks was raised as the president and first lady walked in the Camp David woods. "This was surely the ideal place for the peace talks," Rosalynn Carter remembered, "with a chance for easy informality for the participants." The president agreed, as did his advisers, Powell explained: "We were looking for a place to get the leaders (and their senior advisers) away from really everything," in a location that could be easily secured and had no nearby distractions. The aim, Powell said, was to keep the press at a distance and avoid the kind of public statements and reactions that lead to a hardening of positions and certain stalemate.

The Camp David talks were a risky venture at best. The Middle East seethed with ancient and modern animosities. Tensions were high in the aftermath of the 1973 Yom Kippur War, when

Israel defeated invading Arab armies and seized Egypt's Sinai Peninsula. Carter had decided "it would be best, win or lose, to go all out" in bringing the two principal leaders to the bargaining table.

Carter arrived at Camp David "weighted with maps, briefing books, notes, summaries of past negotiations and my annotated Bible, which I predicted—accurately, as it turned out—would be needed in my discussions with Prime Minister Begin." The summit opened on Tuesday, September 5, 1978. Begin was housed in Birch Lodge, Sadat in Dogwood, both a short walk from the president's quarters at Aspen. It quickly became evident that neither leader would be influenced by being close to nature in relaxed surroundings. Goodwill quickly evaporated. "After three days it became obvious that Begin and Sadat were incompatible," Carter said, "so I acted in between them."

The meeting had required extensive preparation. Vans were rolled in for use as Israeli and Egyptian communications centers, each with direct telephone lines to their respective governments. Because Sadat needed a private place for prayer, the movie theater became a temporary mosque. For his restricted diet, the Egyptian leader brought his own chef to prepare boiled meat and vegetables and the honey-flavored mint tea he favored. Begin ate kosher food, which required a separate preparation area with its own pots, pans, and dishes.

The negotiations were difficult until the end. Carter's go-between role required dogged effort. But on September 17, the president announced that agreement had been reached on a "framework for peace." That led months later to the signing of an Israeli-Egyptian peace treaty. At Camp David, the two leaders offered toasts: Begin with wine and Sadat with orange juice. They were not yet friends. But a historic breakthrough had been achieved.

There were other benchmark moments at Camp David. In July 1979, Carter convened a domestic summit to consider the course of his troubled presidency, and on July 15 he told Americans that the nation suffered from "a crisis of confidence . . . that strikes at the very heart and soul and spirit of our national will." In October at Camp David, Carter decided to permit the ailing shah of Iran to enter the United States for medical treatment. In November, the president was at Camp David when informed that the American Embassy at Tehran had been seized and the staff taken hostage. On March 22, 1980, at Camp David, he authorized reconnaissance of an isolated desert region 200 miles south of Tehran for use in a possible rescue mission. The subsequent failure of the mission cost eight lives and left the hostages in Iranian hands. President Carter negotiated an end to the crisis and the hostages were formally released after President Ronald Reagan's inaugural address on January 20, 1981.

———

Jimmy Carter counted certain Friday afternoons as "among our best-kept secrets in Washington." Taking off from the South Lawn of the White House, *Marine One*, the presidential helicopter, could reach Camp David in about half an hour. The president and first lady walked through the woods to their quarters at Aspen Lodge and changed into outdoor clothes. Then, after the press photographers who had witnessed their arrival departed, they walked back to the helicopter and climbed aboard. Unspotted by outsiders, *Marine One* headed north across the Maryland state line into Pennsylvania. Forty minutes later, the Carters landed in a pasture at Spruce Creek, a four-star trout stream widely regarded as one of the best places to catch trout in the Eastern United States. Visiting repeatedly during and after his presidency, Carter viewed it as "one of my favorite places on earth."

One fishing story President Carter told lived to haunt him. In April 1979, fishing in a farm pond near Plains, he used his oar to shoo away an aggressive rabbit that, he said, seemed intent on climbing into the boat. Several days later, back in Washington, Carter invited several aides to join him for a chat on the Truman Balcony of the White House. Sipping lemonade, the president shared his unusual wildlife experience.

The story itself might have disappeared. But it surfaced several months later during a casual conversation between Associated Press reporter Brooks Jackson and White House press secretary Jody Powell. Jackson confirmed the rabbit story with a second White House source, and used it for a lighthearted AP column called "Jimmy's White House." At the time, he considered it an amusing story and had no notion it would cause a nationwide ruckus.

The *Washington Post* ran Jackson's bylined *AP* story in a box at the bottom of page one with the attention-grabbing headline: "Bunny Goes Bugs, Rabbit Attacks President." They illustrated the article with a cartoon of a toothy, long-eared rabbit gleefully launching itself at the president's boat with the force of an underwater missile. The single-word caption read "PAWS."

Radio stations almost immediately picked up the story and hundreds of news stories, editorials, opinion columns, and cartoons followed. Carter's critics quickly adopted the incident as a symbol of a president under siege from all sides. The press, cartoonists, and comedians poked endless fun at the president and the "Killer Rabbit," seeing it as an anecdote revealing political weakness.

A quarter century later, Carter was asked to reflect again on the aquatic rabbit, and to say whether he thought the story had been overblown. His reply: "It was a simple and routine event in wildlife experience with bunnies."

On October 5, 1980, President Carter enjoyed the solitude of fly-fishing in the wilderness of Spruce Creek, Pennsylvania.

Carter's interest in fly-fishing increased after the Grand Teton vacation. He had invited a dozen noted fly-fishermen to join him at Camp David for a fly-casting seminar. The experts demonstrated casting and fly-tying skills and talked about trout habitat, conservation, and the customs and history of fly-fishing. Rosalynn Carter became as intrigued by the sport as her husband and practiced casting on the surface of the Camp David swimming pool. Before long, at the invitation of the Spruce Creek Hunting and Fishing Club, the president and first lady were casting for hefty brown and rainbow trout, observing the club's catch-and-release rules.

Rising from deep limestone springs, Spruce Creek meanders along the ridges of the Allegheny Mountains for about 13 miles before flowing into the Juniata River. The private stretch that Carter fished included a meadow, woods, a few small waterfalls, a long pool, and a comfortable fishing cabin for spending the night. When word finally got out, some reporters questioned the use of helicopters for fishing trips during an energy crisis. But Carter was unapologetic. He said he needed the "rare opportunity to go fishing or to get out in the woods and swamps and in the fields and on the streams by myself."

There were other angling excursions as well. The Carters fished for bass in the upper regions of the Potomac River and cast for trout not only in Pennsylvania but in Maryland, Virginia, and West Virginia. Fishing took them to streams enjoyed by other angling presidents, including Grover Cleveland, Calvin Coolidge, Herbert Hoover, and Dwight Eisenhower. In the spring of 1979, Carter spent a weekend at the fishing camp Hoover had built in Virginia's Blue Ridge

Mountains, angling for trout in the Rapidan River. Although they sometimes fished with experts, the Carters prized the times when they fished alone. "For a few hours we enjoyed the solitude we badly needed," Carter remembered. "Fishing and tying flies were great for clearing the mind," Carter thought. "My concentration is so intense that for long periods the rest of the world is almost forgotten."

———

In August 1979, Jimmy Carter rode a riverboat down the Mississippi in a 659-mile whistle-blowing, calliope-playing, handshaking, baby-kissing excursion through the heartland. The president drew eager crowds of a size that encouraged and surprised his worried supporters and might have amazed Mark Twain, that old riverboat pilot.

The eight-day tour of the upper river began in St. Paul, ended in St. Louis, and was billed by the White House as a working vacation. Aides explained that Carter would seek rest and relaxation aboard the stern-wheeler *Delta Queen* but would also speak at four rallies along the river to build support for his administration's embattled energy initiatives. It was lost on no one that the 1980 presidential election was a little more than fifteen months away and that the *Delta Queen* would pause at river towns in Wisconsin and Iowa, two states critical to the nominating process.

A 285-foot stern-wheeler, the *Delta Queen* was a vivid reminder of the era when hundreds of steamboats carried thousands of passengers and Twain wrote *Life on the Mississippi*, a book Carter read during the trip. Built in Scotland in 1926, the *Delta Queen* had a steel hull and a wooden superstructure. The Carters had two cabins on the Sun Deck, high on the ship's stern with sweeping views of the river. They used one for sleeping, the other as a presidential office. Carter paid the $1,800 fare himself. Daughter Amy, like other children on board, rode free. The isolation Carter sought on most vacations would prove impossible on a riverboat with a crew of seventy-seven and twice as many paying passengers. The thirty people in Carter's party included White House staff, communications specialists, Secret Service agents, and a small pool of reporters.

President Carter waves to a crowd from the *Delta Queen* on August 19, 1979, the first day of his voyage down the Mississippi.

On the *Delta Queen*, President Carter and his family mingled with fellow passengers and spoke to the crowds gathered along the riverbanks. More than 10,000 came out to see the president. On board, most of the passengers were small-town business people and professionals— middle-aged, middle-class, and Republican. They were good-natured in the face of presidential hubbub. Some slipped on T-shirts that told the world: "I Went Down the River with President Carter."

Fears of meager turnouts and tepid responses evaporated. Few presidents had traveled the river road, and many saw Carter's river-stop tour as not-to-be missed history, even those who did not support him. Lively crowds massed at the boat landings, spread out along the riverbanks, and lined every lock and dam along the legendary watercourse. As many as twenty small craft circled the *Delta Queen*, the boaters waving and shouting greetings.

In his speeches, Carter invariably called the United States the greatest nation on earth, sought support for a windfall-profits tax on energy companies, and advocated gasohol made from corn as an alternative energy source. The plan to speak just four times was soon abandoned. By the time the boat reached St. Louis, Carter had delivered fifty-eight speeches. A reporter calculated that as one speech every three hours. "Don't you people ever go to sleep?" Carter called out in wonderment at one early morning gathering. Forty-seven towns got their presidential moment: eight in Minnesota, six in Wisconsin, eleven in Iowa, fifteen in Illinois, and seven in Missouri, including Hannibal, where the president toured Twain's boyhood home.

The president, Rosalynn, and Amy plunged into friendly crowds, reaching out for hands and kissing babies. A reporter counted eighteen and one-half kissed babies in a single day, discounting one child who refused to be cuddled. At Guttenberg, Iowa, the president shook a cocker spaniel's paw. Once he patted a goat. *Newsweek* called it a revival of the "shirt-sleeve populism" that won voters in 1976. "It really turned into a great campaign swing but that wasn't the intent when we started out," recalled Press Secretary Powell, the senior White House staff member on board. "What we didn't anticipate was the crowds gathering at the locks, even in the middle of the night or the early morning hours. I thought it was a lot of fun; and I was pleased and proud at how people came out to see the president."

The Carters mingled freely on deck and ate in the main dining room. At night they listened to Dixieland, sipped a gin and tonic, and danced as the band played "Sweet Georgia Brown." "He's so common it's hard for me to believe he's that important," a Davenport, Iowa, physician said. Amy enlisted other children in a game of hide-and-seek with Secret Service agents assigned to keep watch on her. Her father, an old submariner, toured the engine room and discussed steamboat history with the captain on the bridge. Heading down the Iowa side of the river from Burlington to Davenport, the president and Amy pecked out tunes on the calliope. On one clear night, Carter pointed out the North Star to passengers gathered at the rail. Before the trip was over he had posed for photographs with all of them.

Some of the exuberance of the trip evaporated when Carter stepped off the stern-wheeler at St. Louis. Organizers had predicted up to 100,000 people would be on hand to greet the president. Despite bands and a fireworks display, only 8,000 showed up, some of them protesters. It was, according to *Newsweek*, "something of a return to reality" after Carter's buoyant excursion through small-town America.

———

Fifteen months later, Carter lost his bid for reelection to Republican Ronald Reagan. He returned to his home in Plains, and also to Altlanta, where he established his presidential library and the Carter Center, dedicated to human rights and the alleviation of human suffering. He has used it to launch international peacekeeping missions, monitor the fairness of elections, improve agricultural productivity, eliminate diseases, and address human rights concerns, mostly in developing countries. In 2002, Carter was awarded the Nobel Prize for Peace for his involvement in those activities and in belated recognition of his role as a mediator between Egypt and Israel at the 1978 Camp David Accords. He has written a shelf of best-selling books, including a novel and a volume of poetry. And he and the former first lady have continued their strong interest in fly-fishing, returning often to Spruce Creek and casting for trout in the Rockies, Alaska, and Canada as well as in Finland, Switzerland, England, Wales, Ireland, New Zealand, Japan, and Russia. An assessment in the *New York Times* said Carter has entered "the hallowed territory of true expertise."

The Jimmy Carter National Historic Site in Plains, Georgia, preserves the key sites and structures associated with Jimmy Carter's life including the Plains High School, where Jimmy and Rosalynn Smith were students (now a visitor center) and the Train Depot that served as Jimmy Carter's presidential campaign headquarters (*below*). The Carters still reside in Plains.

Chapter 35

Ronald Reagan: Ranch in the Sky

For President Ronald Reagan, his ranch, where he loved riding his horses, was restorative. He is shown here with Little Man in 1977. Told by a staff member that he could avoid press criticism by spending less time at the ranch, he responded, "I'm seventy years old and I figure that ranch is going to add some years onto my life, and I'm going to enjoy it."

Narrow, with hairpin turns, Refugio Road's blacktop surface was pitted with potholes and at times awash with floodwater. The road ran nearly 7 miles from California's Pacific Coast Highway into the Santa Ynez Mountains, ascending from lemon groves to a brush-covered canyon. From there it spanned a boulder-strewn stream and twisted upward past sheer cliffs and a grove of live oaks until it reached a gate guarding a single-lane gravel road. That led even higher until it opened into a large green meadow with grass bending in the breeze. Even at low speeds the ride could wrench muscles, jar spines, and test nerves. The reward was in the double view from the top: the Santa Ynez Valley to the east; the Channel Islands and the ever-changing blue of the Pacific Ocean to the west.

Ronald Reagan fell in love with the place moments after he mounted a horse and began to explore. "I took one look at the view and was ready to buy, even before we reached the house." Each time he returned he knew that first, instant decision had been the right one.

Twenty-seven miles north of Santa Barbara and more than 2,200 feet above sea level, the 688-acre ranch had meadows, pastures, oak groves, madrone trees, and dense chaparral. One previous owner called it Tip Top Ranch. Ronald and Nancy Reagan wanted a new name and chose Rancho del Cielo. Reagan translated it from Spanish as "Ranch in the Sky" and was always a bit poetic when he described it: "That particular place casts a spell on you . . . when you get in there, the world is gone," Reagan once told a reporter. Night and day, the ranch reminded him of "an open cathedral." "Rancho del Cielo can make you feel," he said, "as if you are on a cloud looking down at the world."

During his eight years as president, Reagan spent 364 days, a day short of a full year, at Rancho del Cielo. The president visited as often as he could, averaging about 45 days a year. He tended to head to the ranch on Presidents' Day weekend in February, for Easter week in April, and for the Memorial Day weekend at the end of May. He liked to be there to celebrate the first lady's birthday on July 6 and for a longer summer vacation in August. He returned in late November for a family Thanksgiving.

The former movie actor bought the ranch for $526,000 in 1974, shortly before he completed his second and final term as governor of California. The property had already been designated an "agricultural preserve" under a California law designed to protect open land from commercial development. That kept taxes low. The protective zoning meant Reagan paid just $1,148 in annual property taxes in 1981, even though the ranch had greatly increased in value.

While the views were far-reaching, the ranch house was cramped, shabby, and dark. Built in 1872 of plastered adobe, heated with a potbelly stove, it was hardly the place one might expect a wealthy Hollywood star and California's former governor to call home. Nancy Reagan thought the house had "a million problems" and remembered that the master bedroom was originally so small that the only way she could make the bed was to climb on top of it.

The Reagans purchased a ranch at the top of the Santa Ynez Mountains in 1974 and named it Rancho del Cielo— "Ranch in the Sky." In his memoirs, Reagan explained why: "From the house we look across the meadow at a peak crowned with oak trees and beyond it, mountains that stretch toward the horizon. From some points on the ranch, you can watch boats cruising across the Santa Barbara Channel, then turn your head and see the Santa Ynez Valley unfold like a huge wilderness ampitheater before your eyes."

Agreeing that the house "wasn't very pretty," Reagan enlisted the help of two aides who had become close friends. Barney Barnett, a retired California highway patrolman, had been Reagan's driver during his governorship. Dennis LeBlanc, another former state policeman, had worked on Reagan's campaigns and would join the White House military office. The three men replaced the weathered asbestos shingles on the roof with simulated Spanish tiles, giving the house more of the appearance of a nineteenth-century Spanish adobe. They tore out a rough-and-ready screened porch and, with the help of a contractor, replaced it with a large L-shaped family room with a fireplace. New windows opened views across the meadow. Knowing that Nancy was feeling "a little claustrophobic," Reagan enlarged the master bedroom and added a two-bedroom guest house. When the work was done the ranch house itself was still a relatively modest 1,500 square feet. Its small scale, inexpensive materials, and lack of pretension surprised most visitors. But John Barletta, a Secret Service agent and horseman who often rode with Reagan, thought the renovated house with its red tile roof fit into its surroundings, looking "as if it were just a small part of a painting under the vast blue sky."

Inside, the house displayed a decidedly western and personal character: rattan furniture with patterned red fabric, bright red curtains in the living room, Mexican and Indian rugs, collections of Hopi kachina dolls and Indian spirit figures, the mounted head of a favorite bull near the stone fireplace in the den, a Sharps rifle, an Indian peace pipe, and a Kenneth Wyatt painting of a cowboy leading a lame horse through a rainstorm. There were bookshelves with volumes on California history and the American West, an accumulation of miniature elephants, a jar of Reagan's favorite jellybeans, and, in the small bar area, the embodiment of a western joke, a pair of stuffed jackalopes—jackrabbits with antlers added. A rack holding favorite caps and hats stood near the door. The Reagans' bedroom, painted in a favorite soft, bright yellow, had two twin beds pushed together. The walk-in closet had been fortified with steel and concrete, making it the blast-proof "safe room" to which the president would have been taken had the house come under attack.

Like other presidents before him, Reagan felt "cooped up" and fenced in once the comforts and luxuries of the White House were his to enjoy. "You can get a kind of a bird-in-a-gilded-cage feeling," he mused. The first lady agreed: "As much as Ronnie and I loved the White House, we found it very difficult to live in a place where you couldn't ever go out for a walk."

The caged bird flew, nearly free, in the Santa Ynez Mountains. The ranch gave Reagan room to roam, recharged his energies, and allowed him time to think—often on horseback. The ranch freed him from the White House appointments calendar, which measured his working day in fifteen minute slices. But total escape was never possible. Reagan credited his wife with putting it this way: "Presidents don't get vacations; they just get a change of scenery." He continued: "You're still president; the job goes with you."

The ranch's furnishings were decidedly western in character. Here shown on the phone in 1982, President Reagan was regularly in communication with his advisers. He reserved mornings for the paperwork of the presidency.

Reagan first flew to Rancho del Cielo as president in late February 1981, a bare month after his inauguration, setting the pattern for the next eight years. After a five-hour flight across the continent, *Air Force One* landed at Point Mugu Naval Air Station south of Santa Barbara. During the helicopter ride to the ranch, Reagan sat on the edge of his seat, pointing out landmarks to his physician and military aide.

Reporters in the press filing center, at an ocean-side hotel in Santa Barbara, saw almost nothing of the vacationing president. But from that first visit, the president's spokesmen offered a description of Reagan's daily activities that varied only in small details: "The president attended to routine paperwork this morning and is now getting ready to go horseback riding with Mrs. Reagan. After lunch with Mrs. Reagan the president will chop wood and clear brush on the ranch property." After listening to countless reports of what one journalist called the president's "chop-and-clear woodland agenda," reporters wondered how much brush could be left on Reagan's mountaintop and fantasized that tons of new brush were being hauled in before each visit.

Years later, LeBlanc noted that the brush-clearing had a purpose. Reagan cut 12 miles of riding trails on his 688 acres, many of them through dense greasewood. "He liked to be able to ride about ten feet up in the air and he didn't want to bend down all the time, so we'd cut high on the trees, cut back the branches," LeBlanc explained. "We cut the greasewood with handsaws and sometimes gas-run chain saws. . . . It was me and Barney Barnett and the president."

Reagan and his friends also sawed up dead or fallen trees to provide firewood for the two fireplaces that heated the house. At more than 2,200 feet, the temperature was often cold enough to keep the fires going day and night. "You see him out there with all that sweat rolling down and a big grin on his face," an aide reported. "He's very content after an afternoon like that."

There were other chores that worked up a sweat. Reagan replaced a muddy pool in front of the ranch house with a larger, broader pond he called Lake Lucky. It was deep enough to stock with fish and wide enough to build a dock and take Nancy for a ride in a canoe named *Truluv*. He built rail fences of discarded, 15-foot-long telephone poles, splitting them into posts and rails and digging postholes. When roads washed out in rainstorms, he helped repair them by filling the fresh cuts with rock and tamping in dirt to make the roadway level. It was hard work, and at the end of the

While at Rancho del Cielo, President Reagan dug trenches, repaired roads, built fences, cleared brush, and chopped wood. In the beginning he split logs with axes, wedges, and a sledgehammer. Then he bought a hydraulic splitting machine that worked by shoving logs against a wedge. The split logs were sawed into fireplace lengths and stacked; the brush was hauled out and piled in open areas for burning. All these photos were taken by White House photographers during visits to the ranch.

day the president and his helpers often dozed off while watching *Jeopardy* or *Murder She Wrote* on television. LeBlanc called it a refreshing kind of tiredness, and Reagan agreed: "It's the greatest therapy in the world, because it becomes all-important. . . . And you go to bed thinking about, well, now tomorrow you go back to what it was we were doing and finish that up."

Some ranch chores struck outsiders as a bit exotic. Lake Lucky often filled with small black snakes, harmless but unpleasant so close to the house and outbuildings. Not long after he bought the ranch, Reagan and his helpers waded in, bagged more than 180 snakes, and dumped them in a pond bordering the Los Padres National Forest. They dubbed the relocation site "Snake Lake."

The mountaintop ranch also had its share of rattlesnakes. Dr. T. Burton Smith, one of Reagan's White House physicians, planned for emergency treatment and evacuation to a hospital if a snake ever bit the president. His foresight was never needed, and Reagan himself wasn't concerned. He once stomped on a rattler and put it out of action before realizing he was wearing low-cut sneakers, not the tall and heavy boots he usually wore at the ranch. While the rattlesnakes stayed away from the house, they were often seen on the trails.

A devoted and serious rider, Reagan named all the ranch's riding trails—Sunrise, Hanging

Tree, Rock, Main, Snake Lake, Valley Trail. Dubbed "Rawhide" by the Secret Service, Reagan plotted the route of each ride on a map in the tack barn. As Reagan rode, radios might crackle with the announcement that Rawhide had just turned into "Pennsylvania Avenue," the president's name for the main road into the ranch. To pinpoint Rawhide's location, identifying numbers were drilled on rocks along the trails and reported by radio to the Secret Service command post as he rode past. Landing zones were cleared and ready at a number of locations in case a helicopter was needed for an emergency evacuation. Knowing they were going to have to ride with Reagan, agents took riding lessons at the U.S. Park Police stables in Washington so they could control their horses and safely keep up with the president.

President and Mrs. Reagan enjoyed time together alone on Lake Lucky, in their canoe *Truluv*, on August 17, 1983. Responding to a rumor that she did not like the ranch nearly as much as her husband did, she said: "I don't chop wood, but I don't stay on the phone all the time either. . . I really like it up here."

During most of the White House years, Reagan's favorite ranch horse was El Alamein, a spirited, often difficult, Arabian stallion. The horse was light gray, almost white. To confuse a possible sniper, John Barletta, the agent who generally rode next to Reagan, often saddled Gwalianko, a look-alike Arabian. He roughly matched his clothes and cap to those Reagan wore. "From a thousand yards, you couldn't tell those horses or riders apart," Barletta remembered. Nancy Reagan rode No Strings, a sorrel quarter horse. The president saddled the horses near the tack barn, then rang an old locomotive bell mounted on a post to signal his wife ("Rainbow" to the Secret Service) to walk up from the house. They ended each ride with a hug and kiss from husband to wife. While riding, the Reagans were followed by Secret Service agents on horseback. Behind the riders, four-wheel-drive vehicles carried more agents, the president's doctor with emergency medical gear, and the military aide with the "football," the attaché case containing release codes for nuclear weapons. One vehicle, bristling with antennas, served as the mobile outpost of the White House Communications Agency and enabled Reagan to reach out from the riding trail to anywhere in the world.

Although Reagan surrounded himself with western imagery and wore a broad-brimmed Stetson while working, he drew the line when he mounted a horse. He used an English saddle, smoother and lighter than the tooled-leather western saddles used by working cowboys. He wore English riding pants tucked into tall, brown-leather, English-style riding boots. Barletta described his riding style: "His back was ramrod straight, and he was squared up on his horse, confidently in control of his animal. Only when he jumped would he lean forward, and that was to carry the horse over." LeBlanc thought riding English-style had improved Reagan's posture and strength. One of his biographers explained: "To ride English you've got to be in good shape because to stay on the horse you hold yourself in place with your thighs and calves. When things turn wild or surprising you use your body to control things."

On horseback, Reagan identified not with cowboys but with cavalrymen of the American West. When Dr. Smith suggested the president wear a broad-brimmed cowboy hat to keep the sun off his face while riding, Reagan told him he was not a cowboy and wore a billed cap instead. One of his riding caps designated him as "Rancho del Cielo Cavalry Commander." It was an appropriate title. Reagan's riding skills—and his lifelong bond with horses—developed in the 1930s when he joined an army reserve cavalry unit in Des Moines, where he was working as a sportscaster for

a local radio station. "I just fell in love with riding and I began to dream of owning a ranch," he wrote in his memoir. As a Hollywood star, he portrayed cavalrymen in three motion pictures, taking the role of George Armstrong Custer in *Santa Fe Trail*. "Ever since I'd become addicted to Saturday matinees, I'd had an affection for those scenes when a troop of cavalrymen in blue tunics and gold braid, flags raised and bugles blowing, raced across the prairie to rescue beleaguered pioneers," he wrote. At the ranch, Dr. Smith watched as Reagan demonstrated the cavalry dismount: sliding off a horse, landing on both feet, and snapping to attention.

Riding reinforced Reagan's native optimism. On March 30, 1981, while leaving a Washington hotel after a speech, the president was shot in the chest. The would-be assassin's bullet stopped an inch from his heart. Recovering from his wound, Reagan asked his doctors how long it would be before he could ride again. At least two months, they told him. The president held up one finger. It took a little longer than a month. But on May 23, 1981, Reagan saddled Little Man and headed off on a ranch trail. The next day he was chopping wood. The ranch had always been Reagan's sanctuary. But now, hemmed in as he was by heightened security, he found it even more important. "On that first trip after the shooting, we rediscovered a freedom we never had anymore in the White House," he recalled.

At the ranch, President Reagan cultivated his positive image as a westerner, but he genuinely enjoyed riding and had long dreamed of owning a ranch. Above he rides El Alamein, his favorite ranch horse, and below feeds him a a carrot.

———

Knowing that Richard Nixon had been censured in the press and investigated by Congress for the millions of dollars spent by the government on his houses in California and Florida, Reagan ordered the Secret Service to install nothing at the ranch that could not be removed once he left office. By the late spring of 1981 a helicopter landing pad was in place and concrete foundations laid for a helicopter hangar. Soon seven temporary buildings housed a Secret Service command

On a horseback ride with her husband in 1986, First Lady Nancy Reagan held up a sign emblazoned with the motto of her antidrug campaign: "Just Say No." Captured by news photographers with huge lenses trained on the ranch, it could have been interpreted as a message to the watchers and their cameras. To the Reagans, the ranch was a sanctuary, and they tried hard to protect their privacy.

post, workspace for White House communications, a clinic, staff offices, and sleeping space for the few aides whose presence at the ranch was considered essential. Trees and shrubs were planted to mask the new buildings. Motion detectors were installed inside fake boulders to keep them hidden. At the time, overall construction costs were estimated at $750,000. But most of the president's official buisness was conducted from a beach-side hotel at Santa Barbara, where aides were linked to the White House by separate communication lines for routine and classified messages.

The expense of flying the president across the continent for West Coast vacations quickly became an issue. Responding to press questions, the Air Force estimated the fuel cost for *Air Force One* at $5,221 an hour or about $52,000 for the ten-hour round trip. The cost increased to $119,000 when fuel for a backup plane was included. The *Washington Post* quoted expense estimates as high as $250,000 for each trip, including the use of helicopters, autos, and accommodations for the dozens of staff members and support personnel who travel with a president. When reporters raised questions about cost, spokesman Jim Brady joked that Reagan probably considered the trip essential "from a mental health standpoint."

With Reagan's activities at the ranch mostly hidden from view, the national television networks fretted over the lack of film of the president on horseback or clearing brush. So they installed huge lenses, trained at the ranch like cannon from a neighboring mountain. Viewers in the nation's living rooms were provided wavering images of Reagan brushing down his horse and riding off. Initially amused, the president joked that he was tempted to fake a heart attack, clutch his chest, and fall off his horse. "I wonder what they'd do then?" he told aides. But eventually the Reagans complained. "Now the whole world could watch as we walked around the ranch," the president wrote in his memoirs. "We didn't like it very much."

When the Reagans were in a good mood they waved at the distant cameras. The former actor didn't have to be directed. "The president . . . likes to look up suddenly to the precise point where he knows where the cameras are—stage left," the *New York Times* reported during Reagan's 1982 Thanksgiving visit. "Then he simply waves a greeting with the enthusiasm of one of those football

players who are always pantomiming, 'Hi, Mom,' on national television."

Journalists were given a rare close-up look at Rancho del Cielo during a bill-signing ceremony on August 13, 1981. But they found Reagan's mountaintop wrapped in fog so dense they could barely make out the house while standing in the front yard. "I wish the fog would lift so you could see some of the brush piles around here," the president told them. Gloomy or not, it was an important day for the conservative chief executive.

Dressed in a denim jacket and blue jeans, on August 13, 1981, President Reagan signed the 1981 Tax Reconciliation Act at Rancho del Cielo. He used two dozen pens, saving each as a souvenir for a congressional sponsor. That meant a single pen for each letter of his name. "It's times like these I wish I had a middle name," he stated. Correspondent Sam Donaldson replied, "You do, Mr. President. It's Wilson," prompting an uproar of laughter.

Wearing a denim jacket and faded blue jeans, Reagan signed legislation laying the cornerstone of his national economic policy. The two bills on the Mexican-style table on the patio reduced spending on many government programs while sharply cutting taxes. Reagan boasted that they represented "a turnaround of almost a half century of a course this country has been on and marks an end to the excessive growth in the government bureaucracy and government spending and government taxing."

In the wide-ranging news conference that followed, Reagan conceded that continuing deficits meant that his budget might not be balanced by 1984. Then he was asked to comment on angry protests by the Soviet Union over his decision to move ahead with production of the neutron bomb. His reply: "They're screaming like they're sitting on a sharp nail simply because we now are showing the will . . . not to let them get to the point of dominance where they can someday issue to the free world an ultimatum of surrender or die." Outside the gate leading to the Reagan ranch, observed by reporters but unseen by the president, a cluster of demonstrators protested the neutron bomb decision.

Rancho del Cielo was also gloomy when Queen Elizabeth II and Prince Philip came for a visit on March 1, 1983. After riding horseback with the queen at Windsor Castle in June 1982, Reagan invited her to ride with him at his ranch. But the day the royal couple arrived heavy rains and gale-force winds raked the Santa Ynez Mountains. Helicopters were grounded. Refugio Road turned into a treacherous obstacle course of fallen boulders, downed tree limbs, and overflowing streams. Not wanting to disappoint another head of state, the queen insisted on going ahead. Her party transferred from limousines to four-wheel drive vehicles and splashed upward. The clouds were low and mist was swirling as the royal couple arrived at the ranch house.

The promised ride was impossible. "It was raining so hard I thought the horses would sink to their knees in the mud," Secret Service agent Barletta recalled. Instead, Reagan ushered the royal couple inside for a Mexican lunch. When the president apologized for the weather the queen cut him short: "Yes, if it was *just* dreary, but this is an adventure." White House deputy chief of staff Michael Deaver called her "a real trouper and a good sport."

Royal visits were one thing. But for someone as proud of his land as he was, the president was highly selective in showing it to others. "Invitations to outsiders—even to his closest friends and aides—are very rare, and almost never involve an overnight stay," former Treasury Secretary Donald Regan observed in a memoir written after he was dismissed as White House chief of staff. But some lower-ranking White House aides confided that they were not eager to pull ranch duty. "It's pretty damn secluded—just gnats, a few rattlesnakes and every now and then a buzzard flies over," one aide told the *New York Times*.

————

Although the ranch was clearly Reagan's favorite refuge, Camp David in Maryland's rolling Catoctin Mountains was much easier to reach. "Without Camp David, you'll go stir crazy," former First Lady Patricia Nixon told Nancy Reagan. The president soon came to think of Camp David as "a slice of heaven" and spent more time there than any previous chief executive. He visited the retreat 187 times over his eight years in office, for a total of 571 days. Nancy Reagan put it into five words: "Thank God for Camp David!"

The Reagans made one immediate change at Camp David. President Nixon had ordered the riding trails paved to ensure smooth riding for golf carts. The Reagans restored them and brought in horses borrowed from the Park Police. They rode the camp trails and, despite the nervousness of the Secret Service, ventured into parkland outside the fence. The first lady also made changes at Aspen Lodge. Narrow windows were enlarged to open the views. The furniture got new slipcovers. She hung a collection of vintage army, navy, and marine corps posters at Laurel Lodge. The new touches were achieved without the critical comment that followed her decorating efforts at the White House. "For me, one of the best parts about Camp David was that there wasn't a whisper of controversy about the renovations I made there," she recalled. "Because the entire place is off-limits to the press, nobody ever knew what I did." One more permanent change was the construction of a chapel, not completed until the Reagans left the White House. Religious services had formerly been held in the camp's recreation hall. In 1988 the Reagans selected the site and helped break ground for a wood and stone chapel with stained glass and a bell tower, to be built with $1 million in privately raised money.

On Saturdays, shortly after noon, Reagan took a sip of hot water—a throat-clearing suggestion from singer Frank Sinatra—leaned into a microphone at Laurel Lodge, and delivered his weekly five-minute radio address. Topics over the years ranged from relations with Moscow to summer jobs for students. The president had enjoyed radio since he was hired in 1933 as a sportscaster for a

On a rainy March 1, 1983, the Reagans welcomed Queen Elizabeth II of England to Rancho del Cielo. One British reporter was reminded of "a wet afternoon on Dartmoor." Another envisioned "the Hounds of the Reaganvilles, very Basil Rathbone." The queen's American visit ended on a brighter note when she celebrated the Reagans' thirty-first wedding anniversary at a dinner aboard the royal yacht *Britannia*. "I know I promised Nancy a lot when we were married, but how can I ever top this?" the president declared in his toast.

radio station in Davenport, Iowa. He spoke easily, imagining his listeners were a circle of old friends. Over eight years he delivered 150 radio addresses from Camp David.

On weekend evenings, Reagan often revisited his moviemaking past. White House aides and Camp David staff gathered at Aspen Lodge, balanced bowls of popcorn on their knees, and watched a series of "golden oldies," which the president generally preferred to more recent films. The stars on the screen might include Humphrey Bogart, Clark Gable, Katherine Hepburn, Cary Grant, Rita Hayworth, John Wayne, Fred Astaire or, on request, Ronald Reagan and his bride, Nancy Davis Reagan. The Reagan-Davis films

Only rarely were advisers invited to Rancho del Cielo, but on November 25, 1987, Chief of Staff Howard Baker and National Security Adviser Colin Powell met there with the president.

included *Hellcats of the Navy*, which they made in 1957. When the screen went dark, the president offered behind-the-scenes stories about the actors, the movies, and the studios. Before showing *Bedtime for Bonzo*, the 1951 movie in which he shared top billing with a chimpanzee, he advised that the best way to spot Bonzo was to look for the one not wearing a wristwatch.

Nancy Reagan considered Camp David the president's "most private retreat." Senior officials were only rarely invited. Family members came infrequently. No foreign leader stayed overnight. Japanese Prime Minister Yasuhiro Nakasone and Mexican President José López Portillo were guests for lunch. British Prime Minister Margaret Thatcher, a Reagan favorite, came twice. "That was about it," Mrs. Reagan noted. She and her husband relaxed alone, walked, rode horses, exercised, swam in the pool, and watched movies. Nevertheless, she reported, the president always faced a regimen of briefing books, intelligence reports, speechwriting, decision-making, and the Saturday radio address. "You might be off in the mountains, but you're still president, and the world doesn't stop turning," she reflected.

Although squads of squirrels inhabited the White House grounds, there were few oak trees and therefore few acorns for food. Since Camp David's oaks produced plenty of acorns, Reagan scooped them into plastic bags and carried them back to Washington on his helicopter. Each

President Reagan took advantage of the solitude at Camp David to write his State of the Union Address, February 2, 1985.

weekday morning he scattered acorns outside the door to the Oval Office. "Throughout the day he would look up from his desk and see the squirrels scurrying off with their treats from the country," his daughter Maureen remembered.

During the summer of 1988, while the 77-year-old president was recuperating at Bethesda Naval Hospital after successful surgery for colon cancer, the first lady had photographs of Camp David hung in his room. "They really help," Reagan wrote, and paraphrased a line from W. C. Fields: "All in all, I'd rather be at Camp David."

———

At the beginning of each new year, Reagan took a break from horse-riding and brush-cutting to plunge into the social swirl at the verdant estate in the California desert near Palm Springs owned by Walter Annenberg, billionaire publisher and Reagan's ambassador to Great Britain. Observing from the other side of the electronically controlled gate, reporters caught glimpses of an oasis of pools, fountains, and lush gardens. Forty-seven invited guests entered a house with a light-filled atrium and one of the world's great private art collections.

An excursion to sun-drenched Palm Springs had been an annual rite of winter for nearly a decade by the time Reagan became president. The social gatherings were described in news accounts as a much-anticipated opportunity for the first lady to catch up with a wide circle of California friends. There were several parties over the week. Some were elegant but some were casual: turtleneck sweaters and sport coats. Annenberg's private 9-hole golf course provided the venue for what Reagan called his annual golf game. Overall, he played no more than a dozen games during his presidency; no scores were ever released. "I've never been a great aficionado of the desert," Reagan replied when a reporter asked if he liked Palm Springs enough to retire there.

News from the desert oasis was often scarce. Lou Cannon of the *Washington Post* used the Palm Springs dateline to issue a year-end collection of "Reaganisms," humorous presidential misstatements on a variety of somber topics. Cannon's "Reaganism of the Year" for 1983 came from an Oval Office interview on nuclear weapons: "This kind of weapon can't help but have an impact on the population as a whole." Cannon concluded that Reagan's frequent verbal gaffes humanized him while causing opponents to

President and Mrs. Reagan walked together at Camp David, October 2, 1982. Because Marines guarded the outer fences, the Reagans could just step out the front door at Aspen Lodge and go for a walk, something they could not do at the White House. The president called that a freedom only someone in his position could fully appreciate.

Only a few foreign dignitaries were invited to Camp David during the Reagan years. On June 8, 1981, President Reagan and President José López Portillo of Mexico went for a horseback ride 1981 (*left*). In 1986, the president and Prime Minister Margaret Thatcher of Great Britain toured the grounds of Camp David (*below*).

Each December, the Reagans spent the holidays at Sunnylands, the Palm Springs estate of Walter Annenberg. Events were star-studded. At one formal affair, President Reagan danced with Leonore Annenberg and Mrs. Reagan with Walter Annenberg (*left*). At another President Reagan talked with singer Sarah Brightman, composer Andrew Lloyd Webber, and Walter Annenberg, 1988 (*right*).

underestimate his political skills. "It is difficult to show that they have done him any harm," he wrote.

Government business followed Reagan to the desert. While the president was in Palm Springs in 1988 he and Soviet leader Mikhail S. Gorbachev exchanged prerecorded New Year's Day messages to the Soviet and American people. Reagan filled his message with accounts of freedoms and opportunities largely unavailable to Soviet citizens. Gorbachev spoke of hope for more substantial arms control agreements in the coming year and expressed optimism that the two countries were weaving "a tangible fabric of trust and growing mutual understanding." The next year, in their final exchange of New Year's messages, Reagan and Gorbachev cited progress in arms control and in resolving Soviet-American disputes. "The world is safer than it was a year ago," Reagan told the Soviet people from Palm Springs. Gorbachev agreed and said to Americans: "Fears and suspicions are gradually giving way to trust and feelings of mutual liking."

In the summer of 1988, Reagan had jokingly told reporters who had covered his vacations that once he left office he planned to work for passage of a constitutional amendment "to make every president spend his vacation in Santa Barbara." It was a remark appreciated by those who had enjoyed Santa Barbara's sunny beaches, even though they hadn't seen much of the fortieth president at his ranch and refuge. When his two terms ended, the Reagans bought a house in Los Angeles and traveled widely; he gave speeches, met with world leaders, and kept regular office hours. They spent considerable time at the ranch, in some years visiting as often as once a month.

On May 3, 1992, Reagan took Gorbachev for a ranch tour, driving the riding trails in a blue Jeep. Both leaders were out of office by then, and the Soviet Union had been divided into its many parts. Secret Service agent Barletta, who had continued on the Reagan protective detail, thought

The president and
Mrs. Reagan, relaxing
in the sun at Walter
Annenberg's estate,
Sunnylands, 1981.

President Reagan, on horseback (*opposite*), heads for the trail at Rancho del Cielo, accompanied by his faithful friends, Freebo and Victory, 1986.

On May 3, 1992, Mikhail Gorbachev, on a two-week tour of the United States, visited Rancho del Cielo (*left*). The two world leaders were now out of office, and the visit was cordial.

Gorbachev was impressed with the small size and simplicity of the house. Others thought it was evident he had been expecting something far grander. The former president of the United States showed off the saddles in the tack room and introduced his horses, and gave the former president of the Soviet Union a wide-brimmed western hat. No one wanted to embarrass the former Soviet leader by telling him he had put it on backward.

Reagan continued to ride horses, repair fences, and cut brush. But on November 4, 1994, in a letter to the American people, he reported his doctors' finding that he had the early signs of Alzheimer's disease and that his life was about to change. As the months passed, Barletta observed Reagan's riding skills deteriorating and saw him make dangerous "rookie mistakes." With Mrs. Reagan's encouragement, Barletta told the former president he shouldn't ride. "It's OK, John, I know," Reagan told him, and never rode again. As the disease progressed, Barletta realized Reagan was confusing the ranch in the Santa Ynez Mountains with others he had owned. Reagan visited Rancho del Cielo for the last time in the late summer of 1995 and died at his Los Angeles home on June 5, 2004.

In the spring of 1998, Nancy Reagan sold Rancho del Cielo to the Young America's Foundation, a successor to the conservative, college-age coalition, Young Americans for Freedom, active during the Reagan years. The foundation maintains the ranch, its buildings, and a collection of original Reagan furnishings and personal belongings. It holds student conferences in Santa Barbara and conducts tours of the ranch for conferees. The ranch is not open to the broader public.

Chapter 36

George H. W. Bush: Running Hard

GEORGE H. W. BUSH
41st President of the
United States, 1989–1993

George H. W. Bush hurtled through his vacations at Kennebunkport, Maine, as if he were in a high-stakes race with himself. Days began shortly after dawn with a 2-mile run from the family's stone-and-shingle summer home at Walker's Point. That over, the president galloped through 18 holes of stopwatch golf, making the round in less than half the time most players needed. A set or two of fast-paced tennis followed, or a swim in Maine's chilly waters. Most days included a heart-stopping zoom out to sea in *Fidelity*, the president's sleek and powerful 28-foot speedboat. The pace slowed a bit out on the water as Bush trolled for bluefish or cast for striped bass, sometimes using a quiet moment to read a White House memo or consult with advisers. Then he brought *Fidelity* back to full throttle and careened back to Walker's Point, his course marked by a furrow of white foam. If there were fish to clean he'd clean them, then play a fiercely competitive game of horseshoes and romp with the grandchildren. Between jogging, putting, lobbing, casting, trolling, and horseshoe throwing, he made room for his daily intelligence briefing, dealt with paperwork, and reached out around the world by telephone.

"This President Relaxes by Wearing Others Out," a newspaper headline advised in the summer of 1989. Why maintain such a killing pace? a reporter asked. "I always have," the president replied. "I find it relaxing and it clears the mind." Then he added: "You know me, I get restless." Bush "brings to the normal worries of his job an almost abnormal faith in the virtues of perpetual motion," a *New York Times* editorial asserted.

An 11-acre shelf of splintered rock, Walker's Point projects into the Atlantic like a miniature peninsula. It is a place of slapping waves, gliding seagulls, tangy salt air, bobbing lobster pots, and long ocean views. Twenty-five miles south of Portland, the point has been a family enclave since 1903, when George Herbert Walker, a St. Louis banker and the president's grandfather, built two large summer cottages. Ownership transferred over the decades to the president's mother, Dorothy, and his father, Senator Prescott Bush, a Connecticut Republican. Eventually their son, George Herbert Walker Bush, became the point's owner. By the time Bush followed Ronald Reagan to the presidency, he had spent all but one of his sixty-four summers at Walker's Point. He missed only the summer of 1944, when he was on duty as a navy fighter pilot in the Pacific.

"Maine in the summer was the best of all possible adventures," he wrote in his 1987 autobiography, *Looking Forward*. As a boy he searched the rock crevices for starfish and sea urchins, and the natural beauty of the place became a sustaining memory: "There was the wonder of the tidal pools, the smell of cool salt air, the pulsating sound of waves crashing ashore at night, and the natural wonder of storms that suddenly swept across the rocky coastline." He returned every August even as he built his resume: Texas oilman, member of Congress, ambassador to the United Nations, chairman of the Republican National Committee, U.S. envoy to China, director of the Central Intelligence Agency, and vice president.

An avid fisherman, President George H. W. Bush is seen here on his boat *Fidelity* displaying a large bluefish, caught near Walker's Point in 1991.

Walker's Point has been a Bush family enclave since 1903. This pond was set up and stocked by Great-Grandfather Walker. In the background is what President Bush called "the Big House," the original seaside cottage of 1903.

The family compound adjusted to meet changing times during and after Bush's presidency. Eventually there were ten structures providing space for family and guests, the Secret Service, presidential aides, a presidential office, and maintenance facilities. The list of amenities included a workout gym, a boat dock, sauna, hot tub, tennis court, and horseshoe pits.

But Barbara Bush confessed to being stunned when she saw what had been done to accommodate her husband's presidency. She mourned each of the trees and shrubs cut to make room for the new facilities, which included a helicopter landing pad, living quarters for the president's doctor and military aide, and a long chain-link fence. "Suddenly we looked like a prison instead of a beautiful summer home. . . . It hurt to see a ten-foot-high fence when we rounded the drive instead of the ocean." Eventually adjustments were made and part of the fence came down.

———

Reporters almost never saw Ronald Reagan when he vacationed at his mountaintop ranch in California. Television networks were resigned to getting just one shot: the president on horseback seen through shimmering heat waves, an image captured by giant telephoto lenses perched on a neighboring mountain. Variety was not a problem at Kennebunkport. By the end of Bush's first presidential vacation in 1989, television producers had accumulated dozens of tapes of the president racing his golf cart across the greens, cutting a wake in *Fidelity*, catching fish, playing softball, swinging at a tennis ball, jumping off the dock, jogging, and throwing horseshoes. Peaceful Kennebunkport "was turned upside down by a new president eager to show the world that he can play hard at everything while a horde of reporters, photographers and onlookers tried to keep him in their sights," the *Washington Post* reported. "He plunged into the frigid ocean and 20 days of vacation without apologies for leaving the business of the presidency behind."

Bush brought his own offbeat, teasing, intensely competitive, and fast-moving style to all of his activities, including golf. Although he often scored in the 80s, he played with an eye on the stopwatch, zipping around in golf carts, politely playing through slower golfers, and urging others

in his foursome to make each round faster than the one before. The White House physician diagnosed it as "aerobic golf." The Secret Service reportedly called it "power golf." George W. Bush, the president's eldest son, called his father's version of the game "polo." Whatever it was called, the *Washington Post* concluded that Bush and his partners had turned a game of skill and concentration into "a rollicking, accelerated gallop." In 1989 reporters timed the president's circuit through 18 holes at one hour and fifty-one minutes. In 1990 he cut that time to one hour forty-two minutes.

Teeing off one afternoon, Bush mockingly introduced a new character to the gallery. "All right, the crowd is hushed," he gravely announced. "They sense Mr. Smooth is back." Then, having raised expectations, he hooked his shot to the left. He took a shot that was a bit better and just for the moment said nothing further about "Mr. Smooth." But soon he was asking a press aide to round up reporters and photographers "to come see what Mr. Smooth is like on the tennis courts." And on another day, talking nonstop while throwing horseshoes, the normally modest president congratulated himself every time he scored a ringer: "Mr. Smooth does it again!"

Bush kept up a running patter on the course. Mr. Smooth was just one creation of Bushspeak. Observers noted that to Bush, his sons, and other frequent partners, "Wedge City" meant a sand trap. Controlling the "yips and chips" meant dealing with nerves while putting and following through correctly on short strokes. A "power outage" described a putt that faded far short of the cup. Steering the ball to "the dance floor" meant reaching the green. "Vic Damone" described a gratifying win. But "Arnold Farmer" was Bush code for a golfer who had experienced a very bad day. Like many golfers Bush also talked to the ball, but kept his language fit for even the most delicate ears. "Oh, golly darn, get up there," he exclaimed after one drive.

A passion for golf was one of the ornaments on the Bush family tree. The president's maternal grandfather, George Herbert Walker, an excellent golfer and the builder of the house at Walker's Point, established the British-American Walker's Cup amateur match and served as president of

Walker's Point projects out into the Atlantic and is surrounded on three sides by water. President Bush described the point as his "anchor to windward."

the United States Golf Association in 1920. The president's father, Senator Prescott Bush, another proficient amateur, headed the USGA in 1935. Members of the combined families had played at Kennebunkport's Cape Arundel Golf Club, a five-minute drive from Walker's Point, for decades.

Even more than golf, the blue-hulled cigarette boat *Fidelity* met the president's need for speed and constant motion. Newspapers reported that the Secret Service was forced to increase the power of its boats to keep up with him. Press secretary Marlin Fitzwater remembered being aboard for a three-hour run up the coast to Walker's Point when Bush was still vice president:

> He kept it full-throttle all the way, water spraying over the bow, taking every wave with a thud and burst of speed. It was great fun for the first hour, then my back started hurting, my legs began to tire from flexing with the waves, and my fanny ached from bouncing on the back bench. But his face was glued into the wind, hair plastered back so he looked like the hood ornament of a 1956 Oldsmobile, and his windbreaker had long since failed to do its job. As we neared Walker's Point, close enough to see the lights of the house, he found a bit more power in the twin engines and we raced into the cove at full speed. I asked why. He said it was the closest he could come to duplicating the race of the wind from an open-cockpit airplane, the TBM *Avenger* he flew during World War II.

For Bush, a vacation day without a few hours of fishing was a day wasted. "There's no way to describe the excitement I feel when a bass hits the lure or when a sixteen-pound bluefish hits my surface plug," he told a reporter. "You get out there in the chop and the foam, with a school of blues breaking water and birds going nuts, and you're in another world," he told a boating magazine. When he became president a small armada joined the fish and diving birds. *Fidelity* was followed by Secret Service boats, flanked by Coast Guard boats, and pursued by chase boats carrying photographers and television crews. The president enjoyed being out on the water under nearly any circumstance. He was willing to go on fishing even when it was clear the fish were not biting. After Bush caught nothing on an outing in Alabama, a spokesman offered an official explanation: "It says something about the tenacity with which he approaches sports that he is willing to fish under the worst possible conditions."

The walls in President Bush's private office at Walker's Point, seen here in 2004, offer testimony to his love of fishing.

Bush's tenacity was put to the test in August 1989, his first vacation as president. While others caught fish, he caught nothing. Day after day he steered *Fidelity* to one favored fishing spot after the other. Day after day he returned empty-handed. He began muttering about "this jinx." The newspapers posted a daily fish watch: "Fish 13; Bush 0." The long streak of no-luck days became fodder for Johnny Carson and other late-night television quipsters. Reporters arrived at a news conference given by Bush and Canadian Prime Minister Brian Mulroney wearing T-shirts with the words, "No Fish." Bush took it personally, if just a bit facetiously. "My record fishing in these waters is well known," he intoned. "It's a superb record—a record of bountiful catches. And somehow some things have gone wrong for the last thirteen days, something's happened." With just three full days remaining in the vacation, the president made a promise: "Between now and when I leave on Monday, I guarantee you—I positively guarantee you that this jinx will be broken."

On Sunday September 3, just eighteen minutes after he pulled away from the dock and entered the chop off Walker's Point, a bluefish struck at the president's lure. Bush set the hook and reeled

Whenever he could, President Bush took off in his speedboat *Fidelity*, sometimes with family, and always followed by the Secret Service.

in a 2-foot-long fish: estimated weight, 9 pounds. Later in the afternoon he caught two more fish. The press boats sounded horns in salute as he brought *Fidelity* into the dock and posed for photos with his catch. "The jinx is broken!" he exulted. "A long dry summer; but it all worked out." Months later he explained his methods: "I kept the hook in the water. I refused to get too tense. Tense yes, 'too tense,' no. I cast into every swirl I saw; I trolled 'til the sun had sunk. I changed lures and rods for luck; and finally on the second to last day as I began to troll, a good bluefish hit."

The world was at peace that summer. Bush's approval ratings were high. He played hard during what he called "a total vacation" with almost no speeches or public events. But the work of the presidency never entirely stopped. Bush tried to compress that work into a few hours a day, beginning with morning intelligence briefings on the side porch of the old house. On a typical day he took and initiated calls and dealt with correspondence from an office in a cottage at the Secret Service compound.

Bush's world changed on August 2, 1990, when the Iraqi army under Saddam Hussein occupied and plundered Kuwait, threatening the oil reserves of neighboring Saudi Arabia. Bush told the nation that the Iraqi aggression "will not stand" and dispatched tens of thousands of American regular and reserve forces to the Saudi desert.

One decision Bush had to make quickly was whether to go ahead with his long-scheduled twenty-five-day Kennebunkport vacation. Jimmy Carter had widely been seen as captive of the Iranian hostage crisis of 1980, pinned down in the White House as if a hostage himself. Bush vowed not to permit the Iraqi dictator to control the movements and activities of the president of the United States. He believed he had to show he was unworried, confident, in charge and free to go where he wanted. "A relaxed George Bush was the best possible signal to send," he asserted. He contended many years later, as have many other chief executives, that a modern president can function well no matter where he is or what he is doing:

On duty at Walker's Point, President Bush conducted a press briefing on the Middle East crisis in August 1990. At left is Defense Secretary Dick Cheney.

> In truth, a president is never truly on vacation and is never "away" from the office. His responsibilities follow him wherever he goes, day or night, and the office is wherever he happens to be. This is especially true in the modern presidency, where instant communications are easy. . . . In helicopters, airplanes, cars and boats (including the *Fidelity*) the president always has telephones at hand, and the distance from the person on the other end makes no difference. We had secure communications at our home on Walker's Point. . . . What we did was simply move shop from one location to the other.

"The American people want to see life go on so long as they understand their President and top officials are on top of a troubled situation," Bush told reporters as *Air Force One* flew to Maine. He vowed to mix vacation activities with a busy work schedule.

The next day the Pentagon announced that a fourth carrier task force was on its way to the Persian Gulf, and the work-play agenda became an increasingly awkward fit. Television pictures of the president running, fishing, golfing, and boating were paired with shots of troops preparing to

President Bush was surrounded by the press on a classic Walker's Point vacation in July 1991. UPI Reporter Helen Thomas, standing inside the rope line near the president, was ready with a question.

embark for the Persian Gulf and American families ordered detained in Iraq. Aides fretted over images of the president fielding questions about the crisis while sitting in his golf cart. "It looks horrible," one Bush adviser told the *New York Times*. "No one in the Bush inner circle thinks the President is not paying enough attention to the crisis or that he is behaving in a cavalier way," *Times* reporter Maureen Dowd noted. "It is just that the image looks frivolous."

Later Bush reflected that his fishing excursions allowed him to talk to his advisers without inhibition or intrusion. The ocean had become the president's "secure room." He remembered going out with Brent Scowcroft, his national security adviser, on a day when the wide-ranging discussion was more productive than the fishing:

> It was a beautiful, warm August day with a bright blue sky and a handful of clouds.
> Small swells lifted the *Fidelity* and waves lapped against its sleek blue racing hull,
> rocking it as we slowly trolled back and forth. There was a fresh ocean breeze,
> which tamed the heat. We were on the water about four hours under these ideal
> conditions and I put out a couple of lines, but the fish weren't biting. We soon
> became absorbed in a long, philosophical chat as we sat toward the stern of the
> boat with dark glasses and brimmed hats.

The conversation reportedly reviewed the Persian Gulf crisis to date, considered whether Saddam Hussein might retreat without the use of force, and what it would require to expel his forces if he did not. It laid the underpinnings for the decision later in the year to eject the Iraqi army from Kuwait by force.

Still, the flap over the president's vacation continued. Ignoring the criticism as best he could, Bush worked the phones to secure the international alliance he had built and returned to Washington for a day or two when going back seemed important. When reporters asked if he couldn't handle the crisis better staying back in Washington, he responded, "I've been able to keep in very close touch, and of course, we're making a lot of international phone calls that you wouldn't ordinarily expect at

President and Mrs. Bush loved to welcome their grandchildren in their bedroom in the morning. The Halloween Storm of 1991 destroyed the room (*bottom left*) when it blew a hole in the wall of the house, causing extensive interior damage. Family treasures, including photographs, were lost to the three-story waves. The house was soon repaired, and the stunning views of ocean, available from practically every window in the house (*bottom right*), were restored.

the time of a vacation. But I've got a good team, and they've been supportive. A lot of them have been up here."

The pressure had eased by the summer of 1991. The greatest foreign policy crisis of the Bush presidency had come and gone. The U.S.-led international coalition Bush had recruited routed Iraq's armies in Operation Desert Storm. Kuwait had been liberated. That eliminated the threat to Middle East oil reserves, although Saddam Hussein remained in power in Baghdad. Bush felt a strong need to unwind. He planned a four-week stay at Walker's Point. "I think I've earned it," he exclaimed, "and I'm looking forward to it. And it will not be denied."

The vacation began tranquilly enough. Fitzwater remembered going out with the president one August day in pursuit of bluefish. Soon after leaving the dock *Fidelity* passed a house with a large group of young people partying on an outside deck. One of them spotted the president's boat. Fitzwater told the rest of the story: "They started shouting and doing 'the wave,' standing shoulder to shoulder along the porch, arms in the air, swaying from side to side. 'Let's return it,' the president said. All four of us stood side by side in the boat, arms outstretched, and returned the wave."

As the *Fidelity* got farther from land and began trolling for bluefish, a serious conversation began. The president and his aides talked about Saddam Hussein, his continued defiance of United Nations resolutions, and what the United States might have to do about it. "But suddenly we got into a school of fish, and from then on it was all fishing," Fitzwater recalled. Each of the anglers hauled in about ten fish. Returning to Walker's Point, the president retrieved a long knife from his tackle box and cleaned them himself. The jinx had long since vanished. "I love trolling when the big blues hit," Bush informed his tape-recorded diary.

But that summer also held an unpleasant surprise. Shortly after midnight on August 19, Brent Scowcroft, Bush's national security adviser, called Walker's Point from his hotel room in Kennebunkport and awakened the president with the first, preliminary reports of a coup in the Soviet Union. President Mikhail Gorbachev was isolated at his vacation home in the Crimea, his status and personal safety unclear. Bush turned to the telephone as he always did in a crisis, contacting world leaders to deliver the message that there would be no acceptance of the coup. Late in the morning of August 21, Bush and Scowcroft went for a ride in *Fidelity*. A call reached the boat that a head of state was trying to reach the president, and Bush headed into the dock. He walked into his bedroom, picked up the secure phone, and was told Gorbachev was on the line. He thought the Soviet leader sounded jubilant and upbeat. The first few words made the message clear: the coup had failed. "I was just delighted to hear that he was fine, delighted that he appeared to be well," Bush told reporters later. He observed in a diary entry several days later that, despite the unexpected crisis, the vacation had been a success: "Pressures will mount now, but I've got enough of this sea air, ocean and rocks and pools in my soul that it will give me the strength to get on through a long, cold winter, cold politically—who knows about meteorologically wise."

It was a meteorological event that would test the president's soul. Walker's Point's expansive ocean views meant it was vulnerable when the North Atlantic turned ugly. On October 31, 1991, Halloween, a powerful storm struck the New England Coast. Three-story waves overwhelmed the main house, smashed through the front windows, surged through the first-floor rooms, broke out the rear wall, and washed tables, chairs, sofas, and several lifetimes of memories out to sea. Just before evacuating the compound, the Secret Service detail assigned to Walker's Point shot a videotape of a mountainous wave breaking over the house. A day later, visiting in Texas, the president and first lady watched the ocean wreck their house. Fitzwater was with them:

On November 24, 1989, President Bush took British Prime Minister Margaret Thatcher for a snowy ride in a golf cart at Camp David.

> We watched in the bedroom of their hotel suite as the giant wave reached up over the rocks, over the side of the home, appeared over the chimney of the fireplace, then disappeared into the house. Finally we could see the walls of the entire structure bloat outwards, as the fury and pressure of the water sought release through windows and doors. Then it was gone. And everything inside the main floor of the house went with it.

On February 25, 1990, President and Mrs. Bush greeted West German Chancellor Helmut Kohl and his wife, Hannelore Kohl, on their arrival at Camp David.

On Christmas Eve (*top left*), 1991, President Bush read stories to his grandchildren at Camp David.

Pitching horseshoes (*top right*) is a Bush family tradition. Here family members play at Walker's Point, but they also played at Camp David and at the White House, where horseshoe pits were installed for their enjoyment.

Two days later the president flew to Maine to inspect the damage: the shattered wall, the broken glass, the guesthouse heaved off its foundation, the tennis court filled with sand, rocks, and rubble. Bush found a framed photograph of his father on wet ground near the house, its glass broken and the picture stained with seawater. "He held it, stared at it, and carried it with him," Fitzwater noted. But Bush remained upbeat as he wrote to a friend that Walker's Point "had its body bent and broken but its soul is OK. Our ground floor is shot—books, pictures—so many treasures like that gone; but it will bounce back inspite of its truly historic pounding."

Like most presidents since Franklin Roosevelt, Bush used Camp David in Maryland's mountains for pleasant weekend escapes from the White House and as a secure and secluded place to meet with world leaders. Camp David's attraction, Bush wrote, was the quiet mountain setting, the canopy of trees, the nighttime movies at the president's quarters in Laurel Lodge, the tennis courts, swimming pool, putting green, skeet range, and the horseshoe-throwing pits installed during his presidency. He liked to see his dogs Millie and Ranger exploring the Camp David woods, "sniffing and sniffing . . . and turning; and dramatically running after a deer here and there." The president believed that the activities and the informality created the circumstances for frank discussions and provided a chance to get to know guests personally.

Marlin Fitzwater called Camp David the one refuge a president has from twenty-four-hour press scrutiny. "Presidents like it because the press can't get in," Fitzwater wrote. "The press like it because the president can't get out, at least not without being spotted." Thus presidents can swim and go for a walk or play tennis and throw horseshoes and read and think and spend private time with their families. When in 1992 Bush's daughter, Dorothy "Doro" Bush LeBlond, wanted to celebrate her marriage to William Koch with little fuss, the chapel at Camp David offered the privacy needed for a family celebration.

Bush had thrown horseshoes since he was a boy and zealously pursued the sport during his presidency. Two state-of-the art horseshoe pits were installed, one at Camp David and one next to the swimming pool at the White House. The pit areas were outlined in wood, backed with a redwood retaining wall, and filled with synthetic clay. Narrow concrete walks flanked each side of the range.

Newspapers noted that throwing horseshoes was as much a Bush family sport as touch football had been for the Kennedys. The Bushes, the *New York Times* observed, "do it with as much passion, vigor, and spirited competitiveness as that relatively mild sport allows." The aim of the game is to wrap a 2½ pound shoe around an iron stake driven into the ground. Men throw from a distance of 40 feet; women from 30 feet. Each ringer scores three points. Bush made ringers about 30 percent of the time, and experts said that marked him as a credible but not a champion player. His widely reported participation in the sport led to a spurt of sales in the recreational horseshoe industry.

Bush tried to keep the atmosphere at Camp David casual and relaxed, even when conferring with other heads of state. In May 1990, during a meeting with Gorbachev, Bush took it as an achievement when he was able to persuade the Soviet leader to shed his coat and tie and continue the talks in his shirtsleeves. During a break between two working sessions, while Bush was taking a short nap, Gorbachev went for a walk and paused at the horseshoe pits. The next time Bush saw journalists he reported on what happened next: "President Gorbachev picked up a horseshoe, never having played the game to my knowledge, and literally—literally, all you horseshoe players out there—threw a ringer the first time." The horseshoe was retrieved, mounted on a plaque, and presented to the Soviet leader at dinner that evening. Barbara Bush called it an exercise in "horseshoe diplomacy." But the president, apparently still unable to believe what he called Gorbachev's "beginner's luck," joked that the unexpected ringer was "the only thing that went wrong" during the summit. Gorbachev had the last word: "Well, I couldn't give in, after all."

———

Following his presidency, George H.W. Bush oversaw the establishment of his presidential library on the campus of Texas A&M University in College Station, Texas, where his speedboat, *Fidelity*, is on display.

President Bush's Camp David office has been recreated at the George H.W. Bush Presidential Library and Museum at College Station, Texas.

Chapter 37

Twenty-First-Century Escapes

WILLIAM J. CLINTON
42nd President of the
United States, 1993–2001

GEORGE W. BUSH
43rd President of the
United States, 2001–2009

BARACK OBAMA
44th President of the
United States, 2009–

While jetliners, helicopters, and motorcades have long since replaced George Washington's coach and four-horse team, the precedent he set for presidential escapes endures. But even as more recent presidents break free from White House schedules to golf, fish, sail, ski, walk on the beach, or just read a book, they are never free from the responsibilites that come with the Oath of Office.

Three twenty-first-century presidents—Bill Clinton, George W. Bush, and Barack Obama—fit the familiar pattern, each in his own way. These photos show them unwinding, just about everywhere: Obama in Hawaii and Martha's Vineyard; Bush cutting brush and meeting world leaders at his Texas ranch; and Clinton teeing off on golf courses coast to coast.

While spending the summer at Kennebunkport, Maine, President George W. Bush uses a recently introduced method of green transportation—the Segway, 2005 (*top right*).

President Bill Clinton watches his shot off the first tee at the start of his second round of golf at the Farm Neck Golf Club on Martha's Vineyard, 2008 (*opposite*).

President Barack Obama hikes Cadillac Mountain in Acadia National Park, Bar Harbor, Maine, with First Lady Michelle Obama and daughters Malia and Sasha, 2010 (*right*).

At Work on Vacation

President Clinton spoke by telephone with Russian President Boris Yeltsin from his vacation home on Martha's Vineyard, 1998 (*above*). In front of the president's home on his Texas ranch near Crawford, George W. Bush and German Chancellor Angela Merkel addressed the media, 2007. President Barack Obama signed H.R. 847, the James Zadroga 9/11 Health and Compensation Act, in Kailua, Hawaii, 2011 (*below*).

President William J. Clinton:
From Martha's Vineyard to the Teton Mountains

President and Mrs. Clinton rested on a hammock near Beaver Lake (*above*) on a return to their home state of Arkansas in 1993.

President Clinton bought First Lady Hillary Rodham Clinton an orange-pineapple ice cream cone after attending the Martha's Vineyard Agricultural Fair in 1997.

At right, the Clinton family enjoyed a rafting trip down the Snake River south of Jackson, Wyoming, in 1995.

We all needed the time off, and I was really looking forward to the prospect of hiking and horseback riding in the Grand Tetons; rafting the Snake River; visiting Yellowstone National Park to see Old Faithful, the buffalo and moose, and the wolves we had brought back to the wild; and playing golf at the high altitude where the ball goes a lot further. — Bill Clinton, 1996

During a vacation near Wyoming's Jackson Hole in 1996, the Teton Mountains could be seen in the background as President Clinton and daughter Chelsea rode horses and as the president teed off on the golf course.

Retreating to Camp David

Recent presidents have continued to enjoy the solitude of Camp David and often visit the retreat with family.
President Obama played pool (*above*) in the Holly Cabin at Camp David following the conclusion of the G8 Summit, 2012,
President Bush and his family attended an Easter Service at the Camp David chapel with his family, 2006 (*below left*).
President Clinton spent Thanksgiving at Camp David with his family, 1995 (*below right*).

Camp David also continues to be an ideal place for hosting visiting heads of state. President Obama and Russian President Dmitry Medvedev (*left*) enjoyed a break during the G8 Summit at Camp David, 2012. South Korean President Lee Myung-bak and President Bush addressed the press (*above*) at Camp David, 2008. President Clinton met with Palestinian President Yasser Arafat in his cottage at Camp David during a Middle East summit, 2000 (*below*).

393

President George W. Bush:
A Ranch in Texas

President Bush cleared cedar branches during a month-long vacation at his 1,600-acre ranch near Crawford, Texas, 2002.

The press called my time away from Washington a vacation. Not exactly. I received my daily intelligence briefings at the secure trailer across the street, checked in regularly with advisers, and used the ranch as a base for meetings and travel. The responsibilites of the presidency followed me wherever I went. We had just moved the West Wing 1200 miles farther west.
—George W. Bush

President Bush carried his dog Barney into his pickup truck before driving back to his ranch house, after meeting the press on August 13, 2003. He had reported on a meeting with a team of economic advisers during his August vacation.

The wedding of the president's daughter Jenna Bush to Henry Hager was held in outdoor ceremony at the Bush family's Prairie Chapel Ranch in Texas, 2008.

President Bush displayed a striped bass caught while fishing with his father off the coast of Maine in June 2003 (*above*) and teed off at the Crosswater Golf Course at the Sunriver Resort in Sunriver, Oregon, during a two-day visit to the Pacific Northwest in 2003 (*right*).

President George W. Bush, left, began his 56th birthday playing a round of golf with his father, former president George H.W. Bush, right, at the Cape Arundel Golf Club near the Bush family home in Kennebunkport, Maine, July 6, 2002. President Bush sported a cap that said "El Jefe, meaning "the boss" in Spanish.

President Barack Obama:
Hawaiian Interludes

I know you are all eager to skip town and spend some time with your families. Not surprisingly, I am too. . . . I am sure that I will have even better ideas after a couple days of sleep and sun.— Barack Obama

President Obama often vacations in Hawaii, where he was born. During the presidential campaign in 2008, he was photographed body surfing at Sandy Beach in Honolulu (*right*).

President Obama played with Bo, his family's Portuguese water dog, aboard *Air Force One* enroute to Hawaii for the Christmas holidays in 2011 (*above*). During that 2011 vacation, President and Mrs. Obama toured the USS *Arizona* Memorial in Pearl Harbor (*above left*). Upon arriving for the Christmas holidays in 2013, President Obama greets members of the military on the tarmac at Joint Base Pearl Harbor–Hickam, in Honolulu (*left*).

President Obama is often seen enjoying outdoor sports including (*clockwise from top right*): bike riding with Sasha during a 2009 summer vacation on Martha's Vineyard; golfing at the Mid-Pacific County Club in Kailua, Hawaii, 2014; basketball with White House staffers while on vacation on Martha's Vineyard, 2009; and fishing for trout on the East Gallatin River near Belgrade, Montana, August 2009.

Exploring America

Twenty-first century presidents have continued the tradition of exploring America's National Parks during their vacations while highlighting the need to protect the environment. In 1995, President Clinton observed an osprey through a telescope during a visit to Yellowstone National Park, Wyoming, on the 79th anniversary of the National Park Service (*right*). In 2001, President Bush toured Sequoia National Park, in California (*below*). In 2009, President Obama was photographed at the lookout over Hopi Point during a tour the Grand Canyon in Arizona (*opposite*).

Sources, References and Resources

Preface

Page xiii, "We have got so": Walt Whitman, *Walt Whitman's Memoranda During the War: Written on the Spot in 1863–65*, ed. Peter Coviello (Oxford: Oxford University Press, 2004), 41.

Introduction

Page 1, "every inch of mind": Theodore C. Sorensen, *Kennedy* (New York: Harper and Row, 1965), 377.

Page 1, "a bed of thorns": John Tyler, quoted in Jane C. Walker, *John Tyler* (Blacksburg, Va.: McDonald and Woodward, 2001), 37.

Page 1, "splendid misery": Thomas Jefferson, in a letter to Elbridge Gerry, May 13, 1797, Founders Online, http://founders.archives. gov/documents/Jefferson.

Page 1, "a dreadful self-inflicted penance": Grover Cleveland, quoted in Alyn Brodsky, *Grover Cleveland: A Study in Character* (New York: St. Martin's Press), 104.

Page 1, "the loneliest place": Woodrow Wilson, quoted in A. Scott Berg, *Wilson* (New York: G. P. Putnam's Sons, 2013), 277.

Page 1, "This great white jail": Harry S. Truman, in President Harry S. Truman's 1947 Diary Book, transcribed by Raymond H. Geselbracht, Truman Presidential Museum and Library, www.trumanlibrary.org.

Page 1, "You can get": Ronald Reagan, quoted in Lou Cannon, *President Reagan: The Role of a Lifetime* (New York: Simon and Schuster, 1991), 466.

1: George Washington

SOURCES

Page 4, fifteen times: reported by Mary V. Thompson, research historian, and Jennifer Kittlaus, library reference assistant, George Washington's Mount Vernon, Mount Vernon, Va.

Page 4 caption, "No estate in United America": *George Washington, Letters from His Excellency General Washington, to Arthur Young*, 160.

Page 6, 397 days: reported by Thompson and Kittlaus.

Page 6, "I will return immediately": quoted in Henderson, *Washington's Southern Tour*, 38.

Page 6, Once, when his coach: George Washington, *Diaries of George Washington*, ed. Jackson and Twohig, 6:209.

Page 6, one trip to Philadelphia: Smith, *Patriarch*, 72.

Page 6, a horse fell: George Washington, *Diaries of George Washington*, ed. Jackson and Twohig, 6:107.

Page 6 caption, "should like to have": George Washington, *Writings of George Washington*, ed. Fitzpatrick, 29:250.

Page 7, "extremely indifferent": George Washington, *Diaries of George Washington*, ed. Jackson and Twohig, 6:158.

Page 7, "no rooms or beds": ibid., 6:113.

Page 7, "extra exertions": ibid., 6:158.

Page 8, "a fiery trial": quoted in Arnebeck, *Fiery Trial*, 1–2.

Page 8, commercial "emporium": quoted in Bowling, *Creation of Washington, D.C.*, 234.

Page 8 caption, "pointing with her fan": quoted in Miles et al., *American Paintings*, 154.

Page 10, 1,887 miles: editor's note to George Washington, letter to Tobias Leer, June 1[1], 1791, Papers of George Washington Digital Edition, ed. Crackel,

Page 10, thankful he had not been delayed: George Washington, letter to Alexander Hamilton, June 13, 1791, ibid.

Page 10, "relaxation from business": George Washington, letter to Betty Washington Lewis, October 12, 1789, ibid.

Page 10, "as good a salute": George Washington, *Diaries of George Washington*, ed. Jackson and Twohig, 6:114.

Page 10, "elegantly dressed & handsome lad[ies]": ibid., 6:130.

Page 10, "at least 400 ladies": ibid., 6:131.

Page 10, Middletown on the Connecticut River: ibid., 5:467.

Page 10, "a curious piece of mechanism": ibid., 5:481.

Page 10, Arriving at Charleston, and the rest of the visit: ibid., 6:131–32.

Page 11, Portsmouth, New Hampshire: ibid., 5:488.

Page 11, deep-sea fishing off Kittery: ibid., 5:489–90, including editor's note.

Page 11, three-day fishing trip off Sandy Hook: Tebbel, *George Washington's America*, 292.

Page 11, "We are told," "wholesome exercise": quoted in Decatur, *Private Affairs*, 133.

Page 11–13, The president directed and the rest of the paragraph: reported and quoted in Tebbel, *George Washington's America*, 366–67.

Page 13, "more real enjoyment": quoted in Flexner, *Washington: The Indispensable Man*, 360.

REFERENCES AND RESOURCES

Arnebeck, Bob. *Through a Fiery Trial: Building Washington, 1790–1800*. Lanham, Md.: Madison Books, 1991.

Bowling, Kenneth R. *The Creation of Washington, D.C.: The Idea and Location of the American Capital*. Fairfax, Va.: George Mason University Press, 1991.

Clotworthy, William G. *In the Footsteps of George Washington*. Blacksburg, Va.: McDonald and Woodward, 2002.

Collins, Herbert Ridgeway. *Presidents on Wheels*. New York: Bonanza Books, 1971.

Dalzell, Robert F., Jr., and Lee Baldwin Dalzell. "Memory, Architecture, and the Future: George Washington, Mount Vernon, and the White House." *White House History*, no. 6 (Fall 1999): 35–45.

Decatur, Stephen, Jr. *Private Affairs of George Washington: From the Records and Accounts of Tobias Lear, Esquire, His Secretary*. Boston: Houghton Mifflin, 1933.

Ellis, Joseph J. *His Excellency: George Washington*. New York: Alfred A. Knopf, 2004.

Flexner, James Thomas. *George Washington: Anguish and Farewell, 1793–1799*. Boston: Little, Brown, 1969.

———. *George Washington and the New Nation, 1783–1793*. Boston: Little, Brown, 1969.

———. *Washington: The Indispensable Man*. Boston: Little, Brown, 1974.

Garrett, Wendell, ed. *George Washington's Mount Vernon*. New York: Monacelli Press, 1998.

George Washington's Mount Vernon, online materials, www.mountvernon.org.

Freeman, Douglas Southall. *Washington*. New York: Simon and Schuster, 1968.

Harris, C. M. "Washington's Gamble, L'Enfant's Dream: Politics, Design, and the Founding of the National Capital." *William and Mary Quarterly*, 3rd ser., 56, no. 3 (July 1999): 527–64.

Hart, Albert Bushnell. *Washington the Traveler*. Washington, D.C.: George Washington Bicentennial Commission, 1932.

Henderson, Archibald. *Washington's Southern Tour, 1791*. Boston: Houghton Mifflin, 1923.

Miles, Ellen Gross, et al., *American Paintings of the Eighteenth Century*. Washington, D.C.: National Gallery of Art, 1995.

Rhodehamel, John. "Washington's City." *White House History*, no. 6 (Fall 1999): 4–13.

Showalter, William Joseph. "The Travels of George Washington." *National Geographic* 61, no. 1 (January 1932): 1–62.

Smith, Richard Norton. *Patriarch: George Washington and the New American Nation*. Boston: Houghton Mifflin, 1993.

Tebbel, John. *George Washington's America*. New York: E. P. Dutton, 1954.

Thompson, Mary V. "George Washington Slept Here . . . And Ate Here . . . And Talked Here: Adventures in 18th Century Travel with George Washington and Selected Members of His Family," paper presented at the Annual Clothing Symposium on "Travel, Taverns, and Attire," Gadsby's Tavern, Alexandria, Va., Oct. 2, 2004, online at www.mountvernon.org.

Washington, George. *The Diaries of George Washington*. Vols. 5–6. Edited by Donald Jackson and Dorothy Twohig. Charlottesville: University of Virginia Press, 1979.

———. *Letters from His Excellency General Washington, to Arthur Young . . . Containing an Account of His Husbandry, with a Map of His Far; His Opinions on Various Questions in Agriculture; and Many Particulars of the Rural Economy of the United States*. London: Sold by W. J. and J. Richardson, 1801.

———. *The Papers of George Washington Digital Edition*. Edited by Theodore J. Crackel. Charlottesville: University of Virginia Press, 2008, http://rotunda.upress.virginia/edu/founders/ GEWN.html.

———. *The Papers of George Washington: Presidential Series, Vols. 1–12*. Edited by Dorothy Twohig. Charlottesville: University of Virginia Press, 1987.

———. *The Writings of George Washington from the Original Manuscript Sources, 1745–1799*. 39 vols. Edited by John C. Fitzpatrick. Westport, Conn.: Greenwood Press, 1970.

2: John Adams

SOURCES

Page 14, "Yesterday mow'd all the Grass" and other diary entries in this paragraph: John Adams, *John Adams: A Biography*, ed. Peabody, 348.

Page 14, two barrels: ibid., 349.

Page 16, "I think to christen": quoted in McCullough, *John Adams*, 462.

Page 16, "ark of safety": quoted in Smith, *John Adams*, 2:916.

Page 16, "bake house": quoted in ibid., 2:941.

Page 16, "simple, but elegant enough" and the rest of the quotations and figures in this paragraph: Collins, *Presidents on Wheels*, 31.

Page 17, "Our horses go": quoted in McCullough, *John Adams*, 515.

Page 17, "public sentiment": quoted in ibid., 526.

Page 17 caption, "so that no trouble occurs": quoted in Levin, *Abigail Adams*, 354.

Page 18, "absconded," "exceedingly agitated": quoted in McCullough, *John Adams*, 491.

Page 18, "Nothing is done," "The post goes": quoted in Smith, *John Adams*, 2:1005.

Page 18, "I know the president": quoted in Levin, *Abigail Adams*, 353–54.

REFERENCES AND RESOURCES

Adams, John. *John Adams: A Biography in His Own Words*. Edited by James Bishop Peabody. New York: Newsweek, 1973.

Adams National Historical Park, online materials, www.nps.gov/adam.

Burleigh, Anne Husted. *John Adams*. New Rochelle, N.Y.: Arlington House, 1969.

Collins, Herbert Ridgeway. *Presidents on Wheels*. New York: Bonanza Press, 1971.

Ferling, John. *John Adams: A Life*. Knoxville: University of Tennessee Press, 1992.

Levin, Phyllis Lee. *Abigail Adams: A Biography*. New York: St. Martin's Press, 1987.

McCullough, David. *John Adams*. New York: Simon and Schuster, 2001.

"President Adams Moves In." *White House History*, no. 7 (Spring 2000): entire issue.

Smith, Page. *John Adams*. Vol. 2, *1784–1826*. Garden City, N.Y.: Doubleday, 1963.

3: Thomas Jefferson

SOURCES

Page 20, "long and habitual absences": quoted in Malone, *Jefferson the President: First Term*, 63.

Page 20, "I consider it as," "I should not suppose," "But, grumble who will": quoted in ibid., 64.

Page 20 caption, "the most sublime": Jefferson, *Notes on the State of Virginia*, 21.

Page 22, *Columbian Centinel, National Intelligencer*, summarized and quoted in Malone, *Jefferson the President: First Term*, 63–64.

Page 23, "They came": quoted in Fleming, *Man from Monticello*, 354.

Page 23, The president told his daughter: Malone, *Jefferson the President: First Term*, 65 n. 33.

Page 23, Castor and "sopha" where Jefferson left his traveling money: Thomas Jefferson, *Jefferson Himself*, ed. Mayo, 271.

Page 24, "cabinet of curiosities": Robinson, "American Cabinet of Curiosities," 41.

Page 24, "I am panting": Thomas Jefferson, *Jefferson Himself*, ed. Mayo, 274.

Page 26 caption, "autobiographical masterpiece": "Monticello, The House," *Thomas Jefferson's Monticello*, online materials.

Page 26 caption, "essay in architecture": Thomas Jefferson, letter to Benjamin Henry Latrobe, October 10, 1809," National Archives Founders Online, http://founders. archives.gov/documents/Jefferson.

Page 27, "Never did a prisoner": Thomas Jefferson, *Jefferson Himself*, ed. Mayo, 283.

Page 27, "I am retired": ibid., 287.

Page 27 caption, "I cannot live": quoted in McDonald, "Private Villa," 16.

REFERENCES AND RESOURCES

Ellis, Joseph. *American Sphinx: The Character of Thomas Jefferson*. New York: Alfred A. Knopf, 1997.

Fleming, Thomas. *The Man from Monticello: An Intimate Life of Thomas Jefferson*. New York: William Morrow, 1969.

Haas, Irvin. *Historic Homes of the American Presidents*. 2nd ed., rev. New York: Dover, 1991.

Jefferson, Thomas. *Jefferson Himself: The Personal Narrative of a Many-Sided American*. Edited by Bernard Mayo. Charlottesville: University Press of Virginia, 1970.

———. *Notes on the State of Virginia*. Charlottesville: University Press of Virginia, 1970.

———. *The Papers of Thomas Jefferson: Retirement Series*. Vol. 1, *4 March 1809–15 November 1809*. Edited by J. Jefferson Looney. Princeton, N.J.: Princeton University Press, 2004.

McDonald, Travis. "The Private Villa Retreat of Thomas Jefferson." *White House History*, no. 18 (Spring 2006), 4–23.

Malone, Dumas, *Jefferson the President: First Term, 1801–1805*. Boston: Little, Brown, 1971.

———. *Jefferson the President: Second Term, 1805–1809*. Boston: Little, Brown, 1974.

Peterson, Merrill D. *Thomas Jefferson: A Reference Biography*. New York: Charles Scribner's Sons, 1986.

Robinson, Joyce Henri. "An American Cabinet of Curiosities: Thomas Jefferson's Indian Hall at Monticello." *Winterthur Portfolio* 30, no. 1 (1995): 41–58.

Thomas Jefferson: Life and Labor at Monticello, Library of Congress exhibition, www.loc/gov/exhibits /jefferson.

Thomas Jefferson's Monticello, online materials, www.monticello.org.

4: JAMES MADISON

SOURCES

Page 28, "wild and romantic": Anna Maria Thornton, quoted in Ketcham, *James Madison*, 427.

Page 28, "salubrious": among others, Edmund Pendleton. See Hyland, *Montpelier and the Madisons*, 34.

Page 28, 600 days: "Madison Chronology, 1809–1812," also "1813–1817," in James Madison, *Papers of James Madison, ed.* Rutland and Mason.; David B. Mattern, associate editor of *Papers of James Madison*, correspondence with author, October 2006.

Page 28, "keep hold of the thread": quoted in Ketcham, *James Madison*, 600.

Page 28, "We passed two months": Dolley Payne Madison, *Selected Letters*, ed. Mattern and Shulman, 150.

Page 30, "All articles": quoted in Ketcham, *James Madison*, 428.

Page 31, "oweing to the croud": *Dolley Payne Madison, Selected Letters*, ed. Mattern and Shulman, 181.

Page 31, "Hospitality is the presiding genius" and Mrs. Smith's visit: quoted and reported in Ketcham, *James Madison, 479*.

Page 31, "fears & alarms" and the rest of the quotations in this paragraph: *Dolley Payne Madison, Selected Letters*, ed. Mattern and Shulman, 176.

Page 31 caption, "were covered with pictures": quoted in Hunt-Jones, *Dolley and the "great little Madison,"* 75.

Page 31 caption, "I wish you had": quoted in ibid., 74.

Page 32, "our glorious peace": quoted in Ketcham, *James Madison*, 597. See also, generally, 576–99.

Page 33, "profuse and handsome dinner": quoted in ibid., 607.

Page 33, "Work is easy for him," "sweetness, honesty": quoted in ibid.

Page 33, "as playful as a child," "talked and jested": quoted in Ketcham, *James Madison,* 612.

REFERENCES AND RESOURCES

The Digital Montpelier Project, www.digitalmontpelier.org.

Hunt-Jones, Conover. *Dolley and the "great little Madison."* Washington, D.C.: American Institute of Architects Foundation, 1977.

Hyland, Matthew G. *Montpelier and the Madisons: House, Home, and American Heritage*. Charleston, S.C.: History Press, 2007.

Ketcham, Ralph. *James Madison: A Biography*. Charlottesville: University Press of Virginia, 1990.

Madison, Dolley Payne. *The Selected Letters of Dolley Payne Madison*, ed. David B. Mattern and Holly C. Shulman. Charlottesville: University of Virginia Press, 2003.

Madison, James. *The Papers of James Madison: Presidential Series. Vols. 1–5, 1809–1812*, ed. Robert A. Rutland and Thomas A. Mason. Charlottesville: University Press of Virginia, 1984.

Montpelier, online materials, www.montpelier.org.

Rutland, Robert A., ed. *James Madison and the American Nation, 1751–1836*. New York: Simon and Schuster, 1994.

5: JAMES MONROE

SOURCES

Page 37, "so honest": quoted in Cresson, *James Monroe*, 376.

Page 39, "presidential Jubilee," "Era of Good Feelings": quoted in Beschloss, ed., *American Heritage*, 77. See also Ammon, *James Monroe*, 366.

Page 39, "mrs [*sic*] Monroe & yourself": Thomas Jefferson, letter to James Monroe, June 27, 1820, Founders Early Access, http://rotunda.upress.virginia.edu/founders/FOEA.html.

Page 39, "though the moment": John Quincy Adams, *Diary*, ed. Nevins, 198.

Page 39, "The American continents": quoted in Cresson, *James Monroe, 448*.

Page 40, "earliest and best": quoted in ibid., 472.

REFERENCES AND RESOURCES

Adams, John Quincy. *The Diary of John Quincy Adams, 1794–1845*. Edited by Allan Nevins. New York: Longmans, Greene, 1928.

Ammon, Harry. *James Monroe: The Quest for National Identity*. New York: McGraw Hill, 1971.

Beschloss, Michael, ed. *American Heritage Illustrated History of the Presidents*. New York: Crown Publishers, 2000.

Collins, Herbert Ridgeway. *Presidents on Wheels*. Washington, D.C.: Acropolis Books, 1971.

Cresson, W. P. *James Monroe*. Chapel Hill: University of North Carolina Press, 1946.

Cunningham, Noble E., Jr. *The Presidency of James Monroe*. Lawrence: University Press of Kansas, 1996.

Fennell, Christopher. "An Account of James Monroe's Land Holdings," www.histarch.illinois.edu.

Hart, Gary. *James Monroe*. New York: Times Books, Harry Holt, 2005.

Morgan, Elizabeth. "Oak Hill: Historical Inventory." Report for the Works Progress Administration of Virginia, 1937.

Seale, William. *The President's House: A History*. 2nd ed. Washington, D.C.: White House Historical Association, 2008.

Upton, Harriet Taylor. *Our Early Presidents, Their Wives and Children*. Boston: D. Lothrop, 1890.

6: JOHN QUINCY ADAMS

SOURCES

Page 42, "My native air": quoted in Hecht, *John Quincy Adams*, 456.

Page 42, "insupportable," "gasping for breath": quoted in Nagel, *John Quincy Adams*, 256.

Page 42, "one of the greatest": quoted in ibid.

Page 42, "to weak nerves": quoted in ibid., 257.

Page 44, "take a month of holiday": quoted in ibid., 290.

Page 44, "I know not": John Quincy Adams, *Diary*, ed. Nevins, 361.

Page 44, "It is repugnant," "Where else," "This will be a safe": ibid.

Page 44, "upwards of five hours": quoted in Nagel, *John Quincy Adams*, 313.

Page 44, "an uncontrollable dejection," "a sluggish carelessness": quoted in ibid., 315.

Page 44, "doff the world": quoted in ibid.

Page 45 caption, "Soon after breakfast," "I went out": quoted in "Photo Gallery," Adams National Historical Park, online materials.

Page 47, still depressed: reported in Nagel, *John Quincy Adams*, 315–16.

Page 47, "God bless you all!": quoted in Hecht, *John Quincy Adams*, 458.

Page 47, "disorder," "vain or unworthy": quoted in Nagel, *John Quincy Adams*, 316.

Page 47, "the unpardonable sins": John Quincy Adams, *Diary*, ed. Nevins, 384.

Page 47, "A stranger would think": ibid., 484.

Page 47, "This is the last": quoted in Nagel, *John Quincy Adams*, 414.

REFERENCES AND RESOURCES

Adams, John Quincy. *The Diary of John Quincy Adams, 1794–1845*. Edited by Allan Nevins. New York: Longmans, Greene, 1928.

Adams National Historical Park, online materials, www.nps.gov/adam.

Hecht, Marie B. *John Quincy Adams: A Personal History of an Independent Man*. New York: Macmillan, 1972.

Nagel, Paul C. *John Quincy Adams: A Public Life, A Private Life*. Cambridge, Mass.: Harvard University Press, 1997.

Parsons, Lynn Hudson. *John Quincy Adams*. Madison, Wis.: Madison House, 1998.

Remini, Robert V. *John Quincy Adams*. New York: Times Books, Henry Holt, 2002.

7: ANDREW JACKSON

SOURCES

Page 48, "beautiful spot": Andrew Jackson, *Correspondence of Andrew Jackson*, ed. Bassett, 5:149.

Page 48, "from the bustle": ibid., 4:304.

Page 50, just four times: Cole, *Presidency of Jackson*, 93.

Page 50, "I cannot yet determine": Andrew Jackson, *Correspondence of Andrew Jackson*, ed. Bassett, 4:66.

Page 50, hotel charges: ibid., 5:168–69, 362.

Page 50, "Business and company": quoted in Remini, *Andrew Jackson and the Course of American Democracy*, 258.

Page 51, "worn down": Andrew Jackson, *Correspondence of Andrew Jackson*, ed. Bassett, 5:281.

Page 51, "scarcely able": ibid., 5:280.

Page 51, "I am fearful": ibid., 5:418.

Page 51, "You may conclude": ibid., 5:426.

Page 52 caption, "temple & monument": quoted in "The Hermitage, The Mansion and Grounds," The Hermitage, online materials.

Page 53, "We must plow better": Andrew Jackson, *Correspondence of Andrew Jackson*, ed. Bassett, 5:423.

REFERENCES AND RESOURCES

Cole, Donald B. *The Presidency of Andrew Jackson*. Lawrence: University Press of Kansas, 1993.

Edling, Richard. "A Brief History of Fort Wool (1823–1946)," www.civilwaralbum.com.

The Hermitage, online materials, www.thehermitage.com

Jackson, Andrew. *The Correspondence of Andrew Jackson*. Vol. 4, *1829–1832*; Vol. 5, *1834–1836*. Edited by John Spenser Bassett. Washington, D.C.: Carnegie Institution, Washington, 1929, 1931.

James, Marquis. *Andrew Jackson: Portrait of a President*. Indianapolis: Bobbs Merrill, 1937.

Parton, James. *Life of Andrew Jackson*. Vol. 3. New York: Mason Brothers, 1860.

Quarstein, John V., and Julie Steele Clevenger. *Old Point Comfort Resort: Hospitality, Health, and History on Virginia's Chesapeake Bay*. Charleston, S.C.: History Press, 2009.

———, and Dennis P. Mroczkowski. *Fort Monroe: The Key to the South*. Charleston, S.C.: Arcadia, 2005.

Remini, Robert V. *Andrew Jackson and the Course of American Freedom, 1822–1832*. New York: Harper and Row, 1981.

———. *Andrew Jackson and the Course of American Democracy, 1833–1845*. New York: Harper and Row, 1984.

8: MARTIN VAN BUREN

SOURCES

Page 57, "a PALACE as splendid": Ogle, "Speech of Mr. Ogle," 36.

REFERENCES AND RESOURCES

Froncek, Thomas, ed. *The City of Washington: An Illustrated History*. New York: Alfred A. Knopf, 1985.

Kunhardt, Philip, Jr., Philip Kunhardt III, and Peter W. Kunhardt. *The American President*. New York: Riverhead Books, 1999.

Niven, John. *Martin Van Buren: The Romantic Age of American Politics*. New York: Oxford University Press, 1983.

Ogle, Charles. "Speech of Mr. Ogle, of Pennsylvania, on The Regal Splendor of the President's Palace," delivered in the House of Representatives, April 14, 1840, reprinted in *White House History*, no. 10 (Winter 2002), 35–97.

Seager, Robert, II. *And Tyler Too: A Biography of John and Julia Gardiner Tyler*. New York: McGraw-Hill, 1963.

Seale, William. *The President's House: A History*. 2nd ed. Washington, D.C.: White House Historical Association, 2008.

Weeks, Christopher. *Guide to the Architecture of Washington, D.C.* Baltimore: Johns Hopkins University Press, 1994.

Writers' Program of the Work Projects Administration. *Washington, D.C.: A Guide to the Nation's Capital*. Washington, D.C.: Hastings House, for the George Washington University, 1942; reprint, New York: Pantheon Books, 1983.

9: JOHN TYLER

SOURCES

Page 58 caption, details about the Peace-Maker: Blackman, "Fatal Cruise of the *Princeton*."

Page 60, "tempest-tossed": quoted in Kunhardt et al., *American President*, 212.

Page 60, "Though I am": quoted in French, *Witness to the Young Republic*, 159.

Page 61, "I fainted": quoted Knutson, "D.C. Disaster."

Page 61, "I did not know": quoted in Seager, *And Tyler Too*, 206.

Page 61, "After I lost," "He seemed": quoted in ibid., 207.

Page 62, "Wherever we stopped": quoted in ibid., 8. Page 62, "I have commenced": quoted in Peterson, *Presidencies of Harrison and Tyler*, 236.

Page 62, first time: Seale, *President's House*, 242.

Page 62, "True love" and the rest of the quotations in this paragraph: quoted in Seager, *And Tyler Too*, 10.

Page 64, "where to make," "was amazed": quoted in ibid., 12.

Page 65, "Yes," "They cannot say": quoted in Peterson, *Presidencies of Harrison and Tyler*, 259.

REFERENCES AND RESOURCES

Anthony, Carl Sferrazza. *America's First Families*. New York: Touchstone Books, Simon and Schuster, 2000.

———. *First Ladies: The Saga of the Presidents' Wives and Their Power*. New York: William Morrow, 1990.

Blackman, Ann. "Fatal Cruise of the *Princeton*." *Navy History*, September 2005, www.military.com

Crapol, Edward P. John Tyler: *The Accidental President*. Chapel Hill: University of North Carolina Press, 2006.

Fraser, Hugh Russell. *Democracy in the Making: The Jackson-Tyler Era.* Indianapolis: Bobbs-Merrill, 1938.

French, Benjamin Brown. *Witness to the Young Republic: A Yankee's Journal, 1828–1870.* Edited by Donald B. Cole and John J. McDonough. Hanover, N.H.: University Press of New England, 1989.

Haas, Irvin. *Historic Homes of the American Presidents.* New York: Dover Publications, 1991.

Knutson, Larry. "D.C. Disaster Concluded in a Romance." *Los Angeles Times,* March 5, 2000, latimes.com.

Kunhardt, Philip, Jr., Philip Kunhardt III, and Peter W. Kunhardt. *The American President.* New York: Riverhead Books, 1999.

Peterson, Norma Lois. *The Presidencies of William Henry Harrison and John Tyler.* Lawrence: University Press of Kansas, 1989.

Seager, Robert, II. *And Tyler Too: A Biography of John and Julia Gardiner Tyler.* New York: McGraw-Hill, 1963.

Seale, William. *The President's House: A History.* 2nd ed. Washington, D.C.: White House Historical Association, 2008.

Sherwood Forest: Home of President John Tyler, online materials, www.sherwoodforest.org.

Wise, John S. *Recollections of Thirteen Presidents. 1906;* reprint, Freeport, N.Y.: Libraries Press, 1968.

10: James K. Polk

SOURCES

Page 66, details of Polk's morning: James K. Polk, *Diary,* ed. Nevins, 342. Polk wrote that he "drank some of the water" in the morning and "more of the water" in the afternoon.

Page 66, "And during that whole period": ibid., 340.

Page 69, "In truth," "with me": quoted in Bergeron, *Presidency of James K. Polk,* 243.

Page 69, "No president": James K. Polk, *Diary,* ed. Nevins, 360.

Page 69, typical day: Sellers, *James K. Polk,* 301, 306–7.

Page 69, "one of the hottest days": quoted in ibid., 485.

Page 69, "Many objects": James K. Polk, *Diary,* ed. Nevins, 239.

Page 69, Polk's log: Appleton, *North for Union,* ed. Cutler.

Page 69, "lightning line": ibid., 4.

Page 69, poem: quoted in ibid., 35.

Page 70, "We enjoyed facilities for travel": ibid., 81–82.

Page 71, "derangements of the liver": quoted in Frear, *Bedford Springs,* 3.

Page 71, greatest medicinal value: James K. Polk, *Diary,* ed. Nevins, 342.

Page 71, "It is almost too late": ibid., 343.

Page 71, charges for hotel stay: Frear, *Bedford Springs,* 29.

Page 71, "well-meaning old man": James K. Polk, *Diary,* ed. Nevins, 389.

REFERENCES AND RESOURCES

Appleton, John. *North for Union: John Appleton's Journal of a Tour to New England Made by President Polk in June and July 1847.* Edited by Wayne Cutler. Nashville: Vanderbilt University Press, 1986.

Bergeron, Paul H. *The Presidency of James K. Polk.* Lawrence: University Press of Kansas, 1987.

Byrnes, Mark Eaton. *James K. Polk: A Biographical Companion.* Santa Barbara, Calif.: ABC-CLIO, 2001.

Dulles, Foster Rhea. *A History of Recreation: America Learns to Play.* New York: Appleton-Century-Crofts, 1965.

Frear, Ned. *The Bedford Springs.* Bedford, Pa.: Frear Publications, 2000.

Fries, Deborah. "Sustainable Magic: Restoring the Allure of Bedford Springs." *Terrain,* no. 20 (2007), www.terrain.org.

"The History of Bedford Springs," www.omnihotels.com/FindAHotel/BedfordSprings.

James K. Polk Ancestral Home, online materials, www.jameskpolk.com.

Morgart, Brad. "Bedford Springs Hotel: Two Centuries of Rejuvenation." Pennsylvania Center for the Book, fall 2009, www.pabook.libraries.psu.edu.

Polk, James K. *Polk: The Diary of a President, 1845–1849.* Edited by Allan Nevins. London: Longmans, Green, 1929.

Sellers, Charles Sellers. *James K. Polk, Continentalist: 1843–1846.* Princeton, N.J.: Princeton University Press, 1966.

Siegenthaler, John. *James K. Polk.* New York: Times Books, Henry Holt, 2003.

11: James Buchanan

SOURCES

Page 74, rolltop desk: Frear, *Bedford Springs,* 33.

Page 74, "His health was much improved": quoted in ibid., 34.

Page 74, "Dashing through Bedford Town": quoted in ibid.

Page 75, "the wonderful wire": quoted in Curtis, *Life of James Buchanan,* 2:238.

Page 75, telegraph messages: quoted in Frear, *Bedford Springs,* 33.

Page 75, Virginia widow and slave: Klein, *James Buchanan,* 334.

Page 77, *Pittsburgh Post,* "final and irrevocable": reported and quoted in ibid., 340.

REFERENCES AND RESOURCES

Baker, Jean H. *James Buchanan.* New York: Times Books, Henry Holt, 2004.

Curtis, George Ticknor. *Life of James Buchanan, Fifteenth President of the United States.* Vol. 2. New York: Harper and Brothers, 1883.

Frear, Ned. *The Bedford Springs.* Bedford, Pa.: Frear Publications, 2000.

Fries, Deborah. "Sustainable Magic: Restoring the Allure of Bedford Springs." *Terrain,* no. 20 (2007), www.terrain.org.

"The History of Bedford Springs," www.omnihotels.com/FindAHotel/BedfordSprings.

"In James Buchanan's Time." *White House History,* no. 12 (Winter 2003): entire issue.

Klein, Philip Shriver. *President James Buchanan: A Biography.* University Park: Pennsylvania State University Press, 1962.

Morgart, Brad. "Bedford Springs Hotel: Two Centuries of Rejuvenation." Pennsylvania Center for the Book, fall 2009, www.pabook.libraries.psu.edu.

National Park Service, "Wheatland, Pennsylvania," American Presidents: Discover Our Shared Heritage Travel Itinerary, www.nps.gov.nr/travel/presidents/james_buchanan_wheatland.

12: Abraham Lincoln

SOURCES

Page 78, army officer remembered: Pinsker, *Lincoln's Sanctuary,* 5.

Page 78, "he would be up": quoted in ibid.

Page 78 caption, Buchanan retreated: Curtis, *Life of James Buchanan,* 2:241.

Page 80, "I see the president," "entirely unornamental *cortège,*" "deep latent sadness": Whitman, *Whitman's Memoranda,* 39–41.

Page 81, numbers of months, Pinsker, *Lincoln's Sanctuary,* 5.

Page 81, description of cottage: in addition to citations listed in references and resources, David Overholt, preservation projects director, Lincoln Cottage, conversation with author, January 18, 2007.

Page 81, "The drives & walks," "very beautiful," "this sweet spot": Mary Todd Lincoln, *Mary Todd Lincoln,* ed. Turner and Turner, 131, 94, 130.

Page 81, "pretended to produce messages": quoted in Pinsker, *Lincoln's Sanctuary,* 31.

Page 82, find a missing cat: Brownstein, *Lincoln's Other White House,* 75.

Page 82, Nanny, Tad's goat: ibid.

Page 82, peacock story: Pinsker, *Lincoln's Sanctuary,* 151.

Page 82, "get in line": quoted in ibid., 78.

Page 82, game of checkers: ibid., 80.

Page 82, "The trip will cost nothing": Mary Todd Lincoln, *Mary Todd Lincoln,* ed. Turner and Turner, 94.

Page 83, "All along the beach": quoted in New Jersey Writers' Project, *Entertaining a Nation,* 39–40.

Page 83, "intensely warm": Mary Todd Lincoln, *Mary Todd Lincoln,* ed. Turner and Turner, 690.

Page 83 caption, "elegant hospitalities": quoted in New Jersey Writers' Project, *Entertaining a Nation,* 31.

Page 84, "about come to the conclusion": quoted in Welles, *Diary,* 70.

Page 85, One found him: Pinsker, *Lincoln's Sanctuary,* 52.

Page 85, "Am I to have no rest?" "a brute": quoted in ibid., 52–53.

Page 86, visit to the National Observatory, "The president read Shakespeare to me": reported and quoted in Thayer, *Life and Letters of Hay,* 1:198.

Page 86, "You boys remind me": quoted in Pinsker, *Lincoln's Sanctuary,* 153.

Page 86, "The enemy are reported advancing": quoted in ibid., 135.

Page 88, "The lonely situation": Brooks, *Mr. Lincoln's Washington,* 354.

Page 88, "He was in the Fort": Hay, *Lincoln and the Civil War,* 208.

Page 88, "for fear he might," "The chief is evidently disgusted": quoted in Furguson, *Freedom Rising,* 320.

Page 88, "some foolish gunner," "kept quiet": quoted in Pinsker, *Lincoln's Sanctuary,* 163.

Page 89, treasury official encountered: ibid., 204.

Page 89, "How dearly I loved": Mary Todd Lincoln, *Mary Todd Lincoln,* ed. Turner and Turner, 268.

Page 89, restoring the building: Overholt, conversation with author, January 23, 2007.

REFERENCES AND RESOURCES

Armed Forces Retirement Home—Washington, "Historic Preservation Plan," www.afrhdevelopment.com.

Brooks, Noah. *Mr. Lincoln's Washington: Selections from the Writings of Noah Brooks, Civil War Correspondent.* Edited by P. J. Staudenraus. South Brunswick, N.J.: Thomas Yoseloff, 1967.

Brownstein, Elizabeth Smith. *Lincoln's Other White House: The Untold Story of the Man and His Presidency.* New York: John Wiley and Sons, 2005.

Curtis, George Ticknor. *Life of James Buchanan, Fifteenth President of the United States.* Vol. 2. New York: Harper and Brothers, 1883.

Donald, David Herbert. *Lincoln.* New York: Simon and Schuster, 1995.

———. *Lincoln at Home: Two Glimpses of Abraham Lincoln's Domestic Life.* Washington, D.C.: White House Historical Association in cooperation with Thornwillow Press, 1999.

———. *We Are Lincoln Men: Abraham Lincoln and His Friends.* New York: Simon and Schuster, 2003.

Federal Writers Project. *The WPA Guide to Washington, D.C.* Revision of the 1937 Works Progress Administration edition. New York: Pantheon Books, 1983.

Furgurson, Ernest B. *Freedom Rising: Washington in the Civil War.* New York: Alfred A. Knopf, 2004.

Goodwin, Doris Kearns. *Team of Rivals: The Political Genius of Abraham Lincoln.* New York: Simon and Schuster, 2005.

Hay, John. *Lincoln and the Civil War in the Diaries and Letters of John Hay.* Cambridge: De Capo Press, 1988.

"Life in the Lincoln White House." *White House History,* no. 24 (Fall 2008), 25 (Spring 2009): entire issues.

Lincoln, Mary Todd. *Mary Todd Lincoln: Her Life and Letters.* Edited by Justin G. Turner and Linda Levitt Turner. New York: Alfred A. Knopf, 1972.

Klingaman, William K. *Abraham Lincoln and the Road to Emancipation.* New York: Viking, 2001.

National Park Service, "Civil War Defenses of Washington," www.nps.gov.cwdw.

National Park Service, "President Lincoln's Cottage at the Soldiers' Home," American Presidents: Discover Our Shared Heritage Travel Itinerary, www.nps.gov.nr/travel/presidents/lincoln_cottage.

New Jersey Writers' Project. *Entertaining a Nation: The Career of Long Branch.* Bayonne, N.J.: Jersey Printing Company, for the Works Progress Administration, State of New Jersey, 1940.

Pinsker, Mathew. *Lincoln's Sanctuary: Abraham Lincoln and the Soldiers' Home.* Oxford: Oxford University Press, 2003.

President Lincoln's Cottage at the Soldiers' Home, lincolncottage.org.

Randall, Ruth Painter. *Mary Lincoln: Biography of a Marriage.* Boston: Little, Brown, 1953.

Seale, William. *The President's House: A History.* 2nd ed. Washington, D.C.: White House Historical Association, 2008.

———. "The Soldiers' Home: First Presidential Retreat." *White House History,* no. 18 (Spring 2006): 24–31.

Thayer, William Roscoe. *The Life and Letters of John Hay.* Vol. 1. Boston: Houghton Mifflin, 1908.

Tindall, William. *Standard History of the City of Washington.* Knoxville, Tenn.: H. W. Crew, 1914.

Waugh, John C. *Reelecting Lincoln: The Battle for the 1864 Presidency.* New York: Crown Publishers, 1997.

Welles, Gideon. *The Diary of Gideon Welles.* Vol. 1, *1861–1864.* Boston: Houghton Mifflin, 1911.

Whitman, Walt. *Walt Whitman's Memoranda During the War: Written on the Spot in 1863–65.* Edited by Peter Coviello. Oxford: Oxford University Press, 2004.

13: Andrew Johnson

SOURCES

Page 90, hardest-working president: Trefousse, *Andrew Johnson,* 259–60.

Page 90, a recent biographer, contemporaries: Means, *Avenger Takes His Place,* 168–69.

Page 90, "I told him": Welles, *Diary,* 2:329.

Page 90, Welles thought: ibid.

Page 90 caption, "You are President": quoted in Trefousse, *Andrew Johnson,* 194.

Page 93, often-repeated story: Thomas, *First President Johnson,* 596–97.

REFERENCES AND RESOURCES

Andrew Johnson National Historic Site, online materials, www.nps.gov/anjo.

Bushong, William. *"Rock Creek Park, District of Columbia: Historic Resources Study." Report for the* National Park Service, 1990, http://www.cr.nps.gov/history/online_books/rocr1/hrs.pdf.

Means, Howard. *The Avenger Takes His Place: Andrew Johnson and the 45 Days That Changed the Nation.* New York: Harcourt, 2006.

Miller Center, University of Virginia, "Andrew Johnson," American President: A Reference Resource, millercenter.org/president/johnson.

Mr. Lincoln's White House, online materials, www.mrlincolnswhitehouse.org.

National Park Service, "Civil War Defenses of Washington," www.nps.gov.cwdw.

Seale, William. *The President's House: A History.* 2nd ed. Washington, D.C.: White House Historical Association, 2008.

Thomas, Lately. *The First President Johnson: The Three Lives of the Seventeenth President of the United States.* New York: William Morrow, 1968.

Trefousse, Hans L. *Andrew Johnson: A Biography.* Newtown, Conn.: American Political Biography Press, 1968.

Welles, Gideon. *Diary of Gideon Welles, Secretary of the Navy under Lincoln and Johnson.* Vol. 2. Boston: Houghton Mifflin, 1911.

14: Ulysses S. Grant

SOURCES

Page 94, he had never seen: New Jersey Writers' Project, *Entertaining a Nation,* 45.

Page 94, "I have purchased a cottage": quoted in "Farewell Festival," *Baltimore Sun,* August 5, 1869, 1.

Page 96, "It commands a vast sweep": "President Grant at Long Branch," *New York Herald,* July 20, 1870, reprinted as "The President's Summer Home," *Hartford Daily Courant,* July 26, 1870, 1.

Page 96, "The Summer Capital": Hazard, *Long Branch in the Golden Age,* 33–34.

Page 96, "recreation from official duty": Ulysses S. Grant, "Speech on August 3, 1869," in Ulysses S. Grant, *Papers of Ulysses S. Grant,* ed. Simon, 19:223.

Page 96, "What a boon," "gathered new strength": Julia Dent Grant, *Personal Memoirs,* 177.

Page 96, "The full force of the sea": quoted in New Jersey Writers' Project, *Entertaining a Nation,* 56.

Page 96, "glorious drives": Julia Dent Grant, *Personal Memoirs,* 177.

Page 96, "suitable in width and strength": Orville E. Babcock to Brewster & Co., New York City, December 26, 1874, in Ulysses S. Grant, *Papers of Ulysses S. Grant,* ed. Simon, 25:455–56.

Page 96 caption, continued description of house: "President Grant at Long Branch". See also Jones, *Homes of the American Presidents,* 130–32.

Page 97, "As soon as we reached" and the rest of the quotations in this paragraph: Jesse R. Grant, *In the Days of My Father,* 94.

Page 98, "dignified, slow moving": ibid., 130.

Page 98, "Did you see that, Julia": quoted in ibid., 131.

Page 98, "as lightly as Buck": ibid.

Page 98, "delightful sea air," "prolonged his life": Julia Dent Grant, *Personal Memoirs,* 177.

Page 98, "Custer's massacre": quoted in "Gen. Grant," *Chicago Daily Tribune,* September 4, 1876, 1.

Page 99, visitors to Long Branch: ibid., passim. See also Sniffen, *Long Branch,* 64; Frank Pallone Jr., speech, April 21, 2004, *Congressional Record,* 108th Congress, 2nd Session, House of Representatives, E592, online at thomas.loc.gov.

Page 99, "Madam, I had rather": quoted in New Jersey Writers' Project, *Entertaining a Nation,* 47.

Page 99, Grant's travels: "Chronology 1874," in Ulysses S. Grant, *Papers of Ulysses S. Grant,* ed. Simon, 25:xxiii–xxv.

Page 100, "The president left": quoted in Peskin, *Garfield,* 339.

Page 100, "President Grant Left Washington": *Chicago Tribune,* September 16, 1874, 4.

Page 100, $30,000: "Long Branch," *Chicago Tribune,* July 26, 1870, 2.

Page 100, $32,000: "President Grant at Long Branch."

Page 100, "campaign slanders": "Campaign Slanders," *Boston Daily Globe,* September 12, 1872, 4.

Page 100, Blackburn resolution, including "the seat of government established by law" and "incompatible with the public interest": April 3, 1876, *Congressional Record,* 44th Congress, 1st Session, House of Representatives, 2158, online at heinonline.org.

Page 100, Babcock, Belknap, and Grant's salary: "Introduction," in Ulysses S. Grant, *Papers of Ulysses S. Grant,* ed. Simon, 27:xi–xiii. Grant later pardoned Babcock; Belknap was acquitted by the Senate; and the pay reduction did not become law.

Pages 100–102, Grant's response, and all quotations: Ulysses S. Grant, "Message from the President of the United States," May 4, 1876, *Congressional Record,* 44th Congress, 1st Session, House of Representatives, 2999–3000, online at heinonline.org.

Page 102, "severe rebuke," "impudent," "blunder": "The President's Duties," *New York Times,* May 5, 1876, 1.

Page 102, "simple lesson in history": "The President Reads Unsophisticated Democrats a Simple Lesson in History," *Chicago Tribune,* May 5, 1876, 1.

Page 102, "a complete answer," "no sensible person": quoted in Ulysses S. Grant, Ulysses S. *Papers of Ulysses S. Grant,* ed. Simon, 27:107.

Page 103, "the very grandest of grand tours": Young, *Around the World,* ed. Fellman, 424.

Page 103, "an experience that": ibid., 438.

REFERENCES AND RESOURCES

Bunting, Josiah, III. *Ulysses S. Grant.* New York: Times Books, 2004.

Grant, Jesse R., with Henrz R. Grant. *In the Days of My Father General Grant.* New York: Harper and Brothers, 1925.

Grant, Julia Dent. *The Personal Memoirs of Julia Dent Grant (Mrs. Ulysses S. Grant).* Carbondale: Southern Illinois University Press, 1975.

Grant, Ulysses S. *The Papers of Ulysses S. Grant, 1869–1876.* Edited by John T. Simon. Carbondale: Southern Illinois University Press, 1995–2005.

Grant's Cottage, online materials, www.grantcottage.org.

Grant's Tomb, online materials, www.grantstomb.org.

Hazard, Sharon. *Long Branch in the Golden Age: Tales of Fascinating and Famous People.* Charleston: History Press, 2007.

Jones, Cranston. *Homes of the American Presidents.* New York: Bonanza Books, 1962.

McFeeley, William S. *Grant: A Biography.* New York: W. W. Norton, 1981.

New Jersey Writers' Project. *Entertaining a Nation: The Career of Long Branch.* Bayonne, N.J.: Jersey Printing Company, for the Works Progress Administration, State of New Jersey, 1940.

Perret, Geoffrey. *Ulysses S. Grant: Soldier and President.* New York: Random House, 1997.

Perry, Mark. *Grant and Twain: The Story of a Friendship.* New York: Random House, 2004.

Peskin, Allan. *Garfield.* Kent, Ohio: Kent State University Press, 1999.

Smith, Jean Edward. *Grant.* New York: Simon and Schuster, 2001.

Sniffen, Paul. *Long Branch.* Dover, N.H.: Arcadia, 1996.

Young, John Russell. *Around the World with General Grant (1879).* Edited by Michael Fellman. Baltimore: John Hopkins University Press, 2002.

15: Rutherford B. Hayes

SOURCES

Page 104, "Rutherford, the Rover": "Rutherford, the Rover," *Chicago Times,* September 6, 1878, 4.

Page 104, "scenery mad": quoted in Davison, *Presidency of Hayes,* 71.

Page 104, "large pillars," "noble view": Rutherford B. Hayes, *Diary,* ed. Williams, 165.

Page 104, account of tour on the *Tallapoosa,* ibid., 234–45.

Page 104, "an agreeable abode": Rutherford B. Hayes, *Diary,* ed. Williams, 92.

Page 107, "You have no idea": quoted in Hoogenboom, *Rutherford B. Hayes,* 346.

Page 107, "His Fraudulency," "Rutherfraud B. Hayes": Barnard, *Hayes and His America,* 402.

Page 107, "Lemonade Lucy": "Lucy Ware Webb Hayes," The White House, Our First Ladies, www.whitehouse.gov.

Page 107, "the finest car": quoted in Davison, *Presidency of Hayes,* 217.

Page 107 caption, USS *Tallapoosa:* "USS *Tallapoosa* (1)," NavSource Naval History, www.navsource.org.

Page 108, "riding shotgun": ibid., 218.

Page 108, "What beautiful country": quoted in Hoogenboom, *Rutherford B. Hayes,* 443.

Page 108, "The grandeur of the views": quoted in ibid.

Pages 108–9, "We had a whole week": quoted in Davison, *Presidency of Hayes,* 219.

Page 108, "The sea is smooth": quoted in ibid.

Page 108, "Your Mama wishes me": quoted in ibid., 219–20.

Page 109, "We left W[ashington]": Rutherford B. Hayes, *Diary,* ed. Williams, 297.

Page 109, "We will grow old": quoted in Mahan, *Lucy Webb Hayes,* 97.

REFERENCES AND RESOURCES

Barnard, Harry. *Rutherford B. Hayes and His America,* New York: Russell and Russell, 1967.

Davison, Kenneth E. *The Presidency of Rutherford B. Hayes.* Westport, Conn.: Greenwood Press, 1972.

Hayes, Rutherford B. *Hayes: The Diary of a President, 1875–1881.* Edited by T. Harry Williams. New York: David McKay, 1964.

Hoogenboom, Ari. *Rutherford B. Hayes: Warrior and President.* Lawrence: University Press of Kansas, 1995.

Mahan, Russell L. *Lucy Webb Hayes: A First Lady by Example.* New York: Nova History Publications, 2005.

National Park Service, "Spiegel Grove: Rutherford B. Hayes Presidential Center," American Presidents: Discover Our Shared Heritage Travel Itinerary, www.nps.gov.nr/travel/presidents/hayes_spiegel_grove.

New Jersey Writers' Project. *Entertaining a Nation: The Career of Long Branch.* Bayonne, N.J.: Jersey Printing Company, for the Works Progress Administration, State of New Jersey, 1940.

Ohio History Connection, online materials, www.ohiohistory.org.

Rutherford B. Hayes Presidential Center, online materials, www.rbhayes.org.

Seale, William. *The President's House: A History.* 2nd ed. Washington, D.C.: White House Historical Association, 2008.

Taylor, John M. *Garfield of Ohio: The Available Man.* New York: Norton, 1970.

Trefousse, Hans L. *Rutherford B. Hayes.* New York: Times Books, 2002.

16: James A. Garfield

SOURCES

Page 110, singing and handsprings: Leech and Brown, *Garfield Orbit,* 5; Peskin, *Garfield,* 595.

Page 112, healing powers: Leech and Brown, *Garfield Orbit,* 4.

Page 113, "My God!": quoted in Ackerman, *Dark Horse,* 378.

Page 113, "a very loud report": quoted in ibid.

Page 114, "Disappointed Office Seeker": "A Dark Deed," *Boston Daily Globe,* July 3, 1881, 1.

Pages 114–15, "Hot coffee and sandwiches": "Everything Ready at Elberon," *New York Times,* September 6, 1881, 1.

Page 115, "one of the finest" and other details: "Safe on Board the Train: How the Party Embarked for Long Branch," *Washington Post,* September 7, 1881, 1. See also "The President's Special Train," *New York Times,* September 5, 1881, 1.

Page 117, "The rooms are large": "The Preparations at Elberon," *New York Times,* September 5, 1881, 1.

Page 117, "convalescent": quoted in Taylor, *Garfield of Ohio,* 277.

Page 117, "The president's condition": "Further Improvement: The President Surely on the Road to Recovery," *Washington Post,* September 10, 1881, 1.

Page 117, "The medical reports": quoted in ibid.

Page 117, "We had better": quoted in Ridpath, *Life and Work of Garfield,* 626.

Page 117, "Not So Well," "He has held his own": "Not So Well As Saturday," *New York Times,* September 12, 1881, 1.

Page 117, the president had lost ground: reported in "The Latest Bulletins," *Washington Post,* September 18, 1881, 1.

Page 117, "I have no hopes of his recovery": quoted in ibid.

Page 117, "I am in terrible pain": quoted in Ackerman, *Dark Horse,* 426.

Page 117, "It is over": quoted in Clark, *Murder of Garfield,* 109.

Page 117, "joyfully, almost boyishly happy," "that trouble lay behind him": quoted in Ridpath, *Life and Work of Garfield,* 689. On January 25, 1882, after a fifty-four day trial, a jury convicted Charles J. Guiteau of murder. He was executed on June 30, 1882, just days before the first anniversary of his crime.

Page 117 caption, "It is refreshing": quoted in Clark, *Murder of Garfield,* 106.

Page 117 caption, "the fishermen," "I am myself": quoted in Peskin, *Garfield,* 606.

REFERENCES AND RESOURCES

Ackerman, Kenneth D. *Dark Horse: The Surprise Election and Political Murder of President James A. Garfield.* New York: Carroll and Graf, 2003.

Clark, James C. *The Murder of James A. Garfield: The President's Last Days and the Trial and Execution of His Assassin.* Jefferson, N.C.: McFarland, 1993.

Leech, Margaret, and Harry J. Brown. *The Garfield Orbit.* New York: Harper and Row, 1978.

New Jersey Writers' Project. *Entertaining a Nation: The Career of Long Branch.* Bayonne, N.J.: Jersey Printing Company, for the Works Progress Administration, State of New Jersey, 1940.

Peskin, Allan. *Garfield.* Kent, Ohio: Kent State University Press, 1999.

Ridpath, John Clark. *The Life and Work of James A. Garfield.* Cincinnati: Jones Brothers, 1881.

Rutkow, Ira. *James A. Garfield.* New York: Times Books, 2006.

Seale, William. *The President's House: A History.* 2nd ed. Washington, D.C.: White House Historical Association, 2008.

Taylor, John M. *Garfield of Ohio: The Available Man.* New York: Norton, 1970.

17: Chester A. Arthur

SOURCES

Page 118, neglect of duty: "A Roving Lot," *New York Sun,* September 29, 1882, 1.

Page 120, "slender as a carriage whip": "The President Fishing: Going in a Steam Yacht and Catching Fish from a Skiff," *New York Sun,* October 3, 1882, 1.

Page 120, "When he felt a tug" and fishing catch: ibid.

Page 120, "President Arthur has got": "Gen. Arthur's Fishing Over," *New York Sun,* October 8, 1882, 5.

Page 120, "culpable absenteeism" and the rest of the quotations in this paragraph: "Roving Lot," 1.

Page 120, "We propose that Congress": ibid.

Page 121, "about the last man": quoted in Karabell, *Chester Alan Arthur,* 63.

Page 121, "A few able editors," "But, it really seems": editorial, *Washington Post,* September 10, 1882, 2.

Page 121 caption, USS *Despatch*: "*Despatch*," *Dictionary of American Fighting Ships,* www.history.navy.mil.

Page 122, "sudden and violent": "The President Taken Ill," *New York Times,* April 21, 1883, 1.

Page 122, "I am feeling perfectly well": quoted in Reeves, *Gentleman Boss,* 359. See also "The President at Home: He Arrives in Apparently Perfect Health," *Washington Post,* April 23, 1883, 1.

Page 122, "Vacation! That is the way": quoted in "The President's Holiday: Received with Ceremony at Cape May," *New York Times,* July 24, 1883, 1.

Page 122, further and expensive example: *Sun's* response commented upon in "Disagreeing Doctors," *New York Times,* August 9, 1883, 4.

Page 123, "It is not to be": "President Arthur's Yellowstone Trip," *Hartford Daily Courant,* July 19, 1883, 3.

Page 123, "It appears that a junketing expedition": "The Sunday Post," *Washington Post,* July 21, 1883, 2.

Page 124, army dispatch from Buffalo Lake: quoted in "In the Wilderness," *Washington Evening Star,* August 13, 1883, 1.

Page 124, army dispatch from Camp Strong: quoted in "Still Catching Trout," *New York Times,* August 25, 1883, 1.

Page 125, "without a second's delay": quoted in Mares, *Fishing with the Presidents,* 26.

Page 125, "where presidents didn't come fooling about": Eugene Field, "The Indian and the Trout," *Poems of Eugene Field,* 445–46.

Page 125, 350 miles, 100 pounds: "The President on His Way Home," *Washington Evening Star,* September 3, 1883, 1.

REFERENCES AND RESOURCES

Doenecke, Justus D. *The Presidencies of James A. Garfield and Chester A. Arthur.* Lawrence: Regents Press of Kansas, 1981.

Field, Eugene. *Poems of Eugene Field.* New York: C. Scribner's Sons, 1912.

Goodyear, Frank H., III. *A President in Yellowstone: The F. Jay Haynes Photographic Album of Chester Arthur's 1883 Expedition.* Norman: University of Oklahoma Press, 2013.

Hartley, Robert E. *Saving Yellowstone: The President Arthur Expedition of 1883.* Westminster, Colo.: Sniktau Publications, 2007.

Karabell, Zachary. *Chester Alan Arthur.* New York: Times Books, 2004.

Mares, Bill. *Fishing with the Presidents.* Mechanicsburg, Pa.: Stackpole Books, 1999.

Reeves, Thomas C. *Gentleman Boss: The Life of Chester Alan Arthur.* New York: Alfred A. Knopf, 1975.

Saving Yellowstone: The President Arthur Expedition of 1883, online materials, www.savingyellowstone.com.

18: Grover Cleveland

SOURCES

Page 126, "The president had hoped": "Installed at Deer Park: How the First Day of the Honeymoon Was Spent," *Washington Post,* June 4, 1886, 1.

Page 126, "I can see a group": quoted in Nevins, *Grover Cleveland,* 307.

Page 128 caption, details of cottage: "A Mountain Honeymoon," *New York Times,* June 4, 1886, 1.

Page 129, "a pretty dress," "A white morning shawl," "The bride had replaced": ibid.

Page 129, "If I am going to keep": quoted in Mares, *Fishing with the Presidents,* 30.

Page 129, "with more enthusiasm than experience": "Marriage of Grover Cleveland to Miss Frances Folsom Is Recalled by President Wilson's Wedding Plans," *Washington Post,* October 24, 1915, A13.

Page 129, "Mrs. Cleveland Fishes": "Mrs. Cleveland Fishes: But She Does Not Succeed in Catching Anything," *Washington Post,* June 6, 1886, 1.

Page 129, "They have used": quoted in Nevins, *Grover Cleveland,* 307.

Page 129, "Mr. Cleveland wants to know": "Sharp and Pointed," *New York Times,* August 19, 1886, 4.

Page 129, "Let him alone," "The frenzy of public curiosity," "deserve the reprobation": "Let Him Alone," *Washington Post,* August 18, 1886, 2.

Page 130, "Tonight, at Mrs. Cleveland's request": "The President's Vacation: He Arrives at Prospect House and Both He and Mrs. Cleveland Are Delighted with the Place," *Washington Post,* August 18, 1886, 1.

Page 130, "a sensible domestic American wife": quoted in Seale, *President's House,* 544.

Page 130, $21,500 for a house and 23 acres: Nevins, *Grover Cleveland,* 312; Brodsky, *Grover Cleveland,* 175.

Page 131, centerpiece of red roses: "Two Years Married: The President Finds Roses on the Breakfast Table," *Boston Daily Globe,* June 3, 1888, 2.

Page 131, one-room cottage: "The President's New Cottage," *Washington Post,* August 7, 1888, 2.

Page 131, squirrel hunt: "A Presidential Squirrel Hunt," *Washington Post,* November 4, 1888, 5.

Page 131, "We are coming back": quoted in Seale, *President's House,* 549.

Page 131, 134, "If you hit a rock": quoted in Brodsky, *Grover Cleveland,* 313.

Page 133 caption: report on interior of Gray Gables: "Gay at Gray Gables: Changes in President Cleveland's Summer Home," *Chicago Tribune,* May 13, 1894, 35.

Page 134, "What a sigh of intense relief": quoted in Nevins, *Grover Cleveland,* 531.

Page 134, "The assertion that": "The President Is All Right: Alarming Stories About His Illness Without Foundation," *New York Times,* July 9, 1893, 5.

Page 134, a good catch: "Caught Several Fish," *Washington Post,* July 11, 1893, 1.

Page 134, let the word be passed: "Back at Buzzards Bay," *Washington Post,* July 20, 1893, 1.

Page 134, "My day's doings": quoted in "Off for Gray Gables," *Hartford Courant,* August 12, 1893, 1.

Page 135, *Philadelphia Press* story: reported in Brodsky, *Grover Cleveland,* 315–16.

Page 135, Dr. Keen's account: Dr. William Keen, "The Surgical Operations on President Cleveland," *Saturday Evening Post,* September 22, 1917, 24–25, 53, 55.

Page 136, "The facts in this matter": "Keen Men on Watch: Mrs. Cleveland and Her Children Specially Protected," *Chicago Tribune,* August 6, 1894, 1.

Page 136, "His fishing and hunting excursions": Gilder, *Grover Cleveland,* 157.

Page 136 caption, "If we catch fish": Grover Cleveland, *Fishing and Shooting Sketches,* 175.

Pages 136–37, "hunger and heat," "by the worst hail-storm": Gilder, *Grover Cleveland,* 60.

Page 137, Cleveland once said: reported in ibid., 158.

Page 137, "If you want to catch fish": quoted in ibid., 60.

Page 137, "I started the fishing branch": quoted in Jeffers, *An Honest President,* 232.

REFERENCES AND RESOURCES

Brodsky, Alyn. *Grover Cleveland: A Study in Character.* New York: St. Martin's Press, 2000.

Dunlap, Annette M. "Stage Struck: Frances Cleveland and the Theater." *White House History,* no. 30 (Fall 2011): 76–84.

Cleveland, Grover. *Fishing and Shooting Sketches.* New York: Outling, 1906.

Gilder, Richard Watson. *Grover Cleveland: Record of a Friendship.* New York: Century, 1910.

Graff, Henry F. *Grover Cleveland.* New York: Times Books, 2002.

Harper, J. "Gray Gables: Summer Home of President Grover Cleveland," Mass History, www.masshist.com/gray-gables.

Jeffers, H. Paul. *An Honest President: The Life and Presidencies of Grover Cleveland.* New York: William Morrow, HarperCollins, 2000.

National Park Service, "Grover Cleveland Birthplace, New Jersey," American Presidents: Discover Our Shared Heritage Travel Itinerary, www.nps.gov.nr/travel/presidents/grover_cleveland_birthplace.

National Park Service, "Grover Cleveland Home, Westland, New Jersey," American Presidents: Discover Our Shared Heritage Travel Itinerary, www.nps.gov.nr/travel/presidents/grover_cleveland_home.

Nevins, Allen. *Grover Cleveland: A Study in Courage.* New York: Dodd, Mead, 1932.

Peter, Grace Dunlop, and Joyce D. Southwick. *Cleveland Park: An Early Residential Neighborhood of the Nation's Capital.* Washington, D.C.: Cleveland Park Community Library Committee, 1959.

Seale, William. *The President's House: A History.* 2nd ed. Washington, D.C.: White House Historical Association, 2008.

Tugwell, Rexford G. *Grover Cleveland.* Toronto: Macmillan, 1968.

Welch, Richard E., Jr. *The Presidencies of Grover Cleveland.* Lawrence: University Press of Kansas, 1988.

19: Benjamin Harrison

SOURCES

Page 140, "There is my jail": quoted in Socolofsky and Spetter, *Presidency of Benjamin Harrison,* 162.

Page 141, "was greatly surprised": quoted in Sievers, *Benjamin Harrison,* 3:156.

Page 141, "Who are those" "The President who takes a bribe": quoted in ibid.

Page 141, "near the President's home," "It is just possible": [no title], *Los Angeles Times,* June 8, 1890, 4.

Pages 141, 143, "gift cottage," "The big lower hall," "Already excursions": "Mrs. Harrison's New Home," *Washington Post,* June 22, 1890, 13. See also "Mrs. Harrison at Cape May," *New York Times,* July 20, 1890, 5.

Page 143 "I was surprised by the gift," "How others may be benefited," and the interview: quoted in "What Mrs. Harrison Says," *Washington Post,* July 7, 1890, 4, reprinting an interview from the *Philadelphia Press.*

Page 143 caption: "Present Fit for a Queen" and other quotations: *Boston Daily Globe,* June 16, 1890, 4.

Page 144, "Be good enough": quoted in Sievers, *Benjamin Harrison,* 3:157.

Page 144, "So far as the main point": quoted in ibid.

Page 144, "The President's 'Gift Cottage'": "The President's 'Gift Cottage' Bought with Hard Money," *Hartford Courant,* July 23, 1890, 1.

Page 144, "been led into making," "to join the ragged edges": "That Cape May Cottage: Now It Is Said That the President Bought It," *New York Times,* July 24, 1890, 1.

Page 144, "President Harrison's second thought": "Editorial Points," *Boston Daily Globe,* July 27, 1890, 12.

Page 144, "To President Harrison": "The President Goes Crabbing," *New York Times,* July 8, 1891, 1.

Page 144–45, "The president said a vacation he'd take": quoted in Socolofsky and Spetter, *Presidency of Benjamin Harrison,* 168–69.

Page 145, sold the Cape May Point cottage to Wanamaker for the same $10,000: Sievers, *Benjamin Harrison,* 3:157–58.

REFERENCES AND RESOURCES

Benjamin Harrison Presidential Site, online materials, www.presidentbenjaminharrison.org.

"Cape May History," City of Cape May, www.capemaycity.com.

Calhoun, Charles W. *Benjamin Harrison.* New York: Times Books, 2005.

Jordan, Joe J. *Cape May Point: The Illustrated History, 1875 to the Present.* Atglen, Pa.: Schiffer, 2003.

National Park Service, "Benjamin Harrison Home, Indiana," American Presidents: Discover Our Shared Heritage Travel Itinerary, www.nps.gov.nr/travel/presidents/benjamin_harrison_home.

Schaad, Jacob, Jr. "Benjamin Harrison's Cape May Vacation: One for the History Books," *Cape May Gazette,* November 23, 2011, www.shorenewstoday.com.

Seale, William. *The President's House: A History.* 2nd ed. Washington, D.C.: White House Historical Association, 2008.

Sievers, Harry J. *Benjamin Harrison.* Vol. 3, *Hoosier President: The White House and After.* Newtown, Conn.: 1998.

Socolofsky, Homer E., and Allan B. Spetter. *Benjamin Harrison.* Lawrence: University Press of Kansas, 1987.

20: William McKinley

SOURCES

Page 146, "He told me the other day": "As Seen by a Woman: President McKinley As He Appears on Vacation," *Washington Post,* August 23, 1897, 7.

Page 146, curl up on a sofa and nap: "Fairly Basks in Rest: President McKinley Making the Most of His Vacation," *Chicago Tribune,* August 1, 1897, 11.

Page 146, "He enjoys his friends," "But no other form": "In Control from Canton . . . Likes Few Sports," *Chicago Tribune,* July 29, 1900, 48.

Page 146, those who saw him at close range: "As Seen by a Woman," 7.

Page 146 "The pleasant look deepens": ibid.

Page 146 caption, size of the hotel: Snyder, "Hotel Champlain."

Page 148, "This is a fine place," "It is good": quoted in "Never Felt Better in His Life," *Washington Post,* March 26, 1899, 1.

Page 148 caption, USS *Dolphin*: McSherry, "Gunboat *Dolphin*."

Page 148 caption, Solterra: "Solterra: A Jekyll Island Cottage"; McCash and Martin, *Jekyll Island Club Hotel,* 53–59.

Page 149, "In remaining at his post": "A Commendable Example," *Chicago Tribune,* June 28, 1898, 6.

Page 149, "It is simply the home": "The Optimist," *Washington Post,* July 21, 1901, 19.

Page 150, $14,500, $3,000: "The President's Canton Home," *New York Times,* August 7, 1899, 2; "Owns His First Home Again," *Atlanta Constitution,* August 7, 1899, 4.

Pages 150–51, "We began our married life," "Now I shall": quoted in Leech, *Days of McKinley,* 460.

Page 151, "as readily as if," "put him in touch": "In Control from Canton: How the President Runs the Government from His Ohio Home," *Chicago Tribune,* July 29, 1900, 48.

Page 151 caption, election of 1896: Miller Center, "William McKinley, The Campaign and Election of 1896." See also Morgan, *From Hayes to McKinley,* 515–16.

Page 152, "So accustomed did the people": "Averse to Bodyguard: President Always Declared There Was No Danger," *Washington Post,* September 7, 1901, 1.

Page 152 caption, Theodore Roosevelt's opinion of McKinley's home: Gardner, *Departing Glory,* 29.

Page 154, "It is really so comfortable": quoted in Morgan, *William McKinley and His America,* 394.

Page 154, callers in the summer of 1901: "Callers on the President: Their Number Continues to Increase," *New York Times,* July 12, 1901, 2; "Senator Hanna Sees the President," *Washington Post,* July 16, 1901, 1; "The President's Callers," *New York Times,* August 17, 1901, 3; "Secretary Hay at Canton," *Washington Post,* August 22, 1901, 4.

Page 154, "Expositions are the timekeepers": quoted in Leech, *Days of McKinley,* 584.

Page 154 caption, McKinley's speech: William McKinley: "President McKinley's Last Public Utterance to the People in Buffalo, New York," September 5, 1901, American Presidency Project, www.presidency.ucsb.edu.

REFERENCES AND RESOURCES

Anthony, Carl. "McKinley's Home in the Saxton House," National First Ladies Library, www.firstladies.org.

Gardner, Joseph L. *Departing Glory: Theodore Roosevelt as Ex-President.* New York: Charles Scribner's Sons, 1973.

Gould, Lewis L. *The Presidency of William McKinley.* Lawrence: Regents Press of Kansas, 1980.

Leech, Margaret. *In the Days of McKinley.* New York: Harper and Brothers, 1959.

McCash, June Hall, and Brenden Martin. *The Jekyll Island Club Hotel.* Virginia Beach, Va.: Donning, 2012.

McSherry, Patrick. "Gunboat Dolphin," Spanish American War Centennial Website, www.spanamwar.com.

Miller Center, University of Virginia, "William McKinley, The Campaign and Election of 1896," American President: A Reference Resource, millercenter.org/president/mckinley.

Morgan, H. Wayne. *From Hayes to McKinley.* Syracuse: Syracuse University Press, 1969.

———. *William McKinley and His America.* Kent, Ohio: Kent State University Press, 2003.

Phillips, Kevin. *William McKinley.* New York: Times Books, 2003.

Saxton McKinley House, online materials, www.firstladies.org

Snyder, Patricia. "Hotel Champlain," Clinton County Historical Association, Plattsburgh, N.Y., clintoncountyhistorical.org.

"Solterra, a Jekyll Island Cottage," Jekyll Island Club Hotel, Club News, www.jekyllclub.com.

"William McKinley's Home," Suite 101, suite101.com.

21: THEODORE ROOSEVELT

SOURCES

Page 156, July 5, 1902, arrival: "The President Arrives Home in a Storm," *New York Times,* July 6, 1902, 1.

Page 156, 150,000 letters: estimate by National Park Service historian Amy Verone, Sagamore Hill National Historic Site.

Page 156, 12 minutes: John Gable, foreword to Gluck, *TR's Summer White House,* i–ii.

Page 158, "regular business of the administration": quoted in "Spend Day Outdoors: President and Family Have Enjoyable Picnic," *New York Times,* July 5, 1904, 7.

Page 158, "It was the rule": Cheney, *Personal Memoirs,* 76.

Page 158, nomination of Holmes: "Roosevelt Chronology, January 1, 1901–August 31, 1905," in Theodore Roosevelt, *Letters of Theodore Roosevelt,* ed. Morison et al., 4:1353.

Page 159, "The existence at Oyster Bay": Alice Roosevelt Longworth, *Crowded Hours,* 53–54.

Page 160, "old Sagamore Mohannis": Roosevelt, *Autobiography,* 328.

Page 160, "He never takes," "They do not allow": Butt, *Letters of Archie Butt,* 82–83.

Page 160, "and carried away," "watched every hand": "Thousands Guests of the President," *New York Times,* September 16, 1902, 9.

Page 160, "Cousin Theodore" and the rest of the anecdote: quoted and reported in Hagedorn, *Roosevelt Family,* 152.

Page 160 caption, "I always especially welcome": Theodore Roosevelt, *Correspondence of Roosevelt and Lodge,* 2:24.

Page 161, "scrambles," "over or through, but never around": Robinson, *My Brother, Theodore Roosevelt,* 210.

Page 162, "If they came": Amos, *Hero to His Valet,* 81.

Page 162, "Needless to say": Robinson, *My Brother, Theodore Roosevelt,* 211.

Page 162, "Of course I had not": Theodore Roosevelt, *Letters to His Children,* ed. Bishop, 54.

Page 162, "It only kept them dry": Theodore Roosevelt, *Correspondence of Roosevelt and Lodge,* 222.

Page 162, "the kind that knock": quoted in Butt, *Letters of Archie Butt,* 88.

Page 162 caption, "I think Mr. Roosevelt": ibid., 88.

Page 162 caption, "He joked and talked": Amos, *Hero to His Valet,* 85.

Pages 162–63, "a perfect flying squirrel": ibid., 87.

Page 163, reporters exaggerating: Hagedorn, *Roosevelt Family,* 155–56.

Page 163 caption, USS *Mayflower:* "USCGC *Mayflower,*" Navsource Naval History, www.navsource.org.

Page 164, "To the welfare": quoted in Miller, *Theodore Roosevelt,* 446.

Page 164, "I am having": Theodore Roosevelt, *Letters to Kermit,* ed. Erwin, 109.

Page 164, *Plunger's* log: log of the Torpedo Submarine Boat *Plunger,* August 25, 1905, U.S. Naval Historical Center Archives, Washington, D.C. See also "Submarine A-1, History of the Torpedo Submarine Boat *Plunger,*" n.d., ibid.

Page 164, "I have never seen anything": quoted in "President Takes Plunge in Submarine," *New York Times,* August 26, 1905, 1.

Page 164 caption, fifty-five minutes: ibid.

Page 165, "He really ought," "some new-fangled": "Our Submerged President," *New York Times,* August 27, 1905, 6.

Page 165, "I went down": quoted in Busch, *T.R.,* 207.

Page 165, "I've had many": quoted in ibid.

Page 165, "This is splendid!" "It's a mighty good thing": quoted in Miller, *Theodore Roosevelt,* 448.

Page 165, "like lying in a great solemn cathedral": Theodore Roosevelt, *Outdoor Pastimes,* 316.

Page 165, "rare combination": Burroughs, *Camping and Tramping,* 80.

Pages 165, 167–67, numbers of acres, reservations, preserves, parks, and monuments: "Theodore Roosevelt and Conservation," Theodore Roosevelt National Park, online materials.

Page 166 caption, eight-week, twenty-five-state tour: Hein, "President Theodore Roosevelt's 1903 Visit of Wyoming."

Page 166 caption, "The geysers": Theodore Roosevelt, *Compilation of the Messages and Speeches,* ed. Lewis, 274.

Page 167, "All hunters": Theodore Roosevelt, *Outdoor Pastimes,* 339.

Page 167, wildlife, "brushy tailed" pack rat, "There were eagles": ibid., 86.

Page 167, "Simply exasperating": quoted in Morris, *Theodore Rex,* 172. See also Jeffers, *Roosevelt the Explorer,* 125.

Page 168, "Put it out": quoted in Morris, *Theodore Rex,* 173.

Page 168, story of Teddy Bears: ibid., 173–74.

Page 168, "the nicest little place": quoted in Harbaugh, "Roosevelts' Retreat," 10.

Page 168, "rest and repairs": quoted in ibid., 3.

Page 168, "probably quite the most": Walden Fawcett, quoted in ibid., 5.

Page 168, "a rather crude place": "Arrival at Pine Knot," *Washington Post,* May 18, 1907, 3.

Page 168, $280, 15 acres: Harbaugh, "Roosevelts' Retreat," 6.

Page 168, first visit: ibid., 10.

Page 169, "the king of American game birds": Theodore Roosevelt, "Small Country Neighbors," 395.

Page 169, "President Gets His Wild Turkey": *Richmond Daily Progress,* quoted in Harbaugh, "Roosevelts' Retreat," 26. Reporters for the *Richmond Times-Dispatch* reported on the president's progress but apparently missed the moment of his success.

Page 169, "The turkey came out": Theodore Roosevelt, "Small Country Neighbors," 395.

Page 169, Burroughs's visit: Burroughs, *Under the Maples,* 101.

Page 169, "I go armed": quoted in ibid., 106.

Page 169, "She did not let": ibid.

Page 169, "He had killed": ibid.

Page 169 caption, "It was lovely": Theodore Roosevelt, *Letters of Theodore Roosevelt,* ed. Morison et al., 4:1209.

REFERENCES AND RESOURCES

Amos, James E. *Theodore Roosevelt: Hero to His Valet.* New York: John Day, 1927.

Auchincloss, Louis. *Theodore Roosevelt.* New York: Times Books, 2001.

Barber, James C. *Theodore Roosevelt: Icon of the American Century, with an Essay by Amy Verone.* Washington, D.C.: National Portrait Gallery, Smithsonian Institution, 1998.

Beale, Howard K. *Theodore Roosevelt and the Rise of America to World Power.* Washington, D.C.: Johns Hopkins University Press, 1956.

Brands, H. W. *TR: The Last Romantic.* New York: Basic Books, 1997.

Burroughs, John. *Camping and Tramping with Roosevelt.* New York: Houghton Mifflin, 1906.

———. *Under the Maples.* Boston: Houghton Mifflin 1921.

Busch, Noel F. *T.R.: The Story of Theodore Roosevelt and His Influence on Our Times.* New York: Reynal, 1963.

Butt, Archie. *The Letters of Archie Butt.* Garden City, N.Y.: Doubleday, Page, 1924.

C. K. Berryman: The Gentleman Cartoonist, Tudor Place Historic House and Garden exhibition, Washington, D.C., 2001.

Cheney, Albert Loren. *Personal Memoirs of the Home Life of the Late Theodore Roosevelt as Soldier, Governor, Vice President, and President, in Relation to Oyster Bay.* Washington, D.C.: Cheney Publishing Company, 1919.

Gluck, Sherwin. *T.R.'s Summer White House, Oyster Bay.* Oyster Bay, N.Y.: Sherwin Gluck Publisher, 1999.

Hagedorn, Hermann. *The Roosevelt Family of Sagamore Hill.* New York: Macmillan, 1956.

Hammond, John E. *Oyster Bay Remembered.* Huntington, N.Y.: Maple Hill Press, 2002.

Harbaugh, William H. *Power and Responsibility: The Life and Times of Theodore Roosevelt.* New York: Farrar, Straus and Cudahy, 1961.

———. "The Theodore Roosevelts' Retreat in Southern Albemarle: Pine Knot, 1905–1908." *Magazine of Albemarle County History* 51 (1993).

Hein, Rebecca. "President Theodore Roosevelt's 1903 Visit to Wyoming." WyoHistory: A Project of the Wyoming State Historical Society, www.wyohistory.org.

Jeffers, Paul H. *Roosevelt the Explorer.* New York: Taylor Trade Publishing, 2001.

Longworth, Alice Roosevelt. *Crowded Hours.* New York: Charles Scribner's Sons, 1933.

Miller, Nathan. *Theodore Roosevelt: A Life.* New York: William Morrow 1992.

Morris, Edmund Morris. *Theodore Rex.* New York: Random House, 2001.

Morris, Sylvia Jukes. *Edith Kermit Roosevelt: Portrait of a First Lady.* New York: Modern Library, 2001.

Muir, John. *The Life and Letters of John Muir.* New York: Houghton Mifflin, 1924.

Pringle, Henry F. *Theodore Roosevelt.* New York: Harcourt Brace 1931.

Renehan, Edward J. *The Lion's Pride: Theodore Roosevelt and His Family in Peace and War.* New York: Oxford University Press, 1998.

Robinson, Corinne Roosevelt. *My Brother, Theodore Roosevelt.* New York: Charles Scribner's Sons, 1921.

Roosevelt, Theodore. *A Compilation of the Messages and Speeches of Theodore Roosevelt, 1901–1905.* Edited by Alfred Henry Lewis. Washington, D.C.: Bureau of National Literature and Art, 1906.

———. *Letters to Kermit from Theodore Roosevelt.* Edited by Will Erwin. New York: Charles Scribner's Sons, 1946.

———. *The Letters of Theodore Roosevelt.* Edited by Elting E. Morison et al. Cambridge, Mass.: Harvard University Press, 1951.

———. *Outdoor Pastimes of an American Hunter.* New York: Charles Scribner's Sons, 1905.

———. *Selections from the Correspondence of Theodore Roosevelt and Henry Cabot Lodge, 1884–1918.* New York: Charles Scribner's Sons, 1925.

———. "Small Country Neighbors." *Scribner's Magazine* 42, no. 4 (October 1907): 385–95.

———. *The Strenuous Life: Essays and Addresses by Theodore Roosevelt.* New York: Century Company, 1902.

———. *Theodore Roosevelt, An American Mind: Selections from His Writings.* Edited by Mario R. DiNunzio. New York: St. Martin's Press, 1994.

———. *Theodore Roosevelt: An Autobiography.* New York: Macmillan, 1914.

———. *Theodore Roosevelt's Cyclopedia.* Edited by Albert Bushnell Hart and Herbert Ronald Ferleger. New York: Roosevelt Memorial Association, 1941.

———. *Theodore Roosevelt's Letters to His Children.* Edited by Joseph Bucklin Bishop. New York: Charles Scribner's Sons, 1919.

Roosevelt Pine Knot Foundation, online materials, www.pineknot.org.

Sagamore Hill National Historic Site, online materials, www.nps.gov/sahi.

Sagamore Hill National Historic Site: Home of Theodore Roosevelt. Mankato, Minn.: Creative Company, 2000.

Scottsville Museum, "Pine Knot," scottsvillemuseum.com.

Seale, William Seale. *The President's House: A History.* 2nd ed. Washington, D.C.: White House Historical Association, 2008.

Theodore Roosevelt National Park, online materials, www.nps.gov/thro.

Wallace, David H. "Sagamore Hill: Sagamore Hill National Historic Site, Oyster Bay, New York." Report for the National Park Service, 1991.

22: William H. Taft

SOURCES

Page 172, "I didn't think": Helen Herron Taft, *Recollections of Full Years,* 369.

Page 173, "Local police": "Rainbow for Taft in His Beverly Home," *New York Times,* July 5, 1909, 7.

Page 173, 2,000 miles: Garland, *North Shore,* 261.

Page 174, Myopia golf course: "Taft Begins Day with Golf at the Summer Capital," *New York World,* August 8, 1909, 1. See also Charles R. Macauley, "The *World* Cartoonist's Day with Taft at Beverly," *New York World,* July 24, 1910, Sunday Editorial Section, 1.

Page 173, half of each day: Butt, *Taft and Roosevelt,* 1:173.

Page 173, "feels that he has earned": ibid., 1:174.

Page 174, shared one typical day": Macauley, "*World* Cartoonist's Day with Taft at Beverly."

Page 174, "The presidential appetite": ibid.

Page 174, "Nobody found it": Helen Herron Taft, *Recollections of Full Years,* 370.

Pages 175, "have found out": "How Long Should a Man's Vacation Be?" *New York Times,* July 31, 1910, Sunday Feature Section, 3.

Page 175, "the whole army": Macauley, "*World* Cartoonist's Day with Taft at Beverly."

Page 175, "No Automobiles Allowed": Bromley, *Taft and the First Motoring Presidency,* 31.

Page 175, "daredevil," "famous all about": "Taft's Daredevil Chauffeur," *New York Times,* August 15, 1909, Sunday Feature Section, 4.

Page 175 caption, "The President went golfing," "He stands very straight": quoted in Garland, *North Shore,* 260.

Pages 175–76, "He likes to sit": "Taft's Daredevil Chauffeur."

Page 176, "atmospheric champagne": quoted in Bromley, *Taft and the First Motoring Presidency,* 54.

Page 176, "speed trap": "Taft in Auto Speed Trap," *New York Times,* September 5, 1909, 1.

Page 176, "such a hot speed": "Baseball Placard Says 'Go See Taft'," *New York Times,* May 2, 1910, 12.

Page 176 "he sets a rather bad": "Topics of the Times: Setting a Bad Example," *New York Times,* May 3, 1910, 12, reported in Bromley, *Taft and the First Motoring Presidency,* 201.

Page 176, "junkets," "pleasure cruises": "Use of Naval Vessels by Presidents and Others Cost $1,465,261 in 5 Years," *New York World,* July 24, 1910, Sunday Feature Section, 1.

Page 176, "It was one": Butt, *Taft and Roosevelt,* 2:455–56.

Page 177, "One continuous": Butt, ibid., 1:417.

Page 177, "rather pitiful failure": quoted in Manners, *TR and Will,* 170.

Page 177, "I never saw": Butt, *Taft and Roosevelt,* 1:417.

Page 177, "For a full minute": "Roosevelt and Taft in a Warm Embrace; 'Just Like Old Times,' Declare White House Employes [*sic*] When They Meet at Beverly; Many Slaps on the Back; Rumors of Coolness Between Them Effectively Disposed Of as They Laugh and Chat Together," *New York Times,* July 1, 1910, 1.

Page 177, "He was in his best": Butt, *Taft and Roosevelt,* 1:421.

Page 177, "gave us as merry" and quotations in the rest of the paragraph: Helen Herron Taft, *Recollections of Full Years,* 384.

Page 177, "Things have become so bitter": Butt, *Taft and Roosevelt,* 2:515.

Page 177, "I am beginning": ibid., 2:755.

Page 177 caption, different set of calluses: ibid., 2:717.

Page 178, "He was like," quoted in Seale, *President's House,* 2:24.

Page 178–79, "summed up Taft's four summers," "The playing course": "Taft, On Road Again, Here To-morrow," *New York Times,* September 23, 1912, 3.

Page 179, "I have come": quoted in Adler, *Presidential Wit,* 100.

REFERENCES AND RESOURCES

Adler, Bill. *Presidential Wit.* New York: Trident, 1966.

Anderson, Judith Icke. *William Howard Taft: An Intimate History.* New York: W. W. Norton, 1981.

Beschloss, Michael, ed. *American Heritage Illustrated History of the Presidents.* New York: Crown Publishers, 2000.

Bromley, Michael. *William Howard Taft and the First Motoring Presidency.* Jefferson, N.C.: McFarland, 2003.

Butt, Archibald. *Taft and Roosevelt: The Intimate Letters of Archie Butt, Military Aide.* Garden City, N.Y.: Doubleday, Doran, 1930; reprint, Port Washington, N.Y.: Kennikat Press, 1971.

Chace, James. *1912: Wilson, Roosevelt, Taft and Debs: The Election That Changed the Country.* New York: Simon and Schuster, 2004.

Duffy, Herbert S. *William Howard Taft.* New York: Minton, Balch, 1930.

Garland, Joseph E. *Boston's Gold Coast: The North Shore, 1890–1929.* Boston: Little, Brown, 1981.

———. *The North Shore.* Beverly, Mass.: Commonwealth Editions, 1998.

Manners, William. *TR and Will: A Friendship That Split the Republican Party.* New York: Harcourt, Brace and World, 1969.

Pringle, Henry F. *The Life and Times of William Howard Taft.* Norwalk, Conn.: Easton Press, 1968.

Seale, William. *The President's House: A History.* 2nd ed. Washington, D.C.: White House Historical Association, 2008.

Taft, Helen Herron. *Recollections of Full Years.* New York: Dodd, Mead, 1914.

23: Woodrow Wilson

SOURCES

Page 180, "Here we are": Woodrow Wilson, *Papers of Woodrow Wilson,* ed. Link, 24:481–82.

Page 180, "Need you ask?": quoted in McAdoo, *The Woodrow Wilsons,* 153.

Page 180, "ten-inning game": quoted in "Wilson Is Serene As Voting Goes On," *New York Times,* June 29, 1912, 1.

Page 182, "a hard, pounding battle": quoted in Saunders, *Ellen Axson Wilson,* 227.

Page 182, "As it has seemed," "The Little White House": quoted in "Gov. Wilson Not Elated by Victory," *New York Times,* July 3, 1912, 1.

Page 182, "I must choose": quoted in Walworth, *Woodrow Wilson,* 310.

Page 184, "Mrs. Wilson is a serious": "President's Wife Shows Landscapes," *New York Times,* November 15, 1913, 11.

Page 184, outdoor pageant: "President Watches Daughter in Play," *New York Times,* September 13, 1913, 11.

Page 184, "because when you are": Woodrow Wilson, *Papers of Woodrow Wilson,* ed. Link, 28:161.

Page 185, Grayson said: Grayson, *Woodrow Wilson,* 46.

Page 185, "an ineffectual attempt": quoted in ibid.

Page 185, "The fact": ibid., 47.

Page 185, "a fidgety player": quoted in Campbell and Landau, *Presidential Lies,* 37.

Page 186, "I'm nearly frozen": quoted in news reports in Herndon family scrapbook, Woodrow Wilson House, Washington, D.C.

Page 186, "Please take good care": quoted in Grayson, *Woodrow Wilson,* 35.

Page 186, "Oh my God": quoted in Shachtman, *Edith and Woodrow,* 39.

Page 186, "only temporary diversions": Grayson, *Woodrow Wilson,* 48.

Page 186, "Tears came into": Colonel Edward M. House, quoted in Woodrow Wilson, *Papers of Woodrow Wilson,* ed. Link, 30:464.

Page 186, "It is no compliment": quoted in Tumulty, *Woodrow Wilson,* 473.

Pages 186–87, "Things are looking," "The president's daughters": Jaffray, *Secrets of the White House,* 53–54.

Page 187, "music made": Edith Bolling Wilson, *My Memoir,* 71.

Page 187, whistling and dancing: account in Starling, *Starling of the White House,* 62.

Page 187, "We are having": Woodrow Wilson, *Papers of Woodrow Wilson,* 35:399.

Page 187, would not be stampeded: ibid., 424.

Page 188 caption, "awful": Edith Bolling Wilson, *My Memoir,* 103.

Page 189, "soft and fragrant," "a fine, humorous": interview by Ida Tarbell, reprinted in Woodrow Wilson, *Papers of Woodrow Wilson,* 38:327, 324.

Page 190, "How's your game?" "Grayson's got": quoted in Shachtman, *Edith and Woodrow,* 141.

Page 190, "The boss has won": quoted in Starling, *Starling of the White House,* 77.

Page 190, "It was a funny election": ibid. 78.

REFERENCES AND RESOURCES

Aucella, Frank J., and Patricia A. Piorkowski Hobbs, with Francis Wright Summers. *Ellen Axson Wilson, First Lady—Artist.* Washington, D.C.: Woodrow Wilson House, and Staunton, Va.: Woodrow Wilson Birthplace and Museum, 1993.

Bell, H.C.F. *Woodrow Wilson and the People.* Garden City, N.Y.: Doubleday, Doran, 1945.

Campbell, Shepherd, and Peter Landau. *Presidential Lies: The Illustrated History of White House Golf.* New York: Macmillan, 1996.

Colby, Virginia Reed, and James B. Atkinson. *Footprints of the Past: Images of Cornish, New Hampshire and the Cornish Colony.* Concord, N.H.: New Hampshire Historical Society, 1996.

Grayson, Cary T. *Woodrow Wilson: An Intimate Memoir.* Washington, D.C.: Potomac Books, 1960.

Jaffray, Elizabeth. *Secrets of the White House.* New York: Cosmopolitan Book Corporation, 1928.

Lawrence, David. *The True Story of Woodrow Wilson.* New York: George H. Doran Company, 1924.

Link, Arthur S., ed. *Woodrow Wilson: A Profile.* American Century Series. New York: Hill and Wang, 1968.

McAdoo, Eleanor Wilson, with Margaret Y. Gaffey. *The Woodrow Wilsons.* New York: Macmillan, 1937.

McAdoo, William Gibbs. *Crowded Years: The Reminiscences of William G. McAdoo,* Boston: Houghton Mifflin, 1931.

Ross, Ishbel. *Power with Grace.* New York: G. P. Putnam's Sons, 1975.

Saunders, Frances Wright. *Ellen Axson Wilson: First Lady Between Two Worlds.* Chapel Hill: University of North Carolina Press, 1985.

Shachtman, Tom. *Edith and Woodrow: A Presidential Romance.* New York: G. P. Putnam's Sons, 1981.

Smith, Gene. *When the Cheering Stopped: The Last Years of Woodrow Wilson.* New York: William Morrow, 1964.

Starling, Edmund W., with Thomas Sugrue. *Starling of the White House.* New York: Simon and Schuster, 1946.

Tumulty, Joseph P. *Woodrow Wilson as I Know Him.* Garden City, N.Y.: Doubleday, Page, 1921.

Van Natta, Don, Jr. *First Off the Tee: Presidential Hackers, Duffers, and Cheaters, from Taft to Bush.* New York: Public Affairs, 2003.

Walworth, Arthur C. *Woodrow Wilson.* New York: W. W. Norton, 1978.

Wilson, Edith Bolling. *My Memoir.* New York: Bobbs-Merrill, 1938.

Wilson, Woodrow. *The Papers of Woodrow Wilson,* ed. Arthur L. Link. Princeton, N.J.: Princeton University Press, 1978.

24: Warren G. Harding

SOURCES

Page 192, "not heroics, but healing": quoted in Dean, *Warren G. Harding,* 57

Page 192, "With a jack knife": Starling, *Starling of the White House,* 177.

Page 192, "the nature and customs": "Countryside Joins President in Camp," *New York Times,* July 25, 1921, 1.

Page 195, "The Duchess": Seale, *President's House,* 2:95.

Page 195, "The constant adulation of people": quoted in Russell, *Shadow of Blooming Grove,* 421.

Page 196, Drinks were served: see Seale, *President's House,* 2:96, for an account of Harding's attitude toward the private consumption of alcohol.

Page 196, "He played as if": Starling, *Starling of the White House,* 168.

Page 196, "I had to keep accounts," ibid., 169.

Page 196, "Forget that I am President": quoted in ibid.

Page 196, "I may not know everything": quoted in Campbell and Landau, *Presidential Lies,* 53.

Page 196, "After all": quoted in ibid., 65.

Pages 196, 198, "Almost everyone in Washington": "Half Way," *Time,* Mary 10, 1923, 1.

Page 197 caption, "A blind sow": *Springfield Leader,* June, 8, 1922, 15

Page 198, "having been tied down": "Time-Table Barred in President's Trip," *New York Times,* March 8, 1923, 16.

Page 198, "quite tired": "Camera Men Take Ocean Pictures of President on Trip," *Miami Herald,* March 16, 1923, 9.

Page 198, "President Harding will be a candidate": quoted in "Harding Will Run, Nation Wants Him, Says Daugherty," *New York Times,* March 18, 1923, 1.

Page 198 caption, the McLeans: Russell, *Shadow of Blooming Grove,* 262.

Page 199, forcefully dispelled rumors: "Mr. Harding's Hat," *Time,* March 24, 1923, 3.

Page 199, ambitious transcontinental trip: "Anabasis," *Time,* July 2, 1923, 3.

Page 199, Harding couldn't sleep: Starling, *Starling of the White House,* 189.

Pages 199–200, "I want you to promise," "Are you sure": quoted in ibid., 195–96.

Page 200, "cut every program": quoted in ibid., 195.

Page 200, "He looked more weary": ibid.

Page 200, sixty-five people': "Anabasis," *Time*, July 2, 1923, 3.

Page 200, "My passion is for justice": quoted in Mee, *Ohio Gang*, 217.

Page 200, five airplanes: "Anabasis," *Time*, July 2, 1923, 3.

Page 200, "I am seeking American sentiment": quoted in Mee, *Ohio Gang*, 218.

Page 200, "There were only four": Herbert Hoover, *Memoirs of Herbert Hoover*, 2:49.

Page 200–201, "If you knew": quoted in ibid.

Page 201, "Publish it," "abruptly dried up": quoted in ibid.

Page 201, "an apostle of understanding": quoted in "President 'Apostle of Understanding'," *Washington Post*, July 10, 1923, 1.

Page 201, the northernmost point: "Anabasis," *Time*, July 23, 1923, 3.

Page 201, "Just can't get on": quoted in Ferrell, *Strange Deaths*, 12.

Page 205, Alaska's natural resources: "President Insists Alaska's Wealth Shall Be Guarded," *Washington Post*, July 28, 1923, 1.

Page 205, "an exhausted man": quoted in Ferrell, *Strange Deaths*, 13.

Page 205, "grave": quoted in ibid., 17.

Page 205, found the president: Starling, *Starling of the White House*, 198–99.

Page 205, report of Harding's death: Gramling, *AP*, 304–5. Years later Steve Early became press secretary to President Franklin D. Roosevelt, and he announced President Roosevelt's death from the White House, April 12, 1945.

REFERENCES AND RESOURCES

Anthony, Carl Sferrazza. *Florence Harding*. New York: William Morrow, 1998.

Campbell, Shepherd, and Peter Landau. *Presidential Lies: The Illustrated History of White House Golf*. New York: Macmillan, 1996.

Dean, John W. *Warren G. Harding*. New York: Times Books, 2004.

Ferrell, Robert H. *The Strange Deaths of President Harding*. Columbia; University of Missouri Press, 1996.

Gramling, Oliver. *AP: The Story of News*. New York: Farrah and Rinehart, 1940.

Hoover, Herbert. *The Memoirs of Herbert Hoover*. Vol. 2. New York: Macmillan, 1952.

Johnson, Willis Fletcher. *The Life of Warren G. Harding*. Chicago: John C. Winston, 1923.

Mee, Charles L., Jr. *The Ohio Gang: The World of Warren G. Harding*. New York: M. Evans, 1981.

Russell, Frances. *The Shadow of Blooming Grove*. New York: McGraw-Hill, 1968.

Seale, William. *The President's House: A History*. 2nd ed. Washington, D.C.: White House Historical Association, 2008.

Starling, Edmund W., with Thomas Sugrue. *Starling of the White House*. New York: Simon and Shuster, 1946.

Trani, Eugene P., and David L. Wilson. *The Presidency of Warren G. Harding*. Lawrence: Regents Press of Kansas, 1977.

Van Natta, Don., Jr. *First Off the Tee: Presidential Hackers, Duffers, and Cheaters, from Taft to Bush*. New York: Public Affairs, 2003.

25: Calvin Coolidge

SOURCES

Page 206, "as different": Longworth, *Crowded Hours*, 325.

Page 206, so far west: "Coolidges Start Long Rail Journey to South Dakota," *Washington Post*, June 14, 1927, 1.

Page 206, "every street," "Every switch": Coolidge, *Autobiography*, 218.

Page 208, "When he went": ibid., 190.

Page 208 caption, "My father had it": quoted in Fuess, *Man from Vermont*, 352.

Page 209, "the little fellow": Starling, *Starling of the White House*, 204.

Page 209, "Mama! Mama!" quoted in ibid., 242.

Page 209, "You never," "Yes, he did": quoted in "Mosquitos Keep Coolidge Indoors," *New York Times*, July 9, 1926, 3.

Page 209, "Thereafter we fished": Starling, *Starling of the White House*, 204.

Page 210, "the population in and about": quoted in Taliaferro, *Great White Fathers*, 222.

Page 210, "rattler extermination hunt": Starling, *Starling of the White House*, 248.

Page 210, "You can fish all day": ibid.

Page 210, "tag-team of airplanes": "President Is Busy with State Tasks, After Day of Play," *Washington Evening Star*, June 17, 1927, 5.

Page 211, "working vacation": "President's Party Starts Tonight on a Working Vacation," *Washington Evening Star*, June 13, 1927, 1.

Page 211, "It is seldom quiet": quoted in "Tent Community Grows Up Around Coolidge's Lodge," AP, June 30, 1927, available online at newspaperarchive.com, printed in, e.g., *Waterloo (Iowa) Evening Courier*, June 30, 1927, 1.

Page 211, Rebecca: "Coolidge Raccoon Flees," *New York Times*, June 24, 1927, 8.

Page 213, "presents": Taliaferro, *Great White Fathers*, 223; "The Coolidge Week," *Time*, June 27, 1927, 7; "The Coolidge Week," *Time*, August 1, 1927, 7.

Page 213, "pure and wholesome": quoted in "The Coolidge Week," *Time*, June 27, 1927, 7.

Page 213, "Grace Coolidge Creek": "Creek in South Dakota Is Named for Mrs. Coolidge," *New York Times*, July 1, 1927, 1.

Page 213, "Worm": quoted in M. E. Hennessy, "Coolidge Fishes Day and Night," *Boston Globe*, June 17, 1927, 12.

Page 213, "hullabaloo": Starling, *Starling of the White House*, 250.

Page 213, "Nothing but an imbecile trout": quoted in "Worms Trout Bait? 2 Senators Aghast," *Washington Post*, June 18, 1927, 5.

Page 213, "Any trout that would lie": quoted in ibid.

Page 213, "an old, dilapidated Black Gnat," "he tangled his own": Starling, *Starling of the White House*, 251.

Page 213, "The two miles," "became the nation's": quoted In Lathem, *Meet Calvin Coolidge*, 121.

Page 213, 6,801 letters: "The Coolidge Week," *Time*, July 11, 1927, 9.

Page 213, "Still Waters": "The Coolidge Week," *Time*, July 4, 1927, 7.

Page 213, "Sullen Warrior": "Coolidgiana and Heat," *New York Times*, June 29, 1927, 24. See also "New Coolidge Name Picked by Indians," *New York Times*, June 28, 1927, 2.

Page 213, "Man-Who-May-Be-President": "The Coolidge Week," *Time*, July 4, 1927, 2.

Page 213 caption, "the President is attempting": quoted in "La Follette Sees Third Term Fishing," *New York Times*, July 8, 1927, 4.

Page 213 caption: "The Coolidge Week," *Time*, August 15, 1927.

Page 214, "I have been president": quoted in Sobel, *Coolidge*, 369.

Page 214, "Now—I am not" and the rest of the quotations in this paragraph: quoted in Feuss, *Calvin Coolidge*, 392.

Page 214, National Woman's Party: "President Hears Equal Rights Plea," *Washington Evening Star*, July 15, 1927, 4.

Page 214, scheduled morning briefing: Sobel, *Coolidge*, 369.

Page 215, "a twelve-word shock": "Shock," *Time*, August 15, 1927, 7.

Page 215, "I ain't gonna do it": quoted in Ferrell, *Presidency of Coolidge*, 192.

Page 215, "meant everything" and the rest of the quotations in this paragraph: quoted in Taliaferro, *Great White Fathers*, 222.

Page 215 caption, first time he had been photographed: "The Coolidge Week," *Time*, August 22, 1927, 9.

Page 216, "We have come here," "to which future generations": quoted in "Coolidge Dedicates Mountain Memorial to Four Presidents," *New York Times*, August 11, 1927, 1.

Page 216, "His mind was now free": Starling, *Starling of the White House*, 259.

Page 216, "roar with laughter": quoted in "Neronic," *Time*, July 25, 1927, 11.

Page 216, "Well, it's good": quoted in Fuess, *Man from Vermont*, 391.

Page 216, "If he had fallen asleep": Starling, *Starling of the White House*, 254.

Page 216 caption, had learned his fly book: "Summer Sport," *Time*, August 6, 1928, 9.

Page 217, "Charles A. Lindbergh": quoted in "The Coolidge Week," *Time*, September 12, 1927, 9.

Page 217, "I have had": quoted in Starling, *Starling of the White House*, 259.

Page 217, "We lost her": Coolidge, *Autobiography*, 221.

Page 217, "that superman": quoted in Starling, *Starling of the White House*, 263.

Page 217, "The Brule River," "Nature could not": ibid., 265.

Page 218, "Curtains of rain," "All week": "Rain," *Time*, July 2, 1928, 9.

Page 218, "One day he lost" and the rest of the exchange: Starling, *Starling of the White House*, 267.

Page 218, "motorized gawkers": Thibodeau, *Remember, Remember*, 221.

Page 218, "I feel": quoted in Gilbert, *Tormented President*, 237.

REFERENCES AND RESOURCES

Coolidge, Calvin. *The Autobiography of Calvin Coolidge*. New York: Cosmopolitan Book Corp., 1929.

Ferrell, Robert H. *The Presidency of Calvin Coolidge*. Lawrence: University of Kansas Press, 1998.

Fuess, Claude M. *Calvin Coolidge: The Man from Vermont*. Boston: Little, Brown, 1940.

Gilbert, Robert E. *The Tormented President*. Westport, Conn.: Praeger, 2003.

Hannaford, Peter, ed. *The Quotable Calvin Coolidge: Sensible Words for a New Century*. Bennington, Vt.: Images from the Past, 2001.

Jones, Cranston. *Homes of the American Presidents*. New York: Bonanza Books, 1962.

Lathem, Edward Connery. *Meet Calvin Coolidge: The Man Behind the Myth*. Brattleboro, Vt.: Stephen Greene Press, 1960.

Longworth, Alice Roosevelt. *Crowded Hours*. New York: Charles Scribner's Sons, 1933.

Ross, Ishbel. *Grace Coolidge and Her Era: The Story of a President's Wife*. New York: Dodd, Mead, 1962.

Sobel, Robert. *Coolidge: An American Enigma*. Washington, D.C.: Regnery Press, 1998.

Starling, Edmund W., with Thomas Sugrue. *Starling of the White House*. New York: Simon and Schuster, 1946.

Taliaferro, John. *Great White Fathers: The Story of the Obsessive Quest to Create Mt. Rushmore*. New York: PublicAffairs, 2002.

Thibodeau, Lynn, ed. *Remember, Remember*. St. Paul, Minnesota: Carillon Books, 1978. 221.

White, William Allen. *A Puritan in Babylon*. New York: Macmillan, 1938.

26: Herbert Hoover

SOURCES

Page 220, "For these reasons": quoted in Racine, *"Rapidan Camp,"* 15–16.

Page 220, "Washington's exhausting summer heat": Herbert Hoover, *Memoirs*, 322–23.

Page 221 caption, five large sailfish:

Page 222, "He was looking for": "Rejoicing and Gladness," *Time*, April 1, 1929.

Page 222, "That's where I want": quoted in Lambert, *Herbert Hoover's Hideaway*, 19. See also Racine, *"Rapidan Camp,"* 17.

Page 222, "It is really away": Mildred Adams, "Here the President Finds Calm," *New York Times Sunday Magazine*, September 8, 1929, 1.

Page 223, catch enough trout: "Hoover Party Lands Fish for Two Meals," *New York Times*, June 10, 1929, 4.

Page 223, $5 an acre: Racine, *"Rapidan Camp,"* 65.

Page 223, $114,000 of his own money: Lambert, *Herbert Hoover's Hideaway*, 124.

Page 223, Shenandoah National Park: Herbert Hoover to William E. Carson, chairman of the Virginia Conservation Commission, "Letter Proposing Incorporation of Camp Rapidan Into the Shenandoah National Park," August 7, 1929, American Presidency Project. www.presidency.ucsb.edu.

Page 223, "It would have been easier": quoted in Lambert, *Herbert Hoover's Hideaway*, 20.

Page 223, "The fish are close at hand": "Hoover's Fishing Camp a Veritable Village, to Build Which Has Been a Stupendous Job," *Washington Post*, August 11, 1929, M11.

Page 223, "It is the kind": ibid.

Page 225, "I have discovered" and the rest of Hoover's speech: Herbert Hoover, "Remarks to the People of Madison County, Virginia, at the Celebration of 'Hoover Day in Madison'," August 17, 1929, American Presidency Project. www.presidency.ucsb.edu.

Page 225 caption, Hoover School: "The Hoover Week," *Time*, September 16, 1929, 13; "New Hoover School Is Boon to Elders," *New York Times*, February 23, 1930, 33; "Mountains Kids Rush to Attend Hoover School," *Chicago Tribune*, February 25, 1930, 29.

Page 226, medicine ball: Heller, *President's Doctor*, 133–37.

Page 226, "the fresh air": quoted in ibid., 136.

Page 226, "The camp buildings harmonize": Hunter, *President's Camp*, 6.

Page 226 caption, "It required less skill": Herbert Hoover, *Memoirs*, 327.

Page 227, "I had no idea": Irwin H. Hoover, *Forty-Two Years in the White House*, 191.

Page 227, "He always wants to have people": quoted in Richard Norton Smith, *Uncommon Man*, 34.

Page 227, Lindbergh lamp: Racine, "Rapidan Camp," 65.

Page 227, "The President is very fond": quoted in Lambert, *Herbert Hoover's Hideaway*, 46.

Page 228, "Almost as soon as": "President at Camp, Finds Fish Biting," *New York Times*, April 5, 1930, 1.

Page 228, "carries a fly-book": "Hoover at Rapidan, Catches 20 Trout," *New York Times*, May 11, 1930, 2.

Page 228, "drought relief headquarters": "Sticks to His Camp Desk": *New York Times*, August 10, 1930, 1.

Page 228, "place in which to get away": "On the Rapidan," *Washington Post*, April 27, 1930, 51.

Page 228, "His hands would tremble" and the rest of the quotations in this paragraph: Starling, *Starling of the White House*, 284.

Page 229 caption, crest road: Lambert, *Undying Past*, 218. See also Reed Engle, "Skyline Drive: A Road to Nowhere," Shenandoah National Park, online materials.

Page 230 caption, "After all blankets": quoted in Mares, *Fishing with the Presidents*, 70.

Page 230 caption, "The public barely knew him": Richard Norton Smith, *Uncommon Man*, 34.

Page 231, "It was very difficult," "A great opportunity": quoted in Racine, *"Rapidan Camp,"* 64.

Page 231, "The back of the Depression": "A Fearful Price," *Time*, June 30, 1932, 11.

Page 231, "a New Deal": Franklin D. Roosevelt, "Address Accepting the Presidential Nomination at the Democratic National Convention in Chicago," July 2, 1932, *American Presidency Project*, www.presidency.ucsb.edu.

Page 231, "destroy the very foundations": Herbert Hoover, "Address at Madison Square Garden in New York City," October 31, 1932, American Presidency Project. www.presidency.ucsb.edu._

Page 231, packing of personal belongings: "Mrs. Hoover Closes the Rapidan Camp," *New York Times*, December 5, 1932, 14.

Page 231, FDR picnic: "Roosevelt Visits Rapidan on Picnic," *New York Times*, April 10, 1933, 15.

Page 231, Hoover returned: Lambert, *Herbert Hoover's Hideaway*, 135–36.

REFERENCES AND RESOURCES

Fausold, Martin L. *The Presidency of Herbert C. Hoover*. Lawrence: University Press of Kansas, 1985.

Heller, Milton F., Jr. *The President's Doctor: An Insider's View of Three First Families*. New York: Vantage Press, 2000.

Hoover, Herbert. *Fishing for Fun—And to Wash Your Soul*. West Branch, Iowa: Herbert Hoover Presidential Library, 1963.

———. *The Memoirs of Herbert Hoover*. New York: Macmillan Company, 1952.

———. *Public Papers of the Presidents of the United States: Herbert Hoover, 1929–1933*. Washington, D.C.: Government Printing Office, 1974–77.

Hoover, Irwin H. *Forty-Two Years in the White House*. Boston: Houghton Mifflin, 1934.

Hunter, Thomas Lomax. *The President's Camp on the Rapidan*. Roanoke, Va.: Stone Printing and Manufacturing, for the Virginia State Commission on Conservation and Development, 1931.

Lambert, Darwin. *Herbert Hoover's Hideaway: The Story of Camp Hoover on the Rapidan River*. Luray, Va.: Shenandoah Natural History Association, 1971.

———. *The Undying Past of Shenandoah National Park*. Boulder, Colo.: Roberts Rinehart, for the Shenandoah Natural History Association, 1989.

Mares, Bill. *Fishing with the Presidents*. Mechanicsburg, Pa.: Stackpole Books, 1999.

National Park Service, "President Herbert and Lou Henry Hoover's Rapidan Camp, Virginia," American Presidents: Discover Our Shared Heritage Travel Itinerary, www.nps.gov.nr/travel/presidents/hoover_camp_rapidan.

Racine, Laurel A. "Rapidan Camp: The Brown House." Report for Shenandoah National Park, Northeast Museum Services Center, National Park Service, 2001.

Shenandoah National Park, online materials, www.nps.gov/shen.

Smith, Gene. *The Shattered Dream: Herbert Hoover and the Great Depression*. New York: William Morrow, 1970.

Smith, Richard Norton. *An Uncommon Man: The Triumph of Herbert Hoover*. New York: Simon and Schuster, 1984.

Starling, Edmund W., with Thomas Sugrue. *Starling of the White House*. New York: Simon and Schuster, 1946.

27: FRANKLIN D. ROOSEVELT

SOURCES

Page 235, "Perfect navigation": "Roosevelt Battles Seas off Cape Till Forced to Nantucket Refuge," *New York Times*, June 20, 1933, 3. Articles in the *New York Times*, June 16–30, 1933, are a general source for the cruise of the *Amberjack II*. See also Cross, *Sailor in the White House*, 1–46.

Page 235, "That's not yachting": quoted in "Roosevelt Sails to Pulpit Harbor," *New York Times*, June 24, 1933, 3.

Page 235, "I am having": quoted in Starling, *Starling of the White House*, 311.

Page 235, "I remember": quoted in Charles Hurd, "Roosevelt Greeted Royally by Canada at Campobello Isle," *New York Times*, June 30, 1933, 1.

Page 236, landed pompano, bonito: Captain Wilson Brown, Log of the President's Cruise to Hawaii, 1 July–3 August, 1934, Trips of the President, Cruises and Logs, Franklin Delano Roosevelt Library, Hyde Park, N.Y.

Pages 236, "perfect for this mood": Franklin D. Roosevelt, in *Closest Companion*, ed. Ward, 44.

Page 236, "President Roosevelt loves the sea": Mildred Adams, "The President Takes to the Sea Lanes," *New York Times Sunday Magazine*, July 1, 1934, 7.

Page 236, "the woman I love": quoted in "King's Romance Soars Above All Loves of Past," *Chicago Tribune*, December 13, 1936, 4.

Page 237, "tickled him": James Roosevelt and Sidney Shalett, *Affectionately, FDR*, 282.

Page 237 caption, "an exhibition of strength": McIntire, *White House Physician*, 9.

Page 237 caption, "I hadn't been out": Franklin D. Roosevelt, in *Closest Companion*, ed. Ward, 46.

Page 238, "I have a lot," "about half a mile": quoted in John C. Waite Associates, *President as Architect*, 29.

Page 238, "tree grower": quoted in Hassett, *Off the Record*, 219.

Page 238 caption, Roosevelt ritual: Jackson, *That Man*, 142–43.

Page 238 caption, "I think you all": quoted in "Hyde Park To Be Summer Capital," *New York Times*, February 26, 1933, F5.

Pages 240, "No president," "a brief transition": C.W.B. Hurd, "Roosevelt, on Vacation, Feels Capital's Pulse," *New York Times*, July 30, 1933, 106.

Page 240, "He again has become": "Roosevelt Leads Picnickers in Fun," *New York Times*, September 4, 1934, 3.

Page 241, "I found that," "to escape the mob": Franklin D. Roosevelt, memorandum, December 9, 1942, in *FDR: His Personal Letters*, ed. Elliott Roosevelt, 1378–79.

Page 241 caption, Hyde Park in wartime: Hassett, *Off the Record*; Reilly, *Reilly of the White House*, 238.

Page 242, "the nicest hill," "our hill": Daisy Suckley, in *Closest Companion*, ed. Ward, 35–36.

Page 242, "homelike, personal": quoted in John C. Waite Associates, *President as Architect*, 20.

Page 243 caption, "He was conversing," "It was a relief": quoted in Black, *Franklin Delanore Roosevelt*, 524.

Page 244, "people with whom": Daisy Suckley, in *Closest Companion*, ed. Ward, 134.

Page 244, "My mother does not": exchange quoted in Swift, *Roosevelts and the Royals*, 135.

Page 244, Tube Alloys: Meacham, *Franklin and Winston*, 183–84.

Page 244 caption, "our secret base": quoted in Nelson, *President Is at Camp David*, 2.

Page 245, Bear's Den: descriptions from "Roosevelt Hideaway," *Life*, October 15, 1945, 101–4; Rigdon, *White House Sailor*, 214–15.

Page 245, Secret Service hid: Reilly, *Reilly of the White House*, 238–39.

Page 245 caption, "with much interest": quoted in Meacham, *Franklin and Winston*, 224.

Page 246, "There were no luxuries": Rigdon, *White House Sailor*, 215.

Page 246, twenty-two other visits, visitors to Shangri-La: Shangri-La Log Books, President's Personal File, Roosevelt Library.

Page 246, "Thank God. That sounds grand": quoted in Nelson, *President Is at Camp David*, 15.

Page 246, "On this cruise": Shangri-La Log Book, November 6–8, 1942.

Page 246, "much to our regret": ibid., May 14–17, 1943.

Page 246, "The president always knows": Hassett, *Off the Record*, 111.

Page 247, "flush with the ground," "wonderful for sunsets," "a home for all": quoted in Goodwin, *No Ordinary Time*, 561.

Page 247, forty-one times: Compilation of FDR Visits to Warm Springs, Ga., Trip File, Roosevelt Library.

Page 247, "a perfectly good": Franklin D. Roosevelt, "Remarks to Orthopedic Surgeons, Warm Springs, Georgia," December 7, 1935, American Presidency Project, www.presidency.ucsb.edu.

Page 247, Roosevelt told the story: ibid. See also "Remarks at Thanksgiving Day Party at Warm Springs, Georgia," November 29, 1934, American Presidency Project, www.presidency.ucsb.edu.

Page 248, "swimming his way": Cleburne Gregory, "Franklin Roosevelt Will Swim to Health," *Atlanta Journal*, Sunday Magazine, October 26, 1924, 7.

Page 248, "I am deriving": quoted in ibid.

Page 249, 2,900 votes to 37: Carl Vinson Institute of Government, the University of Georgia, "Franklin D. Roosevelt's Visits to Georgia," October 23–24, 1932," Carl Vinson Institute of Government, University of Georgia, http://georgiainfo.galileo.usg.edu/FDRvisit.htm.

Page 249, "absolutely dead weight": Reilly, *Reilly of the White House*, 227.

Page 249 caption, "I am grateful": Franklin D. Roosevelt, "Radio Address at Thanksgiving Dinner, Warm Springs Foundation, Warm Springs, Georgia," November 24, 1938, American Presidency Project, www.presidency.ucsb.edu. See also "Roosevelt Carves Turkey, Not a Map," *New York Times*, November 25, 1938, 1.

Page 250, "Heigh-O, Silver" "His voice was wonderful": Smith, *Thank You, Mr. President*, 186.

Page 250, "The only limit," "Let us move": Franklin D. Roosevelt, "Undelivered Address Prepared for Jefferson Day," April 13, 1945, American Presidency Project, www.presidency.ucsb.edu.

Page 250, "slipping away": Hassett, *Off the Record*, 327.

Page 250, "He has the whole," "The best thing," "Very smiling": Daisy Suckley, in *Closest Companion*, ed. Ward, 414.

Page 250 caption, "Hi-Ya, Neighbor!": quoted in Stevens, *"Hi-Ya Neighbor,"* 64.

Page 251, "But if there is" and the rest of the exchange: quoted in Bishop, *FDR's Last Year*, 572.

Page 251, "exceptionally good color," "That gray look": quoted in Persico, *Franklin and Lucy*, 338.

Page 251, "colour was good," "He looked smiling": Daisy Suckley, in *Closest Companion*, ed. Ward, 417.

Page 251, the president looked ill: Hassett, *Off the Record, 333*–34.

Page 251, in motion for days: Stevens, *"Hi-Ya Neighbor,"* 88–90.

Page 252, "He looked at me": Daisy Suckley, in *Closest Companion*, ed. Ward, 418.

Page 252, "I have a terrific pain": Franklin D. Roosevelt, in ibid.

Page 252, "Why aren't you people": quoted in Smith, *Thank You, Mr. President*, 180.

Page 252, "It is my sad duty": quoted in ibid., 182.

REFERENCES AND RESOURCES

Albee, Peggy A. *"Historic Structure Report: Home of Franklin D. Roosevelt." Report* for Northeast Field Area, National Park Service, 1996.

Bishop, Jim. *FDR's Last Year, April 1944–April 1945*. New York: William Morrow, 1974.

Black, Conrad. *Franklin Delano Roosevelt: Champion of Freedom*. London: Weidenfeld and Nicolson, 2003.

Burns, James MacGregor. *Roosevelt: The Lion and the Fox*. New York: Harcourt Brace and World, 1956.

———. *Roosevelt: The Soldier of Freedom, 1940–1945*. New York: Harcourt Brace, Jovanovich, 1970.

Churchill, Winston. *The Hinge of Fate*. Boston: Houghton Mifflin, 1950.

Cross, Robert F. *Sailor in the White House: The Seafaring Life of FDR*. Annapolis, Md.: Naval Institute Press, 2003.

Daniels, Jonathan. *White House Witness, 1942–1945*. Garden City, N.Y.: Doubleday, 1975.

Davis, Kenneth S. *FDR: The Beckoning of Destiny*. New York: G. P. Putnam's Sons, 1971.

Douglas, William O. *Go East, Young Man: The Early Years*. New York: Random House, 1974.

Ezickson, A. J., ed. *Roosevelt Album*. New York: Knickerbocker Publishing Company, 1945.

Ferrell, Robert H. *The Dying President: Franklin D. Roosevelt, 1944–1945*. Columbia and London: University of Missouri Press, 1998.

Freidel, Frank. *Franklin D. Roosevelt: A Rendezvous with Destiny*. Boston: Little, Brown 1990.

Gallagher, Hugh Gregory. *FDR's Splendid Deception*. New York: Dodd, Mead, 1985.

Goodwin, Doris Kearns. *No Ordinary Time: Franklin and Eleanor Roosevelt: The Home Front in World War II*. New York: Simon and Schuster, 1994.

Gunther, John. *Roosevelt in Retrospect: A Profile in History*. New York: Harper and Brothers, 1950.

Hassett, Wiliam D. *Off the Record with F.D.R., 1942–1945*. New Brunswick, N.J.: Rutgers University Press, 1958.

Hunt, John Gabriel, ed. *The Essential Franklin Delano Roosevelt*. New York: Portland House, a division of Random House, 1995.

Ickes, Harold. *The Secret Diary of Harold L. Ickes*. New York: Simon and Schuster, 1953–54.

Jackson, Robert H. *That Man: An Insider's Portrait of Franklin D. Roosevelt*. Oxford: Oxford University Press, 2003.

John C. Waite Associates, Architects. *The President as Architect: Franklin D. Roosevelt's Top Cottage*. Albany, N.Y.: Mount Ida Press, 2001.

Jones, Cranston. *Homes of the American Presidents*. New York: Bonanza Books, 1962.

Lash, Joseph P. *Eleanor and Franklin*. New York: W.W. Norton, 1971.

Leuchtenberg, William E. *The FDR Years: On Roosevelt and His Legacy*. New York: Columbia University Press, 1995.

Lippman, Theo, Jr. *The Squire of Warm Springs: F.D.R. in Georgia, 1924–1935*. Chicago: Playboy Press Book, 1977.

Mackenzie, Compton. *Mr. Roosevelt*. New York: E. P. Dutton, 1944.

McIntire, Ross T., with George Creel. *White House Physician*. New York: G. P. Putnam's Sons, 1946.

Meacham, John. *Franklin and Winston: An Intimate Portrait of an Epic Friendship*. New York: Random House, 2003.

Miller, Nathan. *FDR: An Intimate History*. Garden City, N.Y.: Doubleday, 1983.

Nelson, W. Dale. *The President Is at Camp David.* Syracuse, N.Y.: Syracuse University Press, 1995.

Perisco, Joseph E. *Franklin and Lucy: Mrs. Rutherfurd and the Other Remarkable Women in Roosevelt's Life.* New York: Random House, 2009.

———. *Roosevelt's Secret War: FDR and World War II Espionage.* New York: New York, 2001.

Reilly, Michael F., with William J. Slocum. *Reilly of the White House.* New York: Simon and Schuster, 1947.

Rigdon, William M., with James Derieux. *White House Sailor.* Garden City, N.Y.: Doubleday, 1962.

Roosevelt, Eleanor. *Eleanor Roosevelt's My Day*, ed. Rochelle Chadakoff. New York: Pharos Books, 1989.

Roosevelt, Elliott, ed. *FDR: His Personal Letters.* New York: Duell, Sloan, and Pearce, 1947–50.

Roosevelt, Elliott, and James Brough. *A Rendezvous with Destiny: The Roosevelts of the White House.* New York: G. P. Putnam's Sons, 1975.

Roosevelt, Franklin D. *The Public Papers and Addresses of Franklin D. Roosevelt.* 13 vols. Various publishers, 1938–50.

Roosevelt, James, and Sidney Shalett. *Affectionately, FDR: A Son's Story of a Lonely Man.* New York: Harcourt Brace, 1959.

Rosenman, Samuel I. *Working with Roosevelt.* New York: Harper and Brothers, 1952.

Rosenau, James N., ed. *The Roosevelt Treasury.* Garden City, N.Y.: Doubleday, 1951.

Sherwood, Robert E. *Roosevelt and Hopkins: An Intimate History.* New York: Harper and Brothers, 1948.

Smith, A. Merriman. *Thank You, Mr. President: A White House Notebook.* New York: Harper and Brothers, 1946.

Starling, Edmund W., with Thomas Sugrue. *Starling of the White House.* New York: Simon and Schuster, 1946.

Stevens, Ruth. "*Hi-Ya Neighbor.*" New York and Atlanta: Tupper and Love, 1947.

Swift, Will. *The Roosevelts and the Royals.* Hoboken, N.J.: John Wiley and Sons, 2004.

Tugwell, Rexford. *The Democratic Roosevelt.* Garden City, N.Y.: Doubleday, 1957.

Tully, Grace. *F.D.R., My Boss.* New York: Charles Scribner's Sons, 1949.

Ward, Geoffrey C., ed. *Closet Companion: The Unknown Story of the Intimate Friendship Between Franklin Roosevelt and Margaret Suckley.* Boston: Houghton Mifflin, 1995.

West, J. B. West, with Mary Lynn Kotz. *Upstairs at the White House.* New York: Warner Books, 1973.

28: Harry S. Truman

SOURCES

Page 254, "The Big White Jail": "The Big White Jail," *New York Times*, April 15, 1958, 32.

Page 254, eleven times, 175 days: Presidential Trip File and Chronology, Harry S. Truman Library and Museum, Independence, Mo., online at "President Truman's Travel Logs," www.trumanlibrary.org.

Page 254, "Truman Beach": William M. Rigdon, oral history interview, July 16, 1970, 11, Truman Library, www.trumanlibrary.org.

Page 254, "Down there," "From the first": Rigdon oral history interview, 10.

Page 256, "If the weather was cool": Rigdon, *White House Sailor*, 257.

Page 256, visiting with friends: ibid., 257.

Page 256, "Wherever I happened to be": Harry S. Truman, "The President's Farewell Address to the American People," January 15, 1953, American Presidency Project, www.presidency.ucsb.edu.

Page 256, "I do not know": Harry S. Truman, *Memoirs*, 2:361.

Page 256, "very useful": ibid.

Page 258, "proved too much": "I Accept Their Verdict," *Time*, November 18, 1946, 24.

Page 258, "My cough," "I am sorry": quoted in Margaret Truman, *Harry S. Truman*, 324.

Page 258, "Don't Go Away Mad": ibid., 333. See also Steinberg, *Man from Missouri*, 357.

Page 258 caption, *The Independence*: Harry S. Truman, *Memoirs*, I:361.

Page 259, "There were quite": Rigdon oral history interview, 24–25.

Page 259, "The sun shines": quoted in Watson, Devine, and Wolz, *National Security Legacy*, 32.

Page 260, "To keep things running": Rigdon, *White House Sailor*, 261.

Page 260, "The President suns": Roger Tubby, oral history interview, February 10, 1970, 96–97, Truman Library, www.trumanlibrary.org.

Page 260, Missouri sidestroke: "Season in the Sun," *Time*, November 22, 1948, 25.

Pages 260–61, "No one, not even me," "This terrible decision": quoted in Margaret Truman, *Harry S. Truman*, 343.

Page 260 caption, fourteen military campaigns: Joseph G. Feeney, oral history interview, September 20, 1966, 99-100, Truman Library, www.trumanlibrary.org.

Page 261, "The reception was perfect": Rigdon, Log of the President's Trip to Key West, Florida, 12–19 March 1947, Truman Library, online at "President Truman's Travel Logs," www.trumanlibrary.org.

Page 261, "a good, choir-average soprano": "Moment for Margaret," *Time*, March 4, 1947, 20.

Page 261, "seemed to be heading": "Little Accident," *Time*, March 15, 1948, 28.

Page 261, "I have been in touch": Harry S. Truman, "The President's News Conference at Key West," March 1, 1948, American Presidency Project, www.presidency.ucsb.edu.

Page 261 caption, International Fishing Tournament: Rigdon, "Log of the President's Trip to Key West, Florida, 12–19 March 1947," 10–11, Truman Library, online at "President Truman's Travel Logs," www.trumanlibrary.org.

Page 262, "The weather here is ideal": quoted in Watson, Devine, and Wolz, *National Security Legacy*, 32.

Page 262, "The little old voter": "The Nation: Independence Day," *Time*, November 8, 1948, 23.

Page 262, 31,700-mile trek, 356 speeches, 16 in one day: Harry S. Truman, *Memoirs*, 2:219.

Page 262, "Why, it can't be anything": quoted in "The Nation: Independence Day," *Time*, November 8, 1948, 23. Truman beat Dewey by more than 2 million votes, 24.1 to 21.9 million, even as Dixiecrat Strom Thurmond and Progressive Party candidate Henry A. Wallace captured more than 1 million votes each. Electoral vote: Truman 303; Dewey 189; Thurmond, 39.

Page 262, "Key West never before": Earl Adams, "Key West Cheers Truman on Arrival for His Vacation," *Miami Herald*, November 8, 1948, 1.

Page 262, "Key West Greets Truman," "election day miracle man": Anthony Leviero, "Key West Greets Truman As a Hero; Vacation Starts," *New York Times*, November 8, 1948, 1.

Page 262, "I didn't know": quoted in Margaret Truman, *Harry S. Truman*, 394.

Page 262, "He had pulled off": Clark Clifford, oral history interview, July 26, 1971, 332–33, Truman Library, www.trumanlibrary.org.

Page 263, "I doubt I've ever been": Clark Clifford, oral history interview, March 16, 1972, 344, Truman Library, www.trumanlibrary.org.

Page 263, "I remember": Clifford oral history interview, July 26, 1971, 332.

Page 263, "one of the few times": Clifford, *Counsel to the President*, 246.

Page 263, "seemed as far as": ibid., 247.

Page 263, "I had never seen" and the following quotations: Rigdon, *White House Sailor*, 254.

Page 263, "No . . . it's a Jeff Davis": quoted in "Truman Grows 'Jeff Davis' Beard But First Lady's Advent Dooms It," *New York Times*, November 11, 1948, 1.

Page 263, "give them the devil," "Give 'em hell," "I'm through": quoted in Anthony Leviero, "Truman Catches Press Off Guard," *New York Times*, November 9, 1948, 23.

Page 263, "like a man": "Holiday's End," *New York Times*, November 21, 1948, E1.

Page 263, "an air of firmness": "Season in the Sun," *Time*, November 22, 1948, 25.

Page 263, "once again his old self," "It was observed": Rigdon, *White House Sailor*, 255.

Page 263, "the most important developments": Hechler, *Working with Truman*, 113.

Page 263, "So there was thinking": George M. Elsey, interview by author, September 2003, White House Historical Association, Washington, D.C.

Pages 263–64, "We needed a rest" and the rest of the quotations in this paragraph: Margaret Truman, *Harry S. Truman*, 395.

Page 264, "In the summer of 1948": ibid., 398.

Page 264, "little better than a fire trap": "Fire Trap," *Time*, November 22, 1948, 26.

Page 264, "By the time we came back": Margaret Truman, *Harry S. Truman*, 399.

Page 264, "Wish you and Margie": Harry S. Truman, *Letters Home*, ed. Poen, 234.

Page 264, "my favorite form of paper work": quoted in McCullough, *Truman*, 511.

Page 264, "Bill, round up": quoted in Rigdon, *White House Sailor*, 258.

Page 264, "Getting together": quoted in McCullough, *Truman*, 510.

Page 265, "Although the conversation": Hechler, *Working with Truman*, 22.

Page 265, "nobody would get hurt": George M. Elsey, oral history interview, July 9, 1970, 434, Truman Library, www.trumanlibrary.org.

Page 265, "He would get": "Time for a Breather," *Time*, March 5, 1951, 22.

Page 265, "transfer his base": quoted in ibid.

Page 265, "Angry grey-green": "Clean House, with Termites," *Time*, March 26, 1951, 21.

Page 265, "All a president": Harry S. Truman, "The President's News Conference at Key West," March 15, 1951, American Presidency Project, www.presidency.ucsb.edu.

Page 265, "no intention": Harry S. Truman, "The President's News Conference at Key West," November 15, 1951, American Presidency Project, www.presidency.ucsb.edu.

Page 266, "I am not a candidate," "In my opinion": quoted in Donovan, *Tumultuous Years*, 171.

Page 266, "New stores are opening": "Fish & Quips," *Time*, November 26, 1951, 24.

Page 266, "All you fellows": Harry S. Truman, "The President's News Conference at Key West," March 20, 1952, American Presidency Project, www.presidency.ucsb.edu.

Pages 266–67, "He managed": "Poverty Poker," *Time*, March 31, 1952, 24.

Page 267, "I shall not": quoted in Donovan, *Tumultuous Years*, 396.

REFERENCES AND RESOURCES

Clifford, Clark, with Richard Holbrooke. *Counsel to the President: A Memoir.* New York: Random House, 1991.

Donovan, Robert J. *Tumultuous Years: The Presidency of Harry S. Truman, 1949–1953.* Columbia: University of Missouri Press, 1996.

Ferrell, Robert H. *Harry S. Truman: A Life.* Columbia: University of Missouri Press, 1994.

———. *Harry S. Truman and the Modern American Presidency.* Boston: Little, Brown, 1983.

Hechler, Ken. *Working with Truman: A Personal Memoir of the White House Years.* New York: G. P. Putnam's Sons, 1982.

McCullough, David. *Truman.* New York: Simon and Schuster, 1992.

Rigdon, William M., with James Derieux. *White House Sailor.* Garden City, N.Y.: Doubleday, 1962.

Seale, William. *The President's House: A History.* 2nd ed. Washington, D.C.: White House Historical Association, 2008.

Steinberg, Alfred. *The Man from Missouri: The Life and Times of Harry S. Truman.* New York: G. P. Putnam's Sons, 1962.

Truman, Harry S. *The Autobiography of Harry S. Truman.* Edited by Robert H. Ferrell. Columbia: University of Missouri Press, 2002.

———. *Dear Bess: The Letters from Harry to Bess Truman, 1910–1959.* Edited by Robert H. Ferrell. New York: W. W. Norton, 1983.

———. *Letters Home.* Edited by Monte M. Poen. Columbia: University of Missouri Press, 1984.

———. *Memoirs.* 2 vols. Garden City, N.Y.: Doubleday, 1955–56.

———. *Off the Record: The Private Papers of Harry S. Truman.* Edited by Robert H. Ferrell. New York: Harper and Row, 1980.

———. *Public Papers of the Presidents of the United States: Harry S. Truman, 1945–1953.* Washington, D.C.: Government Printing Office, 1966.

Truman, Margaret. *Harry S. Truman.* New York: William Morrow, 1972.

Walsh, Kenneth T. *Air Force One: A History of the Presidents and Their Planes.* New York: Hyperion, 2003.

Watson, Robert P., Michael J. Devine, and Robert J. Wolz. *The National Security Legacy of Harry S. Truman.* Kirksville, Mo.: Truman State University Press, 2005

29: Dwight D. Eisenhower

SOURCES

Page 268, "a big green field," "He asked me": Khrushchev, *Khrushchev Remembers*, 406.

Page 268 caption, "But he plodded": quoted in Van Natta, *First Off the Tee*, 70.

Page 270 caption, fifty club members chipped in: Roberts, *Story of the Augusta National Golf Course*, 146.

Page 271, "the greatest thing": quoted in Van Natta, *First Off the Tee*, 57.

Page 271, it was time the president: Smith, *Meet Mister Eisenhower*, 171.

Page 271, 112 days a year: Frank Cormier, "Truman Called Down by 'Boss'," *Washington Post*, May 6, 1957, A3.

Page 271, nearly 800 rounds of golf: Gustafson, "President Eisenhower's Hobby," 98–99.

Page 271, "It is not the criticism": Dwight David Eisenhower to General Alfred Gruenther, September 15, 1956, *Papers of Dwight D. Eisenhower, The Presidency: The Middle Way*, ed. Galambos and Van Ee, 17:2284.

Page 271, "We want the president": quoted in Smith, *Meet Mister Eisenhower*, 172.

Page 271, "mild exercise": Dwight D. Eisenhower, "The President's News Conference," October 15, 1958, American Presidency Project, http://www.presidency.ucsb.edu

Page 272, "working vacation": quoted Adam Clymer, "Merry Month of Going Fishing and Looking Busy," *New York Times*, August 3, 2002, A11.

Page 272, ten days of complete rest: "Presidential Travels," *U.S. News and World Report*, May 4, 1956, 49.

Page 272, "A president is president": Dwight David Eisenhower, *Mandate for Change*, 267.

Page 272, "Every time I see": Dwight David Eisenhower to Arthur S. Nevins, August 31, 1954, *Papers of Dwight David Eisenhower, The Presidency: The Middle Way*, ed. Galambos and Van Ee, 15:1268–69.

Page 272, "without the fear": quoted in "The Presidency," *Time*, December 6, 1953, 23.

Page 272, "chewing on the bow": John Eisenhower, *Strictly Personal*, 212–13.

Page 273, "must bow to the law": "Retreat from Newport," *Time*, September 23, 1957, 13.

Page 273, "Dad had a powerful swing": John Eisenhower, *Strictly Personal*, 8.

Page 273, "Stick your butt out": quoted in Conte, *History of the Greenbrier*, 161.

Page 273, "If the President": quoted in Ben Hogan with Tim Cohane, "How Ike Can Play in the 80s," *Look*, June 3, 1953, 30.

Page 273, "Ben Hogan for President": Van Natta, *First Off the Tee*, 64.

Pages 273, a Bessemer furnace: interview with Bryce Harlow, in *Eisenhower Presidency*, ed. Thompson, 147–48.

Page 274, "His anger": Snyder diary, quoted in Beschloss, *Eisenhower*, 134.

Page 274, "My doctor has given me," "Every time I miss": quoted in "Old Zest Shown by Ike at Golf," *Washington Post*, February 24, 1956, 17.

Page 274, "most even-tempered": Dwight David Eisenhower to Clifford Roberts, April 1, 1957, *Papers of Dwight David Eisenhower, The Presidency: Keeping the Peace*, ed. Galambos and Van Ee, 18:127.

Page 274 caption, "no evidence of fatigue": quoted in "Old Zest Shown by Ike at Golf," 17.

Page 274 caption, "Don't Ask What I Shot!": quoted in "President Joins Under-90 Golfers," *New York Times*, April 21, 1953, 1.

Page 275, "that pair of helicopters," "His face bleached," and the rest of the exchange: "The Presidency: The Case for the Budget," *Time*, April 8, 1957, 20.

Page 275, helicopters: Van Natta, *First Off the Tee*, 64–65.

Page 275, "The answer": Dwight David Eisenhower to Daphne Moaney, January 18, 1961, *Papers of Dwight David Eisenhower, The Presidency: Keeping the Peace*, ed. Galambos and Van Ee, 21:2255.

Page 275, "I think": quoted in Nelson, *President Is at Camp David*, 31. See also West, *Upstairs at the White House*, 160.

Page 275 caption, "was just a little fancy": quoted in Dwight D. Eisenhower, *Ike's Letters to a Friend*, ed. Griffith, 111.

Page 277, "It is a nice green": Slater, *Ike I Knew*, 76.

Page 277, "So deep": Smith, *Meet Mister Eisenhower*, 179.

Page 277, "I get more fun": *Papers of Dwight David Eisenhower, The Presidency: The Middle Way*, ed. Galambos and Van Ee, 16:1955.

Page 277, "a sort of" and the rest of the paragraph: quoted and reported in Nelson, *President Is at Camp David*, 40.

Page 277, "I couldn't," "I was afraid," "far from": Khrushchev, *Khrushchev Remembers*, 371–72.

Page 277, "On the outside," ibid., 407.

Page 278, Khrushchev at Gettysburg:

Page 278, "Mamie's Dream House": "The Eisenhowers: After 38 Years, a Dreamhouse," *Newsweek*, June 28, 1954, 28–30.

Page 278, "What makes it really charming": Slater, *Ike I Knew*, 114.

Page 278, "that conformed": Dwight D. Eisenhower, *At Ease*, 358.

Page 278, "escape from concrete": ibid.

Page 278, "plain fell in love": Weinman, "Mr. Eisenhower Builds His Dream House," 24.

Page 278, "The buildings had seen better days": Dwight D. Eisenhower, *At Ease*, 358.

Page 278, "I must have this place": quoted in David and David, *Ike and Mamie*, 216.

Page 278, $40,000, $16,000: Dwight D. Eisenhower, *At Ease*, 358.

Page 278 caption, "should have been sacked": quoted in "Quotes of President Dwight D. Eisenhower," Eisenhower National Historic Site, online materials.

Page 279, grayish green: "Eisenhower Helps Mix Paint for Barn," *New York Times*, February 26, 1955, 5.

Page 280, "He talks crop rotation": quoted in Weinman, "Mr. Eisenhower Builds His Dream House," 26.

Page 280, "there are enough": Dwight D. Eisenhower, *At Ease*, 194.

Page 280, "Sooooooey": quoted in "The Presidency: The Farmer in the Dell," *Time*, August 22, 1955, 18.

Page 280, "Both Mamie and I": Dwight D. Eisenhower, *At Ease*, 360.

Page 281, putting green: "President's Farm Gets Putting Green," *New York Times*, November 8, 1955, 21.

REFERENCES AND RESOURCES

Adams, Sherman. *Firsthand Report: The Story of the Eisenhower Administration*. New York: Harper and Brothers, 1961.

Allen, George E. *Presidents Who Have Known Me*. New York: Simon and Schuster, 1960.

Ambrose, Stephen E. *Eisenhower: Soldier and President*. New York: Simon and Schuster, 1990.

Bailey, Thomas A. *Presidential Greatness: The Image and the Man from George Washington to the Present*. New York: Appleton-Century, 1966.

Beschloss, Michael R. *Eisenhower: A Centennial Life*. New York: Harper/Collins, Edwin Burlingame Book, 1990.

Burk, Robert F. *Dwight D. Eisenhower: Hero and Politician*. Boston: Twayne Publishers, 1986.

Cohen, Stan. *The Eisenhowers: Gettysburg's First Family*. Charleston, W.Va.: Pictorial Histories Publishing Company, 1983.

Conte, Robert S. *The History of the Greenbrier: America's Resort*. Charleston, W.Va.: Pictorial Histories Publishing Company, 1989.

David, Lester, and Irene David. *Ike and Mamie*. New York: G. P. Putnam's Sons, 1981.

Donavan, Robert J. *The Inside Story*. New York: Harper and Brothers, New York, 1956.

Eisenhower, Dwight D. *At Ease: Stories I Tell to Friends*. Garden City, N.Y.: Doubleday, 1967.

———. *Ike's Letters to a Friend: 1941–1958*. Edited by Robert Griffith. Lawrence: University Press of Kansas, 1984.

———. *Mandate for Change: 1953–1956*. Garden City, N.Y.: Doubleday, 1963.

———. *The Papers of Dwight D. Eisenhower, The Presidency: The Middle Way and Keeping the Peace*. Edited by Louis Galambos and Daun Van Ee. Baltimore: Johns Hopkins University Press, 1996, 2001.

———. *Waging Peace: 1956–1961*. Garden City, N.Y.: Doubleday, 1965.

Eisenhower, John S. D. *Strictly Personal: A Memoir*. Garden City, N.Y.: Doubleday, 1974.

Eisenhower, Milton S. *The President Is Calling*. Garden City, N.Y.: Doubleday, 1974.

Eisenhower National Historic Site, online materials, www.nps.gov/eise.

Greenstein, Fred I. *The Hidden Hand Presidency: Eisenhower as Leader*. New York: Basic Books, 1982.

Gustafson, Merlin. "President Eisenhower's Hobby." *Presidential Studies Quarterly* 13, no. 1 (Winter 1983): 98–100.

Hagerty, James C. *The Diary of James C. Hagerty: Eisenhower in Mid-Course, 1954–1955*. Edited by Robert H. Ferrell. Bloomington: Indiana University Press, 1983.

Khrushchev, Nikita S. *Khrushchev Remembers*. Translated and edited by Strobe Talbott. Boston: Little, Brown, 1974.

Larson, Arthur. Eisenhower: *The President Nobody Knew*. New York: Charles Scribner's Sons, 1968.

MacMahon, Edward B., MD, and Leonard Curry. *Medical Cover-Ups in the White House*. Washington, D.C.: Farragut, 1987.

Morin, Relman. *Dwight D. Eisenhower: A Gauge of Greatness*. New York: Simon and Schuster, an Associated Press Book, 1969.

Nelson, W. Dale. *The President Is at Camp David*. Syracuse, N.Y.: Syracuse University Press, 1995.

Palmer, Norman A., and William V. Levy. *Five Star Golf*. New York: Duell, Sloan and Pearce, 1964.

Perret, Geoffrey. *Eisenhower*. New York: Random House, 1999.

Reston, James Reston. *Deadline: A Memoir*. New York: Random House, 1991.

Ritchie, Donald A. "Waging Publicity: Eisenhower and the News Media." Paper prepared for the Eisenhower Seminar, Gettysburg, Pa., October 28, 2000.

Roberts, Clifford. *The Story of the Augusta National Golf Club*. Garden City, N.Y.: Doubleday, 1976.

Slater, Ellis D. *The Ike I Knew*. N.p.: Ellis D. Slater Trust, 1980.

Smith, Merriman. *Meet Mister Eisenhower*. New York: Harper and Brothers, 1955.

Strout, Richard L. *TRB: Views and Perspectives on the Presidency*. New York: Macmillan, 1979.

Thompson, Kenneth W., ed. *The Eisenhower Presidency: Eleven Intimate Perspectives of Dwight D. Eisenhower*. Lanham, Md.: University Press of America, 1984.

Van Natta, Don, Jr. *First Off the Tee: Presidential Hackers, Duffers, and Cheaters, from Taft to Bush*. New York: Public Affairs, 2003.

Walsh, Kenneth. *Air Force One: A History of the Presidents and Their Planes*. New York: Hyperion, 2003.

West, J. B., with Mary Lynn Kotz. *Upstairs at the White House: My Life with the First Ladies*. New York: Coward, McCann and Geoghegan, 1973.

Weinman, Martha. "Mr. Eisenhower Builds His Dream House." *Collier's Weekly*, September 17, 1954, 23–27.

Wicker, Tom. *Dwight D. Eisenhower*. New York: Henry Holt and Co., Times Books, 2002.

30: John F. Kennedy

SOURCES

Page 282, "You know": quoted in Cassini, *In My Own Fashion*, 327.

Page 282, "the most private place": quoted in Smith, *Grace and Power*, 113.

Page 282, "The President's office": Sorensen, *Kennedy*, 376.

Page 282, nearly thirty-five months in office numbers: Summary of Trips of President John Fitzgerald Kennedy, February 1961–November 1963, 1, John F. Kennedy Library and Museum, Boston, Mass., www.jfklibrary.org.

Page 282 caption, "He must remain always": Sidey, *John F. Kennedy*, 252.

Page 284 caption, "like crossing a frontier": Schlesinger, *Thousand Days*, 62.

Page 285, "Kennedy to Week-End": "Kennedy to Week-End in the White House," *Chicago Tribune*, April 6, 1962, 19.

Page 285, "every inch of mind": Sorensen, *Kennedy*, 377.

Page 285, thirteen successive weekends: Summary of Trips, 3.

Page 285, "We were all": Rose Fitzgerald Kennedy, *Times to Remember*, 355.

Page 286, "Everywhere were roadblocks": Schlesinger, *Thousand Days*, 62.

Page 286, "Off the living room": Salinger, *With Kennedy*, 91–92.

Page 287, "On Friday": quoted in Joseph A. Loftus, "'Uncle Jack' Kennedy Leads Candy Treks," *New York Times*, August 14, 1961, 14. See also "The Treats Are on the President at Hyannis Port," AP, *New York Times*, July 30, 1961, 3; "President Is Host to 18 Children at Candy Story," *New York Times*, September 2, 1961, 1.

Page 287, "heart-pounding," "Since sitting down" and quotations in rest of paragraph: "Nation: Vacation Time," *Time*, August 3, 1962, 12.

Page 288, "Beyond the western bank": Sidey, *John F. Kennedy*, 220.

Page 289, "I got angry": quoted in Oberdorfer, *Senator Mansfield*, 194.

Page 289, "He's under the boat!": quoted in Shepard, *John F. Kennedy: Man of the Sea*, 134.

Page 289, "reached over and grabbed," "Caroline watched": quoted in Meyers, ed., *John Fitzgerald Kennedy: As We Remember Him*, 207. In other accounts the hungry fish is a whale, not a shark.

Page 289, "that when Jack began": quoted in Andersen, *Day John Died*, 72.

Page 290, "He demanded privacy": Thomas, *Dateline*, 25.

Page 290, "With the President," "As soon as she cleared": E. W. Kenworthy, "President Sails in 30-Knot Wind," *New York Times*, July 29, 1962, 32.

Page 290, "The whole top": Shepard, *John F. Kennedy: Man of the Sea*, 135.

Page 290, "I always wondered": quoted in ibid.

Page 291, extra-firm mattress and other details: Sidey, *John F. Kennedy*, 252–55.

Page 291, "I really don't know": John F. Kennedy, "Remarks in Newport at the Australian Ambassador's Dinner for the America's Cup Crews," September 14, 1962, American Presidency Project, www.presidency.ucsb.edu.

Page 291, "The love," "It was good," "gazing out over": Shepard, *John F. Kennedy: Man of the Sea*, 122.

Page 291, "He enjoyed sailing," "He loved": Fanta, *Sailing with President Kennedy*, 50.

Page 291, "She's got rotting": quoted in Bradlee, *Conversations with Kennedy*, 195.

Page 292, "The weather was dreadful": ibid., 198.

Page 292, "tweedy elegance": "Virginia: Social Notes from Glen Ora," *Time*, March 24, 1961, 19.

Page 292, "I appreciate the way": quoted in Smith, *Grace and Power*, 114.

Page 293 caption, fun to play with: Bradlee, *Conversations with Kennedy*, 86.

Page 294, "I'm sorry Jackie" and the rest of the incident: quoted and reported in Moon, *Private Passion of Jackie Kennedy Onassis*, 141, 143.

Page 294, "to an impeccable background": Jones, *Homes of the American Presidents*, 222.

Page 294, fourteen weekends: Summary of Trips.

Page 295, "The idea of the new home": quoted in "No Try for Trianon at Atoka," *Washington Post*, February 21, 1963, C24.

Page 295, "motel shacks": quoted in Andersen, *Jack and Jackie*, 348.

Page 295, "If only I'd realized": quoted in West, *Upstairs at the White House*, 237.

Page 295, sixteen weekends: Summary of Trips.

Page 295, "the separate houses": Bradlee, *Conversations with Kennedy*, 187.

Page 295 caption, "No one knows": quoted in Nelson, *President Is at Camp David*, 53.

Page 297, "Do you think" and the rest of the exchange: quoted in Bradlee, *Conversations with Kennedy,* 199, 201.

Page 297, "nudging the presidential rear end": ibid., 236.

REFERENCES AND RESOURCES

Andersen, Christopher. *The Day John Died.* New York: HarperCollins, 2001.

———. *Jack and Jackie: Portrait of an American Marriage.* New York: William Morrow, 1996.

Bradford, Sarah. *America's Queen: The Life of Jacqueline Kennedy Onassis.* New York: Penguin Books, 2001.

Bradlee, Benjamin C. *Conversations with Kennedy.* New York: W. W. Norton, 1975.

Cassini, Oleg Cassini. *In My Own Fashion: An Autobiography.* New York: Simon and Schuster, 1987.

Clarke, Thurston. *JFK's Last Hundred Days: The Transformation of a Man and the Emergence of a Great President.* New York: Penquin Press, 2013.

Dallek, Robert. *An Unfinished Life: John F. Kennedy, 1917–1963.* Boston: Little, Brown, 2003.

Damore, Leo. *The Cape Cod Years of John Fitzgerald Kennedy.* Englewood Cliffs, N.J.: Prentice-Hall, 1967.

Fanta, J. Julius. *Sailing with President Kennedy: The White House Yachtsman.* New York: Sea Lore Publishing, 1968.

Fay, Paul B., Jr. *The Pleasure of His Company.* New York: Harper and Row, 1966.

Giglio, James N. *The Presidency of John F. Kennedy.* Lawrence: University Press of Kansas, 1991.

John F. Kennedy Library and Museum, online materials, www.jfk.library.org.

Jones, Cranston. *Homes of the American Presidents.* New York: Bonanza Books, 1962.

Kennedy, John F. **Public Papers of the Presidents of the United States: John F. Kennedy, 1961–1963.** Washington, D.C.: Government Printing Office, various years.

Kennedy, Rose Fitzgerald. *Times to Remember.* Garden City, N.Y.: Doubleday, 1974.

Latham, Caroline, and Jeannie Sakol. *The Kennedy Encyclopedia.* New York: New American Library, 1989.

Meyers, Joan, ed. *John Fitzgerald Kennedy . . . As We Remember Him.* Philadelphia: Courage Books, Running Press Book Publishers, 1966.

Moon, Vicky. *The Private Passion of Jackie Kennedy Onassis: Portrait of a Rider.* New York: Regan Books, HarperCollins Publishers, 2004.

Nelson, W. Dale. *The President Is at Camp David.* Syracuse, N.Y.: Syracuse University Press, 1995.

O'Brien, Michael. *John F. Kennedy: A Biography.* New York: St. Martin's Press, 2005.

Oberdorfer, Don. *Senator Mansfield: The Extraordinary Life of a Great American Statesman and Diplomat.* Washington, D.C.: Smithsonian Books, 2003.

Reston, James. *Sketches in the Sand.* New York: Alfred A. Knopf, 1967.

Ritchie, Donald A. "Mike Mansfield and the Vietnam War." In *Vietnam and the American Political Tradition: The Politics of Dissent, ed. Randall B. Woods, 171–203.* Cambridge: Cambridge University Press, 2003.

Salinger, Pierre Salinger. *With Kennedy.* Garden City, N.Y.: Doubleday, 1966.

Schlesinger, Arthur M., Jr. *A Thousand Days: John F. Kennedy in the White House.* Boston: Houghton Mifflin / Cambridge: Riverside Press, 1965.

Shepard, Tazewell, Jr. *John F. Kennedy: Man of the Sea.* New York: William Morrow, 1965.

Sidey, Hugh. *John F. Kennedy, President.* New York: Atheneum, 1963, 1964.

Smith, Sally Bedell. *Grace and Power: The Private World of the Kennedy White House.* New York: Random House, 2004.

Sorensen, Theodore C. *Kennedy.* New York: Harper and Row, 1965.

Thomas, Helen. *Dateline: The White House.* New York: Macmillan, 1965.

———. *Front Row at the White House.* New York: Scribner, 1999.

Van Natta, Don, Jr. *First Off the Tee: Presidential Hackers, Duffers, and Cheaters, from Taft to Bush.* New York: Public Affairs, 2003.

West, J. B. *Upstairs at the White House: My Life with the First Ladies.* New York: Coward, McCann and Geoghegan, 1963.

White, Theodore H. *The Making of the President, 1960.* New York: Atheneum Publishers, 1961.

31: Lyndon B. Johnson

SOURCES

Page 298, "rich inheritance": Cormier, *LBJ: The Way He Was,* 17.

Page 298, "Lonely Acres": Lyndon B. Johnson, "Remarks at the Annual Convention of the International Union of Electrical Workers," September 23, 1964, American Presidency Project, www.presidency.ucsb.edu.

Page 298, "It was the place": Youngblood, *Twenty Years,* 211.

Page 298, "The sight and the feel," "All my life": quoted in Cormier, *LBJ: The Way He Was,* 17.

Page 298, "From now on": Nan Robertson, "The First Lady Takes Huge Guest Lists in Her Stride," *New York Times,* January 4, 1964, 12.

Page 300 caption, "our heart's home": Lady Bird Johnson, ***White House Diary,*** 175.

Page 300 caption, doormat with saying: Bearss, "***Historic Structure Report,***" 105

Page 300 caption, "Friendship Walk": ibid., 46.

Page 301, seventy-five times: LBJ Ranch Reference File, LBJ Presidential Library, Austin, Tex.

Page 301, twenty-nine times: The President's Daily Diary: Sequoia Trips, Camp David Visits, LBJ Library.

Page 301, "Mr. Johnson did almost nothing": Charles Mohr, "Johnson's Mood: Warily Hopeful," *New York Times,* January 3, 1965, 37.

Page 301, "That's where": quoted in "The Union & the World," *Time,* January 8, 1965, 15.

Page 301, "Here the sun": quoted in Miller, *Lyndon,* 403.

Page 301, "I'm going to show you": Jack Valenti, quoted in ibid.

Page 301, "In the long twilight": Lady Bird Johnson, *White House Diary,* 175.

Page 301 caption, "We don't have": quoted in Miller, ***Lyndon,*** 403.

Page 302, "Thank goodness": quoted in Bearss, "*Historic Structure Report,*" 7.

Page 302, "a man who": Caro, *Years of Lyndon Johnson,* 427.

Page 302, "Every man": quoted in ibid., 428.

Page 302, "is an oasis": "The Prudent Progressive," *Time,* January 1, 1965, 26.

Page 302 caption, "I hardly recognized": quoted in "Mrs. Johnson Is Tour Guide of LBJ Ranch," ***Chicago Tribune,*** December 28, 1963, 4.

Page 303, $3.5 million: Cormier, *LBJ: The Way He Was,* 25. See also, for information in this paragraph, Rothman, *LBJ's Texas White House,* 132–33; "'Hot Line'—Never a Busy Signal," *Christian Science Monitor,* June 10, 1965, 1; Bearss, "*Historic Structure Report,*" 61–63.

Page 303, "He could practically": quoted in Rothman, *LBJ's Texas White House,* 127.

Page 304, "a revolving door" and the rest of the quotations in this paragraph: Lady Bird Johnson, *White House Diary,* 27.

Page 304, "Relaxing with LBJ": Carpenter, *Ruffles and Flourishes,* 170.

Page 304, "sound like Texas fables": Clifford, *Counsel to the President,* 393.

Page 304 caption: "No law": Lyndon B. Johnson, "Remarks in Johnson City, Tex., Upon Signing the Elementary and Secondary Education Bill," April 11, 1965, American Presidency Project, www.presidency.ucsb.edu.

Page 305, "The cows are fat": quoted in "Mr. President, You're Fun," *Time,* April 10, 1964, 41.

Page 305 caption, nothing remotely like it: "The President: Sparerib Summit," ***Newsweek,*** January 6, 1964, 12.

Pages 305–6, "and thundered on over," with other quotations in this paragraph: "Mr. President, You're Fun."

Page 307, Lincoln Continentals and other vehicles: "Presidential Vehicles," Lyndon B. Johnson National Historical Park, online materials.

Page 307, "the car started" and quotations from Johnson: Califano, *Triumph and Tragedy,* 22.

Page 307, leaped up onto the back seat: Clifford, *Counsel to the President,* 393.

Page 307, "Slow down!": quoted in Youngblood, *Twenty Years,* 216.

Page 307, "He drove faster": Califano, *Triumph and Tragedy,* 22.

Page 307 caption, "Just as I": Clifford, ***Counsel to the President,*** 393.

Page 308, "Mr. President": quoted in Helen Thomas, UPI, "LBJs Introduce Humphreys to Texas," *Chicago Tribune,* September 1, 1964, B3.

Page 308, "a little zany lady": quoted in Miller, *Lyndon,* 404.

Page 308, "ramshackle" and the rest of the quotations in this paragraph: Thomas, *Thanks for the Memories,* 55.

Page 308, "Cousin Oriole": quoted in Wicker, "LBJ Down on the Farm," 159.

Page 308, "a nothing-wasted layout": Rothman, *LBJ's Texas White House,* 150.

Page 308, "a dime's worth": Dale Malachek, interview, November 22, 1978, Oral History Collection, Lyndon B. Johnson National Historical Park, quoted in Rothman, ***LBJ's Texas White House,*** 150.

Page 308 caption, "no man on horseback", "will do a great deal": *Washington Post,* September 1, 1964, A12.

Page 309, "That's where": quoted in Cormier, *LBJ: The Way He Was,* 23.

Page 309, "the best fertilizer": quoted in James Reston, "Washington: The State of the President and Other Matters," *New York Times,* January 8, 1964, 36.

Page 309, "who stops to telephone": Lady Bird Johnson, *White House Diary,* 333.

Page 309, "He expected": quoted in Rothman, *LBJ's Texas White House,* 154.

Page 310, "riding and talking," "trying to help": Lady Bird Johnson, *White House Diary,* 566.

Page 310, "I shall not seek": Lyndon B. Johnson, "The President's Address to the Nation Announcing Steps to Limit the War in Vietnam and Reporting His Decision Not to Seek Reelection," March 31, 1968," LBJ Library, www.lbjlib.utexas.edu.

Page 310, "hoped, and probably anticipated": Califano, *Triumph and Tragedy,* 320.

Page 310 caption, "the hands were not," "could find nothing": Lady Bird Johnson, *White House Diary,* 330.

Page 310 caption, Hurd's response: reported in Robert J. Donovan, "Angry LBJ Rejects Portrait," ***Los Angeles Times,*** January 6, 1967, 1.

Page 311, "For a moment": quoted in Califano, *Triumph and Tragedy,* 320.

Page 311, "suspended-in-space time": Lady Bird Johnson, *White House Diary,* 705.

Page 311, "the three-ring circus": ibid., 706.

Page 311, "probably as strange": ibid., 705.

Page 311, "There are green velvet": ibid., 745.

Page 311, "at last maybe," "There are just": ibid., 745.

Page 311 caption, "From afar": ibid., 705–6.

Page 312, "Cowboys aren't very good": quoted in Dallek, *Flawed Giant,* 614.

Page 312, any chance Johnson might run: ibid.

Page 312, "We can ride": quoted in Unger and Unger, *LBJ,* 524.

Page 312 caption, "I want each of you": quoted in Anthony Lewis, "Power and Illusion," ***New York Times,*** June 3, 1976, 37.

Page 312 caption, "It's the one place": quoted in Cormier, ***LBJ, The Way He Was,*** 16.

REFERENCES AND RESOURCES

Bearss, Edwin C. "*Historic Structure Report, Texas White House.*" *Report for Lyndon B. Johnson National Historical Park,* National Park Service, 1986.

Bell, Jack. *The Johnson Treatment: How Lyndon B. Johnson Took Over the Presidency and Made It His Own.* New York: Harper and Row, 1965.

Beschloss, Michael. *Reaching for Glory: Lyndon Johnson's Secret White House Tapes, 1964–1965.* New York: Simon and Schuster, 2001.

———, ed. *Taking Charge: The Johnson White House Tapes, 1963–1964.* New York: Simon and Schuster, 1997.

Califano, Joseph A. *The Triumph and Tragedy of Lyndon B. Johnson: The White House Years.* New York: Simon and Schuster, 1991.

Caro, Robert A. *The Years of Lyndon Johnson: Master of the Senate.* New York: Alfred A. Knopf, 2002.

Carpenter, Liz. *Ruffles and Flourishes: The Warm and Tender Story of a Simple Girl Who Found Adventure in the White House.* Garden City, N.Y.: Doubleday, 1970.

Clifford, Clark, with Richard Holbrooke. *Counsel to the President: A Memoir.* New York: Random House, 1991.

Conkin, Paul K. *Big Daddy from the Pedernales: Lyndon Baines Johnson.* Boston: Twayne Publishers, 1986.

Cormier, Frank. *LBJ: The Way He Was.* Garden City, N.Y.: Doubleday, 1977.

Dallek, Robert. *Flawed Giant: Lyndon Johnson and His Times, 1961–1973.* New York: Oxford University Press, 1998.

Goodwin, Doris Kearns. ***Lyndon Baines Johnson and the American Dream.*** New York: Harper and Row, 1976.

Gulley, Bill, with Mary Ellen Reese. *Breaking Cover.* New York: Simon and Schuster, 1980.

Houk, Rose. *Heart's Home: Lyndon B. Johnson's Hill Country.* San Antonio, Tex.: Southwest Parks and Monuments Association, 1986.

Johnson, Lady Bird. *A White House Diary.* New York: Holt, Rinehart and Winston, 1970.

Johnson, Lyndon Baines. ***Public Papers of the Presidents of the United States: Lyndon Baines Johnson, 1963–1969.*** Washington, D.C.: Government Printing Office, various years.

———. *The Vantage Point: Perspectives of the Presidency, 1963–1969.* New York: Holt, Rinehart and Winston, 1971.

Lyndon B. Johnson National Historical Park, online materials, www.nps.gov/lyjo.

Miller, Merle. *Lyndon: An Oral Biography.* New York: G. P. Putnam's Sons, 1980.

Newlon, Clarke. *L.B.J.: The Man from Johnson City.* New York: Dodd, Mead, 1968.

Rothman, Hal K. *LBJ's Texas White House: Our Heart's Home.* College Station: Texas A&M University Press, 2001.

Sidey, Hugh. *A Very Personal Presidency: Lyndon Johnson in the White House.* New York: Atheneum, 1968.

Thomas, Helen. *Thanks for the Memories, Mr. President.* New York: Scribner, 2002.

Unger, Irwin, and Debi Unger. *LBJ: A Life.* New York: John Wiley and Sons, 1999.

Wicker, Tom. "LBJ Down on the Farm." **Esquire,** October 1964.

Youngblood, Rufus. *Twenty Years in the Secret Service: My Life with Five Presidents.* New York: Simon and Schuster, 1973.

32 : RICHARD M. NIXON

SOURCES

Page 314, "the great decisions": Richard M. Nixon, "Letter to the Citizens of New Hampshire," January 31, 1968, Presidential Campaigns and Candidates, 4President, www.4president.org.

Page 314, one night out of every three: Hugh Sidey, quoting UPI, "The Presidency," *Time*, September 10, 1973, 22.

Page 314, "For a man": Safire, *Before the Fall*, 617.

Page 314, "to change the pace": Nixon, *In the Arena*, 162.

Page 314, "thinking great thoughts": William Safire, "Shake-Up in Shangri-La," *New York Times*, July 2, 1973, 27.

Page 314, "band-box crisp": Donnie Radcliffe, "Nixons Like Privacy in an 'Extrovert's Job," *Washington Post*, January 20, 1973, G5.

Page 314, "He's the kind": quoted in Safire, *Before the Fall*, 606.

Page 316, "with more support troops," "He goes away": James Reston, "Fiery Run, Va—Who's for a Vacation?" *New York Times*, June 7, 1970, 166.

Page 316, "What do we do": quoted in Julie Nixon Eisenhower, *Pat Nixon*, 319.

Page 316 caption, "he's resting to work": quoted in Dan Oberdorfer, "The Presidency: Still Very Private after the First Year," *Washington Post*, January 18, 1970, A1.

Page 317, "Nixon has always," "does not gossip": Ehrlichman, *Witness to Power*, 67.

Page 317, "We do some fishing," "We work, too": quoted in Lukas, *Nightmare*, 362–63.

Page 317, twenty-one side trips, Abplanalp said later: Cordtz, "Imperial Life Style," 222.

Page 317 caption, "While he was": Hugh Sidey, "Seeking a Magical Vista," *Time*, September 10, 1973, 24.

Page 318, "Guards sat," "one had to speak": Julie Nixon Eisenhower, *Pat Nixon*, 319.

Page 318, "Operation Gemstone": Emery, *Watergate*, 89.

Page 318, "We feared": quoted in ibid., 195.

Page 318 caption, "A perfect day": Julie Nixon Eisenhower, *Pat Nixon*, 226.

Page 319, "I scanned": Richard Nixon, *RN*, 625–26.

Page 319, "The Watergate break-in": ibid., 626.

Page 319, "stupid": ibid., 627.

Page 319, "The Camp David air," "There you are": Safire, *Before the Fall*, 618.

Page 320, "I find that up here," "think objectively": Richard Nixon, "Remarks on Plans for the Second Term," November 27, 1972, American Presidency Project, www.presidency.ucsb.edu.

Page 320, 149 times and other figures: Nelson, *President Is at Camp David*, 86; Aldo Beckman, "Nixon Uses His Mountain Retreat Often," *Chicago Tribune*, November 19, 1972, A15.

Page 320 caption, "I came back": Nixon, *In the Arena*, 162

Page 320 caption, "In general": quoted in Frank Cormier, "Nixon Prefers Solitude in Deciding Issues," *Los Angeles Times*, November 16, 1972, H1.

Page 321, "Camp Three," "Camp David": Julie Nixon Eisenhower, *Pat Nixon*, 318.

Page 321, "All day": ibid. See also "Can't Go Where She Likes, Pat Nixon Says," *Los Angeles Times*, December 14, 1969, 3.

Page 321, "Working until five": Safire, *Before the Fall*, 621.

Page 321, "It was designed": Maxine Cheshire, "The High Cost of Operating Camp David," *Washington Post*, October 25, 1973, E4.

Page 321 caption, King Timahoe: Nelson, *President Is at Camp David*, 87; "Nixon's Setter Balks at Flying," *Washington Post*, April 13, 1969, 15.

Page 322, "It's like a resort hotel": quoted in Packard, *American Monarchy*, 104.

Page 322, "A hideaway": Safire, *Before the Fall*, 618–19.

Page 322, "I feel like I'm": Colson, *Born Again*, 75.

Page 322, "the smoking gun": Rowland Evans and Robert Novak, "'They Had Been Betrayed and Deceived,'" *Washington Post*, August 7, 1974, A15.

Page 322, "very muddy," "the unbelievable battle," "is just to treat": Richard Nixon, *RN*, 1007.

Page 322, "You sense": Magruder, *American Life*, 3.

Page 323, "Government is not," "The San Clemente operation": quoted in Ambrose, *Nixon: Triumph of a Politician*, 371.

Page 323, "insisted he never": Kissinger, *Years of Upheaval*, 184.

Page 323 caption, "aura of power": Magruder, *American Life*, 3.

Page 324, "The Nixon in the backseat": Kissinger, *Years of Upheaval*, 1186.

Page 324, "Each room": Julie Nixon Eisenhower, *Pat Nixon*, 271–72.

Page 324, "Nightly, along with": ibid., 272.

Page 324 caption, "Cushman One": "Nixon: The Beach and the Budget," *Time*, August 10, 1970, 11.

Page 324 caption, "the contrast": Cordtz, "Imperial Life Style," 224.

Page 325, three dozen demonstrations: William Claiborne, "U.S. Pays Half San Clemente Police Cost," *Washington Post*, December 4, 1973, A13.

Page 325, "It was amusing": Richard Nixon, *RN*, 882.

Page 325, "we're-too-busy": Fred L. Zimmerman, "As Watergate Unfolds, President Pretends the Scandal Is Behind Him," *Wall Street Journal*, July 3, 1973, 11.

Page 325, "frozen melancholy": Kissinger, *Years of Upheaval*, 3.

Page 325, "As details of": Price, *With Nixon*, 318.

Page 326, "He remarked": ibid., 318.

Page 326, Press reports: Ambrose, *Nixon: Ruin and Recovery*, 153, quoting a May 14, 1973, report in the *Santa Ana Register*. See also Reeves, *President Nixon*, 114; Ambrose, *Nixon: Ruin and Recovery*, 215; Kenneth Bredemeier, "Nixon Mortgage Still $300,000," *Washington Post*, May 27, 1973, A20; Ronald J. Ostrow and Robert C. Toth, "Nixon Lists Details of Home Financing," *Los Angeles Times*, August 28, 1973, A3; Lou Cannon, "Rebozo Aided Nixon Land Purchase," *Washington Post*, August 28, 1973, A1; Cordtz, "Imperial Life Style," 145.

Page 326, White House claims: "Richard Nixon, Mortgagee," *Time*, September 10, 1973, 22.

Page 326, series of disclosures: sources for figures in this paragraph: "Government Paid $39,525 to Improve Nixon's Home," *New York Times*, May 27, 1973, 1; "Coast Records Show $100,000 Government Outlay on Western White House," *New York Times*, May 29, 1973, 17; Kenneth Reich and Jack Nelson, "Federal Spending on Western White House Set at $413,246," *Los Angeles Times*, June 14, 1973, A2; "Can't Anybody in There Count?" *Time*, July 2, 1973, 22; William Claiborne, "$10 Million Spent on Nixon Homes," *Washington Post*, August 7, 1973, A1; "Now It's $10 Million," *Time*, August 20, 1973, 24.

Page 326, $17.1 million: "Report Sets Nixon Homes' Cost to U.S.," *Washington Post*, May 10, 1974, B21; "House Unit, 36 to 0, Approves Report on Nixon's Homes," *New York Times*, May 15, 1974, 94; Mary Russell, "Hill Panel Hits Nixon Homes' Costs," *Washington Post*, March 22, 1974, A2. The *Washington Post* calculated the salaries of all U.S. presidents from Washington's $25,000 a year to Nixon's $200,000 at about $9.7 million over 185 years.

Page 326 caption, "card-carrying Communist": quoted in John Herbers, "Brezhnev Leaves the West on a Note of Informality," *New York Times*, June 25, 1973, 69.

Page 327, "they were the routine": Price, *With Nixon*, 272.

Page 327, "that nothing hastened": Julie Nixon Eisenhower, *Pat Nixon*, 387–88.

Page 327, "The deliberate expansion": Cordtz, "Imperial Life Style," 224.

Page 327, "avoid the appearance": ibid, 145.

Page 327, "Unfortunately, the American people," "at the time," "help maintain": Richard Nixon, "Statement About Financial Affairs During Tenure As President," December 8, 1973, American Presidency Project, www.presidency.ucsb.edu.

Page 329, $2,300 check: "Nixon Sends U.S. a $2,300 Check for His Flagpole," *Washington Post*, September 7, 1979, A7.

Page 329, "requested by the U.S. Secret Service": quoted in ibid. See also "Nixon Requests Restoration of Property," *Los Angeles Times*, September 7, 1979, C5.

REFERENCES AND RESOURCES

Ambrose, Stephen E. *Nixon: The Triumph of a Politician, 1962–1972*. New York: Simon and Schuster, 1989.

———. *Nixon: Ruin and Recovery, 1973–1991*. New York: Simon and Schuster, 1991.

Colson, Charles W. *Born Again*. Grand Rapids, Mich.: Chosen Books, a division of Baker Book House, 1976.

Comptroller General of the United States. "Report to the Congress: Protection of the President at Key Biscayne and San Clemente." U.S. General Accounting Office, 1973.

Cordtz, Dan. "The Imperial Life Style of the U.S. President," *Fortune*, October 1973.

Dean, John. *Blind Ambition: The White House Years*. New York: Simon and Schuster, 1976.

Drew, Elizabeth. *Washington Journal: The Events of 1973–1974*. New York: Random House, 1974.

Ehrlichman, John. *Witness to Power: The Nixon Years*. New York: Simon and Schuster, 1982.

Eisenhower, Julie Nixon. *Pat Nixon: The Untold Story*. New York: Simon and Schuster, 1986.

Emery, Fred. *Watergate: The Corruption of American Politics and the Fall of Richard Nixon*. New York: Times Books, Random House, 1994.

Gulley, Bill, with Mary Ellen Reese. *Breaking Cover*. New York: Simon and Schuster, 1980.

Haldeman, H. R., with Joseph DiMona. *The Ends of Power*. New York: Times Books, 1978.

———. *The Haldeman Diaries: Inside the Nixon White House*. New York: G. P. Putnam's Sons, 1994.

Kissinger, Henry. *Years of Upheaval*. Boston: Little, Brown, 1982.

Lukas, J. Anthony. *Nightmare: The Underside of the Nixon Years*. New York: Viking Press, 1976.

Magruder, Jeb Stuart. *An American Life: One Man's Road to Watergate*. New York: Atheneum, 1974.

McCarthy, Dennis V. N., with Philip W. Smith. *Protecting the President: The Inside Story of a Secret Service Agent*. New York: Dell, 1985.

Nelson, W. Dale. *The President Is at Camp David*. Syracuse, N.Y.: Syracuse University Press, 1995.

Nixon, Richard. *In the Arena: A Memoir of Victory, Defeat, and Renewal*. New York: Simon and Schuster, 1990.

———. *RN: The Memoirs of Richard Nixon*. New York: Grosset and Dunlap, 1978.

———. *The Public Papers of the Presidents of the United States: Richard M. Nixon, 1969–1974*. Washington, D.C.: U.S. Government Printing Office, various years.

Packard, Jerrold M. *American Monarchy: A Social Guide to the Presidency*. New York: Delacorte Press, 1983.

Price, Raymond Price. *With Nixon*. New York: Viking Press, 1977.

Reeves, Richard. *President Nixon: Alone in the White House*. New York: Simon and Schuster, 2001.

Safire, William. *Before the Fall: An Inside View of the Pre-Watergate White House*. Garden City, N.Y.: Doubleday, 1975.

Woodward, Bob, and Carl Bernstein. *The Final Days*. New York: Simon and Schuster, 1976.

33 : GERALD R. FORD

SOURCES

Page 330, "super!" "just perfect!": "At Play in the 'Dallas Alps'," *Time*, January 6, 1975, 50.

Page 330, "absolutely gorgeous": quoted in Carroll Kilpatrick, "President Is Awaiting Full Report," *Washington Post*, December 26, 1974, A2.

Page 330, "like a coat of marshmallow frosting": ibid.

Page 330, "He constantly shoves himself": "Ford Termed an Aggressive Skier," AP, December 25, 1974, available online at newspaperarchive.com, or printed in, e.g., *San Mateo (California) Times*, December 25, 1974, 6.

Page 330, "the kind of guy": quoted in James P. Sterba, "Ford's Instructor at Vail, Colo., Says the President is 'All for Skiing' and 'Doesn't Fall Down Much'," *New York Times*, December 23, 1974, 10.

Page 330, "When he goes": ibid.

Page 330, the most athletic: Fred Emery, "A Spring Break for Nation's Best-Known Athlete," *U.S. News and World Report*, April 14, 1975, 50–51.

Page 330, "the most strenuously physical man": "At Play in the 'Dallas Alps'."

Page 330 caption, "by far the most athletic president": quoted in Van Natta, *First Off the Tee*, 97.

Page 332, "Off to a Fast": "Gerald Ford: Off to a Fast, Clean Start," *Time*, August 26, 1974, 11.

Page 332, "our long national nightmare": Gerald R. Ford, "Remarks on Taking the Oath of Office," August 9, 1974, American Presidency Project. www.presidency.ucsb.edu.

Page 332, "ugly passions": Gerald R. Ford, "Remarks on Signing a Proclamation Granting Pardon to Richard Nixon," September 8, 1974, American Presidency Project. www.presidency.ucsb.edu.

Page 332, "efforts to restore confidence": "The Pardon That Brought No Peace," *Time*, September 16, 1974, 20.

Page 332, 21 points: Clifton Daniel, "Ford's Gallup Rating Off 21 Points After Pardon," *New York Times*, October 13, 1974, 1.

Page 332, in his best form, "skimming the powder": "Tough Choices in the Snow," *Newsweek*, January 6, 1975, 15.

Page 332, Gallup poll: reported in John Herbers, "Ford Rating in Poll Slips to Low of 42%," *New York Times*, December 26, 1974, 1.

Page 332, Ford told reporters: Fran Lewine and Helen Thomas, "Pool Report Aboard *Air Force One*—Washington to Vail, Colorado, December 22, 1974," Gerald R. Ford Library and Museum, Ann Arbor and Grand Rapids, Mich., www.fordlibrarymuseum.gov.

Page 332, "mandatory," "We were still": Susan Ford Bales, interview by author, June 19, 2006.

Page 332, "They were all," "a great place": Gerald R. Ford, interview by author, October 15, 2004.

Page 332, "Cold. Fun": Susan Ford Bales interview.

Page 332, "Ski Biscayne": Press Dispatches, December 29, 1974, available online at newspaperarchive.com, or printed, e.g., as "Vail Not Snowed by Ford's Visit," *Milwaukee Journal*, December 29, 1974, 10.

Page 332–33, "Why couldn't he": Aldo Beckman, "Ford on Slopes, Finds 'Ski Legs'," *Chicago Tribune*, December 25, 1974, 3.

Page 333, Local businesses: "Guess Who's Coming to Ski?," *Newsweek*, December 30, 1974, 41.

Page 333, "the Fords in Basshaus": Betty Ford, *Times of My Life*, 153, 200. See also Peter Eichstaedt, "At a Village in the Snow," *Washington Post*, December 16, 1974, B1; "Guess Who's Coming to Ski?"; "Tough Choices in the Snow"; "Presidential Breather: Downhill Fun After Some Uphill Struggles," *U.S. News and World Report*, January 6, 1975, 66–67.

Page 333, "the lap of luxury": Susan Ford Bales interview.

Page 333, "quite austere": James P. Sterba, "It's Not Exactly a 'Winter White House'," *New York Times*, January 1, 1975, 28.

Page 333, presidential pressures: Gerald R. Ford, *Time to Heal*, 225.

Page 333, "Rumsfeld has a lot": quoted in "Ford Skis, Opens Gifts with Family," AP, December 26, 1974, online at newspaperarchive.com, or printed in, e.g., *Lewiston (Maine) Daily Sun*, December 26, 1974, 20.

Page 334, "He could get out": Susan Ford Bales interview.

Page 334, "fluorescent orange": Robert P. Dalton, AP, December 26, 1974, available online at newspaperarchive.com, or printed, e.g., as "Ford Skis, Summons Advisers," *Schenectady (New York) Gazette*, December 26, 1974, 1.

Page 334, "Flash Gordon": James Deakin and Roger Gittines, "Pool Report: Thursday Morning," December 26, 1974, White House Press Release, available online at Gerald R. Ford Library, www.fordlibrarymuseum.gov.

Page 334, "it's strictly thermal underwear": Carroll Kilpatrick, "An Open, Relaxed Presidential Retreat," *Washington Post*, January 1, 1975, A2.

Page 334, No presidential holiday: ibid. See also Don Irwin, "Vail Is Costly But Not Exclusive," *Los Angeles Times*, December 29, 1974, 4.

Page 334, "was always giving me": Gerald R. Ford interview.

Page 334–36, "an amiable, vacillating": Philip Shabecoff, "Aides Say Ford Ignores Skepticism About Ability," *New York Times*, December 29, 1975, 53.

Page 335 caption, "You make me": quoted in John Hebers, "Ford Jest That He'd Trade Presidency for Job in Vail," *New York Times*, December 25, 1974, 8.

Page 336, "I had skied": Gerald R. Ford, *Time to Heal*, 343.

Page 336 "Every picture": quoted in Greene, *Fraternity*, 203.

Page 336, "not the stumbling": David Broder, "A President with His Chin Out, Defiantly," *Washington Post*, January 4, 1976, F7.

Page 336, the first time: "President Takes to Camp David Like a Duck to Water," *Los Angeles Times*, September 2, 1974, H7.

Page 336, "nice place": quoted in Frank Cormier, AP, September 2, 1974, available online at newspaperarchive.com, or printed, e.g., as "Ford Finds Camp David a Great Place," *Hope (Arkansas) Star*, September 2, 1974, 10.

Page 336, "If I get," "The air": Betty Ford, *Times of My Life*, 168.

Page 336, "It was a beautiful location": Gerald R. Ford interview.

Page 336, "Camp David was convenient," "What Camp David meant": Susan Ford Bales interview.

Page 336, seventeen times: Nelson, *President Is at Camp David*, 104.

Page 336, "Liberty got to": Susan Ford Bales interview.

Pages 336, 338, cabinet members: details in this paragraph from Nelson, *President Is at Camp David*, 104–5.

Page 339, "I had a helluva drive": quoted in Van Natta, *First Off the Tee*, 86. See also Kenneth Denlinger, "18-Handicapper Ford Displays Dedication to Golf," *Washington Post*, September 12, 1974.

Page 339, "Can't say that much": Gerald R. Ford interview.

Page 339, signs: quoted in Van Natta, *First Off the Tee*, 83.

Page 339, "I have never seen": Gerald R. Ford: "Remarks at a Dinner Honoring Inductees Into the World Golf Hall of Fame," September 11, 1974, American Presidency Project, www.presidency.ucsb.edu.

Page 339, "Ford Uses Golf," "was much": Marjorie Hunter, "Ford Uses Golf as Example in 'Reconciliation' Plea," *New York Times*, September 12, 1974, 28.

Page 339, "Any connection": Gerald R. Ford interview.

Page 339, "We have all heard," "a very wild swing": Gerald R. Ford, "Remarks at a Dinner Honoring Inductees Into the World Golf Hall of Fame," September 11, 1974, American Presidency Project, www.presidency.ucsb.edu.

Page 339, "Jerry, we all have," "just another Sunday duffer": quoted in Aldo Beckman, "Duffer Ford Earns Nicklaus' Praise," *Chicago Tribune*, February 27, 1975, C16.

Page 339, "He's very strong": quoted in "The Gallery Is Charitable Toward Ford's Golfing," *New York Times*, February 27, 1975, 73.

Page 339, "Ford was the first," "Ford doesn't really": quoted in Van Natta, *First Off the Tee*, 94.

Page 339, "The last time": quoted in Macintosh, *Everything You Ever Wanted*, 81.

Page 339, "The almost inevitable": Campbell and Landau, *Presidential Lies*, 171.

Page 341, "I enjoyed golf": Gerald R. Ford interview.

Page 341, "He plays for fun," "I've seen him": quoted in Fred Emery, "A Spring Break for the Nation's Best-Known Athlete," *U.S. News and World Report*, April 14, 1975, 50–51.

Page 341, "first family jitterbugging": James M. Naughton, "2 miles Up, Ford Relaxes with Golf," *New York Times*, August 13, 1975, 1.

Page 341, eleven numbers: "Fords Go Nightclubbing in Vail," AP, August 12, 1975, available online at newspaperarchive.com, or printed in, e.g., *Racine (Wisconsin) Journal Times*, August 12, 1975, 2B.

Page 341, 44 hours and the rest of the figures in this paragraph: Don Irwin, "Ford Touring as President and Politician," *Los Angeles Times*, August 24, 1975, 4.

Page 341, "Relax, have a good time": quoted in Dorothy Townsend, "Ford Swims, Golfs, Does Paperwork on Vacation," *Los Angeles Times*, November 9, 1976, B3.

Page 341, "Where were all": quoted in Campbell and Landau, *Presidential Lies*, 181.

Page 341, most satisfying experience: Gerald R. Ford interview.

References and Resources

Campbell, Shepherd, and Peter Landau. *Presidential Lies: The Illustrated History of White House Golf.* New York: Macmillan, 1996.

Cannon, James. *Time and Chance: Gerald Ford's Appointment with History.* New York: HarperCollins, 1994.

Ford, Betty, with Chris Chase. *The Times of My Life.* New York: Harper and Row, 1978.

Ford, Gerald R. *Humor and the Presidency.* New York: Arbor House, 1987.

———. *Public Papers of the Presidents of the United States: Gerald R. Ford, 1974–1977.* Washington, D.C.: United States Government Printing Office, various years.

———. *A Time to Heal: The Autobiography of Gerald R. Ford.* New York: Harper and Row, 1979.

Greene, Bob. *Fraternity: A Journey in Search of Five Presidents.* New York: Crown Publishers, 2004.

Hartmann, Robert T. *Palace Politics: An Inside Account of the Ford Years.* New York: McGraw-Hill, 1980.

Macintoch, Iain. *Everything You Ever Wanted to Know About Golf (But Were Too Afraid to Ask).* London: A&C Black, 2010.

Nelson, Dale W. *The President Is at Camp David.* Syracuse, N.Y.: Syracuse University Press, 1995.

Nessen, Ron. *It Sure Looks Different from the Inside.* Chicago: Playboy Press, 1978.

Reeves, Richard. *A Ford, Not a Lincoln.* New York: Harcourt Brace Jovanovich, 1975.

terHorst, Jerald F. *Gerald Ford and the Future of the Presidency.* New York: Third Press, 1974.

Van Natta, Don, Jr. *First Off the Tee: Presidential Hackers, Duffers, and Cheaters, from Taft to Bush.* New York: Public Affairs, 2003.

34: Jimmy Carter

Sources

Page 342, "Plains, Ga." billboard: "Demonstrators in Plains Decry Carter's Human Rights Policy," *Washington Post*, July 5, 1978, A6.

Page 342, was already ruined: "Candidate Billy Carter Against Commercialization," AP, December 6, 1976, available online at newspaperarchive.com, or printed in, e.g., *South Mississippi Sun*, December 6, 1976, B7.

Page 342, "Things in Plains": Jimmy Carter, *Christmas in Plains*, 111.

Page 342, media in Plains: "When a Sleepy Georgia Town Plays Host to Georgia White House," *U.S. News & World Report*, November 22, 1976, 25–26.

Page 342 caption, "A president should": quoted in Nelson, *President Is at Camp David*, 129.

Page 344, "They've got all": quoted in Don Irwin, "Likes 'New Look': President Tours Downtown Plains," *Los Angeles Times*, December 23, 1977, B10.

Page 344, "This is better," Murray Smith, "I wish the hell": recorded in author's notes, Plains, Ga., December 23–25, 1978.

Page 344, "The cameras were always," a reporter, "It was on": Jimmy Carter, *Sharing Good Times*, 74.

Page 345, "It was almost impossible": ibid., 73.

Page 345, "despite our love": ibid., 74.

Page 345, needless expense: "Carter Puts 'Sequoia' Up for Sale," *UPI*, *Washington Post*, April 1, 1977, B13.

Page 345, "There might be": Jimmy Carter, interview by author, April 16, 2004.

Page 345, "pleasure comes in being": Jimmy Carter, *Sharing Good Times*, 70.

Page 347, "We would drive": Jimmy Carter interview.

Page 347, "This morning": quoted in Harry Kelly, "Presidents Need Some Privacy, Too: Carter Chafes at Public Interest in Personal Life," *Chicago Tribune*, April 18, 1979, 1.

Page 347, "There's no doubt," "Anyone who goes": quoted in Edward Walsh, "Carter on Vacation: Intense Pursuit of Solitude He Craves," *Washington Post*, April 16, 1979, A2.

Page 347, "It was a good vacation": Jimmy Carter interview.

Page 347, "Deacon is fishing": Harry Kelly, "Carter Family Goes Rafting, Runs into Foul Weather," *Chicago Tribune*, August 23, 1978, 3.

Page 347, 80-mile, whitewater run: Maureen Santini, "Carters Have Stormy Raft Ride," AP, available online at news.google.com, or printed in, e.g., *Sarasota Herald-Tribune*, August 22, 1978, 1A.

Page 347 caption, "We were all": Jimmy Carter, *Sharing Good Times*, 76.

Page 348, "Keep the Canal": Judith Frutig, "Ford, Reagan Factions Split on Panama," *Christian Science Monitor*, October 4, 1977, 3.

Page 348, 39 percent: George Gallup, "Carter's Popularity Is at a Low Point," *Boston Globe*, August 21, 1978, 2.

Page 348, "I need time": quoted in "The Raft of State," *Newsweek*, September 4, 1978, 16–17.

Page 348, "one of the most": quoted in Santini, "Carters Have Stormy Raft Ride," AP, available online at news.google.com, or printed in, e.g., *Sarasota Herald-Tribune*, August 22, 1978, 1A.

Page 348, "I have issued": quoted in ibid.

Page 348, "It was a nice day": quoted in "Rafting in the Rockies: The Carters, Like Anyone Else, Enjoy a Vacation," *Time*, September 4, 1978, 12.

Page 349, 111 trout: Jimmy Carter: "Salmon River in Idaho Informal Exchange with Reporters at the Conclusion of the President's Raft Trip," August 24, 1978, American Presidency Project, www.presidency.ucsb.edu.

Page 349, "We came in": quoted in ibid.

Page 349, "I don't want": "Carter, Family to Spend Week in Wyoming," AP, August 25, 1978, available online at newspaperarchive.com, or printed in, e.g., *Odessa (Texas) American*, August 25, 1978, 14A.

Page 349, "the best three days": quoted in Jimmy Carter: "Salmon River in Idaho."

Page 349, "If he is simply going": quoted in Ellen Hume, "Carter Will Cut Vacation Short to Fight for Gas Bill," *Los Angeles Times*, August 28, 1978, 1.

Page 349, "I went back": Jimmy Carter interview.

Page 349, Richard Nixon: Nixon, *In the Arena*, 159.

Page 349, "glowing" report, "close to near": Jimmy Carter interview.

Page 349, "one of the most": Carter, *Sharing Good Times*, 71.

Page 349, "very attractive": Jimmy Carter interview.

Page 351, "typical of," "The ability of": ibid.

Page 351, averaged 40 miles: ibid.

Page 351 caption, "He seemed to know": Jimmy Carter, *Keeping Faith*, 372.

Page 352, visits to Camp David: Nelson, *President Is at Camp David*, 130.

Page 352, "This was surely": Rosalynn Carter, *First Lady from Plains*, 257.

Page 352, "We were looking": Jody Powell, interview by author, March 29, 2004.

Page 352, "it would be best": Jimmy Carter, *Keeping Faith*, 316.

Pages 352, 354, "weighted with maps": ibid., 322.

Page 353, Killer Rabbit story: Mares, *Fishing with the Presidents*, 131.

Page 353, "Bunny Goes Bugs": Brooks Jackson, "Jimmy's White House: Bunny Goes Bugs, Rabbit Attacks President," AP, *Washington Post*, August 30, 1979, 1.

Page 353, "It was a simple": Jimmy Carter, letter to author, April 20, 2004.

Page 354, "After three days": Jimmy Carter interview.

Page 354, "a crisis of confidence": Jimmy Carter, "Address to the Nation on Energy and National Goals: 'The Malaise Speech'," July 15, 1979, American Presidency Project, www.presidency.ucsb.

Page 354, "among our best-kept secrets": Jimmy Carter, *Outdoor Journal*, 7.

Page 354, "one of my favorite": Carter, *Sharing Good Times*, 79.

Page 355, "rare opportunity": Jimmy Carter, "The President's News Conference," May 29, 1979, American Presidency Project, www.presidency.ucsb.edu.

Page 355, "For a few hours": Carter, *Outdoor Journal*, 71.

Page 355, "Fishing and tying flies": Jimmy Carter letter.

Page 355, "My concentration": Jimmy Carter, *Outdoor Journal*, 8.

Page 355, Aides explained: Don Irwin, "Carter to Steam Down the Mississippi," *Los Angeles Times*, August 10, 1979, B4.

Page 356, Built in Scotland, paid the $1800 fare: "Carters Begin Their Trip Cruisin' Down the River," *Washington Post*, August 18, 1978, A6.

Page 356, crew of 77: Don Erwin, "Working Vacation on Stern-Wheeler," *Los Angeles Times*, August 10, 1970, B4.

Page 356, fifty-eight speeches, one speech every three hours: Bill Peterson, "After 659 Miles and 58 Speeches, Carter Plans a Rest," *Washington Post*, August 25, 1979, A3.

Page 356, "Don't you people": quoted in "Life on the Mississippi," *Newsweek*, September 3, 1979, 30.

Page 356, Forty-seven towns: Peterson, "After 659 Miles and 58 Speeches."

Page 356, eighteen and one-half: Raymond Coffey, "President Sets a Baby-Bussing Record in Iowa," *Chicago Tribune*, August 21, 1979, 11.

Page 356, "shirt-sleeve populism": "Life on the Mississippi," *Newsweek*, September 3, 1979, 31.

Page 356, "It really turned into" "What we didn't": Jody Powell interview.

Page 356 caption, more than 10,000 people: "Crowds Growing as Sternwheeler Continues Tour," *New York Times*, August 23, 1979, A22.

Page 356 caption, "I Went Down": Bill Peterson, "Carter at Ease on Slow Boat to St. Louis," *Washington Post*, August 19, 1979, A1.

Page 357, "He's so common": quoted in Bill Peterson, "Trappings of a Campaign," *Washington Post*, August 20, 1979, A1. Other sources for the details in this paragraph are Coffey, "President Sets a Baby-Bussing Record in Iowa"; "Life on the Mississippi"; "My Spirits Restored, Carter Says," *Los Angeles Times*, August 22, 1979, A2.

Page 357, "something of a": "Life on the Mississippi."

Page 357, "the hallowed territory": Howell Raines, "In Fly Fishing, Carter's Record Can't Be Assailed," *New York Times*, May 5, 1991, 32.

REFERENCES AND RESOURCES

Bourne, Peter G. *Jimmy Carter: A Comprehensive Biography from Plains to Post-Presidency*. New York: Scribner, a Lisa Drew Book, 1997.

Brzezinski, Zbigniew. *Power and Principle: Memoirs of the National Security Adviser, 1977–1981*. New York: Farrar, Straus, Giroux, 1983.

Carter, Jimmy. *Christmas in Plains: Memories*. New York: Simon and Schuster, 2001.

————. *Keeping Faith: Memoirs of a President*. New York: Bantam Books, 1982.

————. *An Outdoor Journal: Adventures and Reflections*. New York: Bantam Books, 1988.

————. *Public Papers of the Presidents of the United States: Jimmy Carter, 1977–1981*. Washington, D.C.: Government Printing Office, various years.

————. *Sharing Good Times*. New York: Simon and Schuster, 2004.

Carter, Rosalynn. *First Lady from Plains*. Boston: Houghton Mifflin, 1984.

Germond, Jack W., and Jules Witcover. *Blue Smoke and Mirrors: How Reagan Won and Why Carter Lost the Election of 1980*. New York: Viking Press, 1981.

Jimmy Carter National Historic Site, online materials, www.nps.gov/jica.

Jordan, Hamilton. *Crisis: The Last Year of the Carter Presidency*. New York: G. P. Putnam's Sons, 1982.

Kaufman, Burton I. *The Presidency of James Earl Carter, Jr*. Lawrence: University Press of Kansas, 1993.

Mares, Bill. *Fishing with the Presidents*. Mechanicsburg, Pa.: Stackpole Books, 1999.

Meck, Charles R. *Trout Streams and Hatches of Pennsylvania*. Woodstock, Vt.: Countryman Press, 1999.

Nelson, W. Dale. *The President Is at Camp David*. Syracuse, N.Y.: Syracuse University Press, 1995.

Nixon, Richard. *In the Arena: A Memory of Victory, Defeat and Renewal*. New York: Simon and Schuster, 1990.

Powell, Jody. *The Other Side of the Story*. New York: William Morrow, 1984.

Quandt, William B. *Camp David: Peacemaking and Politics*. Washington, D.C.: Brookings Institution, 1986.

Sabato, Larry J. *Feeding Frenzy: How Attack Journalism Has Transformed American Politics*. New York: Free Press, 1991.

35: RONALD REAGAN

SOURCES

Page 358, "I took one look": Ronald Reagan, *American Life*, 193.

Page 358, "Ranch in the Sky": ibid.

Page 358, "That particular place": "Interview with Jerry Rankin of the *Santa Barbara News-Press*," February 13, 1985, American Presidency Project, www.presidency.ucsb.edu.

Page 358, "an open cathedral": quoted in Noonan, *When Character Was King*, 176.

Page 358, "Rancho del Cielo": Ronald Reagan, *American Life*, 194.

Page 358, 364 days, 45 days: Hannaford, *Ronald Reagan and His Ranch*, 11.

Page 358, $526,000, $1,148: Lou Cannon, "President's Low-Key Itinerary Designed to Protect His Privacy," *Washington Post*, February 21, 1981, A1.

Page 358, "a million problems": Nancy Reagan, *My Turn*, 98.

Page 358 caption, "I'm 70 years old", "I'm going to enjoy it": quoted in Cannon, *President Reagan*, 528.

Page 360, "wasn't very pretty": Ronald Reagan, *American Life*, 194.

Page 360, "a little claustrophobic": ibid.

Page 360, "as if it were": Barletta, *Riding with Reagan*, 7.

Page 360 caption, "From the house": Ronald Reagan, *American Life*, 194.

Page 361, "cooped up": Nancy Reagan, *My Turn*, 90.

Page 361, "You can get": Cannon, *President Reagan*, 466.

Page 361, "As much as": Nancy Reagan, *My Turn*, 253.

Page 361, "Presidents don't get vacations," "You're still president": quoted in Lou Cannon, "Reagan Says He Needs Escape from White House's 'Gilded Cage'," *Washington Post*, February 18, 1985, A15.

Page 361, During the helicopter ride: "'Homesick' Reagan Flies to Ranch," *Nashua Telegraph*, February 20, 1981, 3.

Page 361, "chop-and-clear": Francis X. Clines, "Duty and Mortality Shadow Vacation," *New York Times*, February 13, 1984, A16.

Page 361, "He liked to be able": quoted in Noonan, *When Character Was King*, 115.

Page 361, "You see him," "He's very content": George Skelton, "President Returns to the Saddle and the Saw," *Los Angeles Times*, May 24, 1981, A1.

Page 362, "It's the greatest": quoted in Steven B. Weisman, "On Holiday Back at the Reagans' Ranch," *New York Times*, November 26, 1981, A1.

Page 362, "Snake Lake": Smith, *White House Doctor*, 140; Cannon, "Reagan Says He Needs Escape."

Page 362, stomped on a rattler: Smith, *White House Doctor*, 141.

Page 363, "Rawhide": Barletta, *Riding with Reagan*, 183.

Page 363, "From a thousand yards": ibid., 116.

Page 363, "His back was": ibid., 73.

Page 363, "To ride English": Noonan, *When Character Was King*, 110.

Page 363, "Rancho del Cielo Cavalry Commander": see photo 46 in Hannaford, *Ronald Reagan and His Ranch*.

Page 363 caption, "I don't chop wood": quoted in "Transcript of the President's News Conference on Foreign and Domestic Matters," *New York Times*, August 14, 1981, A10.

Page 364, "I just fell in love": Ronald Reagan, *American Life*, 75.

Page 364, "Ever since": ibid. In 2005 the Ronald Reagan Presidential Foundation and Library presented an exhibition titled *Lieutenant Ronald Reagan and the U.S. Cavalry: Hollywood and History*.

Page 364, how long: Lee Lescaze, "Reagan Takes Trail Ride, Returns to Ranch Routine," *Washington Post*, May 24, 1981, A1.

Page 364, "On that first trip": Ronald Reagan, *American Life*, 275–76.

Page 365, temporary buildings: Steven R. Weisman, "Reagan Aides Call New Ranch Facilities Temporary," *New York Times*, May 24, 1981, A19.

Page 365, $750,000: Lescaze, "Reagan Takes Trail Ride."

Page 365, $5,221 an hour: Terence Hunt, "'Caged Bird' Flies to Calif.," *Lewiston (Maine) Daily Sun*, February 20, 1981, 8.

Page 365, "$250,000 for each trip": Cannon, "President's Low-Key Itinerary."

Page 365, "from a mental health standpoint": quoted in Hunt, "'Caged Bird' Flies to Calif."

Page 365, brushing down his horse: Terence Hunt, "'Privacy Peak' Annoys Staff," *Boca Raton News*, September 1, 1982, 5A.

Page 365, "I wonder": quoted in Steven R. Weisman, "Reporter's Notebook: At Home on the Rancho . . . ," *New York Times*, August 17, 1981, B8.

Page 365, "Now the whole world": Ronald Reagan, *American Life*, 503.

Pages 365–66, "The president . . . likes," "Then he simply": Francis X. Clines, "The White House Notebook: The Story of a 'Thanksgiving Turkey'," *New York Times*, November 28, 1982, B6.

Page 366, "I wish the fog," "a turnaround": quoted in "Transcript of the President's News Conference."

Page 366, "They're screaming": quoted in Bernard Gwertzman, "A Week of Tough Choices in Defense and Diplomacy," *New York Times*, August 16, 1981, E1.

Page 366, "It was raining": quoted in Hannaford, *Ronald Reagan and His Ranch*, 69.

Page 366, "Yes, if it was": quoted in Ronald Reagan, *American Life*, 387.

Page 366, "a real trouper": quoted in George Skelton and Patt Morrison, "'Trouper' Queen Braves Storm Peril to Visit Reagans," *Los Angeles Times*, March 2, 1983, A13.

Page 366, "Invitations to outsiders": Regan, *For the Record*, 22.

Page 366 caption, "It's times like these," "You do": quoted and reported in Speakes, *Speaking Out*, 116.

Page 367, "It's pretty damn secluded": quoted in Howell Raines, ". . . And Meantime, Back in the Capital," *New York Times*, August 17, 1981, B8.

Page 367, "Without Camp David": quoted in Ronald Reagan, *American Life*, 396.

Page 367, "a slice of heaven": quoted in ibid.

Page 367, 187 times, 571 days: Nelson, *President Is at Camp David*, 134–35.

Page 367, "Thank God": Nancy Reagan, *My Turn*, 253.

Page 367, "For me," "Because the entire place": ibid., 258.

Page 367, chapel at Camp David: Nelson, *President Is at Camp David*, 143.

Page 367 caption, "a wet afternoon": quoted in Skelton and Morrison, "'Trouper' Queen Braves Storm Peril," A13.

Page 367 caption, "the Hounds of Reaganville": Francis X. Clines, "Queen's Party Fords Streams in Rain," *New York Times*, March 2, 1983, A1.

Page 367 caption, "I know I promised Nancy": Reagan, *American Life*, 388.

Page 368, 150 radio addresses: Nelson, *President Is at Camp David*, 134.

Page 368, "most private retreat," "That was about it," "You might be off": Nancy Reagan, *My Turn*, 253–54.

Page 368, "Throughout the day": Maureen Reagan, *First Father, First Daughter*, 326.

Page 368, "They really help," "All in all": Ronald Reagan, *American Life*, 501.

Page 369, reporters caught glimpses: James Gerstenzang, "If This Is New Year's Day, It Must Be Palm Springs," *Lakeland Ledger*, January 2, 1983, 14A.

Page 369, "I've never been": quoted in Cannon, "Reagan Says He Needs Escape."

Pages 369–70, "Reaganism of the Year": Lou Cannon, "In the Sun, a Search for the Presidential Utterance of the Year," *Washington Post*, January 2, 1984, A3.

Page 370, "a tangible fabric": "Transcripts of New Year's Greetings from Reagan and Gorbachev on TV," *New York Times*, January 2, 1988, 6.

Page 370, "The world is safer," "Fears and suspicions": "Leaders Trade Smiles on U.S. and Soviet TV," *New York Times*, January 1, 1989, 11.

Page 370, "to make every president": quoted in Hannaford, *Ronald Reagan and His Ranch*, 91.

Page 372, Gorbachev was impressed: Barletta, *Riding with Reagan*, 146–48.

Page 372, "rookie mistakes": ibid., 212.

Page 372, "It's OK": quoted in ibid., 213.

REFERENCES AND RESOURCES

Barletta, John R., with Rochelle Schweizer. *Riding with Reagan: From the White House to the Ranch*. New York: Citadel Press, Kensington Publishing, 2005.

Barrett, Lawrence I. *Gambling with History: Ronald Reagan in the White House*. New York: Doubleday, 1983.

Cannon, Lou. *President Reagan: The Role of a Lifetime*. New York: Simon and Schuster, 1991.

Hannaford, Peter. *Ronald Reagan and His Ranch: The Western White House, 1981–1989*. Bennington, Vt.: Images from the Past, 2002.

Morris, Edmund. *Dutch: A Memoir of Ronald Reagan*. New York: Random House, 1999.

Nelson, W. Dale. *The President Is at Camp David*. Syracuse, N.Y.: Syracuse University Press, 1995.

Noonan, Peggy. *When Character Was King: A Story of Ronald Reagan*. New York: Viking, 2001.

Reagan, Maureen. *First Father, First Daughter*. Boston: Little, Brown, 1989.

Reagan, Nancy, with William Novak. *My Turn: The Memoirs of Nancy Reagan*. New York: Random House, 1989.

Reagan, Ronald. *An American Life*. New York: Simon and Schuster, 1990.

Reeves, Richard. *President Reagan: The Triumph of Imagination*. New York: Simon and Schuster, 2005.

Regan, Donald T. *For the Record: From Wall Street to Washington*. New York: Harcourt Brace Jovanovich, 1988.

Smith, T. Burton, MD, with Carter Henderson. *White House Doctor*. Lanham, Md.: Madison Books, 1992.

Speakes, Larry. *Speaking Out: The Reagan Presidency from Inside the White House*. New York: Charles Scribner's Sons, 1988.

Van Natta, Don, Jr., *First Off the Tee: Presidential Hackers, Duffers, and Cheaters, from Taft to Bush*. New York: Public Affairs, 2003.

36: GEORGE H. W. BUSH

SOURCES

Page 374, "This President Relaxes": Maureen Dowd, "This President Relaxes by Wearing Others Out," *New York Times*, July 4, 1989, 34.

Page 374, "I always have," "I find it relaxing," "You know me": quoted in ibid.

Page 374, "brings to the normal worries": "Perils on the Mountaintop," *New York Times*, May 6, 1991, A14.

Page 374, "Maine in the summer," "There was the wonder": George Bush and Gold, *Looking Forward*, 27, 29.

Page 376, "Suddenly we looked": Barbara Bush, *Barbara Bush*, 311–12.

Page 376, "was turned upside down," "He plunged": David Hoffman, "See How He Plays," *Washington Post*, September 3, 1989, F1.

Page 376 caption, "anchor to windward": quoted in David Hoffman, "Bush's Maine Event," *Washington Post*, May 28, 1988, C1.

Page 377, "aerobic golf": quoted in Maureen Dowd, "Bush Is Yipping and Chipping in Wedge City," *New York Times*, August 24, 1989, A1.

Page 377, "power golf": Van Natta, *First Off the Tee*, 288.

Page 377, "golf-polo": quoted in Dowd, "Bush Is Yipping and Chipping in Wedge City," *New York Times*, August 24, 1989, A1. See also Hoffman, "See How He Plays."

Page 377, "a rollicking, accelerated": Hoffman, "See How He Plays."

Page 377, golf times: Maureen Dowd, "A Grim Bush Golfs and Boasts as Aides Fret About Image," *New York Times*, August 20, 1990, A1.

Page 377, "All right": quoted in Hoffman, "See How He Plays."

Page 377, "Mr. Smooth": quoted in Maureen Dowd, "Bush Bats .500 and Settles Old Score," *New York Times*, August 28, 1989, A12.

Page 377, "to come see": quoted in ibid.

Page 377, "Wedge City," "a power outage," "on the dance floor," "Vic Damone," "Arnold Farmer": Van Natta, *First off the Tee,* 288.

Page 377, "yips and chips": Dowd, "Bush Is Yipping and Chipping in Wedge City," *New York Times*, August 24, 1989, A1.

Page 377, "Oh, golly darn": quoted in Ibid.

Page 378, "He kept it": Fitzwater, *Call the Briefing!*, 373.

Page 378, "There's no way": quoted in Parmet, *George Bush*, 13.

Page 378, "You get out there": quoted in Maureen Dowd, "It's a Rare Sport That Bush Doesn't Like," *New York Times*, January 2, 1989, 1. The magazine was *Motor Boating and Sailing*.

Page 379, "It says something": quoted in ibid.

Page 379, "this jinx": quoted in David Hoffman, "Sportsman Bush Knows Record Is on the Line," *Washington Post*, September 1, 1989, A5.

Page 379, ongoing reports of fish scores: ibid. See also Barbara Bush, *Barbara Bush*, 326–27.

Page 379, "No Fish": Barbara Bush, *Barbara Bush*, 308.

Page 379, "My record fishing," "It's a superb record": quoted in Hoffman, "Sportsman Bush."

Page 379, "Between now": ibid.

Page 380, "The jinx is broken!" "a long dry summer": quoted in Bernard Winraub, "Bush Ends a Vacation by Getting His Fish," *New York Times*, September 4, 1989, 7.

Page 380, "I kept the hook": George Bush, *All the Best*, 464.

Page 380, "a total vacation": quoted in David Hoffman, "Despite 'Total Vacation,' Demands on President Never Cease," *Washington Post*, August 27, 1989, A4.

Page 380, "will not stand": quoted in "This Aggression Will Not Stand," *New York Times*, March 1, 1991, A26. See also George Bush and Scowcroft, *World Transformed*, 333.

Page 380, "A relaxed George Bush": quoted in George Bush and Scowcroft, *World Transformed*, 343.

Page 380, "In truth, a president": ibid., 343.

Page 380, "The American people": quoted in Maureen Dowd, "Aides Worry About How Bush's Vacation Looks in a Crisis," *New York Times*, August 11, 1990, 8.

Page 381, "It looks horrible": quoted in Maureen Dowd, "A Grim Bush Golfs and Boats as Aides Fret About Image," *New York Times*, August 20, 1990, A1.

Page 381, "No one in the Bush inner circle": ibid.

Page 381, "secure room": Sidey, "Walker's Point," 70.

Page 381, "It was a beautiful": George Bush and Scowcroft, *World Transformed*, 69–70.

Page 381, "I've been able": George Bush, "Remarks and a Question-and-Answer Session with Reporters in Kennebunkport, Maine, Following a Meeting with Prime Minister Brian Mulroney of Canada," August 27, 1990, American Presidency Project, www.presidency.ucsb.edu.

Page 382, "I think I've earned it": quoted in Marshall Ingwerson, "President Plans Serious Vacation," *Christian Science Monitor*, August 8, 1991, 7.

Page 382, "They started shouting": Fitzwater, *Call the Briefing!*, 373.

Page 382, "But suddenly": ibid., 374.

Page 383, "I love trolling": George Bush, *All the Best*, 532.

Page 383, "I was just delighted": quoted in "Bush and Gorbachev Talk," *New York Times*, August 22, 1991, A15.

Page 383, "Pressures will mount": George Bush, *All the Best*, 537.

Page 383, "We watched": Fitzwater, *Call the Briefing!*, 371–72. See also "3-Story Waves Heavily Damage Bush Vacation Compound in Southern Maine," *New York Times*, November 1, 1991, B4.

Page 384, "He held it": Fitzwater, *Call the Briefing!*, 372.

Page 384, "had its body bent": George Bush, *All the Best*, 540–41.

Page 384, "sniffing and sniffing": ibid., 439–40.

Page 384, "Presidents like it": Fitzwater, *Call the Briefing!*, 273–74.

Page 384, Bush's daughter's marriage: "Bush's Daughter Marries with 'a Minimum of Fuss'," *New York Times*, June 28, 1992, 14.

Page 384, "do it with as much passion": "Where Bush Throws Weight Around," *New York Times*, August 21, 1988, 26.

Page 385, "30 percent": "Bush's Horseshoe Hobby Rings Up Sales," *Washington Post*, August 13, 1989, A3.

Page 385, "President Gorbachev": quoted in Anne Devroy, "At Camp David, Bush's Emphasis Is on Informality," *Washington Post*, June 3, 1990, A23.

Page 385, "horseshoe diplomacy": Barbara Bush, *Barbara Bush*, 303.

Page 385, "beginner's luck," "the only thing": George Bush and Scowcroft, *World Transformed*, 287.

Page 385, "Well, I couldn't": quoted in Maureen Dowd, "Smiles, Golf Carts, and 2 Lethal Footballs," *New York Times*, June 3, 1990, 1.

REFERENCES AND RESOURCES

Bush, Barbara. *Barbara Bush: A Memoir.* New York: Macmillan, 1995.

Bush, George. *All the Best, George Bush: My Life in Letters and Other Writings.* New York: Touchstone Books, Simon and Schuster, 2000.

———. *Public Papers of the Presidents of the United States: George Bush, 1989–1993.* Washington, D.C.: Government Printing Office, various years.

———, and Victor Gold. *Looking Forward: The George Bush Story.* New York: Doubleday, 1987.

———, and Brent Scowcroft. *A World Transformed.* New York: Alfred A. Knopf, 1998.

Duffy, Michael, and Dan Goodgame. *Marching in Place: The Status Quo Presidency of George Bush.* New York: Simon and Schuster, 1992.

Fitzwater, Marlin. *Call the Briefing! Reagan and Bush, Sam and Helen: A Decade with Presidents and the Press.* New York: Random House, Times Books, 1995.

George Bush Presidential Library and Museum, online materials, www.bushlibrary.tamu.edu.

Greene, John Robert. *The Presidency of George Bush.* Lawrence: University Press of Kansas, 2000.

Killian, Pamela. *Barbara Bush: A Biography.* New York: St. Martin's Press, 1992.

Parmet, Herbert S. *George Bush: The Life of a Lone Star Yankee.* New York: Scribner, 1997.

Sidey, Hugh S. "Walker's Point: A Visit to the Maine Retreat of President George H. W. Bush." *White House History*, no. 18 (Spring 2006): 66–89.

Smith, Jean Edward. *George Bush's War.* New York: Henry Holt, 1992.

Van Natta, Don, Jr. *First Off the Tee: Presidential Hackers, Duffers, and Cheaters, from Taft to Bush.* New York: Public Affairs, 2003.

37: TWENTY-FIRST CENTURY ESCAPES

Page 391, "We all needed the time off": Bill Clinton, *My Life* (New York: Vintage Books, 2005), 667–68.

Page 394, "The press called": George W. Bush, *Decision Points* (New York, Crown, 2010), 313.

Page 396, "I know you all": Barack Obama, "Press Conference by the President," December 20, 2013, The White House, Office of the Press Secretary, www.whitehouse.gov.

ILLUSTRATION CREDITS

All illustrations in this book are copyrighted as listed below and may not be reproduced without permission of the copyright owner.

ILLUSTRATION CREDITS KEY:

Adams, NPS—Adams National Historical Park (National Park Service)
AP—Associated Press
API—Associated Press Images
BEP—Bureau of Engraving and Printing
Harrison—Benjamin Harrison Presidential Site
Beverly Historical—Beverly Historical Society and Museum
Eisenhower—Dwight D. Eisenhower Presidential Library, Museum, and Boyhood Home
FDR Library—Franklin D. Roosevelt Presidential Library and Museum
Bush Library—George Bush Presidential Library and Museum
Ford Library—Gerald R. Ford Presidential Library and Museum
Truman Library—Harry S. Truman Presidential Library and Museum
Hoover Library—Herbert Hoover Presidential Library and Museum
Carter Library—Jimmy Carter Library and Museum
JFK Library—John F. Kennedy Presidential Library and Museum
LBJ Library—Lyndon Baines Johnson Library
LOC—Library of Congress
Montpelier—The Montpelier Foundation
MVLA—Mount Vernon Ladies' Association
NARA—National Archives
NPS—National Park Service
Nixon Library—Richard Nixon Presidential Library and Museum
Reagan Library—Ronald Reagan Presidential Foundation and Library
Monticello—Thomas Jefferson Foundation at Monticello
Sagamore Hill—Sagamore Hill National Historic Site
WH—White House Photo
WH Collection—White House Collection
WHHA—White House Historical Association
Wilson Library—Woodrow Wilson Presidential Library